Indigenous Firsts

A History of Native American Achievements and Events

ALSO FROM VISIBLE INK PRESS

African American Almanac: 400 Years of Triumph, Courage and Excellence
By Lean'tin Bracks, Ph.D.
ISBN: 978-1-57859-323-1

The American Women's Almanac: 500 Years of Making History
By Deborah G. Felder
ISBN: 978-1-57859-636-2

Black Firsts: 4,500 Trailblazing Achievements and Ground-Breaking Events
By Jessie Carnie Smith, Ph.D.
ISBN: 978-1-57859-688-1

Black Heroes
By Jessie Carnie Smith, Ph.D.
ISBN: 978-1-57859-136-7

Freedom Facts and Firsts: 400 Years of the African American Civil Rights Experience
By Jessie Carnie Smith, Ph.D., and Linda T. Wynn
ISBN: 978-1-57859-192-3

The Handy African American History Answer Book
By Jessie Carnie Smith, Ph.D.
ISBN: 978-1-57859-452-8

The Handy American History Answer Book
By David L. Hudson, Jr.
ISBN: 978-1-57859-471-9

The Handy Christianity Answer Book
By Stephen A. Werner, Ph.D.
ISBN: 978-1-57859-686-7

The Handy Islam Answer Book
By John Renard, Ph.D.
ISBN: 978-1-57859-510-5

Native American Almanac: More Than 50,000 Years of the Cultures and Histories of Indigenous Peoples
By Yvonne Wakim Dennis, Arlene Hirschfelder, and Shannon Rothenberger Flynn
ISBN: 978-1-57859-507-5

Native American Landmarks and Festivals: A Traveler's Guide to Indigenous United States and Canada
By Yvonne Wakim Dennis and Arlene Hirschfelder
ISBN: 978-1-57859-641-6

Originals! Black Women Breaking Barriers
By Jessie Carney Smith, Ph.D.
IBSN: 978-1-57859-759-8

Trailblazing Women: Amazing Americans Who Made History
By Deborah G. Felder
ISBN: 978-1-57859-729-1

PLEASE VISIT US AT WWW.VISIBLEINKPRESS.COM.

ABOUT THE AUTHORS

Yvonne Wakim Dennis attempts to wind the world well through her books, presentations, and workshops. She interweaves environmental and social justice into all she writes and credits her diverse family (Sand Hill/Cherokee/Syrian) for her resolve to create an inclusive and multicultural world. She is a consultant, lecturer, curriculum developer for publishers, schools, museums, organizations seeking to improve their image and content of First Nations peoples, and serves on several boards. Her publications have received several awards like the Independent Publishers Gold Moonbeam; Silver Ippy; National Arab American Museum's Best Children's Book of the Year; Bank Street College Best Children's Books of the Year; CCBC Choice; and IRA Notable Book for a Global Society. Dennis has been an advocate/educator for Native youth (Native American Education Program) and founder/director of Nitchen, an advocacy organization for Indigenous families. In 2020, Dennis was presented a Lifetime Achievement Award for her service to the Native community from the Tomaquag Museum.

Arlene Hirschfelder (1943–2021): In deepest gratitude and with love, we dedicate *Indigenous Firsts: A History of Native Achievements* to Arlene Hirschfelder, our sister-friend, mentor, adventure partner, collaborator, co-facilitator, and co-author. Arlene has been a stellar example of how to be an ally for Indigenous people. Throughout her lifetime, she advocated for Native people to be represented fairly, equally, accurately, and inclusively. Her legacy and struggles will continue through her books, papers, and all the people she influenced and guided to have a better understanding of Native cultures and civil rights. Arlene's thoughts and research are very much a part of this book, and we will miss her forever.

Paulette F. Molin, a citizen of the Minnesota Chippewa Tribe from White Earth, is an award-winning author and curator. Her writings include *The Encyclopedia of Native American Religions* and *The Extraordinary Book of Native American Lists*, both authored with Arlene Hirschfelder, as well as *American Indian Themes in Young Adult Literature.* She and Hirschfelder also co-curated exhibits such as *Contemporary Native Women Opening Doors to Change* at the Mitchell Museum of the American Indian. She lives in Hampton, Virginia, where she has served as an educator and completed writings and curatorial work on boarding school history.

Indigenous Firsts

A History of Native American Achievements and Events

Yvonne Wakim Dennis ◆ Arlene Hirschfelder ◆ Paulette F. Molin

INDIGENOUS FIRSTS

A History of Native American Achievements and Events

Visible Ink Press®
43311 Joy Rd., #414
Canton, MI 48187-2075

Visible Ink Press is a registered trademark of Visible Ink Press LLC.

Most Visible Ink Press books are available at special quantity discounts when purchased in bulk by corporations, organizations, or groups. Customized printings, special imprints, messages, and excerpts can be produced to meet your needs. For more information, contact Special Markets Director, Visible Ink Press, www.visibleink.com, or 734-667-3211.

Managing Editor: Kevin S. Hile
Art Director: Cinelli Design
Cover Design: John Gouin
Typesetting: Marco Divita
Proofreaders: Larry Baker and Shoshana Hurwitz
Indexer: Shoshana Hurwitz

Cover images: Billy Frank (Wikicommons), Nadine Caron (University of the Fraser Valley), Jim Thorpe (Wikicommons), Nancy B. Jackson (Science History Institute), Anneliese Satz (U.S. Marine Corps), Robbie Robertson (KingKongPhotos/www.celebrity-photos.com), Maria Tallchief (Dance Magazine), Ben Nighthorse Campbell (U.S. Congress), Camille Seaman (Camille Seaman), Queen Lili'uokalani (Wikicommons), John Bennett Harrington (NASA).

Cataloging-in-Publication Data is on file at the Library of Congress.

ISBN (paperback): 978-1-57859-712-3
ISBN (library hardback): 978-1-57859-807-6
ISBN (ebook): 978-1-57859-806-9

10 9 8 7 6 5 4 3 2 1

Printed in the United States of America.

CONTENTS

PHOTO SOURCES

AbsconditumEtIncognitum (Wikicommons): p. 32.

Ahsaki: p. 147.

Akta Lakota Museum & Cultural Center: p. 107.

Alaska State Library, Historical Collection: p. 238.

Alaska State Senate: p. 305.

AMD, Inc.: p. 44 (bottom).

American Anthropologist: p. 348 (bottom).

Ammodramus (Wikicommons): p. 348 (top).

The Architect of the Capitol (www.aoc.gov): p. 245.

Arizona Republic: p. 304 (middle).

Associated Press: p. 396.

ASU Department of English: p. 113 (bottom).

Aurora Observer: p. 227.

David Benbennick: p. 129.

b-matsunaga9758 (Wikicommons): p. 163 (top).

Julia Keen Bloomfield: p. 332 (top).

Bowers Museum: p. 83.

Romain Bréget: p. 281.

British Library: p. 403.

Bwark (Wikicommons): p. 315.

CeeX (Wikicommons): p. 398 (bottom).

Cherokee Phoenix: p. 10.

Gert Chesi: p. 44 (top).

Chocktawnation.com: p. 259.

Christophe95 (Wikicommons): p. 398 (top).

College Football Hall of Fame: p. 386.

Crimsonedge34 (Wikicommons): p. 40 (top).

Daderot (Wikicommons): p. 67.

DAVilla (Wikicommons): p. 20.

Mark Dayton: p. 214 (bottom).

Ada Deer: p. 200.

Jacob Deitchler: p. 410.

Yvonne Wakim Dennis: pp. 39, 100 (middle), 142, 400.

Herman Derman: p. 26.

Djembayz (Wikicommons): p. 155.

Dr vin7201 (Wikicommons): p. 185.

Dschwen (Wikicommons): p. 205 (middle).

DThompson1313 (Wikicommons): p. 146.

Eclectek (Wikicommons): p. 197.

The Eloquent Patient (Wikicommons): p. 172.

Fort Worth Public Library Archives: p. 41 (bottom).

Bernard Gagnon: p. 327 (top).

Lisa Gansky: p. 389 (top).

Gen. Quon (Wikicommons): p. 279.

George Grantham Bain Collection, Library of Congress: p. 51.

Getty Images: p. 395 (top).

Gillfoto (Wikicommons): p. 334.

Greatness21 (Wikicommons): p. 406.

GualdimG (Wikicommons): p. 280.

Dan Harasymchuk: pp. 100 (bottom), 118.

Hasselblad500CM (Wikicommons): p. 328.

Hawaii State Archives: p. 98 (bottom).

Hawaii Journal of History: p. 191 (top).

HazteOir.org: p. 338.

Heritage Auctions: p. 395 (bottom).

HHSgov (Wikicommons): p. 356.

Carol Highsmith: p. 282.

Historic American Buildings Survey: p. 79.

Idahomiller (Wikicommons): p. 103 (bottom).

Instituto Nacional de Antropología e Historia: p. 40 (bottom).

J. Paul Getty Museum: p. 327 (bottom).

Jackalopearts.org: p. 198 (bottom).

Johnmaxmena2 (Wikicommons): p. 390.

Jon698 (Wikicommons): p. 212 (top).

Lehua Kane: p. 239 (bottom).

D. B. King: p. 65.

KingKongPhoto & www.celebrity-photos.com: p. 43 (top).

Patar Knight: p. 176.

Kurtwfan13: p. 212 (bottom).

Irma-Estel LaGuerre: p. 38.

Lakeland PBS: p. 214 (middle).

Ldleman2008: p. 204 (bottom).

The Leader-Post (Saskatchewan, Canada): p. 262.

Library and Archives Canada: pp. 37, 95.

Library of Congress: pp. 17, 42 (second and third from top), 50, 97 (bottom), 132, 174, 192 (top and bottom).

Library of Congress Life: p. 113 (top).

Littlecarls (Wikicommons): p. 302.

Donna M. Loring/Jane Peasley: p. 213.

Los Alamos National Laboratory: p. 183 (bottom).

"The Mala Collection," University of Alaska, Anchorage: p. 4 (top).

Marinainusa (Wikicommons): p. 186.

McGhiever (Wikicommons): p. 330 (top).

Jim McIntosh: p. 244.

Metropolitan Museum of Art, New York City: pp. 74, 84.

Military Sealift Command: p. 267 (top and bottom).

Minnesota Senate: p. 214 (top).

Montanabw (Wikicommons): p. 31.

Ray Montgomery: p. 387 (bottom).

Larry D. Moore: p. 97 (top).

Michi Moore: p. 204 (top).

MT Education Advocate: p. 170.

Murray State College: p. 203 (bottom).

Musical Courier: p. 41 (third from top).

Naa (Wikicommons): p. 397 (bottom).

Narademo.umiacs.umd.edu: p. 199.

NASA: pp. 375 (top), 377.

National Anthropological Archives, Smithsonian Institution: p. 41 (top).

National Endowment for the Arts: p. 82 (bottom).

National Marine Sanctuaries: p. 183 (top).

National Museum of the American Indian: p. 82 (top).

National Photo Company Collection: p. 278.

National Portrait Gallery (U.S.): pp. 41 (second from top), 93.

Native Truth (Wikicommons): p. 111 (top).

Navajo Nation Zoological and Botanical Park: p. 309.

Navajoindian (Wikicommons): p. 295.

Nebraska State Historical Society La Flesche Collection: p. 103 (top).

Erik Neills: p. 116.

Donna J. Nelson: p. 184.

New York Herald-Tribune: p. 419.

New York World-Telegram and Sun: p. 33.

Ser Amantio di Nicolao: p. 47.

Obamawhitehouse.archives.gov: p. 196.

Office of Greg Stanton, United States Congress: p. 173.

Office of the United States President, Barack Obama: p. 304 (bottom).

Oklahoma Historical Society: p. 330 (bottom).

Oklahoma State University Library: p. 337.

Oregon Historical Society: p. 399 (bottom).

Parabluemedic (Wikicommons): p. 21.

Paramount Records: p. 42 (top).

Michael Perrin: p. 253.

Pete for America: p. 135.

John Phelan: p. 233.

Photoplay: p. 42 (bottom).

Radioboy14 (Wikicommons): p. 218 (bottom).

Ravenstrick (Wikicommons): p. 412.

Rmajzels (Wikicommons): p. 111 (bottom).

Rupaul Dragcon: p. 52.

Salish Kootenai College: p. 188.

San Francisco Public Library: p. 112.

Lisa Savage: p. 300.

Camille Seaman: p. 80.

Andrew Scheer: p. 128.

Science History Institute: p. 378.

Seattle Municipal Archives: p. 432.

Senate Democrats: p. 388.

Shakespeare (Wikicommons): p. 430.

Lorie Shaull: p. 205 (top).

Shutterstock: pp. 6, 9, 22, 36, 43 (middle and bottom), 48, 56, 59, 61, 122, 126, 127, 144, 237, 239 (top), 241, 242, 243, 306, 345 (top and bottom), 382, 399 (top), 404, 418, 422.

Preston Singletary: p. 69.

Gage Skidmore: pp. 218 (top), 221.

Martin Cruz Smith: p. 108.

Smontooth (Wikicommons): p. 424.

St. Louis World's Fair Album: p. 383.

State Archives of Florida, Florida Memory: p. 296.

Gelvin Stevenson: p. 139.

Sarah Stierch: p. 78.

Jamescita Peshlakai: p. 210.

Peter Stockdale: p. 5.

Technical World Magazine: p. 3.

ThisIsIndianCountry (Wikicommons): p. 313.

Aaron Thomas: p. 143.

Tiddled (Wikicommons): p. 218 (middle).

Toronto Maple Leaves: p. 389 (bottom).

Marty Two Bulls: p. 2.

UCLA Library Special Collection: p. 4 (bottom).

Phil Uhl: p. 391.

University of the Fraser Valley: p. 355.

U.S. Air Force: p. 252 (bottom), 261.

U.S. Army: pp. 269, 270, 271 (bottom), 298.

U.S. Army Institute of Heraldry: p. 276 (bottom).

U.S. Army National Guard: p. 268.

U.S. Bureau of Indian Affairs: p. 264.

U.S. Congress: pp. 193, 195, 409.

U.S. Department of Agriculture: p. 231.

U.S. Department of the Interior: pp. 189, 201 (top).

U.S. Department of Transportation: p. 86.

U.S. Embassy Canada: p. 397 (top).

U.S. Embassy London: p. 387 (top).

U.S. Government: pp. 201 (bottom), 414.

U.S. House Office of Photography: p. 194 (top and bottom).

U.S. Marine Corps: p. 274 (top).

U.S. Mint: p. 265.

U.S. National Archives and Records Administration: pp. 260, 276 (top), 303, 321, 323 (top).

U.S. National Guard: p. 274 (bottom).

U.S. National Library of Medicine: p. 13.

U.S. Navy: p. 252 (top).

U.S. Office of War Information: p. 263.

U.S. War Department: p. 271 (top).

Uyvsdi (Wikicommons): pp. 63, 100 (top), 138.

Vintagecardprices.com: p. 381.

Ansgar Walk: p. 70.

The White House: pp. 205 (bottom), 284, 373.

White House Photo Office Collection (Nixon Administration): p. 307.

White House Television: p. 297.

G. B. Wittick: p. 71.

Womeninwisconsin.org: p. 169.

YouTube.com: pp. 203 (top), 379.

Stephen Zeigler: p. 228.

Public domain: pp. 19, 45, 49, 73, 87, 94, 98 (top), 106, 157, 160, 163 (bottom), 166, 191 (bottom), 198 (top), 255 (top and bottom), 256, 304 (top), 320, 323 (bottom), 326 (top and bottom), 329 (top and bottom), 332 (bottom), 349, 375 (bottom).

ACKNOWLEDGMENTS

Yvonne Wakim Dennis: I am deeply grateful to all the people who granted me interviews, helped check facts, and allowed us to use their photographs. Special thanks to Tom Giago, Nadema Agard, Beverly Singer, Marty Two Bulls, Kris Easton, Mike Mabin, Ahsaki Báá LaFrance-Chachere, Chip Thomas, Tlisza Jaurique, Irma Laguerre, Lorén Spears, Mike DeMunn, Mary and James Fraser, Marty Montano, Paul Deo, the Big Crow family, Martha Berry and Camille Seaman. Gratitude to Paulette Fairbanks Molin for being a fabulous coauthor; Dennis Hirschfelder for being such a loving caretaker of our coauthor, Arlene; Roger Jänecke for letting me speak the truth, and to Kevin Hile for putting it all together.

Paulette F. Molin: Many thanks to all those who helped with this project. Your generosity is beyond measure. With appreciation to Yvonne Wakim Dennis for inviting me to join her and Arlene as a coauthor; also to Dennis Hirschfelder for his ongoing friendship and support. Thank you to Roger Jänecke and Kevin Hile at Visible Ink Press for their many contributions and editing work. With appreciation to everyone who responded to questions concerning "firsts," including individuals at agencies, libraries, and other organizations, and for their help maneuvering around restrictions stemming from Covid-19 shutdowns. Thank you, too, to all those who answered queries via email and phone and helped with information as well as photographs (Larry, Jacob, Racheal, and Jason among them). I am especially grateful to family (and friends who are family), past and present, including my siblings, nieces, and nephews (too many to list without leaving someone out), and other relatives. Many thanks to Larry Molin for his daily love and support; also to Todd and the rest of the Molin family. With heartfelt appreciation, too, to all the lives represented in this work.

DEDICATION

We dedicate this book to our coauthor, sister-friend, and ally, Arlene Hirschfelder (1943–2021). A lifelong educator, respected scholar, activist, award-winning author, and champion of Native American and children's rights, Arlene wrote and edited almost 100 nonfiction books and curricula and curated museum exhibitions. For more than two decades, Arlene was the scholarship director and education consultant for the Association on American Indian Affairs; her research was integral in the creation and passing of the 1978 Indian Child Welfare Act. She was key in debunking stereotypes and inaccurate information locally and nationally and was considered a fearless and compassionate advocate in Indian country, sometimes called upon to be an expert witness for Native American tribes and organizations challenging institutional racism.

Arlene was key in helping a vast array of institutions, agencies, and corporations improve their portrayal, awareness, and presentation of Indigenous peoples. She served as consultant, lecturer, teacher trainer, curriculum developer, and workshop facilitator for institutions like the National Museum of the American Indian, Nitchen, Inc., Fordham University, Aquinnah Cultural Center, New York City Department of Education, New York City Mental Health Department, various tribal nations, and many other education and cultural establishments. For several years, Arlene was a faculty member at the New School for Social Research, where she taught contemporary Native American literature.

An ally and mentor to many, Arlene championed Native American writers, enabling several to break into the publishing industry. Among those whom she chose as writing partners were Dr. Paulette Fairbanks Molin for this book as well as *The Extraordinary Book of Native American Lists* and other publications, Dr. Beverly Singer (Tewa/Navajo) for *Rising Voices*, and Yvonne Wakim Dennis (Cherokee/Sand Hill/Syrian) for this book, other VIP publications, children's books for Charlesbridge and Chicago Review Press publishers, and other publications.

An ardent supporter of justice for children, Arlene Hirschelder was the founding editor of Rowman and Littlefield's award-winning series "It Happened to Me," which includes almost 50 books for teenagers, helping them find answers to life's most difficult questions related to social issues, health matters, and lifestyles. She chronicled the arduous journey of the little-known Sephardic Jewish photographer, Solomon Nunes Carvalho, on the 1853 western expedition of Colonel John Charles Frémont. The book, *Photo Odyssey: Solomon Carvalho's Remarkable Western Adventure 1853–54,* was the basis of the award-winning documentary film *Carvalho's Journey,* directed by Steve Rivo. The Hirschfelder–Molin Stereotype Collection is one of the largest of its kind and is housed at the Sequoyah National Research Center at the University of Arkansas at Little Rock. The collection illustrates the racist and inaccurate representation of Indigenous peoples in children's toys, books, and games for almost a century.

Arlene's thoughts and research are very much a part of *Indigenous Firsts: A History of Native American Achievement and Events,* and we are heartbroken that she is not around to see the finished product. We are honored to be part of her legacy and miss her every day. In deepest gratitude and with love, we dedicate this book to Arlene Hirschfelder.

INTRODUCTION

"People often like to describe Native people as invisible. We're not invisible. If you look for us, we're here. We have our own tribal governments, our own constitutions, our own police departments, our own land, our own hospitals, our own treaties with the United States, and so on. We have a rich and vibrant culture...." —Jodi Rave Spotted Bear (Mandan, Hidatsa and Minneconjou Lakota), Director of The Indigenous Media Freedom Alliance

Consider that there are 574 federally recognized tribal nations in the United States, including 347 within the contiguous 48 states and 227 within the state of Alaska as published in the Federal Register on January 28, 2022. These tribal nations each have government-to-government relationships with the United States. There are also state-recognized tribes as well as those who are without either federal or state recognition. Although our emphasis is on Native people in the United States, including Native Hawaiians, we have also added a number of First Nations entries to this book. According to the Crown-Indigenous Relations and Northern Affairs Canada, the Canadian Constitution recognizes three Aboriginal groups: Indians (generally referred to as First Nations), Inuit, and Métis. This agency cites more than 630 First Nation communities in Canada representing more than 50 Nations and 50 Indigenous languages. Adding to the richness and complexity, some Indigenous peoples whose traditional homelands may be traced to other parts of the Americas, are now U.S. citizens.

This book focuses on selected Indigenous firsts, organized into fourteen chapters, in fields such as art, business, government, health, literature, media, military, religion, science, urban life, and sports. We include firsts that extend beyond individuals to tribal nations, businesses, organizations, legislative acts, teams, and more. Readers will find individual achievements but also events associated with wartime service, the Covid-19 pandemic, and tribal government. We drew from sources such as almanacs, biographies, chronologies, journals, memoirs, newspapers, interviews, and websites. We also include quotes from Indigenous people to introduce or supplement chapters and sections. Some firsts are well documented and well publicized, others are not. Some are lost to history, others go unheralded. Not every first could be included, given the number and range.

Sometimes we found individuals repeatedly cited as firsts, but the information turned out to be inaccurate. In a number of cases, we included more than one person as first, especially in fields with few Native individuals represented. Father Philip B. Gordon (Ojibwe) comes to mind. Identified as the second Native American to become a Catholic priest in the United States, he was the first from his tribal nation to be ordained to the priesthood. He also served as the only Native Catholic priest in the country for many years. The same is true of early medical doctors and other health practitioners. We also included selected founders of organizations, businesses, and various initiatives. Many individuals have multiple firsts, including some in more than one field. Others continue to achieve groundbreaking accomplishments.

When possible, we noted reflections by individuals concerning their experiences. "I'm often asked what it feels like to be the first female First Nations graduate from UBC School of Medicine, and that means a lot," Dr. Nadine Caron (Sagamok Anishnawbe) commented. "I was the first not because I was special, but because of where we are as a society in Canada." The same could be said for the United States. Dr. Caron's comments help shed light on perspectives often missing in discussions of "firsts." In 2017, she gave a TEDxUNBC talk, "The Other Side of 'Being First,'" raising a number of important questions. While being first is an individual achievement that should be celebrated, she notes, what about the responsibility of society? Why was there never a first before?

Why, indeed? We know, for example, that it took from 1849 to 2021 for the first Native American to become Secretary of the U.S. Department of the Interior (DOI), actually even longer when reaching back to earlier cabinets established in 1789.

The impact of that immense gap in time is hugely consequential for Native Americans. When she was nominated to head the DOI, Congresswoman Deb Haaland (Pueblo of Laguna) commented: "This moment is profound when we consider the fact that a former secretary of the interior once proclaimed his goal to 'civilize or exterminate' us. I'm a living testament to the failure of that horrific ideology. I also stand on the shoulders of my ancestors and all the people who have sacrificed so that I can be here." The DOI is highly significant as the primary federal agency charged with carrying out the U.S. trust responsibility to American Indians and Alaska Natives as well as other critical roles, including managing public lands and natural resources.

In another example, in 2009, 308 years after Yale University's founding as Collegiate College, award-winning historian Dr. Ned Blackhawk (Western Shoshone) became the first tenured Native American professor at the school. Gabriella Blatt (Chippewa Cree), a student at Yale, wrote an article published in *The Yale Herald* in 2019, "Why Do None of My Professors Look Like Me?" Besides her title question, Blatt asks: "What does it mean to be the only Native your university thinks is doing work worthy of Yale tenure? How does it feel when you're often the only Native voice in faculty meetings? Further, how does it feel to know that the Native students you teach have only one tenured Native professor at their university?" The same questions could be asked of any number of other institutions, including those with huge endowments and located on lands seized from Indigenous people.

Raquel Montoya-Lewis (Pueblo of Isleta), the first Native American to serve on the Washington Supreme Court, commented to a reporter that she expected some people would think that she was appointed to the office because of her heritage. "People have said that about my successes since I was in high school," she stated. As Judge Montoya-Lewis pointed out, "My record says otherwise." Her record includes serving as chief judge for the Nooksack and Skagit tribes, winning election and reelection on the Whatcom County Superior Court, and serving as an associate professor. Other individuals noted similar experiences of having their qualifications questioned or undermined, even when they were clearly overqualified.

What needs to be examined includes the length of time it took Indigenous people to be represented, what prevented them from having seats at the table, and the resulting impact on individuals, families, communities, and nations. It also means scrutinizing the paths individuals followed and what their experiences were once they became firsts. Dr. Susan La Flesche Picotte (Omaha), the first Native American woman to become a medical doctor, had to overcome obstacles of both race and gender. The arduous conditions under which she worked to provide care to those in need ultimately undermined her own health and wellbeing.

A number of individuals do not speak of their own accomplishments. As Karen Gayton Swisher and AnCita Benally point out in their 1998 book, *Native North American Firsts*: "We must also consider that in many indigenous cultures, humility is a value that is strictly adhered to, so it is inappropriate for individuals to speak of, or bring attention to, her/his deeds or accomplishments." Consistent with that, the *New York Times* reported that Carol J. Gallagher (Cherokee Nation), first Native American female bishop of a major Christian church, "seemed hesitant to speak much about being a first. 'There aren't a whole lot of "I" statements in the Indian community,' she said." Dr. Kona Williams (Cree/Mohawk), another first, commented: "I don't want to be the only First Nations forensic pathologist in 10 years." She mentors young Indigenous students to travel on her journey with her and pursue the arduous training required in her chosen field.

A number of firsts come with loneliness, sacrifice, perseverance, and bravery in the face of racist taunts, isolation, obstacles, imposter syndrome, limitations, trauma, and/or being treated as "other" or undeserving of place. As Dr. Caron points out, in terms of achievement, the first must not be the last. Instead, she says, "We need to focus on increasing the numbers" and representation. We must also fight for firsts yet to come. Our hope is that this book will help in that effort.

We also hope to put to rest the belief that the only firsts that matter are those that impact or improve the dominant society. In this book, you will discover contributions that Indigenous people continue to make to their own communities, to their professions, to their callings, or to their art. We have also chronicled some "first" events that put into motion systemic racism, land loss, and continuing brutality and destruction.

Indigenous Firsts: A History of Native American Achievements and Events

Organizing the material was challenging and some entries could have fit into more than one category. "Arts" was such an immense subject that we broke it up into five chapters and we incorporate public art, such as murals, into the section "Indigenous Spaces and Public Places." It was important to us to include relationships among and within tribal nations, which are featured in "Sovereignty, Land and the Environment." Since most Native people reside in cities, there is also a chapter on "Urban Life."

MEDIA ARTS

"Since the founding of America, just the word 'founding' is superficial to Native Americans because we were already here. We didn't need to be found. We never had a voice in the nation's media. We had no place to express our opinions because most of the media did not want to hear our opinions because they often found it disagreeable. I started my own newspaper to offer a forum for Native American voices. Soon I found that some of the great writers were Native American and the process of educating my readers began. We addressed the racism that so many South Dakotans failed to recognize. When we found out Indians were being charged higher interest rates at the local banks, we wrote about it and the Justice Department came to South Dakota and brought it to a halt. We addressed the profiling of Natives by the Highway Patrol and local police departments. And by our very presence, we forced the state's media to emulate us and start addressing issues important to Native Americans."

—*Tim Giago, editor,* Native Sun News Today

CARTOONS/COMICS

"My work was published in the *Washington Post, L.A. Times,* and *Chicago Tribune* in the late 1980s and I'm nationally syndicated through Universal Press syndicate, but I would never be so presumptuous to say. I'm the 'first.' That distinction goes to a female Native (Taos Pueblo), Eva Mirabal, a cartoonist who created *GI Gertie* that was syndicated in the *Stars and Stripes* newspaper, during World War II. In reality we Native cartoonists stand upon the shoulders of the Native artists who came before us—they struggled through poverty and racism; they deserve any credit for being the 'first.'"

—*Marty Two Bulls, Oglala Sioux artist*

Indigenous Firsts: A History of Native American Achievements and Events

1943: Eva Mirabal (Eah Ha Wa, Green Corn, or Fast Growing Corn) (1920–1968), Taos Pueblo, was commissioned to create a comic strip for the Corps newsletter after enlisting in the Women's Army Corps (WAC). Her strip, *G.I. Gertie,* was the first to be written from a woman's perspective, and Mirabal is credited with being the first female Native American cartoonist. Mirabal was commissioned to create military posters advertising war bonds, murals, and other artwork during her military service.

1994: Sam Campos, Native Hawaiian, developed the Hawaiian superhero Pineapple Man. Isamu Pahoa, a young Hawaiian man who turned to a life of crime, is Pineapple Man's secret identity. After a near-fatal attack, Pahoa is metamorphosed into Kukailimoku, having both superhuman strength and agility. Learning to control his newfound powers, he grudgingly decides to use them for good and takes on the alter ego of Pineapple Man due to his pineapple-like appearance. The series ran four successful issues, locally outselling Batman and X-Men comics, becoming the first Native Hawaiian superhero series. Campos, a successful Hollywood film graphic artist, returned to his Native Hawaii to develop *Dragonfly,* a supernatural martial arts series set in Hawaii. His work combines action movies, Native Hawaiian tradition, the inclusivity of Hawaii's multicultural customs, and science fiction.

1996: Writer Jon Santaanta Proudstar (1967–), Yaqui, and artist Ryan Huna Smith (1967–), Chemehuevi/Navajo, published *Tribal Force,* the first comic book to present a team of Native American superheroes. The comics present five people whose superpowers were granted by Thunderbird to protect native lands from a powerful, high-tech government.

2006: Ricardo Caté (1964–), Kewa, became the first Native to publish cartoons regularly

in the *Santa Fe New Mexican,* dubbed the "oldest newspaper in the West." He continues to contribute the daily cartoon *Without Reservations* in the *Taos News* as well and pokes fun at serious subjects that make people laugh and then think. *Without Reservations* is also the name of his book featuring his cartoons. In 2020, Caté was named New Mexico's reigning clown prince of COVID-19 awareness and worked with the New Mexico Department of Health to develop a humorous brochure and TV campaign to get out the word. One of his most memorable images was of his character "Chief" in a face mask with the motto: "Face mask or face fine!"

2011: Marty Two Bulls Sr., Oglala Lakota, political cartoonist, was the first Native recipient of the Society of Professional Journalists' Sigma Delta Chi Award for Editorial Cartooning. The nationally recognized artist is known for his distinctive and sharp-witted political cartoons that highlight issues in contemporary Native America. Two Bulls took the prize for his portrayal of the United

A political cartoon by Marty Two Bulls illustrates the power of his political commentary.

Nations Declaration on the Rights of Indigenous Peoples. His art has been published internationally in newspapers and magazines and is syndicated through Universal Press syndicate (https://www.gocomics.com/m2bulls). Two Bulls served as graphic editor for South Dakota's two largest daily newspapers, the *Rapid City Journal* and the *Sioux Falls Argus Leader*. He was a 2021 Pulitzer Prize finalist for editorial cartooning, the first time an Indigenous person was selected.

James Young Deer

2014: Tatum Begay (1990–), Navajo, started *The Pretty Okay Adventures of Tatum*, a webcomic series that has attracted thousands of views. She has also self-published comics, including *Nanaba's Summer* (2016) and *Spiral* with Damon Begay (2017).

FILM

"I create media that connects American Indian people with each other, to reduce the noise, to get back to inherent values and practices that keep people belonging to a community, locally and globally, as full partners in what is the creative economy at this moment in history."

—Dr. Beverly Singer, Tewa/Diné, from November 10, 2010, presentation for Grand Valley State University American Indian Heritage Month series

1909: James Young Deer (1876–1946), Winnebago, was the first Native man to act in a film. He appeared in *The Mended Lute* and *The True Heart of an Indian*. He was married to actress Lillian St. Cyr, Winnebago, known on stage as Princess Red Wing, and the two appeared together in *The Yaqui Girl* (1911).

1911: Native activists expressed their disapproval of the inaccurate portrayal of Native Americans in the film and entertainment industry. They took their concerns to Bureau of Indian Affairs (BIA) commissioner Robert G. Valentine, who promised to assist in eliminating racist presentations of Indians as well as the film industry's practice of casting non-Indians in Native roles. It was the first time Natives collectively protested the entertainment business. In 1914, Native actors threatened to strike if the motion picture companies did not improve their stereotypic presentations. In 1979, the American Indian Theatre Guild reported that little had changed since those first protests. Native peoples were still being represented in an inaccurate and racist way, and non-Native actors were still being cast in Native roles. And in 2015, actor Loren Anthony, Diné, and eight others quit the production of Adam Sandler's Netflix project *The Ridiculous 6* after producers ignored their concerns over the film's portrayal of Apache culture.

1912: For the first time, a large number of Native people were employed by the film industry. The Bison-10 Motion Picture Co. got permission from the U.S. government to transport Oglala Sioux from Pine Ridge, South Dakota, to a film studio in the Santa Monica Mountains of California. For three years, the group acted in more than 80 westerns.

1913: Lillian St. Cyr (1873–1974), Winnebago, whose stage name was Princess Red Wing, starred in Cecil B. DeMille's film *Squaw Man*, Hollywood's first full-length feature film.

1926: Chief Yowlachie (born Daniel Simmons; 1891–1966), Yakama, was the first Native film actor to portray a non-Native.

He was cast as a Chinese man in *Tell It to the Marines*.

1932: Ray Mala (born Ray Agnaqsiaq Wise; 1906–1952) became the first Inupiaq—and first Alaska Native—lead actor in Hollywood. He starred in the film *Igloo* for Universal Pictures.

Ray Mala

1966: The first documentaries produced by Native people about Native people were part of an experiment by Professors Sol Worth and John Adair and their student Richard Chalfen. The trio traveled to Pine Springs, Arizona, and gave 16mm cameras to interested Navajo to make films based on their culture. Participants were Mike Anderson, Al Clah, Susie Benally, Johnny Nelson, Mary Jane Tsosie, Maxine Tsosie, and later Benally's mother, Alta Kahn. The film series is known as *Navajo Film Themselves*, and it became world renowned, as did the researchers. The burgeoning documentarians covered several aspects of Native life, and for the first time, Native people were totally in charge of the complete filming process. In 1972, the researchers published *Through Navajo Eyes*, which has become a cornerstone textbook for teaching visual anthropology.

Sacheen Littlefeather

1970: "Chief" Dan George (1899–1981), Squamish, was nominated for a Best Supporting Actor Academy Award for his role in *Little Big Man*. He was the first known Native American to be nominated.

1973: Sacheen Littlefeather (1946–), White Mountain Apache/Yaqui actress and activist for Native American rights, represented Marlon Brando at the 45th Academy Awards. On his behalf, she declined the Best Actor Oscar for *The Godfather* in a speech protesting Hollywood's racist portrayal of American Indians and the media industry's blackout of events at Wounded Knee. At the time, Oglala and AIM activists were occupying the town of Wounded Knee, on the Pine Ridge Indian Reservation in South Dakota. They were trying to bring attention to the corrupt reservation police force, the deplorable living conditions on the reservation, and the abrogation of treaty rights. For 71 days, the protesters were besieged by the National Guard and the FBI. Wounded Knee was also the site of the 1890 massacre of nearly 300 Lakota people by soldiers of the U.S. Army. Although the occupation was a call to the dominant culture to resolve past and present injustices, the gravity of the situation was underreported. But Brando used his position to gain access to Americans via the Oscars, one of the most watched events on television. The audience's response to Brando's boycotting was divided between jeers and applause, but the incident resulted in more news coverage of the Wounded Knee protests as well as a new ruling by the Academy of Motion Picture Arts and Sciences banning future proxy acceptance of Academy Awards. Littlefeather's bravery has long been an inspiration for others who criticize the media for racist and sexist policies and practices. Coretta Scott King called Littlefeather to thank her for the speech. In 2014, the 87th ceremony of the Academy Awards drew criticism for lack of inclusivity in nominations; actress Jada Pinkett Smith boycotted the ceremony, citing Littlefeather as her inspiration to do so.

1980: It is thought that Bob Hicks (1924–2014), Creek/Seminole of Oklahoma, was the first Native American to graduate from the American Film Institute. He was cofounder and first president of First Americans in the Arts, an organization honoring Native American filmmakers.

1980: George Burdeau (1944–), Blackfeet Nation, was the first Native American director to belong to the Director's Guild of America. He was a founding board member of the Native American Public Broadcasting Consortium, known today as Native American Public Telecommunications. Burdeau received an Emmy Award for *The Native Americans* and a Peabody Award along with Diane Reyna, Taos/San Juan Pueblos, for *Surviving Columbus*.

1982: Singer/songwriter Buffy Sainte-Marie (1941–), Cree, won an Academy Award for Best Original Song, "Up Where We Belong," from *An Officer and a Gentleman*. She is the first known Native American to win an Oscar.

1991: Norman Patrick Brown (c. 1990–) was the first Navajo to write and direct a film, *Awakening*, which is entirely in the Navajo language. "I'm not going after Hollywood," he said in an interview. "My audience is my elders. If I can make Grandma smile, it's worth it to me."

Buffy Sainte-Marie

1992: The first major international platform of Indigenous American cinema was held in Munich, Germany, at the Tenth Annual Munich Filmfest. Films included *Surviving Columbus* (directed by Diane Reyna, Taos Pueblo), *Wiping the Tears of Seven Generations* (directed by Fidel Moreno, Huichol/Chichimica), and *Itam Hakim Hopiit* (directed by Victor Masayesva Jr., Hopi).

1996: *Grand Avenue,* a two-part mini-series, was HBO's first-ever production about Native people set in contemporary times. Based on the collection of short stories by Gregory Sarris (1952–), Federated Indians of Graton Rancheria, *Grand Avenue* is a real place located in the South Park district of Santa Ana, California, and the stories are based on Sarris's own life. Sarris served as coexecutive producer, and it was shot entirely on location in Santa Rosa, not far from where Sarris grew up. The stellar cast of *Grand Avenue* included Sheila Tousey, Menominee; Tantoo Cardinal, Cree/Métis; A Martinez, Apache/Piegan Blackfeet/Mexican; August Schellenberg, Mohawk/Swiss-German; and Zahn Tokiya-ku McClarnon, Hunkpapa Lakota. *Grand Avenue* was awarded the Best Picture at the 1996 American Indian Film Festival.

1997: *Naturally Native*, the first motion picture starring and written, directed, and produced by Native women, was also the first film financed by a Native nation. The Mashantucket Pequot Tribal Nation of Connecticut worked with writer/director Valerie Red-Horse (1959–), Cherokee, to bring the contemporary drama to the screen. The storyline follows three sisters in their quest to start a natural skincare line based on old remedies handed down in their family. They are met with racism and sexism but are victorious and do it all with humor, feistiness, and grace. The stellar cast included Irene Bedard, Inupiat/French Canadian/Cree/Métis; Valerie Red-Horse; Yvonne Russo, Sicangu Lakota; Mary Kay Place; Max Gail; Floyd Red Crow Westerman, Dakota; and Pato Hoffmann, Aymara/Quechua. Naturally Native products were real and offered at the same time the movie premiered.

1998: *Smoke Signals* premiered and was the first major feature film to be written, directed, coproduced, and acted by American Indians with a mainstream distributor. It was directed by Chris Eyre (1968–), Cheyenne/Arapaho, and based on the book *The Lone*

Ranger and Tonto Fistfight in Heaven (1993), by Sherman Alexie (1966–), Spokane/Coeur d'Alene. The all-star cast includes Adam Beach Anishinaabe; Evan Adams, Coast Salish; Irene Bedard, Inuit/Cree; Gary Farmer, Cayuga; Tantoo Cardinal, Cree/Métis; Elaine Miles, Cayuse/Nez Perce; and John Trudell, Santee Dakota. The film took many awards, including the Sundance Filmmakers Trophy and Audience Awards and Best Film honors at the American Indian Film Festival.

2000: Joanelle Romero (1957–), Apache/Cheyenne/Sephardic Jewish, is an award-winning director and producer of film, television, and new media. To date, she has been the only North American Native director, producer, and writer shortlisted for an Academy Award by the Documentary Branch for her award-winning film *American Holocaust: When It's All Over I'll Still Be Indian,* the documentary that addresses the American Indian and the Jewish Holocausts. In 1995 Romero founded the Red Nation Celebration Institute (RNCI), which hosts the Red Nation International Film Festival held annually in Los Angeles, California. In 2006 Romero launched Red Nation TV as the world's first online streaming company. The service offers several genres of programming through Native- and non-Native-produced and -themed original shows for both adults and families, including hundreds of documentaries and feature films, drama series, film festivals, award shows, sports, trending news, comedy specials, the first Native women's talk show, music videos, and Native fashion shows. Red Nation TV portrays lifestyles and cultures of Native American and Indigenous peoples from around the world.

Joanelle Romero

2000: Filmmaker and stage and screen actor Gary Farmer (1953–), Cayuga, was the first recipient of the Bernie Whitebear Community Service award for his work in Native cinema and media. He also won the Taos Mountain Award (2001) given by the Taos Talking Pictures Film Festival to an outstanding Indigenous film professional.

2001: *Atanarjuat/The Fast Runner* was the first Native language feature film produced entirely in Inuktitut. The Canadian film was written and directed by Zacharias Kunuk (1957–), Inuk, and featured an Inuit cast. The film won the Caméra d'Or (Golden Camera) at the 54th Cannes Film Festival and six Canadian Genie Awards, including Best Motion Picture.

2001: Beverly Singer, Tewa/Navajo, associate professor of anthropology and Native American studies at the University of New Mexico and noted documentarian, published *Wiping the War Paint Off the Lens,* the first chronicle of Native American filmmaking as a larger struggle for "cultural sovereignty" as the right to maintain tribal perspectives when filming cultures and traditions. Singer is also a founding member of the Native American Producers Alliance.

2004: *G: Methamphetamine on the Navajo Nation,* a documentary film created by Navajo filmmakers Shonie De La Rosa and Larry Blackhorse Lowe, explored the effect that methamphetamine has had on the Navajo Nation. The drug could be legally sold until the film raised awareness and the tribal council banned it. It was the first Navajo film to win at the American Indian Film Festival, earning the Best Public Service Award (2004).

2006: Chris Eyre (1968), Cheyenne/Arapaho, won the Directors Guild of America Award for Outstanding Directorial Achievement in Children's Programs for *Edge of America.* He was the first Native to win the honor.

2006: *Alanis Obomsawin: The Vision of a Native Filmmaker* by Randolph Lewis was published, the first book devoted to any Native filmmaker. Obomsawin (1932–), Abenaki, who has produced more than 50 films, is one of the most acclaimed Indigenous directors in the world, central to the development of Native media in North America. Her films include *Incident at Restigouche* (1984) and *Kanehsatake: 270 Years of Resistance* (1993). Obomsawin's work was showcased in a retrospective at the Museum of Modern Art in New York in 2008.

2007: *Mile Post 398* debuted as the first feature film in cinema history that an all-Navajo team wrote, produced, directed, starred in, and filmed. Navajo filmmakers Shonie and Andee De La Rosa created the drama of a Navajo man facing challenging life-altering decisions, and the film won many awards.

2011: The short film *Rocket Boy* was selected for the Sundance Festival, one of only 84 out of almost 6,500 entries. The filmmaking trio of Diné youth, aged 20–22, became the youngest Native Americans to ever take part in the festival. Donavan Seschillie, Jake Hoyungowa, and Deidra Peaches premiered their 16-minute film in Park City, Utah.

2015: "Queer Horror" premiered, a bimonthly film screening series programmed and hosted by Portland, Oregon's premier drag clown, Carla Rossi (Anthony Hudson), Confederated Tribes of Grand Ronde, at the historic Hollywood Theatre in Portland. It is the only LGBTQ program of its kind in the United States. Hudson was named a 2018 National Artist Fellow from the Native Arts and Cultures Foundation, a 2018 Western Arts Alliance Native Launchpad Artist, a 2019 Oregon Arts Commission Fellow, a 2021 First Peoples Fund Fellow, and has received project support and fellowships from the National Endowment for the Arts, National Performance.

2019: For the first time, a Native nation created its own film office. Jennifer Loren, Cherokee and recipient of nine Emmy Awards, was key in the development of the Cherokee Nation Film Office and serves as its director.

2020: Actor Wes Studi (1947), Cherokee Nation, became the first Native American actor to win an honorary Academy Award for Lifetime Achievement. He had key roles in several films, including *Dances with Wolves*, *The Last of the Mohicans*, *Geronimo: An American Legend*, *Heat*, and *Avatar*. Also in 2020, Studi was named one of the top 25 actors of the 21st century by the *New York Times* and was the only Native person on the list.

PODCASTS, THE INTERNET, AND SOCIAL MEDIA

"A lot of powwow folks, even dancers and drummers, have been affected by what's going on [the pandemic]. There wasn't any kind of group, to the level that I envisioned on any kind of social media platforms, so I wanted to make a group that could embrace the drums, the dancers, the singers, the artists, the vendors, and our whole community so that we had a place we could go to be seen and heard."

—*Dan Simonds, Mashantucket Pequot, founder of the Facebook page "Social Distance Powwow"*

2016: *UNHhhh* premiered on YouTube, starring drag persona Trixie Mattel (Brian Firkus, Ojibwe) and Katya Zamolodchikova (Brian McCook). After both were eliminated from *RuPaul's Drag Race*, they created the comedy series with themes like crying, trav-

Google Doodles

The homepage for Google Search is one of the most-viewed web pages in the world as it powers billions of searches on a daily basis. The Google logo usually appears above the search box, but occasionally, special art pops up, known as a Google Doodle. Google Doodles have been around since the founding of the company in 1998. They highlight world issues, historic events, and celebrations around the globe; Google employs an entire department of illustrators—called doodlers. And for the last few years, Native-themed Google Doodles have been added.

- FIRST Native-themed Doodle: "Three Sisters" on Thanksgiving Day, November 26, 2015

- FIRST Doodle of a Native American person: Blackfeet/A'aninin author James Welch's 76th birthday, November 18, 2016

- FIRST Doodle of a Native artist: Edmonia Lewis, Ojibwe/African American, depicted sculpting *The Death of Cleopatra*, February 1, 2017

- Mohawk activist Richard Oakes's 75th birthday, May 22, 2017

- FIRST Doodle of a Native American doctor: Omaha physician Susan La Flesche Picotte's 152nd birthday, June 17, 2017

- FIRST Doodle of a First Nations/Canadian person: Onondaga record-setting long distance runner Tom Longboat's 131st birthday, June 4, 2018

- Cherokee First Native woman engineer Mary G. Ross's 110th Birthday, August 9, 2018

- FIRST video Doodle to honor a Native American: Cherokee woodcarver/educator Amanda Crowe, November 9, 2018

- FIRST Doodle to honor a Native Hawaiian: Award-winning surfer Eddie Aikau's 73rd birthday, May 4, 2019

- FIRST Doodle by a Native guest artist: Joshua Mangeshig Pawis-Steckley, Wasauksing First Nation, "Celebrating the Jingle Dress Dance," June 15, 2019

- Cherokee Will Rogers's 140th Birthday, November 4, 2019

- Israel Kamakawiwo'ole's 61st Birthday, in honor of Asian Pacific Heritage Month in the United States, May 20, 2020

- Tlingit artist Michaela Goade doodles Tlingit activist Elizabeth Peratrovich, December 30, 2020

- Chris Pappan, Kaw Nation, doodles Yankton Sioux writer, teacher, musician, and suffragist Zitkála-Šá (Red Bird) on her 145th birthday, February 22, 2021 eling, and space. Part of the popularity of *UNHhhh* was that the "plot never drags because there is no plot." The two cranked out 68, 10-minute episodes that impressed Viceland producers so much that the enterprise was turned into a bona fide TV program in 2017, called *The Trixie & Katya Show*. In the span of two years, Firkus went from lip-synching for tips in Midwestern gay bars to cohosting, in drag, a national TV show.

Trixie Mattel

2018: *Gaylords of Darkness* premiered as the only queer feminist horror podcast. Stacie Ponder and Anthony Hudson, Confederated Tribes of Grand Ronde, present the mysterious world of horror through a queer lens—with occasional visits from ghouls and goblins.

2019: Sivan Alyra Rose (1999–), San Carlos Apache, was the first Native American woman to star in a Netflix series. The thriller, *Chambers*, featured a young Native woman (Sasha Yazzie), who receives a heart transplant and must contend with the psychological, spiritual, and otherworldly influence of a potentially evil heart from an Anglo donor.

2020: For the first time, social media broadcasted and tweeted petitions urging President-elect Joe Biden to appoint U.S. representative Deb Haaland, Laguna Pueblo, of New Mexico as U.S. secretary of the interior, a position that had never been held by a Native person. Indigenous leaders, advocates, and allies declared "Deb for Interior Week" with a flurry of hashtags, memes, and a twitterstorm. Biden subsequently nominated her to the post, and she was confirmed by the U.S. Senate on March 15, 2021.

2020: In response to the pandemic, Dan Simonds, Mashantucket Pequot, Stephanie Hebert, Mi'kmaw, and Whitney Rencountre,

Crow Creek Sioux, founded Social Distance Powwow (SDP) on Facebook to keep Indian people connected virtually. SDP promotes community and cultural preservation by posting cultural knowledge through Indigenous songs, dance, and arts. In addition to being a forum for Native singers and dancers, the SDP page is a venue for people to overcome fear of the coronavirus and to show support for ending the epidemic of missing and murdered Indigenous women and other issues affecting Native Americans. More than 250,000 members meet up to share videos, discussions, art, photos, and a marketplace.

JOURNALISM

"Long before today there has been a great need for a newspaper for the northern Natives of Alaska.... [*Tundra Times*] will be the medium to air the views of the Native organizations. It will reflect their policies and purposes as they work for the betterment of the Native peoples of Alaska.... It will strive to keep informed on matters of interest to all Natives of Alaska, whether they be Eskimos of the Arctic, the Athabascans of the Interior, [or] other Indians and Aleuts of the Aleutian Islands. We have also realized that an unbiased presentation of issues that directly concern the Natives is needed. In presenting those things that most affect Natives, we will make every effort to be truthful and objective. The *Tundra Times* is your paper. It is here to express your ideas, your thoughts and opinions on issues that vitally affect you. When you have a subject that you feel needs to be written about, pass that subject along. If you have something to offer, such as a good photograph, you think would add to the paper, pass that along too. Each offering will be carefully considered and much appreciated. They will aid the success of the paper."

—*Howard Uyaġak Rock (1911–1976), Inupiat, from his first editorial of the first issue of the* Tundra Times, *October 1, 1962*

1826: *The Literary Voyager,* or *Muzzenie-gun,* a literary magazine, was established as the first publication to present information by and about American Indians on a weekly basis. Henry Rowe Schoolcraft, non-Native, published many articles written by his Ojibwe wife, Jane Johnston Schoolcraft.

1834: Newspapers *Ka Lama Hawaii* and *Ke Kuma Hawaii* were the first periodicals published in the Hawaiian language.

1835: *Siwinowe Kesibwi* (Shawnee Sun) was the first periodical published entirely in a North American Native language.

1844: The *Cherokee Messenger,* first issued in August 1844, was the first periodical published in Indian Territory (Oklahoma). It was published by the Reverend Jesse Bushyhead at the Baptist Mission he established near present-day Westville, Oklahoma.

1844: The first newspaper published in Arkansas was the *Cherokee Messenger,* started

Cherokee Phoenix

May 21, 1828, front page of the *Cherokee Phoenix*

"As the *Phoenix* is a national newspaper, we shall feel ourselves bound to devote it to national purposes. 'The laws and public documents of the Nation,' and matters relating to the welfare and condition of the Cherokees as a people, will be faithfully published in Cherokee and English." —Elias Boudinot

The *Cherokee Phoenix* was the first tribal newspaper in North America and the first to be published in an Indigenous language. The first issue was published in English and Cherokee on February 21, 1828, in New Echota, capital of the Cherokee Nation (present-day Georgia). The first editor, Elias Boudinot, aka Buck Watie, Cherokee (1802–1839), ran the newspaper as a way to educate Cherokee citizens and to protest the state of Georgia's attempts to extend its laws over the Cherokee Nation. The newspaper was under constant attack from Georgia lawmakers and proponents of Indian removal to Indian Territory (present-day Oklahoma). In 1829, Boudinot renamed the *Cherokee Phoenix* as the *Cherokee Phoenix and Indians' Advocate,* to influence an audience beyond the Cherokee. He addressed issues that Indians across the United States and its territories faced related to assimilation and removal from their traditional homelands. Boudinot featured stories about debates over Indian removal and U.S. Supreme Court cases that affected Indian life. The paper was published intermittently after Cherokee removal to Indian Territory, and today it has been revived by the Cherokee Nation as a monthly broadsheet, available in print and online in Tahlequah, Oklahoma.

a few months after the Oklahoma *Cherokee Messenger*, but with very different content. Edward Wilkerson Bushyhead, Cherokee, one of the founders, eventually launched the *San Diego Union* newspaper.

1844: The *Cherokee Advocate,* established by the Cherokee National Council as the official newspaper of the Cherokee Nation, was the first newspaper published in Indian Territory (present-day Oklahoma). The weekly publication was published in Tahlequah, the Cherokee capital, in both Cherokee and English, and featured current events, laws, editorials, foreign news, fiction, inspirational pieces, and general articles. William Potter Ross (1820–1891), Cherokee, who graduated from the College of New Jersey (later Princeton) in 1842, was the first editor.

1848: The *Choctaw Telegraph* was the first Choctaw newspaper published in Indian Territory (present-day Oklahoma). Its purpose was to "to advocate and disseminate morality, education, agriculture and general intelligence."

1851: *Copway's American Indian* was published in New York City by a single individual, George Copway (Kahgegagahbowh, He Who Stands Forever) (1818–1869), Ojibwa hereditary chief. He owned and edited the weekly, publishing it between July 10 and October 4, 1851. The August 9, 1851, issue incorporated a motto on the nameplate: "Devoted to the General History of the North American Indian and American Literature. Neutral in Politics and Creeds." The publication also promoted Copway's plan for establishing an Indian tract of land bound by the Missouri River, where Indian people from Great Lakes tribal nations could remove and live free from outside interference.

1854: The *Chickasaw Intelligencer,* published in Indian Territory (present-day Oklahoma), was the first newspaper of the Chickasaw Nation to be created by private Native citizens rather than a tribal government.

1854: Students at the Cherokee Female Seminary founded the first Native American student publication, *A Wreath of Cherokee Rose Buds.* The periodical featured student literary works.

1857: John Rollin Ridge (1827–1867), Cherokee author, was the founding editor of the *Daily Bee* in Sacramento, California. The publication became known as the *Sacramento Bee,* one of the most prominent newspapers in the nation today. Ridge also edited several other newspapers, including the *Weekly California Express,* the *Daily National Democrat,* the *San Francisco Evening Journal,* the *San Francisco Herald,* and the *Red Bluff Beacon.* He was a partner in the National Printing Company in California and served as editor at the time of his death in 1867.

1860: The *Fort Smith Picayune,* a monthly publication founded by John C. Wheeler, Cherokee, was the first-ever American Indian periodical to feature humor.

1868: The *San Diego Union* was created by Edward Bushyhead, Cherokee, and was the first newspaper privately owned by a Native person that did not focus primarily on Indian issues.

c. 1871: The *Halaquah Times* was a manuscript magazine published by students at the Wyandotte Mission School in Indian Territory (present-day Oklahoma). Written by an all-female staff and edited by Ida Johnson and Julia Robitaille, it was a publication of the Halaquah, a literary society, and published until about 1875.

1872: William F. Wheeler and his son John C. Wheeler, Cherokee, created the *Wheeler's Independent,* the first nontribal, but Native-owned, publication to address the concerns of the Native American community.

1873: *Our Monthly*, a community newsletter, was the first publication devoted to concerns of two Indian nations, the Creek and the Choctaw. Printed in Muskogee, the common language of both groups, it was published at Tallahassee Creek Nation, Indian Territory.

1875: Elias C. Boudinot (1835–1890), Cherokee, established the first independent Cherokee-owned newspaper, the *Indian Progress*. The paper expressed his political views, which often disagreed with those of the Cherokee Nation.

1876: With the motto "We Seek to Enlighten," the *Indian Journal* became the first newspaper published in the Creek Nation at Muskogee, Indian Territory. It represented the interests of the Five Civilized Indian Tribes: Cherokee, Choctaw, Creek, Seminole, and Chickasaw.

1878: The *Choctaw News*, one of the first Native American dailies, was the first Choctaw tribal newspaper. Short lived, it reported daily on the deliberations of the Choctaw Nation. In 1884, it was replaced by the *Indian Champion*.

1886: The *Progress* was the first Minnesota newspaper published on a reservation by members of the tribe. Gus H. Beaulieu and Theodore H. Beaulieu, both White Earth tribal citizens, were the publisher and editor, respectively, of the weekly. After its initial publication on March 25, 1886, the next issue of the *Progress* did not appear until October 8, 1887. In the interim, the Indian agent, Timothy J. Sheehan, had taken punitive actions against the tribal press. Sheehan was opposed, in part, to the paper's stance against policies and practices of the Bureau of Indian Affairs. Ultimately, the commissioner of In-

dian Affairs ordered the expulsion of the publisher from the reservation "as being an unfit person to remain among Indians" and the printing press was seized. The matter was taken up by a U.S. Senate subcommittee in Washington, D.C., which finally determined that distributing the paper was a "lawful occupation" without a need for "surveillance and restrictions." The *Progress* then resumed publication but was later suspended while tribal land allotment negotiations were underway; its final issue was July 13, 1889. In 1903, the paper was reintroduced by Gus Beaulieu as the *Tomahawk*. "Believing the pen is mightier than the sword," Beaulieu wrote, "we start on the war-path with a paper tomahawk." The paper's motto was "Truth before Favor."

1889: The *Daily Capital* was the only daily newspaper published in Indian Territory at the time and was based in the Cherokee capital of Tahlequah.

1893: For the first time, the Osage had an independent newspaper directed at their issues. The *Wah-sha-she* was founded by George E. Tinker and other Osage people.

1893: Norma E. Standley Smiser (1865–1955), Choctaw, became associate editor of the *Indian Citizen* at Atoka, Choctaw Nation, acquiring her father's interest in the paper, the first Native woman to edit and publish a newspaper. She and her husband, Butler Stonestreet Smiser, served as owners and editors of the *Indian Citizen*, covering Choctaw interests. In 1900, Norma Smiser became editor and manager of the newspaper, serving until 1905, when it was sold.

1903: The *Tomahawk* became one of the first tribal newspaper of the Chippewa of White Earth, Minnesota. It was founded by Gustave H. Beaulieu and took strong stands on issues of political and economic importance to the tribe.

1908: The *Quileute Independent* (1908), followed by the *Quileute Chieftain* (1910), were founded by Webster H. Hudson, Quileute, in La Push, Washington. Hudson, who served as editor and publisher, was a graduate of Chemawa Indian School in Oregon. Both publications were short-lived, the first ending in 1909 and the other in 1910.

1911: As the earliest-known attempt to produce an intertribal publication focusing on pan-Indian activism, the *Indian Observer* was established in Washington, D.C., by August Breuninger, Menominee. He was one of the first to propose the founding of an "Indian University" to preserve "Indianess," which would offer Native-oriented courses, including Indian "law, music, and dramatic art." Because of the special emphasis on culture, Breuninger wanted the university connected to an Indian museum.

1913: The Society of American Indians (1911–1923), the first national American Indian rights organization run by and for Indians, founded the *Quarterly Journal* in 1913 and renamed it the *American Indian Magazine* in 1916. Arthur Parker, Gertrude Simmons Bonnin, Sherman Coolidge, Charles Eastman, Henry Roe Cloud, and Carlos Montezuma were among the distinguished intellectuals and leaders who served as editors and writers.

1913: The *Rossville Reporter* was created by Peter Navarre, Prairie Band Potawatomie, and was the first newspaper owned by a member of his nation.

1916: Dr. Carlos Montezuma (1867–1923), Yavapai, founded *Wassaja* (the Yavapai word for "signaling" or "beckoning" and also his birth name), an antigovernment newspaper that chronicled Indian issues and publicly attacked the government for the conditions imposed upon Natives. He became an outspoken opponent of the Bureau of Indian

Affairs (BIA). Montezuma was a cofounder of the Society of American Indians in 1911, the first Indian rights organization created by and for Indians. He used *Wassaja* as a platform to spread his views of the BIA and Native American education, civil rights, and citizenship.

1935: The first urban Indian newspaper was launched. *Talking Leaf,* published by the American Indian Center in Los Angeles, California, featured poetry, local and national news, and educational and career opportunities.

1937: Alice Lee Jemison (1901–1964), Seneca, published the *First American,* the first political newsletter edited by a Native woman. Her strong views opposed the Bureau of Indian Affairs (BIA) and advocated to dissolve the institution. Jemison was key in establishing the American Indian Federation (1934), and the *First American* became its signature publication. The paper supported Indian rights and denounced the Indian Reorganization Act. She protested stereotypical images in popular culture like Horatio Greenough's *The Rescue,* a sculpture depicting a Native man killing a white woman and

Dr. Carlos Montezuma is pictured here with some of the nurses he trained at the Carlisle Indian School.

prominently installed on the steps leading to the Capitol rotunda. Jemison was strongly influenced by Carlos Montezuma.

1943: William Morgan (1915–2001), Navajo, translated *Ádahooníligíí*, the first Navajo newspaper. It covered current Navajo news as well as national and international articles.

1945: The National Congress of American Indians (NCAI) published a newsletter and, in 1947, a bulletin. Both publications were the first postwar efforts by American Indians to address Native issues.

1947: The *Smoke Signal*, established in Sacramento, California, was the first Native newspaper in Sacramento, home to thousands of Native people representing dozens of tribes.

1959: Dillon Platero (1926–2003), Navajo, chairman of the Navajo Tribal Council's Education Committee, became the first editor and publisher of the *Navajo Times*, a monthly newsletter published by the education committee in Window Rock, Arizona. The inaugural issue of the publication, in 1959, stated the paper's primary goal was to serve Navajo children attending off-reservation schools to keep them informed about news on the reservation. Over the years, the publication evolved into the current weekly *Navajo Times*, independent from the Tribal Council, with the subheading *Diné Bi Naaltsoos*, "Newspaper of the Navajo People."

1960: Marshall Tome (c. 1922–2007) became noted as the first known Navajo journalist who transformed the *Navajo Times* from a tribal education newsletter into a full-fledged newspaper centered on Navajo news. Tome, a U.S. Marine Corps enlistee, served in the South Pacific in an amphibious unit during World War II. Following his military discharge, he completed a bachelor's degree in journalism at the University of Missouri in 1952. While working as assistant city editor at the *San Francisco Chronicle*, Tome was asked by Dillon Platero, chairman of the Navajo Education Committee, to return home and turn the tribal newsletter into a newspaper. Tome ran the *Navajo Times* from 1960 to 1965, eventually serving as director of communications at Arizona State University. He also worked at the *Albuquerque Tribune* and *Kansas City Star* and worked in other leadership positions in the Navajo Nation.

1961: The *Journal of American Indian Education*, established at Arizona State University's Center for Indian Education, was the first periodical devoted exclusively to Indian education issues.

1962: Howard Uyagak Rock (1911–1976), Iñupiaq from Point Hope, founded the *Tundra Times* (Fairbanks, AK), the first Alaska Native newspaper. As Rock indicated in the first issue, the biweekly paper would be the medium for airing the views of Native organizations and would strive to keep informed on matters for interest to all Natives of Alaska. The *Tundra Times*, published from 1962 to 1997, played a role in the development of the Alaska Federation of Natives and the passage of the Alaska Native Claims Settlement Act. In 1975, it was nominated for a Pulitzer Prize. Besides being the first Inuit to found a newspaper, Rock was an acclaimed artist who also contributed to the establishment of the World Eskimo Indian Olympics and the Institute of Alaska Native Arts.

1966: The *American Indian News* was born on the Wind River Reservation in Wyoming, becoming the first such publication on the reservation.

1968: The *Indian Archives* was the first newsletter established for prison inmates. It addressed culture, religion, history, and the socioeconomic conditions among Native people. In 1969, it was followed by the *American Indian Cultural Group Newsletter*, established by Indigenous inmates at San Quentin Prison, California.

1969: The *Council of Women* was the first urban periodical published exclusively by women. The idea began as a protest against the male-dominated *Talking Leaf* (Los Angeles American Indian Center) and addressed issues of equality as well as Native news.

1969: Charles Trimble (1935–2020), Oglala Lakota, born and raised on the Pine Ridge Indian Reservation in South Dakota, was the principal founder of the American Indian Press Association, the forerunner of the Native American Journalists Association. He served as the organization's executive director, leaving to serve as executive director of the National Congress of American Indians from 1972 to 1978. Trimble attended Holy Rosary Mission at Pine Ridge and completed a bachelor of fine arts degree from the University of South Dakota in 1957. After serving in the U.S. Army, he pursued studies in journalism at the University of Colorado. Trimble's leadership included work in international affairs, serving as a U.S. delegate at the United Nations Sub-commission on Prevention of Discrimination and Protection of Minorities in Geneva, Switzerland, and in other roles. Before retiring in 2001, he was president of Charles Trimble Company, a national consulting firm specializing in economic development on reservations. He was also the president of Red Willow Institute, a nonprofit corporation that he founded to help Native American nonprofit organizations.

1969: Ernest Kaientaronken Benedict, Akwesasne Mohawk, founded the *Akwesasne Notes*, the first newspaper on the reservation in upstate New York. It became the most influential and largest Native newspaper in the world. It chronicled Native American activism and featured a poster with quotes from Native authors in each edition. Benedict also established the White Roots of Peace, a traveling college that educated the public on Native American issues and cultures.

1973: The first issue of *Wassaja* (not to be confused with a paper of the same name published by Carlos Montezuma in 1916) was published by Rupert Costo (1906–1989), Cahuilla. The newspaper's platform was to advocate for American Indians and included articles on self-determination, land and water rights, housing, treaties, and other significant issues, as well as poetry, book reviews, cartoons, and feature stories.

1979: Brandon Clark, Choctaw, founded Oklahoma's largest weekly newspaper, the *Friday Newspaper*.

1981: The *Lakota Times*, a small, weekly newspaper, was launched on the Pine Ridge Reservation in South Dakota by Oglala Lakota visionary journalist/publisher Tim Giago (1934–), also known as Nanwica Kciji. It soon became the largest weekly newspaper in the state, the first time a Native newspaper outgrew a publication owned by the dominant culture. It was also the first time in the state's history that a Native-owned paper covered subjects about and by Native people in great detail. The *Lakota Times* eventually became the largest national Indian newspaper, and in 1992, the name was changed to reflect the broad scope of the paper's coverage: *Indian Country Today (ICT)*. In 1998 Giago sold the paper to 4 Directions Media, owned by the Oneida Nation of New York. In 2011, *ICT* became Indian Country Today Media Network (ICTMN), an online multimedia news platform.

1986: *News from Indian Country (NFIC)* was launched by Ojibwe/Oneida journalist Paul DeMain (1955–) on the Lac Courte Oreilles (LCO) reservation in Wisconsin. *NFIC* was an independent Native American newspaper, growing to achieve national and international reach. DeMain's company, Indian Country Communications, eventually published special publications, a website, and an internet news broadcast. At times, it was the largest employer at LCO. *NFIC* included national, cultural, and regional sections, covering stories about Native communities across the country and beyond. DeMain, the managing editor as well as owner, also took on controversial topics, including investigating murders on the Pine Ridge Reservation in South Dakota during the 1970s. In 2002, DeMain received the Wassaja Award for courage by journalists covering Indian Country, and in 2003, he was honored with the Payne Award for Ethics in Journalism by the University of Oregon. After 33 years, *News from Indian Country* published its last issue in August 2019.

2002: *SAY (Spirit of Aboriginal Youth)*, an Indigenous lifestyle magazine, was founded by Leslie Lounsbury (1947–2018), Métis, to celebrate First Nations, Métis, and Inuit ingenuity by sharing success stories and narratives of resilience.

2005: *Rez Biz*, a monthly magazine, was founded by Navajo Nation members George Joe and Michael Clani. It was the first regional and free publication targeted to Native American businesspeople or those interested in running their own businesses. It is also used for instructional purposes in high schools and colleges with predominantly Native student populations in Arizona and New Mexico. With a vision of improving the economic conditions of Native Americans, *Rez Biz* has won two journalism awards from the Native American Journalism Association (2007).

c. 2006: *Independent Voices* was conceived. It is an open access digital collection of alternative press newspapers, magazines, and journals drawn from the special collections of participating libraries. These periodicals were created by feminists, dissident GIs, campus radicals, Native Americans, antiwar activists, Black Power advocates, Hispanics, LGBT activists, the extreme right-wing press, and alternative literary magazines during the latter half of the 20th century.

2012: *Native Max* became the nation's first Native American fashion magazine and is available in print and online. The publication also features arts, cuisine, entertainment, and culture for well-rounded coverage of contemporary Native Americans.

2013: Cherokee Nation citizen America Meredith published the inaugural issue of *First American Art Magazine (FAAM)*, the first art periodical owned by Native people. Meredith's vision was "to provide a common platform for Native and non-Native academics, art professionals, artists, collectors, and other interested readers to seriously investigate and celebrate Indigenous American art—from ancestral to 21st century artwork." The bimonthly magazine has earned critical acclaim in the publishing and art world. *Library Journal* ranked it in its Best Magazines 2013 list, and Feedspot chose *FAAM* as one of its "Top 10 Art Magazines and Ezines to Follow in 2018."

RADIO

"Native Hawaiians, my very precious nation with me tonight, youth of our University of Hawai'i who are passionate about the Hawaiian language, yes, tell me now the things that you have in mind."

—*John Kameaaloha Almeida, elder and Native Hawaiian musician, from the first broadcast (1972) of the first all Hawaiian language radio show (Ka Leo Hawai'i), hosted by Native Hawaiian language professor Larry Lindsey Kimura*

c. 1924: Ora V. Eddleman Reed (1880–1968), Cherokee, became the first Native host of a radio show on Wyoming's first radio station. Her half-hour daily talk show, *The Sunshine Lady*, was filled with commentaries on how to achieve contentment in everyday life. Reed answered listeners' calls and letters on the wildly successful program, which ran until she moved from Casper, Wyoming, to Tulsa, Oklahoma, in 1932.

1929: Will Rogers (1879–1935), Cherokee, launched *The Gulf Headliners* and became the first Native to host a weekly national radio program. The successful show highlighted Rogers's candid, engaging style as he jumped from topic to topic. He was often so engrossed that he forgot the time and was cut off in mid-sentence when the half-hour show ended. To correct this bad habit that left his audience hanging, he brought in a wind-up alarm clock, and its on-air buzzing reminded him to wrap up his comments. By 1935, Rogers's show was being announced as *Will Rogers and His Famous Alarm Clock*. Rogers died in a plane crash the same year the title of his show changed. He is often called the first king of media.

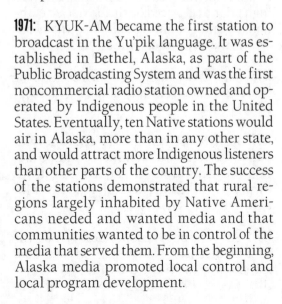

Will Rogers

1934: Sadie Brower Neakok (1916–2004), Inupiaq, was the first radio announcer to broadcast the news in the Iñupiat language. She also was the first female magistrate in Alaska, serving in Alaska's Second Judicial District in Utqiagvik.

1957: KNDN-AM began the *All Navajo, All the Time* radio program broadcasting in Navajo and English under KWYK-AM. Today the show is mainly in the Navajo language, and it is the first and only radio station to use the Navajo language so extensively.

1968: *Seeing Red*, the first regularly broadcast Native news program in the United States, aired on WBAI-FM (public radio station) in New York City. Producers and hosts Suzan Shown Harjo (1945–), Cheyenne/Hodulgee Muscogee, and husband Frank Ray Harjo (1947–1982), Muscogee, moderated the show until 1975.

1970: WYRU-AM became the first commercial Native-licensed radio station. Owned by the Lumbee Tribe, it was broadcast from Red Springs, North Carolina, for a general audience.

1971: Radio Tuktoyakuk began broadcasting in Inuktitut and English and became the first Native language program on the radio in Canada.

1971: American Indian students participated in Columbia University's first broadcast journalism summer program for members of minority groups. Lorraine Edmo, Shoshoni/Bannock, Tanna Beebe, Cowlitz, and Donald Savage, Chippewa, had all worked for radio-TV stations and completed the eleven-week training session located on Columbia's New York City campus.

1971: KYUK-AM became the first station to broadcast in the Yu'pik language. It was established in Bethel, Alaska, as part of the Public Broadcasting System and was the first noncommercial radio station owned and operated by Indigenous people in the United States. Eventually, ten Native stations would air in Alaska, more than in any other state, and would attract more Indigenous listeners than other parts of the country. The success of the stations demonstrated that rural regions largely inhabited by Native Americans needed and wanted media and that communities wanted to be in control of the media that served them. From the beginning, Alaska media promoted local control and local program development.

1972: KTDB-FM was the first Navajo-owned, Navajo-operated, Navajo-language noncommercial radio station and was broadcast from Ramah, New Mexico, on the Navajo Reservation. Today, it is in nearby Pinehill, also on the reservation.

1972: *Ka Leo Hawai'i,* a public Hawaiian language radio program, was first broadcast. The popular show featured interviews of Native Hawaiian–speaking elders and phone calls from listeners. The program sparked interest in the revival of the Hawaiian language. *Ka Leo Hawai'i* founder Professor Larry Kimura, Native Hawaiian, is called the grandfather of the Hawaiian language's revitalization. In 2020, he received the honor of Living Treasure of Hawai'i from the Honpa Hongwanji Mission of Hawai'i for his extraordinary commitment to the preservation and use of the Hawaiian language.

1975: KBRW-AM, licensed to Silakkuagvik Communications, Inc., a nonprofit membership organization whose board of directors is controlled by Alaska Natives, was the first and only station to serve Barrow, Alaska, as well as eight villages scattered across the North Slope. Most listeners are Inupiat, and a high priority is placed on the broadcast of the language programming. *Silakkuagvik* means "voices that fly through the air" in Inupiat.

1976: The Navajo Radio Network became the first radio station entirely under Navajo control.

1977: KMDX-FM became the first individually Native-owned commercial radio station. Broadcast from Parker, Arizona, it was owned by Gilbert Leivas, Colorado River Indian Tribes.

1977: Akwesasne Freedom Radio (AFR), the first nonlicensed, Native-run private radio station, was established by Ray J. "Wahnitiio" Cook (1956–2019), Mohawk. It was made possible by a small 20-watt FM transmitter located in a small Mayan village in Guatemala and then transmitted to "The Farm" in Tennessee, which directed it to the Mohawks. Later, Cook created CKON—Mohawk Nation Radio.

1978: Four Native stations were added to the electronic communication venue of Native America: KINI-FM, Rosebud Sioux Reservation, South Dakota; KNDN-AM, Farmington, New Mexico; KSHI-FM, Zuni Pueblo, New Mexico; and KNCC-FM, Tsaile, Arizona, making the Navajo Reservation the first to have two radio stations.

1978: Gary Fife, Cherokee/Creek, became the first Native American Ford Fellow in Educational Journalism. He produced and hosted *National Native News,* a national radio news service featuring Indigenous issues.

1979: Rosemarie Kuptana (1954–), Inuvialuk, was the first host on the Canadian Broadcasting Corporation's (CBC) Native language program and reported on issues that were relevant to the Inuvialuit and in Inuvialuktun. Kuptana served as president of the Inuit Broadcasting Corporation from 1983 until 1988 and ensured that programs were in Inuktitut. She was involved in developing Television Northern Canada, later to become the Aboriginal Peoples Television Network.

1980: KIDE-FM, a noncommercial station, began broadcasting from the Hoopa Valley Reservation in California.

1982: Two more stations were born in Indian Country: KNNB-FM broadcast to the Fort Apache Indian Reservation in Whiteriver, Arizona; WOJB-FM covered the Lac Courte Oreilles Reservation in Hayward, Wisconsin.

1983: KILI-FM, owned and operated by Lakota Communications, was launched, the first station to broadcast in the Lakota language. KILI serves 30,000 people on three reservations in South Dakota, along with the large American Indian urban community in Rapid City, South Dakota. Many feel the station has been key in preserving and teaching Lakota. Two other stations had their inaugural broadcasts: KABR-AM from the Alamo Reservation in New Mexico; and KMHA-FM, which reached the Mandan, Hidatsa, and Arikara Nations on the Fort Berthold Reservation, North Dakota.

1984: The Mohawk Council of Chiefs became the first and only sovereign Indian nation to award an operating radio license. The founders of CKON-FM, Mohawk citizens Ray Cook and Doug George-Kanentiio, did not seek approval from the U.S. Federal Communications Commission and the Canadian Radio and Television Commission, asserting their right to recognize the Mohawk Nation as their governing body. The commercial community 24-hour radio station is self-sufficient and the only international radio station operated by Native people. Today CKON can be streamed online.

1986: KTNN-AM, a commercial station owned by the Navajo Nation and based in Window Rock, Arizona, was the first to broadcast in the Navajo, Hopi, Apache, Pueblo, and Ute languages. Broadcaster Ernie Manuelito, Navajo, scored another first with his play-by-play coverage in Navajo of the 1996 Super Bowl (Dallas Cowboys vs. Pittsburgh Steelers) for both KTNN Radio and TV. In the same year, Selena Manychildren and Deenise Becenti, both Navajo newscasters and reporters for KTNN, received first prize for best newscast in a small market by the New Mexico Broadcasters. In 1999, KTNN received a Native American Music Award (Nammy) for the best radio station, the first radio station honored by the organization.

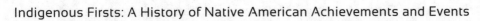

Kenneth Maryboy

1987: National Native News (NNN), the nation's first daily radio news service covering Indigenous issues for both Native and non-Native listeners, was created. Content is from a Native perspective and available on public radio stations across the country. Produced by Gary Fife, Creek/Cherokee, the program has won several awards.

1990: KCIE-FM began broadcasting for the first time to the Jicarilla Apache people in Dulce, New Mexico.

1991: KGHR-FM was the country's first Native high school radio station and was broadcast from Tuba City, Arizona. The station is one of three on the Navajo Nation.

1991: K-TWINS began broadcasting from the Kah-Nee-Ta Resort on the Confederated Tribes of Warm Springs Reservation and Bend, Oregon. The station was a merger between two commercial FM stations (KTWI and KTWS).

1993: Kenneth Maryboy (1961–), Navajo, started covering Phoenix Suns basketball games in the Navajo language on KTNN 660 AM from Window Rock, Arizona. Maryboy also founded the organization Navajo Santa to help serve the needs of the Navajo people all year long. The program provides gifts of food, clothing, blankets, and toys, medical care, and other services, including hope, to some of the country's most impoverished communities.

1995: *Native America Calling* (NCC) was launched on American Indian Radio on Satellite (AIROS), the first-ever daily all-Native live radio talk show programming. Today, the show is available online.

1996: KNBA, a project of Koahnic Broadcast Corporation, became the first urban Native radio station in Alaska. Based in Anchorage, Koahnic, which means "live air" in Ahtna, one of the eleven Athabaskan languages, also operates the National Training Center, once known as the Indigenous Broadcast Center (founded in 1992), providing training opportunities for Alaska Natives and Native Americans interested in a broadcasting career.

2006: Native Voice One (NV1) was born after the Koahnic Broadcast Corporation won the contract to use the satellite network American Indian Radio on Satellite (AIROS), the service that distributed Native American programming to radio stations. In 2014, the Smithsonian Institution listed two organizations as operating Native American networks via satellite: Native Voice One and Satellite Radio Bilingüe. The latter serves Spanish language radio listeners in the United States, many of whom are Indigenous.

Jay Silverheels

2008: *Raven's Radio Hour* (KNBA in Anchorage, Alaska) began airing. The format paid homage to 1940s radio variety shows, and host Ed Bourgeois, Mohawk, described the show as a "tundra home companion." He blends the vintage format with the diversity of Native Alaska and features Indigenous timeless stories, traditional songs, and jokes "that'll make you blow moose milk through your nose!" Bourgeois, a humorist and performer, was in the first group of six artists to be awarded an Advancing Indigenous Performance Fellowship (2018).

TELEVISION

"Our culture is vibrant with storytelling; that's what reporting is. I often talk to Native American kids and encourage them to go into the news business. That's our culture; we are storytellers."

—Hattie Kauffman, Nez Perce, CBS News correspondent and a four-time Emmy Award–winning journalist

1949: Jay Silverheels/Harry Smith (1912–1980), Mohawk, was the first Native American to be featured in a television series and the first Native to be awarded a star on the Hollywood Walk of Fame (1979). He starred as Tonto in the popular ABC show *The Lone Ranger* until 1957, appearing in over 220 episodes. Before Smith turned to acting, he was a professional lacrosse player and a Golden Gloves Middleweight Champion. He objected to the name "Tonto" and the character's use of pidgin English. It is rumored that he sometimes used derogatory words in Mohawk that escaped the censors. Silverheels founded and ran the Indian Actors Workshop in Los Angeles in the 1960s, becoming a strong advocate for Indigenous people in film and television. Probably his most important role was off-screen in curtailing the entertainment industry's tradition of casting non-Natives in Indigenous roles, rather than Native actors.

1962: Wayne Newton (1942–), Powhatan/Cherokee, was the first Native entertainer to be featured on televised variety shows.

c. 1963: Mary Jane Giago (c. 1928–2016), Oglala Lakota, was probably the first Native woman and maybe the first Native to work on the staff of *The Tonight Show*, starring Johnny Carson, in Burbank, California. She was the first in her family to join the military, and when she was discharged, she was the first to go to college. Journalist Tim Giago credits his big sister with being his role model. When he was a teenager, Mary Jane "rescued" him from boarding school and enrolled him in a public high school in Texas, where she was living. He followed in her footsteps by joining the military, going to college, and fashioning a career in media arts.

1971: Inuit villages in the Arctic received television broadcasting for the first time.

1972: Randolph Mantooth (1945–), Seminole, was the first Native actor to star in an ensemble cast for a television medical drama. He appeared on NBC's *Emergency* until 1979.

1975: Buffy Sainte-Marie (1941–), Cree, became the first Native American to star on *Sesame Street* (PBS). She played Buffy (a fictionalized version of herself) until 1981 and performed some of her own songs on the show, such as "Cripple Creek," as well as tunes written for the series (including "Country Song," "Dog Song," and the music to "Wynken, Blynken and Nod"). Sainte-Marie said that she hoped her role on the show would teach children that "Indians still exist."

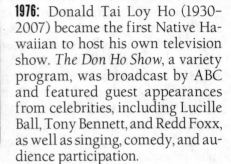
Randolph Mantooth

1975: Sandra Sunrising Osawa, Makah Indian Nation, produced *The Native American Series*, a groundbreaking ten-part series for KNBC-TV. She was the first Native American to have a series on commercial television. Twenty years later in 1995, Osawa produced *Lighting the 7th Fire* for Point of View (POV), the first Native filmmaker to do so. The film chronicled the Ojibwe prophesy of the Seven Fires and details leading up to contemporary times in northern Wisconsin. The first Six Fires foretold the beginnings of the Anishinaabe and their journey to the Great Lakes area, the arrival of fair-skinned people, a time of intense struggle, and a period of great loss and suffering. The Seventh Fire tells of the restoration of lost traditions. In a 1983 court decision, which restored Ojibwe treaty rights to hunt and fish on ceded territory off the reservations, the belief was that the time of the Seventh Fire had begun. However, as the Ojibwe people tried to engage in their traditional custom of fishing for walleye, white protesters showed up in force, threatening and harassing the Native fishermen. The angry mob flashed racist signs like "Spear a Pregnant Indian Squaw and Save Two Walleye."

1976: Donald Tai Loy Ho (1930–2007) became the first Native Hawaiian to host his own television show. *The Don Ho Show*, a variety program, was broadcast by ABC and featured guest appearances from celebrities, including Lucille Ball, Tony Bennett, and Redd Foxx, as well as singing, comedy, and audience participation.

1976: Six Native producers in public television chartered the Native American Public Broadcasting Consortium (NAPBC), later known as Native American Public Telecommunications (NAPT) and now Vision Maker Media. Since its founding, Vision Maker Media and its predecessor organizations have created more than 500 films, awarded $11 million to independent producers, and held hundreds of film-screening events across the nation.

1978: The Oglala Sioux Tribe (Pine Ridge Sioux Reservation, South Dakota) began to construct the first Indian-owned and -operated television station in the country.

1980: Inuit Tapirisat (Inuit Brotherhood) founded Inukshuk, an experimental television station, and gained access to a Canadian Broadcasting Corporation (CBC) satellite channel. Both the station and satellite access were a first.

1981: The Inuit Broadcasting Corporation was the first Native-language television network in North America. Programs included *Super Shamou*, a children's show, plus dramas of Inuit stories and information shows.

1982: *Spirit Bay*, the first aboriginal family television show, premiered on CBC Television and TVOntario. It was rebroadcast in the United States on the Disney Channel and chronicles the lives of townsfolk on a fictional Ojibwe reservation town near Macdiarmid, Ontario. Episodes detail the spiritual kinship among Spirit Bay families, nature, and contemporary life on the reservation from a young person's viewpoint. It set the stage for all other Native Canadian programming (such as *The Rez*, *North of 60*, and *Moccasin Flats*) and paved the way for many famous First Nations actors including Graham Greene (Oneida), Tom Jackson (Cree), Tantoo Cardinal (Cree/Métis), Gary Farmer (Cayuga), Shirley Cheechoo (Cree), Monique Mojica (Kuna/Rappahannock), and Margo Kane (Cree-Saulteaux).

1983: *I'd Rather Be Powwowing* was the first television documentary produced by an entirely Native crew. Al Chandler, Gros Venture Nation, is followed from his mainstream job as a senior technical representative for the Xerox Corporation to his travels to powwows with his family. The film was directed by Larry Littlebird, Laguna/Santo Domingo.

1987: Nancy Tuthill, Quapaw/Shawnee, was the first Native person to hold the position of editor in the Broadcast Standards and Practices department for ABC Television.

1987: Shirley G. Cuffee (1932–2018), Powhatan/Arrohateck/Cherokee, made headlines in the New York City metro area by producing and hosting a television show titled *A Touch of Native America*. The theme of the show was new territory for Queens and Manhattan Public Access stations; twice a

Chuck Norris

week fans tuned in to see Cuffee interview Native guests on a vast array of subjects. She brought awareness about Indigenous peoples to a diverse audience. In 1998, her decade of programming was celebrated when she received the Queens Public Access's highest award for programming. Cuffee was also an educator, poet, and activist in the Native community.

1989: Hattie Kauffman, Nez Perce, of ABC News, was the first Native reporter on national television. Her foray into national broadcasting was as a special correspondent and substitute anchor for *Good Morning America* in 1987. In 1990, Kaufmann moved to CBS News as a correspondent and substitute anchor on *CBS This Morning*. At CBS she reported for *48 Hours*, *Street Stories*, *Sunday Morning*, *CBS Radio*, *CBS Special Reports*, *The Early Show*, and *CBS Evening News*. Kaufmann published her memoir, *Falling into Place*, in 2013; during her career, she received four Emmy awards.

1990: CBS premiered *Walker, Texas Ranger*, starring Chuck Norris (1940–), Cherokee. It was the first time a Native American played the title character; the hit series aired until 2001. Storylines sometimes featured Native themes and actors like Floyd Red Crow Westerman, Dakota; Frank Sotonoma "Grey Wolf" Salsedo, Wappo; and Nick Ramus, Blackfoot.

1992: *Heartbeat Alaska* was launched by Jeanie Greene, Inupiaq. It was the first Native-owned, -produced, and -staffed news program to air nationally and internationally. Greene has dedicated her life to featuring the Native people and communities of Alaska, sharing their heritage, news, and issues. The veteran journalist has won several awards, and in 2013, the program began airing on ABC.

1992: The Aboriginal Peoples Television Network (APTN), based in Winnipeg, Manitoba, Canada, was the first network that aired and produced programs made by, for, and about Indigenous peoples in Canada and the United States. APTN offers a variety of programming including documentaries, news magazines, dramas, entertainment specials, children's series, movies, sports events, educational shows, and more. Programming is broadcast in 56% English, 16% French, and 28% Aboriginal languages.

1996: *Grand Avenue* was HBO's first-ever production about Native people set in contemporary times. Written by Greg Sarris, Federated Indians of Graton Rancheria (Coast Miwok), the film featured a cast of stellar Indigenous actors like Irene Bedard, Inupiat/Métis; Tantoo Cardinal, Cree/Métis; Cody Lightning, Cree; A Martinez, Apache/Piegan Blackfeet; August Werner Schellenberg, Mohawk; Sheila Tousey, Menominee/Stockbridge-Munsee; and Zahn Tokiya-ku McClarnon, Hunkpapa Lakota.

1996: Lena Carr, Navajo, won an Emmy Award for Outstanding Historical Programming, the first Native woman to receive an Emmy in that category. She earned the prestigious honor for *War Code: Navajo*, a National Geographic Television Explorer episode broadcast on TBS.

2007: David Eugene Mills (1961–2010), Pamunkey, was an award-winning journalist and television writer/producer. He was the first Powhatan person to win two Emmy Awards, which he earned for writing and producing the HBO miniseries *The Corner* (2007/2008). He was the creator, executive producer, and writer of the NBC miniseries *Kingpin*. Mills earned top honors from the Writers Guild of America (2009), the Edgar Award (2007) for *The Wire*, and Humanitas Prize (1997) for *NYPD Blue* as well as being nominated for several other awards. In 2010,

just 12 days before the premiere of his award-winning HBO series *Treme*, he died of a brain aneurysm. Eighty members of the show's cast and crew dedicated a tree in New Orleans's City Park to Mills's memory as the Rebirth Brass Band played and the group ate apple-filled Hubig's Pies from wrappers on which the lines "David Mills 1961–2010/ Won't Bow, Don't Know How" had been stamped.

2008: The Tulalip Tribes in Washington State became the first Native Nation to own a cable channel, KANU-TV 99.

2009: 'Ōiwi Television became the first Native Hawaiian TV station, providing news, language lessons, documentaries, and cartoons focusing on Indigenous Hawaiian culture and issues. It was founded by Native Hawaiian cinematographer Nā'ālehu Anthony.

2011: Stacy Layne Matthews (1984–), Lumbee, was the first-ever Native American to compete in *RuPaul's Drag Race*. She was the sixth contestant to be eliminated.

2016: The first annual Native American TV Writers Lab was held. The talent development program aims to boost the careers of Native American writers and is sponsored by the LA Skins Fest, a Native American film festival, in partnership with Comcast/NBCUniversal, CBS Entertainment Diversity, and HBO. The five-week curriculum, taught by seasoned writing executives, consists of daily workshops, seminars, and one-on-one mentoring to help each writer develop and complete a pilot in five weeks and hone skills to become staff writers. The first participants selected were Joseph Clift, Cowlitz Indian Tribe; Kelly Lynne D'Angelo, Tuscarora; William Jehu Garroutte, Cherokee Nation of Oklahoma; Tom Hanada, Cherokee Nation of Oklahoma; Khadijah Holgate, Nipmuc; Jason Levinson, Northern Cherokee

Nation Organization; and Carlee Malemute, Athabascan.

2017: Lucas Brown Eyes, Oglala Lakota, sold the pilot of his situation comedy, *Reservations*, to 20th Century Fox. It was the first time this genre featured Native people. The story line follows a Native American family that relocates to Los Angeles from their South Dakota reservation, a move inspired by the dreams of their 14-year-old boy to live in Hollywood and based on Brown Eyes's life. The teenager has a dad and three "moms" (mother, grandmother, and aunt), who all find city life to be even weirder and more complicated than what they were expecting. The scripts debunk stereotypes about Indians while raising issues of invisibility and racism. Brown Eyes has written for Freeform's *Young and Hungry* and the Disney Channel's *K.C. Undercover* and is also the founder of Brown Eyes Media Corp.

2019: PBS premiered *Molly of Denali*, its first animated series featuring mostly Indigenous characters and themes. The protagonist, Vlogger Molly, and her community, the fictional village of Qyah, are Alaskan Native. Her family runs the Denali Trading Post, managed by her dad, and her mom is a bush pilot. The show's theme song is sung by Phillip Blanchett and Karina Moeller from the Yup'ik band Pamyua. Portions of the show's dialogue are in the Gwich'in language, and the main cast members are Indigenous. Molly is voiced by Sovereign Bill, Gwich'in/Koyukon/Dena'ina Athabascan. Molly films videos on her phone to share with viewers in the other states and Washington, D.C. about life in Alaska. She is loyal, kind, brave, and loves basketball and animals; her native name is Shahnyaa, which means "one who informs us." Over 60 Alaska Native writers, producers, voice talents, advisors and musicians develop the series, and the advisers are from every region of Alaska where the show takes place. *Molly of Denali* earned several

accolades: Television Critics Award for Outstanding Achievement in Youth Programming (2020); Peabody Award for Best Children and Youth Programming (2020); Kidscreen Award for Best Inclusivity (2021); and Youth Media Alliance Best Program, Animation, Ages 6–9 (2021).

2020: HBO's *We're Here* focused on Native Americans for the first time. Navajo Nation citizens fashion designer Darin Jamal Tom, photographer Nate Lemuel, and drag queen Lady Shug are featured in Season 1, Episode 4.

2020: Alaqua Cox, Menominee, was the first deaf Native American to be cast in a major role in a series. Her character is Maya Lopez, the alter-identity of Echo, a deaf Native American Superhero in the Disney+ series *Hawkeye*.

2020: MTV aired the "Hanna Harris Story" on *True Life Crime*. Harris, Northern Cheyenne, is just one of several hundred Native women who has disappeared or has been found murdered. This was the first time the murder of a Native American woman was profiled on any true crime show. Dometi Pongo, journalist and host, was shocked to learn about the crisis of missing and murdered Indigenous women.

2021: The ABC drama series *Grey's Anatomy* was set in Seattle, Washington, and sets were often decorated with Indigenous art of the region. On May 10, 2021 (Season 17, Episode #15), the storyline incorporated Suquamish parents, whose child was born at the hospital. A stunning red cradleboard, made by Tulalip artist Taylor Henry, was an integral prop. It was the first time a cradleboard had been made specifically for a television show, and Henry constructed it in the same way as if he had made it for real-life use. He is a teacher of traditional arts for the Hibulb Cultural Center's Rediscovery Project, Tulalip, Washington.

ORGANIZATIONS

1974: Nā Maka o ka ʻĀina ("The Eyes of the Land") was founded as the first independent video production team to focus on the land and people of Hawaiʻi and the Pacific. They have created over 100 documentary and educational programs aired on PBS, Hawaiʻi public and commercial television stations, public access cable channels, and broadcast/cable networks in Canada, Aotearoa (New Zealand), Japan, Mexico, and Europe. Covering history, culture, and current issues of Indigenous Hawaiians, their work has won or been nominated for almost 30 awards.

1977: Native American Public Telecommunications, now named Vision Maker Media (VMM), was incorporated and became the premiere source of media by and about Native Americans. The organization's impressive list of films explore a variety of issues and include *Blood Memory*, *For the Rights of All: Ending Jim Crow in Alaska*, *Skindigenous*, and *Searching for Sequoyah*. VMM provides Native filmmakers with professional workshops, funding, internships, and mentorship programs.

1983: Over two dozen Native journalists were called together at Penn State University by Tim Giago (1934–), Oglala Lakota, the owner and editor of the *Lakota Times*. The historic gathering eventually formed the Native American Press Association. The first convention was held in the summer of 1984 at Warm Springs, Oregon. The name was changed to the Native American Journalists Association (NAJA) and offers a variety of services including the "Red Press Initiative to better understand the value of an Indigenous free press to the wellbeing of Indigenous people, communities and nations,"

legal support, youth projects, industry news, and training.

1990: The National Film Board of Canada created Studio One, a project designed for use by Indigenous peoples to develop media that portrays Native peoples and culture accurately. It was the first organization to devote its attention exclusively to training Natives in the film industry.

2004: Native Public Media (NPM) was founded "to empower Native people ... to participate actively in all forms of media and to do it on our own terms." The organization holds an annual summit featuring an intensive, two-week media training session. NPM's contributions include *New Media, Technology and Internet Use in Indian Country* (2009), a report that "contains the first valid and credible data gathered from the ground up on technology use, access, and adoption in Native American Lands."

2004: Sundance Institute, created by Robert Redford and headquartered in Utah, founded the Indigenous Program to support Indigenous filmmakers. The efforts include searching for and identifying Native artists, providing support at Sundance to get their work made and shown, and then bringing the filmmakers and their work back to Indian Country. The Native Filmmakers Lab has been vital to supporting Indigenous filmmakers since the inception of the program.

2005: Longhouse Media was launched in Washington State to support and encourage new media works by Indigenous artists and communities, debunk negative stereotypes of Native people in the media, and train youth in all aspects of digital media.

2015: The Hawaiian Comic Book Alliance, founded by Sam Campos (Native Hawaiian), was a group of independent creators collaborating to cultivate the comic book culture in Hawai'i.

FESTIVALS

1975: The first annual American Indian Film Festival (AIFF) opened in Seattle, Washington. Founder and director Michael Smith (1951–2018), Fort Peck Sioux, had a vision to create a broader media culture of Native voices, viewpoints, and stories that have been historically excluded from mainstream media. To accomplish this goal, AIFF advocates for Natives to be represented accurately and authentically in the industry and for opportunities for Native Americans to be part of filmmaking in front of and behind the camera. AIFF is the oldest and the best-known international film forum devoted to the presentation of American and Canadian Indians in cinema and is now held in San Francisco, California.

1981: The Hawai'i International Film Festival (HIFF) was inaugurated and has become a premiere cinematic event in the Pacific. Along with Asian films from around the Pacific, Native Hawaiian films are showcased to a broader audience.

1997: The Native American Film and Video Festival, held biennially in New York City until 2011, was the first to feature Native productions from throughout the Americas and the Arctic Circle. Indigenous media makers participated from Bolivia, Brazil, Canada, Chile, El Salvador, Mexico, and the United States. It was sponsored by the National Museum of the American Indian and included Indigenous filmmakers such as Chris Eyre, Randy Redroad, and Nora Naranjo Morse, and Native American cultural experts and academics such as G. Peter Jemison, Beverly Singer, and Paul Apodaca.

2000: The annual imagineNATIVE Film + Media Arts Festival kicked off in Toronto, Ontario. It is the largest showcase for Canadian and international Indigenous filmmakers and media artists.

2006: Vision Maker Media hosted its first annual festival in Lincoln, Nebraska.

2007: The Monument Valley Film, Blues & Arts Festival was launched by Navajo filmmakers Shonie and Andee De La Rosa on the Navajo Nation in Kayenta, Arizona. It is the only film festival of its kind on the Navajo Nation. The De La Rosas are best known for their collaborative effort in the groundbreaking documentary film *G* (2004) and the release of their first full-length feature film *Mile Post 398* (2007).

2008: "Bringing the Circle Together" was the first monthly film series by and about Indigenous peoples of Americas. The influential free film series in downtown Los Angeles was a central gathering place for Indigenous peoples and their supporters to discuss issues and share historical narratives, art, and traditions. It ran for four years.

2010: Ōiwi Film Festival was the first to feature only Native Hawaiian filmmakers.

The logo of the Hawaii International Film Festival, which was founded in 1981.

2012: The Garifuna International Indigenous Film Festival (GIIFF) was founded by Freda Sideroff, Indigene of the Garifuna. The annual event held in Santa Monica, California, showcases Garifuna culture and seeks to support the preservation of all Indigenous cultures in the world through art and film.

2015: May Sumak, a film festival celebrating Indigenous and community filmmaking in the Quechua languages spoken throughout the diaspora, from the Andes to the United States, kicked off in New York City. The annual event features documentaries and dramas that are interconnected through the Quechua language.

2016: Indigenous Comic Con debuted in Albuquerque, New Mexico, to promote Native American comic creators. In 2019, the festival was expanded to include Indigenous people around the world and renamed IndigiPop X.

2016: The annual Smithsonian's Mother Tongue Film Festival celebrated cultural and linguistic diversity by showcasing films and filmmakers from around the world, highlighting the crucial role languages play in daily lives. Indigenous-language films are integral to the festival.

PERFORMING ARTS

"Let me try to stimulate your imagination. There are 512 or so Indian tribes in the United States today. If each one were to establish and sponsor its own theater company, and produce just one new work based on its history, culture, and heritage, we would have 512 new works for the theater. And if only half of them were to do this— in some fantastical dream-come-true—then there would be 256 new Indian plays. The theater can help us in so many good ways. Theater is one of the most accessible of the performing arts, and we should begin immediately to create new Indian theaters."

—Hanay Geiogamah, Kiowa/Delaware, director, Project HOOP

COMEDY AND MAGIC

"I put a box on Jeramy's head. It's got a little door in the front. You can open the door & see Jeramy's face. I will stick a napkin over his face & I will shoot the top of that box full of lighter fluid & set it on fire. When I open that door, his face is burnt to a skull. Then the magic is I've got to bring his head back."

—Bobby Neugin, Cherokee magician

1974: Charles "Charlie" Allan Hill (1951–2013), Oneida Nation of Wisconsin, was the first Native American comedian to appear on *The Tonight Show Starring Johnny Carson.* Over his long career, he was an actor in many films and television shows and also a writer on *Roseanne.* Hill hosted an evening of Native American comedians for Showtime and was the subject of the PBS documentary *On and Off the Res' with Charlie Hill* (1999), directed by Sandra Osawa, Makah.

2008: Reuben Fast Horse (1971–), Standing Rock Sioux, became the first known Lakota magician. He has performed across the country for thousands of schools as well as abroad. Fast Horse is also a juggler, flautist, comedian, and street performer and has taken his unique act abroad, often with his significant other Vivian Billy, Pomo, a professional face painter, psychic, and tarot card reader.

2009: The 1491s, a sketch comedy group, first appeared in a YouTube video, "The Wolf Pack Auditions," a satire about the casting of Natives for the *Twilight* movies. The group's name is a reference to the year 1491, the year before Christopher Columbus brought the European invasion of the Western Hemisphere.. The "take no prisoners" Indian act uses videos, improvisation, and sketch comedy to depict contemporary Native American life in the United States. Humorous and satirical sketches explore issues such as stereotypes and racism (internal and external), tribal politics, the conflict between traditional and contemporary life, and taboo topics within their own communities. Members, based in Minnesota, Montana, and Oklahoma, include Dallas Goldtooth, Mdewakanton Dakota/Diné, Keystone XL campaign organizer for the Indigenous Environmental Network, Dakota language-instructor, writer, and artist; Sterlin Harjo, Seminole/Muscogee, filmmaker; Migizi Pensoneau, Ponca/Ojibwe, television and film writer and producer; Ryan Red Corn, Osage Nation, graphic artist and photographer; and Bobby Wilson (aka Bobby Dues), Sisseton Wahpeton Dakota, visual artist and actor. They describe themselves as a "gaggle of Indians chock full of cynicism and splashed with a good dose of indigenous satire."

2010: The *American Indian Comedy Slam: Goin Native No Reservations Needed* aired on television, hosted by Charlie Hill. Not only was it a first, but it was also the first time so many legendary Native American comedians were on one stage together: Charlie Hill, Oneida; Larry Omaha, Yaqui Zapotec; Howie Miller, Cree; Marc Yaffee, Navajo; Jim Rule, Bay Mills Ojibwe; Vaughn Eaglebear and JR Redwater, Standing Rock Sioux.

2014: The Ladies of Native Comedy was formed, the first collaboration of Native female comedians. The group is composed of Adrianne Chalepah, Kiowa/Apache, who opened for First Lady Michelle Obama in 2012; Teresa Choyguha, Tohono O'odham, winner of the 2012 Winnipeg Aboriginal Film Festival Best Actress Award for her role in *More Than Frybread*; and Deanna M.A.D., Tonawanda Seneca, recipient of the Embrey Women's Leadership Fellowship.

2016: Jeramy Neugin and his father, Bobby Neugin, started the first-known Native American father-son magic act, Lost City Magic (named after their Oklahoma Cherokee community). Their novel routines brim with all the thrills and excitement of disappearing and reappearing acts while exposing the audience to Cherokee heritage. Their illusions are linked to Cherokee traditions (including the "little people"), and they include tricks like bringing live swarms of wasps to life from a handful of dirt and pulling live snakes from drawings. Encouraged by their fans, they auditioned for *America's Got Talent.*

2018: The Los Angeles County Board of Supervisors replaced Columbus Day with Indigenous People's Day to honor the vibrant culture and historical resilience of Native people. To kick off the celebration, the storied LA comedy club and the Upright Citizens Brigade presented *The Ghost of Christopher Columbus Theater Smudging Spectacular,* featuring an all–Native American lineup including Jana Schmieding, Cheyenne River Lakota; Joey Clift, Cowlitz; and Kaitlyn Jeffers, Dakota.

2018: The Oregon Shakespeare Festival and New Native Theatre cocommissioned the comedy troupe 1491s to create a play for their *American Revolutions* series of new works about U.S. history. The play, *Between Two Knees,* covers events between the Wounded Knee massacre of 1890 and the Wounded Knee incident of 1973 with an infusion of accurate accounts and humor.

DANCE

"Through dance I am able to express my dreams, visions and stories, both historical and contemporary."

—*Tekaronhiáhkhwa Santee Smith, Mohawk, artistic director of Kaha:wi Dance Theatre*

c. 1918: The Jingle Dress Dance has been traced to the period of the global pandemic of 1918–1919, when it was created by Anishinaabe (Ojibwe) people as a healing dance. Oral histories vary on where it first appeared but generally identify tribal communities in Minnesota, Wisconsin, and/or Ontario. The dresses are embellished with metal cones that make tinkling sounds as dancers move to the music of the drum. In 2019, an exhibit at the Mille Lacs Indian Museum in Minnesota, "Ziibaaska'iganagooday: The Jingle Dress at 100," curated by historian Brenda Child, celebrated the dress's centennial. Child points out that the dance remained a regional tradition until the 1980s, "when it became wildly popular and spread among many tribal nations on powwow circuits across North America." On June 15, 2019, Google featured a doodle of Jingle Dancers created by Ojibwe guest artist Joshua Mangeshig Pawis-Steckley.

1926: The first large, intertribal, off-reservation powwow dance organized by American Indians was held at the Haskell Institute (now Haskell Indian Nations University) in Lawrence, Kansas.

c. 1920s and 1930s: The Fancy Dance was originated by members of the Ponca Nation working to preserve their culture and religion. The U.S. and Canadian governments had outlawed historical dance traditions to eradicate Native religions. Some dances, part of Indigenous ceremonies, went "underground," to avoid government detection. The new Fancy Dance was loosely based on the traditional War Dance but was advertised as performance art. It became a popular feature of powwows and spread from tribe to tribe. The fast-paced energetic dance often includes trick steps and very complicated athletic movements. Male dancers wear flashy regalia of brightly colored twin feather bustles, fringed and beaded bodice, leggings, fringed breech cloth, bells, moccasins, a head piece (called a roach) with two

Young women dance in jingle dresses at the Last Chance Community Pow Wow in Helena, Washington, in 2007.

feathers (which bob to the dancer's steps), beaded cuffs, beaded headband, and other feathered or beaded accessories. In the late 1930s, women created their own version of the Fancy Dance and also have colorful outfits, generally composed of a beaded dress, fringed shawl, beaded moccasins, and other accoutrements like headwear and jewelry.

c. 1935: Tony White Cloud, Jemez Pueblo, is generally credited as the founder of the modern Hoop Dance. In his stylized version, he used five hoops made of willow wood bent to form a circle 24 inches in diameter. Today dancers use a lighter material like reed from Vietnam and often perform with 22–40 hoops. In 1942, White Cloud brought the

A man in traditional dress performs a hoop dance using five hoops made of bent willow wood.

hoop dance to the big screen when he made his debut in *Valley of the Sun*, starring Lucille Ball. White Cloud also traveled and performed throughout America and Europe with Gene Autry (the "singing cowboy") to promote World War II war bonds. It soon spread to other tribes. In 1991, the World Championship Hoop Dance Contest began at the New Mexico State Fair, and Eddie Swimmer, Eastern Band Cherokee/Chippewa Cree, was the first world champion. In 1992, the contest moved to the Heard Museum in Phoenix, Arizona, where it is still held. Lisa Odjig, Odawa/Anishinaabe, became the first female champion in 2000. In 2021, the event was held online for the first time because of the ongoing impact of the COVID-19 pandemic.

Marjorie Tallchief

c. 1942: Maria Tallchief (1925–2013), Osage, was the first Native American and the first American to dance with the Paris Opera. Tallchief was also the first American to receive the title of prima ballerina in the United States. Before that, prima ballerinas were always "imported" from Europe. Tallchief was the first Native American to dance with the Ballet at the Bolshoi Theater in Moscow (1947). George Balanchine created ballets for her, including *Firebird*. Over her lifetime, she received many honors and was the first Native woman to be honored at the Kennedy Center (1967). She was one of the "Five Moons," along with ballerinas Marjorie Tallchief, Rosella Hightower, Yvonne Chouteau, and Moscelyne Larkin.

1957: Moscelyne Larkin (1925–2012), Shawnee/Peoria, established the Oklahoma Indian Ballerina Festival. Larkin was one of the celebrated Oklahoma Native ballerinas referred to as the Five Moons. She also created a ballet school and founded the Tulsa Civic Ballet (1957), more firsts. It became a major company in the Southwest and made its premier in New York in 1983. Larkin introduced area schoolchildren to the art and taught ballet to more advanced students at the University of Tulsa.

1957: Marjorie Tallchief (1926–2021), Osage, and younger sister of Maria Tallchief, was the first American and first Native American to be named "première danseuse étoile" in the Paris Opera Ballet. She was known for her great expressive powers and her acrobatic elasticity and high speed *fouettes* that became her trademark. Both sisters were part of the famous Five Moons.

1962: Rosella Hightower (1920–2008), Choctaw, and one of the Five Moons of Oklahoma, founded her own dance school in Cannes, France, the first Native American to do so. She was both the first American and Native American to direct major companies, including the Marseilles Ballet from 1969 to 1972, the Ballet of the Grand Théâtre of Nancy in 1973–74, the Paris Opéra Ballet from 1980 to 1983, and the La Scala Ballet of Milan in 1985–86. Hightower was the first to discard the hierarchical star system and devised a controversial practice that gave all dancers a time to shine and develop their skills. Like the other Native ballerinas, Hightower was world-famous and danced with prestigious companies in the United States and Europe and was awarded many honors.

1963: Louis Mofsie (1936–), Hopi/Winnebago, founded the American Indian Thunderbird Dancers in New York City, the first professional Native dance troupe in the metro area. The intertribal group has performed in almost every state and in many different countries. Their annual powwow held at Queens Farm in Queens, New York, draws thousands of visitors.

1967: Kenneth Harris, Gitxsan, and his wife, Margaret Harris, Cree, founded the Dancers of Damelahamid in Prince Rupert, British Columbia, Canada. The couple did so to preserve Northwest Coast Indigenous dance styles. Such dances were banned in Canada between 1884 and 1951, part of repressive Euro-Canadian assimilation efforts by the federal government. In 2019, the Harrises were inducted into the Dance Collection Danse Hall of Fame in Toronto. Their daughter Margaret Grenier continues their work, serving as the executive and artistic director of Dancers of Damelahamid.

1977: Marla Bingham (1953–), Mashpee Wampanoag, was the first Native principal dancer with the prestigious Alvin Ailey American Dance Theater. She has performed in 14 countries and became the first Native to be the artistic director of Austria's Vereinigte Bühnen Wien's Musical Theater School (Tanz Gesang Studio), heading up successful productions of *Cats, Phantom of the Opera, Les Misérables,* and *A Chorus Line.* Bingham has choreographed for the American Indian Dance Theatre, the Joffrey Ballet Concert Group, the Mississippi Ballet, and Disneyland's "The Spirit of Pocahontas," the first time Disney used a Native American choreographer for a live production (1995). She founded the Marla Bingham Contemporary Ballet Company (1996), based in Southern California. In 2000, she was featured in *Dance Spirit* magazine and *Native People's Magazine* for the world premiere of a Native version of Stravinsky's *The Firebird,* an original ballet she choreographed and performed with her company. Bingham was the first Native dancer and choreographer for MTV music videos, appeared on several television programs, and has received many awards for her work, including the Native American Youth Educator of the Year from the Tri-County Native American UMC Circle of Life (2000) and the First American in the Arts award for outstanding

achievement in dance (2002). She is the first known American Indian to own her own Pilates studio (Los Angeles).

1980: Rosalie Jones (1941–), Blackfeet/Chippewa, founded Daystar, the first dance company in the United States to feature all-Native performers. Daystar encourages and trains Native Americans in the performing arts and teaches non-Indians how to respect the dance, music, and art of Native Americans. The company has performed nationally and internationally.

1985: Jock Soto (1965–), Navajo/Puerto Rican, became the first Native man and the youngest-ever man to be the principal dancer with the New York City Ballet. He danced featured roles in over 40 ballets, of which more than 35 were created for him. In 2007, the documentary *Water Flowing Together* was released. The film explores Soto's connection to his heritage and follows him through the last two years of his career up to his retirement on June 19, 2005. His memoir, *Every Step You Take,* was published in 2011.

1990: The American Indian Dance Theatre was the first Native dance troupe to be featured on a prime-time television special, PBS's *Great Performance Series.*

1997: Yvonne Chouteau (1929–2016), Shawnee, was the first dancer to be designated as an Oklahoma Cultural Treasure, an award given by the state's governor. Her storied career included many milestones: she was the youngest dancer ever accepted to the Ballet Russe de Monte Carlo (1943), where she taught for 14 years; she launched the first Oklahoma City Civic Ballet (1956); and founded the first fully accredited university dance program in the United States, the School of Dance at the University of Oklahoma (1962). Chouteau is portrayed in the mural *Flight of Spirit,* by Chickasaw artist Mike Larsen, in the Oklahoma Capitol Ro-

East and West Meet

Kamala Cesar (1948–), Mohawk, received a National Endowment for the Arts Folk Art Grant in 1986. She was the first and only Native American to be awarded the honor to study Bharata Natyam, a South Indian traditional dance. Cesar is also one of the few American disciples to study in the style of the world-celebrated dancer T. Balasaraswati. She has performed extensively in the United States, Europe, and India. In 1989, Cesar founded Lotus Music & Dance, a not-for-profit organization that produces multicultural programs that promote the understanding, appreciation, and preservation of traditional arts and the creation of new works that evolve from traditional art forms. Some of her productions include *Mohawk Heartsong: Journey through the Longhouse; The New York Ramayana; Eagle Spirit—A Tribute to the Mohawk High Steelworkers; Message of Peace—An Excerpt from the Peacemaker's Journey; World in the City; Dancing across Cultural Borders; World Dance Passport; and Lotus—the Energy Within.* Since 2002, Cesar has directed Drums along the Hudson: A Native American Festival and Multicultural Celebration, held annually in Manhattan's Inwood Hill Park.

tunda, and in *The Five Moons,* a set of bronze sculptures by artist Gary Henson at the Tulsa Historical Society. In 2004, she was honored with the inaugural National Cultural Treasures Award at the opening of the Smithsonian Institution's National Museum of the American Indian in Washington, D.C.

2000: Red Sky Performance was founded by Sandra Laronde (Misko Kizhigoo Migizii Kwe, "Red Sky Eagle Woman"), Teme-Augama Anishinaabe, in Toronto, Ontario, Canada. The company, with Laronde serving as the executive and artistic director, incorporates aboriginal culture, contemporary dance, theater, and music into each production. Red Sky has toured since 2003, with international performances in 17 countries on four continents. The company has also delivered over 2,700 performances across Canada. It is the recipient of 16 Dora Mavor Moore awards and nominations, two Canadian Aboriginal Music Awards, three International Youth Drama Awards, the Smith-sonian Expressive Award, and other recognitions.

2004: Coopdanza, Inc. was founded by Cristina Cortes (1955–), Muisca, to expose environmental conflicts affecting Native communities of the Americas and the implications for all peoples. Through contemporary and Native dance performance, Coopdanza engages in local and international collaborations to create ARTivism, community projects and public education programs that generate environmental awareness while reinforcing Indigenous knowledge and heritage. It is the first dance troupe of its kind and is based in New York City.

2006: Christopher K. Morgan became the first Native Hawaiian director of the Dance Residency at Art Omi, an annual collaborative choreographers' residency located in Ghent, New York. He is the executive artistic director of his own company, Christopher K. Morgan & Artists (CKM&A) as well as the executive artistic director of Dance Place, based in Washington, D.C. In 2018, Morgan was one of three artists to be awarded a Launchpad in a new initiative for Native artists sponsored by the Western Arts Alliance.

2010: Nicole Prescovia Elikolani Valiente Scherzinger (1978–), Native Hawaiian, was the first Indigenous person to win *Dancing with the Stars*. Scherzinger went on to achieve other Native firsts: the first to serve as a judge on *British X Factor* (2010), where she helped form One Direction; the first Native to win the variety show *I Can Do That* (2015); the first to perform the national anthem at a Special Olympics World Summer Games (2015); and the first to appear as a panelist on *The Masked Singer*. Scherzinger is best known as the lead singer of the Pussycat Dolls, who are credited for becoming one of the world's best-selling girl groups of all time. In 2019, she took part in the protests against the building of the Thirty Meter Telescope on Mauna Kea, a place considered a holy site for Indigenous Hawaiians.

Nicole Scherzinger

2015: Carla Drumbeater (1971–), Leech Lake Band of Ojibwe, became the first Indigenous competitor in the Minnesota Madness "Smooth Category of Ballroom Dance" (waltz, tango, and foxtrot). In 2016, she was once again the first Native dancer to participate in the Minnesota Starball "Rhythm Category," performing rumba, salsa, cha cha, bachata, and swing, held in Bloomington.

2017: Edwin (1951–), Taino, and Nick Garcia-Cleveland (1951–), Creek/Seminole/Arapaho/Kiowa/Cheyenne, were the first and only Native couple to perform a disco routine on the Manhattan Neighborhood Network (MNN) TV show *No Boundaries: Up Close and Personal*, hosted by Ron Balaguer.

They are known throughout the NYC Metro area for their innovative dance routines. The first Native and also the first two-spirit couple to be featured on the front page of the *Staten Island Advance* (October 2014), the article chronicled their Native background, love story, experiences dancing in Manhattan clubs for 40 years, and their 40th anniversary jubilee.

2017: "Powwow Sweat" was launched by the Coeur d'Alene Tribe in Idaho. In the demonstrations of the intense exercise program based on traditional dances like the rigorous and high-stepping crow hop and jingle dance, tribal member and exercise leader Shedaezha Hodge commands, "Drop the Pringles and let's jingle." The tribe also supports a community garden on the reservation and a project that stocks the gas station market with healthy food options.

2017: The Intermountain All-Women Hoop Dancing Competition was held, the first of its kind. The event was held at This Is the Place Heritage Park in Salt Lake City, Utah. Sandra Yellowhorn, Piegan Nation, won first place.

2020: Margaret Grenier, Gitxsan/Cree, was the first Indigenous recipient of the Canada Council for the Arts' prestigious Walter Carsen Prize for Excellence in the Performing Arts. She was also the first dance artist outside of Ontario and Quebec to win the $50,000 prize. Grenier is the executive and artistic director of Dancers of Damelahamid.

2020: Indigenous Enterprise, an all-Native dance group, became the first act to perform Native dances on the hit NBC show *World of Dance*. The dance collective started performing in 2015 at local community colleges to educate people on the traditions and culture of Native Americans and soon achieved worldwide fame. They were also the first Native American group to perform at the Sydney Opera House in Australia. Dancers are from the Diné and Salt River Maricopa Pima nations.

George Henry

DRAMA, DRAMATISTS, AND THEATER

"We are the oldest Native feminist theater in the world, as far as we know. That's important. The stories that we tell are from many nations, but mostly from the spirit, which is really important to us."

—Muriel Miguel, Kuna/Rappahannock, Spiderwoman Theater

1844: George Henry (1811–1888), Ojibwa, also known as Maungwudaus, formed the first all-Native acting troupe, Wild Indian. They traveled extensively internationally performing Native dances and exhibitions. Henry also wrote a travelogue, *Remarks Concerning the Ojibway Indians by One of Themselves, Called Maungwudaus, Who Has Been Traveling in England, France, Belgium, Ireland and Scotland* (1847). It is thought to be the first written by an American Indian.

c. 1880: Emily Pauline Johnson (1861–1913), also known by her Mohawk stage name, Tekahionwake ("double-life"), was the first Native woman to support her family with a stage career. She was also a critically acclaimed poet/author and thought to be the

first Native woman to publish poetry. Johnson created a two-part act that would confuse the contrast between her Mohawk and English background. In act 1, she would come out as Tekahionwake, the Mohawk name of her great-grandfather, wearing a generic "Indian" outfit, and perform dramatic "Indian" lyrics. During intermission, she would wear a fashionable English dress. For act 2, her persona was a Victorian English North-West Mounted Police officer (now known as the Royal Canadian Mounted Police [RCMP]) performing in "English" verse. Johnson graced the stages of many theaters in North America, often being the only female actor.

1931: *Green Grow the Lilacs*, written by Rollie Lynn Riggs (1899–1954), Cherokee, was produced by the Theatre Guild in New York City. It was the first time the Guild had presented a work by a Native playwright. The play was later adapted by Richard Rodgers and Oscar Hammerstein into the musical *Oklahoma!* Riggs is considered one of the greatest writers of folk drama.

1956: Arthur Smith Junaluska (1912–1978), Cherokee, organized the first American Indian drama company. He was also the first Native to perform in a Shakespearean repertory company. In addition, he founded the American Society for Creative Arts. Junaluska wrote and produced many plays, including *The Grand Council of Indian Circle;* was a choreographer (*Dance of the Twelve Moons*); and was a consultant for radio, television, and stage. Junaluska's talents were not limited to theater. In 1966, he cofounded the Indian Actors Workshop in Los Angeles, with Jay Silverheels, Mohawk; George Pierre, Colville; and Noble "Kid" Chissell, Cherokee. The Workshop, the first of its kind, aimed to promote Native American writing and acting talent in Hollywood, train Native American actors in theater, arts, and advocate a more accurate representation of Native Americans in theater, television, and film.

1971: Hanay Geiogamah (1945–), Kiowa/Delaware, founded the American Indian Theatre Ensemble at the La MaMa Experimental Theatre Club in New York City. It was the first all-Native repertory theater company in the country and toured Europe and the United States. In 1980, Geiogamah published *New Native American Drama: Three Plays.* He is a professor in the School of Theater, Film, and Television at the University of California, Los Angeles. He also served as the director of the UCLA American Indian Studies Center from 2002 to 2009. From 1993 to 1996, Geiogamah produced the TNT series *The Native Americans: Behind the Legends, Beyond the Myths.* He is a cofounder and director of Project HOOP, based in L.A., which is a national, multidisciplinary initiative to advance Native theater artistically, academically, and professionally.

1976: Spiderwoman Theater was founded in New York City by sisters Muriel Miguel, Gloria Miguel, and Lisa Mayo (née Elizabeth Miguel), Kuna/Rappahannock, and was the first Native American women's theater troupe in the country. Blending Indigenous art forms with Western theater, their work questions gender roles, sexual and economic oppression, and cultural stereotypes and promotes Indigenous performance practice. Spiderwoman has toured New Zealand, Europe, Australia, China, Canada, and the United States presenting satires filled with slapstick humor, Indigenous issues, and a feminist perspective, like their critically acclaimed *Winnetou's Snake Oil Show from Wigwam City.*

Irma-Estel LaGuerre

1977: Vivia Nail Locke (1916–1987), Choctaw/Chickasaw, became the first person of her nation to be awarded an Oklahoma Governor's Arts Award. A drama professor at Oklahoma State University (1950–1981), she was also the first Native in the state to have a university theater named for her. She was an integral part of the theater department's growth. In 2019, actor Gary Busey credited Professor Locke with his success as an actor.

1982: Native Earth Performing Arts was founded in Toronto, Ontario, and is Canada's oldest professional Indigenous theater company. It develops, produces, and presents professional artistic expressions of the Indigenous experience in the country. Some of Native Earth's key productions are Tomson Highway's award-winning *The Rez Sisters* and *Dry Lips Oughta Move to Kapuskasing,* Daniel David Moses's *Almighty Voice and His Wife,* Drew Hayden Taylor's *Someday,* and Cliff Cardinal's *Huff.* Native Earth hosts the annual Weesageechak Begins to Dance festival, which showcases emerging Indigenous theater, dance, and multidiscipline artists.

1985: Irma-Estel LaGuerre (1953–), Taino/Azteca, actress/singer, won the Institute of Puerto Rico Excellence in Art and Service to the Community for her role as Lady Thiang opposite Yul Brynner in the Broadway revival of *The King and I.* She was the first Indigenous person to play the role and receive the award. She was also the first Native performer to work with celebrated director Julie Taymor, in the critically acclaimed *Juan Darien: A Carnival Mask.* For her outstanding performance in that production, LaGuerre was nominated for a San Francisco Bay Area Theatre Critic Circle Award for lead actress in a musical (1990), another first. She is the director of the Children's Cultural Center of Native America, a New York City educational organization that works with schools to debunk stereotypes about American Indians.

2000: Leaf Arrow Storytellers was created by Donna Coteau Cross, Sac and Fox, and Joe Cross, Caddo Tribe of Oklahoma in New York City. They produce interactive shows based on traditional accounts and filled with tribal family values. It is the first Native theater troupe in the New York Metro area to present to intergenerational audiences.

2018: The Arena Theater (Washington, D.C.) produced its first play written by a Native American. The drama, *Sovereignty*, by playwright and attorney Mary Kathryn Nagle, Cherokee, revolves around Cherokee lawyer Sarah Ridge Polson's battle to reinstate the Cherokee Nation's sovereignty and jurisdiction.

2019: Moses Goods, Native Hawaiian, wrote, produced, and starred in the one-man show *My Name Is 'Ōpūkaha'ia*, presented from an Indigenous perspective for the first time at the Maui Arts and Cultural Center. Henry 'Ōpūkaha'ia (c. 1792–1818) was a complex figure in Hawaiian history, both celebrated and denounced for being the first Hawaiian Christian. An orphan, the teen hopped aboard a trading ship in 1807, landing on the American East Coast two years later. 'Ōpūkaha'ia ended up in New Haven, Connecticut, living in the home of Timothy Dwight, president of Yale University and cofounder of the American Board of Commissioners for Foreign Missions (ABCFM). He was tutored in many subjects, including Christian principles, and became an exceptional scholar. 'Ōpūkaha'ia mastered English and Hebrew, learned Greek and Latin, and graduated from the Foreign Mission School in one year. Goods also founded the 'Inamona Theatre Company, dedicated to reintroducing traditional Hawai'ian stories to the community.

2020: For the first time, the Smith Prize for Political Theater went to an American Indian. Recipient Vickie Ramirez, Tuscarora,

Joe Cross and Donna Coteau Cross of the Leaf Arrow Storytellers

is a founding member of Chukalokoli Native Theater Ensemble and Amerinda Theater. Her work has been developed at the Public Theater, the LAByrinth Theater, the Roundabout Theatre's Different Voices, the Missoula Writer's Colony, and the Black Swan Theatre at the Oregon Shakespeare Festival.

MUSIC

"Look, I'm an Indian right off the reservation and I got to play with Louis Armstrong."

—*Russell "Big Chief" Moore, Pima, jazz trombonist*

1888: Composer Juventino Rosas (1868–1894), Otomí, became the first Indigenous person to write a waltz, "Sobre las Olas." The iconic tune

Te Ata the Treasure

Mary Frances Thompson (1895–1995), best known as Te Ata, was named Oklahoma's first State Treasure (1987). An actress and citizen of the Chickasaw Nation, she was known for telling Native American stories and was the first Native performer to entertain at a state dinner during President Franklin D. Roosevelt's time in office (c. 1930s). Te Ata performed in several Broadway productions; her most notable role was Andromache in *The Trojan Women*. Her career focus became her one-woman performances of Native American songs and stories. Te Ata was an American favorite and has been featured in many books, plays, and magazines, including in "Types of American Beauty" in a 1924 issue of *McCall's Magazine*. She is the namesake for Lake Te Ata in New York, was the *Ladies' Home Journal* Woman of the Year (1976), and was inducted into the Oklahoma Hall of Fame (1957) and the Chickasaw Hall of Fame (1990). Te Ata's alma mater, the University of Science and Arts of Oklahoma (formerly Oklahoma College for Women), honored her in many ways. She was the first inductee into the University of Science and Arts of Oklahoma Hall of Fame (1972); had a building named for her—Te Ata Memorial Auditorium (2006); and had a statue of her dedicated in the campus center (2014).

Statue of Te Ata (Mary Frances Thompson), University of Science & Arts of Oklahoma

was also the first of Rosas's works to be recorded on a double-faced, 78 rpm record. The song received international acclaim and is usually credited to Johann Strauss, the Waltz King. Rosas died when he was just 26 years old while on tour in Cuba. In 1950, *Sobre las olas*, a biopic film about his life, premiered. The brilliant young musician wrote in many genres, including polka.

Juventino Rosas

1889: Teenager Joseph Kekuku (1874–1932) invented the steel guitar while attending the Kamehameha School for Native Hawaiian Boys in Honolulu, Hawaii. The lilting sound of the Hawaiian steel guitar captivated Americans, and Kekuku became a world-touring guitar soloist. The instrument influenced various genres of American music; the guitarist holds it on his lap, plucks the cords instead of strumming them, and runs a steel bar over the neck.

1893: The monograph *A Study of Omaha Indian Music* was published, the first of its kind. Francis La Flesche (1857–1932), Omaha/Ponca, worked closely with musicologist John Comfort Fillmore to produce the work. La Flesche, a lawyer, is thought to be the first Native ethnologist and worked with the Bureau of American Ethnology from 1910 until his retirement in 1929. During his tenure with the bureau, he recorded traditional Osage ceremonies on wax cylinders. Contemporary Osage tribal members have compared the effect of hearing the recordings of their traditional rituals to that of Western scholars reading the newly discovered Dead Sea Scrolls.

1895: For the first time, Native music was used by the dominant culture in a classical piece. Antonín Dvořák used Omaha music as the foundation for his masterpiece, *The New*

World Symphony. However, the music was anglicized and turned into a stereotype of Native music.

1913: Zitkála-Šá (Lakota for Red Bird), also known as Gertrude Simmons Bonnin (1876–1938), Yankton Dakota, wrote the libretto and songs for *The Sun Dance Opera*, the first American Indian opera. Composed in a romantic musical style, the story featured Sioux and Ute cultural themes. Zitkála-Šá was also an activist, writer, editor, translator, and musician. From 1897 to 1899 Zitkala-Ša studied and played the violin at the New England Conservatory of Music in Boston and may have been the first American Indian woman to do so.

1914: Soprano Ada Navarrete (c. 1885–1967), Maya, was the first Indigenous person from the Americas to be known internationally as an opera star. She debuted with the Boston Opera Company in 1917.

1916: For the first time, 78 rpm records featuring an Indigenous Hawaiian instrument (steel guitar) outsold every other genre of music in the United States.

1926: Tsianina Redfeather Blackstone (1882–1985), a Creek/Cherokee singer and performer, was the first Native to sing a title role in the first American opera with a modern setting. She starred in *Shanewis: The Robin Woman* at the Metropolitan Opera in New York City.

c. 1926: The Nez Perce jazz band Harmony Chiefs gave a premier performance in Lap-

Francis La Flesche

Zitkála-Šá

Ada Navarrete

Tsianina Redfeather Blackstone

wai, Idaho. Dressed in outfits blending Indigenous and non-Native styles, the group kicked off an era of Indian jazz and dance bands. Boarding schools educated Indian students in European-style music, hoping the young musicians would favor it over Indigenous music. Although the young musicians had learned to play marching band songs and hymns, they were drawn to the "new" African American music of jazz and blues. When they returned to their homes, they kept the instruments but used them to play jazz music, much to the dismay of their boarding school pro-assimilation music teachers. The Harmony Chiefs, along with Nez Perce bands like the Nezpercians, Lollipop Six, and ensembles from other reservations across the Northwest, played the popular big band music to audiences from the Canadian border to Southern California. The bands gave musicians an opportunity to travel off the reservations, earn money and respect, and still embrace their Indian identities.

1929: Charley Patton (1891–1934), Cherokee/Choctaw/African American, recorded his first album for Paramount Records, which included "Pony Blues," his trademark tune. Considered by consensus the Father of Delta Blues, he is one of the most important American musicians of the twentieth century. Patton described his mixed heritage in "Down the Road Blues" with the lyrics of having gone down to "the Nation" and "the Territo," which was the Cherokee Nation of Indian Territory (now the eastern half of Oklahoma).

1935: Russell "Big Chief" Moore (1912–1983), Pima, first played with the Lionel Hampton Orchestra, becoming the first Native American to be recognized as a jazz trombonist with a non-Native band. During his storied career, he performed with the great Louis Armstrong for several years as well as other luminaries like Ruby Braff, Pee Wee Russell, Eddie Condon, Wild Bill Davison, Jimmy McPartland, Tony Parenti, Mezz Mezzrow, Sidney Bechet, and Buck Clayton. Moore also had his own Dixieland band and toured extensively in Canada. In 1960, he played at the inaugural ball for President John F. Kennedy, another first for him. Moore was also the first Native American jazz musician to be memorialized at St. Peter's Church in Manhattan (1983), which is known as the first jazz church in the world.

1938: Mildred Bailey (1907–1951), Coeur d'Alene, became the first Native American jazz vocalist to have a number one song on the *Hit Parade* with "Please Be Kind." Later that year, she earned the top spot again with her song "Says My Heart." In 1940, Bailey's "Darn That Dream," recorded with the Benny Goodman Orchestra, reached number one on the U.S. pop singles chart. She was also the first Native American jazz singer to have a postage stamp in her honor (1994).

c. 1949: Oscar Pettiford (1922–1960), Choctaw/Cherokee/African American, was the first musician to use the cello in a solo jazz performance (with Woody Herman's band). Born in the Muscogee Creek capital—Okmulgee, Oklahoma—he

Charley Patton

Mildred Bailey

Oscar Pettiford

Keely Smith

came from a musical family and began performing with the family band as a child. By 14, he was playing the bass, and his growing skill would soon change the way the instrument was heard and played. Pettiford played and recorded with several jazz greats like Duke Ellington, John Coltrane, Thelonious Monk, Coleman Hawkins, Roy Eldridge, Erroll Garner, and Max Roach and was one of the earliest musicians to work in the bebop style. Although he was a double bassist, he began to substitute the cello while recovering from a broken arm and birthed the cello onto the jazz scene.

1951: Ed Lee Natay (?–1967), Navajo, was the first Native to record for Canyon Records in Phoenix, Arizona. The album, *Natay, Navajo Singer,* featured traditional songs and built a reputation for Canyon Records as a brand for Native music. Natay was also one of the first Native teachers in New Mexico public schools.

1959: Keely Smith (1928–2017), Cherokee, along with Louis Prima, won the first Grammy awarded for Best Performance by a Vocal Group or Chorus with the Top Twenty hit "That Old Black Magic."

1962: Louis Ballard (1931–2007), Quapaw/Cherokee, graduated from the University of Tulsa, becoming the first American Indian to receive a Ph.D. in music composition. In 1969, Ballard's *Ritmo Indio*, a three-movement work for woodwind quintet, won the Marian Nevins MacDowell Award for American Chamber Music. His second work for ballet,

Desert Trilogy, was nominated for a Pulitzer Prize in 1971. He was also the first American composer to have an entire concert dedicated to his music at Beethovenhalle in Bonn, Germany (1999). During his tenure as national curriculum specialist for the Bureau of Indian Affairs (1968–1979), Ballard published the seminal multimedia curriculum *American Indian Music for the Classroom*. He received the National Indian Achievement Award four times. Ballard was also awarded the Distinguished Service Award from the U.S. Central Office of Education, a citation in the U.S. *Congressional Record*, a Lifetime Musical Achievement Award by the First Americans in the Arts, and the Cherokee Medal of Honor.

Robbie Robertson

1962: Wayne Newton (1942–), Powhatan/Cherokee, was the first Native entertainer to be featured on televised variety shows: *The Jackie Gleason Show, The Ed Sullivan Show,* and *The Danny Kaye Show.* Newton went on to become the most successful and popular nightclub performer in Las Vegas and is referred to as Mr. Las Vegas. In 1975, he was the first Native person to ever be honored by being named "Entertainer of the Year" by the Academy of Variety and Cabaret Artists.

1967: Loretta Lynn (1932–), Cherokee, became the first woman of Native American descent to be named the Country Music Award's Female Vocalist of the Year. She has won more accolades than any other woman in the country music industry, and in 1980, her biography, *Coal Miner's Daughter*, was made into a film.

c. 1969: Robbie Robertson (1943–), Mohawk, was the first Native American to become a prominent

Wayne Newton

Loretta Lynn

rock musician and was also the first Indian rock musician to win several honors for his music. His band, called The Band, released an album named for the group, which went gold. Robertson is credited with composing several songs, including the Joan Baez hit "The Night They Drove Old Dixie Down." He and The Band played with folk/rock great Bob Dylan. As a film soundtrack producer and composer, Robertson is known for his collaborations with director Martin Scorsese for several films: *The Last Waltz* (1978); *Raging Bull* (1980); *Casino* (1995); *The Departed* (2006); *The Wolf of Wall Street* (2013); and *The Irishman* (2019). He has worked on many other soundtracks for film and television and was featured prominently in the documentary *Rumble: The Indians Who Rocked the World* (2017). Robertson's memoir, *Testimony*, a *New York Times* bestseller, was published in 2016.

1969: The hit single "Witchi Tai To" is the first and only song based on a Native American chant to hit the Billboard charts. Jazz saxophonist, composer, and singer Jim Pepper (1941–1992), Kaw/Muscogee Creek, derived it from a peyote song of the Native American Church that he had learned from his grandfather. He was the first person to mix traditional Indigenous music with jazz and was one of the early proponents of jazz fusion. Director Sandra Osawa, Makah, produced the biographical film *Pepper's Powwow* in 1996. Pepper was posthumously granted the Lifetime Musical Achievement Award by First Americans in the Arts in 1999, and in 2000 he was inducted into the Native American Music Awards Hall of Fame. In 2013, the annual Jim Pepper Native Arts Festival was founded in his hometown of Portland, Oregon. The festival increases access to music education and honors this remarkable musician's legacy.

1971: Willie Dunn (1941–2013), Mi'kmaq, produced the first music video in Canada for his song "The Ballad of Crowfoot." He was also a singer-songwriter, film director, and politician.

1971: XIT released its album *Plight of the Redman,* becoming the first American Indian band to be produced by the iconic Motown record company. The rock songs chronicle the history of American Indian struggles with European colonial settlers. The album garnered critical acclaim and Grammy consideration. XIT was the first Native rock band to play at the International Music Festival in Venice, Italy (1972). The original band members, A. Michael Martinez (guitar and vocals), Lee Herrera (drums), Jomac Suazo (bass), and R. C. Gariss (guitar and piano), represent the Colville, Isleta Pueblo, Diné, and Muscogee Creek Nations.

1978: Jeff "Cherokee" Bunn, Haliwa-Saponi, became the first Native American to play with George Clinton of Parliament-Funkadelic. He was the principal bassist for Clinton's Brides of Funkenstein group. Bunn continues to serve as "on call" bassist for George Clinton as well as sharing the bass chair at Second Baptist Church in Richmond, Virginia.

1980: John Kim Bell (1952–), Mohawk, produced, directed, cocomposed, and conducted *In the Land of Spirits,* the first all-Indigenous ballet to tour nationally; it premiered at the National Arts Centre in Ottawa, Ontario, Canada. As a teen he played piano for the Ken-

Jim Pepper

Marty Robbins

ley Players Summer Theatre Company, which led to his appointment as associate conductor of the international company of *A Chorus Line.* By the age of 18, Bell was conducting numerous Broadway, ballet, and operatic productions, which included headliners Gene Kelly and Lauren Bacall. He apprenticed with Zubin Mehta at the New York Philharmonic and conducted for the Dance Theater of Harlem.

1982: Martin David Robinson (1925–1982), known professionally as Marty Robbins, became the first American Indian elected to the Country Music Hall of Fame. A Paiute from Arizona, he was also the first Native named Artist of the Decade (1960–1969) by the Academy of Country Music. Robbins's songs often topped the country charts and were successful crossover pop hits. In 1998, he was given a Grammy Hall of Fame Award for his song "El Paso." Robbins was inducted into the Nashville Songwriters Hall of Fame in 1975 and earned a star on the Hollywood Walk of Fame at 6666 Hollywood Boulevard. In addition to his recordings and performances, Robbins was an avid race car driver, competing in 35 career NASCAR races with six top-10 finishes, including the 1973 Daytona 500. In 1967, Robbins played himself in the car racing film *Hell on Wheels.*

1982: Buffy Sainte-Marie (1941–), Cree, was the first known Native American to earn an Oscar. She, Jack Nitzsche, and Will Jennings won for composing "Up Where We Belong," the theme song from the film *An Officer and a Gentleman.*

1989: Tom Bee, Dakota, the manager of the all-Native rock band XIT, founded the first American Indian record company, Sounds of American Records (SOAR), in New Mexico. SOAR comprises three publishing companies and five different labels: SOAR, Natural Visions, Warrior, Dakotah, and Red Sea. With over 300 titles of both contemporary and traditional music, SOAR was the first company to release traditional Native American music on compact disc.

1990: The art of Inuit "throat singing" was included in popular music for the first time in the world premier of *Tornrak,* by Welsh composer John Metcalf, performed at the Banff Centre for Arts and Creativity in Banff, Alberta, Canada.

1992: Gary Paul "Litefoot" Davis (1969–), Cherokee, released his album *The Money EP,* the first rapper from a federally recognized tribe to do so. He was the first rap artist to take the Native American Music Association (NAMA) Native Artist of the Year category with his song "Native American Me." Davis is also an actor and an entrepreneur.

Gary Paul "Litefoot" Davis

1993: Paula Washington (1952), Cherokee, earned her Ph.D. from the New York University School of Education, Health, Nursing and Arts Professions, becoming the first Native American to earn a doctorate in the neuropsychology of musical performance. Her dissertation, "An Electroencephalographic Study of Musical Performance: Imagined versus Actual Playing and Solo versus Chamber Playing," was a milestone in the study of the brain and music performance. Washington taught lower strings at her alma mater, Fiorello H. LaGuardia High School of Music & Art and Performing Arts in New York City, and for over ten years, served as the United Federation of Teachers chapter leader. She is the first and only Native violist with three different orchestras: Adelphi; Broadway Bach Ensemble; and

Centre City Orchestra, all based in the New York City Metro area.

1996: Robert Moore (1963–2010), Sicangu Lakota, sang the National Anthem at the Democratic National Convention in Chicago, becoming the first Native American to sing at a national political convention. A European classically trained musician, he was instrumental in the founding of the Lakota Music Program, which started in 2005.

1997: Israel "Iz" Ka'ano'i Kamakawiwo'ole (1959–1997), Native Hawaiian musician and sovereignty activist, was the first nongovernment person to lie in state at the Hawaiian capitol building. Over 10,000 fans attended his funeral. "Iz" became the voice of Hawaii; his medley of "Somewhere over the Rainbow/What a Wonderful World" was featured in several films. A talented ukulele player, he artfully incorporated Indigenous Hawaiian, jazz, reggae, and other styles into his music. In May 20, 2020, Google celebrated "Iz" Ka'ano'i Kamakawiwo'ole's 61st birthday with a doodle video of his music.

1997: James Stephen "Big Chief" Wetherington (1922–1973), tribal affiliation unknown, became the first person of Native descent to be inducted into the Southern Gospel Music Hall of Fame.

1997: R. Carlos Nakai (1946–), Navajo, was the first Native flautist to sell more than five hundred thousand copies of an album. The Gold album, *Canyon Trilogy,* was recorded in 1989.

1998: The First Annual Native American Music Awards Show (NAMA) was held at the Mashantucket Pequot Tribal Nation's Foxwoods Resort in Ledyard, Connecticut. Hosted by Wayne Newton, Powhatan/Cherokee, the event featured 20 categories and dozens of musicians. The first winners: Artist/Group of the Year—Black Lodge Singers; Debut Artist of the Year—Walela; Best Male Artist—R. Carlos Nakai; Best Female Artist—Joanne Shenandoah; Best Rap Artist—Litefoot; Best Folk/Country Group—Apache Spirit; Song of the Year—"The Warrior" by Walela; Record of the Year—*American Warriors: Songs for Indian Veterans*; Best Traditional Recording—"Peyote Songs" by Primeaux & Mike; Best Instrumental Recording—*Two World Concerto* by R. Carlos Nakai; Best Compilation Recording—*American Warriors: Songs for Indian Veterans*; Best New Age Album—*Two World Concerto* by R. Carlos Nakai; Best Pow Wow Album—*Enter the Circle* by the Black Lodge Singers; Lifetime Achievement—Frederick Whiteface and Robbie Robertson; Hall of Fame—Jimi Hendrix and Buddy Red Bow.

2000: For the first time, a chanter was inducted into the Hawaiian Music Hall of Fame. Keaulumoku (1716-1784) was fluent in many forms of chant (Oli), including genealogical, war, praise, and love, but was best known for his prophetic chants. He foretold the union of the islands under King Kamehameha, the extinction of the monarchy, the domination of the white race, the destruction of the temples, and the probable extinction of the Hawaiian people. Elaborate chants were composed to record important information, such as births, deaths, triumphs, losses, and both good and bad times.

2001: Brent Michael Davids (1959-), Stockbridge Munsee, founded the Native American Composer Apprenticeship Project of the Grand Canyon Music Festival in Arizona and became the first composer in residence. A composer and flautist, Davids is known internationally for his innovative music that features elements of Native American traditional music combined with Western compositional techniques. He often designs his own instruments, including flutes made of quartz crystal. In 2006, the National Endowment for the Arts named Davids among the nation's most celebrated choral composers in its project "American Masterpieces: Three Centuries of Artistic Genius," along with Leonard Bernstein, Stephen Foster, and 25 others.

2001: For the first time, the Grammys included the Best Native American Music Album category. The first winner was the compilation album *Gathering of Nations Pow Wow*, produced by Tom Bee (Dakota) and Douglas Spotted Eagle. In 2011, the category was eliminated along with 30 others, and Native American works became eligible for the Best Regional Roots Music Album category.

2002: The Native American Music Awards (NAMA) added a Gospel/Christian Recording category. The first album to win the award was *Voices of the Creator's Children* by the Cherokee National Children's Choir sung in the Cherokee language.

2003: Mary Youngblood (1958-), Seminole, became the first Native American solo female musician to win a Grammy Award. She received the prize for her work *Beneath the Raven Moon*, in the Native American Music Album category.

2004: Lillian Little Soldier Klaudt (1906-2001), Arikara-Mandan, was the first Native American woman to be inducted into the Southern Gospel Music Hall of Fame. She was the matriarch of the Klaudt Indian Family, a professional music group popular on the gospel circuit in the South.

2004: Charly Lowry (1984-), Lumbee, became the first Native contestant on *American *Idol* to make it into the top 32. Today, she is the lead vocalist in the band Dark Water Rising, and in 2019, they performed in "The Music at the Mansion," part of "Come Hear North Carolina," at the North Carolina's governor's mansion, another first.

2005: The Lakota Music Program kicked off in South Dakota. Cosponsored by Lakota/Dakota communities and the South Dakota Symphony Orchestra, the project addresses racial tension and seeks to create an open and sharing environment for Native and white musicians to enhance cultural understanding.

2005: For the first time, the Grammys included the Best Hawaiian Music Album category. The winning album was *Slack Key Guitar, Volume 2*, performed by 10 slack key artists, each with his own tuning and style ranging from traditional to contemporary: Bryan Kessler, Ken Emerson, Keoki Kahumoku, Randy Lorenzo, Sonny Lim, John Keawe, John Cruz, Jeff Peterson, Charlie Recaido, and Charles Michael Brotman. Brotman received the award for producing the album.

2008: The San Francisco Symphony Chorus performed and recorded Jerod Impichchaachaaha' Tate's *Iholba*, the first time the chorus had sung any work in Chickasaw or any other American Indian language. Tate (1968–), a Chickasaw classical composer and pianist, has several firsts in his impressive career. He founded Music Composition Academy (2017) sponsored by the Lakota Music Program to teach both

Jerod Impichchaachaaha' Tate

Native and non-Native students together. He is the founder and artistic director of the Chickasaw Chamber Music Festival and cofounder and composition instructor for the Chickasaw Summer Arts Academy. In addition, Tate is the first Native American classically trained musician to be a three-time

commissioned recipient of the American Composers Forum, a Chamber Music America's Classical Commissioning Program recipient, a Cleveland Institute of Music Alumni Achievement Award recipient, a governor-appointed Creativity Ambassador for the State of Oklahoma, and an Emmy Award winner for his work on the Oklahoma Educational Television Authority documentary *The Science of Composing*.

2009: Grammy Award–winning musician Bill Miller (1955–), Mohican, performed his cocomposed symphony, *The Last Stand*, in Israel with the Israel Kibbutz Orchestra, the first time a Native American symphony was performed in that country. The music, which commemorates the Battle of Little Bighorn, was initially performed by the La Crosse Symphony at a world premiere in 2008. Photos from the debut are now in the permanent collection of the National Museum of the American Indian.

2011: Signal 99, an all-Navajo heavy metal band, became the first Indian music group to win the Rockstar Energy Drink Uproar Festival (Albuquerque).

2013: Pawnee/Choctaw brothers Lil Mike and Funny Bone appeared on *America's Got Talent* and made it to the Vegas round. It was the first time Native American rappers finished that far in the competition.

2015: Bass player and vocalist Robert "Freightrain" Parker, Seneca, was the first Indigenous person inducted into the Buffalo, New York, Music Hall of Fame. He and his band are known for their compelling live performances across the United States, Europe, Asia, and the Caribbean.

2016: VIZIN, Arikara, from the Fort Berthold Reservation in North Dakota, was the first

Native American drag queen to hit the Billboard Dance Club Charts. Her rendition of "You Make Me Feel (Mighty Real)," debuted in the 24th position, ahead of pop star Taylor Swift. VIZIN is also a trained opera singer.

2017: Kane Brown (1993–), Cherokee descent, became the first artist to have simultaneous hits on all five main *Billboard* country charts.

2019: The world premiere of musical compositions by high school musicians from Sisseton, Pine Ridge Reservation, Oelrichs, Mission, and Rapid City, participating in Music Composition Academies sponsored by the South Dakota Symphony Orchestra's Lakota Music Project, was held at Black Hills State University, South Dakota.

Kane Brown

◆◇◆
PERFORMANCE ART, WILD WEST SHOWS, CIRCUSES, DRAG SHOWS, AND PUPPETRY

"Back in the day anyone that was gay or transsexual or transgendered were considered by a broad term called 'Two Spirits.' It's more of a male and a female spirit inhabit our bodies. We basically experience life as both. We get the best of both worlds. Back in the day we were more regarded than frowned upon like now."

—*VIZIN, Arikara, drag queen*

c. 1910: Carpas (tents in Spanish), "a cross between vaudeville and a circus," began to be popular in the Southwest and were the in-

vention of Mexican Indigenous Americans; most were family-owned. The performances drew working-class Spanish-speaking audiences. Many featured Indigenous performers from Mexico as well as Indigenous performance traditions, some centuries old, like the Danza de los Voladores. Believed to have originated with the Nahua, Huastec, and Otomi peoples of central Mexico, the "dance" is part of a ritual featuring five performers who climb a 30-meter pole. Four are tied with ropes and launch themselves to the ground, twirling, spinning, and doing death-defying tricks in the air. The fifth remains on top of the pole, dancing and playing a flute and drum. The Maromeros, tightrope performers, were also seen in Mexican American circuses. They do daring tricks on the tightrope while a brass band plays the typical music for the occasion. Normally there is also a clown reciting verses, bringing laughter to the audience. This daredevil feat comes from ancient Aztec traditions. After World War II, most of the carpas were disbanded and many performers joined other circuses.

1960: Circus owner D. R. Miller purchased a section in the town cemetery of the Choctaw Nation community of Hugo, Oklahoma, to memorialize his brother, Kelly, and other circus performers. Hugo has long been winter headquarters for various circus companies and bears the nickname "Circus Town, USA." The Showmen's Rest section in Hugo's Mount Olivet Cemetery pays tributes to "all showmen under God's big top," from animal trainers to jugglers to high-wire artists. A popular tourist attraction, it is also the only such cemetery located in a Native community.

1984: Buddy Big Mountain (1955–), Mohawk, became the first nationally known American Indian Ventriloquist. His show, the Mini Pow Wow and Gifts & Legends, grew into

Will Rogers: The Immortal Vaudeville Star

"I don't make jokes. I just watch the government and report the facts." "Ten men in our country could buy the whole world and ten million can't buy enough to eat." "There is no trick to being a humorist when you have the whole government working for you." These are just a few of the famous quips by Will Rogers.

William "Will" Penn Adair Rogers (1879–1935), Cherokee, became a vaudeville star in 1905. A citizen of Indian Territory (now Oklahoma), his adventures took him to South America and South Africa, where he worked as a gaucho and a wrangler. Rogers was on the vaudeville circuit as a trick roper, rising to fame at a show in Madison Square Garden in New York City. A wild steer broke out of the arena and began to climb into the viewing stands, and to the crowd's delight, Rogers roped the steer and saved the day. Newspapers headlined the feat on their front pages, and he gained valuable publicity. Theater manager Willie Hammerstein booked Rogers's act, and for the next decade he was featured in a myriad of New York City theaters. Along with his pony and fancy roping, his act featured his sharp wit and humor, often mocking the dominant culture. His witty criticisms of the government and politicians are as apropos today as they were a century ago. As an entertainer and humorist, Rogers traveled around the world three times, made 71 films (50 silent films and 21 "talkies"), and wrote more than 4,000 nationally syndicated newspaper columns. By the mid-1930s, "Oklahoma's favorite son" was hugely popular in the United States for his leading political wit, and he was the highest paid Hollywood film star. He died in 1935 with aviator Wiley Post when their small airplane crashed in northern Alaska. Will Rogers's legacy lives on, and his political satire is as relevant today as it was in the last century. "If you ever injected truth into politics, you would have no politics."

Will Rogers

the Buddy Big Mountain Variety Comedy Show with ventriloquist figures such as Iron Horse and Awesome Fox, vocals, magic, and a performing cast of marionette dancers. In 1993, Big Mountain won two awards as a master puppeteer for filming one of his marionettes in the video *Stumbling Bear,* which won best short film at the Native American Film Awards in San Francisco and at the Wind and Glacier Voices II in New York City's Lincoln Center. He grew up in a performing family that had engagements all over the world. Besides being a master puppeteer, Big Mountain is a champion fancy dancer and actor. In 1967, Big Mountain landed his first acting role on the TV series *Gentle Ben.* He has shared the stage with many great performers such as Willie Tyler, Sinbad, Charlie Hill, Buffy Sainte-Marie, Floyd Westerman, Foster Brooks, Seals and Crofts, and Riders in the Sky. In 2009, Big Mountain received the Japanese Ventriloquist Association Award for his many years of contribution to the art.

2009: World champion hoop dancer Nakotah LaRance (1989–2020), Hopi, Navajo and Assiniboine, became the first Native American man to join the Cirque du Soleil. In the almost four years he performed with the

Wild Westing

Buffalo Bill's Wild West, an internationally known traveling extravaganza that toured North America and Europe from the late 1800s into the twentieth century, was produced by scout and showman William Frederick ("Buffalo Bill") Cody. It was the best known of a genre that also included medicine shows. Cody's first such show was held in Omaha, Nebraska, in 1883 and featured mainly members of the Pawnee Tribe. Ultimately promoted as "America's National Entertainment," Buffalo Bill's depictions of "authentic" life on the Great Plains incorporated dramatic plays, circus and vaudeville themes, sharpshooting and archery demonstrations, mock battles between cavalry and Indians, buffalo-hunting exhibitions, and other theatrics. Teepees, Plains traditional clothing, and other Native cultural belongings dotted the sets. Cody hired thousands of American Indians to lend authenticity or convey "actual scenes, genuine characters" to his portrayals of America's western frontier, always from the view of Euro-American expansionism. At the same time, Plains Indians were pushed onto reservations. Their traditional lifeways and economy, centered on the great bison herds, were being destroyed as the buffalo were hunted to near extinction by white sport hunters. This contributed to catastrophic conditions as land, food, culture, and religion were threatened.

Buffalo Bill Cody hired Chief Sitting Bull of the Hunkpapa Lakota to be in his show.

The Wild West shows underscored the message that the story of the Wild West was one of heroic conquest by Euro-Americans, the triumph of "civilization" over "savagery." Yet for many Native people, participation in the Wild West shows offered an alternative to the harsh conditions on Indian reservations, where Indian agents ruled. Hired by Cody, Indian participants could earn wages to help their families. They could also travel, interact with other showmen and women, and experience new places and customs. Federal officials opposed Cody, informing him that as wards of the government, Indians were not allowed off their reservations. The showman had to obtain bonds for the Indians' safe return at the end of the season and make contractual arrangements through the Indian agency as required, practices that he continued to follow to hire Indians. Government officials especially opposed Indian participation in the shows because they wanted no interference or backsliding in their efforts to turn Indians into "civilized" English-speaking people who embraced Euro-American culture and religion.

Ultimately, Plains Indians, especially Lakota from Pine Ridge and Rosebud reservations in present-day South Dakota, participated in Buffalo Bill's Wild West. The renowned Oglala holy man Black Elk later commented on his travels with the show: "I did not see anything to help my people. I could see that the Wasichus [white people] did not care for each other the way our people did before the nation's hoop was broken. They would take everything from each other if they could, and so there were some who had more of everything than they could use, while crowds of people had nothing at all and maybe were starving."

Cirque, he traveled to many countries. Today, his younger sister, ShanDien LaRance (1993–) is also a hoop dancer and the first Native woman to be part of Cirque du Soleil.

2015: *Queer Horror*, a bimonthly screening series, debuted at the historic Hollywood Theatre in Portland, Oregon. Programmed and hosted by Portland's premier drag clown, Carla Rossi (Anthony Hudson), Confederated Tribes of Grand Ronde, it is the only LGBTQ program of its kind in the United States. Hudson was named a 2018 National Artist Fellow from the Native Arts and Cultures Foundation, a 2018 Western Arts Alliance Native Launchpad Artist, a 2019 Oregon Arts Commission Fellow, a 2021 First Peoples Fund Fellow, and has received project support and fellowships from the National Endowment for the Arts, National Performance.

2020: Ilona Verley, Nlaka'pamux, was the first Indigenous, two-spirit, and Los Angeles–based drag queen to earn a place on the reality show *Canada's Drag Race*.

PAGEANTS

"Did you really think I was going to just sit there and look pretty? Definitely not. I have a title, a platform, and a voice to make change and bring awareness to First Nations issues here in Canada.... They don't expect a pageant girl to say political things."

—*Ashley Callingbull, Enoch Cree Nation, Mrs. Universe (2015–2016)*

1926: Norma Smallwood (1909–1966), Cherokee, became the first Native American to win

Norma Smallwood

the title of Miss America. She was also Miss Tulsa and captain of her college hockey team.

1951: Lucy Yellow Mule (1935–), Crow, was chosen as Wyoming's first Native American rodeo queen. The crowning of Yellow Mule set in motion a series of events that healed some of the damaging effects of anti-Indian racism in Sheridan. The community began to foster better cross-cultural relations, which inspired the first All-American Indian Day and National Miss Indian America Pageant in 1953.

1953: Arlene Wesley, Yakama, was crowned the winner in the first ever Miss Indian America pageant. It ran from 1953 to 1984 and was a feature of the annual All-American Indian Days festival in Sheridan, Wyoming. Contestants were judged on appearance; communication skills; knowledge and practice of Native culture; and knowledge of tribal, federal, and state governments.

1953: For the first time, a department store held an "Indian Beauty Contest." S. Klein's featured an "Indian Village" at their store located at Union Square in Manhattan, New York. Artisans and exhibitors showed off Indian jewelry and other artwork. The draw of the show was the Miss Indian Queen pageant, and eight Native women paraded across the stage in regalia. The judges, mostly Haudenosaunee chiefs, made their choice of 38-year-old "She Who Is Single," a tall and buxom Seneca woman weighing almost 200 pounds. However, the store manager disregarded the choice and announced his winner: "Little Sunshine," a 117-pound, 19-year-old petite Tsimshian contestant. It was reported in the *Daily News*, using the most stereotypic verbiage, "Tempest in a Teepee: Indians on the Warpath over a Queen." Chief Cornplanter and supporters retreated into the longhouse display, and the celebration almost came to an end. In the end, the chiefs' selection prevailed, and She Who Is Single became Miss Indian Queen.

1971: Sacheen Littlefeather (1946–), White Mountain Apache/Yaqui, was the winner of the first Miss American Vampire contest, an event promoting the TV series *Dark Shadows*.

Stacy Layne Matthews

1983: Codi High Elk, Cheyenne River Sioux, was crowned Miss Indian World at the Gathering of Nations Powwow in Albuquerque, New Mexico. It was the first time the competition had been held.

1987: Judy Tallwing (1945–), Apache/Tewa/African American, won the first International Ms. Leather contest held in San Francisco. Tallwing is also an artist whose works appear in the Heard, Smithsonian, and American Visionary Arts museums. An activist for human rights, women's equality, and animals, Tallwing was severely punished in Indian boarding school for her attraction to girls. She ran away as a young teenager and eventually earned a college degree, directed an advocacy agency for victims of domestic violence, and founded a no-kill animal shelter in Washington State. After Hurricane Katrina, Tallwing spent six weeks rescuing people and their pets in Louisiana.

1997: Brook Mahealani Lee (1971–), Native Hawaiian, was the first American Indigenous person, as well as the oldest person, to be crowned Miss Universe.

2012: Shaylin Shábi, Navajo/Diné, was crowned the first Miss Native American USA in Tempe, Arizona. During her reign, she promoted healthy lifeways among Native American communities.

2013: Stacy Layne Matthews, Lumbee, was the first Native American to be crowned Miss Illusion Continental Plus. The pageant is for plus-size female impersonators.

2015: Ashley Callingbull (1989–), Enoch Cree Nation, became the first Native woman and the first Canadian ever to win the Mrs. Universe Pageant. The pageant honors the beauty and accomplishments of married women. She has used her status to promote awareness and rights of Indigenous peoples.

FESTIVALS, ORGANIZATIONS

1904: The annual Crow Fair was created by Crow leaders and an Indian government agent to present the Crow Tribe of Indians as culturally distinct and modern peoples in an entrepreneurial venue. The event is held the third week of August on land surrounding the Little Big Horn River near Billings, Montana, and resembles a county fair. It is also called the "the teepee capital of the world, over 1,500 teepees in a giant campground." During the week, there are several celebrations of dance and two powwows a day. A rodeo and a parade almost two miles long also make the fair a remarkable event.

1929: The Choctaw Indian Fair, an annual event, began on Choctaw homelands in Mississippi. Since then, it has become a huge annual celebration of Choctaw culture and gives homage to the traditional Green Corn Ceremony.

1952: The first Cherokee National Holiday Powwow kicked off in Tahlequah, Oklahoma, capital of the Cherokee Nation. Today, over 100,000 people attend the festivities to celebrate and to commemorate the signing of the 1839 Cherokee constitution. The nation's holiday, held every Labor Day weekend, also coincides with the annual State of the Nation address from the Cherokee principal chief.

1959: The first annual Eastern Shoshone Indian Days and Pow Wow was held at Fort Washakie, Wyoming. The June event features food, arts, traditional Indian games, a parade, carnival games, and traditional dancing to the sounds of several drum groups.

1964: The first Merrie Monarch Hula Festival, held in Hilo, Hawaii, included events such as a King Kalākaua beard look-alike contest, a barbershop quartet contest, a relay race, a re-creation of King Kalākaua's coronation, and a Holokū Ball. The April festival features a premier hula competition and a Miss Aloha Hula pageant. It is named for King David La'amea Kalākaua, nicknamed the Merrie Monarch, who ruled from 1874 to 1891 and advocated for a renewed sense of pride in all things Hawaiian, such as the arts, medicine, music, and hula.

1971: Native students at Stanford University in California hosted a powwow to protest the school's racist mascot. They were successful, and the "Indian" imagery was officially eliminated the next year. Today the annual Mother's Day weekend event has 10,000 visitors a day with 250 dancers and is the largest college powwow.

1982: The first biennial celebration was held in Juneau, Alaska, and has become the largest cultural event in the state. Held every other June, it is organized by the Sealaska Corporation to pass on cultural knowledge to Native Alaskan children. Besides dance events, regular activities include workshops on the Tlingit, Haida, and Tsimshian languages, Northwest Coast art, and Southeast Alaska Indian cultures and historical events;

canoe racing; film screenings; poetry gatherings; and a Native fashion show.

1983: The first annual Gathering of Nations Powwow took place in Albuquerque, New Mexico. Founded by Derek, Lita, and Melonie Mathews (Santa Clara Pueblo), it has become the biggest Indigenous festival in the world, attracting almost 200,000 people. The April event features aisles of shopping in the Indian Trader's Market, Native foods, Horse & Rider Parade, music on Powwow Alley's Stage 49, and the Miss Indian World Pageant.

1991: The Ganondagan Indigenous Music and Arts Festival began. Highlights of the annual event are a juried Hodinöhsö:ni' Art Show and traditional and contemporary music and dance performances. It is held at the Ganondagan State Historic Site in Victor, New York, which became a National Historic Landmark in 1987 and is the only New York State Historic Site dedicated to a Native American theme. It is the original site of a seventeenth-century Seneca town and home to the Seneca Art & Culture Center.

1994: The Mashantucket Pequot Tribal Nation in Mashantucket, Connecticut, hosted its first annual Schemitzun Powwow—the Feast of Green Corn and Dance. It was a significant event as the Pequot had struggled for centuries for the right to reestablish their community. It is one of the oldest continuously occupied Indian reservations in North America.

2006: The first annual Flute Quest was held in Washington State to celebrate Native flute music, particularly styles from the Pacific Northwest.

2011: The Bay Area American Indian Two-Spirits (BAAITS) hosted the first annual Two-Spirit powwow, and it has become the largest event of its kind in the nation. "Two-spirit" is often used as a term to describe a Native person who is lesbian, gay, bisexual, transgender, queer, or questioning (LGBTQ). The term was adopted in 1990 at the Indigenous lesbian and gay international gathering in Winnipeg, Manitoba, Canada, and "specifically chosen to distinguish and distance Native American/First Nations people from non-Native peoples." It was also offered as an alternative to the offensive anthropological French/Persian word *berdache*, which can mean anything from passive homosexual to slave to boy prostitute. Although "two-spirit" has become a pan-Indian word, each tribal language has its own words for gender-variant members, and the belief is that people were accepted and safe whatever their identities. Based in San Francisco, California, BAAITS seeks to restore Native traditions of acceptance and respect for two-spirit people by creating a forum for spiritual, cultural, and artistic expression.

2013: The 1st Annual Native Hip-Hop Festival was held at the Musqueam Cultural Centre in Vancouver, British Columbia, Canada. The three-day event draws hip-hop artists from all over the United States and Canada and features Native Graf artists, b-boys, DJs, MCs, and others.

2021: The first-ever International Indigenous Hip Hop Awards took place in a two-day virtual celebration broadcast from Winnipeg, Manitoba. Performers represented Indigenous groups from Canada, the United States, Australia, the Caribbean, and India. The event was hosted by Pawnee/Choctaw rapper brothers Lil Mike and Funny Bone.

VISUAL ARTS

"You're Indian youngsters, make the most of that, but don't feel you have to do your art a certain way. Grow with the times. Don't forget your heritage, and with it you can find enough material to be the greatest artists in the world."

—Allan Houser, Chiracahua Apache, artist

ARCHITECTURE

"With the uptick in Native American architects working with tribes and increase in architects involving tribal clients in the design process, cultural appropriation is thankfully becoming less common in architecture. Recognize that the culture of tribal people is thriving every day. When a culture can speak for itself, authenticity will result."

—Tamara Eagle Bull, Oglala Lakota, the first Native woman to be a licensed architect

1971: Dennis C. Numkena (1942–2010), Hopi, founded Numkena Architects, the first all-Native-owned architectural firm in the United States. His award-winning designs include the Anasazi Resort Condominiums in Phoenix, Arizona, and the Pyramid Lake Paiute Tribe Museum in Nixon, Nevada.

1971: Thalden Boyd Emery (TBE) Architects was founded and has had over 100 tribal nations as clients. The firm is guided by Charles "Chief" Boyd, Cherokee, and known for designing resorts, hotel rooms, convention centers, restaurants, retail spaces, and casinos. Boyd also designed the Cherokee Cultural Center in Tahlequah, Oklahoma (1963).

1978: The United Nations Educational, Scientific and Cultural Organization (UNESCO) designated a Native American community a World Heritage Site for the first time. The massive cliff apartment dwellings, ancestral Pueblo homes, constructed from stone and built from the sixth to twelfth centuries, are located on the Mesa Verde plateau in southwest Colorado.

An 1890 photograph of 'Iolani Palace.

'Iolani Palace: America's Only Royal Residence

Construction began in 1879 on the 'Iolani Palace, home of the Hawaiian royal family in Honolulu, Hawaii. The palace is the only building in the world referred to as "American Florentine," characterized by features found in Italian Renaissance style blended with elements iconic to Hawaiian architecture like a koa wood grand staircase. The new structure boasted indoor plumbing, electricity, and telephones long before the White House had such modern amenities. King Kalākaua and Queen Kapi'olani moved into their new home in 1882.

Queen Lili'uokalani succeeded them, and when the Americans illegally overthrew the Hawaiian monarchy in 1893, the queen was imprisoned for nine months in a small room on the upper floor. She was later transferred to house arrest in a different building, and believing that those Native Hawaiians who had been incarcerated for defending Hawaii would be executed, she abdicated the throne in exchange for their freedom. The troops of the newly formed Provisional Government of Hawai'i renamed 'Iolani Palace the Executive Building for the Republic of Hawai'i. Their plan was to annex the country to the United States. Whatever the interlopers felt was not suitable for their operations was sold at public auctions, including Hawaiian antiquities and cultural belongings. When Queen Lili'uokalani was released from house arrest, she unsuccessfully led Indigenous Hawaiians in opposing the annexation treaty, which was signed into law in 1898. The palace is the only official state residence of royalty on U.S. soil.

'Iolani Palace: America's Only Royal Residence (contd.)

In 1930 the 'Iolani Palace was remodeled, and wood framing was replaced with steel and reinforced concrete. The name 'Iolani Palace was officially restored in 1935, and during World War II, it was the headquarters for the military governor in charge of martial law in the Hawaiian Islands. Hawaiian soldiers of Japanese ancestry who were accepted for U.S. Army service became the core of the 442nd Infantry Regiment and were sworn in during a mass ceremony on palace grounds.

The palace was a functioning yet neglected government building for over 70 years, until Hawaii became a state in 1959. 'Iolani Palace was designated a National Historic Landmark in December 1962 and added to the National Register of Historic Places listings in Oahu in 1966. That same year, the government vacated the building, and the nonprofit, nongovernmental organization Friends of 'Iolani Palace, founded by Lili'uokalani Kawānanakoa Morris, grandniece of Queen Kapi'olani, stepped up to ensure its restoration. The group researched the original construction plans, furnishings, and palace lifestyles in nineteenth-century newspapers, photographs, and archival manuscripts and restored the palace rooms to their monarchy-era appearance. A quilt made by Queen Lili'uokalani is on display. Through efforts of many individuals and organizations, several original palace objects were repatriated. 'Iolani Palace opened to the public in 1978 and features a photographic display of the palace, orders and decorations given by the monarchs, and an exhibit outlining restoration efforts. The grounds of 'Iolani Palace are managed by the Hawai'i State Department of Land and Natural Resources, but the palace itself is managed as a historical house museum by the Friends of 'Iolani. Birthdays of Hawaiian luminaries are celebrated at the palace, and it is one of the only places in Hawaii where the flag of Hawaii can officially fly alone without the American flag.

On January 17, 1993, thousands attended an observation held on the grounds of 'Iolani Palace to mark the 100th anniversary of the overthrow of the Hawaiian monarchy. And on November 23, 1993, President Bill Clinton signed Public Law 103-150, the "Apology Resolution" to Native Hawaiians, for the overthrow of the Hawaiian Kingdom.

1981: The Native American Center for the Living Arts (the Turtle) opened the doors to its 60,000-square-foot building constructed in the shape of a giant turtle, based on the Haudenosaunee creation account that the world came to be perched on the back of a turtle. One of the founders, Dennis Sun Rhodes, Arapaho, was also the architect of the stunning building in Niagara Falls, New York. The monolithic turtle's head faces the famous falls as if on guard. Developed from the collaboration of Native artists, it was the first time a project of this size had been erected to house all fields of Indigenous arts. Unfortunately, the Turtle had to close in 1995 because of financial difficulties and faces an uncertain future.

1989: Our Lady of Fatima Catholic Church was constructed on the Navajo Reservation in Chinle, Arizona. It is the first church built by Navajo people that reflects traditional

Navajo architecture. Resting on a pedestal evoking a Navajo prayer pile, it is a hogan-shaped octagon structure of rough-hewn logs. The juniper log altar is covered with deerskin, and there is a six-foot-wide depression in the center of the building that represents the Navajo cosmic axis. Walls are adorned by paintings of the four sacred mountains.

1991: Cornell University's Akwe:kon (uh-GWAY-go) in Ithaca, New York, opened its doors, making it the nation's first university residence hall that celebrated American Indian culture and heritage. In the Mohawk language, Akwe:kon means "all of us." The distinctive eagle-shaped building and landscape were designed with input from Haudenosaunee (Iroquois) people, incorporating wampum belt symbols on the exterior that reflect Haudenosaunee history, politics, culture, and cosmology .

1992: The Childers Architect firm, owned and operated by James Childers, Cherokee, built the Wilma Mankiller Health Center in Stilwell, Oklahoma, for the Cherokee Nation. It is the first health facility designed to incorporate Cherokee culture. Since then, the firm has partnered with several Native nations to create culturally appropriate medical buildings, including the first Native-owned medical school (Oklahoma State University College of Osteopathic Medicine at the Cherokee Nation, 2020).

1994: Tamara Eagle Bull, Oglala Lakota, became the first Native woman to be a licensed architect. In 2018, she scored another big first when she became the first American Indian to earn the American Institute of Architects Whitney M. Young Jr. Award. The prestigious honor is granted to an individual or architectural organization that "embodies social responsibility and actively addresses a relevant issue, such as affordable housing, inclusiveness, or universal access." Her Lincoln, Nebraska, company, Encompass Architects, pc, is known for culturally relevant, sustainable/energy-efficient and responsible design projects. Eagle Bull is a community advocate and puts her stamp on both urban and reservation buildings.

1995: Red Feather Development Group was founded in Seattle, Washington, by Robert Young, who wanted to address the lack of homes as well as sub-standard housing, particularly for elders on reservations. He developed a more affordable construction approach using straw bales. The first straw-bale house was built on the Pine Ridge Reservation in South Dakota for elder Katherine Red Feather, Lakota; the company bears her name. The organization operates similarly to Habitat for Humanity, and prospective homeowners and volunteers erect the environmentally sustainable homes. The straw bales are comprised of stalks that are left after the food from wheat, rice, and other plant materials has been extracted. After a home is completed, it is impossible to tell that the main material, hidden behind the walls, is straw bales. Native community representatives serve on the board and as staffers for Red Feather.

2001: Indigenous Community Enterprises (ICE) at Northern Arizona University launched its Navajo Hogan/Roundwood Manufacturing Project on the Navajo Nation. The energy-efficient homes are based on traditional Navajo architecture and are built using environmentally friendly building techniques. Designed to be affordable, the hogans ($30,000 to $40,000) provide maximum heat efficiency and minimal maintenance. Six-to-nine-inch-diameter logs, often burned as part of the U.S. Forest Service's prescribed burn program, form the frames.

2004: Tamarah Begay became the first Navajo woman to be a licensed architect. She is the founder and owner of the award-winning Indigenous Design Studio + Architecture in Albuquerque, New Mexico.

Acoma Pueblo in New Mexico was designated a National Historic Trust Site in 2007.

2007: Acoma Pueblo, New Mexico, was the first Native American community to be designated a National Trust Historic Site. Built around 1100, Acoma is home to what are considered the first and oldest continuously occupied apartment buildings in the United States.

2010: For the first time, a Native Hawaiian location was declared a World Heritage Site by UNESCO. Papahānaumokuākea is a vast and isolated cluster of small, low-lying islands and atolls northwest of the main Hawaiian Archipelago and extending over some 1,200 miles. The area has deep cosmological and traditional significance for Native Hawaiian culture. On two of the islands, Nihoa and Makumanamana, there are archaeological remains of Native Hawaiian communities/culture before European contact.

2018: Architect David Fortin, Métis, was appointed director of the McEwen School of Architecture at Laurentian University in Sudbury, Ontario, Canada, making him the first Native head of an architecture school in Canada or the United States. Through hands-on projects, Indigenous teachings, and the highest-level professional standards, students are guided to design sustainable buildings for cold climates worldwide.

2018: The Indigenous Scholars of Architecture, Planning and Design (ISAPD) was established at Yale University School of Architecture in New Haven, Connecticut. The student group seeks to increase the knowledge, consciousness, and appreciation of Indigenous architecture, planning, and design. Founding members were architecture students Summer Sutton, Lumbee; Anjelica Gallegos, Santa Ana Pueblo/Jicarilla Apache; and Charelle Brown, Kewa Pueblo.

2019: Operation MEMIMEN TOKW (Tiny Home) was launched on the Lummi Reservation in Washington. Tribal members learn to construct the tiny homes for Eagle Haven Village.

BASKETRY

"All human communities from times out of memory have created things which have made their individual lives easier. Pottery was made to cook in or to contain ceremonial or religious offerings; baskets were woven to carry things or to prepare food; cloth was woven to wear; houses were built to shelter mankind from ever-present nature. These things, among many others, which people have made become things of 'art' and beauty when they are produced, not just for utility, but to the best of each individual's ability in order to enrich his or her life."

—Claude Medford, Choctaw,
basket maker and traditional arts teacher

c. 1895: Detsolatee (c. 1835–1925), Washo, began to sell her baskets in her employers' store at the beginning of the Arts and Crafts Movement and during the basket craze of the earliest part of the twentieth century. She was the most noted basket maker of the time, and she elevated Washo basketry to a high art form. Detsolatee is credited with the Washo basket art revival, and in 1919 she exhibited and demonstrated basket making at the St. Louis Exposition. Others made much more money on her baskets than she did. In 1930, five years after her death, one of her baskets sold for $10,000. Today, the Washo Tribe owns most of Detsolatee's valuable baskets.

1924: Lucy Parker Telles (c. 1870/1885–1955/6), Miwok/Paiute, was the first Miwok basket weaver to combine new and traditional techniques. Using red and black colors, she wove realistic designs of birds, flowers, butterflies, and other motifs into baskets, the largest ever made. In 1924, Telles was regarded as the best basket weaver in Yosemite Valley and maintained that honor until her death. Her baskets are on display in museums like the Autry Museum of the American West. Telles taught her art to her grandson's wife, Julia Peter Parker, Kashaya Pomo, another famous artist.

1935: Elsie Allen (1899–1990), Ukiah Pomo, was the first Pomo basket weaver to teach Pomo basketry to those not related to her. She broke the tradition of only teaching other Pomo because of the encroachment of Anglo society on Pomo lands and wanted to ensure that the art would continue. Her mother, Annie Burke (1876–1962), founded the Pomo Indian Women's Club to promote basketry.

1982: Marjorie Abbey Battise (1942–), Koasati (or Coushatta), was the first basket maker to be inducted into the Louisiana Folklife Center's Hall of Master Folk Artists.

1983: Ada Thomas (1924–1992), Chitimacha, was the first Native American basket weaver to receive a National Endowment for the Arts Fellowship. Known for her traditional double-weave baskets, she used swamp cane and natural dyes. The centuries-old designs reflect the Chitimacha relationship to the environment in the Louisiana bayous and have such descriptive names as Alligator Entrails, Bull's Eye, Rabbit Teeth, Snake Design, Bear's Earrings, Fish, and Muscadine Peel.

1995: Mary Holiday Black (1934–), a Navajo basket maker from Utah, became the first Utah artist as well as the first Navajo artist to receive a National Heritage Fellowship from the National Endowment for the Arts. Also called "the matriarch of Navajo basketry," Black helped revive Navajo basket weaving and added her own designs and techniques. She expanded the size of the traditional baskets, incorporated motifs from ancient pottery, and used Navajo religious

Basket weaving is an art practiced by numerous artists of various nations, many of whom have been nationally and internationally recognized for their work.

imagery to weave visual narratives into her baskets. She is also known as the pioneer of Navajo "story baskets."

2002: The Louisiana Regional Folklife Program cohosted the first gathering of the Southeastern Indian Basketweavers. Held in Natchitoches, Louisiana, on the campus of Northwestern State University, Native artisans had the opportunity to exchange ideas and create strategies to preserve traditional basketmaking techniques. Some of the styles demonstrated were from the Choctaw, Houma, Koasati, Chitimacha, Seminole, and Cherokee.

2007: Pat Courtney Gold (1939–) was the first Wasco person to be granted a National Endowment of the Arts National Heritage Fellowship. She was a mathematician, and then in 1991, through the Oregon Traditional Arts Apprenticeship Program, Gold began to study the making of "sally bags," flexible cylindrical baskets created by Wasco-Wishram people for gathering medicines, nuts, and mushrooms. She mastered the full-turn twining basket weaving technique and now teaches basketry. Gold is recognized internationally for her art and received a Community Spirit Award (2003) and Cultural Capital Fellowship from the First People's Fund (2004).

2010: The Southwest Museum of the American Indian (part of the Autry Museum of the American West) in Los Angeles, California, opened the "The Art of Native American Basketry: A Living Tradition." It was the first time an exhibition of this size and scope was

Claude Medford, Cultural Preservationist

Claude Medford (1941–1989), Choctaw, was passionate about preserving and teaching traditional arts. As a child, he learned to weave cane splint baskets from his grandfather, a traditionalist, and it sparked his lifelong dedication to conserving the time-honored art forms of Indigenous peoples, particularly of those from the southeastern United States. After earning a BA in anthropology and art history from the University of New Mexico, Medford took to the road and traveled from state to state and tribe to tribe to immerse himself in Native heritage. He lived with the Alabama, Tunica-Biloxi, Coushatta, Pamunkey, Caddo, Delaware, and Yuchi and learned to speak many languages, including Alabama, Coushatta, and Choctaw. Medford became skilled in creating each nation's style of basketry as well as their particular type of pottery, woodworking, shell working, metal working, finger weaving, bead work, feather work, horn and hoof work, brain tanning of deer hide, leather working, and gourd work. He became an encyclopedia of southeastern arts and went on to share all the knowledge he had acquired. Medford helped develop instructional programs so that these centuries-old traditions would continue with current and future generations.

Medford taught at the American Indian Museum in New York City; the American Indian Archaeological Institute in Washington, Connecticut; the Clifton Choctaw Indian community in Louisiana; and many other places. Medford was especially delighted to receive a fellowship from the Louisiana State Arts Council of the Louisiana Division of the Arts as it provided him the resources to teach members from the five surviving tribes of Louisiana. He was also an artist-in-residence for the Williamson Museum and the Louisiana Folklife Center at Northwestern State University. Medford participated in several festivals, including the New Orleans Jazz and Heritage Festival and the Natchitoches-NSU Folk Festival, and his work is in many museum collections. Because of his contribution to preserving the heritage of his people and his talent in basketry, Medford was inducted into the Louisiana Folklife Center's Hall of Master Folk Artists in 1983, the first Choctaw to be so honored.

dedicated to baskets. The display was organized into 11 different regions. Thirteen basket makers from all over the country were on hand as cultural interpreters.

2014: Henry Jake Arquette (1931–2015) from the Akwesasne Reservation, New York, was the first Mohawk to be awarded an NEA National Heritage Fellowship. He specialized in Mohawk pack, laundry, picnic, wedding, and other utility baskets woven of black ash. A retired Mohawk ironworker, Arquette began making baskets full time in 1993 and mentored others at the Akwesasne Cultural Center in Hogansburg, New York. He was recognized twice with a Traditional Arts of Upstate New York's North Country Heritage Award (1994 and 2004). Arquette's baskets are in the National Museum of the American Indian as well as part of prized collections all over the world.

2018: Iva Honyestewa (1964–), Hopi/Navajo, won first place for contemporary basketry at the Santa Fe Indian Market for her *pootsaya* creation. The unique style is her own and a combination of sifter and coiled baskets.

BEADWORK, QUILLWORK, LEI, WHIMSIES

"My hope for the future of Cherokee and Southeastern beadwork is for there to be a good, strong, market for it. That will only happen if people know what they are looking at when they see it. Currently, the average person can recognize Plains beadwork on sight. They see it as being Native American and they have come to expect this look when they look to buy a piece of beadwork. What I would like to see is for Cherokees, and other Southeastern descendants, to be able to see a piece of Southeastern Woodlands beadwork and know that it is the beadwork of their own grandmothers. I would love for a bandolier bag to be as indicative of Southeastern Woodlands nations as a totem is of Northwestern nations or a kachina is of the Southwestern nations. We need this visual identity."

—*Martha Berry, Cherokee, beadwork artist*

c. 1821: Beadwork was a major source of income for the Mohawk, Tuscarora, and Seneca of New York, and novelties or "whimsies" appealed to the Euro-American Victorian-era decorating style. Native artists put the two together and invented a new art form of Native-inspired beaded souvenir whimsies that thrilled the thousands of tourists who flocked to Niagara Falls after the opening of the Erie Canal. Utilitarian pieces like picture frames, pin cushions, match holders, and coin purses were given a distinctly Indian flair. Other whimsies seemed to poke fun at the non-Native customers: a canoe had "fast boat" beaded on it, and a box spelled out "BOX." Today, whimsies are very

Marcus
Amerman

collectable, with some items valued at hundreds of dollars. The art continues. The late Mohawk artist Barbara Little Bear Delisle (1945–2017) was known for her beaded velvet "worry birds" and picture frames with raised beadwork, a distinctive Haudenosaunee technique. Grant Jonathan (1961–), Tuscarora and beadwork artist, has spent years repatriating beadwork sold to tourists by his Tuscarora artist-ancestors. He has almost 3,000 historical whimsies in his collection. Jonathan's own whimsies have earned him multiple ribbons from the Santa Fe Indian Market.

c. 1950s: Alice New Holy Blue Legs (1925–2003), Oglala Lakota, was the first to revive the ancient art of quillwork. It had almost been lost as most beaders preferred the easier-to-attain glass beads. Preparing porcupine quills is an arduous task; the process is quite time-consuming even before the actual quillwork can begin. Throughout the generations, the New Holy women continued to do outstanding quillwork, and as her grandmother taught her, New Holy Blue Legs taught the art to her five daughters. She facilitated workshops and demonstrations across the nation including Dartmouth College, Brown University, the Children's Museum in Indianapolis, the Buffalo Bill Historical Center, and the University of South Dakota's Indian Studies program. New Holy Blue Legs was chosen to demonstrate quilling for the opening of the Sacred Circles exhibit in Kansas City (1977). It is ironic that most Native artists use European-type beads, yet New Holy Blue Legs's quillwork was and is desired by European collectors, who appreciate its beauty as well as the laborious method used to create it.

1985: Marcus Amerman (1959–), Choctaw, became the first beadwork artist to have his work published in *Playboy* magazine. He is also an award-winning glass artist, painter, fashion designer, and performance artist.

1990: Maude Kegg (Naawakamigookwe; "Centered upon the Ground Woman") (1904–1996), Ojibwe, was the first person to receive a National Heritage Fellowship for beadwork. She was a master of Ojibwe floral designs and geometric loom beadwork techniques and was known for her fully beaded traditional bandolier bags. Kegg was also a cultural preservationist, and Minnesota governor Rudy Perpich honored her by declaring August 26, 1986, as "Maude Kegg Day" for the state of Minnesota. In 1991, she was featured in the book *Portage Lake: Memories of an Ojibwe Childhood*, published by the University of Alberta Press.

1990: Marie McDonald (1926–2019), Native Hawaiian, was the first lei maker to receive a National Heritage Fellowship. One of Hawaii's most respected floral Kupuna (elders) and well-known kapa makers, she was named one of the 10 "Living Treasures of the Hawaiian People" by the Office of Hawaiian Affairs. She authored books on the art of the lei tradition.

1994: Martha Berry, Cherokee, brought back the traditional form of Cherokee beadwork for the first time in over a century. Her pursuit of the original styles took her to the Smithsonian Museum of the American Indian, where she researched photographs and beadwork in the collections, figuring out how to re-create the lavish art form, which had almost been lost. Berry fashions beaded bandolier bags, moccasins, belts, knee bands, purses, and sashes with the distinctive ancient Cherokee designs of floral and geometric patterns. She has won several awards for her artwork as well as being honored in 2013 as a Cherokee National Living Treasure.

2002: Ruth Waukazo, Ojibwe, was chosen to be a Community Spirit Award Honoree by

the First Peoples Fund. She was the first Ojibwe beadworker to be honored.

2014: Yvonne Walker Keshick (1946–), Odawa/Anishinaabe, received an NEA National Heritage Fellowship and became the first porcupine quill artist and the first Odawa to win the honor. From the Little Traverse Bay Bands of Odawa Indians in Michigan, her designs incorporate traditional elements from her culture as well as animal and plant designs passed down through the generations. In 1992, she was honored with a Michigan Heritage Award for her "mastery of her tradition, attention to authenticity, and commitment to sharing her cultural knowledge within her community" by Michigan State University. Her work has been displayed in the National Museum of the American Indian and in many other museums. Keshick was a featured participant in the 2006 Smithsonian Folklife Festival's Carriers of Culture Native Weaving Traditions program.

CARVING AND WOODWORKING

"The totem poles are a symbol of something that all of us have within us. We have the power to heal, the power to love each other, the power to unite—that's what the symbol is about. The totem pole [itself] isn't a sacred thing; it's the sacredness of love joining us together. If we believe in God, then it seems to me that we need to protect the world that He created."

—*Master carver Jewell Praying Wolf James, director of the Lummi Sovereignty and Treaty Protection Office and head of the House of Tears Carvers*

1945: Inuit artists in Alaska began using soapstone for carving, replacing the traditional ivory.

1978: For the first time in more than a century, a totem was raised at the village of Skidegate, Alaska. Bill Reid (1920–1998), Haida, carved the pole for his mother's village.

1990: David Boxley (1952–), Tsimshian, is the world's most prolific totem pole carver, having created over 70 poles, which have been displayed in places like Disney World, Florida, and the Smithsonian National Museum of the American Indian (Washington, D.C.), where his work is on permanent exhibition. His poles are owned by various museums around the world and have been commissioned by royal families and nobles across Europe and Asia. For the 1990 Goodwill Games, he carved a "Talking Stick," the first Native person to design one for the international games. The crown of the stick depicted the American eagle and the Russian bear together as a symbol of peace between the United States and Russia. He even engraved messages from the leaders of the two countries, President George H. W. Bush and President Mikhail Gorbachev. The event was held in Moscow, Russia, and Seattle and other Washington locations. Similar to the Olympic Torch, the stick was carried across the United States.

1991: George Blake (1944–), Hupa-Yurok, was the first carver to be awarded a National Heritage Fellowship (NEA). From 1980 to

This Lummi totem pole, carved by Jewell Praying Wolf James, was donated to the 9/11 Memorial Groves project in Washington, D.C.

1983, Blake was curator of the Hupa Tribal Museum, teaching traditional arts like featherwork and antler carving to younger tribal members as well as re-creating a traditional Hupa canoe. Although several of his boats are exhibited in museums, he also carves them to be seaworthy, and they have been used for voyaging in the Pacific. He also makes jewelry, combining many styles and materials. In 2016, he received an honorary doctorate of humane letters from California State University and Humboldt State University for his role in the resurgence of Native California traditional cultural life since the 1970s.

1992: Bel Abbey (1916–1991), Koasati, was the first Native blowgun maker, wood carver, and storyteller to be inducted into the Louisiana Folklife Center's Hall of Master Folk Artists.

1993: Nicholas Charles (1910–1995) and his wife, Elena Charles (1918–2007), were the first Yup'ik artists to be awarded an NEA National Heritage Fellowship. They were honored for their part in preserving and restoring traditional Yup'ik cultural arts. Nicholas Charles is credited with reviving Yup'ik mask making; both he and Elena Charles also made other carvings, skin clothing, and baskets.

2011: Jewell Praying Wolf James, Lummi, was the only artist to carve an inaugural totem pole for the U.S. National Library of Medicine's exhibit "Native Voices: Native Peoples' Concepts of Health and Illness." The library, part of the National Institutes of Health, created the exhibition under the advisement of Indigenous groups throughout the United States. The 20-foot Healing Pole, raised in Bethesda, Maryland, was transported by truck from Lummi homelands in Washington State to Maryland. It stopped on dozens of Indigenous homelands to receive blessings. In 2021, James and his Lummi community sent another pole to Washington, D.C., from their Lummi Reservation, near Bellingham, Washington. He and his team of artists, aged 4 through 70, carved it from a 400-year-old red cedar as a reminder to honor the rights of Indigenous people and their sacred sites. The journey, called the "Red Road to D.C.," passed sacred sites before arriving in the nation's capital. Once there, it was gifted to President Joe Biden and featured in a special exhibition developed by the Natural History Museum and House of Tears Carvers.

DOLL MAKING

"I feel that my dolls, intentionally or unintentionally, often resemble me in various ways. However, if I were to consciously create a portrait of myself in a doll, I would hope that it would depict a woman who was in touch with her culture and traditions. I would want it to depict the dignity of one, like my grandmother, who had knowledge and was a keeper of stories. I would like the face to convey the wisdom of one who had asked questions and had listened to and learned from the wisdom of her elders. I would hope that this doll would ultimately depict the kind of woman that younger generations would come to, seeking knowledge."

—*Rhonda Holy Bear,*
Cheyenne River Sioux, doll artist

c. 1952: Ethel Washington (1889–1967), Inupiaq from Kotzebue, Alaska, was often referred to as "the mother of modern Alaska doll makers." Although she began making dolls in 1930, it wasn't until after her husband died that she created finely crafted doll families to support her family. Washington was the first Native doll maker known to

A display of Native American dolls from various regions of North America is seen here on display at the Robbins Museum in Middleborough, Massachusetts.

non-Native customers. She dressed her dolls in fur parkas and outfitted them with tools, utensils, or hunting equipment. She used a Boy Scout knife to whittle the faces from reclaimed wood from the Kobuk River. The dolls were often carved to resemble community members. Washington was an inspiration to others, and Kotzebue women took up the art, including Lena Sours, Rose Francis, Emma Black Lincoln, and Dolly Spencer.

1985: Rhonda Holy Bear (1960–), Cheyenne River Sioux, was the first doll maker to receive the Southwestern Indian Association of Indian Affairs' Fellowship. Her world-famous dolls are historically accurate and detailed from the underclothes to the intricately beaded traditional outfits. Holy Bear's

lifelike creations seem like miniature people from their exquisite facial expressions to their precisely constructed footwear. She has won countless awards for her masterpieces.

1996: Dolly Spencer (1930–2005) became the first Inupiaq artist/doll maker to be awarded an NEA National Heritage Fellowship. She was also the first to be known internationally, and her dolls are in collections around the world. Spencer used all traditional materials—carved beechwood heads, skin bodies stuffed with caribou hair, and fur and skin garments sewn with sinew. She reproduced traditional dress and customs, hoping that each creation preserved her memories of Inupiat life and served to educate the general public.

Indigenous Firsts: A History of Native American Achievements and Events

2002: American Girl Dolls released its Nez Perce Kaya doll, after collaborating with the Nez Perce over six years. Kaya is a historical character from the 1700s and has a series of books that tell her story. The books focus on traditional Nez Perce values such as compassion, responsibility, friendship, and family.

2007: Susie Silook (1960–), Yupik/Inupiaq writer, carver, and sculptor, was the first in her art form to be awarded a United States Artist award. Ancestral ivory dolls of Saint Lawrence, traditionally carved by men, are the basis of her work. Although Silook creates art in the traditional media of ivory and whalebone, her themes are the contemporary issues confronting Native Alaskans, particularly women, with a specific focus on violence against Native women.

2016: The Florida Museum of Natural History, which has the world's largest holding of Seminole and Miccosukee dolls, exhibited its collection. Comprised of over 170 dolls, the collection covers nearly 70 years of history from the 1930s to early 2000s. The dolls are constructed of palmetto fiber stuffed with cotton and accurately portray the traditional hairstyle and patchwork clothing. The patchwork art that is the hallmark of Seminole fashion was invented out of necessity. The Seminoles are composed of various culturally related tribes, which began to migrate south into northern Florida sometime before 1750, fleeing the harsh conditions created by colonialists. Most had already replaced their traditional clothing with outfits made from European trade goods, often adopting European styles. As resources dwindled and cloth sellers were far from where people lived in relative safety from Europeans and later Americans, seamstresses got creative, wasting not one bit of material. They salvaged as much fabric as they could, often cutting it into strips and dis-carding the damaged pieces. Then they sewed the usable parts together into beautiful designs that created a new tradition. Dolls were dressed in the same outfits as the people, and soon tourists began clamoring for the colorfully clad figures. The sale of dolls helped support many Seminole and Miccosukee families before the arrival of the gaming industry and are highly prized today by collectors around the world.

2017: Joyce Laporte, Ojibwe from Fond du Lac (Minnesota), conducted a "Faceless Dolls" workshop, the first "Sister Site Visit" event sponsored by the American Indian College Fund and held at Leech Lake Tribal College.

GLASS AND MOSAICS

"My work with glass transforms the notion that Native artists are only best when traditional materials are used. It has helped advocate on the behalf of all indigenous people—affirming that we are still here—that we are declaring who we are through our art in connection to our culture."

—*Preston Singletary, Tlingit*

1999: Tony Jojola (1958–), Isleta Pueblo, established the Taos Glass Workshop in northern New Mexico to teach at-risk youth the process and art of glass blowing. Considered one of the top glass artists in the country, he was one of the first Native artists to work in the discipline. Jojola creates hand-blown, one-of-a-kind pieces in an array of colors, combining striking abstract and traditional Native designs.

2003: The first collaborative exhibition of Native American glass artists, "Fusing Traditions: Transformations in Glass," opened at the Museum of Craft and Folk Art in San Francisco, California. Eighteen artists contributed 37 artworks blending cultural heritage and individual creativity into stunning new glass forms, and for two years the show traveled to other sites: the Los Angeles Museum of Craft and Folk Art; the Heard Museum in Phoenix, Arizona; the Santa Cruz Museum of Art and History in California; the Anchorage Museum of Art and History in Alaska; the Alaska State Museum in Juneau; and the Mashantucket Pequot Museum and Research Center in Ledyard, Connecticut. The dazzling art was created by Susan Point, Coast Salish; Tony Jojola, Isleta Pueblo; Marcus Amerman, Choctaw; Larry Ahvakana, Inupiaq; Michael Carius, Siberian Y'upic; Conrad House, Navajo; Clarissa Hudson, Tlingit; Ramson Lomatewama, Hopi; Ed Archie NoiseCat, Salish; Marvin Oliver, Quinalt; Joe David, Nuu-Chah-Nulth; John Hagen, Alaskan Native; Wayne Price, Tlingit; Shaun Peterson, Salish; Robert Tannahill, Mohawk/Métis; Brian Barber, Pawnee; Preston Singletary, Tlingit; and C. S. Tarpley, Choctaw.

2007: Glass artist Preston Singletary (1963–), Tlingit, stunned the art world when he collaborated with Maori artist Lewis Tamihana Gardiner to create the piece "Devilfish Prow," blown and sandcarved glass with steel connections, pounamu (New Zealand jade), Australian black jade, Siberian jade, and paua shell inlays. His unique designs incorporate traditional Tlingit themes and are part of several museum collections, including the Handelsbanken in Stockholm, Sweden; the Corning Museum of Glass in Corning, New York; and the National Museum of the American Indian, Smithsonian Institution, in Washington, D.C.

Preston Singletary

Singletary has blown glass in Sweden, Italy, and Finland.

GRAPHIC DESIGN

"I am passionate about the intersection of Native cultures and graphic design. Graphic design, art, philosophy, and cultural movements have long gone hand in hand. I very much believe that Native outlooks and art forms can inform the process of design. I believe that the practice of graphic design can be used to positively promote Native communities and identities. I think it's important that Native people speak for themselves, especially in a time when Native cultures and art forms continue to be co-opted."

—Neebinnaukzhik Southall, Chippewas of Rama First Nation, graphic artist

1996: For the first time, the *AIGA Journal of Graphic Design* (vol. 14, no. 1, the Property Issue) published an article about the abuse of Indigenous cultures by the graphic design industry. "Get Crazy Horse Off That Beer Can and Let Pocahontas Go Home," written by Yvonne Wakim Dennis (then known as Yvonne Wakim Beamer), Cherokee/Sand Hill/Syrian, addressed the cultural misappropriation and stereotypes of Native religions, languages, historical figures, customs, icons, and other aspects of Indian heritage for commercial design purposes.

2010: Encore Vision in Spokane, Washington, launched its Native Vision line of eyeglass-wear featuring Indigenous-inspired designs. Virgil "Smoker" Marchand, an artist

Kenojuak Ashevak

Kenojuak
Ashevak

Kenojuak Ashevak (1927–2013) was one of Canada's most celebrated graphic artists. Born on south Baffin Island, she lived in several areas of the Arctic, particularly the Nunavik territory in northern Quebec. In the late 1950s, Ashevak and her husband began experimenting with carving and drawing and worked together until his death. Starting in 1959, she was represented in almost every annual print collection, and her artwork has also been included in numerous special projects and commissions, including World Wildlife Print Portfolio, 1978. Via Rail Canada commissioned her for a large mural for its Club Car series, 1998; Indian and Northern Affairs Canada commissioned *Nunavut Qajanatuk (Our Beautiful Land)* to commemorate the signing of the Inuit Land Claim Agreement, 1990; and for the final signing agreement, she created the large lithograph entitled *Nunavut*, 1994. The National Film Board documented her traditional life and art in the film *Eskimo Artist: Kenojuak*, which received an Oscar nomination in 1963. Ashevak has a long list of awards and honors: Companion in the Order of Canada, honorary degrees from Queen's University and the University of Toronto, Lifetime Achievement Award from the National Aboriginal Achievement Awards, and the first Inuit artist to be inducted into the Canada's Walk of Fame. Ashevak traveled the world representing Inuit art, and in 2004, her major stained-glass piece was installed at the John Bell Chapel at Appleby College near Toronto. Her simple compositions, bold lines, and strong colors define the classic drawing Cape Dorset style (now named Kinngait, an Inuit hamlet at the southern tip of Baffin), and Ashevak's art is distinguished by a central component—often an animal, bird, fish, or human—positioned on the paper without landscape or narrative devices.

and member of the Colville Confederated Tribes known for his stunning monuments, created the line.

2013: Neebinnaukzhik Southall of the Chippewas of Rama First Nation launched the Native Graphic Design Project to promote and showcase North American Indigenous graphic designers.

2019: Joshua Mangeshig Pawis-Steckley (1989–), Ojibwe from Wasauksing First Nation, designed a Google Doodle depicting the Jingle Dress tradition. It was the first time a Native dance had been honored on the Google website.

METALSMITHING

"I've never had a helmet or a hubcap ordered yet, but I'm sure in time one will come along."

—*Bruce Caeser, Pawnee, Silversmith*

1853: Blacksmith Atsidi Sani (c. 1830–c. 1870 or 1918) made his first silver objects and was the first known Navajo silversmith. He learned ironmaking from a Mexican friend and became so adept at making bridles that most Navajo relied upon him to fit their horses. His silver work consisted of conchas, bracelets, and a variety of other jewelry pieces. In addition to being a silversmith and a blacksmith, Sani was also a medicine man, spiritual leader, ceremonial singer, and a Navajo chief. Today, Navajo metalsmiths make buckles, bridles, buttons, rings, canteens, hollow beads, earrings, crescent-shaped pendants (called *najas*), bracelets, crosses, powder chargers, tobacco canteens, and conchas (or conchos)—typically used to decorate belts—from copper, steel, iron, and most commonly, silver.

Atsidi Sani

c. late 1870s: The Navajo were the first to design the iconic squash blossom necklace, which had appeared centuries before in their rock art. Created from silver, turquoise, and other material, the necklace depicts squash, an important Navajo crop. However, the Navajo word *naja* was given to the design on the bottom of the necklace. The symbol itself is believed to have originated in the Middle East during ancient times; the Moorish horses were outfitted with the symbol for good luck. There are several theories on how an Arabian ancient cultural design ended up as an icon in the southwestern United States.

1974: Award-winning jewelry artist Charles Loloma (1921–1991), Hopi, was the first Native to have an artist residency in Japan as well as the first to have work commissioned by President Lyndon B. Johnson, the queen of Denmark, and the first lady of the Philippines. His jewelry is among the most distinctive and prized in the world, and he is lauded for dismantling barriers that barred Indian jewelers from creating what non-Natives considered to be Indian art. Loloma was the first to use materials other than turquoise and silver; his designs popularized the use of gold and gemstones

not previously used in Hopi jewelry. The first to hide designs and stones on the inside of jewelry, Loloma said that they were symbols of inner strength and beauty possessed by each person. He was also a stellar potter; he and his wife operated a ceramics shop in Scottsdale, Arizona. A true renaissance man, Loloma painted murals for the Federal Building on Treasure Island in San Francisco Bay as part of the Golden Gate International Exposition (1939) and for New York's Museum of Modern Art. He was a camouflage expert for the U.S. Army, received a Whitney Foundation Fellowship to study clays in the Hopi area, and headed the Plastic Arts and Sales Departments at the Institute of American Indian Arts in Santa Fe, New Mexico. He received many awards, including first prize seven years in a row at the Scottsdale National Indian Arts Exhibition. Loloma has been featured in the films *Three Indians* (1972) and *Loloma* (1974) and inspired and taught many other artists.

1998: Bruce Caesar (1952–), Pawnee, was the first silversmith to be awarded an NEA National Heritage Fellowship. In 2019, the exhibition "How It Was Handed to Me: The Caesar Family Legacy" was featured at the Coe Center in Santa Fe, New Mexico. It was the first time in the area that a show focused on Plains jewelry created from German (or nickel) silver. German silver is an alloy of copper, zinc, and nickel and actually contains no silver—despite its name and appearance. It is widely used across Plains communities for dance regalia and for Native American church ceremonies. Caesar learned the art form from his father and then went on to teach his children as well as others. The family and those they have trained make stunning and collectable pieces that include detailed tiaras, earrings, armbands, and cuffs.

PAINTING AND COLLAGE

"Sacred feminine iconography and spirituality is the subject matter of much of my work. Our Native peoples have always respected the feminine creative Power and so I continue this tradition with my works as devotional pieces made in reverence to the earth, sky, sun, moon, and stars—all the creative and regenerative forces of the universe. They are also metaphors for the cosmic relationships between the sacred feminine and sacred masculine and the harmonious balance of those powers."

—*Nadema Agard,*
Lakota/Cherokee/Powhatan, artist

c. late 1800s: Amos Bad Heart Bull (1869–1913), Oglala Sioux, was one of the early Native Americans to develop ledger drawings. An artist and historian, Bad Heart Bull, who inherited the position of band historian from his father, learned about daily life and important tribal events, which he drew in a ledger book. He eventually created a series of 415 drawings in which he recorded battles, especially the Battle of the Little Big Horn, the Ghost Dance, and the massacre at Wounded Knee. He drew with black pen; pencils; blue, yellow, green, and brown crayons; and red ink. His drawings provide multiple perspectives of the same event, using a view from above, topographic views, and closeups of a participant from a crowded scene. The book passed to his sister when he died.

1939: Pablita Velarde (born Tse Tsan, meaning "Golden Dawn"; 1918–2006), Santa Clara Pueblo, was commissioned to create artwork depicting Pueblo life for the first museum at the U.S. Park Service's Bandelier National Monument near Los Alamos, New Mexico. She combined her unique style with her intimate knowledge of Pueblo culture to create over 70 intricate paintings of the Pueblo world. Her works depict in detail the traditional clothing and hairstyles, ceremonial dances, gender roles, architecture, and activities of daily life. Velarde was a pioneer as a woman artist in an era and community where painting was a male art form. Her painting began in a traditional manner but evolved into many original styles. She became well known for her "earth colors." She grounded rocks and minerals into a powdery substance on a metate and mano and mixed them with water and glue. Velarde's work won many awards and made her internationally famous.

1949: An artist and culture bearer, Fred Kabotie (1900–1986) was the first Hopi to receive the Indian Achievement Award given by the Indian Council Fire of Chicago. He is recognized as being the first professional Hopi artist. Kabotie reproduced traditional Hopi designs in his paintings to preserve the tradition. He combined his desire to record his culture with his goal to preserve genuine Hopi designs by establishing the Hopi Silvercraft Cooperative Guild. Kabotie was also a renown silversmith, illustrator, potter, author, curator, and educator.

1954: For the first time, a foreign government recognized Native American art when France awarded the Ordre des Palmes académiques for outstanding contributions to art to painter Pablita Velarde, Santa Clara Pueblo; sculptor Allan Houser, Apache; and potter Maria Montoya Martinez, San Ildefonso.

1957: Oscar Howe (1915–1983), Yanktonai Dakota, became the first recipient of the South Dakota Governor's Award for Creative Achievement. Among his many other awards, in 1966 he received the Waite Phillips Trophy for outstanding contributions

One of Amos Bad Heart Bull's many drawings depicting the Battle of the Little Big Horn.

to American Indian Art by the Philbrook Art Center in Tulsa, Oklahoma. Howe is considered a pioneer who expressed himself through innovative techniques and styles such as cubism and abstract expressionism rather than through traditionally perceived art forms.

1958: The first commercial Navajo sandpaintings were created for sale. Traditionalists vehemently opposed the reproductions of sacred subject matter.

1962: The Institute of American Indian Arts (IAIA) was founded in Santa Fe, New Mexico. The institution has played a key role in educating contemporary Native American artists. Some of the most prominent Indian artists assisted in establishing the art school and taught there as well, including such notable artists as Allan Houser and Charles Loloma.

1963: George Morrison (Wah Wah Teh Go Nay Ga Bo [Standing in the Northern Lights]; 1919–2000), Grand Portage Chippewa Band, was the first Native artist appointed assistant professor of art at a major art school, the Rhode Island School of Design. In 1997, he was honored in a ceremony held in the nation's capital for an exhibition entitled "Twentieth Century American Sculpture at the White House," which included his work. His paintings evoked various styles from Surrealism to Impressionism to Abstract Expressionism. Morrison also created monumental and compositionally complex wood collages.

1972: Joseph Kabance (1945–), Prairie Band Potawatomie Nation, received the Grand Award at the Philbrook Art Museum's annual Indian Art Exhibition in Tulsa, Oklahoma. The winning painting, *Of the Sioux*, was the first-ever circular canvas work to

This ledger drawing is an example of a Cheyenne work circa 1880.

Ledger Drawings

Native people of the Plains region were known for their paintings. Men worked in groups to paint their tipi linings, buffalo robes, and pictographic (picture writing) historical accounts. As the U.S. government tried to subdue resistance, they imprisoned many Native men far from their homelands. Nearly every one of the jailed men was an artist; they expressed their loneliness in drawings that had long been their medium of expression and chronicling events. In precontact days, the painters used natural pigments and porous buffalo-bone brushes. They soon adopted non-Indian crayons, pencils, watercolors, and inks to fill army commissary books, trader ledgers, and pieces of muslin with traditional images of the world from which they came. The drawings became known as ledger art and depicted both the daily and important historic events in which they participated, including battles, hunting, and ceremonies. Soldiers recorded their exploits on what were sometimes called "brag skins."

There is an unknown number of pictographic records of winter counts, buffalo hunts, raids, biographies, and historic events in public museums. In many cases, the ledger art was produced out of necessity to buy food as the artists soon learned they had a market value to souvenir-hungry American soldiers, travelers, and others. Original ledger drawings from the early period (1870s) are highly prized.

Today, many artists still use this medium. Ledger art has influenced the development of painting by young Plains Indian artists. One such award-winning painter, Dwayne Wilcox (1957–), Oglala Lakota, is a master contemporary Plains ledger artist. His work emphasizes the contemporary life of Native peoples, although he often does visit "older

Ledger Drawings (contd.)

subjects" with emotional sarcasm and wit. Wilcox's themes present vignettes of Indian life infused with humor and depicts scenes of powwows, social dances, families, and everyday mundane activities. Some of his humorous works include *Picking George Out of the Line Up; Under the Microscope;* and *Wow! Real Blooded White People.*

receive the honor in the prestigious national Native art competition. Kabance continues to create the circular canvases and a unique style termed "oil on circular canvas, with mixed media and 3-dimensional elements, based on Native/Indigenous themes." The paintings range from 24 inches to 60 inches in diameter and are in private collections as well as the Philbrook and Heard Museums. He has been an artist in residence at the National Museum of the American Indian and part of many shows around the country. In 2011, Tapwe Production Projects produced a film about Kabance and his work as an Indian/Native artist living and working in New York City.

1973: R. C. Gorman (1931–2005), Navajo, became the only living artist to be honored in the "Masterworks of the American Indian" exhibition at the Metropolitan Museum of Art in New York City. In 1975, he became the first artist to be selected for a series on contemporary American Indian artists at the National Museum of the American Indian in New York City. Gorman primarily painted Native American women characterized by fluid forms and vibrant colors. He also worked in sculpture, ceramics, and stone lithography.

1974: Joan Hill (1930–2020), Muskogee Creek Nation (Chea-Se-Quah, or Redbird), was given the title Master Artist by the Five Civilized Tribes Museum in Muskogee, Oklahoma. She received almost 400 awards and honors, including the Waite Phillips Special Artists Trophy from the Philbrook Museum of Art. Hill was known most for her stylized, acrylic paintings of historical and cultural scenes. She predominately painted Creek and Cherokee women. In 1978, Hill participated in the first Painters Cultural Interchange with the People's Republic of China and is the only known Indian artist to have her work exhibited in that country.

1976: Kevin Red Star (1943–), Crow, was the first graduate of IAIA to return as artist-in-residence. The same year, he was selected as Artist of the Year by the *Santa Fean* magazine.

1980: David Bradley (1954–) Minnesota Chippewa, was the only artist to win the top awards in the Fine Art categories of both painting and sculpture at the Santa Fe Indian Market. For the past four decades, Bradley has been a recognized voice from Indian Country, confronting through his art questions of identity, self-determination, and self-representation, as well as definitions of "traditional" Indian art. Influenced by diverse sources such as Santa Fe–style painting of the 1930s and 1940s, Renaissance art, pop culture, advertising, and film, Bradley's work is at once serious and fun, historical and contemporary. His paintings especially address issues of stereotype, cultural appropriation, and Native social and political justice. His activism has impacted federal and state policies that protect Native artists from frauds who pass off their work as authentic Native arts.

1985: Clifford Bahnimptewa, Hopi, was the only Hopi to receive the Anisfield-Wolf Book Award for Race Relations for his paintings of 286 Kachinas featured in Harold S. Colton's book *Hopi Kachina Dolls*. He never received the royalties promised him.

1985: The largest exhibition of art devoted to the topic of Native HIV/AIDS was held at the American Indian Community House Gallery, New York City's only Native-owned and -operated gallery.

1985: Artists Jaune Quick-to-See Smith (1940-), French-Cree/Shoshone/Salish, and Harmony Hammond (1944-) curated the first exhibition of contemporary Indian women's art. "Women of Sweetgrass, Cedar and Sage" was presented at the American Indian Community House Gallery in New York City and featured a variety of artists, from photography and painting to basketmaking, quilting, clay and silver, to beads and mixed media. In 2020, Quick-to-See Smith became the first Native artist to have a painting on canvas—*I See Red: Target*—in the National Gallery of Art.

1991: Rolland D. Lee, Navajo, exhibited his paintings in the Skylight Gallery of the Wheelwright Museum in Santa Fe, New Mexico. At only age 14, he was the youngest person to do so. Lee was also the regional spelling bee champion for years.

1994: Dan Lomahaftewa (1951-2005), Hopi and Choctaw, was the first visiting artist at the Rainmaker Gallery in Bristol, England. Lomahaftewa created distinctly spiritual works of art that sought to communicate the strong continuum that connects ancient ancestors to the peoples of today, to future generations, and beyond. In his extensive research of petroglyphs and pictographs, Lo-

mahaftewa visited many sites of ancient rock art created by Indigenous ancestors. These timeless forms often appeared as subjects of his paintings and prints.

1995: Harrison Begay (Haskay Yahne Yah [Warrior Who Walked Up to His Enemy]; 1917-2012), a renowned Navajo painter, was awarded the Native American Masters Award by the Heard Museum in Phoenix, Arizona. He specialized in silkscreen prints and paintings in tempera, watercolor, and acrylics of Navajo Indian figures and other Southwest scenes regarded as "quiet and peaceful" in tone. In 1954 Harrison was the first Navajo artist to be awarded the Ordre des Palmes académiques, a special commendation from the French government, for his contributions to the arts. Painting into his 90s, Begay was awarded the 2003 Lifetime Achievement Award by the Southwestern Association of Indian Artists, organizers of the annual Santa Fe Indian Art Market.

1995: Don Montileaux (1948-), Oglala Sioux artist, was commissioned by the South Dakota School of Mines & Technology to create a piece that would fly aboard the space shuttle *Endeavour*. Titled *Looking Beyond One's Self*, the painting was the first created by a Native artist to be launched into space. Montileaux has won many honors and accolades for his work and considers his favorite the First Place and Best of Division awards at the internationally known Santa Fe Indian Art Market in 2006.

1996: The art exhibition "Plains Indian Drawings 1865-1935: Pages from a Visual History" opened at the Drawing Center in New York City. It was the first time the most extensive study of ledger drawings was presented as a separate and unique art genre. The show, cosponsored with the American Federation of Arts, featured ledger drawings by the Lakota, Cheyenne, Kiowa, and Arapaho warriors, often incarcerated, in the late nineteenth and early twentieth centuries. Done on discarded lined ledger papers, the art depicted a variety of subjects from everyday life to battle scenes.

1996: Virgil "Smoker" Marchand (1951–), Colville Arrow Lakes Band Salish, was the first Native artist to have his work, *Trail Talk*, featured on the Hamilton Collection plates.

2005: For the first time, the Ellis Island National Museum of Immigration at the Statue of Liberty National Monument hosted an all-Native women's art exhibition, "An Artistic Perspective: Lady Liberty as a Native American Icon." The vision of award-winning artist/curator Nadema Agard (Winyan Luta/Woman Holy Red), Cherokee/Lakota/Powhatan, was to promote healing from the September 11, 2001, World Trade Center tragedy. Agard invited Native women artists, who also view the Statue of Liberty as having an Indigenous spirit that predates the great American icon, to join her. The multimedia works by these "artists imbued Lady Liberty with a Native feminine presence that reflected a nurturing and fiercely protective warrior mother of America." The artists included Annalisa Agard, Lakota—Standing Rock Sioux; Nadema Agard, Cherokee/Lakota/Powhatan; Glory Tacheenie Campoy, Diné—Navajo; Katsitsionni Fox, Bear Clan Mohawk; Shelley Niro, Turtle Clan Mohawk; Ina McNeil, Hunkpapa Lakota—Standing Rock Sioux; Beverly Singer, Tewa/Diné; Laura Ortman, White Mountain Apache; and Barbara James Snyder, Paiute/Washoe. Nadema Agard is also a writer and illustrator; her work has appeared in books, museums, and festivals. She has curated many exhibits, including *Manahatta Today: Indigenous Art of N.Y.C.* (2014).

2006: The "Arthur Amiotte: Collages, 1988–2006" exhibition opened at the Wheelwright Museum of the American Indian in Santa Fe, New Mexico. Arthur Amiotte (Wanblí Ta Hócoka Washté, or Good Eagle Center; 1942–) spent 18 years working on the collages inspired by ledger art that chronicle Sioux life from 1880 to 1930. He is the first artist to focus on the Plains Indians' involvement with the Buffalo Bill and other western shows that toured Europe from 1887 to 1906. After Amiotte was awarded a Lila Wallace Reader's Digest/Arts International Fellowship (1997), he worked and lived for six months in Claude Monet's residence in Giverny, France. He researched old bookstores

The Kiowa Six

The Kiowa Six, a group of Kiowa artists prominent in the development of contemporary American Indian painting, were part of the early "Oklahoma school" of artwork, generally characterized by paintings of ceremonial and social scenes in colorful, flat, two-dimensional styles. Their artistic talent was first recognized and began to be nurtured as students at Saint Patrick's Indian Mission School in Anadarko, Oklahoma. The Kiowa Six studied at the University of Oklahoma, where they were mentored by school art director Oscar B. Jacobson, who promoted their work through international exhibitions and other venues. The Kiowa Six were Spencer Asah (c. 1905–1954); James Auchiah (1906–1974); Jack Hokeah (c. 1902–1969); Stephen Mopope (1898–1974); Monroe Tsatoke (1904–1937); and Lois Smoky (1907–1981), the only woman.

in Paris to find images for the collages. He overpainted photographs from different sources: old family albums; historical collections; laser copies of his own paintings; photos he had taken along with text and advertisements from antique magazines and books; pages from antique ledger books; and photocopies of his drawings or reproductions of original drawings by his great-grandfather, Standing Bear (1859–1933), who illustrated *Black Elk Speaks*, by John Neihardt. The results illustrate the rich diversity and complex lives of late-nineteenth and early-twentieth-century Lakota people from an Indigenous viewpoint. Amiotte debunks one-dimensional stereotypes of Indian identity and shows images that are "inventive, humorous, melancholy, witty, profound, and philosophical."

2009: Fritz Scholder (1937–2005), Luiseno, became the first American Indian and first painter to be inducted into the California Hall of Fame. An enrolled member of his tribe, Scholder often said he was not Indian. His works were recognized for their insight and powerful commentary on the public's stereotypic views of Native Americans. The Fritz Scholder website notes: "His revolutionary paintings broke away from stereotypical roles and forever changed the concept of 'Indian artist.'"

2019: Jim Denomie (1955–2022), Lac Courte Oreilles Band of Ojibwe, became the first Native American artist to be chosen for the Distinguished Artist Award of the McKnight Foundation since the award's inception in 1996. Denomie combined vivid hues and humor in monumental narrative paintings that explore the collisions between Indigenous cultures and European colonizers.

2020: Jaune Quick-to-See Smith, Confederated Salish and Kootenai

Jim Denomie

Tribes, was the first Native artist to have a painting on canvas in the National Gallery of Art, Washington, D.C. Her work was entitled *I See Red: Target.*

2021: Artists Bently Spang, Northern Cheyenne Tribe, and Robert Martinez, Northern Arapaho, were selected to have major pieces of their work displayed in Montana State University's new American Indian Hall, in Bozeman.

PHOTOGRAPHY

"It was a beautiful day when the scales fell from my eyes and I first encountered photographic sovereignty. A beautiful day when I decided that I would take responsibility to reinterpret images of Native peoples. My mind was ready, primed with stories of resistance and resilience, stories of survival. My views of these images are aboriginally based—an indigenous perspective—not a scientific godly order but philosophically Native."

—Hulleah Tsinhnahjinnie, Diné/Seminole/Muscogee, photographer

1890: Benjamin Alfred Haldane (1874–1941) opened the first photography studio in Metlakatla, Alaska, and is thought to be the first Tsimshian professional photographer. He documented community events like potlatches (outlawed at the time), weddings, and his own marching band showing the Tsimshian during a period of great transition. Haldane's work was included in "Our People, Our Land, Our Images," an exhibition of Indigenous photographers at the C.

N. Gorman Museum at the University of California, Davis, curated by Hulleah Tsinhnahjinnie.

c. 1900: Jennie Ross Cobb (1881–1959), Cherokee, the first known Native American woman photographer in the United States, began taking pictures of her Cherokee community in the late nineteenth century. Born in Tahlequah, Cherokee Nation, Indian Territory (present-day Oklahoma), she lived in what was known as the Murrell Home and documented the house and surroundings so well that the Cherokee Nation was able to return it to its original beauty using her photographs as a guide. Cobb supervised the renovation. Her images "defied the stereotypical photographic views" of Native Americans at the time, showing that the Cherokee were educated, fashionable, and proud of their culture. Today the Murrell Home is a state-owned museum named the Hunter's Home; it was declared a National Historic Landmark in 1974. Cobb also was the first Native woman to own her own flower shop (Arlington, Texas).

1941: Jean Fredericks (1906–1990) built a darkroom in his home in Old Oraibi, Arizona, a village located on Third Mesa on the Hopi Reservation. He is thought to be the first Hopi to take both candid and posed photographs of family members and community events on the reservation. Fredericks also focused on documentary images, which have been essential to recording Hopi history. He served as chairperson of the Hopi Tribe (c. 1960s).

The George M. Murrell House (aka Hunter's Home) is located in Cherokee County, Oklahoma.

Indigenous Firsts: A History of Native American Achievements and Events

1967: Photographer Bernie Boston (1933–2008), Tauxenent/Dogue, is thought to be the first Native American to be a runner-up for a Pulitzer Prize in Photography, for his iconic "Flower Power" image. The famous photo was of a Vietnam War protestor putting flowers in the barrels of the National Guard soldiers, who were aiming their weapons at him. Boston was also a Pulitzer Prize finalist for his 1987 photograph of Coretta Scott King unveiling a bust of her late husband, the Rev. Martin Luther King Jr., in the U.S. Capitol. During his career, he worked for various newspapers and captured the image of every sitting president from Harry S. Truman to Bill Clinton. In 1993, the National Press Photographers Association awarded Boston their highest honor, the Joseph A. Sprague Memorial Award, and he was inducted into the Hall of Fame of Sigma Delta Chi, the Society of Professional Journalists.

1998: "Constructing Histories: Portraits of Native Americans" opened at the Ansel Adams Center for Photography in San Francisco, California. The exhibition featured the art of photographer Dugan Aguilar (1947–2018), Maidu/Northern Paiute, one of the first Maidu photographers to chronicle Native life in Yosemite and California.

2000: Photographer Hulleah Tsinhnahjinnie (1954–), Diné/Seminole/Muscogee, was chosen a Community Spirit Award Honoree by the First Peoples Fund. She was the first in the new category of photography.

2005: Zig Jackson (1957–) Mandan/Hidatsa/Arikara, became the first contemporary Native American photographer to be collected by the Library of Congress when 12 of his images were accessioned by its Prints and Photographs Division.

2006: Lee Marmon (1925–2021), Laguna Pueblo, received the Lifetime Achievement Award from the Santa Fe–based Southwestern Association for Indian Arts for the "legacy of integrity" his works inspired during the 59 years that he practiced his craft. Known especially for his black-and-white portraits of tribal elders, he spent his life photographing the people, missions, customs, and landscapes of the Laguna and Acoma Reservations, amassing more than 90,000 negatives. In 1972, Marmon was the first Native photographer to ever be commissioned by a U.S. president when President and Mrs. Richard Nixon displayed his photo collection of tribal pottery from New Mexico at the White House.

Camille Seaman

2006: Photographer Camille Seaman (1969–) was the first Shinnecock to be granted a National Geographic Award. In 2007, she was the first to win a Critical Mass Top Monograph Award from *Photolucida*, an international photography organization based in Portland, Oregon. Seaman's work illustrates the effects of climate change, particularly the polar regions, and has been widely published in *Newsweek, Time,* the *New York Times,* and *Men's Journal.* In 2008, she was honored with a one-person exhibition, "The Last Iceberg," at the National Academy of Sciences. Using portraiture techniques to present the changing environment, Seaman's photographs are known for merging science and art.

2006: Larry McNeil (1955–), Tlingit/Nisga'a, received an international award from the All Roads Film Project sponsored by National Geographic to provide a global platform for Indigenous and under-represented minority-culture filmmakers, photographers, and artists. He has also won numerous other awards including the prestigious Eiteljorg Fellowship and the New Works

Award from En Foco, the national photography organization.

2007: Photographers Walter Tutsi Wai Big-Bee (1958–), Comanche, and Caimi Waiasse, Native Brazilian, presented "Shared Heritage" installed at Centro Universitário Senac University in São Paulo, Brazil. The photography exhibition explored the lives of contemporary urban Indigenous peoples of the United States and Brazil. This collaboration was a first for award-winning BigBee, owner of the Big Picture Studio in Tesuque, New Mexico. Among his many honors are top prizes from the Southwestern Association for Indian Arts (SWAIA) Indian Market and the Institute of American Indian Arts (IAIA) Museum, both in Santa Fe, New Mexico, and the Eiteljorg Museum in Indianapolis, Indiana.

2012: Matika Wilbur (1984–), Swinomish/Tulalip, sold everything in her Seattle apartment and went on the road to create Project 562, a commitment to "visit, engage and photograph all 562 plus Native American sovereign territories in the United States." She has traveled 250,000 miles by RV, train, plane, boat, horseback, and even foot across all 50 states documenting Indigenous peoples and their opinions about tribal sovereignty, self-determination, wellness, healing from historical trauma, decolonization, and revitalization of culture. Her goal is to humanize Native Americans and debunk historical inaccuracies and stereotypical images. Hundreds of Native communities have hosted and supported her; she has recorded them in photographs, videos, and audio recordings. Project 562 is Wilbur's response to Edward Curtis's photographs of Indigenous Americans a century earlier.

2017: Shelly Niro (1954–), Mohawk, took home Canada's top photography prize, the Scotiabank Photography Award, the first given to a Native artist. The groundbreaking multimedia artist has won awards in all of her genres: film, sculpture, photography, and painting, as well as an honorary doctorate from the Ontario College of Art and Design University (2019). Niro's work challenges stereotypes, gender imbalance, and cultural appropriation with a bit of humor. Throughout her career she has always represented Native people in realistic and explorative portrayals.

2019: Salish and Kootenai photojournalist Tailyr Irvine began documenting the complexities of blood quantum and Native identity and how it affects relationships in Indian communities. The project, "Reservation Mathematics: Navigating Love in Native America," explores the "unsustainable, colonial system placed on the shoulders of single Natives who are trying to find a partner in a shrinking pool or who might feel directly responsible for the complete genocide of Native people." This was the first time a Native photographer tackled the consequences of non-Natives defining who is an American Indian. Irvine is a National Geographic Explorer and a We, Women Artist.

POTTERY

"I like to make them [pots] when I feel good. My husband used to get after me.... 'Why don't you quit doing that?' And I said, 'Well, I like to do it.' He says, 'There's a lot of hard work in it.' And I said, 'I know it. It's a lot of fun, too.'"

—*Georgia Harris, Catawba, potter*

c. 1895: Nampeyo (c. 1860–1942), Hopi/Tewa, led the Sikyátki Revival Movement, a renaissance of pottery designs among Hopi potters. That same year, Nampeo and her husband, Lesou, joined the archaeologist Walter Fewkes at the Hopi excavation site at Sikyátki in Arizona, where she recorded designs on excavated pots. Nampeyo experimented with various types of clay and shaped pots like the ones found at the dig site. She was so talented that Fewkes was concerned her pots could pass for the originals. But Nampeyo put a contemporary spin on her designs and became quite famous and appeared at different venues like the U.S. Land and Irrigation Expo in Chicago (1910).

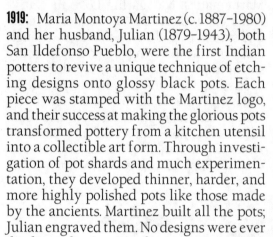

Nampeyo

Hopi educator and writer, but she is best known for her pottery. She was the first person known to have used traditional materials to create new forms. Most of her designs featured raised motifs of an ear of corn or *Kokopelli,* and her clay colors ranged from white to red. Among Qöyawayma's many awards were the Arizona Indian Living Treasure Award (1978) and Department of the Interior Distinguished Service Award (1954). She was inducted into the Arizona Women's Hall of Fame in 1991.

1919: Maria Montoya Martinez (c. 1887–1980) and her husband, Julian (1879–1943), both San Ildefonso Pueblo, were the first Indian potters to revive a unique technique of etching designs onto glossy black pots. Each piece was stamped with the Martinez logo, and their success at making the glorious pots transformed pottery from a kitchen utensil into a collectible art form. Through investigation of pot shards and much experimentation, they developed thinner, harder, and more highly polished pots like those made by the ancients. Martinez built all the pots; Julian engraved them. No designs were ever duplicated. Among her many honors, she won the Indian Achievement Award from the Indian Council Fire (1934), the first woman and only the second person to win; she won the Jane Addams Medal (1959), one of the highest honors ever granted to an American woman; and she was the first to be awarded the SWAI Lifetime Achievement Award (1995). Martinez taught her craft to others, and she and Julian are considered to be the most influential of any potters.

c. 1950s: Polingaysi Qöyawayma (1892–1990), also known as Elizabeth Q. White, was a

1964: Helen Cordero (1915–1994), Cochiti Pueblo, made the first storytelling doll, launching a major art genre, and took first, second, and third prizes at the New Mexico State Fair. She was inspired by the memory of her grandfather telling stories to children and also by the Cochiti women's custom of creating small clay toy figures, called "Singing Mothers," a tradition that had almost died out as the toys were frowned upon by the Catholic missionaries. The small figurine has closed eyes, open mouth, tilted head, and smaller figures sitting atop his lap and shoulders. Each of Cordero's dolls was unique; no two were ever alike.

Georgia Harris

c. 1972: Georgia Harris (1905–1997) was the first Catawba to revitalize the Catawba pottery tradition, which can be traced back over 4,000 years. In 1997, she became the first Catawba to be awarded an NEA National Heritage Fellowship. Harris did not succumb to the tourism demand of mass-produced pots but instead insisted on using the traditional methods she had learned as a child to create a variety of pottery, ranging from the ceremonial wedding jugs to smoking pipes. For millennia, the Catawba have guarded their secret places for gathering clay from South Carolina riverbanks, and Harris continued the tradition. Her apprentices were taught to make pots the old way, including using a fire pit instead of a kiln, and her strict adherence to the ancient heritage of pottery has ensured that the legacy continues. The prized pots are popular internationally, and one is on display in the White House.

1976: Alice Williams Cling (1946–), Navajo, is credited with being the first Navajo potter to use a smooth river stone to polish her pots instead of the traditional corncob method. The pots are created from clay found near the Black Mesa area in Apache-Navajo Counties in Arizona and are then fired outdoors using juniper wood. Cling is a coil potter who changed the pottery from an everyday object to a nonutilitarian art form, which represented a major shift. In 1978, Cling's work was selected by Second Lady Joan Mondale to be displayed in the vice-presidential mansion in Washington, D.C. Cling received many awards, including the Arizona Indian Living Treasures Award (2006).

1984: Margaret Tafoya (1904–2001), Santa Clara, was the first Native potter to receive the National Heritage Fellowship awarded by the National Endowment for the Arts. She was considered the matriarch of Santa Clara Pueblo potters and received many prestigious honors for her work, including the Best of Show Award at the Santa Fe Indian Market (1978 and 1979) and an Honor Award for Outstanding Achievement in the Visual Arts from the national Women's Caucus for Art. Tafoya is the only Native American ever awarded a Lifetime Contribution Award by the National Academy of Western Art at the National Cowboy Hall of Fame and Western Heritage Center in Oklahoma City, Oklahoma.

1991: Jereldine "Jeri" Redcorn (1939–), Caddo/Potawatomie, single-handedly revived traditional Caddo pottery. By researching pre-

A wedding vase designed by Margaret Tafoya, c. 1970.

European contact pots in museums, she figured out how to replicate Caddo methods, which involve coiling the clay and incising traditional Caddo decorations with metal or bone tools. In 2009, First Lady Michelle Obama displayed a pot by Redcorn, "Intertwining Scrolls," in the White House.

2015: Gladys A. Widdiss (1914–2012), Aquinnah Wampanoag of Gay Head, was a historian, potter, and tribal leader. Her work was featured in the first-ever museum exhibit on the history of the area's pottery. Martha's Vineyard Museum's "Made of Clay" showcased the famous style of pottery from the fourteenth to the twentieth century, to show how clay-based production has impacted the island. Widdiss was one of the few artists who constructed the pots the "old" way with clay from the island's iconic multicolored cliffs. To preserve the beautiful rainbow hues, she sun-baked them and was one of the few allowed to dig clay from the protected cliffs.

SCULPTURE

1867: Edmonia Lewis (c. 1844–c. 1907), also called Wildfire, Mississauga Ojibwe, was the first professional Native American and African American sculptor who earned critical praise for her works. One of her most prized sculptures was *Forever Free* (1867), which depicted a Black man and woman emerging from the bonds of slav-

"Hiawatha" by Edmonia Lewis

ery. Another piece, *The Arrow Maker* (1866), which drew on her Native American heritage, shows a father teaching his young daughter how to make an arrow. The sale of copies of her most famous work allowed her to move to Rome, home to a number of expatriate American artists. Her work blended both Native American and African American themes in a Neoclassical style.

1969: Retha Walden Gambaro (1917–2013), Creek, began sculpting in clay, stone, and bronze and quickly became a luminary among Native sculptors. She felt her artistry was as much a miracle as it was art. One of Gambaro's well-known exhibitions is "Attitudes of Prayer," which celebrates the artist's figurative work. Executed in stone and bronze, Gambaro's work was ex-

Michael Naranjo

Michael Naranjo (1944–), Santa Clara Pueblo, who was blinded by a grenade in the Vietnam War in 1968 and lost the use of his right hand, turned to sculpture after losing his sight. People doubted that he could succeed as a sculptor with no sight and only one hand. Naranjo not only succeeded, but he has been recognized internationally as one of the greatest artists of his time. He has met presidents and Pope John Paul II, won countless honors and accolades—including the 2007 Lifetime Achievement Award from the Southwestern Association for Indian Arts—touched Michelangelo's sculptures, and had shows across the globe. In 2012, Nedra Matteucci Galleries in Santa Fe hosted a retrospective of Naranjo's career exhibiting 40 sculptures as well as another 65 pieces owned by private collectors. Much of Naranjo's work comes from childhood memories; other ideas come from books, dreams, or talking to people. His subjects range from an eagle ready to take flight to the timeless relationship between a mother and child in a life-size bronze fountain. In October 2019, Naranjo became the first artist to examine the iconic *End of the Trail* sculpture by James Earle Fraser with just the use of his hands. The National Cowboy and Western Heritage Museum staff arranged for Naranjo to board a scissor lift and examine the monumental giant. He examined Michelangelo's works and other famous pieces the same way. Naranjo's art is included in the collections of the Vatican; the White House in Washington, D.C.; and the Heard Museum in Phoenix, Arizona. Over his lifetime, Naranjo has won countless awards and accolades.

hibited in Phoenix, Arizona's Heard Museum (2012). In the 1970s, Gambaro and her husband purchased a home with an old carriage house in the Capitol Hill area of Washington, D.C. and turned the carriage house into a sculpture studio and gallery. The Via Gambaro Studio became the first gallery in the capital to exclusively exhibit and promote Indigenous artwork and artists and soon became an East Coast focal point for Native American artists and their artwork. An early champion of the National Museum of the American Indian and president of the Amerindian Circle at the Smithsonian Institution, Gambaro was key in organizing the Kennedy Center's "Night of the First Americans" gala in 1982, which launched a fundraising campaign for the Museum.

TEXTILES AND FASHION

"When I first started to design I had a lot of people from the fashion and art industry tell me what people wanted in a Native designer. That the looks had to be very Hollywood or anthropological.... I really had to keep my visions and work on what my heart understood as being Native.... I wanted patrons to wear contemporary clothing that wasn't a fringed buckskin dress or a broom stick skirt. I started to visualize garments by the dozen by the age of eight years old. I can remember this because I thought if they can buy modern Native art they can buy modern Native clothing; it's just not available. So I started experimenting in my room as a little girl on my dolls and anything that I could change—fabric, bead work, leather, silk, velvet, paintings with different pigments and textures. I was working on my work in my room almost every day thereafter as I still do to this day."

—Patricia Michaels, Taos fashion designer, from Chic Galleria, November 24, 2015

1802: It is believed that the first recorded example of ribbon work appliqué was on a Menominee wedding dress made in 1802. Ribbon work reached its peak in the last quarter of the nineteenth century, having moved out from its epicenter in the Great Lakes to several nations in the Prairies, Plains, and Northeast. Ribbon skirt materials are not Native in origin, but the appliqué creations adorning the skirts have become traditional markers of Native identity. Today ribbon skirts have spread across the United States, and many women see them as a connection to their spiritual traditions.

c. 1900: For a few decades, Native men had been wearing their own versions of shirts made with European fabrics gotten through trade. Many of the garments were festooned with shells, metals, and leathers. Then traders brought ribbons, and Native artists creatively adopted the bright colored ribbons into clothing styles. The iconic ribbon shirt worn today appeared around 1900. There are at least three different collar styles, but each artist is totally free to design his or her shirt. As diverse nations fraternized at boarding schools and on reservations, styles were shared, and the ribbon shirt became a "pan-Indian" phenomenon.

1951: Lloyd Kiva New (1916–2002), Cherokee, became the first Indigenous American to exhibit a collection in an international fashion show—the Atlantic City International Fashion Show. He showed there again in 1952 and was the first Native clothing designer to be featured in the *Los Angeles Times*. In 1957, Miss Arizona, Lynn Freyse, wore a Kiva creation at the Miss America Pageant in Atlantic City, New Jersey, another first. For decades, New ran his own boutique in Scottsdale, Arizona, which featured leatherwork and garments with a Native spin. He collaborated with other Native artists like Andrew Van Tsinajinnie, Manfred Susunkewa, and Charles Loloma and is credited for helping make Scottsdale an artistic center. New cofounded the Institute of American Indian Arts in Santa Fe, New Mexico, in 1962.

1962: Josephine Myers-Wapp (1912–2014) was one of the first teachers and the first Comanche to serve on the faculty of the newly created Institute of American Indian Arts (IAIA) in Santa Fe, New Mexico. She taught basket weaving, beading, pottery making, rag dolls, cross-stitch, dyeing, fingerweaving, rag weaving, and spinning. In 1968, Myers-Wapp was one of the coordinators for a dance exhibit at the Mexican Summer Olympic Games. She has work in the permanent collection of the IAIA and has been featured at the Smithsonian Institution. Between 2014 and 2016, she was in an exhibition of Native American women artists at the Museum of Indian Arts and Culture in Santa Fe. Myers-Wapp helped found the National Museum of the American Indian in New York City and the Comanche National Museum and Cultural Center in Lawton, Oklahoma, where her collection of blankets and finger-weavings was part of the opening exhibit. Her art has been shown internationally and in 2013, Myers-Wapp was the recipient of the Santa Fe Indian Art Market's Povi'ka Award, which honors outstanding individuals who have influenced, contributed to, and promoted American Indian Art.

1967: Frankie Welch (1924–2021), Cherokee, was the first Native to design clothing for Washington, D.C., politicians and dignitaries. Her career took off after she created a scarf featuring the Cherokee syllabary as a fundraiser for the Native American Education Service and the Eastern Cherokee higher education fund. The scarf caught the attention of First Lady Lady Bird Johnson, who commissioned Welch to design a scarf promoting Johnson's "Discover America" campaign. The scarf was featured at the first fashion show ever held at the White House. She went on to design scarves for presidential campaigns for Hubert Humphrey, Richard Nixon, Gerald Ford, Jimmy Carter, and Bill Clinton. In 1974, First Lady Betty Ford wore a Welch design to greet the press after Nixon's resignation. Welch designed accessories for several businesses, universities, and organizations, including McDonald's, the Arkansas Democrats Association, the American Medical Association, and the Congressional Wives' Club. One of Welch's dresses designed for Betty Ford is in the collection of the Gerald R. Ford Presidential Library and was part of the touring "Native Fashion Now" exhibit.

1969: The "tear dress" became the official dress of the Cherokee. Virginia Stroud was chosen as Miss Cherokee Tribal Princess and wanted to wear a "traditional" Cherokee outfit, which was problematic since Cherokee women had worn contemporary mainstream fashions for at least two centuries and, before that, wore very little clothing. Chief W. W. Keeler appointed a committee of Cherokee women to design an outfit based on a hundred-year-old dress owned by a tribal member and also by researching regalia from other Southeastern tribes. They

Cherokee women wearing tear dresses for a concert.

fashioned the tear dress, a long shirtwaist dress typically worn by working-class women of European descent. In 1969, Stroud won the Miss Cherokee title; in 1970, she won the Miss National Congress of American Indians title; and in 1971, she was crowned Miss Indian America, wearing the "new" traditional tear dress. Contrary to popular thought and representation in art from the 1800s, the tear dress was not worn until Stroud's reign.

1980: The annual Akwesasne Freedom School Quilt Auction was founded to raise money for the Akwesasne Freedom School, located on the Akwesasne Mohawk Reservation, which sits on the border of New York in the United States and Ontario in Canada. All subjects are taught from a traditional Mohawk perspective along with Mohawk language and culture. The school does not receive government funding, and as part of the year's tuition, each family donates an original full-sized quilt. The masterpieces are auctioned off to pay for school expenses. Parents must either make, pay someone else to make, or buy and donate a quilt. Different quilter groups and quilters from around the country have donated a variety of gorgeous quilts to keep the school running. Dozens of quilts are auctioned off in the friendly competition; some go for several thousand dollars. One of the first parents of the Akwesasne Freedom School was Sheree "Peachy" Bonaparte, who was not convinced the quilt idea was a good one. However, she became an accomplished quilt artist and operated a quilt shop, the Ionkwanikonhriiosne Creative Sewing Centre, until it closed.

1982: Georgeann Robinson (1917–1985) an Osage teacher, artist, and businesswoman, was the first Native American recipient of a National Heritage Fellowship by the National Endowment for the Arts.

She used her ribbonwork art to promote and preserve Osage cultural heritage. Her creations are prized worldwide and part of the permanent collections of the Metropolitan Museum of Art in New York City; the Museum of International Folk Art in Santa Fe, New Mexico; and the Southern Plains Indian Museum in Anadarko, Oklahoma. Robinson was active in the National Congress of American Indians beginning in 1958, serving as its vice president for several years.

1985: Mariah Meali'i Namahoe Lucas (Richardson) Kalama (1909–2004) was the first Native Hawaiian quilter awarded the National Heritage Fellowship. In 1980, the YMCA recognized Kalama "for being responsible for the revival of Hawaiian quilting." In 1950, she left her position as a teacher to become the first director of a newly opened "Papakōlea Playground" (known today as Papakōlea Community Center) and taught children to sew and quilt—or, as one fan stated, she could teach anything.

1986: Jennie Thlunaut, or Shax'saani Kéek' ("Younger Sister of the Girls"; 1891–1986), Tlingit, was the first Indigenous weaver to receive the National Endowment for the Arts National Heritage Fellowship. Known for her blankets and tunics, she is credited with preserving the art of Chilkat weaving. She used the traditional material of mountain goat wool (dyed with tree lichens, oxidized copper, and urine-steeped hemlock bark) and red cedar bark. Thlunaut spun all her own yarn in the time-honored way, twisting the wool against her leg.

1989: Vanessa Paukeigope Morgan Jennings (1952–), Kiowa/Kiowa Apache/Gila River Pima, was the first Regalia Maker to be awarded a National Endowment for the Arts Fellowship. Although she learned the art as a child, she stated that her professional career began when she

Vanessa Jennings

was commissioned by the Museum of International Folk Art in Santa Fe, New Mexico, to make a ceremonial child's dress using traditional Kiowa beadwork on rawhide. Jennings also makes traditional Kiowa saddles, moccasins, beadwork, and cradleboards, which she says are her favorite to create. Over the years, she has won multiple awards at the Santa Fe Indian Market, Red Earth Festival, and Great Plains Rendezvous.

1991: Rose Frank (1912–?) was the first Nez Perce to receive a National Endowment for the Arts Fellowship. She was also the first to preserve the Nez Perce art of cornhusk weaving using found objects and dyed husks to create beautiful and functional objects and accessories.

1996: Aunty Elizabeth Malu'ihi Lee (1929–2016), Native Hawaiian, founded Ka Ulu Lauhala O Kona to perpetuate the traditional weaving arts of Hawaii. Her specialties were intricately woven hats made from Indigenous materials, which are valued around the world. Even as an elder, she taught at Kamehameha schools, spoke in Hawaiian, shared her gift of weaving, and reflected on her humble beginnings. Some of her masterpieces still sell for thousands of dollars.

2006: The United States Artists organization included two Native Alaskan artists in its first-ever fellowship awards. Anna Brown Ehlers, Chilkat blanket weaver, and Teri Rofkar, Tlingit basket maker, received the prestigious honors.

2014: Patricia Michaels, Taos, received the first Arts and Design Award from the Smithsonian National Museum of the American Indian. The fashion designer was also the first Native American contestant on *Project Runway* (2012) and made it to the finals, showing her collection at New York Fashion Week. In 2011, she won the Best of Classification in Textiles 2011 (a first for a modern garment or textile) at the SWAIA Santa Fe Indian Market.

2016: Canadian First Lady Sophie Grégoire Trudeau presented a cape to U.S. First Lady Michelle Obama. It was the first such gift made by an Indigenous fashion designer. Tammy Beauvais, Mohawk, had made a similar cape for Trudeau, who liked it so much she asked Beauvais to make one for Obama. Beauvais has also fashioned creations for many celebrities including Robert De Niro and Eric Roberts.

EXHIBITIONS AND SHOWS

1922: The first annual Santa Fe Indian Market was held in Santa Fe, New Mexico, by the Museum of New Mexico Foundation. Since then, the event has grown and matured into the largest and most prestigious Native American art event in the world. For several decades, it has been under the administration of the Southwestern Association for Indian Arts (SWAIA).

1931: The *Exposition of Indian Tribal Arts* at Grand Central Art Galleries in New York City was billed as "the first exhibition of American Indian art selected entirely with consideration of esthetic value." It was the first exhibition of Native American Art held in New York City.

1941: The *Indian Arts of the United States* exhibition was mounted at the Museum of Modern Art in New York City. For the first time, Indian historical pieces were treated as fine works of art.

1958: The Heard Museum Guild Indian Fair & Market kicked off in Phoenix, Arizona, and continues to be an annual event. More than 100 American Indian and Alaska Native Tribes and Canadian First Nations participate. Artwork includes baskets, beadwork, quillwork, jewelry, lapidary, paintings, drawings, photography, graphics, personal attire, pottery, pueblo carvings, sculpture, weavings, and textiles as well as other artistic media.

1976: *Sacred Circles: Two Thousand Years of North American Indian Art* has been considered a landmark exhibition among scholars of American Indian life. It was acclaimed as the largest assembly of North American Indian art objects (approximately 850) ever put on public view. The major British event in celebration of the American Bicentennial year was at the Hayward Gallery in London.

1981: *Arctic Art: Eskimo Ivories* at the National Museum of the American Indian in New York City displayed 200 works representing the skills of master carvers living in the entire circumpolar region from Siberia to Greenland. Drawn from storage, most of the pieces had never been photographed, published, or exhibited.

1985: The nation's first extensive art exhibition on the topic of Native HIV/AIDS was held in New York City's only Indian-owned and operated gallery, the American Indian Community House Gallery.

1986: *Lost and Found Traditions: Native American Art, 1965–1985* was a major exhibition of contemporary traditional art produced by Ralph T. Coe under the auspices of the American Federation of Arts. This was the first time an exhibition stressed the importance of preserving these arts.

1988: *Crossroads of Continents: Cultures of Siberia and Alaska* at the Smithsonian Institution's National Museum of Natural History was the first exhibition to be jointly sponsored by North American and Soviet museums. Nearly 600 objects presented the first cultural and historical overview of the diverse peoples who live around the northern Pacific Rim.

1991: *Chiefly Feast: The Enduring Kwakiutl Potlach* at the American Museum of Natural History was the first comprehensive survey of Kwakiutl art by a U.S. museum. It was also the first exhibition the museum did with the assistance of Native people since George Hunt (Kwakiutl/English) came to New York in 1901. The display included 120 objects acquired by the museum between 1897 and 1902 by anthropologist Franz Boas, assistant curator at the museum.

1991: The U'Mista Cultural Centre, the oldest and most successful First Nations cultural facility in British Columbia, displayed its first international traveling exhibition, titled *Mungo Martin: A Slender Thread*. The exhibit honored artist Mungo Martin (1879–1962), Kwakiutl, whose accomplishments preserved Kwakiutl art and culture.

1991: *Objects of Myth and Memory: American Art at the Brooklyn Museum* was the first major exhibition to focus on the large American Indian collection that Stewart Culin, the museum's curator of ethnology, acquired in the field between 1903 and 1911. More than 250 treasures illustrated the diversity of Native arts of the Southwest, California, Northwest Coast, and Plains.

1996: *Woven by the Grandmothers: 18th Century Navajo Textiles from the National Museum of the American Museum*, which included 43 blankets and dresses, was exhibited for the first time. The weavings were produced between 1820 and 1880. Unlike most shows in the previous 25 years, which presented blankets like paintings, hung flat on the wall, this exhibit displayed them wrapped around column-like forms almost as though they were worn by Navajo men, women, and children.

2001: The Heard Museum in Phoenix, Arizona, hosted its first annual Gathering of Katsina Carvers and Market Place, which has come to be the largest event for Hopi carvers.

2002: *Changing Hands: Art Without Reservation* was the first in a series of exhibitions at the American Craft Museum in New York City designed to place contemporary Native art in a broad context within mainstream art. *Changing Hands* included approximately 90 Native artists from southwestern cultures.

2008: *The Sacred Native Fashion Show* was started as an annual event at the Explore Navajo Interactive Museum in Tuba City, Arizona.

2014: *Wendy Red Star's Wild West & Congress of Rough Riders of the World* was the first all-Native contemporary art exhibition at Bumbershoot, an annual international music and arts festival held in Seattle, Washington. Wendy Red Star (1981–), Apsáalooke (Crow), is a multimedia artist known for her humorous approach and use of Native American images to confront stereotypes. Ten other Native artists were also part of the exhibit.

2015: *Spirit Lines: Helen Hardin Etchings* was the first time a complete body of work by Helen Hardin (1943–1984), Santa Clara Pueblo, had been assembled and shown in its entirety. Hardin was one of the twentieth century's most significant artists. *Spirit Lines* features all 23 first editions of the artist's collection of copper plate etchings completed from 1980 to 1984.

2017: The National Museum of the American Indian in New York City hosted a Native American fashion show for the first time. *The Power of Native Design* event featured designers Dorothy Grant, Haida; Jamie Okuma, Luiseño/Shoshone Bannock; and Bethany Yellowtail, Apsáalooke/Northern Cheyenne.

2017: The Peabody Essex Museum in Salem, Massachusetts, opened *Native Fashion Now*, the first traveling exhibition featuring contemporary Native American fashion. From vibrant street clothing to exquisite haute couture, the exhibition celebrated the visual range, creative expression, and political nuance of Native American fashion spanning the past 50 years.

2017: The first solo exhibition of Jaune Quick-to-See Smith's work in over a generation took place in her native state of Montana. *Footsteps of My Ancestors* at the Tacoma Art Museum featured an extensive body of her works dating back to the 1970s.

2018: An exhibition of the Charles and Valerie Diker Collection in the American wing of the Metropolitan Museum of Art in New York City constituted the museum's first-ever show of Native art.

2018: Indigenous Fashion Week in Toronto held its inaugural event. Founded by Sage Paul, Denesųłineį, over 20 Indigenous designers presented runway shows. Sustainability and cultural representation are the center of the designs.

ORGANIZATIONS

1946: Qualla Arts and Crafts was founded on the Qualla Boundary in North Carolina by Eastern Band Cherokee artists, becoming the first arts and crafts cooperative founded by Native Americans in the United States.

1971: Southwestern Association for Indian Arts (SWAIA), a not-for-profit organization, was incorporated in New Mexico. SWAIA's mission is to develop, sponsor, and promote the Santa Fe Indian Market, an annual art market held in Santa Fe, New Mexico, on the weekend following the third Thursday in August. The event showcases work from over 1,000 of the top Native American artists from tribes across the country.

1974: The Indian Arts and Crafts Association (IACA), an international organization that promotes, preserves, and protects authentic Native arts and crafts, was incorporated. Its membership is comprised of individuals and businesses that represent the entire Indian arts industry: artisans, retailers, wholesalers, museums, governmental agencies, collectors, suppliers, and supporters.

c. 1975: The Hale Nauā III Society of Maoli Arts was founded by Rocky Ka'iouliokahikikolo'ehu Jensen and other visionaries to promote Hawaii's Indigenous culture through the creative arts. The Bishop Museum in Honolulu hosted the group's first exhibition.

1976: The American Indian Council of Architects and Engineers was established to promote and recognize the roles of American Indian professional engineers, architects, and design professionals in the industry and to encourage American Indians to pursue careers in architecture related disciplines.

1992: Crow's Shadow Institute of the Arts (CSIA), located on the Umatilla Reservation in Pendleton, Oregon, was established to focus on using art as a transformative tool within the Native American community. CSIA is committed to helping people, young and old, develop their artistic gifts and skills.

1993: The Blackfeet Culture Camp and Lodgepole Gallery/Tipi Village was founded by Darrell Norman, Blackfeet, near Browning, Montana. The first of its kind in Montana, its mission is to cultivate Blackfeet culture and to show its beauty to the world by providing overnight accommodations in tipis with exhibitions of Plains historical and contemporary fine works. A traditional and mixed-media artist, Norman was the first Blackfeet to be a First Peoples Fund Community Spirit Honoree (2003).

1993: The California Indian Basketweavers' Association (CIBA) was founded to preserve, promote, and perpetuate California Indian basketweaving traditions while providing a healthy physical, social, spiritual, and economic environment for basketweavers. Based in Woodland, California, CIBA opposes the use of pesticides and is active in protecting indigenous flora.

1993: The Maine Indian Basketmakers Alliance (MIBA), the premier basketmaking organization on the East Coast that fosters the preservation of traditional basketmaking practices, was established. It was the first time that there was a concerted effort to save the traditional art popular to the Maliseet, Mi'kmaq, Passamaquoddy, and Penobscot. At the time, there were fewer than 12 basketmakers under the age of 50.

1995: The Northwest Native American Basketweavers Association (NNABA) was born to perpetuate traditional basket arts in the region.

1995: The First Peoples Fund was founded to support creative-community-centered Native artists and to nurture the collective spirit that allows them to sustain their people. It is based in Rapid City, South Dakota.

1998: The Council for Indigenous Arts and Culture (CIAC), based in Albuquerque, New Mexico, was established to foster, develop, and contribute to the support and understanding of authentic Native American Arts.

2002: The Alaska Native Arts Foundation (ANAF), founded in late 2002, is more than a retail shop as it represents the best of Alaska's Native visual art culture. Representing over 1,100 Alaska Native artists, ANAF offers a broad spectrum of items for sale that range from unique walrus whisker earrings, baleen baskets, and beautifully carved masks, to oil and acrylic paintings and bronze sculpture. The foundation uses the proceeds from sales to support and build the artistic skills of Alaska Native artists and artisans.

2006: Woodland Indian Art, Inc. (WIA) was established to expand the awareness and appreciation of Woodland Indian arts and culture through education, events, and markets. WIA produces the Woodland Indian Art Show and Market on the Oneida Reservation in Wisconsin.

2009: The Native and Arts and Cultures Foundation was launched to support Native American artists, culture bearers, and Native-led arts organizations, providing them with support through fellowships and project funding, Based in Portland, Oregon, the foundation fosters Indigenous arts in American Indian, Alaska Native, and Native Hawaiian communities.

LITERARY ARTS

"In contrast to the inane stereotype of the Indian as soundless, we know from the vast storehouse of our oral traditions that Aboriginal peoples were peoples of words. Many words. Amazing words. Cultivated words."

—*Emma LaRocque, from* Writing the Circle

1663: Caleb Cheeshahteaumuck (c. 1644–1666), Wampanoag, authored one of the first known pieces of writing by a Native North American, *Honoratissimi Benefactores* (Most Honored Benefactors), in Latin while attending Harvard's Indian College. He was the first (and only) Native American to graduate from the early school (class of 1665).

1772: Samson Occom (1723–1792), Mohegan, wrote and published *A Sermon, Preached at the Execution of Moses Paul, an Indian* in 1772. It was a first, an English-language text written and published by a Native American author that was so popular that it appeared in numerous editions and reprintings, including a Welsh-language translation. Occom served as a tribal leader, a Presbyterian minister, in effect a development officer for the school that became Dartmouth

Samson Occom

College, and a literary figure. Occom also wrote *A Choice Collection of Hymns and Spiritual Songs; Intended for the Edification of Sincere Christians, of All Denominations* (1774). On the basis of hymn-texts that Occom published, musicologist Robert Stevenson called him "the first Native American published composer."

1794: Hendrick Aupaumut (1757–1830), Mahican diplomat and leader, wrote *A Short Narration of My Last Journey to the Western Country* about his work as government liaison to American Indian tribes of the frontier west. Published in 1827, it was the first official report by a Native American person reporting on other Native peoples.

1827: David Cusick (c. 1780–c. 1831 or 1840), Tuscarora, was the author of *David Cusick's Sketches of Ancient History of the Six Nations*, initially published as a 28-page pamphlet. It was one of the earliest accounts of tribal history and oral tradition written and published in English by a Native American. In a later edition, Cusick included some of his own engravings. He and his brother, Dennis Cusick, are credited with helping to establish the early Iroquois Realist style of painting. They were the sons of Nicholas Cusick, a veteran of the Revolutionary War. David Cusick served in the War of 1812.

1916: Olivia Ward Bush-Banks (1869–1944), a Montauk/African American writer born in Sag Harbor, New York, founded the Bush-Banks School of Expression and became a drama instructor in Chicago. Her publications included two books of poetry, contributions to journals such as *Boston Transcript, Voice of the Negro,* and *Colored American Magazine*, and plays. She wrote *Indian Trails: Or Trail of the Montauk*, which did not survive in its entirety. Bush-Banks was active with the intellectual and artistic scene associated with the Harlem Renaissance, contributing a story cycle known as "Aunt Viney's Sketches." She also worked under the Works Progress Administration (WPA), serving as a drama instructor at the Abyssinia Community Center in Harlem between 1936 and 1939.

1932: John Joseph Mathews (1894–1979), Osage, published his first book, *Wah'kontah: The Osage and the White Man's Road* (University of Oklahoma Press), the first work by an academic press to be selected by the Book of the Month Club. It became a best-seller. Mathews served in World War I as a flight instructor and second lieutenant. He graduated from the University of Oklahoma with a degree in geology in 1920. He also attended Oxford University, where he completed a degree in natural science in 1923, becoming one of the school's early Native American graduates. Mathews also studied international relations. Additional writings include *Sundown* (1934), *Talking to the Moon*

Jane Johnston Schoolcraft

Jane Johnston Schoolcraft

Jane Johnston Schoolcraft, or Bamewawagezhikaquay (Woman of the Sound the Stars Make Rushing through the Sky; 1800–1842), Ojibwe, is the first known Native American literary writer. She was born in Sault Ste. Marie, Michigan, to Ozhaguscodaywayquay, the daughter of Waubojeeg, a famous leader, and John Johnston, an Irish trader. Jane Johnston married Henry Rowe Schoolcraft, federal Indian agent, in 1823. Around 1815, she had begun writing poems and traditional stories as well as translating Ojibwe songs and texts into English. Much of her work was unpublished or unattributed, appearing in publications such as *The Muzzinyegun or Literary Voyager*, issued by Schoolcraft. Scholar Robert Dale Parker called attention to her life and work with his book *The Sound the Stars Make Rushing through the Sky: The Writings of Jane Johnston Schoolcraft* (2007). Parker identifies a number of firsts for her: the first known American Indian woman writer, the first known American Indian poet to write poems in a Native language, and the first known American Indian to write out traditional tribal stories (as opposed to transcribing or translating from someone else, which she also did).

Gerald Vizenor, Writing Survivance

Gerald Vizenor (1934–), White Earth Nation, prolific writer and literary critic, initially worked as a journalist for the *Minneapolis Tribune*, calling attention to American Indian issues, including the high rate of suicide among young people. As a creative writer, Vizenor has produced novels, poetry, short story collections, essays, edited collections, and film work. A professor emeritus at the University of California, Berkeley, he has held academic appointments at the University of New Mexico, the University of California, the University of Oklahoma, and the University of Minnesota. He is the recipient of the American Book Award, PEN Oakland's Josephine Miles Award, and other honors. Vizenor was named the Mimi and Peter E. Haas 2020 Distinguished Visitor at Stanford University. He was also appointed as the 2021–2022 honorary curator of the American Haiku Archives at the California State Library in Sacramento. The honor recognizes his seven decades of writing and publishing haiku poetry.

(1945), and *The Osages: Children of the Middle Waters* (1961). In 1996, Mathews was posthumously inducted into the Oklahoma Historians Hall of Fame. A biography, *John Joseph Mathews: Life of an Osage Writer*, was written by Michael Snyder (2017).

1961: E. Pauline Johnson, Tekahionwake (1861–1913), Mohawk from the Six Nations of Grand River, author and performer, was celebrated with a commemorative stamp on the centennial of her birth, the first woman (other than the queen), the first author, and the first aboriginal Canadian to be honored in that way. Johnson's works of poetry include *The White Wampum* (1895), *Canadian Born* (1903), and *Flint and Feather* (1912). She also wrote stories, such as *Legends of Vancouver* (1911), *The Shagganappi* (1913), and *The Moccasin Maker* (1913). In 2002, *E. Pauline Johnson, Tekahionwake: Collected Poems and Selected Prose* was published, calling renewed attention to her life and work.

Emily Pauline Johnson

1975: Craig Strete (1950–), Cherokee, was nominated for two Nebula Awards, the first Native American speculative fiction author to be honored. One nomination was for the short story "Time Deer"; the second was for the novelette "The Bleeding Man," both published in 1974. He was one of the first Native speculative writers, and in 1980 he was nominated again for the short story "A Sunday Visit with Great-Grandfather." Strete's work has appeared in several languages and several anthologies, including *Nebula Award Stories Eleven*, edited by Ursula K. Le Guin (1977).

1992: The first North American Native Writers' Festival, called the Returning the Gift Festival, was held in Norman, Oklahoma, in July 1992. Abenaki author Joseph Bruchac, who co-organized the historic event, commented that it brought more Native writers together in one place than at any other time in history. He edited *Returning the Gift: Poetry and Prose from the First North American Native Writers' Festival* (University of Arizona Press, 1994).

1998: The first Hawai'i Fall Celebration of Island Writing was held at the University

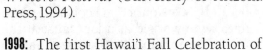

Indigenous Firsts: A History of Native American Achievements and Events

of Hawai'i, Mānoa. Organized by local writers and faculty at UH-Mānoa, the festival produced Try Listen, an audio archive of its participants.

2001: The Native American Literature Symposium (NALS) was organized by an independent group of Indigenous scholars committed to making a place where Native voices can be heard. Since 2001, it has continued to bring together participants to share stories in writing, art, film, and other fields at annual conferences. NALS collaborates with the Association for the Study of American Indian Literatures (ASAIL), a professional academic organization that promotes the study, criticism, and research of Native written and oral literary traditions.

2012: The first Rita Joe Memorial Literacy Day was held at Allison Bernard Memorial High School in Eskasoni First Nation, Nova Scotia, and became an annual event. It honors Rita Joe (1932–2007), who is referred to as the poet laureate of the Mi'kmaq people. Her first book, *The Poems of Rita Joe*, was published in 1978. She wrote six other books and received other honors, including being made a Member of the Order of Canada in 1989 and becoming one of the few nonpoliticians appointed to the Queen's Privy Council for Canada in 1992. Joe's writings include some of her experiences as a residential school student.

2018: Tanya Talaga, Ojibwe, with roots in Fort William First Nation in Ontario, Canada, was the first Anishinaabe woman chosen to deliver the CBC Massey Lectures, an acclaimed annual five-part series of lectures given in Canada by writers and scholars. She is the award-winning author of *Seven Fallen Feathers*, a national bestseller and CBC's Nonfiction Book of the Year. Talaga, who worked as a journalist at the *Toronto Star* for more than twenty years, is also the president and CEO of Makwa Cre-

ative, a production company focused on Indigenous storytelling.

ANTHOLOGIES

"It comes down to this. I believe in each and every Indian woman whose words and pictures lie between the pages of this book. Some hands are comfortable with a typewriter, with a pen. Some hands have only just begun to touch paper and pencil without fear. Our hands are strong. We make baskets, lift heavy machinery, bead earrings, soothe our lovers—female or male—hold our elders. We braid our hair. These hands fight back. We use our fists, our pens, our paints, our cameras. We drive the trucks to the demonstrations, we tie the sashes of our children, dancing for the first time in the circle of the drum. We weave the blankets. We keep us a culture. Our hands live and work in the present, while pulling on the past. It is impossible for us to not do both."

—*Beth Brant,* A Gathering Spirit

1975: *Carriers of the Dream Wheel*, edited by Duane Niatum (1938–), Jamestown S'Klallam, was published, a pathmaking anthology that included work by 16 American Indian poets. Niatum, a former editor for Harper & Row's Native American author series, also edited *Harper's Anthology of 20th Century Native American Poetry* in 1988, a collection with writings by 36 poets. He has authored numerous collections of poetry, such as *Ascending Red Moon Cedar* (1974), *Drawings of the Song Animals: New and Selected Poems* (1991), *The Crooked Beak of Love* (2000), and *Earth Vowels* (2017). Niatum, also a fiction writer and playwright, was nominated for a Pushcart Prize multiple times and is the recipient of the 2017 Lifetime Achievement Award from Native Writers Circle of the Americas.

1979: *The Remembered Earth: An Anthology of Contemporary Native American Literature*, edited by Geary Hobson, Cherokee-Quapaw/Chickasaw, is one of the oldest anthologies of Native literary works. It was first published in 1979 by Red Earth Press and then by the University of New Mexico Press in 1981.

1983: *A Gathering of Spirit: A Collection by North American Indian Women*, edited by Beth Brant (1941–2015), Mohawk, was one of the first anthologies of its kind. It was centered on Native women, from editor to contributors, and brought Brant national recognition. Initially published as a special issue of the periodical *Sinister Wisdom*, it was later published in book form. Brant's other works include *Writing as Witness, Food and Spirits*, and *Mohawk Trail*. She also coedited *Sweet Grass Grows All Around Her: Native Women in the Arts* with arts leader Sandra Laronde.

2010: *Trickster: Native American Tales, A Graphic Collection*, the first graphic anthology of Native American trickster stories, was published. Edited by Matt Dembicki, the award-winning publication pairs 24 Native storytellers with 24 comic artists to depict traditional cultural accounts from across the country.

Heid E. Erdrich

2018: *New Poets of Native Nations*, edited by Heid E. Erdrich, Anishinaabe, an anthology that features 21 poets whose first books were published after 2000.

2020: *When the Light of the World Was Subdued, Our Songs Came*

George Copway

Through: A Norton Anthology of Native Nations Poetry, edited by U.S. poet laureate Joy Harjo, Mvskoke; LeAnne Howe, Choctaw; and Jennifer Elise Foerster, Mvskoke, is considered the first historically comprehensive anthology of Native poetry. It contains the work of 161 poets, representing more than 90 Native nations.

2021: *The Diné Reader: An Anthology of Navajo Literature*, the first comprehensive work of its kind honoring Diné/Navajo literary writings, was published by the University of Arizona Press. It was edited by Esther G. Belin, Jeff Berglund, Connie A. Jacobs, and Anthony K. Webster and includes a diverse array of literary voices and genres.

AUTOBIOGRAPHY

1829: William Apess (1798–1839), Pequot, was the author of *A Son of the Forest*, the first full-length Native American autobiography. Apess was considered one of the most important Native American intellectuals in the country at the time, known to have published more writings than any other Native author before the twentieth century. His history is chronicled in *The Life of William Apess, Pequot*, by Philip F. Gura (2014).

1847: George Copway (Kahgegagahbowh, He Who Stands Forever; 1818–1869), Mississauga (Ojibwa) hereditary chief, Methodist missionary, lecturer, and writer, wrote *The Life, History, and Travels of Kah-ge-ga-gah-bowh*, deemed the first book-length autobiography written by a Native person raised in a traditional Native family. Born near Trenton, Ontario, Canada, Copway has also been described as the first literary celebrity to achieve fame outside the country. Prominent in the United States, he also wrote *The Traditional History and Characteristic Sketches of the Ojibway Nation*.

Sarah Winne-
mucca Hopkins

1883: Sarah Winnemucca Hopkins (Thocmentony, "Shell Flower"; c. 1844–1891), Paiute, published *Life among the Piutes: Their Wrongs and Claims*, the first known autobiography written by a Native American woman. Winnemucca describes Northern Paiute life, the unjust treatment of her people, and her experiences as a female Native American activist. In 1886, she also published a pamphlet, *Sarah Winnemucca's Practical Solution to the Indian Problem*, part of an effort to save a school she helped create. A statue of Winnemucca, sculpted by artist Benjamin Victor, was given to the National Statuary Hall Collection by the state of Nevada in 2005.

Queen
Lili'uokalani

1898: *Hawaii's Story by Hawaii's Queen*, written by Queen Lili'uokalani (1838–1917), the last monarch of the Kingdom of Hawai'i, was published five years after the overthrow of the kingdom. Lili'uokalani recounted her upbringing, her accession to the throne, the overthrow of her government by pro-American forces, her appeals to the United States to restore the Hawaiian monarchy, and her arrest and trial following an unsuccessful 1895 rebellion against the Republic of Hawai'i. The Queen penned the book while she was imprisoned by the U.S. forces after she was deposed. It was the first autobiography written by a Native Hawaiian and the first account of the illegal overthrow and occupation of the Kingdom of Hawaii.

◆◇◆

AWARDS

1952: Carter Revard (1931–2022), Osage, was one of the first American Indians to become a Rhodes Scholar, studying at Oxford University in the United Kingdom. He received

Miracle Hill by Blackhorse Mitchell

Blackhorse Mitchell (1945–) became the first published Navajo writer with the 1967 publication of the landmark work *Miracle Hill: The Story of a Navaho Boy* by the University of Oklahoma Press. The book started as a creative writing assignment at the Institute of American Indian Arts, where Mitchell received an academic degree in 1964 and an MFA in literary writing in 1966. He later earned degrees in education at the University of New Mexico, working as an educator for more than 30 years. A lifelong sheepherder, Mitchell also became known for a number of other avocations, including blues performer, comedian, medicine man, and potter. *Miracle Hill* was reissued by the University of Arizona Press in 2004, assuring its ongoing influence, including a planned stage production in Prague, Czech Republic.

his undergraduate degree at the University of Tulsa, a degree at Oxford, and a doctorate from Yale University. Writer Geary Hobson calls him "by most accounts the most significant American Indian poet from Oklahoma." Revard's poetry books include *Ponca War Dancers* (1980), *An Eagle Nation* (1993), and *How the Songs Come Down* (2005). He was also the author of prose works, including *Family Matters, Tribal Affairs* (1998) and *Winning the Dust Bowl* (2001).

1969: N. Scott Momaday (1934–), Kiowa, became the first Native American to win the Pulitzer Prize for Fiction for his novel *House Made of Dawn*. He has authored novels, poetry, and other works, including *Earth Keeper: Reflections on the American Land*, published in 2020. In 1989, Momaday was the first literary artist honored with the Jay Silverheels Achievement Award from the National Center for American Indian Enterprise. He has received numerous other awards, including the National Medal of Arts, the Golden Plate Award from the American Academy of Achievement, an Academy of American Poets Prize, and the Ken Burns American Heritage Prize. Momaday was named to the National Native American Hall of Fame (2018) and was the subject of *N. Scott Momaday: Words from a Bear*, a film that was released in 2019. Momaday holds more than twenty honorary degrees from American and European colleges and universities. The Poetry Society of America announced that he was the 2021 recipient of the Frost Medal for distinguished lifetime achievement in poetry. Named for Robert Frost and first awarded in 1930, the medal is one of the oldest and most prestigious awards in American poetry. Momaday's works of poetry include *The Death of Sitting Bear: New and Selected Poems*, published in 2020.

1981: Leslie Marmon Silko (1948–), Laguna Pueblo, was the first Native American recipient of a MacArthur Foundation "Genius" Award. By then, she had published her first novel, *Ceremony* (1977), which established her as an important writer and a pioneering Native American female novelist. Silko completed her bachelor's degree at the University of New Mexico in 1969, the same year her first story, "The Man to Send Rain Clouds," was published. She is also the author of *Almanac of the Dead* (1991), a novel that took her more than ten years to complete, and *Gardens in the Dunes* (1999), her third novel. Her friendship with poet James Wright is at the center of *With the Delicacy and Strength of Lace: Letters between Leslie Marmon Silko & James Wright* (1986), which won the Boston Globe Book Prize for nonfiction. Silko is also the author of *Yellow Woman and a Beauty of the Spirit: Essays on Native American Life Today* (1996).

1987: Louis (Little Coon) Oliver (1904–1991), Creek Nation, received the first Alexander Posey Literary Award given by the Este Mvskoke Arts Council at the Symposium of the American Indian at Northeastern State University in Tahlequah, Oklahoma. That year, Oliver was also named the Poet of Honor at Oklahoma Poets Day by the University of Oklahoma's English department.

1992: Robert L. Perea (1946–), Oglala Lakota, won the inaugural Louis Littlecoon Oliver Memorial Prose Award from his fellow writers in the Native Writers' Circle of the Americas for his short fiction, "Stacey's Story."

2006: The Western Literature Association (WLA) began offering the Louis Owens Awards for Graduate Student Presenters at WLA conferences. The awards, which provide a cash prize and a WLA membership, are intended to foster greater diversity within the association. Owens (1948–2002), Choctaw/Cherokee, was the acclaimed author of five novels, four books of literary criticism, and a collection of essays, *I Hear the Train*.

Linda Hogan: A Lifetime of Awards

Linda Hogan

In 1990, Linda Hogan (1947–), Chickasaw, was nominated for a Pulitzer Prize for her first novel, *Mean Spirit* (1990), a book about the oil boom in Oklahoma and its impact on tribal peoples. *Rounding the Human Corners* (Coffee House Press, 2008), a collection of poems, was also a Pulitzer nominee. Internationally acclaimed, Hogan is the author of poetry, fiction, and nonfiction as well as a public reader and speaker. She was inducted into the Chickasaw Nation Hall of Fame in 2007 for her literary contributions. A short time later, Hogan became the Chickasaw Nation's first writer in residence. Her other honors include the American Book Award, Colorado Book Award, Oklahoma Book Award, and the Mountains and Plains Book Award. *Power* and *Solar Storms* were both International Impact Award finalists in Ireland. Hogan has also won the Thoreau Prize from PEN (2016), the *Los Angeles Times* Native Arts and Culture Award (2018), and the Riverside Lifetime Achievement Award (2022).

A scholar of John Steinbeck, he was also a professor of English and Native American studies during his career and headed a creative writing program at the University of California, Davis. Owens was considered the leading critical interpreter of Native American literature in the country. In the words of leading author Gerald Vizenor, "Louis Owens was an inspired, original literary artist, a masterful storier, and he was an exceptional teacher."

Yvonne Wakim Dennis

2006: JudyLee Oliva (1952–), playwright, actress, lyricist, and director of plays, was named the first Chickasaw Nation Dynamic Woman of the Year. Established in 2006, the award honors Chickasaw women who make significant contributions, serve as role models, and exemplify the values, culture, and traditions of the tribal nation. Oliva, who earned a Ph.D. in theater and drama from Northwestern University in Chicago, is the author of articles, books, and plays. She is especially known for her original plays

Richard Wagamese

about actress Te Ata (Mary Frances Thompson Fisher; 1895–1995).

2010: Yvonne Wakim Dennis, Cherokee/Sand Hill/Syrian, was the first Native person to win an Independent Publishers Gold Moonbeam Award in the Activity Book category. She and coauthor Arlene Hirschfelder took top honors for *A Kid's Guide to Native American History* (Chicago Review Press, 2009). The book also won a Silver IPPY Award in the Children's Interactive Book category. In 2014, Dennis's book (coauthored with Maha Addasi, Palestinian) *A Kid's Guide to Arab American History* (Chicago Review Press, 2013) won the Arab American National Museum (AANM) Children's Book of the Year. She was the first and only author of Arab and Native descent to win an award at the AANM.

2013: Richard Wagamese (1955–2017), Ojibwe from northwestern Ontario, was the inaugural recipient of the Burt Award for First Nations, Inuit, and Métis Literature for his book *Indian Horse*.

2015: LeAnne Howe (1951–), Choctaw, received the Modern Language Association inaugural Prize for Studies in Native American Literatures, Cultures, and Languages for *Choctalking on Other Realities* (2013).

2016: Jeannette Armstrong (1948–), Okanagan, became the first Indigenous author to receive the George Woodcock Award, British Columbia's most prestigious literary honor. An author, educator, artist, and activist, Armstrong wrote her path-breaking novel *Slash* (1985) and the nonfiction *Native Creative Process*, in collaboration with architect Douglas Cardinal. Armstrong, bilingual in Syilx and English, was critical to the development of the En'owkin International School of Writing for Native Students in Penticton, B.C., serving as the first director. She was appointed Canada Research Chair in Okanagan Indigenous Knowledge and Philosophy in 2013.

2017: Jamie Natonabah, Diné, was the first recipient of the Sherman Alexie Scholarship at the Institute of American Indian Arts (IAIA). An alumnus of IAIA, Natonabah was also a winner of the New Mexico Slam Poetry Competition. Her work has appeared in *Red Ink: International Journal of Indigenous Literature, Art & Humanities* and in IAIA literary anthologies.

2020: *Fry Bread: A Native American Family Story* (2019), written by Kevin Noble Maillard, a member of the Seminole Nation of Oklahoma, was the first Native-authored book to win the Robert F. Sibert Informational Book Medal. A children's picture book, it was illustrated by award-winning Peruvian-born author-artist Juana Martinez-Neal.

2020: Marcie Rendon (1952–), an enrolled member of the White Earth Nation, became the first Native American woman to receive the McKnight Distinguished Artist Award, a $50,000 award created to honor a Minnesota artist who has made significant contributions to the cultural life of the state. Rendon is the award-winning author of poems, plays, novels, short stories, children's books, and the Cash Blackbear mystery series. She is also the founder of Raving Native Productions Performance Art Theatre, started in 1996, providing a venue for other Native American artists and performers.

2021: Eric Gansworth (1965–), Onondaga, won a Michael L. Printz Honor for his book *Apple (Skin to the Core)* (2020), the first Native American recipient. The Printz awards are given for excellence in literature written for young adults. *Apple* is a young adult memoir-in-verse with images. Gansworth is also the author of *Mending Skins* (2005), *Extra Indians* (2010), *If I Ever Get Out of Here* (2013), and other award-winning works. He is a writer and visual artist whose creative output includes novels, poetry, essays, and drama.

2021: Michaela Goade (1990–), a member of the Tlingit and Haida Indian Tribes of Alaska, won a Randolph Caldecott Medal for outstanding illustration of a children's book, the first Native American illustrator to win the prestigious award. The book, *We Are Water Protectors* (Roaring Brook, 2020), was written by Carole Lindstrom (Turtle Mountain Ojibwe). It was inspired by the opposition to the Dakota Pipeline on the Standing Rock Reservation in 2016 and the fight for clean water by Indigenous peoples in general. The Caldecott Medal, established in 1938, is presented annually at the American Library Association conference.

2021: Jessica (Tyner) Mehta, Cherokee Nation, became the first Native American postgraduate research representative at the Centre for Victorian Studies at the University of Exeter, England, the largest existing institutional grouping of Victorian scholars in the country. Mehta, a multiaward-winning interdisciplinary artist, author, and storyteller, wrote *When We Talk of Stolen Sisters: New and Revised Poems* (2021), *Gimme the Familiars: A Hybrid Short Story Collection* (2019), and numerous other books. In 2012, she founded MehtaFor, a writing services company that serves a range of clients. Mehta was named poet-in-residence at Hugo House in 2021, one of her many residencies. She received a 2021/22 Fulbright U.S. Scholar award to India, which was temporarily suspended because of COVID-19.

2021: David Heska Wanbli Weiden, Sicangu Lakota, became the first Native American to win the prestigious Anthony Award for mystery writers, for *Winter Counts* as best first novel. A Native thriller about a local enforcer on the Rosebud Indian Reservation obsessed with finding a dealer bringing dangerous drugs into his community, it garnered a host of other honors. Besides the Anthony, Weiden won the Thriller, Lefty, Barry, and Macavity awards for best first novel. He was also awarded the Spur Awards for Best Contemporary Novel and Best First Novel and the Tillie Olsen Award for Creative Writing. A bestseller, *Winter Counts* was a *New York Times*

Book Review Editors' Choice and was named one of the Best Books of 2020 by NPR, *Publishers Weekly*, and other outlets. In 2021, the novel was released in France as *Justice Indienne*. It is also being translated into numerous other languages and has been optioned for film production. Weiden is also the author of *Spotted Tail*, a children's book published in 2019.

CHILDREN'S AND YOUNG ADULT LITERATURE

On my blog, I write about books like *Home to Medicine Mountain* and others by Native authors who write books that provide children with accurate information about American Indians. And, I link to websites maintained by Native writers and illustrators...."

—*Debbie Reese*

1881: Susette La Flesche Tibbles (Inshta Theamba, Bright Eyes; 1854–1903), Omaha, writ-

Debbie Reese, American Indians in Children's Literature (AICL)

In 2006, Debbie Reese, Ph.D., Nambe Pueblo, founded American Indians in Children's Literature (AICL), an award-winning internet blog that provides critical analysis of Indigenous peoples in children's and young adult books to parents, teachers, librarians, and other audiences. In 2019, she and Jean Mendoza adapted *An Indigenous Peoples' History of the United States* by Roxanne Dunbar-Ortiz into a book for younger readers. The original publication won an American Book Award, and their version was a 2020 American Indian Youth Literature Young Adult Honor Book with recognition from the National Council for the Social Studies and the Children's Book Council. In 2019, Reese was selected as the first Native American Arbuthnot Honor Lecturer by the Association for Library Service to Children (ALSC). In January of 2021 she was a clue in a *USA Today* crossword puzzle.

ing under the name Bright Eyes, published "Nedawi: An Indian Story from Real Life" in *St. Nicholas: An Illustrated Magazine for Young Folks*. It is believed to be the first nonlegend short story written by a Native American and the first Native-authored work in that publication.

Susette La Flesche Tibbles

2000: Virginia Driving Hawk Sneve (1933–), a member of the Rosebud Sioux Tribe, was the first South Dakotan to be awarded the National Humanities Medal, which was presented to her on December 20, 2000, by President Bill Clinton. She was honored, in part, for bringing "the richness of Native American culture and heritage to thousands of children." Her popular titles include *Jimmy Yellow Hawk* (1972), *The Chichi Hoohoo Bogeyman* (1975), and *High Elk's Treasure* (1995). Sneve is also the author of the autobiographical *Completing the Circle* (1995), which won the North American Indian Prose Award, and *Grandpa Was a Cowboy and an Indian* (2000), a collection of short stories. She coauthored *Too Strong to Be Broken: The Life of Edward J. Driving Hawk* (2020) with her brother.

2006: The American Indian Library Association (AILA) presented its first American Indian Youth Literature Awards (AIYLA) during the Joint Conference of Librarians of Color. Awarded biennially in even-numbered years, the AIYLA honors the best writing and illustrations by Native Americans and Indigenous peoples of North America. The first recipients included *Beaver Steals Fire: A Salish Coyote Story* by the Confederated Salish and Kootenai Tribes, *The Birchbark House* by Louise Erdrich, and *Hidden Roots* by Joseph Bruchac.

2007: The inaugural Red Fern Festival was held in Tahlequah, Oklahoma, commemorating and celebrating "something uniquely Tahlequah." The annual event celebrates the classic novel *Where the Red Fern Grows*, written by Woodrow Wilson Rawls (1913–1984), Cherokee. A coming-of-age story about a boy and his two coon dogs, it was first published under the title "The Hounds of Youth" as a three-part serial in the *Saturday Evening Post* in 1961. A movie adaptation was produced in 1974 set and filmed in Cherokee and Adair counties with local participants. A Disney remake of the title was issued in 2003. A sculpture created by Marilyn Hoff Hansen depicts characters from *Where the Red Fern Grows* and appears outside the Idaho Falls Public Library in Idaho. Another monument, also sparked by the novel, was completed by chainsaw artist Dean Anson and unveiled at Floyd H. Norris Park in downtown Tahlequah in 2008.

2014: First Nation Communities READ (FNCR) and Periodical Marketers of Canada (PMC) announced jointly that Julie Flett, Cree-

The statue at the public library in Idaho Falls, Idaho, by Marilyn Hoff Hansen honoring the novel *Where the Red Fern Grows*.

Cynthia Leitich Smith:
Bestselling Author for Young Readers

Cynthia Leitich Smith, Muscogee Nation, is a *New York Times* bestselling author of books for young readers, including *Hearts Unbroken*, which won the American Indian Library Association's Youth Literature Award. In 2021, she released *Ancestor Approved: Intertribal Stories for Kids* and *Sisters of the Neversea*, a novel. Leitich Smith is also the bestselling author of the *Tantalize* series and *Feral* trilogy. In addition, she is the author-curator of Heartdrum, a Native-focused imprint at HarperCollins Children's Books, the first Indigenous imprint of a major publisher. Leitich Smith was named as the inaugural Katherine Paterson Endowed Chair on the faculty of the MFA program in Writing for Children and Young Adults at Vermont College of Fine Arts in 2020. Her many other honors include being named winner of the 2021 NSK Neustadt Prize for Children's Literature. Nominator Monica Brown said of her: "How rare it is that a writer who has given us so many important, beautiful, entertaining, and empowering books has also given such an enormous gift to other writers, educators, and to children's literature as a whole." Leitich Smith's online presence includes a blog called *Cynsations: Reflections & Conversations about the World of Books for Young Readers*.

Métis, author-illustrator of *Wild Berries/Pakwa che Menisu*, was the first-time recipient of PMC's new Aboriginal Literature Award. Flett has received many other awards, such as the 2017 Governor General's Award for Children's Literature for her work on *When We Were Alone* by David Robertson and the 2016 American Indian Library Association Award for Best Picture book for *Little You* by Richard Van Camp, and is a three-time recipient of the Christie Harris Illustrated Children's Literature Award.

2021: *Firekeeper's Daughter*, a groundbreaking young adult book by Angeline Boulley, a member of the Sault Ste. Marie Tribe of Chippewa Indians in Michigan, debuted at the number one spot on the *New York Times* bestselling book list. The book was also selected for adaptation on Netflix as an original TV series under Barack and Michelle Obama's production company, Higher Ground Productions.

LITERARY JOURNALS

1989: *Red Ink*, a Native American, student-run publication at the University of Arizona, was established in 1989. Its primary mission is to highlight Native American intellectual and creative expression through poetry, short stories, creative nonfiction, scholarly articles, artwork, photography, and reviews.

1998: *'Ōiwi: A Native Hawaiian Journal* was founded by Mahealani Dudoit and ku'ualoha ho'omanawanui as the first contemporary journal dedicated to the literary and artistic expression of Native Hawaiians. The writers as well as the artist and production team are Kanaka Maoli. *'Ōiwi* is produced by Kuleana 'Ōiwi Press and 'Āina Momona, a nonprofit organization.

2012: *As/Us: A Space for Women of the World* was cofounded by poets Tanaya Winder (1985–), a member of the Duckwater Shoshone Tribe, and Casandra Lopez (1978–), Cahuilla/Tongva/Luiseño. The magazine initially focused on Indigenous women and women of color but expanded to *As/Us: A Space for Writers of the World*, publishing work to showcase literary expressions of emerging and scholarly work by writers regardless of gender, race, or ethnicity. Winder is also the founder of Dream Warriors Management, a company created to bring together artists, speakers, and educators.

2015: *Transmotion: An Online Journal of Indigenous Studies*, a Cal State San Bernardino–sponsored publication, was launched. Produced in collaboration with the University of Kent, European University Cyprus, and Portland State University, it is published biannually.

2018: *Hairstreak Butterfly Review*, an online literary journal at Colorado College, was founded by Natanya Ann Pulley, Diné author and educator, who also serves as the journal's managing editor.

2020: *The Massachusetts Review* published its first issue devoted to Native American writing (Winter 2020, vol. 61, issue 4), "A Gathering of Native Voices." It was guest-edited by Laura Furlan, Toni Jensen, and Tacey M. Atsitty.

NATIVE LANGUAGE WORKS

1977: Nia Francisco (1952–), Navajo, wrote "táchééh" in the spring of 1977, a poem published in the journal *College English*, one of the first poems published in the Navajo language. Francisco's writings include her books of poetry *Blue Horses for Navajo Women* (1988) and *Carried Away by the Black River* (1994).

1980: *The South Corner of Time: Hopi, Navajo, Papago, Yaqui Tribal Literature*, a landmark work, was published by the University of Arizona Press. Edited by Larry Evers, it has been praised as "conceptually and theoretically ahead of the time," especially for emphasizing literary traditions within specific tribal cultural contexts.

1982: *Mat hekid o ju/When It Rains: Papago and Pima Poetry*, edited by Ofelia Zepeda and published by the University of Arizona Press in 1982, was introduced at the first poetry reading of contemporary O'odham and English poetry for an O'odham audience. The groundbreaking work is a first book of O'odham poetry. Zepeda also served as poet laureate of Tucson, Arizona.

2020: *Ogimaans* is the first translation of *The Little Prince* by Antoine de Saint-Exupéry in an Indigenous language of North America. It was translated into Anishinaabemowin by Angela Mesic, Margaret Noodin, Susan Wade, and Michael Zimmerman Jr. and published by Edition Tintenfass.

NOVELS

1854: John Rollin Ridge (1827–1867), a member of the Cherokee nation, published *The Life and Adventure of Joaquín Murieta, the Celebrated California Bandit*, considered the first novel written by a Native American. Ridge wrote it under the name Yellow Bird, the English translation of Cheesquatalawny, his Cherokee name. He was also a noted newspaper editor and journalist. Following

Ridge's death, his wife posthumously published his poetry in 1868 (Henry Payot & Company).

1891: Sophia Alice Callahan (1868–1894), Muscogee/Creek, wrote *Wynema: A Child of the Forest*, considered to be the first novel by a Native woman in the United States. Callahan added an account of the 1890 Ghost Dance of the Lakota and the Wounded Knee massacre at Pine Ridge, events in Dakota Territory that occurred shortly before her book was published. Callahan's novel provided the first fictional treatment of the ghost dance religious movement and the horrific massacre of Lakota men, women, and children.

1899: Simon Pokagon (1830–1899), Potawatomi, wrote *Ogimawkwe Mitigwaki* (*Queen of the Woods*), one of the first novels about Indian life by an American Indian author. Pokagon is also known for delivering his *Red Man's Greeting* at the Chicago World's Columbian Exposition in 1893, an address that became widely disseminated. The Simon Pokagon Memorial Research Library is named in his honor by the Pokagon Band of Potawatomi in Michigan. A new edition

Simon Pokagon

of his novel was published by Michigan State University in 2011 with new accompanying materials.

1927: Mourning Dove/Christine (or Christal) Quintasket (Hum-ishuma) (c. 1885–1936), Okanagan/Colville, wrote *Cogewea, The Half-Blood: A Depiction of the Great Montana Cattle Range*, considered the first novel published by a Native American woman in the twentieth century. In 1933, Mourning Dove also published *Coyote Stories*, a collection of legends. Additional writings by her have been issued more recently, among them *Tales of the Okanogans* (1976) and *Mourning Dove: A Salishan Autobiography* (ed. Jay Miller, 1990).

1933: Todd Downing (1902–1974), Choctaw, became Oklahoma's first successful author of detective novels, with his first, *Murder on Tour*. Born George Todd Downing in Indian Territory (present-day Oklahoma), he studied languages at the University of Oklahoma, earning bachelor's (1924) and master's degrees (1928). Downing also studied Spanish, French, and anthropology at the National University of Mexico. *Murder on Tour*, written when a trip was cancelled, became a

First Native American Woman to Win the Pulitzer Prize

In 2021, Louise Erdrich (1954–), a member of the Turtle Mountain Band of Chippewa in North Dakota, became the first Native American woman to win the Pulitzer Prize for fiction with her novel *The Night Watchman* (Harper, 2020). The book is based on the life of her grandfather, who worked as a night watchman and fought against termination, one of the worst federal policies enacted by the U.S. government. Erdrich's writings include sixteen novels, poetry books, children's books, and nonfiction. She has won the National Book Award and the National Book Critics Circle Award, and was an earlier finalist for the Pulitzer Prize. Erdrich has also received the Library of Congress Prize in American Fiction, the PEN/Saul Bellow Award for Achievement in American Fiction, and the Dayton Literary Peace Prize. She lives in Minneapolis, Minnesota, and owns Birchbark Books, an independent bookstore.

Ella Cara Deloria, *Waterlily*

Ella Deloria (1889–1971), Anpetu Washte-win (Beautiful Day Woman), Dakota, was an anthropologist, linguist, educator, and author. She was the daughter of the Reverend Philip Deloria and Mary Sully Deloria and grew up at Wakpala on the Standing Rock Reservation in South Dakota. Ella Deloria attended Oberlin College in Ohio and then Columbia University in New York, where she met anthropologist Franz Boas. At Columbia, she began to work with him on Lakota linguistics, a lasting professional association that extended to other studies. Deloria authored many works, among them *Dakota Texts* (1932) and *Speaking of Indians* (1944). She completed *Waterlily*, an ethnographic novel, in 1948, but was unable to find a publisher. It was not until 1988 that it was finally published, becoming her best-known book. Author Philip J. Deloria called it her "most visible text, considered a landmark both in terms of its postcolonial subjectivity and its turn from ethnography to fictional narrative." The Ella C. Deloria Undergraduate Research Fellowship was established in her honor at Columbia University in 2010.

Ella Deloria

popular radio play. Downing's second novel, *The Cat Screams* (1934), his first work to be published in England, was translated into German, Italian, and Swedish. Other Downing titles include *Murder on the Tropic* (1935), *Night over Mexico* (1939), and *The Case of the Unconquered Sisters* (1936). He also wrote *Chata Anampa*, a series of ten lessons on the Choctaw language and heritage. In 1940, his nonfiction book *The Mexican Earth* was published and later released in a new edition by the University of Oklahoma Press in 1996.

1936: D'Arcy McNickle (1904–1977), a member of the Confederated Salish and Kootenai Tribes in Montana, wrote his first novel, *The Surrounded*, which is often credited as the beginning of a Native American renaissance in contemporary literature. It was initially published by Harcourt, Brace & Company and was republished by the University of New Mexico Press in 1978. *The Surrounded* was influenced by McNickle's own life experiences during the period, exploring issues of race, identity, and politics. McNickle also wrote two more novels, short stories, a biography of

Oliver La Farge, historical monographs, articles, and reviews. In 1961, he chaired the steering committee of the American Indian Chicago Conference and served as the primary author of the Conference's influential "Declaration of Indian Purpose." McNickle served as the founding director of the Newberry Library Center for the History of the American Indian in Chicago from 1972 to 1976, renamed the D'Arcy McNickle Center for American Indian and Indigenous Studies in his honor. The Salish Kootenai College Library was also renamed for him, becoming the D'Arcy McNickle Library in 1987. His life and work are depicted in *The Legacy of D'Arcy McNickle: Writer, Historian, Activist*, edited by John Lloyd Purdy (University of Oklahoma, 1996)

1970: Markoosie Patsauq (1941–2020), Inuk, authored *Harpoon of the Hunter*, the first-known published Inuit novel. Patsauq wrote the story in 1969 while working as a pilot; he was also the first Inuk to get a pilot's license. His manuscript was written in Inuktitut and initially serialized in *Inuttitut*, an Inuit publication, before it was translated into English. It became a sensation, a bestseller at McGill/Queen's University Press, eventually garnering translations into at least twelve languages. In 2020, a new version of the book was released, *Hunter with Harpoon*, and is considered closer to Patsauq's own words.

Martin Cruz Smith

1977: Martin Cruz Smith (1942–), Pueblo/Yaqui descent, was the author of *Nightwing*, one of the first Native thrillers. A crime and horror novel, it was set on a reservation in the Southwest. Smith also authored *The Indians Won* (1970), possibly the first alternate Native history novel, depicting a world where Indian nations worked together to defeat the American military and created their own independent country.

1984: Mitiarjuk Nappaaluk (1931–2007), Inuit author and educator based in the northern Quebec territory of Nunavik, authored *Sanaaq*, one of the first novels published in Inuktitut syllabics. Nappaaluk started writing the book in the 1950s, earlier than Markoosie Patsauq's novel *Harpoon of the Hunter*, but it was published later. A French translation of Nappaaluk's novel was published in 2002 and an English edition came out in 2014. Nappaaluk authored over twenty books, compiled an encyclopedia of Inuit knowledge, translated a prayer book, and helped to develop curriculum materials. She received a National Aboriginal Achievement Award in 1999 and in 2004 was appointed to the Order of Canada.

ORGANIZATIONS

1971: The Association for the Study of American Indian Literatures (ASAIL) was founded to promote the study, criticism, and research on the oral traditions and written literatures of Native Americans. *Studies in American Indian Literatures* (SAIL), the official journal of the organization, has published for over forty years. ASAIL's sister organization is the Indigenous Literary Studies Association (ILSA), which is based in Alberta, Manitoba, Canada.

1986: The Committee to Re-Establish the Trickster (CRET) was founded by First Nations authors Tomson Highway, Cree; Lenore Keeshig-Tobias, Anishinaabe; and Daniel David Moses, Delaware in Canada. As Highway has pointed out, "The title said it all." CRET's activities included publication of the *Magazine to Re-Establish the Trickster* (1988–1997), readings, performances, and workshops.

1992: Native Writers Circle of the Americas (NWCA) was formed as an outgrowth of Returning the Gift, the first North American Native Writers' Festival, which was held in 1992. Its work has included presenting awards to Native American writers in the categories of First Book of Poetry, First Book of Prose, and Lifetime Achievement, voted upon by Native writers. The first recipients were Gloria Bird, Spokane, *Full Moon on the Reservation*, poetry; Robert L. Perea, Oglala Lakota, for *Stacey's Story*, prose; and N. Scott Momaday, Kiowa, who received a lifetime achievement award.

1993: Wordcraft Circle of Native Writers and Storytellers was founded by Lee Francis III, Laguna Pueblo, after he attended the first Returning the Gift Festival of Native writers and storytellers in Norman, Oklahoma, in July 1992. Francis, who also served as Wordcraft's first director, worked to build the organization and an extensive circle of Native writers and storytellers. After he passed away in 2003, Kimberly Roppolo and Lee

Francis IV assumed leadership responsibilities. In 2010, Francis IV was appointed the full-time executive director and president of the board to continue his father's legacy and work.

1996: Carole LaFavor (1948–2011), Ojibwe, is believed to have written the first novel with an Indigenous lesbian protagonist in *Along the Journey River: A Mystery*. It is one of two detective novels she wrote; the other was *Evil Dead Center*. LaFavor, who identified as two-spirit and lesbian, was also known as a Native American rights activist and nurse. Diagnosed with HIV/AIDS in 1986, she became a founding member of Positively Native, an organization supporting Native Americans with the illness. LaFavor served on the President's Advisory Council on HIV/AIDS from 1995 to 1997, the only Native American member.

2010: Robert J. Conley (1940–2014), a member of the Cherokee Nation, was named president of the Western Writers of America, becoming the first American Indian in the role. The organization promotes literature of the American West and has hundreds of members. Conley, prolific award-winning author of fiction and nonfiction, also served as the Sequoyah Distinguished Professor of Cherokee Studies at Western Carolina University.

2011: The First One Hundred Institute, founded by William Mehojah Jr., a member of the Kaw Nation of Oklahoma, held its first summer institute in Albuquerque, New Mexico, in June 2011. The organization works with tribal nations to develop community-based early literacy books, with workshops focused on the development of digital books that can be published locally and distributed to communities to promote Native language and culture. The First One Hundred Institute uses software and literacy tools developed by Unite for Literacy, a company with experience creating culturally and linguistically relevant books.

2017: Saad Bee Hózho, the Diné Writers' Collective, was created at Navajo Technical University in Crownpoint, New Mexico. It was formed from "Diné tséékos haz'ánigi: A Gathering of Dine Writers," an event organized by Diné writers and educators Irvin Morris and Manny Loley in 2017. The name Saad Bee Hózho was inspired by the poetry of acclaimed Diné writer Rex Lee Jim.

POETRY

1960: Ralph Salisbury (1926–2017), of Cherokee and Shawnee descent, was one of the first Native American poets to receive national attention when his poem "In the Children's Museum in Nashville" was published in the *New Yorker*. Two of his books of poetry, *Rainbows of Stone* (2000) and *Like the Sun in Storm* (2012), were finalists for the Oregon Book Award. Salisbury's published works also include three collections of short fiction and a memoir, *So Far, So Good* (2013), which received the River Teeth Book Award for Literary Nonfiction. He completed his twelfth book of poems, *Living in the Mouth*, shortly before his death in 2017. In 2020, the international literary journal *Transmotion* devoted a special issue to Salisbury, dedicating its pages to the work of a single author for the first time.

1972: *Kalala Poems* (Daylight Press), written by Skyros Bruce (c. 1952–), was the first book of poetry written by a British Columbia-born Native woman. Bruce, a member of the Sleil Waututh Nation in BC, was named Kalala (meaning butterfly in the Squamish language), Mary Bruce, and later, Mahara All-

Benjamin Larnell, A Poem in Latin

Benjamin Larnell (c. 1694–1714), Nipmuc, the final colonial-era student to attend Harvard Indian College, wrote "Fable of the Fox and the Weasel," a poem in Latin. It was discovered in 2012 by Stuart M. McManus, a Ph.D. student in history at Harvard, while he was doing research at the Massachusetts Historical Society. Larnell turned an Aesop fable into Latin verse, a school assignment possibly written to gain entrance to Harvard. His writing was undated and appeared on a single page. The young Nipmuc student died before graduating with Harvard's Class of 1716.

brett. Her book was published in a limited edition when she was twenty years old.

1992: Elise Paschen (1959–), a member of the Osage Nation, cofounded Poetry in Motion, a nationwide program that places poetry posters in subway cars and buses. While attending Harvard University, she won the Garrison Medal for Poetry. At Oxford University, where she studied twentieth-century British and American literature and earned her M.Phil. and D.Phil., Paschen cofounded the journal *Oxford Poetry*. She is the former executive director of the Poetry Society of America and the author of award-winning books of poetry and anthologies.

1993: Mark Turcotte (1958–), Anishinaabe, won the first Gwendolyn Brooks Open Mic Poetry Award shortly after moving to Chicago. He grew up on the Turtle Mountain Reservation in North Dakota and later lived in and around Lansing, Michigan. Turcotte's work, which has been nominated for Pushcart Prizes, includes *The Feathered Heart* (1995), *Songs of Our Ancestors* (1995), and *Exploding Chippewas* (2002).

1994: Haunani-Kay Trask (1949–2021), award-winning Hawaiian author, educator, and leader, wrote *Light in the Crevice Never Seen*, the first book of poetry by an Indige-

nous Hawaiian to be published in North America. Trask was the cowriter and coproducer of the documentary *Act of War: The Overthrow of the Hawaiian Nation* (1993). She was also the developer of *Haunani-Kay Trask: We Are Not Happy Natives*, a CD-ROM on the Hawaiian Sovereignty movement. Besides her poetry, she is the author of *From a Native Daughter: Colonialism and Sovereignty in Hawai'i* (1993) and other works. Trask, professor emerita at the University of Hawai'i at Mānoa, was named one of the most influential women in Hawaiian history by *Hawai'i Magazine* in 2017.

1999: Janet McAdams (1957–), of Creek (Muscogee) descent, joined the Kenyon College faculty as the first Robert P. Hubbard Professor of Poetry. Her poetry collections are *The Island of Lost Luggage* (2000), which won the American Book Award in 2001, *Feral* (2007), and a chapbook, *Seven Boxes for the Country After* (2016). In 2005, she became the founding editor of the award-winning Earthworks Poetry Series for Salt Publishing in the United Kingdom.

2005: Kurt Schweigman, Oglala/Lakota, was the first spoken-word poet to receive an Archibald Bush Foundation individual artist fellowship in literature. Although now retired from competition, he has won poetry slams. His writings appear in *Shedding Skins: Four Sioux Poets* (2008). He also coedited *Red Indian Road West: Native American Poetry from California* (2016) with Lucille Lang Day, Wampanoag.

2009: Jamaica Heolimeleikalani Osorio (1991–), Kanaka Maoli, was invited by President Barack and First Lady Michelle Obama to perform at the White House's first poetry jam. Then 18 years old, she performed a piece titled "Kumulipo," honoring her Hawaiian roots, to a standing-room-only crowd. Osorio, who earned her Ph.D. in 2018, serves as a faculty member and teaches Indigenous and Native Hawaiian politics at the University of Hawai'i at Mānoa. She is a three-time national poetry champion and published author. Her book *Remembering Our Intimacies: Mo'olelo, Ahoha 'Āina, and Ea* was published in fall 2021.

2011: Santee Frazier (1978–), Cherokee poet, was the inaugural School for Advanced Research (SAR) Indigenous Writer in Residence fellow in Santa Fe, New Mexico. Other honors include the Lannan Foundation Residency Fellowship, the Fine Arts Work Center's Archie D. and Bertha H. Walker Foundation Scholarship, and a 2014 Native Arts and Cultures Foundation Fellowship. He is the author of *Dark Thirty* (2009) and *Aurum* (2019).

2013: Luci Tapahonso (1953–), Navajo, was named the inaugural poet laureate of the Navajo Nation, serving in the position until 2015, when she was succeeded by writer Laura Tohe. While attending the University of New Mexico (UNM), Tapahonso was influenced by novelist Leslie Marmon Silko, a member of UNM's faculty, who encouraged her to pursue creative writing. Ta-

Luci Tapahonso

pahonso worked on her first book of poetry, *One More Shiprock Night*, while still an undergraduate. Her literary works include *A Radiant Curve*, her sixth book of poetry, which received the Arizona Book Award for Poetry in 2009. Tapahonso has also authored children's books. She retired in 2016, becoming professor emerita of English literature at UNM. Tapahonso was selected as "2016 Best of the City—Our City and State's Prolific Authors" by *Albuquerque the Magazine*. The award-winning author is also a recipient of a 2018 Native Arts and Culture Foundation Artist Fellowship.

2015: Marie "Annharte" Baker (1942–), Anishinabe from the Little Saskatchewan First Nations, was awarded the inaugural Blue Metropolis First People's Literary Prize for her poetry collection, *Indigena Awry* (New Star Books, 2012). She received the $5,000 prize at the Blue Metropolis International Literary Festival in Montreal, where she was interviewed by scholar Taiaiake Alfred. The author also cofounded the Regina Aboriginal Writers Group.

2016: Billy-Ray Belcourt (c. 1996–), who is from the Driftpile Cree Nation, became Canada's first First Nations Rhodes Scholar. He is the author of the poetry collections *NDN Coping Mechanisms* and *This Wound Is a World*. He also wrote a memoir, *A History of My Brief Body*. Belcourt earned his Ph.D. in English at the University of Alberta.

2016: *Red Indian Road West: Native American Poetry from California*, edited by Kurt Schweigman and Lucille Lang Day (Scarlet Tanager Books), is identified as "the first poetry anthology encompassing the entire range of Native American experience in California." It includes the work of 31 poets from 29 tribes.

Marie Annharte Baker

2016: Rebecca Thomas (c. 1986–), M'ikmaw from New Brunswick, became the first Indigenous poet to serve as the Halifax Regional Municipality's poet laureate, serving as an ambassador and advocate for literacy, literature, and the arts for a two-year term. She coordinated the Halifax Slam Poetry team from 2014 to 2017, leading to three national competitions with the Canadian Festival of Spoken Word. Thomas's poetry collection, *I Place You into the Fire*, was a CBC Best Canadian Poetry pick of 2020.

2018: Joan Naviyuk Kane (1977–), Inupiaq, became the first Indigenous poet to be named a John Simon Guggenheim Fellow. Kane, a graduate of Harvard College and Columbia University, is the award-winning author of poetry collections including *The Cormorant Hunter's Wife* (2009), *Hyperboreal* (2013), *The Straits* (2015), *Milk Black Carbon* (2017), *Sublingual* (2018), and *Dark Traffic* (2021). In 2014, Kane, who writes in both English and Inupiaq, became a founding faculty member in the MFA program in creative writing at the Institute of American Indian Arts in Santa Fe, New Mexico.

2018: Matthew Jake Skeets (1991–), Diné poet and teacher, became the first Native American to win the prestigious National Poetry Series for his collection *Eyes Bottle Dark with a Mouthful of Flowers* in 2019. Skeets is also the recipient of a 92Y Discovery Prize, a Mellon Projecting All Voices Fellowship, an American Book Award, and a Whiting Award. He received an MFA in poetry from the Institute of American Indian Arts in Santa Fe and became a faculty member at Diné College on the Navajo Nation. Skeets is also the founding editor of *Cloudthroat*, an online publication for Indigenous writing and art.

2019: Kim Shuck (1966–), Cherokee Nation, poet laureate of San Francisco, California, was awarded an

Kim Shuck

inaugural National Laureate Fellowship from the Academy of American Poets. The author of *Deer Trails* (City Lights Books, 2019) and other works, she received $75,000 to launch "Seeds: Creating Poetic Activism," a seed program for poets to grow writing and reading series and audiences in their own communities across the city.

2019: Prairie Fire made history as the first all-Indigenous poetry team to compete at the poetry slam flagship event hosted by the Canadian Festival of Spoken Word held in Guelph, Ontario, Canada. The four Cree poets—Alexandra Jarrett, Keccia Cook, Alex Alary, and Shawn Joseph—are members of the Saskatoon Indigenous Poets' Society.

2020: Kimberly Blaeser (1955–), poet, photographer, and scholar, who is a member of the White Earth Nation, founded In-Na-Po, Indigenous Nations Poets, a literary organization. Blaeser is the author of *Gerald Vizenor: Writing in the Oral Tradition*, identified as the first Native-authored book-length study of an Indigenous author. She is a professor at the University of Wisconsin–Milwaukee and on the MFA faculty for the Institute of American Indian Arts in Santa Fe, New Mexico. Blaeser, who served as Wisconsin poet laureate from 2015 to 2016, is the author of *Copper Yearning*, *Apprenticed to Justice*, and other poetry collections.

2020: Duncan Mercredi (1951–), Cree/Métis, was named Winnipeg's second poet laureate, a one-year term. In 2020, as well, Wilfred Laurier University Press released *mahikan ka onot: The Poetry of Duncan Mercredi*. It includes work from Mercredi's first book in 1991 to recent unpublished poems.

2021: Natalie Diaz (1978–), Mojave and enrolled member of the Gila River Indian Community, was awarded a Pulitzer Prize for poetry

Joy Harjo, U.S. Poet Laureate

Joy Harjo, a member of the Muscogee Creek Nation and an award-winning poet, musician, playwright, and author, was appointed as the poet laureate consultant to the Library of Congress on June 19, 2019, becoming the first Native American to serve in the position. She is the second U.S. poet laureate to serve three terms. In 2019, she was also elected a chancellor of the Academy of American Poets. Harjo, who attended the Institute of American Indian Arts in Santa Fe, New Mexico, completed her undergraduate degree at the University of New Mexico and a Master of Fine Arts degree in creative writing at the University of Iowa.   Joy Harjo
She is the author of numerous books of poetry, including *An American Sunrise* (2019), a national bestseller; *Conflict Resolution for Holy Beings* (2015); *The Woman Who Fell from the Sky* (1994), which received the Oklahoma Book Arts Award; and *In Mad Love and War* (1990), which received an American Book Award and the Delmore Schwartz Memorial Award. Her memoir *Crazy Brave* (W. W. Norton, 2012) won the 2013 PEN Center USA literary prize for creative nonfiction. She has also written a children's book, *The Good Luck Cat* (Harcourt, Brace 2000), and a young adult book, *For a Girl Becoming* (University of Arizona Press, 2009). Harjo, also known for playing alto saxophone, performed with the band Poetic Justice. Her third term as poet laureate focused on her signature project, "Living Nations, Living Words" (also a published book), mapping 47 contemporary Native American poets across the country. Harjo's *Poet Warrior: A Memoir* was published in 2021.

for her book *Postcolonial Love Poem.* In the same year, she also became the youngest poet ever elected to the Board of Chancellors of the Academy of American Poets. Her election is also the first time the board of chancellors comprised a majority of poets of color and a majority of women, among them U.S. poet laureate Joy Harjo. Diaz is the author of *When My Brother Was an Aztec,* which won an American Book Award. *Postcolonial Love Poem* was also a finalist for the National Book Award and the Forward Prize in Poetry. In 2018, Diaz was named a MacArthur Fellow and the Maxine and Jonathan Marshall Chair in Modern and Contemporary Poetry at Arizona State University. She is also known for playing basketball at Old Dominion University in Virginia and as a professional

Natalie Diaz

player in Europe and Asia. Diaz is known, too, for her work to recover the Mojave language. In 2020, she launched the Center for Imagination in the Borderlands, which garnered support from the Andrew W. Mellon Foundation for a mentorship program for Native students.

2021: Sherwin Bitsui (1975–), Diné, was the first Native American poet featured in the history of Gannon University's Writing Awards ceremony in Erie, Pennsylvania. He served as the guest poet at the 44th annual event, which was held virtually. Bitsui's poetry collections include *Shapeshift, Flood Song,* and *Dissolved.*

2021: Louise Bernice Halfe (1953–), also known by her Cree name Sky Dancer, was

Firsts, Native American State Poet Laureates

Term	Name	Tribal Affiliation	State
1944–45	Anne Semple	Choctaw	Oklahoma
2004–8	Denise Sweet	Anishinaabe	Wisconsin
2007–9	Denise Low	Delaware/Cherokee	Kansas
2007–9	N. Scott Momaday	Kiowa	Oklahoma Centennial
2009–11	Henry Real Bird	Crow	Montana
2012–	Kealoha	Hawaiian +	Hawaii
2012–14	Nora Marks Dauenhauer	Tlingit	Alaska*
2016–18	Elizabeth Woody	Navajo	Oregon
2021	Rena Priest	Lhaq'temish (Lummi)	Washington
2021	Gwen Nell Westerman	Dakota/Cherokee	Minnesota

Alaska's designation changed from state poet laureate to state writer laureate in 1996, broadening the position to all genres of writing.

named the parliamentary poet laureate of Canada, the first appointee to hail from an Indigenous community. The renowned poet, who was raised on Saddle Lake Reserve and attended Blue Quills Residential School in St. Paul, Alberta, previously served as poet laureate in Saskatchewan. Halfe's books include *Bear Bones and Feathers* (1994), *Blue Marrow* (2004), *The Crooked Good* (2007), *Burning in This Midnight Dream* (2016), and *Sôhkêyihta* (2018). Appointed for a two-year term, the parliamentary poet laureate writes poetry for use in Parliament, sponsors poetry readings, advises the parliamentary librarian on collections and acquisitions, and performs related duties at the request of the Speaker of the Senate, the Speaker of the House of Commons, or the parliamentary librarian.

2021: Deborah Miranda (1961–), poet and professor who is a member of the Ohlone-Costanoan Esselen Nation of California, was honored with a new collection in her name at the University Library at Washington and Lee University in Lexinton, Virginia. The Miranda Collection for Native American Library Acquisitions will feature books by Native American and Indigenous authors and literature. The honor was announced for the first time at an on-campus poetry reading by Miranda as a surprise to her. Miranda's collections of poetry include *Indian Cartography*, *The Zen of La Llorona*, and *Raised by Humans*. Miranda is the Thomas H. Broadus Jr. Professor of English at Washington and Lee.

2021: The James Welch Prize, a new annual Indigenous poetry prize, was started by *Poetry Northwest*, a literary magazine located in Portland, Oregon. The prize honors James Welch (1940–2003), esteemed Blackfeet/A'aninin author from Montana. The inaugural prize will be awarded to two Indigenous poets, each of them slated to receive $1,000 and to travel for readings in Missoula and Seattle.

2021: No'u Revilla became the first Native Hawaiian poet to win the National Poetry Series competition. She received a publishing offer from Milkweed Editions after topping more than 1,600 other poets in the event. Revilla, a queer poet and educator, serves as an assistant professor of creative writing at the University of Hawai'i–Mānoa. "I feel very lucky that my works gets to be recognized like this," she said. "When I was young, I didn't have access to poetry written by Hawaiians, and there were definitely no books being published by openly gay Hawaiian women. It is a dream come true." Revilla is the author of *Say Throne* (Tinfish Press, 2011).

PUBLISHING

1971: The Navajo Community College Press (later changed to Diné College Press) was established, becoming the publisher of writings in American Indian and Navajo studies. One of its early publications was *Navajo Stories of the Long Walk Period*, edited by Ruth Roessel and Broderick Johnson, in 1973.

1971: Sun Tracks Series at the University of Arizona Press was launched in 1971, becoming one of the first publishing programs to focus exclusively on creative works by Native Americans. Edited by scholar and poet Ofelia Zepeda since 1992, the series has produced more than 80 works of poetry, prose, art, and photography by distinguished writers such as Joy Harjo, N. Scott Momaday, and Luci Tapahonso.

1980: Pemmican Publications was incorporated in October 1980 by the Manitoba Métis

Federation. Located in Winnipeg, Manitoba, the press provides opportunities for Métis and Aboriginal people to tell their own stories from their own perspectives. Pemmican has become a leading publisher of children's books, also publishing fiction and nonfiction aimed at general audiences. It is committed to publishing works that depict Métis and Aboriginal cultures in positive, accurate ways.

1980: Theytus Books, the oldest Indigenous publishing house in Canada, was founded by Randy Fred (Nuu-chah-nulth). First Nations–owned, it is located in Syilx territory on the Penticton Indian Reserve in British Columbia. "Theytus," which means "preserving for the sake of handing down," operates in partnership with the En'owkin Centre, an Indigenous cultural, educational, ecological, and creative arts organization. Theytus Books has been a leading proponent for Indigenous authors, illustrators, and artists since its inception.

1989: The Tribal Writers Chapbook Series was established under the direction of James W. Parins at the Sequoyah National Research Center at the University of Arkansas in Little Rock with the mission of publishing up-and-coming Native writers. The first series included the publication of five chapbooks from 1989 to 1993, followed by the start of the second series in 2005.

1990: *The Singing Spirit: Early Short Stories by North American Indians*, edited by Bernd C. Peyer and published by the University of Arizona Press, features late-nineteenth- and early-twentieth-century writings. Initially published mainly in small journals or American Indian newspapers and mostly inaccessible to general readers, they represent forerunners of short fiction by contemporary Native American authors. The book includes selections by Gertrude Bonnin, Angel De Cora, Charles Alexander Eastman, E. Pauline

Johnson, William Jones, Francis La Flesche, Susette La Flesche, and Alexander Posey.

1990: Gerald Vizenor, Ojibwe, served as the founding series editor of American Indian Literature and Critical Studies at the University of Oklahoma Press, 1990–2007. During that period, more than fifty books were published.

1993: Kegedonce Press was founded by author Kateri Akiwenzie-Damm, a band member of the Chippewas of Nawash, on the Cape Croker Reserve in Ontario. The books involve Indigenous people at all levels of production. Akiwenzie-Damm serves as the managing editor.

1994: Salina Bookshelf, specializing in publishing Navajo-language books, was founded in Flagstaff, Arizona, by Eric and Kenneth Lockard.

1996: Tribal College Press (TCP), the academic press for the nation's tribal colleges and universities (TCUs), traces its roots to 1996 with the publication of its first title, *Touching Home: Stories, Essays, and Poems by Tribal College Students.* The press, an imprint of *Tribal College Journal*, is interdisciplinary but grounded in American Indian studies, publishing books focused on TCUs or those authored by tribal college faculty, students, and leaders.

2006: The Chickasaw Press was established as an entity of the Chickasaw Nation in Oklahoma, the first tribal publishing house of its kind. Academic in nature, its vision includes "preserving, perpetuating and providing an awareness of Chickasaw history and culture." White Dog Press, which was later established as a secondary imprint under the Chickasaw Press, focuses on literary categories such

Cynthia Leitich Smith

as historical fiction, children's books, and young adult literature.

2007: Kahuaomānoa Press, the first student-run press at the University of Hawai'i, was founded by Native Hawaiian poets Brandy Nālani McDougall and Ann Inoshita. Located on the Mānoa campus as a nonprofit organization and a registered independent organization, it was created "to increase student interest in literature, creative writing, visual art, and editing." *Honua*, the first poetry collection of Sage U'ilani Takehiro (Kanaka Maoli), was the first book published by Kahuaomānoa Press.

2011: Ala Press, an independent publisher of Indigenous Pacific Islander literature, was cofounded by Brandy Nālani McDougall, Kanaka 'Ōiwi/Chinese/Scottish, and Craig Santos Perez, Chamoru. The cofounders, who also serve as coeditors, publish a range of writings, including poetry, fiction, creative nonfiction, and children's books.

2015: Native Realities, an Indigenous Imagination Company, was founded by Dr. Lee Francis IV, Pueblo of Laguna, also the CEO, to unleash the Indigenous imagination through popular culture, including comic books, graphic novels, games, and toys. It has published a range of Indigenous-centric comic books. Francis also founded the Indigenous Comic Con in 2016 and opened Red Planet Books and Comics in Albuquerque, New Mexico, in 2017. In 2018, his first comic, *Tales of the Mighty Code Talkers Vol. I*, won the American Indian Library Association's American Indian Youth Literature Award.

2017: Black Bears and Blueberries Publishing was founded by author Thomas Peacock, Fond du Lac Band of Lake Superior Ojibwe, and educator Elizabeth Albert-Peacock, Red Cliff Band of Lake Superior

Ojibwe, in Duluth, Minnesota. The Native-owned nonprofit company publishes children's fiction and nonfiction paperback books and ebooks on Native topics serving a regional audience, including the Dakotas, Michigan, Minnesota, and Wisconsin.

2019: HarperCollins Children's Books Launched Heartdrum, the first imprint from a major publisher focused exclusively on Indigenous works. Award-winning writer Cynthia Leitich Smith, Muscogee Creek, credits Ellen Oh, cofounder of We Need Diverse Books, as the inspiration for Heartdrum's creation. Leitich Smith serves as the imprint's author-curator and Rosemary Brosnan, vice president, editorial director, HarperCollins Children's Books, as its editor. *The Sea in Winter* by Christine Day, Upper Skagit, Heartdrum's first title, was published in January 2021. Other titles on the list include *Ancestor Approved: Intertribal Stories for Kids*, a middle grade anthology of stories edited by Leitich Smith, novels, and a chapter book series.

READING PROGRAMS

2003: First Nation Communities READ was launched by the Ontario First Nation Public Library community, with support from Southern Ontario Library Service, to promote a community-based approach to reading. Each year, the program rewards excellence in Indigenous literature.

2004: *Night Flying Woman: An Ojibway Narrative* (Minnesota Historical Society Press, 1983) by Ignatia Broker, a member of the White Earth Nation, was chosen for St. Paul Reads One Book in 2004. The title was the program's first selection written by a Native American, the first by a Minnesotan, the first by a woman, and the first published by a local press. St. Paul Reads, a partnership between the city and the school system, encouraged students and community members to read a book in common to discuss together. In 1984, Broker received a Wonder Woman Award for the book and for her activism in the Native community.

2019: First Nations Development Institute, a nonprofit organization in Longmont, Colorado, announced its new Indigenous reading campaign called #NativeReads to honor and celebrate writers from a specific tribal nation or region. First Nations selected the Oak Lake Writers Society, a society of Dakota/Nakota/Lakota writers, to serve as its inaugural grant partner for the first year of the project. Its activities are outlined in a brochure called *Stories of the Oceti Sakowin* and included compiling a list of some 200 books, picking 10 books featured in the #NativeReads campaign and selecting one

Kaona and Contemporary Hawaiian Literature

Brandy Nālani McDougall wrote *Finding Meaning: Kaona and Contemporary Hawaiian Literature*, published by the University of Arizona Press in 2016, the first extensive study of contemporary Hawaiian literature. McDougall, who won the Beatrice Medicine Award for Scholarship in American Indian Studies for the work, examines fiction, poetry, and drama by emerging and established authors.

book, *Our History Is Our Future*, for the community to read and discuss together in 2020.

TEACHING/WRITING PROGRAMS

2016: Debra Magpie Earling (1957–), member of the Confederated Salish and Kootenai Tribes, became the first Native American to be named director of the University of Montana's creative writing program. Her novel *Perma Red* (Putnam, 2002) won the Western Writers Association (WWA) Spur Award, WWA's Medicine Pipe Bearer Award for Best First Novel, a WILLA Literary Award, the Washington State Fiction Award, and the American Book Award. Earling collaborated with photographer Peter Rutledge Koch on *The Lost Journals of Sacajawea* (Koch editions, 2010), a museum piece book exhibited at the New York Public Library, the Beinecke Rare Book & Manuscript Library at Yale, and other venues.

2017: The Emerging Diné Writers' Institute (EDWI) was created as the result of a partnership between the Navajo Women's Commission and Navajo Technical University (NTU) to develop a creative writing summer program. EDWI is funded by the Office of the President at NTU and various grants and directed by Diné cofounder Manny Loley, who received an MFA in creative writing–fiction from the Institute of American Indian Arts in 2018.

2020: The Native Authors Program was launched as a project of All My Relations Arts in Minneapolis, Minnesota. The program was created in response to the underrepresentation of Native authors and books in publishing and in literary grants and awards. The first cohort of eight writers completed *Voices Rising: Native Women Writers*, edited by Diane Wilson and Zibiquah Denny, published by Black Bears and Blueberries in 2021.

WRITERS IN RESIDENCE

Cherie Dimaline

2015: Cherie Dimaline (1975–), award-winning author and editor from the Georgian Bay Métis community, was named Toronto Public Library's first Writer in Residence—Aboriginal Experience, a four-month residency from March to June 2015. Her book *The Marrow Thieves* won the Governor General's Literary Award in 2017.

2019: Bojan Louis (1980–), Diné poet, fiction writer, and essayist, was the inaugural Virginia G. Piper Fellow-in-Residence at Arizona State University. The program, a one-year stint, combines an artistic residency with an academic fellowship. Besides teaching one course per semester, the Fellow-in-Residence presents readings and other literary events for the larger community. The candidates are drawn from alumni of ASU's creative writing program.

2021: Seattle Rep announced it had selected Arianne True, Choctaw/Chickasaw, as its first Native Artist-in-Residence, a local poet and folk artist. True teaches and mentors with Writers in the Schools, the Seattle Youth Poet Laureate program, and the Young Writers Cohort.

BUSINESS AND ECONOMICS

"Once we got the bingo hall open (Foxwoods Casino), nobody thought we'd be successful with it, but we paid off our note early. We're very happy to be able to do and share all of this—housing, a beautiful museum and provide good jobs for our people...."

—*Richard (Skip) Arthur Hayward (1947–), tribal chairman of Mashantucket Pequot Tribe (1975–1998)*

TRIBALLY OWNED BUSINESSES

"I made it my business to bring money, lots of money, into the Seminole Tribe and its citizens."

—*James Billie (1944–), chief of the Seminole Tribe of Florida (1979–2001 and 2011–2016)*

c. 1900: In present-day Oklahoma, the Kiowa-Comanche-Apache (KCA) Reservation Business Committee was formed to blend "traditional" methods with modern economics and politics to produce a uniquely "Native way." Its first order of business was a milestone in tribal entities handling their own economic affairs. It approved a gypsum-mining lease with a non-Native cement company, sold quarry rights to a white community, and used $60,000 of its "grass money" (payment for leasing land to cattle companies) to buy young heifers for the reservation population so they could create their own herds. Unfortunately, the KCA lost its power almost immediately as the U.S. government prohibited the committee from choosing its own business ventures. Land allotment also severely weakened the KCA as "surplus" lands were sold to Anglos by individual Indians instead of going through collective tribal channels.

1912: The Osage Nation of Oklahoma held the first public auction for oil leases on its land. The sale profited one million dollars.

1932: The Pamunkey Pottery School & Guild was founded on the Pamunkey Indian Reservation in Virginia to develop tourist trade

The Four Wealthiest Native American Nations

1. The Shakopee Mdewakanton Sioux Community (SMSC) of fewer than 1,000 members and located near the Twin Cities of Minneapolis and St. Paul, Minnesota, has an annual revenue of $1 billion. Their income is derived from two casinos that attract thousands, the 18-hole Meadows at Mystic Lake golf course, a 2,100-seat concert venue, a 600-room hotel, five restaurants, and an 8,350-seat outdoor amphitheater. Their JW Marriott Minneapolis Mall of America Hotel is just 11 miles from downtown Minneapolis and close to the Mall of America. Voted best RV Park in Minnesota by *Midwest Gaming & Travel Magazine*, the tribe's Dakotah Meadows RV Park offers complete services for recreational vehicles. Mazopiya, a natural foods market, provides a wide selection of local and organic foods grown in the Wozupi Tribal Gardens. The SMSC Organics Recycling Facility supports the Dakota tradition of earth stewardship by recycling organic waste into useful materials, and SMSC Water Bottling is a pure water distributer. The water is also donated across the country.

The Hoćokata Ti [ho-cho-kah-tah-tee] are the SMSC cultural center and gathering space, where heritage, language, and history are preserved for tribal members and also offered to the public. SMSC has had many struggles and challenges, but today, it is able to prosper financially while protecting its lands and culture.

2. The Mohegan Tribe located in Uncasville, Connecticut, has an estimated annual income of $992 million. The tribe operates the Mohegan Sun Casino, ranked the second-largest casino in the United States with 6,200 slot machines. Because of the nearby casino competition from the Mashantucket Pequot, they began to diversify and launched Mohegan Gaming & Entertainment (MGE), a master developer and operator of premier global entertainment resorts. In 2003, the Mohegan Tribe became the first Native nation to own a professional sports team after purchasing the Connecticut Sun, a Women's National Basketball Association (WNBA) team. The tribe was also co-owner of the New England Black Wolves of the National Lacrosse League from 2014 to 2020. The Mohegan bought a horse-racing track in Pennsylvania (2005), becoming the first tribe to run a gaming venture outside its home state and the first to own a nontribal gaming asset. They named it Mohegan Sun at Pocono Downs and built a major casino, the first in Pennsylvania. MGE owns the INSPIRE Entertainment Resort in Incheon, South Korea, which is due to open in 2023, and Niagara Casinos in Niagara, Ontario, Canada. They are the first Native Nation to construct the first integrated resort and casino gaming site in Greece, INSPIRE Athens. In 2021, the Mohegan opened the Mohegan Sun Casino at Virgin Hotels Las Vegas, the first Native American casino in Las Vegas, Nevada. They own several food franchises of Jersey Mike's Subs and Pasta Vita plus Mohegan Renewable Energy, LLC (MRE). MRE provides wood pellets and other biomass products to the global market and operates plants in Alabama, Indiana, Tennessee, and Mississippi.

The Mohegan Tribe of 2,500 members financed the $35 million access road that enables visitors to reach Mohegan Sun without creating local traffic. They fund a re-

The Four Wealthiest Native American Nations (contd.)

gional water project and contribute financially to their town and state. The Mohegan Tribe is the only nonbank investor in Connecticut to partner with the Community Economic Development Fund, a revolving loan program that helps regional businesses create jobs.

3. The Seminole Tribe of Florida has an estimated annual revenue of $853.84 million. In 1979, it launched the first-ever high-stakes bingo hall and casino in the United States, eventually changing the Seminole Nation from impoverished to economically comfortable on its six urban and rural southern Florida reservations. It initiated the Indian gaming movement, and by 2001, 201 nations were operating high-stakes casinos.

The tribe founded its MICCO Aircraft Company in 1994, becoming the first Indigenous nation to own and operate an airplane manufacturing company. *Micco* is the Miccosukee word for "leader" or "superior one." Chief James Billie's love of flying was the driving force in starting the enterprise; he is a longtime pilot who holds single, multiengine, instrument, and helicopter ratings and understands the flight qualities pilots desire. Chief Billie (1944) served 22 years, the second-longest tenure of any elected head of state in the Western Hemisphere, behind only Cuba's Fidel Castro. The Seminole Tribe of Florida was the first nation to venture into international holdings after purchasing the Hard Rock International, Inc. for $965 million in 2006. The acquisition included 160 Hard Rock Cafes in some 45 countries, five hotels, several Hard Rock Live concert venues, and the world's largest collection of rock and roll memorabilia.

In 2019, the Seminole Nation scored another first when it opened its 450-foot guitar-shaped, 35-floor hotel that towers over Hollywood, Florida. And in 2020, the Gaming Empire became the first to offer "live slots," where players control physical slot machines located inside a casino—direct from their laptop, tablet, or mobile device. The tribe created the Seminole Real Estate Fund (SEMREF), a sovereign wealth fund for the financial benefit for future generations. Its first real estate purchase was in 2020, when it acquired the McKinney Uptown Apartments, a 144-unit residential complex located in Dallas, Texas. The tribe generates income by being a key Florida travel destination for families as well as a gambling and nightclub hub for adults. It operated the Everglades Billie Swamp Safari located on grounds that feature thousands of plant and animal life species. Everglades airboat rides, live animal shows, tours of a historic Seminole village, the Ah-Tah-Thi-Ki Museum, and a full-service RV resort are part of the Billie Swamp Safari entertainment package.

Each Seminole citizen receives a substantial yearly allotment plus free access to private schools and college tuition, senior citizen care, and universal health care.

The Guitar Hotel (part of the Hard Rock chain) in Hollywood, Florida, was financed and built by the wealthy Seminole Nation.

The Four Wealthiest Native American Nations (contd.)

4. The Mashantucket Pequot, located in Mashantucket, Connecticut, takes in an annual revenue of $539.2 million. In 2009, it was regarded as the world's richest tribe, and its 800 members were comfortable financially. However, it went through some difficult financial times and has worked hard to recover. The Foxwoods Resort Casino has 300 game tables, the largest poker table on the East Coast, a 3,600-seat bingo hall, a state-of-the-art race book, and is one of the largest employers in the area. The casino has hosted more than 330 million visitors since 1992. In 1993, the tribe established a first-of-its-kind agreement to give slot revenue payments to Connecticut and, so far, has contributed more than $4 billion. Like the other wealthy nations, the Mashantucket Pequot diversified and branched out into unexpected industries: real estate, pharmaceuticals, golf courses, restaurants, high-speed ferries, sand and gravel sales, retail, museums, a bed-and-breakfast, and a spa.

The Pequot Pharmaceutical Network® (PRxN®) began as a pharmacy service for tribal members and employees of the Mashantucket Pequot Tribal Nation in 1999. Now, PRxN® is a major provider of pharmacy benefits management, network pharmacy ac-

The Four Wealthiest Native American Nations (contd.)

cess, and an on-site, state-of-the-art, and wholly owned mail-service pharmacy. Over 65,000 retail chain and independent pharmacies across the country participate in PRxN®.

In 2010, the Mashantucket Pequot Gaming Enterprise and 2,500 dealers, members of the UAW Local 2121 Union, reached the first labor contract negotiated under tribal law. The landmark decision set the precedent that sovereign Indian nations are subject to the National Labor Relations Act.

The Mashantucket Pequot Museum and Research Center is a tourist destination and offers a variety of experiences for all ages. The stunning 308,000-square-foot facility opened in 1998 and features life-size walk-through dioramas that transport visitors into the past, changing exhibits and live performances of contemporary arts and cultures. Extensive interactive exhibits depict 18,000 years of Native and natural history, while two libraries, including one for children, archive a diverse selection of materials on the histories and cultures of Indigenous peoples of the United States and Canada.

and provide employment for Pamunkey affected by the Great Depression. Euro-American instructors focused on the mass production of nonutilitarian, souvenir, tourist art, very different from the traditional Pamunkey style. There were many changes, including the use of the pottery wheel, squeeze molds, and kiln firing as well as painted pictographs and southwestern motifs, but potters still gathered clay from traditional deposits along the Pamunkey River. The guild continues to manage both the artistic and the business side of production.

1969: The Family Employment Training Center for Indians opened in Bismarck, North Dakota. Founded by the United Tribes of North Dakota Development Corporation, the center was the first to be initiated by Natives and the first such enterprise to have an Indian firm, the Bendix Field Engineering Corporation, as contractor.

1969: The Mississippi Band of Choctaw Indians began its "industrial revolution" when it opened its first company, Chahta Development, to build houses for tribal members. Not only were the homes constructed for Choctaws, but Choctaws were hired and trained to build the homes. In the 1970s, when businesses were relocating to the South to avoid unionism and taxes, Chief Phillip Martin sent out 500 letters to companies asking them to relocate their plants to the tribe's newly developed industrial park. His endeavors paid off when Packard Electric committed to opening a factory on the reservation. In 1979, Chahta Enterprise became the first tribally owned company producing wiring harnesses for the automotive industry.

1971: The Rocking Horse Regional Manpower Center opened near Ronan, Montana, becoming the first all-Indian Job Corps Center. Staffed mainly by Indian people, the center was sponsored by the Confederated Salish and Kootenai Tribal Council of the Flathead Reservation.

1972: The Blackfeet Indian Pencil Company was established by the Blackfeet Indian Tribe in Browning, Montana. The successful brand included all-natural cedar pencils as well as colored pencils for the art market. The factory received a special designation for U.S. government bids but lost to the Industries of the Blind in Milwaukee, Wisconsin. However, the pencils were so popular that there is talk about reestablishing the company.

1974: The Shinnecock Tribe opened the first shellfish geothermal/solar hatchery on the East Coast. Tribal members had studied at the Lummi Indian School of Aquaculture in Bellingham, Washington, and brought the technical training back to their reservation in Southampton, New York.

1975: The first tribally owned eighteen-hole golf course was built by the Mescalero Apache Tribe of New Mexico. The professional course is at an elevation of seven thousand feet.

1985: The Jicarilla Apache Tribe of New Mexico became the first Indian nation to issue a tax-free bond using the provisions of the Indian Tribal Governmental Tax Status Act of 1982. The bond was worth over $30 million.

1986: The Eastern Band of Cherokee Indians in North Carolina purchased Carolina Mirror Company, the largest mirror-producing factory in the country.

1995: The Las Vegas Paiute Tribe opened the Las Vegas Paiute Golf Resort in Nevada. It was the first master-planned, multicourse facility of its kind built on Native land. Today there are almost 100 courses on Native lands; many have earned the highest ranking from golf magazines and professional golfers.

1996: The Chamber of Commerce in Marysville, Washington, changed its name to the Greater Marysville Tulalip Chamber of Commerce, the first time a U.S. chamber of commerce has partnered with an Indian nation. Although the Tulalip Nation was a member of the organization, the change of name recognized the Tulalip's role in the region's economy.

1999: The Morongo Band of Mission Indians opened a Coco's Bakery on its lands in Cabazon, California, becoming the first tribe to own one.

1999: S&K Technologies, Inc., a preeminent professional services firm, was formed to provide opportunity and prosperity to the people of the Confederated Salish and Kootenai Tribes (CSKT) on the Flathead Reservation in St. Ignatius, Montana. Its International Towers LLC business manufactures and erects towers and antennas worldwide for broadcasters, cellular providers, and governments. A founding member of the industry's National Association of Tower Erectors (NATE), the company is nationally certified for safety and management practices. S&K Technologies operates ten subsidiary companies that support federal and commercial customers worldwide with operating locations throughout the United States and the Kingdom of Saudi Arabia.

2000: Bedré Fine Chocolate was purchased by the Chickasaw Nation (Oklahoma), the first such enterprise owned by a Native nation. Chocolate was first produced centuries ago by the Olmec, indigenous to what is now southern Mexico. Bedré offers handcrafted candy in a variety of shapes, sizes, and flavors.

2001: A&S Diversified opened as the first Native-owned machining company in Montana. Based in Poplar on the Fort Peck Assiniboine & Sioux Tribes Reservation, the business specializes in machining, assembly,

Elouise Cobell ("Yellow Bird Woman")

An entrepreneur, advocate, and member of the Blackfeet Nation, Elouise Pepion Cobell ("Yellow Bird Woman"; 1945–2011) was a leading force in the struggle for Native control over their own finances. After the only bank on the reservation closed, Cobell was key in the founding of the first tribally owned bank (1985), the Blackfeet National Bank, now the Native American Bank and went on to direct the Native American Community Development Corporation, the bank's nonprofit affiliate. She was in the forefront of demanding fiscal accountability from the Bureau of Indian Affairs (BIA) and other government agencies, especially when Indians were denied their funds held by the BIA. Cobell questioned certain discrepancies in accounting: the money the tribe was supposed to get was far below what actually came into tribal coffers. Cobell was told she didn't know how to read ledgers and financial documents although she had a degree in business from the University of Montana, where she also studied accounting. She was also the tribal treasurer, which required expertise in accounting and other fiscal responsibilities. Despite her findings being dismissed, she was not deterred.

On June 10, 1996, Cobell, along with the Native American Rights Fund (NARF), filed a class-action lawsuit against the U.S. Department of Interior for the mismanagement of the Indian Trust Funds belonging to over 300,000 individual tribal members. *Cobell v. Salazar* is one of the largest class-action lawsuits ever filed against the U.S. government. The lawsuit alleged that the BIA had been mishandling and abusing the Indian Trust Funds for more than a century, causing Native Americans to live in poverty and restricting them from other options to manage their own finances. Cobell was not only the lead plaintiff, but she also helped fund the case, donating part of the $310,000 from her "Genius Grant" as well as other monies. The lawsuit dragged on for 13 years of contentious court battles, but it was successful. Cobell and her lawyers agreed to a $3.4 billion settlement with the U.S. government in December 2009. The settlement included $1.5 billion for the members of the lawsuit, $1.9 billion for a Land Consolidation Program, and $60 million for a college scholarship fund for Native American youth. The settlement was given the final stamp of approval on June 21, 2011, a few months before Cobell's death.

Cobell won countless awards for her activism and accomplishments. After she received a "Genius Grant" from the John D. and Catherine T. MacArthur Foundation in 1997, she joked "about having made the leap from 'dumb Indian' to 'genius' in one lifetime." The Blackfeet Nation honored her with warrior status in 2000, and in 2002 she received an honorary doctorate from Montana State University. But of all Yellow Bird Woman's honors, she is best remembered for taking on the U.S. government and winning.

welding, and metal fabrication, handling several contracts for the U.S. Department of Defense.

2004: Yakama Juice, owned by the Yakama Nation of Washington, was founded. It became the first Native-owned juice company in the nation.

2005: The Sun Kings basketball team was purchased by the Yakama Nation of Washington State and renamed the Yakama Sun Kings. It was the first time a Native nation bought a pro basketball team in the Continental Basketball Association (CBA).

2007: Pojoaque Pueblo of New Mexico and Hilton Hotels embarked on a joint enterprise to create the Buffalo Thunder Resort in the Sangre de Cristo Mountains, 15 minutes from downtown Santa Fe. It was the first time the famous hotel chain teamed up with a tribal government.

2008: The Coushatta Tribe of Louisiana was the first Indian tribe to import and market Aya Natural skin care products from Israel.

2009: The Residence Inn in Washington, D.C., was the first hotel to be owned jointly by four different tribes: Oneida Nation of Wisconsin; Forest County Potawatomi Community; Viejas Band of Kumeyaay Indians; and the San Manuel Band of Mission Indians.

2009: For the first time, a farmers' market was approved to be held on U.S. Forest Service land. Nuui Cunni Farmers' Market, operated by the Kern River Paiute Council, opened in Isabella, California. Nuui Cunni ("Our House" in Paiute), at the Forest Service French Gulch Recreation Area, features local products such as fresh produce, beans, seeds, and honey.

2010: The Forest County Potawatomi Community (Wisconsin) built an $18.5 million biogas energy plant that not only heats its Menomonee Valley Casino but also produces enough electricity to sell to the local utility company. Biogas, sustainable energy, is produced by breaking down raw organic waste, plant material, or food scrap. Using anaerobic digestion, organisms digest or ferment materials whose byproduct produces methane-based gas that can be used to create heat and electricity. In 2007, the community created Project Greenfire, to establish its goal of energy independence using only renewable carbon-neutral or carbon-free resources.

2011: The Yocha Dehe Wintun Nation of California debuted its state-of-the-art sustainable olive oil enterprise, Séka Hills Olive Oil, the first of its kind in the United States.

2011: The Squaxin Island Tribe in western Washington opened its Salish Cliffs Golf Club, becoming the first-ever U.S. property to earn Salmon-Safe golf course certification.

2011: Salt River Fields at Talking Stick became the first Major League Baseball spring training stadium erected on land owned by Indigenous people. The Salt River Pima-Maricopa Indian Community in the Phoenix,

The lobby of the Buffalo Thunder Hotel in Pojoaque, New Mexico.

Arizona, area hosts the training stadium for the Arizona Diamondbacks and the Colorado Rockies.

2012: The 'Namgis First Nation opened Kuterra (derived from *kutala,* 'Namgis for salmon, and *terra,* meaning land), North America's first land-based salmon farm, located on Northern Vancouver Island, close to the Pacific Ocean. The facility was the second in the world to prove the viability of raising salmon at commercial scale through aquaculture. The Kuterra mission is to supply environmentally sound, safe, and healthy farmed salmon.

2013: The Rincon Band of Luiseño Indians became the first California tribe to renegotiate a tribal-state gaming compact with federal courts.

2015: Energy Keepers Inc., a corporation owned by the Confederated Salish and Kootenai Tribes of Montana, acquired the Kerr Dam, becoming the first Native nation to possess a major hydroelectric power plant.

2015: The Weddingwire 2015 Couples Choice Award for Best Venue went to the Event Center at Sandia Golf Club in Albuquerque, New Mexico. The club is owned by Sandia Pueblo, and it was the first time a Native site won the award.

2016: The Salt River Pima-Maricopa Indian Community near Tempe, Arizona was the

Located on the Flathead Indian Reservation in Montana, the Selĭ'š Ksanka Qlispe' Dam (formerly Kerr Dam) is owned by the Confederated Salish and Kootenai Tribes of Montana.

Indigenous Firsts: A History of Native American Achievements and Events

headquarters of the Phoenix Rising professional soccer team. It became the first partnership between a tribe and professional soccer team.

2017: The Poarch Band of Creek Indians in Alabama unveiled the OWA Amusement Park in Foley, the largest such business owned by an Indian nation. The 520-acre resort celebrates local Southern fare and offers thrilling rides and attractions for kids and families. The nation also created the Natural Resources Department, which oversees its Magnolia Branch Wildlife Reserve, a camping and outdoor activity enterprise, and Perdido River Farms, the tribe's cattle business.

2017: The Iowa Tribe of Oklahoma became the first Native nation to be granted an international online gaming license, Ioway Internet Gaming Enterprise Limited. Its first international contract was with the Isle of Man Gambling Supervision Commission in Great Britain.

2018: Kahnawake Brewing Company (KBC) became the first microbrewery to open on a Native Reserve in Canada. With a debut lineup of ten beers and a selection of pizzas, KBC opened its doors to the public on St. Patrick's Day in 2018. The owners worked with the Alcoholic Beverage Control Board, the Mohawk Council of Kahnawake, and attorneys to create the laws and regulations needed. The first permit of its kind was issued to KBC in January 2018 at the end of a year-and-a-half process.

2019: The Jamestown S'Klallam Tribe broke ground for the first four-diamond resort/casino property on Washington's Olympic Peninsula.

2019: SoFi Stadium and Hollywood Park announced that the Pechanga Resort Casino,

owned and operated by the Pechanga Band of Luiseño Indians, would be the official casino partner of the Los Angeles Rams, Los Angeles Chargers, SoFi Stadium, and Hollywood Park. The Luiseño's Pechanga Development Corporation was the first Southern California–headquartered company to partner with the Rams' new 70,000-seat stadium and 298-acre development.

Clarence Louie

2019: Clarence Louie, chief of the Osoyoos Indian Band, became the first Indigenous person to be inducted into the Canadian Business Hall of Fame, which recognizes and celebrates the accomplishments of Canada's most distinguished business leaders. For over 30 years, Louie has led his band, and he started the Osoyoos Indian Band Development Corporation (OIBDC) in 1988. The 460-member community was once impoverished and now controls 32,000 acres of land and owns nine businesses, including tourism, construction, recreation, and Nk'Mip Cellars, the first tribally owned winery in North America. The Osoyoos Band employs 700 people.

2020: The Shinnecock Nation in Long Island, New York, teamed up with tribal gaming giant Seminole Hard Rock Entertainment to start planning for their first casino.

2020: Kevin Nephew was appointed the first Seneca president and CEO of the Seneca Gaming Corporation, the first time in the corporation's 18-year history that a tribal member held the position. Nephew oversees the operation of Seneca Gaming Corporation's properties in upstate New York—Seneca Niagara Resort & Casino in Niagara Falls; Seneca Allegany Resort & Casino in Salamanca; and Seneca Buffalo Creek Casino in downtown Buffalo. The corporation has almost 3,000 employees and hosts millions of visitors each year.

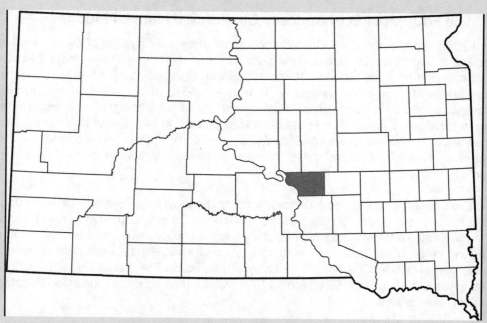

Buffalo County in South Dakota (highlighted) is the poorest county in the United States. Fewer than 2,000 people live there, and the county seat of Gann Valley only has 14 people.

The Four Most Economically Challenged Native Nations

Popular opinion is that gaming and energy businesses have made all Native Americans wealthy. In 2015, casinos created an average of 25 jobs and energy projects created 12, which barely had an effect on reservations with more than 2,000 residents. But neither has been a panacea for decades of abject poverty. The poverty cycle of Indigenous peoples began with European colonization when tribes with healthy economies and food abundance were forced onto remote reservations that had few natural resources or arable land. Millions of animals that were essential to the well-being of communities, like the great bison herds, were slaughtered. Traditional agricultural areas were destroyed or appropriated by Europeans and later Euro-Americans. Tribal nations were prohibited from making their seasonal migrations to procure game, medicines, and other food plants that sustained them. The trading networks that had existed for thousands of years were curtailed, as were the annual gatherings of people from diverse areas to exchange goods and ideas and share camaraderie. And then to exacerbate the situation, centuries of government policies left reservations with limited economic opportunities.

As a result, one of every four Native Americans lives in poverty, the highest poverty rate and the lowest labor force rate (61.1%) of any ethnic group in the United States.

The Four Most Economically Challenged Native Nations (contd.)

In a 2020 study of the top 100 poorest counties in the country, four of the top five—all located in South Dakota—and ten of the top 20 are on reservations throughout the country. Many tribal citizens cope with food insecurity and its accompanying health problems, high unemployment rates (sometimes a whopping 85%), inadequate fuel and clothing, transportation scarcity, and severe housing shortages. Forty percent of reservation housing is considered substandard compared to 6 percent in the rest of the country. Less than half of Native homes are connected to a public sewer system; 16 percent lack indoor plumbing; and 23% of Native households pay 30 percent or more of their household income to housing.

Buffalo County in central South Dakota, home to the Crow Creek Sioux Tribe, is the poorest county in the United States. Second is Shannon County, South Dakota, entirely on the Pine Ridge Reservation, which for the previous twenty years had been the poorest county in the United States. The third poorest county is Ziebach, South Dakota, most of which lies within the Cheyenne River Lakota Reservation. The rest of Ziebach County is within the Standing Rock Sioux Indian Reservation, making it the fourth poorest place in the United States.

In a 2020 study prepared for the Institute for Policy Research, sociologist and Northwestern professor Dr. Beth Redbird, Oglala Lakota/Oklahoma Choctaw, explored factors contributing to Native poverty. She suggested that to generate more employment, tribes should invest in a variety of job initiatives to diversify economic opportunities, rather than putting all their capital into one project. Big projects offer hope, but they also bring a lot of debt and not enough well-paying jobs. Her research pointed out that since 1980, more tribal nations have invested heavily in education. However, the employment and wage rates have continued to decline. Although poverty tends to be higher in rural areas, the poverty gap between Native Americans living in rural and urban areas is larger than the white rural and urban gap, meaning that poverty is not determined by a rural lifestyle. Also, a large number of construction and manufacturing jobs have been lost, the minimum wage has declined, and unstable employment is on the upswing. Redbird feels hopeful despite the challenges. She advises that tribes tailor federal and state policy to meet the needs of their own communities.

2020: The Rincon Band of Luiseño Indians opened the Rincon Reservation Road Brewery (3R Brewery), the first certified Native American owned and operated brewery on tribal land in Southern California. "We plan on bringing recipes that infuse our native plants and agriculture," Ruth-Ann Thorn, chairwoman for the Rincon Economic Development Corporation (REDCO), commented. "All of our beers are made from the water sourced on our reservation." Featuring several beers and a tasting room, 3R now has two locations: Valley Center and Ocean Beach.

2020: The FireKeepers Casino and Hotel, owned by the Nottawaseppi Huron Band of the Potawatomi, became the first of 24 tribally owned gaming establishments in Michigan to open a sportsbook. Patrons of the Battle Creek casino can bet on a variety of professional sports at Dacey's Sportsbook & Taphouse.

2020: The Confederated Tribes of the Chehalis Reservation, home to members of the Chehalis, Klallam, Muckleshoot, Nisqually, and Quinault, was the first tribal entity to legally operate a distillery and produce bourbon, vodka, and gin in the United States. Named Talking Cedar after the iconic trees, it is situated in a 35,000-square-foot complex and includes a restaurant, brewery, and the largest liquor distillery in Washington state.

2020: The Prairie Island Indian Community (Mdewakanton Sioux) began a three-year plan to become the first Native net-zero emissions community in Minnesota, operating on renewable energy only.

2020: The Pamunkey Indian Tribe of Virginia signed a development agreement with the City of Norfolk to build Virginia's first casino and hotel.

2020: The Agua Caliente Resort Casino Spa Rancho Mirage was the only casino property in California to win three Forbes Four-Star Awards at the same time.

2020: A Seattle Seahawks–themed table game pit was the latest collaboration between the NFL team and Snoqualmie Casino in Washington. It is the first casino to contract an official partnership with the Seattle franchise following the Supreme Court's 2018 decision to overthrow the Professional and Amateur Sports Protection Act of 1992 and the NFL's subsequent decision to allow NFL franchises to partner with casinos.

2021: Angel of the Winds Casino Resort contracted to be the exclusive casino partner of the Seattle Storm of the Women's National Basketball Association (WNBA), the first such collaboration in the team's history. While its regular home, the Climate Pledge Arena in Seattle, was closed for renovations in 2019, the Storm played five of its games at the Angel of the Winds Arena, owned by the Stillaguamish Tribe in Everett, Washington.

2021: The Nambé Pueblo, just north of Santa Fe, New Mexico, partnered with the Tesla Company to open a service center on its land. A defunct casino was repurposed into a gleaming building that attracts customers from around the state to the only Tesla store in New Mexico. Carlos Vigil, president of the Nambé Pueblo Development Corporation, called Tesla's Service Center "a renewable business that lines up with our belief system."

INDIVIDUALLY OWNED BUSINESSES

"We are far more powerful when we are united, supporting and encouraging one another as Native entrepreneurs, and as Native people buying the goods and services of other Native people…. We stand to become the partners and allies that we have been looking for."

—Carmen Davis, Makah Nation/Chippewa-Cree/Yakama, publisher of Native Business Magazine, president of Davis Strategy Group, and owner of Native Style

c. 1890s: Wallace Altaha, White Mountain Apache, was known as the most successful Apache cattle rancher. As a young man, he obtained a beef contract from the military

Jackson Barnett is shown here with his wife while visiting Washington, D.C., in 1923.

The First Native American Millionaire (Who Never Was)

Jackson Barnett was born in 1856, almost 20 years after the Muscogee Creek tribe had been forcibly removed from its Georgia and Alabama homelands to Indian Territory (present-day Oklahoma). His first language was Muskogee Creek, but he became a fluent English speaker. Like many other Creek, Barnett supported himself any way he could. He was a ferryman, a cowboy, and sometimes a bootlegger. He sustained a serious leg and head injury while herding cattle, and witnesses reported that it left Barnett in constant pain and "a bit slow." He most probably suffered the effects of a traumatic brain injury (TBI). In spite of Barnett's disability, he was well-liked and known for his kindness and hard work.

The U.S. government did not honor its promises to not interfere with the lifeways and cultures of the tribal nations it removed to Indian Territory beginning in the early 1800s. Although Indian Territory was supposed to remain in Indian control according to treaties and as compensation for tribal lands taken away in the East, it did not. Following the Civil War, intense pressure was put on tribes to give up their land, their governments, their religions, and their traditional ways. The plan was to convert Natives to Christianity and turn them into individual farmers instead of communal farming communities. Individualism, rather than tribalism, was espoused.

Indians did not agree. In 1897, the Crazy Snakes, a Creek group, advocated for retaining traditional ways, including common ownership of land and a government in-

The First Native American Millionaire (Who Never Was) (contd.)

dependent of the United States. The Americans sent in the cavalry and incarcerated 100 traditionalists. Five years later the Crazy Snakes gathered at the Hickory Ground, a sacred area. Again the government intruded; officials arrested the participants and cut off their long hair. Although Barnett was not arrested in either raid, he was a Crazy Snakes sympathizer. He, like other Creeks, protested the breaking up of Creek lands by refusing to take an allotment. The government went ahead anyway and assigned each Creek a 160-acre allotment, best for "growing rocks." Although Indians were given private parcels, the U.S. government deemed them as incompetent, and they became "wards of the state." They were not allowed to make their own decisions regarding any part of their finances and property. Both the federal government and the Oklahoma courts appointed guardians when valuable resources such as oil or natural gas were discovered on Creek allotments.

In 1912, the Department of the Interior approved oil leases on Jackson Barnett's property; soon the wells earned him a monthly royalty of $15,000. Because he was a ward of the government, the money was collected by the Department of the Interior and deposited into his Individual Indian Money (IIM) account. Barnett was only allowed a few hundred dollars a year; his growing fortune was managed by the Department of the Interior and later the Bureau of Indian Affairs (BIA). Indian agents did not allow Natives to buy labor-saving devices as they wanted them to do hard manual labor instead of living off their royalties. To access the money in their IIM accounts, Indians had to prove they really needed the money and that it wasn't going to be spent on something "foolish" or labor-saving.

The press labeled Jackson Barnett as the World's Richest Indian and told the story of his limited "allowance" doled out sparingly by the government, partly because he was a bachelor. As his millions accumulated in the Treasury Department, many people became interested in spending his fortune for him. The First Baptist Church of Henryetta showed up for donations. Barnett was neither literate nor a Christian but still signed a document giving the building church fund $25,000, which the BIA approved. The door opened widely as charities rushed in to secure millions that were of no benefit to Indians. The commissioner of Indian Affairs was a Baptist who helped church groups obtain donations from oil-wealthy Natives.

Anna Lowe, a 39-year-old non-Indian, set her sights on Barnett and seduced him into eloping to Kansas. The marriage was opposed by both the BIA and the Baptist Church. However, if they argued that the marriage should be annulled because Barnett was not mentally competent to make such a decision, then they could be scrutinized for the riches he had unwittingly signed away to them. A Kansas court upheld the marriage.

The First Native American Millionaire (Who Never Was) (contd.)

The U.S. government hired a private investigator to expose Lowe's reputation; the report depicted Barnett's bride as a prostitute, blackmailer, and con woman. When harassed about his marriage, Barnett replied, "Indians get married like other people. Why don't you let us alone?"

Lowe rallied to get Barnett's monthly allowance increased. She wanted an extravagant lifestyle, and the couple purchased a large home in California, where he would stand in the street and direct tourist traffic. This was one of several activities that branded him as an eccentric.

The BIA objected to Barnett spending his money on his wife rather than the church charities it had approved. In 1926, Barnett was seized by U.S. marshals and the Secret Service. His wife told the press that her husband had been kidnapped in a gross abuse of power by the Justice Department. Barnett was taken back to Oklahoma against his will, where he was finally released to his wife's custody. The millionaire was harassed and treated like a criminal. Federal agents again kidnapped him in broad daylight on Muskogee's principal street; again the courts released him into the custody of his wife.

In 1927, Oklahoma judge John C. Knox struck down the government-established trust for the Creek millionaire, citing the years of Barnett's abuse at the hands of the government, charities, and his wife. He had been swindled out of $1,100,000. The judge found that the rationale by the Department of the Interior in creating the trust for Barnett did not justify its redistribution of his money.

The BIA, the state of Oklahoma, and the Baptist Church fought a long and loud legal struggle for control of Barnett's money. He remained calm and amiable as he sat through the numerous court and congressional hearings listening to people degrade him. Despite Barnett's loyalty to his wife, the BIA finally succeeded in getting his marriage annulled in 1934 on the grounds that because of diminished mental capacity, he had selected an inappropriate bride. Lowe was ordered to return all property she had gained through marriage. Soon after, Barnett died in his sleep of heart disease at 78. The BIA refused to release his money to purchase a marble headstone for his grave.

Almost a thousand people claimed a portion of Barnett's estate, and the court proceedings filled 25 volumes and lasted for five years. The judge refused to consider the Creek custom of matrilineality, imposing his own belief in patriarchal inheritance. In his lifetime, Jackson Barnett only used 15 percent of his wealth. Only 25 percent of his fortune was distributed among his heirs as determined by the court, 30 percent went to lawyers, and the remainder just disappeared.

base located at Fort Apache in Arizona and bought land near the fort to have his herds nearby. By 1901, Altaha's R-14 brand was the main supplier to butchers in the Southwest. He grew to be wealthy but was generous and taught many other Indians the trade.

1958: Virginia Ali (1933–), Rappahannock, and her husband, Ben, opened Ben's Chili Bowl in Washington, D.C. This first Native-owned eatery became one of the city's most iconic restaurants serving locals as well as tourists from around the world. It was frequented by both police and protesters during the 1968 Washington, D.C., uprising; Presidents Barack Obama and George W. Bush; and dozens of celebrities, including Anthony Bourdain, Serena Williams, Bono, and Chris Tucker. In 2007, the owners led a coalition of ten small local businesses to broker a deal with a local energy company to convert operations to 100 percent wind energy, another first.

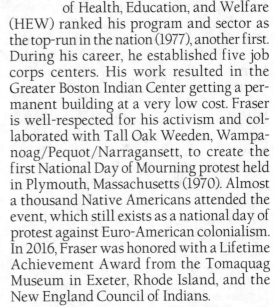

Virginia Ali

1959: Kenneth Stanley "Bud" Adams Jr. (1923–2013), Cherokee, became the first Native American to found and own a football league—the American Football League (AFL). He was also the first Native to own a National Football League franchise—the Tennessee Titans (originally the Houston Oilers). Adams was also an owner of the Houston Mavericks of the American Basketball Association.

c.1960s: Christine "Nunny" Ruben (1910–1989), Karok, was the first Native American to own an FTD florist shop. Based in California, she won national and international awards for her artistry with floral arrangements.

1969: Jim Fraser, Cherokee/Edisto and a long-term federal employee, was appointed as the first director of the Office of Special Programs, Employment and Training Administration (ETA), U.S. Department of Labor (DOL), Region 1. He negotiated grant contracts for Northeast tribes and was the first DOL representative to the first Federal Regional Council Indian Task Force. He arranged for Northeast Native Youth to attend Talking Leaves (Oklahoma) and Kicking Horse (Montana) Job Corps Centers for the first time. Fraser helped create the Massachusetts Commission for Indian Affairs and rallied for more DOL services for tribes. He was first to supervise a Work Incentive Program (WIN) unit. Representatives from the DOL and the Department of Health, Education, and Welfare (HEW) ranked his program and sector as the top-run in the nation (1977), another first. During his career, he established five job corps centers. His work resulted in the Greater Boston Indian Center getting a permanent building at a very low cost. Fraser is well-respected for his activism and collaborated with Tall Oak Weeden, Wampanoag/Pequot/Narragansett, to create the first National Day of Mourning protest held in Plymouth, Massachusetts (1970). Almost a thousand Native Americans attended the event, which still exists as a national day of protest against Euro-American colonialism. In 2016, Fraser was honored with a Lifetime Achievement Award from the Tomaquag Museum in Exeter, Rhode Island, and the New England Council of Indians.

1972: ACKCO, Inc., named for the initials of its Navajo founders, was launched and was the first Indian-owned business to offer a vast array of professional services like conference planning, personnel training, tribal infrastructure development, and tribal health services. It is based in Phoenix, Arizona.

1972: Momi Cazimero, Native Hawaiian, a renowned graphic artist, founded Graphic

House, Inc., the first graphic arts firm owned by a woman in Honolulu. In addition to Cazimero's trailblazing business accomplishments, she is known for volunteering countless hours of service to her community, having served on the Hawaii State Judicial Selection Commission, on the University Community Partnership, and as the vice chairperson of the University of Hawaii Board of Regents.

1977:   Kane S. Fernandez (1938–2001), Native Hawaiian, received the newly created 'Ō'ō Award presented to Native Hawaiians who have made significant contributions to the advancement of the Native Hawaiian community. He inherited the showman's mantle from his late father, E. K. Fernandez, who introduced movies, carnivals, circuses, and Wild West shows to Hawaii and propelled the family business into a multimillion-dollar industry. Fernandez was called the King of the Carnival Midway.

1978:   Frank Bonamie (1951–), an enrolled member of the Cayuga Indian Nation of New York, established the Ongweoweh Corporation in Ithaca, New York, the first Cayuga-owned business in the area. Ongweoweh Corp. is a management company providing pallet and packaging procurement, recycling services, and supply-chain optimization programs. It has grown to be one of the most successful privately owned Native American companies in the country. Bonamie was a founder and supporter of Cornell University's American Indian and Indigenous Program.

1980:   Mary "Smoki" Fraser, Rappahannock, joined the Human Resources Department of textbook publisher D. C. Heath and Company in Lexington, Massachusetts. She became the first Native person to serve as senior human resources administrator for 350 employees for Heath and in 1995 for Houghton Mifflin Company in Boston, also a first.

She serves on the Diversity and Inclusion Committee of the New England Deaconess Association.

1988:   Richard Mike (c. 1941–), Navajo, established the first Burger King franchise on the Navajo Reservation in Kayenta, Arizona. The restaurant features a Code Talker Museum in honor of Mike's father, King Mike, a Navajo Code Talker.

1993:   Iron Eagle Environmental Services debuted in Wantagh, New York, the first Native-owned company in New York State to provide remediation services for environmental hazards like asbestos. Founder and CEO Benedict Peter Reyes (1945–2013), Oklahoma Creek, was known for his community service.

1994:   Dave Anderson (1953–), Chippewa/Choctaw, founded the first Famous Dave's BBQ Shack in Hayward, Wisconsin. A year later, the restaurant was the first-place winner for its Rich and Sassy BBQ sauce at the American Royal Barbecue Sauce Contest held in Kansas City, Missouri—the most prestigious barbecue competition in the world. Since then, Anderson's restaurants have amassed many other awards; as of 2018, there are over 180 Famous Dave's Restaurants in 37 states. Anderson also served as assistant secretary of the interior for Indian affairs from 2004 to 2005.

1994:   Kevin Thornton, Cherokee, started KP Gaming Supplies, Inc. in California, supplying Indian casinos with high-quality gaming supplies. A former "hotshot" wildland firefighter for the U.S. Forest Service, he sustained an injury in 1992 that ended his career. He started making tables, eventually creating special gaming furniture, and developed a lucrative market selling to Indian casinos.

1995:   J. C. Seneca, Seneca, built the Native Pride Plaza and Tallchief Territory, the first travel center on the Seneca Reservation in Irving, New York. The 50-acre property sports a smoke shop, gas station, high-speed diesel pumps, and a diner. Seneca developed his own brand of cigarettes, Buffalo Cigarettes, produced at his Six Nations Manufacturing tobacco plant. In 2020, he was named the *Native Business Magazine* Entrepreneur of the Year and was featured in the 2021 Business First Power 250, a list of Buffalo's most powerful businesspeople.

1996: Rebecca L. Adamson, Cherokee, founder and president of the First Nations Development Institute, was honored with the Robert W. Scrivner Award for Creative Grantmaking by the Council of Foundations. It was the first award to recognize Adamson's framework for Indigenous economic strategies that include traditional knowledge and values. She also received the Jay Silverheels Achievement Award from the National Center for American Indian Enterprise Development for her work in Native communities the same year.

1996: Bill McClure, Muscogee Creek, became the first Native American to own a coffee company. He and his daughter, Ellie, were also the first Indians to have an online coffee company when they started Coffee.org in 2008. The Arkansas business employs mostly Native Americans; customers include the Muscogee (Creek) Nation, airlines, Campbell's Soup, several Fortune 500 companies, hospitals, and hotels.

1998: Valerie Red-Horse (1959–), Cherokee, founded the first female Native-owned investment bank, now called Red-Horse Securities, to assist tribes in raising capital. She is also an award-winning writer/director/actor and has her own company, Red-Horse Native Productions, Inc. Based in Los Angeles, Red-Horse serves on the Texas Cherokee Tribal Council.

1998: Native Vines Winery, located in Lexington, North Carolina, was incorporated by Darlene Gabbard, Lumbee. It is the first wine business in the nation owned by a Native American.

1998: Inventor Thomas David Petite (1956–), Fond du Lac Band of Lake Superior Chippewa, started StatSignal Systems, Inc. (now known as SIPCO, LLC), the first company to patent and introduce wireless mesh technology (SMART CLOUD) to the utility and health care industries. With over a hundred patented inventions, he is best known for developing wireless mesh technology and the networking, remote control, activation, and monitoring of wireless enabled devices.

1998: Loretta Barrett Oden (1932–), Citizen Potawatomi Nation, and her son, Chef Clayton Oden, opened the Corn Dance Cafe in Santa Fe, New Mexico. It was deemed the first restaurant west of the Mississippi to showcase the bounty of indigenous foods. Oden is also known for her five-part PBS television series, *Seasoned with Spirit: A Native Cook's Journey.*

1999: Hui Ku Maoli Ola, owned by Native Hawaiians Matthew Schirman and Richard Barboza, set up shop in Kāne'ohe, Hawai'i. It was the first nursery to repatriate Indigenous Hawaiian plants and sell to stores like Home Depot. Hui Ku Maoli Ola largely acts as a wholesaler, supplying native plant material for large developments and government projects. Their services also include habitat restoration, alien species removal, site planning, and out-planting of special materials. Ongoing restoration projects are located in Kalaeloa, Hamakua Marsh, Waimanalo Stream, and Kahana Pond on Maui.

2000: Alex White Plume (1952–), Oglala Sioux, was the only farmer to openly plant, cultivate, and produce industrial hemp crops within the borders of the United States following the crop's prohibition by federal antidrug laws in 1968. Hemp products could be sold in the United States, but not cultivated. Although hemp is related to cannabis, it does not have psychoactive properties and is in demand worldwide for a variety of uses, including cloth and food. From 2000 to 2002, U.S. Drug Enforcement Administration (DEA) agents destroyed White Plume's industrial hemp crop before he could harvest it for seed. White Plume believed that since he was a member of a sovereign nation and lived on the Pine Ridge Reservation, he was exempt from the antihemp laws. He and his extended family tried growing alfalfa, barley, and corn; they also tried to raise horses and bison, but the reservation's poor agricultural lands and harsh climate were impediments. Hemp is a sustainable product with a short growing season, and during World War II, the U.S. government encouraged its cultivation for qualities of "hardiness, utility and low cost." White Plume lost his case against the DEA, but eventually the movement to legalize and decriminalize marijuana worked in his favor. Today Alex White Plume produces his own line of extracts and is optimistic that the hemp industry can bring prosperity to the people on the Pine Ridge Reservation, which is located in the poorest counties in the United States.

2000: Oweesta became the first national Native institution to be certified as a Community Development Financial Institutions (CDFI) Fund intermediary through the U.S. Department of the Treasury, dedicated to providing technical assistance, training, research, and lending in every state for Native CDFIs.

2000: Sam McCracken, Assiniboine/Sioux, a former high school basketball coach, became the manager of Nike's Native American Program and developed a plan for building re-lationships between Nike and the 250 Indian tribes that had received diabetes education grants and 188 schools that are enrolled in the Office of Indian Education Programs (OIEP). Nike's program collaborates with Indian Health Service (IHS) and the National Indian Health Board (NIHB) on their "Just Move It" program, which promotes physical fitness on reservations. McCracken received Nike's Bowerman Award (2004), which honors the Nike employee who best exemplifies the legacy of tireless motivation, innovation, and inspiration.

2000: Victoria Vasques, Diegueno of the San Pasqual Band of Mission Indians, started her management and technical services company, Tribal Tech, in the Washington, D.C., metro area. To date, she is the only Native businesswoman to receive over 15 awards for her business practices, and Tribal Tech has more than any other Native business and possibly the most for any business. Some of her awards are *Inc.* 5000 Fastest Growing Company (seven years in a row), named to the *Inc. Magazine* 5000 Hall of Fame, 4th Fastest Growing Women-Led Companies in D.C., 50 Fastest-Growing Women-Owned/Led Companies in America (two years in a row); and *Financial Times* 500 Fastest Growing Companies in the Americas (2020).

Douglas Miles

2001: Apache Skateboards was started by San Carlos Apache-Aki-mel/O'odham painter, printmaker, and photographer Douglas Miles, on the San Carlos Apache Reservation in Arizona. It was the first company to offer Indigenous art on skateboards. Miles also founded the Apache Skateboard Team, which gives demonstrations on reservations across the country. The business's success has gone beyond skateboards, and Miles has worked in film, photography, fine art, skateboarding, murals, multimedia projects, community projects, skate park planning, skateboard events, apparel design, television, film, youth conferences, and speaking engagements. The company produced a documentary, *Walk Like a Warrior: The Apache Skateboards Story* in 2008. Apache Skateboards collaborated with iPath Footwear to create the I-PACHE collection of sneakers, fitted hats, and T-shirts, featuring Miles's original designs.

2002: Stephen M. Mills, Chumash, launched AQIWO (Chumash word for "shooting star"), the first Chumash-owned securities company. He calls himself an "Indianpreneur" and uses traditional Indigenous values to operate his successful Virginia-based business.

2004: Kekuli Cafe was launched by Sharon Bond-Hogg, Nlaka'pamux Territory, Nooaitch Indian Band, Merritt, British Columbia, and her husband, Darren Hogg, in West Kelowna, British Columbia. It was one of the first First Nations cafes in Canada. It later became the first Canadian Indigenous restaurant franchise. It's known for its slogan "Don't panic ... we have bannock!" (Bannock is a type of bread native to Indigenous Canadians.)

2004: Henry Red Cloud, Lakota, started Lakota Solar Enterprises on the Pine Ridge Reservation in South Dakota to manufacture solar heaters and alternative energy and conservation devices. It is the first renewable energy business fully owned and operated by Native Americans.

2004: Wade Burns, Comanche, established Beaver Creek Archaeology, Inc. in Bismarck, North Dakota, with a novel idea in mind. The company preserves the Indigenous cultural material and history of the area while helping alternative energy, mining, and transportation projects move forward. Its services include archaeological inventories,

digital solutions, historic preservation, preservation compliance, interpretive planning, and architectural history.

2006: Bethel, Alaska, triplets Michelle, Amy, and Cika Sparck, Cup'ik, started ArXotica, the first skincare company owned by Alaskan Native women. They develop healthy, award-winning skin products from tundra medicinal plants in southwest Alaska.

2006: Gelvin Stevenson (1944–), Oklahoma Cherokee Nation, was appointed manager of international business development for AgriPower, Inc. He is the only Native to ever be in a managerial position for the company, which manufactures and sells a clean, safe, biomass combustion technology that generates heat and electricity from a wide range of organic waste. It operates in the United States, Asia, Africa, and Latin America. Stevenson was also the first Native financial advisor for the Oneida Tribe of Indians of Wisconsin, the first Native to teach environmental economics in Pratt Institute's Sustainable Environmental Systems program, and the first Native to earn a doctorate in economics from Washington University in St. Louis, Missouri. He serves on the boards of First Nations Development Institute and

Dr. Gelvin Stevenson; his wife, Dr. Clara Rodriguez; and their children, Gelvina and Jose

the Cherokee National Historical Society and lives in New York City.

2006: Laura Clelland opened Salt Woman, LLC in Winslow, Arizona, becoming the first Navajo to operate a professional foot service business. She also may be the first Native person to be certified in pedorthics; her practice offers holistic treatment for issues from diabetes, fungal infections, and other foot maladies.

2008: Eighth Generation was launched by designer Louie Gong, Nooksack, known for his vibrant Native designs on Vans Sneakers, in Seattle, Washington. The company eventually became the first Native-owned business to produce high-end wool blankets featuring stunning Indigenous designs. Considered one of the fastest growing Native companies, Eighth Generation and Gong have received numerous awards. In 2019, Gong sold the business to the Snoqualmie Indian Tribe and remained the CEO.

2008: Métis entrepreneur Sean McCormick had no intention of creating an international business. But when celebrities like Kate Moss and Megan Fox were photographed in his calf-high, fur-trimmed mukluks, customers demanded the boots, and Manitobah Mukluks was born and soon became the fastest growing footwear line in Canada. High-end retailers such as Holt Renfrew and Nordstrom stocked Manitobah Mukluks products, and in 2013, McCormick moved his business operations to a 40,000-square-foot building on Métis-owned land in Winnipeg, Manitoba, producing over 4,000 pairs a year. The company's Storyboot Project seeks Indigenous mukluk makers across the country to create original shoes; artisans receive 100 percent of the profits.

2008: Native American Natural Foods introduced its first food product, the Tanka Bar. Based on traditional wasna and pemmican recipes, the Tanka Bar combines high-protein, prairie-fed buffalo and tart-sweet cranberries. Karlene Hunter and Mark Tilsen founded the company on Hunter's homelands, the Pine Ridge Indian Reservation in South Dakota.

2009: Regina Lettau, Coeur d'Alene, launched NNAC, a specialty contracting construction firm geared toward serving military installations and federal customers nationwide. She is the first Idaho Native woman, and possibly the first Native U.S. woman, to do so. Headquartered in Coeur d'Alene, Idaho, NNAC serves customers nationwide.

2009: Jessica Metcalfe, Turtle Mountain Band of Chippewa Indians, established Beyond Buckskin, a company dedicated to promoting Native artists and original designers. As the business grew, she extended micro-loans to Native artists for materials. In 2018, Metcalfe launched the first-ever Native subscription box service, Club BB; subscribers receive a monthly delivery of Native hand-produced products.

2010: Margo Gray-Proctor, Citizen of the Osage Nation, was elected to chair the National Center for American Indian Enterprise Development, which represents thousands of business owners. She was the first woman to serve in the position. Gray-Proctor is the president of the Horizon Engineering Services Company, a certified 8(a) SBA, award-winning, Native American, and woman-owned civil engineering firm.

2010: Virginia Boone's Medicine of the People was the first Native-owned skin care company featured in Whole Foods. Products are created from Boone's herbal knowledge and sold internationally as well as in the United States. She is Navajo.

2011: NativeOne Institutional Trading LLC became the first Native-owned business admitted to the New York Stock Exchange. The California financial firm offers services and products to tribal nations in the United States and Canada in many areas: investors, state treasurers, pension funds, and endowments.

2011: Off the Rez, the first Native food truck in Seattle, Washington, was opened by owners Mark McConnell, Blackfeet Nation, and Cecilia Rikard. The award-winning business features fry bread tacos and other choices on the menu. Off the Rez Café, the first brick-and-mortar location, opened at Seattle's Burke Museum of Natural History and Culture at the University of Washington on October 12, 2019.

2011: Safe and Secure Products Inc. was created after inventor Brad Rousseau, Turtle Mountain Chippewa, designed the Easy Lifter, a device that attaches to a wheelchair for easy transportation. Easy Lifter helps caregivers safely lift people with mobility impairments and gives them greater safety and freedom of movement, particularly in case of an emergency.

2012: The Google American Indian Network (GAIN), led by Kris Easton, Cherokee, hosted the first summit of Native leaders, educators, and policy makers to discuss how Google can help technology in Indian country. The gathering resulted in the creation of a technology task force at the National Congress of American Indians (NCAI), acknowledging that Natives need deeper engagement and influence in technology application and development. Easton joined Google in 2011 and resurrected GAIN, a group of Native employees that influences products built by Google and leverages Google's tools to assist Native peoples, like the inclusion of Indian lands on Google Maps (2014) and support for Indigenous languages with help from Google linguists and translation engineers. Under Easton's leadership, connections have

been established with other Native organizations in the business world: IBM Amazon (Indigenous Network); Facebook (Native@); and Salesforce (WindForce).

2012: Symbiotic Aquaponic, LLC was founded by Choctaw brothers Kaben and Shelby Smallwood in Oklahoma. They combined their years of farming experience, keen understanding of traditional agricultural practices, respect for the Earth, and education to design and build aquaponic farming systems for individuals, tribes, communities, schools, and commercial operations. USDA-certified organic foods are produced with a 99 percent decrease in farming water. *Native Business Magazine* placed the company on its list of top Native-owned businesses (2019).

2012: The Fry Bread House in Phoenix, Arizona, was the first Native restaurant to win a James Beard Foundation American Classic Award, one of only five restaurants chosen that year. Cecilia Miller, Tohono O'odham, opened the eatery in 1992 and serves up a variety of Native American staples from traditional stews to "Indian" tacos using fry bread. In 2005, South Dakota governor Mike Rounds approved a bill designating fry bread as the state's official bread. Supporters said it was time for South Dakota to officially recognize a symbol of American Indian culture.

2012: Wahpepah's Kitchen was opened by Chef Crystal Wahpepah, Kickapoo Nation of Oklahoma, becoming the first Native woman-owned catering company in California. Traditional and holistic Indigenous foods are served. Wahpepah was also the first Native American to appear on the Food Network show *Chopped* (2016).

2012: Robert J. Miller, Eastern Shawnee Tribe, published *Reservation "Capitalism": Economic Development in Indian Country,* an In-

The Fry Bread House in Phoenix, Arizona, was the first Native restaurant to win a James Beard Foundation American Classic Award.

dian perspective on the economy. He contends that Native people need to find their way home financially by returning to their economic cultural roots. An attorney and professor, Miller's areas of expertise are civil procedure, federal Indian law, American Indians and international law, American Indian economic development, and Native American natural resources. He is the chief justice of the Court of Appeals of the Confederacy of Grand Ronde Tribe in Oregon.

2013: Inspired by the Indigenous-led movement "Idle No More," Joey Montoya, Lipan Apache from San Francisco, started Urban Native Era (UNE) to increase visibility of Native peoples and issues. UNE has grown into an internationally recognized clothing and music brand employing green business practices and sustainability. Its products have been featured in *Vogue* and *Cosmopolitan*.

2014: Big Elk Energy Systems, LLC was founded by Geoff Hager, Osage, in Tulsa, Oklahoma. The pipeline equipment manufacturing company is situated in its 140,000-square-foot, 12-acre headquarters. Hager commented, "I am opposed to pipeline infrastructure being laid anywhere that does damage to Indigenous people."

2014: Trickster Company was founded by Tlingit artist Rico Worl in Juneau, Alaska. He started with his hand-painted skateboards and a Kickstarter campaign that funded a deck of playing cards designed with Northwest Coast formline art. Rico's sister, Crystal Worl, became his business partner, and in 2020 the company became part of the National Parks new platform, "Meet the Artisans," a program featuring artists in communities near national parks. "We preserve and celebrate Northwest formline art, a prestigious and distinctive artform," Rico commented, "to explore themes and issues in Native culture in fresh and creative ways that celebrate how Northwest culture is lived today."

2015: Mike Mabin (1959–), Chippewa/Métis, created Shutter Pilots, Inc., an aerial imaging company specializing in using unmanned aircraft systems (UAS), known as drones, to capture photographs and video footage. It was the country's first business to receive a 333 exemption from the Federal Aviation Administration (FAA) to operate UAS for the purpose of aerial imaging and computer animation to provide two-dimensional and three-dimensional visualization services. Shutter Pilots' first client was *National Geographic* for a project featuring aerial footage of the Prairie Pothole Region of the Great Plains. The Harlem Globetrotters hired Shutter Pilots to document record-breaking Anthony "Buckets" Blakes making a 242-foot shot from the top of the North Dakota State Capitol in Bismarck (2017), another first. In 2001, Mabin founded Agency MABU, a marketing/consulting firm providing clients with a vast array of services from branding to marketing strategies; the National Congress of American Indians (NCAI) is one of its biggest clients.

2015: Stephanie Conduff (1980–), Cherokee, needed to have privacy in a public place to pump breast milk. The dilemma inspired her to create the Leche Lounge, a modular and portable lactation station. An attorney for the Cherokee Nation, Conduff now focuses on her lucrative business with both American and international customers. Her 30 Cherokee staff members produce the 36-square-foot modules made of food-grade materials; they are also ADA-accessible for wheelchairs. Some lactation suites are equipped with a multiuser, hospital-grade breast pump.

Aaron Thomas

2016: Metcon, started by Aaron Thomas, Lumbee, president and CEO, completed construction of the first energy-positive building in the Carolinas—the Lumbee River Electric Membership Corporation (LREMC) North Center in Raeford, North Carolina. Metcon is headquartered in Pembroke, North Carolina with regional offices in Raleigh, Charlotte, and Fayetteville, North Carolina; Columbia, South Carolina; and Oxon Hill, Maryland, serving the D.C. and Maryland area. Metcon has been recognized by the U.S. Department of Commerce as the 2011 and 2013 U.S. Minority Construction Firm of the Year, and the *Engineering News and Record* awarded its school projects as the Best K–12 Projects in the U.S. for 2013, 2016, and 2018.

2017: Yahuaca Knowledge Distribution, LLC was launched by Adrian and Michael Lerma, Navajo, based in Tsaile, Arizona. It is the first Arizona Native-owned company to offer "rez tested, grandma approved" affordable solar products for Diné (Navajo) and Kisaani (Hopi) families who live off-grid.

2017: Red Planet Books and Comics opened its doors in Albuquerque, New Mexico. According to owner Lee Francis 4, Laguna Pueblo, head "Indigenerd" and CEO of Native Realities, Red Planet is the only Indigenous

Love's Travel Stops & Country Stores comprise a huge chain that can be found along highways and freeways across the United States.

A Billionaire's "Love" Story

Thomas E. Love (1937–), Chickasaw, is the owner, founder, and executive chairman of Love's Travel Stops & Country Stores. Most customers who patronize the hundreds of Love's locations have no idea that America's 17th largest private company is Native-owned.

In 1964, Tom Love and his wife, Judy, borrowed $5,000 from her parents to lease an abandoned gas station in Watonga, Oklahoma. The venture was successful, and Love went on to open another 30 gas stations. In 1971, he came up with a unique idea. Until then, gas stations only sold gas, and Love thought that there was an opportunity to open small food stores connected to the gas stations. That way, while filling up the tank, customers could be filling up on snacks. Love also created self-service gas stations and merged them with convenience stores, usually open 24 hours. He is responsible for the first known gas-station mini-mart.

The corporation, headquartered in Oklahoma City, has acquired other businesses and has grown into the Love's Family of Companies. Its operations include the Musket Corporation, which specializes in commodity supply, trading, and logistics across North America and handles billions of gallons of crude oil, natural gas liquids (NGL), natural gas, petroleum products, and renewable fuels. Its Gemini Motor Transport operates a fleet of more than 1,050 trucks supplying fuel to Love's locations nationwide and ethanol to terminals throughout the United States and remains one of the industry's safest transportation companies. In 2016, the company purchased Trillium, a leading provider of alternative fueling solutions, specializing in fuel supply, design, installation, and operation for innovation energy solutions. Combined, Love's and

A Billionaire's "Love" Story (contd.)

Trillium own 65 public-access compressed natural gas facilities. The subsidiary Speedco offers comprehensive lube, tire, and light mechanical services for professional drivers. Love's and Speedco make up the largest oil change and preventative maintenance nationwide network on the road today with more than 400 locations. For over 25 years, Speedco has been a leader in lube services and high-speed preventative maintenance (PM) services at highway locations across the United States and provides professional truck drivers and motorists with 24-hour access to clean and safe places to purchase gasoline, diesel fuel, compressed natural gas (CNG), travel items, electronics, snacks, restaurant offerings, and more. Love's Truck Care offers heavy-duty tire care, including TirePass, light mechanical services, and roadside assistance. Love's Hospitality offers an increasing number of hotels and storage rental locations, and Love's Financial offers freight bill factoring and back-office support to professional drivers. Love's Travel Stops & Country Stores has more than 550 locations in 41 states, employs 32,000 people, and has estimated annual revenues of $20.6 billion. The business remains family-operated. Tom is Love's chairman, Judy is the executive secretary, and three of their four children work in the company. Love and his wife have also been leaders in philanthropy, and between personal donations and corporate giving, they have supported institutions of higher education as well as local charities across the country. Since 1999, they have partnered with the Children's Miracle Network, raising more than $28 million for children's medical research. Tom Love's many accomplishments also include induction into the Chickasaw Hall of Fame (2019); the 2000 Outlook Award for innovation and outstanding contribution to the future of the convenience store industry; *Forbes Magazine* rank of No. 9 on its list of America's largest private companies (2012); and the acquisition of 20 Pilot Travel Centers locations and six Flying J locations (2010). According to 2018 U.S. Census data, the highest poverty rate by group is found among Native Americans, so it is a rare occurrence that Native entrepreneur Tom Love placed 61 on *Forbes'* list of richest Americans.

comic shop in the world. He hopes to change the perceptions of Native people through dynamic and imaginative pop culture representations. The store boasts an array of comics, books, games, toys, and collectibles for all the Indigenerds in the crowd and is also the headquarters for both the Indigenous Comic Con and Wordcraft Circle of Native Writers and Storytellers.

2018: Airbnb teamed up with Utah in a first-of-its-kind partnership with a U.S. state for a project named Experiences. The Utah Office of Tourism and Airbnb offer "unique-to-Utah" events for tourists seeking off-the-beaten-path, authentic adventures. The partnership provides "micro-entrepreneurship opportunities" for knowledgeable locals (like members of Utah's five tribes) who sign up to host an Experience. Entrepreneur Carol Talus, Navajo, runs her Experiences venture in her own backyard. She guides clients on a 4.5-hour intermediate and interpretative hike through Monument Valley.

After the hike, Talus serves up a traditional Navajo meal in a hogan.

2018: Former firefighter Stephan Cheney (1990–) introduced his High Rez Wood Company, creating one-of-a-kind furniture pieces salvaged from burned trees. A member of the Kul Wicasa Oyate (Lower Brule Sioux) in South Dakota, Cheney lives in northern California, where he honors fallen trees by turning them into furniture art. He has created tables, benches, cutting boards, serving trays, spoons, paddles and eel hooks (a traditional fishing tool). Cheney donates some of his masterpieces to raise funds for Native causes.

2018: *Native Business Magazine* was founded by Carmen Davis, Makah/ Chippewa-Cree/Yakama, and Gary Davis, Cherokee. Based in Bellevue, Washington, it is the first 100 percent Native-owned-and-operated business magazine.

2018: Jason Cummings, Lumbee/Coharie, became the first Native director of the Process Development and Technology Department at Grifols, a global healthcare company specializing in bioscience. He earned a Ph.D. in chemical engineering from Princeton University (2007) and holds several patents in biotechnology and related fields.

2018: Teara Fraser, Métis, established Iskwew (Cree word for woman) Air, the first-ever Indigenous woman–owned airline in Canada. The company offers charter and destination flights from Vancouver International Airport. Fraser started Give Them Wings, a nonprofit organization that gives Indigenous youth the opportunity to explore what she calls a "career that's really cool" and to earn their pilot's wings, to both address the coming pilot crisis that she says is worsening and to give Indigenous people a path to prosperity.

2018: Mr. Bannock, the first Indigenous food truck in Vancouver, British Columbia, was launched by chef/owner Paul Natrall, Squamish Nation. Indian tacos, bannock calzones, waffle bannock, and a plant-based bowl were among the menu items. Heiltsuk artist KC Hall did the artwork on the Mr. Bannock food truck. Natrall, who trained in the Aboriginal cooking program at Vancouver Community College, had earlier launched a catering company, PR Bannock Factory. In 2012, he went to Germany as a member of Aboriginal Culinary Team Canada for the Culinary Olympics.

2019: Sacred Circle Gift Shop, owned and operated by United Indians of All Tribes Foundation, opened at Seattle-Tacoma International Airport. It is the first partnership between the Port of Seattle and an Indigenous group. The store offers authentic, Native-designed items from Northwest Coast and Coast Salish, including jewelry, clothing and accessories, art, glassware, and gifts.

2019: Sean Sherman (1974–), an Oglala Lakota Sioux chef and promoter of Indigenous cuisine, became the first Native American to win the prestigious James Beard Foundation Leadership Award. He is owner of the Sioux Chef, an Indigenous food education business and catering company and the nonprofit North American Traditional Indigenous Food Systems. Sherman's 2017 cookbook, *The Sioux Chef's Indigenous Kitchen*, won the 2018 James Beard Award for Best American Cookbook.

Sean Sherman

2019: Alexander Mabin (1989–), Chippewa/Métis, founded InnovatAR, Inc., the first Indigenous-owned-and-operated web-based augmented reality (AR) company. Mabin's user-friendly products are unlike other AR businesses, as they can be accessed without application downloads or custom hardware and are available to everyone. In 2020, InnovatAR launched Yondar, its proprietary software used for navigating outdoor events and attractions.

2019: Feather Bear LLC was registered in Tyonek, Alaska, as the first Native-owned company to focus on children's clothing. Through fashion, proprietor KC Elvis, Athabascan, seeks to be a cultural ambassador, helping teach children about meaningful traditions worldwide. Feather Bear offers graphic tee-shirts celebrating cultures around the globe.

2019: *Native Business Magazine* premiered the first-ever "Native Business Top 50 Entrepreneurs" issue in May. Entrepreneurs and businesses across the country are highlighted in the annual list.

2020: Carla F. Fredericks, Mandan/Hidatsa/Arikara of North Dakota, was named executive director of The Christensen Fund (TCF), becoming the first Native American to lead a nonprofit private foundation of its worth. Fredericks, an attorney, established and serves as director of First Peoples Worldwide at the University of Colorado, a cross-campus program that engages tribal leaders, Indigenous peoples, investors, companies, financial institutions, and policy makers to promote implementation of Indigenous rights.

Ahsaki

2020: *Gather*, a documentary about Native food sovereignty and entrepreneurship, premiered online (because of the pandemic). Produced by award-winning film director Sterlin Harjo, Seminole/Muskogee, and directed by Sanjay Rawal, *Gather* highlights the growing movement across Indigenous North America to reclaim sovereignty over their ancestral food systems and food economies.

2020: Kanatan Health Solutions Inc. was founded by a Canadian Plains Cree family based in Edmonton, Alberta. The company creates Indigenous-specific personal protective equipment, designed and formulated with natural traditional materials.

2020: Linda Marie Arredondo was named the first-ever chief information officer (CIO) at Express Employment Professionals. She also served as the director of information technology for her tribe, the Citizen Potawatomi Nation, where she provided IT leadership throughout all areas of the nation, including executive, government, and judicial branches, healthcare, enterprise, gaming, and hospitality.

2020: For the first time ever, *Harper's Bazaar* magazine featured a Native-owned cosmetics/skincare company, Ah-Shí Beauty. The upscale business is owned and operated by Ahsaki Báá LaFrance-Chachere, Navajo. Founded in 2018, Ah-Shí is the Diné phrase for "this is me" and "this is my beauty."

2020: Brian Decorah, Ho-Chunk, landed the position of general manager of Pechanga Resort Casino in southern California, becoming the first Native person to do so.

2020: Dawn Madahbee Leach, Aundeck Omni Kaning First Nation, was awarded an Indspire Award for Business and Commerce; she is the first Indigenous woman in Canada to head a commercial lending institution, Waubetek. "Waubetek" means "the future" in the Ojibwe language, a fitting name for the Aboriginal-owned-and-controlled financial institution that provides business services and commercial financing to Aboriginal businesses in a variety of industries across Ontario. Under Leach's leadership, the company has invested over $80 million in 3,600 First Nation companies with a 94 percent success rate. Leach also advocates globally for Indigenous economic development. She was named one of Canada's top 100 most powerful women by the Women's Executive Network (WXN), listed as a Trailblazer and Trendsetter in honor of women who are first in their field and who have made a great contribution to Canadian society. She was also a recipient of the Anishinabek Nation's Lifetime Achievement Award and the MNP-AFOA Canada Excellence in Aboriginal Leadership Award (2017).

2020: Women in Business New Brunswick (WBNB) launched Nujintuisga'tijig E'pijig ("Indigenous women salespeople or vendors" translated from Mi'kmaq), an online platform where Indigenous female entrepreneurs, vendors, and artisans can sell their traditional products, crafts, and artworks. Natasha Martin-Mitchell from WBNB's development office hopes the platform will help counteract economic losses stemming from changes brought by COVID-19. The platform is exclusive to New Brunswick's Mi'kmaq and Wolastoqey communities.

FESTIVALS AND CONFERENCES

2004: The annual "Trading at the River" was initiated by the Oregon Native American Business and Entrepreneurial Network and takes place at the iconic Celilo Falls in Oregon, traditional trading area on the Columbia River. The agenda included networking opportunities, business support, and product exhibits.

2013: American Indian Alaska Native Tourism Association (AIANTA) launched its industry awards as part of its annual conference. The first "Enough Good People Award" for the Tribal Destination of the Year went to Cherokee Nation Cultural Tourism; Best Cultural Heritage Experience was awarded to the Chickasaw Cultural Center; and Dawn Melvin, Navajo/Hopi, won the Excellence in Customer Service category for her work with the Arizona Department of Tourism.

2018: Native Women's Business Summit was held in Albuquerque, New Mexico, and organized by Native Women Lead. It was the first and largest gathering of Native American female entrepreneurs in history.

ORGANIZATIONS

1969: The National Center for American Indian Enterprise Development (NCAIED) became the first national nonprofit corporation created and directed by American Indians whose sole purpose is to develop American Indian economic self-sufficiency through business ownership. NCAIED is based in Mesa, Arizona. It held its first annual Native American Economic Development Conference in 2007.

1974: The Native Hawaiian Chamber of Commerce was formed to meet the needs of Native Hawaiians struggling to open and maintain their own businesses with Indigenous values.

1974: The National American Indian Housing Council (NAIHC) was founded to support tribal housing entities in their efforts to provide safe, decent, affordable, and culturally appropriate housing for Native people by providing training and technical assistance and apprise Congress of tribal challenges with housing, infrastructure, and community development.

1975: The Council of Energy Resource Tribes (CERT), a consortium of Native American tribes in the United States, was established to increase tribal control over natural resources.

1980: The First Nations Development Institute began its mission to assist Native American tribes, their communities, and Native nonprofits in economic development by providing technical assistance, training, policy, and the awarding of grants. Its slogan is "Strengthening Native American Communities and Economies."

1986: Lakota Funds was established in Kyle, South Dakota, on the Pine Ridge Oglala Lakota Reservation. It became the best-known example of, and is thought to be the first, Native community development financial institution in the country. The number of businesses on the reservation grew from two to almost 400.

1987: The Intertribal Agriculture Council, headquartered in Billings, Montana, was founded to pursue and promote the conservation, development, and use of Native agricultural resources for the betterment of Indigenous communities.

1989: Indian Dispute Resolution Services, Inc. (IDRS, Inc.), a national nonprofit organization headquartered in Plymouth, California, was instituted by California Indian Legal Services, First Nations Development Institute, the Seventh Generation Fund, Northern Circle Indian Housing Authority, and Round Valley Indian Reservation to create sustainable Native communities throughout Indian Country, including Alaska and Hawaii. IDRS provides business coaching, the Side Hustle

Program (to train youth how to create a successful business), training for small farms operations, and dispute resolution skills.

1990: Joel M. Frank, Seminole, became the first commissioner to head the National Indian Gaming Commission (NIGC). NIGC's primary purpose is to work within the framework created by the Indian Gaming Regulatory Act (IGRA) for the regulation of gaming activities conducted by sovereign Indian tribes on Indian lands to fully realize IGRA's goals: (1) promoting tribal economic development, self-sufficiency, and strong tribal governments; (2) maintaining the integrity of the Indian gaming industry; and (3) ensuring that tribes are the primary beneficiaries of their gaming activities.

1994: The American Indian Business Leaders (AIBL) was organized to support and promote the education and development of future Indigenous business leaders and is based on the University of Montana campus in Missoula.

1995: The National Tribal Development Association (NTDA) was initiated to provide services to American Indians and Alaska Natives in all aspects of business. It is based on the Rocky Boy's Indian Reservation in Montana.

1995: The Native American Business Alliance (NABA) was formed to link private, public and Native American businesses. It is headquartered in Dearborn, Michigan.

1999: American Indian Alaska Native Tourism Association (AIANTA), based in Albuquerque, New Mexico, was founded to "define, introduce, grow and sustain American Indian, Alaska Native and Native Hawaiian tourism that honors and sustains tribal traditions and values." AIANTA offers technical assistance to Native communities and creates opportunities for tribes to develop responsible and profitable tourism. AIANTA oversees extensive global outreach programs. AIANTA is the only organization dedicated to advancing Indigenous tourism across the country and recognizes the best of Indian Country travel and tourism at its "Enough Good People Industry Awards" ceremony, held every year during the American Indian Tourism Conference.

2001: The Council for Native Hawaiian Advancement (CNHA), a nonprofit organization, was established to enhance the cultural, economic, political, and community development of Native Hawaiians. CNHA provides access to capital, financial education, and individualized financial counseling services with a focus on low- and moderate-income families, serving as a National Intermediary, providing grants and loans targeting underserved communities in Hawaii.

2003: The American Indian Business Network (AIBN) was started by the National Indian Gaming Association to introduce products and provide networking opportunities with other business owners, customers, and tribal leaders. It is based in Washington, D.C.

2003: The Native American Contractors Association (NACA) was formed to advocate on behalf of community-owned Alaska Native Corporations (ANC), Native Hawaiian Organizations (NHO), and tribal corporations engaged in federal contracting. NACA's mission is to protect the rights of Native American communities to create economic development through government contracting, as a result of the unique nation-to-nation trust relationship between the federal government and Natives.

2004: Native American Capital (NAC) was incorporated in the Washington, D.C., Metro area. Cofounded by Walter Hillabrant (1942–), Citizen Potawatomi Nation of Oklahoma, NAC is a consultancy serving a wide range of Indian Country clients—tribes, Indian-owned businesses, businesses seeking partnerships with tribes, and investors seeking to capitalize Native American–owned enterprises.

2005: The Indigenous Internet Chamber of Commerce (IICC), based in Minneapolis, Minnesota, became the first Western Hemisphere chamber of commerce uniting Indigenous peoples from Greenland to Argentina. IICC provides a connecting place for Native businesses to market their products and services globally.

2007: Hi'ilei Aloha LLC is a state nonprofit subentity of the Office of Hawaiian Affairs (OHA). Its goal is to identify, promote, develop, and support culturally appropriate, sustainable business opportunities that benefit Native Hawaiians, blending modern lifestyles with traditions, customs, practices, activities, values, and beliefs (including, by way of example, agriculture and farming, hunting, gathering, fishing, nourishment, housing, language, music, dance, religion, economic, trade, and social and governmental practices).

2009: Inventor David Petite, Fond Du Lac Chippewa, launched the Native American Intellectual Property Enterprise Council (NAIPEC) to support innovation among Indigenous peoples. NAIPEC, headquartered in Atlanta, Georgia, seeks to protect and promote rights of Native inventors, assist in patent and trademark filings, help develop business plans and feasibility, conduct research and prototypes, and create income for individuals and tribes.

2012: Native American Enterprise Initiative (NAEI) was founded as part of the U.S. Chamber of Commerce in Washington, D.C. The NAEI addresses a host of issues important to Indian Country that seek to drive economic development and reinforce tribal sovereignty.

2012: Based in Washington, D.C., the Native American Financial Services Association (NAFSA) was initiated as a trade association to provide better economic opportunity in Indian Country. NAFSA advocates for the sovereign rights of tribal nations and their economic subdivisions to pursue economic development opportunities within the financial services.

2014: New Mexico Community Capital's Native Entrepreneur in Residence Program (NEIR) was formalized, becoming a flagship nonprofit program. Emerging Native-owned businesses are provided tools for financial literacy, business skills, and a vibrant network. NEIR has served 46 participants from over 28 tribal nations in New Mexico.

2017: Native Women Lead, a support organization for Native women entrepreneurs, was founded by Kalika Davis, Navajo/European; Kim Gleason, Navajo; Jaime Gloshay, Navajo/White Mountain Apache/Kiowa; Alicia Ortega, Santa Clara/Pojoaque Pueblo; Stephine Poston, Pueblo of Sandia; Vanessa Roanhorse, Navajo; and Jaclyn Roessel, Navajo. In 2020, Native Women Lead hired staff. Ortega and Poston became its first codirectors.

2017: Native Women Entrepreneurs in Arizona (NWEAZ) was born to provide Native women business owners with advocacy, leadership, and data.

EDUCATION

"Education is your greatest weapon. With education you are the white man's equal; without education you are his victim and so shall remain all of your lives. Study, learn, help one another always."

—*Chief Plenty Coups (1848–1932), Apsáalooke (Crow Nation)*

NATIVE AMERICAN STUDIES

1969: Acting on input from Native American and other representatives, the Minnesota Board of Regents approved the Department of American Indian Studies at the University of Minnesota. It became the oldest program in the nation with autonomous departmental status. In 1970, W. Roger Buffalohead, Ponca, assumed the position of its first director. Besides administering the new department, he taught and counseled countless students. Working with Dakota and Ojibwe tribal members, Buffalohead also nurtured the development of one of the first accredited Native language programs in the country at the university.

1969: Trent University in Peterborough, Ontario, became the first university in Canada to establish a Native studies program. Called the Indian-Eskimo Studies Program, it was cofounded by Dr. Harvey McCue of the Georgina Island First Nations and Dr. Tom Symons. It was later called Indigenous Studies.

1970: Walter Soboleff (1908–2011), Tlingit spiritual leader and educator, was the founder and first chairman of the new Department of Alaska Studies at University of Alaska Fairbanks (UAF). Under his administration, the department grew over time to offer bachelor's degrees in Alaska Native Studies and bachelor's and master's degrees in rural development. Earlier, Soboleff was the first Alaska Native to be nominated by then-Governor Walter J. Hickel to Alaska's State Board of Education, where he served as chairman.

1975: The American Indian Studies (AIS) Center at UCLA, founded in 1969, was endowed with five faculty full-time equivalent positions and charged with recruitment and

Treaties and American Indian Education

A treaty between the United States and the Oneida, Tuscarora, and Stockbridge Indians dated December 2, 1794, was the first treaty to include a provision for education. Subsequent treaties with other tribal nations commonly included educational provisions as well.

A treaty with the Pawnees, negotiated on September 24, 1857, and ratified by the U.S. Senate in 1858, included the first compulsory school-attendance provision affecting American Indians. A number of later treaties between the U.S. government and other tribal nations also included compulsory attendance provisions.

development of scholars working in AIS. In 1982, the center faculty created the Interdepartmental Program's master's degree in AIS and developed a series of core courses.

1979: The University of Arizona inaugurated a master's degree with a concentration in American Indian Policy in the Political Sciences Department. In 1982, an interdisciplinary master's degree in American Indian Studies was formally approved.

1997: The University of Arizona (UA) became the first educational institution in the nation to offer a Ph.D. in American Indian Studies. It is an interdisciplinary program designed to prepare graduate students for academic careers, conduct scholarly research from a cross-cultural perspective, develop theoretical and innovative theories, methodologies, and research tools useful to tribal nations, and prepare for leadership and policy-making roles. UA also began a concurrent juris doctor (law degree) and master's degree in American Indian Studies in 1997. It is cited as the first program of its kind in the United States and Canada.

1997: Ron Welburn (1944–), Gingaskan/Assateague/Cherokee/African American, co-founded the Certificate Program in Native American Indian Studies (via anthropology)

at the University of Massachusetts Amherst and served as its first director until 2006. Welburn, a professor emeritus in the UMass-Amherst Department of English, is the author of some seven volumes of poetry and a nonfiction collection of essays, *Roanoke and Wampum: Topics in Native American Heritage and Literatures* (2001). He is also the author of *Hartford's Ann Plato and the Native Borders of Identity* (2015). Renowned for his research on Native American jazz musicians, Wellburn coordinated the Jazz Oral History Project at Rutgers University's (Newark) Institute of Jazz Studies and contributed the chapter "Native Americans in Jazz, Blues, and Popular Music" for *IndiVisible: African-Native American Lives in the Americas* (2009).

2000: Henrietta Mann (1934–), Cheyenne, became the first to occupy the Katz Endowed Chair in Native American Studies at Montana State University, Bozeman, later becoming professor emeritus and continuing to serve as special assistant to the president. Based at the University of Montana, Missoula, for some twenty-eight years, she was director/professor of Native American Studies. Mann also was the founding president of the Cheyenne and Arapaho Tribal College in Weatherford, Oklahoma. In 1991, *Rolling Stone* magazine named her as one of the ten leading professors in the nation. In 2001, she joined Chairman Earl Old Person of the Blackfeet Nation in delivering the Montana Tribal Nations Address to the Joint Session of the Senate and House of the Montana 57th Legislative Assembly. Mann was an interviewee and consultant for numerous television and movie productions such as *In the White Man's Image* and *How the West Was Lost*. She has lectured across the United States as well as internationally, and her writings include *Cheyenne-Araphao Education: 1871–1982* (1998).

2010: The Payne Family Native American Center at the University of Montana in Missoula (UM) was dedicated as the first facility in the nation built specifically to accommodate a Department of Native American Studies (NAS) and American Indian Student Services. Located on the site of a historic Salish encampment, it reflects the heritages and cultures of all Montana tribal nations. The Payne Center was also the first LEED (Leadership in Energy and Environmental Design) building constructed on the UM campus.

2015: The Native Nations Center was officially established at the University of Oklahoma, with Amanda Cobb-Greetham, Chickasaw, chair of the Department of Native American Studies, as the founding director. The center was later endowed by the Chickasaw Nation to ensure its future.

2020: The Dana Naone Hall Endowed Chair in Hawaiian Studies, Literature and the Environment at the Hawaiʻinuiākea School of Hawaiian Knowledge, a new Hawaiian Studies chair, was created at the University of Hawaiʻi

The Payne Family Native American Center is located at the Missoula campus of the University of Montana.

Indigenous Firsts: A History of Native American Achievements and Events

White House Conference on Indian Education

The first White House Conference on Indian Education was held in 1992. It was authorized in the Augustus F. Hawkins–Robert T. Stafford Elementary and Secondary School Improvement Amendments of 1988, Public Law 100-297 on April 28, 1988. The conference explored the feasibility of establishing an independent Board of Indian Education and developed recommendations for making educational programs more relevant to the needs of American Indians. A two-volume final report was later issued, documenting recommendations and examining aids and barriers to realizing conference resolutions.

at Mānoa (UH). It was made possible by a $3.2 million donation from the Laurence H. Dorcy Hawaiian Foundation. Hall, a revered Native Hawaiian poet and environmental activist, is the author of *Life of the Land: Articulations of a Native Writer* (2017), which won an American Book Award in 2019. She edited "Malama, Hawaiian Land and Water" in the winter 1985 issue of the journal *Bamboo Ridge*. Hall also was editor of the *Hawai'i Review*, UH Mānoa's literary journal.

BOARDING SCHOOLS/RESIDENTIAL SCHOOLS

"If we can raise a generation of First Nations kids who never have to recover from their childhoods, and a generation of non-Indigenous children who never have to say they're sorry, then I think we have made a major step in co-creating a society that our ancestors always dreamed of, and that our great-great-great grandchildren would be proud of...."

—*Cindy Blackstock, Gitxsan*

1831: Lahainaluna Seminary in Lahaina, Maui, founded by Protestant missionaries, was the first mission school in Hawaii. Today it is the public Lahainaluna High School.

1860: The first federal boarding school was opened at the Yakima (Yakama) Indian Agency in Washington State, the outcome of an 1855 treaty between the United States and the Yakama.

1878: The first group of American Indian students began attending Hampton Normal and Agricultural Institute in Virginia, a private school that had been established ten years earlier to educate newly freed African Americans in the aftermath of the U.S. Civil War. Former prisoners of war who had been incarcerated at Fort Marion in St. Augustine, Florida, following war on the Southern Plains made up the initial group of Native students. All adult men, they were under the supervision of Richard Henry Pratt, who later founded the Carlisle Indian Industrial School with some of the same students. Hampton's American Indian program was funded by the U.S. government until 1912, when controversy over educating Indians and blacks together contributed to the loss of federal support. Native students continued to attend Hampton on their own until 1923, but with dwindling numbers.

The Lahainaluna Seminary in Maui was founded in 1831 by Protestant missionaries.

1879: The Carlisle Indian Industrial School in Carlisle, Pennsylvania, was established as the first federally funded off-reservation boarding school. Created by Richard Henry Pratt, a former military officer who became an architect of family separation, the school served Native children who were removed from their families and communities and indoctrinated with Euro-American language, religion, and culture in settings far from home. Carlisle became a model for the boarding schools that followed.

1900: Francis La Flesche's *The Middle Five: Indian Schoolboys of the Omaha Tribe* was one of the earliest published memoirs of a boarding school graduate. La Flesche (1857–1932), Omaha, wrote of his experiences as a student at the Presbyterian mission school on the Omaha Reservation in Nebraska. He also became known as the first Native American ethnologist; his specialties centered on Omaha and Osage culture and music. La Flesche, who earned undergraduate and master's degrees at George Washington University Law School in Washington, D.C., worked with anthropologist Alice C. Fletcher for decades.

2000: *Remembering Our Indian School Days: The Boarding School Experience* opened at the Heard Museum in Phoenix, Arizona. It was the first major exhibition to explore the history of the education and assimilation of American Indian children in the nineteenth and twentieth centuries. Curated by Margaret Archuleta, Brenda Child, and K. Tsianina Lomawaima, the exhibit incorporated first-hand accounts, archival photographs, artwork, and a range of other materials. The curators also co-edited *Away from Home: American Indian Boarding School Experiences 1879–2000* (Heard Museum, 2000) in conjunction with the exhibit. The exhibition evoked such a response from visitors that it has remained on view as a long-term display. In 2018, the Heard Museum updated it, incorporating new technologies and information, calling it *Away from Home: American Indian Boarding School Stories.*

2008: The Truth and Reconciliation Commission of Canada (TRC) was launched as part of the Indian Residential Schools Settlement Agreement. In 2015, the commission released its final report, documenting the experiences of thousands of First Nations residential school students. The TRC labeled the residential school system as cultural genocide, defining the practice as the "destruction of those structures and practices that allow the group to continue as a group." More recently, countless unmarked graves have been found near residential schools.

2013: Orange Shirt Day was created by alumni of the St. Joseph Mission Residential School in Williams Lake, British Columbia, Canada, to promote awareness about the Indian residential school system and its reverberating impact on Indigenous people through subsequent generations. Participants of the St. Joseph Mission Residential School Commemoration Project and reunion events honored the healing journey of survivors and their families and committed to the ongoing process of reconciliation. Former student Phyllis Webstad recounted her first day at the residential school, when the new orange shirt her grandmother had bought for her was taken away by school officials. Now every September 30, Orange Shirt Day, the National Day of Remembrance, is observed across Canada.

COLLEGES AND UNIVERSITIES

"We collectively acknowledge that Michigan State University occupies the ancestral, traditional, and contemporary Lands of the Anishinaabeg—Three Fires Confederacy of Ojibwe, Odawa, and Potawatomi peoples. In particular, the University resides on Land ceded in the 1819 Treaty of Saginaw. We recognize, support, and advocate for the sovereignty of Michigan's twelve federally recognized Indian nations, for historic Indigenous communities in Michigan, for Indigenous individuals and communities who live here now, and for those who were forcibly removed from their Homelands. By offering this Land Acknowledgement, we affirm Indigenous sovereignty and will work to hold Michigan State University more accountable to the needs of American Indian and Indigenous peoples."

—*Excerpt from Michigan State University's Land Acknowledgement*

1665: Caleb Cheeshahteaumuck (c. 1644–1666), Wampanoag from Martha's Vineyard, became the first American Indian to graduate from Harvard College, which by its 1650 charter was charged with providing for the education of both Native American and English youth. During his tenure at Harvard, he authored *Honoratissimi Benefactores* in Latin, thanking benefactors. Cheeshahteaumuck's classmate Joel Iacoombs, also Wampanoag, died shortly before graduating. In 2011, Harvard University presented a special posthumous degree for him at its commencement exercises.

1840: Maris Bryant Pierce (Hadyanodoh, Swift Runner; 1811–1874), born on the Allegany Seneca Reservation in New York, became the first American Indian to graduate from Dartmouth College in New Hampshire since 1781.

1842: William Potter Ross (1820–1891), Cherokee and an honor student, was the first Native American to graduate from Princeton University in New Jersey. In 1844, he became the first editor of the *Cherokee Advocate*, the first newspaper published in Indian Territory. Ross, a nephew of Chief John Ross, also served as a Confederate colonel, Cherokee principal chief, and in other roles on the Cherokee National Council. He was also a merchant, lawyer, and editor of other newspapers. William Potter Ross's brother, Robert Daniel Ross, also graduated from Princeton (class of 1843), continuing on to complete studies at the University of Pennsylvania Medical School in 1847.

1846: Eleanor Susan Boudinot, Cherokee, has been identified as the first Native American woman to graduate from Mount Holyoke College, then Mount Holyoke Female Seminary, in South Hadley, Massachusetts. She was followed by her sister, Mary Harriet Boudinot, who graduated in 1849. In 1925, Ruth Muskrat Bronson, Cherokee, became the first American Indian graduate during the institution's college years.

1887: Croatan Normal School was established by legislation enacted by the General Assembly of North Carolina to train American Indian teachers. The school opened with one teacher and 15 students in the spring of 1888, and the first diploma was awarded in 1905. In 1909, the school was moved to the center of the Lumbee community in Pembroke, North Carolina, and in 1911, the General Assembly changed the name to the Indian Normal School of Robeson County. In 1913, it was called the Cherokee Indian Normal School of Robeson County. By 1941, the General Assembly changed the name to Pembroke State College

for Indians and, in 1949, to Pembroke State College. In 1969, the school was renamed Pembroke State University, and in 1972, it became a constituent of the newly established 16-campus University of North Carolina.

1898: John Milton Oskison (1874–1947), Cherokee, was the first Native American to graduate from Stanford University, where he was president of the Stanford Literary Society. He became an author, editor, and journalist, working for many years at *Collier's*. Oskison also served with the American Expeditionary Force in World War I. His writings include short stories, several novels, a biography of Sam Houston, and a history of Tecumseh. With Angie Debo, Oskison also edited *Oklahoma: A Guide to the Sooner State* (1941), which was compiled by the writers' program of the Works Progress Administration (WPA). In 1995, Stanford University established the annual John Milton Oskison Writing Competition in his honor.

1904: William Jones (Megasiawa, Black Eagle) (1871–1909), Sac and Fox, Oklahoma, became the first American Indian student to earn a Ph.D. in anthropology at Columbia University. Earlier, he had attended schools at Sac and Fox Agency; Wabash, Indiana; and Newton, Kansas. Jones also attended Hampton Institute, where he graduated in 1892. After graduating from Phillips Academy, he also earned a degree at Harvard University in 1900. Following his tenure at Columbia University, Jones undertook research among his own people for the American Museum of Natural History in New York as well as among Chippewa for the Carnegie Institution. In 1909, he was reported to have been murdered while conducting field research in the Philippines.

1915: Henry Roe Cloud (1884–1950), Winnebago Tribe of Nebraska, founded and became superintendent of the Roe Indian Institute (later American Indian Institute) in Wichita, Kansas, the first college preparatory school for American Indians in the United States. He received his undergraduate degree from Yale University in 1910, a bachelor of divinity degree from Auburn Theological Seminary in 1913, and a master's degree in anthropology from Yale in 1914. He had an instrumental role in preparing the Meriam Report (1928), an influential study that documents the failings of federal Indian policy. In 1933, Roe Cloud was appointed as the first American Indian superintendent of the Haskell Institute in Lawrence, Kansas. He later served as superintendent of the Umatilla Reservation in Oregon. Roe Cloud was married to Elizabeth Bender (White Earth Nation), a leader in her own right. Their granddaughter, Renya K. Ramirez, wrote *Standing Up to Colonial Power: The Lives of Henry Roe and Elizabeth Bender Cloud* (2018). Yale University awarded the first Henry Roe Cloud Medal to Philip "Sam" Deloria, Standing Rock Sioux, in 2005.

Henry Roe Cloud

1926: Archie Phinney (1904–1949), Nez Perce, was the first Native American to graduate from the University of Kansas in Lawrence, earning a bachelor of arts degree. He later pursued anthropology studies at George Washington University, New York University, and Columbia University. Phinney also studied at the Museum of Ethnography and Anthropology of the Soviet Academy of Science (1932–1937). While in Leningrad, he worked on the bilingual *Nez Percé Texts* (1934) based on accounts provided by his mother, Mary Lily Phinney (Wayi'latpu). Although it was not published, he also penned the work *Nez Percé Grammar*. After returning to the United States, Phinney became a field agent for the Bureau of Indian Affairs. He was a founding member of the National Congress of American Indians (NCAI). In 2004, the *Journal of Northwest Anthropology* devoted an issue to his life and work.

1959: The Indian Education Center (IEC), which changed its name to the Center for Indian Education, was created at Arizona State University, the first of its kind nationally. Robert A. Roessel Jr. became the founding director, serving from 1959 to 1966.

1963: George A. Gill (1925–2007), Omaha, was the first American Indian to receive a master's degree in Indian education at Arizona State University (ASU). He later served as the director of ASU's Center for Indian Education (formerly Indian Education Center). Gill served in the U.S. Navy during World War II and the Korean War. In his long education career, he helped establish the *Journal of American Indian Education* and served as its editor. Gill was active in community outreach and research efforts as well as teaching.

1970: The first Convocation of American Indian Scholars was held at Princeton University in New Jersey, bringing together Native American teachers and administrators actively involved in Indian education. It was organized by Rupert Costo, Cahuilla, and his wife, Jeannette Henry Costo, Cherokee.

1970: In response to the need for more Native Americans with training in educational administration, the Office of Economic Opportunity (OEO) funded training programs at Arizona State University, Harvard University, Pennsylvania State University, and the University of Minnesota. The program was initiated by Dr. Jim Wilson, Oglala Lakota, director of the Indian Desk at OEO, whose leadership and initiatives made a difference in changing the underrepresentation of Native Americans and services in critical areas.

1971: Gerald E. Gipp (1941–), Standing Rock Sioux Tribe, was the first American Indian to graduate with a master's degree from Pennsylvania State University through its newly created American Indian Leadership Program (AILP) in the Department of Education and then, in 1974, the first to earn a Ph.D. through the program. After completing his doctorate, he became AILP's first American Indian director, serving in the position until 1977. Gipp then became a deputy commissioner of the Office of Indian Education in the U.S. Office of Education (USOE). With the creation of the Department of Education, he served as the only deputy assistant secretary for Indian education. Following that position, he became the first American Indian president of Haskell Indian Junior College (now Haskell Indian Nations University) in Lawrence, Kansas, from 1981 to 1989. Gipp is coeditor of *American Indian Stories of Success: New Visions of Leadership in Indian Country* (2015).

1975: Ruth A. Myers (1926–2001), Grand Portage Band of Lake Superior Chippewa, became the first American Indian appointed to the Minnesota State Board of Education. Earlier, in 1971, she won a seat on the Duluth School Board, becoming the first nonwhite elected to public office in that city. In 1973, Myers joined the Education Department at the University of Minnesota, Duluth (UMD), starting 16 of 17 programs for American Indian students. She later codirected the Center of American Indian and Minority Health at UMD's School of Medicine. After retiring from UMD in 1994, the university established the Ruth A. Myers Endowed Chair of American Indian Studies. The library at the Fond du Lac Tribal and Community College in Cloquet, Minnesota, where she chaired a task force, is named the Ruth A. Myers Library in her honor.

1976: Elaine Abraham (Chuu Shah; 1929–2016), Tlingit, was named the vice president of rural education affairs, the first woman and the first Native to hold a senior statewide administrative position in the University of Alaska system. Abraham graduated from the Sage Memorial School of Nursing in Ganado, Arizona (1952), and worked in that state before returning to Alaska, becoming the first Tlingit registered nurse in the state. She played a leading role in improving health services. After retiring from nursing in her 40s, Abraham earned associate, bachelor's, and master's degrees and moved into key positions at Sheldon Jackson College, including vice president for institutional development. Abraham was also the cofounder of the Alaska Native Language Center at the University of Alaska. Her honors included becoming the first Alaska Native to receive the American Indian Achievement Award in 1973. Abraham was elected to the Alaska Women's Hall of Fame in 2011.

1984: Elizabeth "Betty" Parent (1941–), Athabascan, was the first Alaska Native to receive a Ph.D., earning it in education from Stanford University (CA). She was also the first Alaska Native woman to obtain tenure as a full professor. Parent earned a B.A. in anthropology with minors in English and education at the University of Alaska. She continued her studies at Harvard University, earning an M.A. in education administration and becoming the first Alaska Native to serve on the editorial board of the *Harvard Educational Review*. Parent accepted a tenure-track appointment at San Francisco State University, where her work included guiding American Indian Studies to department status. She became the department's first full professor. Following her retirement, San Francisco State established the Elizabeth Parent Achievement Award in her honor. She was inducted into the Alaska Women's Hall of Fame in 2017.

1986: Rupert Costo (1906–1989), Cahuilla, and his wife, Jeannette Henry Costo (1909–

2001), Cherokee, endowed the nation's first academic chair in the field of American Indian history at the University of California, Riverside (UCR). Rupert Costo founded the American Indian Historical Society in 1950 and was also key to the establishment of UCR, which was dedicated in 1954. He and his wife, a reporter for the *New York Times* and *Detroit Free Press*, founded the Indian Historian Press in San Francisco. They published *Textbooks and the American Indian* (1970) and numerous other influential works. UCR's Costo Hall is named in the couple's honor, and their extensive books and papers, which they donated to UCR, became known as the Rupert Costo Library for the American Indian.

1988: Karen Gayton Comeau (Swisher) (1943–), Standing Rock Sioux, became the first woman to direct the Center for Indian Education at Arizona State University (ASU) and the first woman to serve as editor of the *Journal of American Indian Education*. Comeau (then Swisher) was also the first female president of Haskell Indian Nations University in Kansas, officially named to the position in 2000 after serving in an interim capacity. Comeau received her Ph.D. in educational administration from the University of North Dakota and retired from Haskell in 2006. She coauthored *Native North American Firsts* (1997) with AnCita Benally.

1991: Akwe:kon (pronounced uh-GWAY-go), which opened at Cornell University in Ithaca, New York, in 1991, became the nation's first university residence hall created to celebrate American Indian culture and heritage. The name *Akwe:kon* means "all of us" in the Mohawk language. Akwe:kon's building and landscape were designed with input from Native people, incorporating design elements symbolic of communal spirit. The 35 residents, roughly half of whom are Native American, represent diverse cultures and backgrounds.

1992: Viola F. Cordova (1937–2002), Jicarilla Apache, became one of the first two Native Americans to earn a Ph.D. in philosophy, completing her doctorate at the University of New Mexico. She taught at the University of Alaska–Fairbanks, University of New Mexico, Idaho State University, Oregon State University, Colorado State University, and other schools. Cordova's writings include *How It Is: A Native American Creation Story* and *Who We Are: An Exploration of Identity*. *Ways of Seeing*, another publication, was devoted to a series of her lectures. Some of Cordova's colleagues organized her pioneering contributions into *How It Is: The Native American Philosophy of V. F. Cordova* (2007).

1992: Anne S. Waters, Seminole/Choctaw/Chickasaw/Cherokee, earned a Ph.D. in philosophy at Purdue University in Indiana, one of the first two Native Americans to earn a doctorate in that field. She also earned a juris doctorate (J.D.) at the University of New Mexico School of Law in 1992. In 2004, Waters served as editor of the first American Indian philosophy anthology, *American Indian Thought: Philosophical Essays*. She was coguest editor of a special issue of *Hypatia— A Journal of Feminist Philosophy: Indigenous Women in the Americas*; the past editor of the *American Philosophical Association Newsletter on Native Indian and Indigenous Philosophy*; and editor of other writing series.

1993: Laura Tohe (1952–) became the first Navajo to earn a Ph.D. in English when she completed her degree at the University of Nebraska, Lincoln. The daughter of a Navajo Code Talker, she was fluent in her language and a successful educator and writer. Her books include *No Parole Today*, about boarding schools; *Sister Nations: Native American Women Writers on Community*, coedited with Heid E. Erdrich; and *Code Talker Stories*, an oral history book. In 2015, Tohe became the Navajo Nation Poet Laureate. She is also a librettist, whose libretto *Nahasdzáán* *in the Glittering World/Mother Earth in the Glittering World* premiered at L'Opera de Rouen Normandie in France in 2019.

Laura Tohe

1996: Regis Pecos (1953–), Cochiti Pueblo, became the first American Indian member of the Princeton University Board of Trustees. Three years later, he was named New Mexico's Distinguished Public Servant. From 2003 to 2013, Pecos served as New Mexico Legislature's House Majority Office chief of staff. He received his bachelor's degree from Princeton University in 1977 and his Ph.D. at the University of California–Berkeley.

2001: David Beaulieu, White Earth Nation, was appointed the first Electa Quinney Endowed Professor of American Indian Education in the University of Wisconsin–Milwaukee School of Education (UWM). The professorship, named in honor of Quinney, Stockbridge-Munsee, Wisconsin's first public school teacher, is UWM's first endowed professorship in the School of Education. It was made possible by a $1 million gift from the Milwaukee Indian Community School.

2001: Princeton University conferred its first honorary degree on a Native American, Kevin Gover (1955–). Gover, a citizen of the Pawnee Nation of Oklahoma, also received his bachelor's degree from Princeton in 1978 and was the assistant secretary of the interior for Indian affairs..

2002: W. Richard West Jr. (1943–), a citizen of the Cheyenne and Arapaho Tribes in Oklahoma, became the first Native American named to the Stanford University Board of Trustees. West, a graduate of Stanford Law School, served as the founding director of the National Museum of the Ameri-

W. Richard West Jr.

can Indian before becoming president and CEO of the Autry National Center of the American West in Los Angeles.

2006: Loriene Roy (1954–), Anishinaabe, White Earth Nation, professor at the University of Texas at Austin's School of Information, was elected president of the American Library Association (ALA) for the 2007–2008 term, becoming the first Native American elected to the position in the organization's 131-year history.

2007: Clara Sue Kidwell (1941–), White Earth Nation/Choctaw, was the founding director of the American Indian Center at the University of North Carolina Chapel Hill, serving in the position until 2011. Kidwell, who earned her Ph.D. from the University of Oklahoma in 1970, is considered a "major figure in the development of American Indian Studies programs." Her work in the field includes serving as a professor of Native American Studies at the University of California at Berkeley, as a visiting assistant professor in Native American Studies at Dartmouth College, and as an assistant professor of American Indian Studies at the University of Minnesota. Kidwell also served as assistant director of cultural resources at the National Museum of the American Indian. A scholar, historian, and author, her books include *Choctaws and Missionaries in Mississippi, 1818–1918* (1997) and *The Choctaws in Oklahoma: From Tribe to Nation, 1855–1970* (2008).

2007: The Hawaiʻinuiākea School of Hawaiian Knowledge became the first new school or college established on the Mānoa campus of the University of Hawaiʻi (UH) since 1982. UH describes it as "the only college of indigenous knowledge in a Research 1 institution in the

United States." The school's stated mission is to pursue, perpetuate, research, and revitalize all areas and forms of Hawaiian knowledge.

2007: Cassandra Manuelito-Kerkvliet (1954–), Navajo, became president of Antioch University Seattle, the first Native American woman to serve as president of an accredited university outside of the tribal college and university system. She held the position until her retirement in 2013. Prior to her tenure at Seattle, Manuelito-Kerkvliet was the first female president of Diné College, on the Navajo reservation in Tsaile, Arizona, the first tribally controlled college. She earned her doctorate in educational policy and management with a special emphasis in higher education administration at the University of Oregon. Manuelito-Kerkvliet, who lives in Corvallis, Oregon, sewed an estimated 5,000 face masks through a program she named Nizhoni, meaning beautiful in the sense of a balanced life in Diné, to help the Navajo Nation during the COVID-19 pandemic.

2007: Wayne Newell (1942–), Passamaquoddy, was the first Native American appointed to serve on the University of Maine's Board of Trustees. In 1970, he was among the largest single group of Native American students to attend Harvard University since the 1600s. At that time, Newell and ten other Native Americans were recruited to attend a federally funded program at Harvard's Graduate School of Education. That program grew into the university-wide Harvard University Native American Program (HUNAP). After earning his master's degree, Newell returned to Maine, where he directed the first bilingual/bicultural education program for the Passamaquoddy Tribe. He contributed to *The Passamaquoddy-Maliseet Dictionary* and other publications.

2008: LuAnn Leonard, Hopi/Tohono O'odham, was the first Native American appointed to the Arizona Board of Regents (ABOR). ABOR oversees Northern Arizona University, Arizona State University, and the University of Arizona, all having large Native student populations. Governor Janet Napolitano cited Leonard's outstanding work as executive director of the Hopi Education Endowment Fund, which flourished under her leadership and enhanced funding for scholarships and aid for students. Leonard, a 1983 graduate of Northern Arizona University (NAU) in applied sociology, was awarded an honorary Doctor of Philosophy from NAU in 2017. Her term on ABOR lasted until 2016.

2009: The Native American Contemplative Garden, an outdoor reflective space, was dedicated at the University of California, Davis (UCD) in honor of the original Patwin inhabitants of lands encompassed by UCD's campus. The garden is believed to be the first of its kind at any public university in the United States. In 2019, a marker titled "Voices, Drums, Whistles. Sing, Dance, Remember" and inscribed with tribal history was unveiled at UCD, another phase of memorializing the early Patwin.

2009: Kishan Lara-Cooper (1979–), Yurok of Northern California, became the first member of her tribal nation to earn a Ph.D. in education. She graduated from Arizona State University, where she wrote a dissertation exploring her community's concepts of giftedness, which differ from Western concepts of the topic. "If anyone is going to research our people," Dr. Lara-Cooper was told by a Yurok elder, "it should be one of our own, someone that respects our way and wants to do right by us. We have things we want to say, things that we want remembered." Serving as a professor in the Department of Child Development, Dr. Lara-Cooper was named 2019/2020 Distinguished Faculty Outstanding Professor in Teaching at Humboldt State University (now known as California State Polytechnic University, Humboldt) in Arcata, California.

2010: Edmund Manydeeds III (1950–), Standing Rock Sioux, was the first Native American appointed to the University of Wisconsin System Board of Regents. A graduate of the University of Wisconsin–Superior, he received his law degree from the University of Wisconsin–Madison. Manydeeds, an attorney working in Eau Claire, Wisconsin, served on the Board of Regents until 2017 and was reappointed in 2019 to serve a second seven-year term. In 2021, he was elected president of the University of Wisconsin System's Board of Regents, the first Native American to serve in the position.

2011: Tiffany Smalley became the first Wampanoag to graduate from Harvard College since 1665, when fellow tribal member Caleb Cheeshahteaumuck received his degree.

2017: Connor Veneski, Cayuga Nation of New York—Bear Clan, was the first tribal colleges and universities (TCU) graduate to be accepted into Harvard Law School. He graduated from Haskell Indian Nations University in 2017. He served as the copresident of the Harvard Native American Law Students Association; Veneski graduated in 2021.

2018: Chance Fletcher, a member of the Cherokee Nation, became the first recipient of the three-year American Indian College Fund Law School Scholarship at Harvard Law School (HLS). Fletcher, who graduated from Princeton University, served as the president of the HLS chapter of the Federalist Society, a conservative legal network.

2019: Aaron Bird Bear, a member of the Three Affiliated Tribes of the Fort Berthold Reservation, was named tribal relations director at the University of Wisconsin–Madison, a newly created position. The role includes fostering strong ties between the tribal nations of Wisconsin and the university as well as representing the UW-Madison Division of Extension leadership in collaboration with tribes. In 2003, Bird Bear, an alumnus of UW-Madison, helped develop the First Nations Cultural Landscape Tour, an experiential education tour of American Indian landmarks on the campus, the ancestral home of the Ho-Chunk.

2019: Tadd Johnson, a member of the Bois Forte Band of Chippewa, was named the University of Minnesota's first senior director of American Indian Tribal Nations Relations. In this inaugural position, Johnson serves as a liaison between the entire U of M system and regional tribal nations. A longtime tribal attorney, he earned his law degree at the U of M and has served as a tribal court judge, tribal administrator, and lecturer on federal Indian law. Johnson also spent five years with the U.S. House of Representatives, becoming staff director and counsel to the Subcommittee on Native American Affairs.

2020: In the 2020–21 academic year, the Intertribal Agriculture Council (IAC) and the Inter-Institutional Network for Food, Agriculture, and Sustainability (INFAS) collaborated to pilot the first Native American graduate student fellowship program in tribal food systems. The Agricultural Sustainability Institute at UC Davis is the hosting institution for INFAS.

2020: The University of Montana (UM) approved the establishment of the American Indian Governance and Policy Institute (AIGPI) with the goal of addressing the core causes of poor socioeconomic health on Indian reservations in the state. Heather Cahoon (1976–), a member of the Confederated Salish and Kootenai Tribes, created the institute and became its first director. The AIGPI is housed within UM's Department of Native American Studies and is affiliated with the Margery Hunter Brown Indian Law Clinic and the Department of Public Administration and Policy.

2021: The University of Minnesota (U of M) launched a new position, senior advisor to the president for Native American affairs, appointing Karen Diver, a member of the Fond du Lac Band of Lake Superior Chippewa, to the post. Earlier, Diver served as the inaugural Faculty Fellow for Inclusive Excellence for Native American Affairs at the College of St. Scholastica in Duluth. In 2007, she became the first woman elected to serve as tribal chair at Fond du Lac. Diver, who earned a master's degree in public administration from the John F. Kennedy School of Government at Harvard, was appointed by President Barack Obama to be a special assistant to the president on Native American affairs, holding the position from 2015 to 2017.

2021: Samantha Maltais became the first member of the Aquinnah Wampanoag in Massachusetts to attend Harvard Law School. A 2018 graduate of Dartmouth College and a former Peace Corps volunteer, she is the recipient of a full scholarship from the American Indian College Fund's American Indian Law School Scholarship at Harvard Law School.

William Whipple Warren

HISTORIANS AND HISTORY BOOKS

1885: William Whipple Warren (1825–1853), Ojibway, completed his *History of the Ojibways, Based upon Traditions and Oral Statements* in the winter of 1852–53, and it was first published years later, in 1885, by the Minnesota Historical Society (MHS). Warren attended schools in Michigan, Wisconsin, and New York. Fluent in Ojibway and Eng-

lish, Warren worked as an interpreter. In the fall of 1850, he was elected as a member of the Minnesota Territorial House, taking his seat in 1851. Warren's book has been called "perhaps the most important history of the Ojibway (Chippewa) ever written." He collected firsthand accounts from tribal leaders and other individuals, providing oral history from the mid-nineteenth century. Other editions of Warren's book have been published by the MHS, including *History of the Ojibway People* (1984).

1921: Rachel Caroline Eaton (1869–1938), Cherokee, is believed to be the first Oklahoma Indian woman to receive a Ph.D. and the first woman county superintendent of schools in Rogers County, Oklahoma. After graduating from the Cherokee Female Seminary in 1887, Eaton attended Drury College (class of 1895) in Springfield, Missouri. She continued her studies at the University of Chicago, where she specialized in history and earned a master's degree, followed by a Ph.D. in history. Her dissertation, *John Ross and the Cherokee Indians,* was published by Banta Publishing Company.

1951: Muriel Hazel Wright (1889–1975), Choctaw, published *A Guide to the Indian Tribes of Oklahoma* (1951), which remains a standard source of information about tribal nations in the state. Descended from the Reverend Allen Wright and other distinguished family members, Wright completed a teacher education course at East Central Normal School in Ada, Oklahoma, in 1912. She also studied at Wheaton Seminary in Norton, Massachusetts, and Barnard College in New York City. Wright collaborated with journalist Joseph B. Thoburn on a four-volume work, *Oklahoma: A History of the State and Its People* (1929). She wrote *The Story of Oklahoma* (1929), *Our Oklahoma* (1939), and

The Oklahoma History (1955) as history textbooks for use in public schools. Wright had a long association with *The Chronicles of Oklahoma*, producing articles and serving as editor. Unofficially called the "Historian of Oklahoma," she was one of the first four inductees of the Oklahoma Historians Hall of Fame when it was launched by the Oklahoma Historical Society in 1993.

1976: Veronica E. Velarde Tiller, who attended the University of New Mexico, was the first Jicarilla Apache to earn a Ph.D., graduating with a doctorate in history. After teaching in Utah, she began pursuing research and writing full time. Tiller became renowned for her writings, including *The Jicarilla Apache Tribe: A History, 1846–1970* and her monumental reference guide to federally recognized tribes, *Tiller's Guide to Indian Country: Economic Profiles of American Indian Reservations*. The *Guide*, first published in 1996 and updated periodically, became an indispensable resource across Indian Country. Following retirement, Tiller has engaged in path-breaking work to preserve her tribal language.

1977: Olive Dickason (1920–2011), Métis, was the first scholar in Canada to receive a Ph.D. in Indigenous history. Her doctoral dissertation, *The Myth of the Savage and the Beginnings of French Colonialism in the Americas*, was published by the University of Alberta Press in 1984. Another book, *Canada's First Nations: A History of Founding Peoples from Earliest Times* (1992), won the Sir John A. Macdonald Prize for best scholarly book in Canadian history in 1993.

1982: Joe S. Sando (Paa Peh; 1923–2011), Jemez Pueblo, wrote *Pueblo Nations: Eight Centuries of Pueblo Indian History* (1992), a book the *New York Times* called "the first insider's story of the 800-year history of the 19 pueblos in New Mexico." Following service in the U.S. Navy during World War II, Sando

studied at Eastern New Mexico University and Vanderbilt University in Tennessee. He taught Pueblo history at institutions that included the University of New Mexico and the Institute of American Indian Arts in Santa Fe. Sando also served as the cofounder and first director of the American Indian Graduate Center in Albuquerque, New Mexico. Additional writings by him include *Nee Hemish: A History of Jemez Pueblo* (1982) and his memoir *Pueblo Recollections: The Life of Paa Peh* (2008).

1994: Steven J. Crum, Western Shoshone scholar, wrote *The Road on Which We Came: A History of the Western Shoshone/Po'i Pentun Tammen Kimmappeh* (University of Utah, 1994), the first comprehensive history of the Great Basin Shoshone.

2005: Robert J. Conley (1940–2014), a member of the Cherokee Nation, wrote *The Cherokee Nation: A History* (University of New Mexico Press, 2005), noted as the first history of the tribal nation to appear in over four decades, the first to be endorsed by the tribal nation, and the first to be written by a Cherokee author. It was named one of the American Library Association's Outstanding Academic Titles in 2005.

2008: *The History of the Assiniboine and Sioux Tribes of the Fort Peck Indian Reservation, Montana, 1800–2000*, the first comprehensive history of the Fort Peck Reservation commissioned by the tribal nations themselves, was published by Montana Historical Society Press in 2008. The authors include David Miller, Dennis Smith, Joseph R. McGeshick, James Shanley, and Caleb Shields. A second edition was published in 2012.

2009: Ned Blackhawk (c. 1970–), Western Shoshone, became the first tenured Native American professor at Yale College in the Department of History and American

Studies, 308 years after Yale was founded. Blackhawk, a graduate of McGill University, holds graduate degrees in history from UCLA and the University of Washington. His award-winning writings include *Violence over the Land: Indians and Empires in the Early American West* (Harvard, 2006), which won the Frederick Jackson Turner Prize from the Organization of American Historians and other honors.

2013: Josephine McCarthy Waggoner (1871–1943), Standing Rock Lakota historian, recorded the lifeways of her people during the 1920s and 1930s but was unable to get her extensive research and writings published during her lifetime. Her work was edited by Emily Levine and published for the first time in 2013 as *Witness: A Húŋkpapha Historian's Strong-Heart Song of the Lakotas* (University of Nebraska). Waggoner, who attended Hampton Normal and Agricultural Institute in Hampton, Virginia, from 1881 to 1884 and 1885 to 1888, married and raised a family after returning home to Dakota Territory. *Witness* includes firsthand accounts and a rare participant's perspective on nineteenth- and early-twentieth-century Lakota and Dakota life.

2015: Anton Treuer (1969), professor of Ojibwe at Bemidji State University in Minnesota and award-winning author, wrote *Warrior Nation: A History of the Red Lake Ojibwe* (Minnesota Historical Society Press, 2015), the first history of the Red Lake Nation. Treuer, a graduate of Princeton University (B.A., Woodrow Wilson School of Public and International Affairs) and the University of Minnesota (M.A. and Ph.D. in history), is also the editor of the *Oshkaabewis Native Journal*, the only academic journal of the Ojibwe language. In 2016, *Warrior Nation* won the Caroline Bancroft History Prize as well as the Award of Merit from the American Association for State and Local History.

2018: Philip J. Deloria (1959–), Lakota, became the first tenured professor of Native American history at Harvard University. He received his Ph.D. in American studies from Yale University and then served on the faculty at the University of Colorado and at the University of Michigan. At Michigan, Deloria served as the associate dean for undergraduate education, director of the Program in American Culture, and director of the Native American Studies Program. He is the author of *Playing Indian* (1998), tracing the tradition of white "Indian play" from the Boston Tea Party to the New Age movement, and *Indians in Unexpected Places* (2004), upending the notion of American Indians as frozen in time and place. Deloria, recipient of numerous honors, coedited *The Blackwell Companion to American Indian History* (with Neal Salisbury) and other works. He is a trustee of the Smithsonian Institution's National Museum of the American Indian, former president of the American Studies Association, and an elected member of the American Academy of Arts and Sciences.

JOURNALS

1961: The *Journal of American Indian Education* (JAIE) was established at the Center for Indian Education at Arizona State University (ASU) by Robert A. Roessel Jr., Bruce Meador, and George A. Gill, Omaha. Published continuously since its founding, JAIE's editorial office is housed at ASU and is now published by the University of Minnesota Press.

1985: *Wičazo Ša Review: A Journal of Native American Studies* was cofounded by Elizabeth Cook-Lynn, Crow Creek Sioux Tribe, who served as its first editor. Other founders included W. Roger Buffalohead, Ponca; Beatrice Medicine, Standing Rock Sioux Tribe; and William Willard. *Wičazo Ša Review* ("Red Pencil" in Lakota) was originally published at Eastern Washington University, where Cook-Lynn served on the faculty. It was acquired by the University of Minnesota Press in 1999.

1989: The *Tribal College Journal (TCJ)*, a quarterly publication on tribal colleges and universities (TCUs). It was established by the American Indian Higher Education Consortium (AIHEC) and journalist Paul Boyer, who served as the founding editor during the journal's early years. *TCJ* was a critically important communication vehicle for the developing tribal college movement. In 2011, the publication went digital, providing online access and further expanding networks between TCUs and beyond.

1998: The First International Conference on Indigenous Literature, held in Guatemala, awarded José Barreiro, editor in chief of *Native Americas*, the inaugural Committed Plume Award. *Native Americas*, a journal published by the Akwe:kon Press at Cornell University's American Indian Program (now named American Indian and Indigenous Studies Program), also won five media awards at the 1998 Native American Journalists Association's (NAJA) annual conference held in Tempe, Arizona.

2013: Jean M. O'Brien, White Earth Ojibwe, University of Minnesota, and Robert Warrior, Osage, University of Kansas, served as the founding coeditors of the Native American and Indigenous Studies Association's *NAIS Journal*. The *NAIS Journal*, which publishes interdisciplinary scholarship, is pub-

lished twice a year by the University of Minnesota Press.

EARLY CHILDHOOD EDUCATION TO GRADE 12

"The prophecies say that the time will come when the grandchildren will speak to the whole world. The reason for the Akwesasne Freedom School is so the grandchildren will have something significant to say."

—*Sakokwenionkwas Tom Porter, Mohawk*

1784: Western schooling was first introduced in Alaska at Three Saints Bay, Kodiak Island, where the first Russian settlement, a fur trading site, was located.

Electa Quinney

1828: Electa Quinney (c. 1798–1885), a member of the Stockbridge-Munsee band of Mohicans, became Wisconsin's first public school teacher, founding the first school without an enrollment fee in what later became the state of Wisconsin. Born in Clinton, New York, Quinney attended schools in New York and Connecticut, relocating to the Wisconsin part of Michigan Territory around 1827, following the removal of her people from New York. In 2010, the Electa Quinney Institute for American Indian Education was founded in her honor at the University of Wisconsin–Milwaukee (UWM). It developed out of an endowed professorship in American Indian education at UWM established as a gift from Milwaukee's Indian Community School in Quinney's name in 1999.

1841: Stephen Foreman (1807–1881), Cherokee, served as the Cherokee Nation's first su-

Denise Juneau, Superintendent of Public Instruction in Montana

Denise Juneau

In 2008, Denise Juneau (1967–), Mandan/Hidatsa/Arikara, was elected superintendent of public instruction in Montana, becoming the first Native American woman elected to statewide office in Montana. In 2012, she won election for a second term in office. Juneau, a Democrat, ran for election to the U.S. House of Representatives in 2016 but was defeated by incumbent Ryan Zinke, a Republican, in the general election. In 2018, Juneau was unanimously selected to lead the Seattle School District, the first American Indian superintendent in the city's history. The district then served some 53,000 children, including 2,000 Native Americans. Juneau remained in the position until 2021.

perintendent of education, holding the position until 1843. Foreman, a Presbyterian minister, attended Union Theological Seminary in Virginia and Princeton Theological Seminary in New Jersey. In 1829, he served as assistant editor of the *Cherokee Phoenix*, where he translated news into the Cherokee language. In 1836, Foreman was a delegate to the U.S. government protesting the New Echota treaty of removal. Following his move to Indian Territory in 1839, he assisted the Reverend Samuel A. Worcester in translating the Bible into the Cherokee language. Foreman also served as an associate justice of the Supreme Court of the Cherokee Nation and held other offices.

1842: The Choctaw General Council enacted legislation to create a national education system. It consisted of day and boarding schools to serve both girls and boys. Wheelock Seminary, already in operation, was incorporated into the newly enacted system.

1909: Madeline Czarina Colbert Conlan (1871–1958), Chickasaw/Choctaw, became the first woman elected to the school board in Oklahoma. She served for two years—prior to women's suffrage—but was ruled ineligible by the state attorney general. She was educated at Baird College in Missouri and Mary Baldwin College in Virginia. In 1896, Conlan organized the Pioneer Club, the first women's club in Atoka, Choctaw Nation. She served as curator at the Oklahoma Historical Society from 1919 to 1942. In 1923, Conlan became the first Indian woman to be honored with a tree planted on Oklahoma's Capitol grounds.

1972: The "Survival School" philosophy was initiated by the American Indian Movement to address the holistic needs of urban Indian children, including life skills. The Heart of the Earth and Red School House survival schools were established in Minneapolis and St. Paul, Minnesota, to provide educational opportunities and support services for Native students from preschool to the 12th grade living in the Twin Cities. Both were alternative Indian-controlled community schools started by parents seeking to curb the high drop-out and push-out rates of Native American students. A key purpose was to teach academics from a Native perspective and with culturally appropriate curriculum. Red School House closed in 1996; Heart of Earth closed in 2010.

1973: Lloyd M. Elm (1934–2019), Onondaga, became the first Native American principal of the Onondaga Indian School in New York, working to expand the number of grades from six to eight. He was given the name Gah Nonh Sah Se, "New House," for his ability to improve the school. Elm was an award-winning athlete, becoming the Kansas State High School mile champion in 1953 and being inducted into the College of Emporia Athletic Hall of Fame. Returning home from Kansas, he attended Syracuse University (SU) and played lacrosse on a squad that include football's famed Jim Brown. In 1978, Elm was among the Onondaga leaders who successfully petitioned SU to remove its Saltine Warrior symbol and mascot, Big Chief Bill Orange. In 1984, Elm became the founder of Native American Magnet School 19 in Buffalo, New York, serving as principal until 1997. He was also a professor at Cornell University and at SUNY Buffalo State. Elm was the recipient of honors that included an Educator of the Year and a Lifetime Achievement Award by the National Indian Education Association.

1975: The Indian Self-Determination and Education Assistance Act, Public Law 93-638, was enacted by the U.S. Congress. The legislation provided American Indian tribal nations with greater autonomy, including the means to assume responsibility for programs and services through contractual agreements. It helped empower tribes to exercise their sovereignty, taking control over services that the federal government had previously provided, controlled, and implemented exclusively.

1979: The Akwesasne Freedom School (AFS) was started by parents and community members on the Akwesasne Reservation in upstate New York, bordering Canada. At the time, only about 5 percent of people on the reservation spoke Mohawk. The community saw a need to preserve traditions and direct the education of the nation starting with the children. They wanted their young people to be educated in the language, to be raised with ceremony and culture on the land of their ancestors without the influence and interference of the Western world, and to develop positive values and healthy self-esteem. AFS has had remarkable success with the total Mohawk immersion program in the K–8 school. There has been an increase in Mohawk language speakers, rejuvenation of cultural strength and familiarity, and the continuance of intergenerational hands-on learning.

1981: The National Native American Honor Society was founded by acclaimed geneticist Dr. Frank C. Dukepoo (1943–1999), the first Hopi to earn a Ph.D. The society's purpose included recognizing Native American students across the country who are achieving straight As in their academic work.

Rough Rock Demonstration School

Rough Rock Demonstration School, founded by educators Robert Roessel Jr. and Ruth Roessel (Navajo) in 1966, was established by the Navajo Nation, the first tribal nation in the United States to assume control of a Bureau of Indian Affairs school. The offerings included bilingual education in English and Diné Bizaad (Navajo language) and other changes under tribal control, direction, and implementation. Rough Rock, located in Chinle, Arizona, served as a model for other American Indian schools to become tribally controlled. It was later renamed the Rough Rock Community School.

The Kamehameha Schools include three campuses: Kapālama, Honolulu, O'ahu (pictured); Pukalani, Maui; and Keaëau, Hawai'i.

Kamehameha Schools

Princess Ke Ali'i Bernice Pauahi Bishop (1831–1884), great-granddaughter of Kamehameha the Great, recognized the power of education to uplift Native Hawaiians and offer hope for their future. She left a will that would finance the Kamehameha Schools in perpetuity and provide any Native Hawaiian with a free private school education. Bishop established the Bernice Pauahi Bishop Estate trust, Hawai'i's largest private landowner. The Kamehameha Schools opened in 1887 and today operate 31 preschools statewide and grade K–12 campuses in Kapālama, O'ahu; Pukalani, Maui; and Kea'au, Hawai'i. The largest is Kapālama Heights in Honolulu, which boards students from other islands and has more than 70 buildings and extensive athletic facilities, including a 3,000-seat stadium, an Olympic-size swimming pool, three gymnasiums, and several tennis courts. Some notable graduates from the Kamehameha Schools include Brook Mahealani Lee (1971–) American actress, television host, and Miss Universe 1997; Isabella Aiona Abbott (1919–2010), the first Native Hawaiian woman to receive a Ph.D. in science; Daniel Akaka (1924–2018), the first Native Hawaiian U.S. senator, who served from 1990 to 2013; and Auli'i Cravalho (2000–), an American actress and the titular character in the 2016 Disney computer animated musical feature film *Moana*. It is the only private school system in the country for Indigenous people.

1989: Wisconsin passed a law known as Act 31 that requires all public-school students in the state to learn the history, culture, and tribal sovereignty of Wisconsin's federally recognized tribal nations. *The Story of Act 31: How Native History Came to Wisconsin Classrooms* (2018) examines the landmark legislation and its implementation.

1997: Dorothy Tabbyyetchy (Sunrise) Lorentino (1909–2005), Comanche, became the first American Indian and the first person from Oklahoma to be named to the National Teachers Hall of Fame. She taught elementary and special needs children for 34 years at schools in Arizona, New Mexico, Oregon, and Oklahoma. In 1918, her father won a landmark case in her name, *Dorothy Sunrise v. District Board of Cache Consolidated School District No. 1.* This public school had refused to admit her on the basis of race, believing American Indians were filthy and would bring lice or disease to white students. Her father's legal victory made it possible for Native American children to attend public schools rather than being restricted to Indian schools, many of which were far from the home communities of students. In 1996, the Dorothy Sunrise Lorentino Award was initiated at Cache High School to annually honor an American Indian graduating senior best exemplifying Lorentino's qualities.

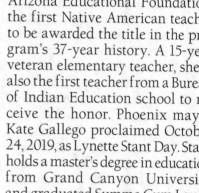

Lynette Stant shown here with U.S. Representative Greg Stanton (D-AZ).

2005: Southern Ute Indian Academy in Ignacio, Colorado, was the first tribal school to earn certification as a National Wildlife Schoolyard Habitat site.

2009: Teach for America's (TFA) Native Achievement Initiative was launched to improve educational outcomes for Native students, initially serving communities in Hawaii, South Dakota, New Mexico, and Oklahoma. In 2013, the name was changed to Native Alliance Initiative and, in 2019, shortened to Native Alliance. TFA was named the best place to work in STEM by *Winds of Change* magazine for the sixth consecutive year in 2019. Robert Cook, Oglala Lakota, directs TFA's Native Alliance, working to provide an additional source of teachers, advance student achievement, and increase opportunities through culturally responsive teaching.

2019: Lynette Stant, a citizen of the Navajo Nation and third-grade teacher at Salt River Elementary School in the Salt River Pima-Maricopa Indian Community, was named 2020 Arizona Teacher of the Year by the Arizona Educational Foundation, the first Native American teacher to be awarded the title in the program's 37-year history. A 15-year veteran elementary teacher, she is also the first teacher from a Bureau of Indian Education school to receive the honor. Phoenix mayor Kate Gallego proclaimed October 24, 2019, as Lynette Stant Day. Stant holds a master's degree in education from Grand Canyon University and graduated Summa Cum Laude with a bachelor's degree in elementary education from Arizona State University. She is also the cofounder of Indigenous Educators Unite, an online support platform.

2020: Carletta Tilousi (1970–) became the first Havasupai tribal leader appointed to First Things First (FTF) Coconino Regional Council. FTF, Arizona's early child-care agency, helps define priorities for services and support for families with children from birth to age five. Its collaborative efforts provide opportunities for youngsters to get a strong start in life. Tilousi, who earned a bachelor of science degree in justice studies from Arizona State University, has more than 25 years of experience working for social and environmental justice for Indige-

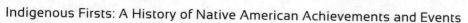

nous peoples of the Grand Canyon. Besides her longtime service on the Havasupai Tribal Council, Tilousi is the president of Red Rock Foundation, a nonprofit organization focused on educational and environmental issues affecting tribes.

◆◇◆
LAW SCHOOLS AND LEGAL WORKS

1823: James McDonald (1801–1831), Choctaw, completed his legal training in Ohio, becoming the first American Indian in the United States to be professionally trained as an attorney. Unable to secure a position at a law firm, he returned to his tribal homeland in Mississippi. McDonald became his tribe's legal advisor, drawing on his training to defend their rights. Enlisted to accompany a tribal delegation to Washington, D.C., in 1824, he assumed a critical role in treaty sessions. "For the first time," author Frederick Hoxie points out, "a tribal attorney would conduct tribal negotiations with the United States." The delegation secured a number of its objectives in a new treaty signed in early 1825. McDonald also drafted an open letter to Congress that foreshadowed the fight for Indian rights across time.

1914: Marie Louise Bottineau Baldwin (1863–1952), Turtle Mountain Band of Chippewa Indians in North Dakota, graduated from Washington College of Law (now part of American University in Washington, D.C.), becoming the first Native American woman to graduate from law school in the United States. She had been a legal clerk for her father, Jean Baptiste Bottineau, whose work included litigating

Marie Louise Bottineau Baldwin

treaty rights on behalf of the Turtle Mountain Chippewa in Washington, D.C. Bottineau Baldwin, who spoke Anishinaabemowin, English, and French, attended law school at night, completing the three-year course in two years, while continuing to work as a legal clerk. She served as a clerk in the Office of Indian Affairs, an agency within the U.S. Department of the Interior, and was appointed to the position by President Theodore Roosevelt in 1904, the first Native woman in the office. Bottineau Baldwin also served on the executive committee of the Society of American Indians, speaking at the organization's first convention in Columbus, Ohio, in 1911. A suffragist, she marched in the 1913 Suffrage Parade, fighting for voting rights for women.

1968: The Hawai'i State Legislature established the William S. Richardson School of Law at the University of Hawai'i at Manoa, located in Honolulu. It remains the only law school in Hawai'i and the only law school in the country named for a Native person. Chief Justice William S. Richardson, Native Hawaiian, of the Hawai'i State Supreme Court (1966–1982), also served as a trustee of what is now Kamehameha Schools/ Bishop Estate. Prior to his tenure as the top jurist in Hawai'i, Richardson was lieutenant governor under John A. Burns. In both the law school and the court, Richardson advocated for Native Hawaiian rights, including teaching and integrating laws created by the Hawaiian Kingdom. Since admitting its first students in 1973, the school has become a top-rated institution, particularly for its success with Native Hawaiian, Asian American, and female students. Students can earn certificates in Native Hawaiian law, Pacific-Asian legal studies, international law, and environmental law; many graduates hold prominent positions, including governor of Hawai'i; lieutenant governor; president of a Hawai'i university; a federal magistrate; and justices for the Hawai'i Supreme Court and intermediate court of appeals. In a 2020 *preLaw Magazine* survey of best law schools for people of color, Richardson School of Law was named the top school for both Asian and Native Hawaiian students.

1990: Rennard Strickland (1940–), Cherokee Nation/Osage, founded the Center for the Study of American Indian Law and Policy at the University of Oklahoma's College of Law, a center that provides counsel to tribal, state, and national policymakers and a forum to address issues facing Native communities. A legal historian, he is considered a pioneer in introducing law into higher education curriculum. Strickland is the first person to have served both as president of the Association of American Law Schools and as chair of the Law School Admissions Council. An authority on federal Indian law, he has served as a law professor, law school dean, and legal historian as well as an author and collector.

1994: Christine Zuni Cruz, Isleta Pueblo/Ohkay Owingeh, became the first tenured Native law professor at the University of New Mexico (UNM). In 2000, she assisted law students in establishing the first electronic public-access journal dedicated solely to the law of Indigenous peoples (UNM School of Law's *Tribal Law Journal*).

2003: The Oneida Indian Nation Professorship of Law was established at Harvard Law School by the Oneida Indian Nation in New York, becoming the first endowed chair in American Indian studies at Harvard and the only professorship of its kind east of the Mississippi River. The professorship was created with a three-million-dollar gift "to help create a better understanding of the complex legal issues faced by all American Indians today and in the future." Robert A. Williams Jr., Lumbee, was named the first Oneida Indian Nation Visiting Professor of Law.

2009: Kevin K. Washburn (1967–), a citizen of the Chickasaw Nation, was named professor and dean of the University of New Mexico School of Law, the first American Indian to serve in the position. A graduate of Yale Law School, he served as Regents Professor of Law at the University of New Mexico School of Law and its dean from 2009 to 2012, when he became assistant secretary of Indian affairs at the U.S. Department of the Interior. Washburn also worked as a trial attorney and then a prosecutor with the U.S. Department of Justice and served as the general counsel of the National Indian Gaming Commission. His work in academia includes faculty positions in Minnesota and Arizona and a year of teaching at Harvard University. Washburn is the author of *Gaming and Gambling Law: Cases and Materials* (2010) and other writings.

2011: Matthew L. M. Fletcher, a member of the Grand Traverse Band of Ottawa and Chippewa Indians, authored *American Indian Tribal Law* (Aspen, 2011), the first casebook for law students on tribal law. Fletcher, professor of law at Michigan State University College of Law and director of the Indigenous Law and Policy Center, is also the coauthor of the sixth edition of *Cases and Materials on Federal Indian Law* (Thomson West, 2011) with David Getches, Charles Wilkinson, and Robert Williams. Other writings include coediting *The Indian Civil Rights Act at Forty* with Kristen A. Carpenter and Angela R. Riley (UCLA American Indian Studies Press, 2012). Fletcher is the primary editor and author of *Turtle Talk*, the leading law blog on American Indian law and policy.

2011: Stacy L. Leeds (1971–), citizen of the Cherokee Nation, served as dean of the University of Arkansas School of Law until

2018, the first American Indian woman to lead a law school. Leeds, who holds law degrees from the University of Wisconsin (LLM) and University of Tulsa J.D., was also the first woman to serve as a justice on the Cherokee Nation Supreme Court. She was the inaugural vice chancellor for economic development at the University of Arkansas from 2017 to 2020. As dean emeritus, Leeds also planned and implemented the new Office of Economic Development there. Earlier academic roles include Salt River Pima–Maricopa Indian Community Distinguished Visiting Professor of Law at Arizona State University, director of the Tribal Law and Government Center at the University of Kansas, and director of the Northern Plains Indian Law center at the University of North Dakota. Leeds serves as the Foundation Professor of Law and Leadership at Sandra Day O'Connor College of Law at Arizona State University.

2018: John Borrows (1963–), a member of the Chippewas of the Nawash First Nation in Ontario, Canada, cofounded the joint common law and Indigenous law degree program at the University of Victoria Faculty of Law. It is the first program in a Canadian law school that provides for an integrated study of Canadian common law and Indigenous legal traditions.

John Borrows

Borrows, who earned his doctor of law at the University of Toronto Faculty of Law and his doctor of philosophy at Osgoode Hall Law School at York University in Toronto, serves as Canada Research Chair in Indigenous Law at the University of Victoria. He is a leading authority on Canadian law.

2019: Elizabeth Kronk Warner, Sault Ste. Marie Tribe of Chippewa Indians, became the first woman named a law school dean at the University of Utah's S. J. Quinney College of Law. Kronk Warner earned her juris doctorate from the University of Michigan Law School, an undergraduate degree in communications from Cornell University, and also studied at Nanyang Technological University in Singapore. She served as associate dean of academic affairs, professor, and director of the Tribal Law and Government Center at the University of Kansas School of Law. Kronk Warner is considered a national expert in environmental and tribal law.

2020: The Sandra Day O'Connor College of Law at Arizona State University became the first law school in the United States to offer both Indian Gaming and Tribal Self-Governance programs as part of its Indian Legal Program. The Indian Gaming program was planned to provide an in-depth curriculum focused on the legal developments associated with Indian gaming. The Tribal Self-Governance program identified areas of study such as federal Indian policy, negotiation of contracts and compacts, and evolving trends in tribal self-governance. The programs were envisioned as a degree emphasis in the Master of Legal Studies (MLS) degree program and Master of Laws (LLM) degree program, and as a certificate.

2021: Elizabeth Reese, Yunpovi (Willow Flower), a member of the Nambé Pueblo in New Mexico, became the first Native American faculty member at Stanford Law School (SLS) and the first enrolled citizen of a tribal nation to secure a tenure-track appointment at a top three law school. Reese, who received her JD from Harvard Law School in 2016, has worked at the NAACP Legal Defense and Education Fund and the National Congress of American Indians. Reese wrote "The Other American Law," an article published in the *Stanford Law Review* that was critical of the exclusion of tribal law from the mainstream curricula of law schools.

LEGISLATIVE ACTIONS

1819: The Civilization Fund Act was enacted by Congress to introduce "the habits and arts of civilization" among Indian tribes. The legislation indicated "that the means of instruction can be introduced with their own consent, to employ capable persons ... to instruct them in the mode of agriculture suited to their situation; and for teaching their children in reading, writing, and arithmetic...." The legislation provided for the annual sum of ten thousand dollars for the purpose of carrying out the provisions of the act.

1928: The Meriam Report, officially called The Problem of Indian Administration, was the first government study to illustrate with extensive data that federal Indian policy had failed Native Americans, including in education. For instance, the report criticized boarding schools for inadequate medical services, overcrowded dormitories, deficient diets, rigid routinization, reliance on student labor, and other measures. Lewis Meriam, from the Institute for Government Research, directed the survey of conditions of Native Americans nationally. Data and findings from the Meriam Report were used to help reform U.S. Indian policy.

1989: American Indian Studies in Wisconsin, often called Act 31, requires that all public school districts and preservice education programs provide instruction on the history, culture, and tribal sovereignty of the eleven federally recognized American Indian nations in the state.

2005: The Navajo Sovereignty in Education Act of 2005 was enacted by the Navajo Nation Council, marking the first time that the Navajo Nation linked sovereignty with education in such a manner. The legislation established the Navajo Nation Board of Education and the Navajo Nation Department of Diné Education. It also confirmed the Navajo Nation's commitment to the education of the Navajo people and updated applicable existing language of the Navajo Nation Code.

2020: U.S. representative Deb Haaland (D-NM) and U.S. senator Elizabeth Warren (D-Mass.) introduced the Truth and Healing Commission on Indian Boarding School Policy in the United States Act, which would establish the first formal commission in U.S. history to investigate, document, and acknowledge past injustices of the federal government's Indian boarding school policies. The commission would also develop recommendations for Congress to aid in healing the historical and intergenerational trauma in Native American families and communities and provide a forum for victims to speak about experiences tied to these human rights violations.

NATIVE LANGUAGE

1886: The Cherokee Nation was the first to establish a phone line west of the Mississippi River. Phone lines connected Tahlequah and Ft. Gibson, Oklahoma, roughly 30 miles apart, and tribal members were able to speak to each other in Cherokee. It was noted that this technology "speaks our language" and was quickly adopted by the tribe.

1887: Commissioner of Indian Affairs J. D. C. Atkins mandated that mission and government-run schools provide English-only instruction. Native languages were banned from being spoken or taught.

c. 1965: The Hermes company developed the Hermes 3000 typewriter, the first to feature

a		e	i	o	u	v [ə]
a		e	i	o	u	v
ga ka		ge	gi	go	gu	gv
ha		he	hi	ho	hu	hv
la		le	li	lo	lu	lv
ma		me	mi	mo	mu	
na hna nah		ne	ni	no	nu	nv
qua		que	qui	quo	quu	quv
s sa		se	si	so	su	sv
da ta		de te	di ti	do	du	dv
dla tla		tle	tli	tlo	tlu	tlv
tsa		tse	tsi	tso	tsu	tsv
wa		we	wi	wo	wu	wv
ya		ye	yi	yo	yu	yv

The first typewriter using a Cherokee syllabary ball was an IBM Selectric in the 1970s. Later, in the 1990s, computer word processing software introduced the characters as well.

the Cherokee syllabary, but there was not enough room on the keyboard for all of the 85 syllabary characters. In the mid-1970s, the Cherokee Nation worked with IBM to create an IBM Selectric Typewriter ball in syllabary, which could accommodate all the characters as well as different size fonts. When word processers became popular in the 1980s, the Cherokee Nation contracted with a company to develop word processing software in Cherokee, and the first word-processed document in syllabary was presented to Chief Wilma Mankiller in 1987. Cherokee fonts for computers began to appear in the 1990s, and in 1999 the Cherokee Nation developed its own font. Because the Cherokee character set was not initially Unicode compliant, many issues arose, but after Cherokee was formally encoded into Unicode (2000), the communication barriers were resolved. In 2003 Apple added a Cherokee keyboard and font to the Macintosh operating system, and in 2007, the Cherokee Immersion Charter School in Park Hill, Oklahoma, began using MacBooks in the no-English-spoken school. Although the Nation did not ask for a Cherokee font, it is thought that Apple founder Steve Jobs liked typographic design and calligraphy and was fascinated with the syllabary. In 2009, Cherokee Nation Language Technology teamed up with Apple to develop a font and keyboard for the iPhone, and in 2010 over 40 million iPhones had the ability to display and type in Cherokee. The technology has encouraged both young people and elders to text and communicate in Cherokee, proving that Cherokee is very much a contemporary and viable language.

1978: Hawai'i became the first state in the nation to recognize an Indigenous language, Native Hawaiian, as its official language along with English. The legal wording states: "The Hawaiian language is the native language of Hawaii and may be used on all emblems and symbols representative of the State, its departments, agencies and political subdivisions." The state motto and state song are in Native Hawaiian.

1978: The American Indian Language Development Institute (AILDI) was founded in 1978 with support from the National Endowment for the Humanities. Lucille Watahomigie, Hualapai educator and language activist, with Leanne Hinton, linguist at the University of California Berkeley, developed a Yuman language workshop focused on Digueno, Havasupai, Hualapai, Mohave, and Yavapai language communities. The first workshop was held at San Diego State University and then the work rotated to other schools. In 1990, AILDI found a permanent home at the University of Arizona. It continues to offer Indigenous language education experience to a range of audiences.

1983: The grassroots organization Pūnana Leo (Hawaiian: "voice nest"; often translated as "language nest") was formed to lift the 90-year ban on teaching Hawaiian in public and private schools. In 1984, the first Pūnana Leo preschool opened in Kekaha, Kaua'i, even though it did not have government approval. Instruction is based on the practices of nineteenth-century Hawaiian-language schools, as well as the Kohanga reo Māori language kindergartens in New Zealand. The Pūnana Leo was the first Indigenous language immersion preschool project in the United States. Graduates from the Pūnana Leo schools have achieved several measures of academic success in later life. Over the past several decades, 'Aha Pūnana Leo established and built numerous programs throughout the islands, inspiring other Indigenous people to revitalize their languages and to raise awareness about the consequences of the loss of Indigenous languages.

1987: The Piegan Institute, a nonprofit organization, was cofounded by educator Dar-

rell Robes Kipp on the Blackfeet Indian Reservation in Browning, Montana. Its work centers on revitalizing the Blackfoot language within the tribal nation. In 1992, the Piegan Institute established the Nizi Puh Wah Sin Blackfoot Language Schools Immersion Program for K–8 students. In 1995, the Institute built a one-room private school, Moccasin Flat, for all-day instruction exclusively in the Blackfoot language.

1990: The Native American Languages Act, Public Law 101-477, was enacted by the U.S. Congress. It repudiated past policies, declaring that "acts of suppression and extermination directed against Native American languages and cultures are in conflict with the United States policy of self-determination for Native Americans." The legislation noted that the United States has the responsibility to help ensure the survival of these unique cultures and languages. The act declared as U.S. policy to "preserve, protect, and promote the rights and freedom of Native Americans to use, practice, and develop Native American languages."

1992: The Indigenous Language Institute (ILI) was founded as the Institute for the Preservation of the Original Languages of the Americas (IPOLA) in Santa Fe, New Mexico. In 1997, the organization became a national center to serve all tribes and individuals working to revitalize Indigenous languages in the Americas. In 2000, IPOLA was changed to Indigenous Language Institute (ILI) to reflect new leadership, expanded services, and working relations internationally.

1998: The University of Hawaii at Hilo established the College of Hawaiian Language, Ka Haka 'Ula O Ke'elikōlani, the first college immersed in the medium of Hawaiian. The college's mission is to assure the revitalization and continued growth of the language, striving for it to once again become commonplace in Hawai'i.

1999: Albert White Hat (1938–2013), a member of the Rosebud Sioux Tribe in South Dakota, became the first Native Lakota speaker to publish a Lakota textbook, *Reading and Writing the Lakota Language* (University of Utah Press, 1999). White Hat was the grandson of prominent leader Chief Hollow Horn Bear and grew up speaking Lakota as his first language. He taught the Lakota language at Sinte Gleska University at Rosebud, where he became the head of the Lakota Studies Department. White Hat also translated the Hollywood movie *Dances with Wolves* into Lakota for the film's actors. He was the recipient of many honors for his dedication to preserving his tribal nation's language and culture, including the Living Indian Treasure Award in 2007.

2003: Lynette Stein-Chandler (1975–2017), member of the Aaniiih Nation (Gros Ventre), founded the White Clay Language Immersion School (WCLIS), a private school under the umbrella of the Aaniiih Nakoda College on the Fort Belknap Indian Reservation in Montana. Stein-Chandler, who completed her doctorate in education at the University of Montana, was nationally and internationally known for her language revitalization work. She was the recipient of the Montana Indian Educator of the Year award in 2012 and the Educational Leadership Excellence Award in 2013. The Fort Belknap Indian Community honored her by declaring May 7, 2012, as Dr. Lynette Chandler Day in recognition of her achievements. In 2017, she was posthumously awarded an honorary doctorate in letters from Montana State University.

2006: A Mohawk community and Rosetta Stone, a software company headquartered in Arlington, Virginia, developed the first-ever Mohawk immersion software. It was the first endangered language software to be developed through Rosetta Stone's Endangered Language Program, founded in 2004. The work was sponsored by Kanien-'kehák Onkwawén:na Raotitióhkwa the Mohawk language and cultural center in Kahnawake, Quebec, Canada. Mohawk Level 1 of the program was released in 2006, followed by Mohawk Level 2 in 2009.

2006: The University of Hawaii at Hilo established a Ph.D. program in Hawaiian and Indigenous language and culture revitalization, the first doctorate in a Hawaiian studies field and the first doctorate in the world specific to the field of Indigenous language and culture revitalization. UH-Hilo's program started with provisional status in 2006 and was approved as an established program in 2015. The doctoral program and the master's (established in 2002) are both recognized as pioneering in the work of revitalizing Native languages.

2008: New Mexico became the first state to adopt a Navajo language textbook for use in the state's public schools. The book, *Diné Bizaad Bináhoo'aah: Rediscovering the Navajo Language*, was written by Evangeline Parsons Yazzie, Ed.D., a Navajo professor at Northern Arizona University, and Margaret Speas, a linguist and founding member of the Navajo Language Academy.

2009: Nkwusm, a Salish language immersion school that opened in the fall of 2002 on the Salish-Kootenai Reservation in Arlee, Montana, had its first graduation. It provides a complete academic program and emphasizes Salish language, culture, and history.

2011: A 20-episode Lakota language edition of the Berenstain Bears, the popular children's literature franchise, became the first Native American language cartoon series. The project was made possible as a joint venture of the Standing Rock Sioux Tribe and the Lakota Language Consortium with the permission of Berenstain Enterprises. The series, Mathó Wauŋšila Thiwáhe (the Compassionate Bear Family), sought to enhance the use of Lakota language by audiences in North and South Dakota and beyond.

2014: Alaska amended its 1998 act designating English as the official state language in 2014, adding 20 Alaskan Native languages as co-official languages. The languages are Inupiaq, Siberian Yupik, Central Alaskan Yup'ik, Alutiiq, Unángax, Dena'ina, Deg Xinag, Holikachuk, Koyukon, Upper Kuskokwim, Gwich'in, Tanana, Upper Tanana, Tanacross, Hän, Ahtna, Eyak, Tlingit, Haida, and Tsimshian.

2019: Organized by Quechua and Spanish professor Americo Mendoza-Mori, the University of Pennsylvania hosted its first Indigenous Languages Week to emphasize, in part, the study of Indigenous languages and cultures as modern. The event was inspired by the United Nations declaration of the International Year of Indigenous Languages in 2019. Penn's Quechua Language Program was created in 2015, becoming the only Quechua program in the Ivy League.

2021: The University of British Columbia-Okanagan announced the bachelor of Nsyilxcn language fluency program, becoming the first university in Canada to offer a bachelor's degree in Indigenous language fluency. Created in collaboration with the Nicola Valley Institute of Technology and the En'owkin Centre, the program selected the language spoken by members of the Syilx Okanagan Nation.

ORGANIZATIONS

1969: The National Indian Education Association (NIEA) was formed in Minneapolis, Minnesota, by Native American educators and formally incorporated in 1970. It was founded to improve the education system for Native children. NIEA's founding principles include bringing Native educators together to explore ways to improve schools and schooling, promoting the maintenance of Native languages and cultures, and developing and implementing strategies for influencing policy and policymakers. The organization hosts an annual convention that provides a national forum for exchanging ideas and influencing policy. Currently based in Washington, D.C., NIEA has become the oldest and largest national education organization dedicated to the educational issues of American Indians, Alaska Natives, and Native Hawaiians.

1973: The American Indian Higher Education Consortium (AIHEC) was founded by the presidents of the first six tribal colleges in the nation to serve as a means of collaborating among member institutions. Gerald One Feather, Oglala Lakota, served as AIHEC's first president, followed by Lionel Bordeaux and then David M. Gipp, Hunkpapa Lakota, who helped establish AIHEC and served as the organization's first executive director. An AIHEC office in Denver, Colorado, was made possible with offerings of start-up support from the Ford, Carnegie, and Donner foundations in 1973. Today, AIHEC has grown to represent some 38 tribal colleges and universities across the country.

1989: The American Indian College Fund (AICF) was established by the American Indian Higher Education Consortium (AIHEC) to provide private funding for tribal colleges and universities (TCUs) and to provide financial assistance to Native students to help make it possible for them to attend TCUs.

2002: The World Indigenous Nations Higher Education Consortium (WINHEC) was launched with the signing of the Declaration on Indigenous People's Higher Education in Calgary, Alberta, Canada during the World Indigenous Peoples Conference on Education in August 2002. Founding members present included Australia, Hawaii, Alaska, the American Indian Higher Education Consortium (AIHEC), Canada, the Wānanga of Aotearoa (New Zealand), and Saamiland (North Norway).

2007: The Native American and Indigenous Studies Association (NAISA) was formed as an interdisciplinary, international membership-based organization to provide a gathering place for Native studies scholars to exchange ideas and work. It was cofounded by Inés Hernández-Ávila, Nimipu/Nez Perce and Tejana; J. Kēhaulani Kauanui, Native Hawaiian; K. Tsianina Lomawaima, Mvskoke/Creek Nation; Jean M. O'Brien, White Earth Nation; Robert Warrior, Osage Nation; and Jace Weaver, Cherokee.

2010: The Association of Tribal Archives, Libraries, and Museums (ATALM) was incorporated as a nonprofit organization in 2010, building upon earlier work at national conferences. Based in Oklahoma City, Oklahoma, ATALM provides culturally relevant programming and services, encourages collaborative work among tribal and nontribal institutions, and offers advocacy measures.

2012: The National Native American Boarding School Healing Coalition (NABS) was incorporated as a nonprofit organization in June 2012 under the laws of the Navajo Nation. It was created to develop and implement a national strategy to increase public awareness and cultivate healing for the ongoing trauma experienced by American Indians and Alaska Natives resulting from U.S. Indian boarding school policies.

2018: IllumiNative was founded as a national, Native-led racial justice organization. It works in areas that include pop culture, media, and K–12 education. IllumiNative partnered with the National Congress of American Indians (NCAI), National Indian Education Association (NIEA), National Education Association (NEA), and Wend Collective to release a comprehensive report on Native American K–12 curricula, *Becoming Visible: A Landscape Analysis of State Efforts to Provide Native American Education for All* (NCAI, 2019).

2019: The Auntie Project: Native Women of Service was founded in Norman, Oklahoma, with educator and author Amanda Cobb-Greetham, Chickasaw, serving as the founding president. The nonprofit organization is dedicated to helping Native American and Indigenous children in need.

SCIENCE AND TECHNOLOGY GRADUATES

1950: Isabella Aiona Abbott (1919–2010) graduated from the University of California, Berkeley, the first Native Hawai'ian woman to earn a Ph.D. in science. She became a full professor in Stanford University's biology department, a first for a woman as well as a member of a minority. Abbott was one of the world's foremost authorities on limu, or the 70-plus edible varieties of seaweed, winning her the accolade "First Lady of Limu." She was also considered the leading expert on Pacific algae. Through her work teaching Hawai'ian ethnobotany at the University of Hawai'i at Manoa, the university created a bachelor's degree in the subject. Abbott's many honors include receiving the National Academy of Science's highest award in marine botany, being named a Living Treasure of Hawaii, and receiving the opportunity to name a National Oceanographic and Atmospheric Administration research ship, the *Hi'ialakai*. Her writings include *La'au Hawai'i: Traditional Hawaiian Uses of Plants*.

1971: Fred Begay (Clever Fox) (1932–2013), Navajo/Ute, became the first member of the Navajo Nation to earn a Ph.D. in nuclear physics, achieving his doctorate at the University of New Mexico (UNM) in 1971. From 1960 to 1963 and 1965 to 1972, he was part of a NASA-supported space physics research team at UNM that conducted studies on the origin of high-energy gamma rays and solar neutrons. Begay began working at Los Alamos National Laboratory as part of its physics staff in 1971. During his career, he held research and teaching fellowships at Stanford University and the University of Maryland. Begay also provided expertise to an extensive number of institutions. His life has been featured in films such as *Nation within a Nation* (Hearst Metrotone News, 1972), *In Our Native Land* (Sandia Laboratory 1973), *The Long Walk of Fred Young-Begay* (BBC and NOVA, 1978), and *Dancing with Photons* (KNME-TV, 1997). He has also appeared in a range of print publications, including *National Geographic*, *Notable Twentieth-Century Scientists* (Gale Research, 1994), textbooks, and various journals and newspapers. Begay was the recipient of numerous awards, including the Ely Parker Award from the American Indian Science & Engineering Society, the Lifetime Achievement Award from the National Science Foundation, and the Distinguished Scientist Award from the Society for the Advancement of Chicanos/Hispanics and Native Americans in Science. He also served as president of the Seaborg Hall of Science, an independent nonprofit education and research institution, in Los Alamos, New Mexico.

Isabella Aiona Abbott

Fred Begay

1973: Frank Dukepoo (1943–1999) graduated from Arizona State University with a Ph.D. in zoology (genetics), becoming the first Hopi to receive a doctorate. He also became known as the first Native American geneticist, one of two in the country. Dukepoo was one of the founding members of the Society for Advancement of Chicanos/Hispanics and Native Americans in Science (SACNAS) and the American Indian Science and Engineering Society (AISES). In 1982 he founded the National Native American Honor Society to recognize high achieving students from fourth grade through graduate and professional school.

1977: A. T. (Andy) Anderson, Mohawk, was a cofounder and the first executive director of the American Indian Science & Engineering Society (AISES), which was established to enhance the number of Native students in engineering and science-related fields. Anderson was a chemical engineer who was awarded an honorary doctor of science degree. His early career included working on the Manhattan Project at the onset of World War II. AISES launched the A. T. Anderson Memorial Scholarship Program in 1983 to honor his memory. It provides financial assistance to qualifying undergraduate and graduate students who are majoring in engineering and other designated fields.

1977: Lorena Hegdal (1954–), Inupiaq, was the first Native woman to graduate from the University of Alaska Fairbanks with a bachelor's degree in civil engineering. Following 24 years with the Alaska Department of Transportation, she joined the Alyeska Pipeline Service Company in 2000. Her leadership responsibilities have included serving as director of right-of-way and emergency preparedness and compliance of the 800-mile-long pipeline. Hegdal, the recipient of numerous awards, also mentors Alaska Native students toward careers in science and engineering.

1977: Al Qöyawayma (1938–), Hopi, a mechanical engineer and potter who earned his master's degree in engineering from the University of Southern California, was a cofounder and first chairman of the American Indian Science & Engineering Society (AISES). "If you have flown internationally or were a pilot in the Gulf War," one biographical account notes about him, "you would have already entrusted yourself to his creativeness." He holds patents worldwide on inertial guidance systems. His pottery is also acclaimed. Astronaut John Herrington, Chickasaw, took one of Qöyawayma's ceramic pots into orbit aboard Space Shuttle Mission STS-113. It is now in the collection of the National Museum of the American Indian.

1980: Donna J. Nelson (1954–), Muscogee Creek Nation, earned her Ph.D. in chemistry at the University of Texas at Austin and then became the first woman to do post-doctorate work with Nobel Prize winner Herbert Charles Brown at Purdue University. Nelson was also the first woman on the tenure track as a professor of chemistry at the University of Oklahoma. Her contributions include pioneering research into the disparity in representation of minorities and women in science and engineering fields. In 2002, she published the first Nelson Diversity Survey, which documented the number of faculty in science and engineering by gender, ethnicity, and rank in higher education. Other such surveys followed. Nelson also served as the science advisor to the popular AMC television series *Breaking Bad*, which aired from 2008 to 2013. She is the coauthor of *The Science of Breaking Bad* (MIT Press, 2019).

1992: Suzanne Van Cooten (1968–), Chickasaw Nation, is considered to be the first

Dr. Donna J. Nelson had her photo appear on the Times Square JumboTron in New York City for her work as an advisor on the TV series *Breaking Bad*.

Native female meteorologist in the country. She worked in a range of weather-related roles while pursuing her master of science degree in engineering and her Ph.D. in engineering and applied science at the University of New Orleans. Van Cooten is identified as the only woman of Native American descent to have obtained a Ph.D. within the National Oceanic and Atmospheric Administration (NOAA).

2005: Powtawche Williams Valerino (1973–), Mississippi Band of Choctaw Indians, became the first Native American to earn a Ph.D. in engineering at Rice University in Houston, Texas. Born to a Choctaw mother and African American father, Valerino earned a bachelor's degree in mechanical engineering from Stanford University and completed master's and doctoral degrees at Rice. In 2005, she joined the NASA Jet Propulsion Laboratory's Mission Design and Navigation Section. Her work has included serving as a navigator with the maneuver and trajectory team on the Cassini mission.

She also worked on the Parker Solar Probe spacecraft, which launched on August 12, 2018. Valerino, who received the NAACP's Education Award in 2016, actively encourages the participation of underrepresented groups in STEM fields.

2006: Otakuye Conroy-Ben (1976–), Oglala Lakota, who graduated from the University of Arizona, became the first Lakota to complete a Ph.D. in environmental engineering. She also completed two master's degrees there, her research interests including wastewater epidemiology. Conroy-Ben served on the faculty at the University of Utah for five years before returning to Arizona to teach civil, environmental, and sustainable engineering at Arizona State University. She also continues to mentor Native American and female students to counteract their underrepresentation in STEM fields.

Marcos Moreno

2011: Sophia Natalia Cisneros, a member of the Confederated Tribes of Coos, Lower Umpqua, and Siuslaw Indians of Oregon, became the first Native American woman to receive her Ph.D. in physics, graduating from New Mexico State University. She also participated in a postdoctoral fellowship at the Massachusetts Institute of Technology from 2011 to 2014. Her work includes research, teaching, and actively mentoring Native youth through the Native Education Science Initiative. Cisneros is also one of the cofounders of the Math, Culture, Environment Academy in Massachusetts.

2012: Shannon Seneca (1978–), Mohawk, became the first female Native American to earn a Ph.D. in engineering from the School of Engineering and Applied Sciences at the University of Buffalo in New York.

2012: Kamuela Yong, Native Hawaiian, who graduated from the University of Iowa, be-

came the first Native Hawaiian to earn a Ph.D. in applied mathematics. After serving as a postdoctoral research scholar at Arizona State University from 2012 to 2015, Yong began teaching at the University of Hawai'i–West O'ahu. His research interests include mathematical modeling of biological, ecological, and epidemiological systems using diffusion.

2017: Marcos A. Moreno (1994–), Pascua Yaqui, who graduated with honors with a bachelor of science degree in neuroscience from Cornell University in Ithaca, New York, became the first person from his tribe to graduate from an Ivy League university. In 2016, he received the Morris K. Udall Award, which recognizes undergraduate students for their work in environmental activism, public policy, or healthcare.

HIGHER EDUCATION

"Higher education ... taught Western European culture and values with no recognition of tribal language and culture beyond a few negative references in history courses. By 1970 less than one half of one percent of adult Indians in the United States held a bachelor's degree, 80 percent of adult Indians did not complete high school, and the Indian college student dropout rate exceeded 90 percent. How could Salish Kootenai College do any worse?"

—From "Education, Leadership, Wisdom": The Founding History of Salish Kootenai College, 1976–2010, by Michael O'Donnell, Joseph McDonald, and Alice Oechsli (Salish Kooenai College Press, 2018)

1962: The Institute of American Indian Arts (IAIA) was established as a high school formed under the Bureau of Indian Affairs in the U.S. Department of the Interior, becoming a two-year college in 1975 and offering associate degrees in studio arts, creative writing, and museum studies. In 1986, IAIA became chartered as a college by Congress. It is the nation's only four-year-degree fine arts institution devoted to contemporary Native American and Alaska Native arts. IAIA, a 1994 tribal college/land grant institution, offers AA, AFA, BA, and BFA degree programs as well as an MFA in creative writing. It also operates the Center for Lifelong Education and the Museum of Contemporary Native Arts.

1968: Navajo Community College (NCC) was founded, becoming the first tribal college in

The Institute of American Indian Arts is located in Santa Fe, New Mexico. The architecture clearly serves as an inspiration to its students.

the United States. Its founders were educators Robert Roessel Jr. and his wife, Ruth Roessel, Navajo. Located in Tsaile, Arizona, NCC was renamed Diné College in 1997. Ruth Roessel became known as the "Mother of Diné College"; she was first referred to in that manner in 2009 when she gave a commencement address at the college. In 2013, Diné College named a new archive building the Ruth and Bob Roessel Archival Center in honor of the college's founders.

1968: Joseph F. McDonald (1933–), Salish-Kootenai, became the first tribal member to administer a public school when he was hired as high school principal at Ronan on the Flathead Reservation in Montana. During his tenure, he created an Indian studies program, a Salish language course, and the nation's first high school Indian historical periodical, *The Dovetail*. McDonald also became the founding president of Salish Kootenai College (SKC), which began in 1976 on the Flathead Reservation, growing it into an institution with an array of educational achievements. In 1994, he helped tribal colleges gain land grant status. In 1999, he became the first Native American and the first tribal college president to serve in the Northwest Association of Schools and Colleges (now known as the Northwest Commission on Colleges and Universities), the regional accrediting body, opening the door for others. That year, Lee Enterprises deemed him one of Montana's 100 most influential people of the century. McDonald guided SKC until his retirement in 2010. He coauthored *"Education, Leadership, Wisdom": The Founding History of Salish Kootenai College, 1976–2010* (with Michael O'Donnell and Alice Oechsli, 2018).

1970: Sherry Red Owl (Anpo Inajin Win, Stands at Dawn Woman), a member of the Rosebud Sioux Tribe in South Dakota, was the first employee of the Rosebud College Center, later renamed Sinte Gleska University

(SGU), and helped to build one of the first tribal colleges in the nation. Red Owl was also a classroom teacher at a time when school systems employed few Native teachers. When the tribal college opened in 1971, there was only one Lakota teacher on the Rosebud reservation. She is also known for leading the development of the first tribal education code in the country, formalized by her tribal nation in 1992. In 1994, President Bill Clinton appointed her to the National Advisory Council on Indian Education (NACIE), and she served as chair from 1995 to 2000. In 2002, Red Owl became the first education director for the Rosebud Sioux Tribe. Following her return to SGU, she became director of the Scott Bordeaux Leadership Institute and vice president of community development and tribal national building.

> "Our vision is to create the next generation of competitive students who are grounded in not only science, technology, engineering and math, but also their culture and language. It's the dream of our people. We want to cultivate innovation and address inequities to keep up with modern technology and advance our nation to provide a better quality of life for our people. We want to lead the way."
>
> —Greg Bigman,
> Diné College Board of Regents president

1971: The Navajo Community College Act, P.L. 92-189, was passed by the U.S. Congress in 1971. The legislation was designed to assist the Navajo Tribe in providing education to tribal members and other qualified applicants at the Navajo Community College. It authorized the secretary of the interior to make grants for assisting the tribe in the construction, maintenance, and operation of the college.

1978: The first Tribally Controlled Community College Act, P.L. 95-471, was signed into law by President Jimmy Carter. The legislation was an effort to provide resources to American Indian tribes for establishing and improving tribal colleges.

1982: Janine Pease (1949–), Apsaalooke (Crow)/Hidatsa, became the first president of Little Big Horn College (LBHC) on the Crow Reservation in Montana, a college that was chartered as a public, two-year community college in 1980. Pease held the LBHC presidency until 2000. Her other leadership roles include president of the American Indian Higher Education Consortium for two terms and serving on the board of directors for the American Indian College Fund (AICF) for seven years. President Bill Clinton appointed Pease to the National Advisory Council on Indian Education and the White House Initiative on Tribal Colleges and Universities. An award-winning educator, she was a National Indian Educator of the Year and the recipient of a MacArthur Fellowship Award and the ACLU Jeannette Rankin Award. Pease is also known for serving as lead plaintiff in a groundbreaking Crow voting rights case against Big Horn County in Montana. More recent endeavors include serving as principal of the Apsáalooke Chickadee Immersion School for young students, focusing on language revitalization for the Crow.

1983: Oglala Lakota College (OLC) on the Pine Ridge Reservation and Sinte Gleska College (SGC) on the Rosebud Reservation, both in South Dakota, became the first two tribal colleges accredited to offer bachelor's degrees. In 1988 Sinte Gleska became the first tribal college to be accredited at the master's degree level with a master of science in elementary education, graduating its first master's degree students the following year. By 1992, SGC had become a university (SGU). Two years later, it offered seven baccalaureate programs, including the first bachelor's degree in Lakota language, history, and culture.

1984: Salish Kootenai College (SKC) in Montana was the first tribal college in the northwest to receive regional accreditation at the associate degree level. The Northwest Commission on Colleges and Universities (NWCCU) accredited SKC as a two-year institution of higher education. It was also the first institution of higher education in the northwest to be accredited in just four years. Other firsts include being the first tribal college in the country to offer a state and regionally accredited associate degree in registered nursing in 1989, the nation's only tribal college to offer a bachelor's degree in a STEM discipline (environmental science) in 1995, and the first tribal college to receive accreditation through the National League for Nursing for the bachelor's degree in nursing in 2000.

1992: Carol Murray, a member of the Blackfeet Tribe with a master's degree in education, was the first tribal college graduate to become a tribal college president. She served as president of Blackfeet Community College, overseeing new growth, including the construction of new buildings.

1994: The Equity in Educational Land-Grant Status Act was enacted by Congress, providing land-grant status for American Indian tribal colleges and universities identified in the legislation. The act directed the U.S. secretary of the treasury to establish a 1994 Institutions Endowment Fund and the U.S. secretary of agriculture to make capacity-building grants to these institutions.

1995: The W. K. Kellogg Foundation launched an initiative to help colleges and universities across the United States create new educational opportunities for Native Americans. During its first phase, the foundation awarded $1,050,000 to 29 tribal colleges, the American Indian Higher Education Consortium, and the American Indian College Fund.

1996: Executive Order 13021, which directed federal agencies to create new partnerships

The entrance to Salish Kootenai College, a private, tribal, land-grant college in Pablo, Montana.

with tribal colleges and/or strengthen old ones, was signed by President Bill Clinton.

1998: Carrie Billy, a member of the Navajo Nation and graduate of the Georgetown University Law Center, was appointed by President Bill Clinton to serve as the first executive director of the White House Initiative on Tribal Colleges and Universities (WHITCU). She held the position, which President Clinton created by Executive Order, until 2001. By then, Billy had already worked for U.S. senator Jeff Bingaman of New Mexico for nearly ten years, including assisting with legislation. In 1996, she served as federal relations counsel at the American Indian Higher Education Consortium (AIHEC). After the Clinton administration ended, Billy returned to AIHEC in 2001, serving as technology director and later as deputy director before being appointed president and CEO of the organization in 2008.

2003: United Tribes Technical College (UTTC) in Bismarck, North Dakota, became the first tribal college to receive accreditation for online programs offering associate of applied sciences degree programs.

2010: The First Nations Launch: Tribal College High-Powered Rocket Competition was initiated through the College of Menominee Nation and the Wisconsin Space Grant Consortium with support from NASA. Held near Burlington, Wisconsin, the inaugural national tribal college competition centered on rocket building and launching.

2010: Salish Kootenai College (SKC) in Pablo, Montana, became the first tribal college or university in North America to offer hydrology and geoscience degree programs. SKC received approval for the associate and bachelor of science offerings from the Northwest Commission on Colleges and Universities.

Sitting Bull College is located in Fort Yates, North Dakota, where it was founded by the Standing Rock Sioux in 1973.

Indigenous Firsts: A History of Native American Achievements and Events

2013: Navajo Technical College in Crownpoint, New Mexico, became Navajo Technical University, the first university established on the Navajo Nation.

2013: Tina Deschenie (1955–), Navajo educator and poet, was the first Diné woman to serve as provost at Navajo Technical University. She also served as the first Native editor of *Tribal College Journal*, a position she held for three years.

2013: During a major conference at Navajo Technical University in Crownpoint, New Mexico, the World Indigenous Nations Higher Education Consortium (WINHEC) officially launched the World Indigenous Nations University (WINU), the first Indigenous international degree-granting institution. During the conference, WINU conferred four Ph.D. degrees on professors from aboriginal Australia.

2014: Sitting Bull College on the Standing Rock Reservation was the first North Dakota tribal college to be approved to offer a Master of Science degree in environmental science. The program was developed out of a growing need for environmental scientists to assess problems and find solutions.

2017: Connor Veneski, Cayuga, a graduate of Haskell Indian Nations University in Lawrence, Kansas, became the first student admitted to Harvard Law School (HLS) from a tribal college or university. He and another student, Chance Fletcher, a member of the Cherokee Nation, are the only two Native Americans in the HLS class of 2021.

2020: Nueta Hidatsa Sahnish College on the Fort Berthold Reservation in New Town, North Dakota, became the first tribal college approved to offer an associate of science degree in sustainable energy technologies. The program will provide students with opportunities to become installers, technicians, and operators of solar and wind technologies.

2020: Salish Kootenai College in Pablo, Montana, became the first tribal college in the United States to offer a Bachelor of Science in nursing (BSN), adding the degree in fall 2020. The college has offered an associate's degree in nursing since 1989.

2021: Diné College held a groundbreaking ceremony for its new state-of-the-art math and science building, scheduled for construction beginning in July 2021 for a completion date of March 2022. It was envisioned to provide space for STEM departments, instructional classrooms, laboratories, and other facilities.

GOVERNMENT

U.S. CONGRESS

1870: Hiram R. Revels (1827–1901), Croatan/Lumbee/African American, was the first person of either Native or Black descent to be elected to the U.S. Senate. A Republican representing the state of Mississippi, he served as a U.S. senator until 1871. The Mississippi legislature had elected Revels, then serving in the state senate to which he was elected in 1869, to fill a vacancy in the U.S. Senate. His education included studies in religion at Beech Grove Quaker Seminary in Union County, Indiana, and Knox College in Galesburg, Illinois. Revels, a chaplain during the Civil War, also worked as an educator, minister, and Freedmen's Bureau worker. Following his tenure as a U.S. senator, he became the first president of Alcorn University

Robert William Kalanihiapo Wilcox

Hiram R. Revels

(now Alcorn State University) in Mississippi, the oldest public historically black land grant institution in the United States.

1900: Robert William Kalanihiapo Wilcox (1855-1903), nicknamed the Iron Duke of Hawai'i, was the first Native Hawaiian elected to the U.S. Congress for the Territory of Hawaii. He served as a delegate to the U.S. House of Representatives from Hawaii Territory's at-large congressional district from November 6, 1900, to March 3, 1903. However, delegates from U.S. territories do not have voting privileges.

1907: Charles David Carter (1868-1929), Chickasaw/Cherokee, Democrat, became the first person to represent Oklahoma's Fourth District in the U.S. House of Representatives following admittance as a state, holding the office until 1915. After redistricting, he represented the Third District from March 4, 1915, to March 3, 1927. He had served as auditor of public accounts (1892–1894), tribal council member (1895), and superintendent of schools (1897) for the Chickasaw Nation. Carter was appointed mining trustee of Indian Territory (present-day Oklahoma) by President William McKinley, and he served from 1900 to 1904. He also became secretary of the first Democratic Party executive committee of the proposed state of Oklahoma in 1906. During his tenure in Congress, Carter served as chair on the Committee on Indian Affairs (1917–1919) and as ranking minority member (1919–1921). He was also a member of the Appropriations Committee (1921–1927).

1907: Robert Latham Owen (1856–1947), Cherokee, Democrat, was elected one of the first two U.S. senators (with Thomas P. Gore) in Oklahoma after statehood in 1907, serving until 1925. Prior to that, Owen taught school at a Cherokee orphanage and was supervisor of

Senator Robert Latham Owen

the Cherokee National School System. An administrator, journalist, federal Indian agent in Indian Territory (present-day Oklahoma) and an attorney, he won the first major Indian land claims cases on behalf of Cherokee and other tribal nations. He also founded and became the first president of a community bank. During his tenure in the U.S. Senate, Owen cosponsored the Federal Reserve Act, considered the most important banking legislation of the twentieth century and his crowning achievement as a legislator. He also became known for the Keating-Owen Child Labor Law of 1916.

1960: Benjamin Reifel (Lone Feather; 1906–1990), Brule Sioux from the Rosebud Reservation, Republican, became the first Lakota elected to serve in the U.S. Congress, South Dakota's only American Indian congressman. Reifel represented the First District for five terms in the U.S. House of Repre-

Charles Curtis, First Native American Vice President

Charles Curtis

Charles Curtis (1860–1936), a member of the Kaw Nation, was the first Native American elected to serve as vice president of the United States. A Republican, he served in the vice presidency alongside President Herbert Hoover from 1929 to 1933. Curtis, who was born in Kansas, worked as a horse racing jockey and newspaper reporter when he was a teenager. After studying law in an attorney's office, he was admitted to the Kansas Bar at the age of 21. In 1892, Curtis became the first Native American elected to the U.S. House of Representatives. In 1907, he was elected to the U.S. Senate, where he became the first Kansas senator to serve as Republican majority leader. While in Congress, Curtis was an advocate of Native American policies that turned out to be disastrous for tribal nations, such as the Dawes Act of 1887, with provisions that resulted in catastrophic tribal land losses. As a member of the Committee on Indian Affairs, he sponsored what became known as the Curtis Act of 1898, with measures adverse to the governments and lands of the Cherokee, Chickasaw, Choctaw, Muscogee (Creek), and Seminole in Indian Territory (present-day Oklahoma). Following his time in government, Curtis practiced law in Washington, D.C.

sentatives, until 1971. Reifel, who was bilingual in Lakota and English, completed his bachelor's degree at South Dakota State College and master's and doctoral degrees in economics and government at Harvard University. He was an Army lieutenant colonel during World War II. Reifel worked for the Department of the Interior for over 20 years, retiring as an area administrator of the Bureau of Indian Affairs in 1960 and then winning a seat in Congress. As a congressman, he was instrumental in having the Earth Resources Observation Systems Center located near Sioux Falls, South Dakota, and in keeping Ellsworth Air Force Base an active military facility in the state.

1973: Forrest J. Gerard (1925–2013), Blackfeet Nation, who conceived and authored the Indian Self-Determination and Education Act, was the first Native American to draft and facilitate passage of American Indian legislation through Congress. In 1971, he began serving as a key advisor on Indian affairs to U.S. senator Henry Jackson of Washington and was instrumental in having him introduce legislation for the policy by the end of that year. In 1977, Gerard was appointed assistant secretary for Indian affairs by President Jimmy Carter, becoming the first person to hold that office. In 2013, Congress honored Gerard as "one of the key architects" of the Indian Self-Determination and Education Assistance Act.

1975: Spiritual leader Frank Fools Crow (c. 1890–1989), Oglala Lakota, became the first Native American holy man to lead the opening prayer for a session of the U.S. Senate.

Senator Daniel Kahikina Akaka

1986: Ben Nighthorse Campbell (1933–), Northern Cheyenne, was the first American Indian to be elected to the U.S. Congress from Colorado. He served as a U.S. representative from 1987 to 1993 and as a U.S. senator from 1993 to 2005. Prior to that, Campbell served two terms in the Colorado State Legislature. In 1989, he authored the bill, which became Public Law 101-185, to establish the National Museum of the American Indian. Campbell was the first Native American elected to serve in the U.S. Senate since Charles Curtis in the 1920s. During his tenure, he was also the only Native American serving in Congress. Initially elected as a Democrat, Campbell switched parties and became a Republican in 1995. In 1997, he became the first Native American chairman of the Senate Committee on Indian Affairs and has also served as one of 44 members of the Council of Chiefs of the Northern Cheyenne. A veteran of the U.S. Air Force during the Korean War, Campbell was awarded the Korean Service Medal and the Air Medal. He was also an award-winning athlete who served as captain of the American judo team at the 1964 Summer Olympics in Tokyo, Japan. His jewelry artistry is renowned as well and has garnered national and international accolades.

1990: Daniel Kahikina Akaka (1924–2018), Native Hawaiian, Democrat, was appointed to the U.S. Senate to fill the vacancy caused by the death of Spark Masayuki Matsunaga, becoming America's first senator of Native Hawaiian ancestry and the only Chinese American member of the U.S. Senate. He won a special election on November 6, 1990. Akaka had previously served in the U.S. House of Representatives from 1977 until 1990. During his tenure as senator, from 1990 to 2013, he served on committees that included Energy and Natural Resources, Veterans' Affairs, Governmental Affairs, Banking, Housing, and Urban Affairs, and the Permanent Select Committee on Indian Affairs. Akaka cosponsored the Native Hawaiian Government Reorganization Act, which became known as the "Akaka Bill" and sought to establish a Native

Debra Haaland, U.S. Secretary of the Interior

Debra Haaland (1960–), a member of the Pueblo of Laguna and a 35th generation New Mexican, made history when she became the first Native American to serve as a cabinet secretary, sworn in as U.S. secretary of the interior on March 16, 2021. At the time of her nomination by President Joe Biden, she was serving as the U.S. representative for New Mexico's 1st congressional district, one of the first two Native American women elected to the U.S. Congress.

Debra Haaland

A child of a military family, Haaland's mother, Mary Toya, Pueblo, served in the U.S. Navy, and her father, John David Haaland, Norwegian Minnesotan, was a 30-year combat Marine who was awarded the Silver Star Medal for saving six lives in Vietnam. Reflecting the military family's many moves, Haaland attended 13 public schools before graduating from Highland High School in Albuquerque, New Mexico. She earned a bachelor's degree in English from the University of New Mexico (UNM) in 1994. Haaland also became a single mother, running her own small business, a salsa company, to support herself and her daughter. She earned a law degree from UNM's School of Law in 2006.

Haaland served as the first woman elected to the Laguna Development Corporation Board of Directors, overseeing the second largest tribal gaming enterprise in New Mexico. She also served as a tribal administrator at San Felipe Pueblo.

Following a run for lieutenant governor of New Mexico in 2014, Haaland became the first Native American woman to be elected to lead a state party, serving as chair of the New Mexico Democratic Party from 2015 to 2017. With her election to Congress in 2018, she focused on environmental justice, climate change, missing and murdered Indigenous women, and family-friendly policies.

Hawaiian tribal unit similar to tribal nations with government-to-government status. He also was key in developing the National Museum of the American Indian. Deciding against running for reelection in 2012, he retired from Congress at the age of 88.

2018: Sharice Davids (1980–), Ho-Chunk, a Democrat, won election as the U.S. representative for the 3rd congressional district of Kansas. She and Debra Haaland of New Mexico are the first Native Ameri-

Sharice Davids

can women elected to Congress. Davids, an attorney educated at the University of Missouri and Cornell Law School, is also the first openly LGBTQ Native American elected to the U.S. Congress and the first openly gay person elected to the U.S. Congress from Kansas. She is the second Native American (after Charles Curtis) to represent Kansas in Congress. Davids, who won reelection in 2020, is the author of *Sharice's Big Voice: A Native Kid Becomes a Congresswoman* (Harper, 2021).

2020: Yvette Herrell (1964–) became the first Cherokee woman and the first Republican Native woman elected to Congress, serving as the U.S. representative for New Mexico's 2nd congressional district. She served four terms representing District 51 in New Mexico's House of Representatives from 2011 to 2019. Herrell, who assumed national office on January 3, 2021, used her first speech in the U.S. House of Representatives to object to some states' electoral votes for President-elect Joe Biden. Following the violent insurrection at the U.S. Capitol on January 6, 2021, she joined other House Republicans in objecting to the certification of Electoral College results for Biden in Arizona and Pennsylvania. Herrell also voted against the impeachment of President Donald J. Trump in the U.S. House of Representatives on January 13, 2021.

Yvette Herrell

THE EXECUTIVE BRANCH

1801: Indian Peace Medals created during the presidency of Thomas Jefferson were the first to include the official portrait of an American president.

1865: Native Americans participated in an inaugural parade for the first time at the second inauguration of President Abraham Lincoln. Chief Iron Whip, Ponca, who signed a treaty with Lincoln, was the first Native American to participate in a presidential inaugural parade.

1915: Attorney Houston Benge Teehee (1874–1953), Cherokee Nation, appointed by President Woodrow Wilson, was the first American Indian to serve as register of the U.S.

Treasury. Serving until 1919, his signature appeared on all federal notes and bonds during World War I. One account notes that "during one five-month period he was signing nearly 2,000 war bonds every single day."

1969: Brantley Blue (1925–1979), Lumbee, was appointed by President Richard Nixon as the first (and only) American Indian to serve as a commissioner on the Indian Claims Commission (ICC). The ICC, which existed from 1946 to 1978, was established by the U.S. Congress to hear and determine longstanding claims by tribal nations against the United States. Blue was also the first Lumbee to become an attorney, earning law degrees in 1946 and 1949.

1969: The American Indian Society (AIS) in Washington, D.C., held its first American Indian Inaugural Ball and formed its first parade unit, marching in the Richard M. Nixon inaugural event.

1980: LaDonna Harris (1931–), Comanche, became the first Native American woman to run for vice president of the United States, running as a candidate for the Citizens Party alongside Barry Commoner. She founded Oklahomans for Indian Opportunity (OIO), the state's first intertribal organization, in 1965 and, nationally, cofounded Americans for Indian Opportunity (AIO) in 1970. During her marriage to Senator Fred Harris from Oklahoma, she became the first wife of a senator to testify before Congress.

1994: President Bill Clinton became the first U.S. president to invite the leaders of all federally recognized tribes to the White House. At the gathering, the president pledged that his administration would work with tribal leaders to establish a true government-to-government relationship. During the meeting, he addressed questions on a range of issues, including economic development, tribal sovereignty, health care, and education.

2009: Kimberly Teehee (1966–), Cherokee Nation, was named the first White House senior policy advisor for Native American affairs by President Barack Obama, remaining in that office until 2012. A member of the Domestic Policy Council, her role included advising the president on issues affecting Indian Country. Teehee, fluent in the Cherokee language, grew up in Claremore, Oklahoma, and earned her juris doctor degree in 1995. She served as the first deputy director of Native American Outreach for the Democratic National Committee and director of Native American outreach for President Bill Clinton's 1997 inauguration.

Kimberly Teehee with President Barack Obama

2009: Jodi Archambault Gillette (1969–), Standing Rock Sioux, appointed by President Barack Obama, became the first Native American to serve as deputy associate director of the Office of Intergovernmental Affairs, the administration's primary liaison to more than 560 federally recognized tribes. Gillette received her undergraduate degree from Dartmouth College in 1991 in government/Native American studies. The recipient of a Bush Foundation Leadership Fellowship in 2002, she earned a Master of Public Administration degree at the University of Minnesota. Gillette also served as the director of the Native American Training Institute, a nonprofit organization. She was the North Dakota First American Vote director for the Obama Campaign for Change as well.

2011: Brad Carson (1967–), Cherokee Nation, was nominated by President Barack Obama and confirmed by the U.S. Senate to serve as general counsel of the Army, serving from 2012 to 2014, the first Native American to hold the position. A Rhodes Scholar, he re-

ceived an MA degree from Trinity College at Oxford University and completed his JD at the University of Oklahoma College of Law. Carson was awarded a Bronze Star for his military service in Iraq (2009–2010). Prior to his deployment, he was the president, CEO, and business development director for Cherokee Nation businesses. In 2000, Carson was elected as a Democrat to the U.S. House of Representatives from Oklahoma's 2nd congressional district (2001–2005). On January 6, 2014, President Obama again nominated Carson, this time to be under secretary of the Army, and his nomination was confirmed by the U.S. Senate. He was sworn in as the 31st under secretary of the Army on March 27, 2014. Carson later served as the acting under secretary of defense for personnel and readiness from April 2015 to April 2016. After federal service, he became a professor at the University of Virginia and a senior advisor at the Boston Consulting Group.

2013: Jack Jackson Jr. (Navajo) became the first liaison to Native American tribal nations on environmental issues in a newly created post in the U.S. Department of State. A Democrat, he had been serving in the Arizona Senate representing the state's 2nd district, starting on January 20, 2011, and ending on July 1, 2013, when he left to take his new position. Earlier, Jackson had served as a member of the Arizona House of Representatives from January 12, 2003, to January 10, 2005. His father, Jack Jackson Sr., had served in the Arizona House until 2004, the first father and son to serve together in the state legislature.

2014: Keith M. Harper (1965–), Cherokee Nation, became the first member of a federally recognized tribe to achieve the rank of U.S. ambassador. A graduate of the New York School of Law, he served as a litigator for the Native American Rights Fund, and he became known for his work in the *Cobell v. Kempthorne* case, a large class action lawsuit. A Democrat who was appointed by President Barack Obama and confirmed by the U.S. Senate, Harper served as U.S. ambassador to the United Nations Human Rights Council in Geneva from June 5, 2014, to January 20, 2017.

2015: More than 1,000 Native youth participated in the first White House Tribal Youth Gathering, which was held in Washington, D.C. It was hosted by the Obama administration as part of the president's Generation Indigenous initiative aimed at improving outcomes for Native youth.

2016: Faith Spotted Eagle (Tunkan Inajin Win; Standing Stone; 1948–), Yankton Sioux, became the first Native American to receive a vote for president of the United States in the U.S. Electoral College. Puyallup tribal member Robert Satiacum Jr., Washington State delegate, in an act of defiance against the status quo, cast his vote for Spotted Eagle, an elder and activist known for her leadership against the Keystone XL and Dakota Access pipelines.

2016: Winona LaDuke (1959–), White Earth Nation, became the first Native American woman and the first Green Party member to receive an electoral vote for vice president of the United States. She was also the first to run as vice president on the Green Party ticket with Ralph Nader (1996 and 2000).

2019: The Frank LaMere Native American Presidential Forum, the first-ever such forum to focus entirely on Native American issues, was held August 19–20, 2019, in Sioux City, Iowa. The nonpartisan event, cohosted by the Native American Rights Fund, was named

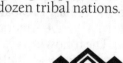

Winona LaDuke

in honor of Frank LaMere, a Winnebago civil rights activist from the Sioux City area.

2019: Montana governor Steve Bullock became the first presidential candidate to visit a Native newsroom. The one-on-one interview was conducted by journalist Mark Trahant at the *Indian Country Today* headquarters in the Walter Cronkite School of Journalism and Mass Communication at Arizona State University on September 25, 2019.

2019: Senator Bernie Sanders (D-VT) became the first presidential candidate to visit the Comanche Nation in over 100 years; as president, Theodore Roosevelt had visited Comanche chief Quanah Parker's home in Fort Sill, Oklahoma, in 1905. During his September 22, 2019, appearance, Sanders participated in the grand entry of the Comanche Nation's Powwow and spoke to attendees of the 28th annual Comanche Nation Fair in Lawton, Oklahoma. While campaigning for president in 2016, he visited over a dozen tribal nations.

◆◇◆

FEDERAL INDIAN LAW

"In our every deliberation, we must consider the impact of our decisions on the next seven generations."

—*Iroquois*

1831: *Cherokee Nation v. Georgia* became the first U.S. Supreme Court case to address tribal sovereignty, defining American Indian tribes as "domestic dependent nations with an unquestionable right to the lands which they occupy."

Chief Standing Bear

Chief Standing Bear

In 1878, Chief Standing Bear (c. 1829–1908), Ponca, was the first Native American declared "a person within the meaning of the habeas corpus act" in the United States. He sued for freedom from U.S. Army custody on behalf of himself and others. In *United States, ex rel. Standing Bear, v. George Crook*, the U.S. government argued "that [Standing Bear] was neither a citizen, nor a person, so he could not sue the government." Standing Bear's attorneys argued that under the Fourteenth Amendment, the Ponca leader and his people were entitled to the same constitutional rights as other citizens of the United States. Judge Elmer Dundy ultimately agreed, a landmark civil rights decision. In 2019, a statue of Chief Standing Bear donated to the National Statuary Hall of the U.S. Capitol by the State of Nebraska was installed in 2019. It includes some of Standing Bear's words: "This hand is not the color of yours, but if I pierce it, I shall feel pain. If you pierce your hand, you also feel pain. The blood that will flow from mine will be of the same color as yours. I am a man. The same God made us both."

1889: Hiram Chase (1861–1928), Omaha attorney and activist, became the first Native American admitted to the Nebraska Bar Association. He had studied law at the Cincinnati Law School, graduating with a bachelor of law degree. In 1892, he and fellow Omaha Thomas Sloan formed Chase & Sloan Attorneys-At-Law, the first Native American law firm in the nation. The following year, Chase was elected county judge of Nebraska's Thurston County, serving one term. In 1898, he was elected county attorney and was reelected in 1901. Chase was active in the Society of American Indians, the pioneering national rights organization.

1904: Thomas L. Sloan (1863–1940), Omaha, was the first Native American to argue a case before the U.S. Supreme Court. After graduating as the valedictorian from Hampton Institute in Virginia in 1889, he read for the law with Hiram Chase, Omaha, a childhood friend and attorney. "I took up the study of law," Sloan commented, "in

order to enable myself to make fights against the [Indian] agent [and] to protect myself and my people...." He was admitted to the Nebraska bar in 1892, initially practicing with Chase but later establishing a legal practice in Washington, D.C. Sloan also helped found the Society of American Indians, an American Indian rights organization that began in 1911, and served as its first president.

1976: Lawrence R. Baca (1950–), Pawnee, was the first American Indian lawyer hired at the U.S. Department of Justice through the Attorney General's Honors Law Program. He was also the first American Indian attorney hired into the Civil Rights Division. In 2008, the Federal Bar Association, Indian Law Section, created the Lawrence R. Baca Lifetime Achievement Award for excellence in Federal Indian Law.

Thomas L. Sloan

1984: Arlinda Faye Locklear (1951–), Lumbee, became the first Native American woman to successfully argue a case before the U.S. Supreme Court. In that case, *Solem v. Bartlett*, she challenged the State of South Dakota's authority to prosecute a member of the Cheyenne River Sioux Tribe for on-reservation conduct. Locklear, considered a pioneer in federal Indian law, appeared before the Supreme Court again in 1985, arguing *Oneida Indian Nation v. County of Oneida* on behalf of Wisconsin's Oneida Tribe.

2002: New Mexico became the first state in the country to add federal Indian law as a subject on its state bar exam, the state's Supreme Court approving the addition in February 2002. University of New Mexico law professor Kenneth Bobroff said, "You can't practice law in New Mexico without understanding the importance of Indian law, the importance of tribal sovereignty."

2005: Philip "Sam" Deloria, Standing Rock Sioux Tribe, was awarded the first Henry Roe Cloud Medal, an honor named for the first American Indian to graduate from Yale University. Deloria also attended Yale, both as an undergraduate and for law school. For 35 years, he directed the American Indian Law Center in Albuquerque, New Mexico, the oldest Indian-controlled legal public policy organization in the country. Deloria was a founder and first secretary-general of the World Council of Indigenous People at the United Nations and a founder of the Commission on State-Tribal Relations.

2010: Leo Brisbois (1961–), White Earth Nation, became the first American Indian to be appointed as a magistrate judge in Minnesota and the second American Indian to hold the position in the United States. He received his undergraduate and law school degrees from Hamline University in St. Paul. He was also an Army captain on the staff of the senior legal advisor to the four-star general commanding U.S. Army forces in Europe.

2018: Tobi Merritt Edwards Young, Chickasaw Nation, accepted a one-year term as a law clerk for U.S. Supreme Court justice Neil Gorsuch. Young is believed to be the first enrolled citizen of a Native American tribe, and the first woman from Oklahoma, to serve as a Supreme Court clerk.

◆◇◆

INDIAN AFFAIRS

1824: Congress established the Office of Indian Affairs (later renamed Bureau of Indian Affairs) in the U.S. War Department. In 1849, it was moved to the newly established Department of the Interior, where it remains to this day.

Ely Samuel Parker

1869: Ely Samuel Parker (1828–1895), Tonawanda Seneca, appointed by President Ulysses S. Grant, was the first American Indian to serve as U.S. commissioner of Indian affairs (1869–1871). He had been an officer and aide to General Grant in the Civil War, fulfilling a historic role that included writing out the terms of the Confederate army's surrender at Appomattox Court House, Virginia, on April 9, 1865. Earlier, Parker studied law, became a civil engineer, and served as a tribal leader. He also collaborated with ethnologist Lewis Henry Morgan on his studies of the Iroquois.

1966: Robert Bennett (1912–2002), Oneida, became the first Native director of the Bureau of Indian Affairs (BIA) since Ely Parker under the Ulysses S. Grant administration. Bennett, born on the Oneida Reservation in Wisconsin, directed the BIA until 1969.

1970: Helen L. Peterson (1915–2000), Oglala Sioux, became the first female assistant to the Commissioner of Indian Affairs. In 1972, she established the first Bureau of Indian Affairs intergovernmental relations office in Denver, Colorado. In 1948, Peterson was appointed as the first director of the Mayor's Committee on Human Relations in Denver. From 1953 to 1961, she was executive director of the National Congress of American Indians. Peterson also founded the Ecumenical Indian Congregation, which became the Church of the Four Winds in 1989.

Ada Deer

1974: Claudeen Bates Arthur (1942–2004), Navajo, graduated from Arizona State University College of Law, becoming one of the first two Navajo and the first Navajo woman to be a licensed lawyer in the United States. In 1978, she became the first Native American woman to attain the rank of field solicitor for the U.S. Department of the Interior (DOI), serving until 1981. Arthur, the first female attorney general of the Navajo Nation in 1983, was also legislative counsel to the Navajo Nation Council, general counsel to the White Mountain Apache Tribe, and director of litigation for Legal Services Corporation in Window Rock, Arizona. In 2003, she was confirmed as Navajo Nation Supreme Court chief justice, the first female chief justice on the tribal nation's high court. During the confirmation proceedings before the Navajo Nation council, she said: "Our Navajo court system must not only be good, it must be outstanding beyond question."

1974: Shirley Trimble Plume (1920–2004), Lakota, was the first female superintendent for the Bureau of Indian Affairs to serve on the Standing Rock Reservation in North Dakota and the first to serve at a major agency.

1993: Ada Deer (1935–), Menominee, was the first woman to serve as assistant secretary for Indian Affairs in the U.S. Department of the Interior. Nominated by President Bill Clinton and confirmed by the Senate, she was sworn into office on July 16, 1993. By then, Deer had also run for the U.S. House of Representatives from Wisconsin's second district, becoming the first American Indian woman to win a major party primary in 1992. Deer, a Democrat, lost in the general election. Her political slogans included "running like a deer" and "me nominee." Deer's autobiography, *Making a Difference: My Fight for Native Rights and Social Justice*, written with Theda Perdue (University of Oklahoma, 2019), chronicles her life growing up on the Menominee Reservation in Wisconsin, her education at the University of Wisconsin and Columbia University, her training and work as a social worker, her efforts to reverse the Menominee Termination Act of 1974, and other aspects of her life and work. In January 2020, Deer received the City-County Reverend Dr. Martin Luther King Jr. Humanitarian Award given to Madison, Wisconsin, area community members who reflect the values of Dr. King.

2009: Hilary Tompkins (c. 1968–), Navajo, became the first Native American to serve as solicitor for the U.S. Department of the Interior. A graduate of Dartmouth College and Stanford Law School, she was appointed to the position by President Barack Obama and confirmed by the U.S. Senate. During her tenure, between 2009 and 2017, Tompkins led over 300 attorneys in 16 offices nationwide in areas such as energy development, water projects, conservation, and public land law. A leader in federal Indian law, she also led the historic settlement of the Cobell tribal trust litigation, the largest class action lawsuit in U.S. history. After leaving her federal position, Tompkins became a partner with Hogan Lovells in Washington, D.C., with a practice in environmental, energy, and federal Indian law. In

The Embassy of Tribal Nations

The Embassy of Tribal Nations opened in Washington, D.C. in 2009. "For the first time since settlement," Chickasaw leader Jefferson Keel said, "tribal nations will have a permanent home in Washington, D.C., where they can more effectively assert their sovereign status and facilitate a much stronger nation-to-nation relationship with the federal government." The embassy serves as the headquarters of the National Congress of American Indians and the center for advocacy work on behalf of tribal nations.

2019 she was elected to the Dartmouth Board of Trustees, the first Native American to serve in that position.

2018: Tara Sweeney (1973–), Iñupiaq, became the first Alaska Native to serve as assistant secretary for Indian affairs, overseeing the Bureau of Indian Affairs and the Bureau of Indian Education at the U.S. Department of the Interior. A Republican, she was nominated by President Donald Trump and unanimously confirmed by the U.S. Senate in June 2018. Sweeney became the 13th person to hold the position. She had worked for Arctic Slope Regional Corporation in various capacities, including as executive vice president of external affairs. From 2015 to 2017, Sweeney served as chairman of the Arctic Economic Council as a representative of the Inuit Circumpolar Council.

Tara Sweeney

Diane Humetewa

U.S. District Court for the Eastern District of Oklahoma, serving as chief judge from 1980 to 1986. Judge Seay learned of his Native ancestry, believed to be Cherokee, when he was in his 50s.

1991: Billy Michael Burrage (1950–), Choctaw Nation, appointed by President Bill Clinton, became the first enrolled tribal member to serve as a federal judge.

2014: Diane Humetewa (1964–), Hopi, nominated by President Barack Obama, became the first Native American woman to serve as a federal judge when the U.S. Senate confirmed her to serve as U.S. district judge of the U.S. District Court for the District of Arizona in 2014. Earlier, nominated by President George W. Bush and confirmed by the Senate, she was the first Native American woman to become a U.S. attorney, serving for the District of Arizona until August 2009.

2021: Lauren J. King (1982–), a citizen of the Muscogee (Creek) Nation, was nominated by President Joe Biden to become a federal district judge for the U.S. District Court for the Western District of Washington State. She was confirmed by the U.S. Senate on October 5 and received her judicial commission

FEDERAL JUDICIARY

1979: Frank Howell Seay (1938–), who was appointed by President Jimmy Carter to the

First Nations Justice on the British Columbia Supreme Court

In 2020, Ardith Walpetko We'daix Walkem (Nlaka'pamux First Nation) became the first First Nations woman to be named a justice on the British Columbia Supreme Court. Walkem, who grew up in Spences Bridge, B.C., earned a bachelor of arts degree from McGill University and law degrees from the University of British Columbia, where she also taught in the faculty of law. Called to the bar in 1996, she has practiced in Indigenous law since then, focusing much of her legal work on land and resource use as well as the rights of children. Walkem, the longtime owner of her own firm, Cedar and Sage Law, also cochaired the Law Society of B.C.'s Truth and Reconciliation Committee advisory committee.

two months later, making her the first Native American federal judge in the Western District of Washington. King also became the third active Native American federal district court judge in the United States (the other two were Diane Humetewa and Ada Brown). A 2008 graduate of the University of Virginia School of Law, she practiced as a principal at Foster Garvey in Seattle from 2012 to 2021 and chaired the firm's Native American Law Practice Group.

> "Indians are the only race in the United States that has experienced the deliberate, official governmental effort over decades to wipe out its way of life, language, and culture. They were conquered, colonized, and subjected to social engineering, culture shock, relocation, and forced negative education."
>
> —*Indians in Minnesota, 4th edition (1985)*

to be counted in the 2010 census. The first person counted was Clifton Jackson, a World War II veteran and the community's oldest resident. The village celebrated the launch of the census with traditional festivities.

2013: Steve Begay (c. 1976–), Navajo, was the youngest and the first Native American to become postmaster for the 134-year-old Farmington Post Office in New Mexico. After serving in the U.S. Marine Corps from 1993 to 1997, Begay began working as a mail carrier in Tempe, Arizona, in 1999.

2020: The Federal Bureau of Investigation (FBI) issued its first poster in a Native American language, Navajo, seeking information on the death of an elderly man, Wilson Joe Chiquito, in 2014 on the New Mexico portion of the Navajo reservation. The FBI offered a reward of up to $10,000 for information leading to an arrest and conviction for the crime, the beating death of the victim at his home.

FEDERAL GOVERNMENT: OTHER FIRSTS

2010: The Inupiat village of Noorvik, Alaska, became the first place in the United States

INTERNATIONAL AFFAIRS

1923–24: Deskaheh (Levi General; 1873–1925), Cayuga chief and activist, traveled to the

League of Nations to take sovereignty claims to an international forum, signifying the first efforts by First Nations to do so in such an assembly.

1971: M. Franklin Keel (1946–), Chickasaw, became the first Native American commissioned as a foreign service officer by the U.S. Diplomatic Corps. His first assignment was to the U.S. Embassy in Athens, Greece.

Mary Simon

> "Indigenous people have the right to revitalize, use, develop and transmit to future generations their histories, languages, oral traditions, philosophies, writing systems and literatures, and to designate and retain their own names for communities, places, and persons."
>
> —*United Nations Declaration of the Rights of Indigenous Peoples*

1977: The Inuit Circumpolar Conference (ICC) was founded by Alaska Native leader Eben Hobson, with the first official gathering of Inuit from Alaska, Canada, and Greenland held in Barrow, Alaska. The ICC grew to become a major international non-government organization and holds Consultative Status II at the United Nations. It represents some 180,000 Inuit from Alaska, Canada, Greenland, and Chukotka (Russia).

2021: Sheryl Lightfoot, Anishinaabe with dual American and Canadian citizenship, was appointed United Nations representative for the rights of Indigenous peoples, the first Native woman from Canada to hold the position. Lightfoot, from the Lake Superior Band of Ojibwe, tribally enrolled at Keweenaw Bay Indian Community in Michigan, serves as a Canada research chair and associate professor in First Nations and Indigenous Studies and the Department of Po-

litical Science at the University of British Columbia.

2021: Mary Simon (1947–), Inuk leader and former Canadian ambassador, became the first Indigenous person appointed governor general, to serve as the representative of Queen Elizabeth II in Canada. Simon, born in Nunavik in northern Quebec, was recommended to the position by Prime Minister Justin Trudeau. She is the first Inuk to hold ambassadorial positions, including Canada's ambassador for circumpolar affairs and Canada's ambassador to Denmark. Her work on behalf of Inuit rights and culture has been recognized with numerous honors: the National Aboriginal Achievement Award (1996), the National Order of Quebec (1992), the Order of Canada (2005), and the High North Hero Award (2018). Simon has also received numerous honorary doctorates of law from Canadian universities.

GOVERNOR AND LIEUTENANT GOVERNOR OFFICES

1951: Johnston Murray (1902–1974), Chickasaw, Democrat, was the first person of Native American descent to be elected governor in the United States, holding the office in Oklahoma from 1951 to 1955. After losing a run for Oklahoma state treasurer in 1962, he worked as a consulting attorney for that state's department of welfare.

Johnston Murray

1959: James Kealoha (1908–1983) was the first Native Hawaiian and Chinese American to be elected as a lieutenant governor in the United

States, emerging victorious in the state of Hawaii's first gubernatorial election. A Republican, he served in the administration of Governor William F. Quinn from 1959 to 1962. Earlier, in 1934, Kealoha had been elected to the Territorial House of Representatives, where he served as speaker pro tem. In 1938, he won a seat in the Territorial Senate and served as president pro tem, the same year he left the Democrats and became a Republican. In 1940, Kealoha was elected to the Hawaii County Board of Supervisors, serving several terms. He later challenged Quinn in the Republican gubernatorial primary in 1962 but was defeated. In 1966, Kealoha ran for a seat in the U.S. House of Representatives but did not win.

John David Waihe'e III

1977: Molly Shi Boren (1943–), Choctaw, was the first person to have served as both First Lady of the State of Oklahoma and First Lady of the University of Oklahoma (OU). She became Oklahoma's First Lady upon her marriage to Governor David Boren in 1977 and First Lady of OU when her husband became OU's president in 1994. Molly Shi Boren received a juris doctorate from the OU School of Law in 1974. She was also the first woman to serve on the Board of Trustees of the Oklahoma Bar Foundation and the first woman elected to the Board of Directors of Ada, Oklahoma's Chamber of Commerce.

Loren Leman

1982: Paul DeMain (1955–), Oneida/Ojibwe, became the first Native American to be appointed as a policy advisor on Indian Affairs in the state of Wisconsin. He served in the position from 1982 to 1986 under Governor Anthony S. Earl. Following that work, DeMain, who became a renowned journalist, served as editor and CEO of Indian Country Communications.

1986: John David Waihe'e III (1946–), Democrat, became the first Native Hawaiian governor of Hawaii as well as the first Native Hawaiian to be governor of any state and served until 1994. He was a member of the first graduating class of the University of Hawaii's Law School in 1976. Two years later, Waihe'e served as a delegate to the Hawai'i State Constitutional Convention and helped establish the Office of Hawaiian Affairs (OHA). He became a state representative in 1980, followed by lieutenant governor from 1982 to 1986.

2002: Loren Leman (1950–), Alutiiq/Russian-Polish, was the first Alaska Native to be elected lieutenant governor, holding the office from 2002 until 2006. Earlier, from 1989 to 1993, he served as a member of the Alaska House of Representatives from the 9th district. Leman also served in the Alaska Senate from 1993 to 2002.

2011: Leroy "J. R." LaPlante Jr. (c. 1969–), Cheyenne River Sioux, was named South Dakota's first secretary of tribal relations, a cabinet level position, by Governor Dennis Daugaard. A graduate of the University of South Dakota School of Law, LaPlante later served as an assistant U.S. attorney. He also served as Cheyenne River Sioux Tribe's chief administrative officer and as chief judge and court administrator for the Crow Creek Sioux Tribe. In 2015, LaPlante was named director of tribal relations by Avera Health in South Dakota, its primary liaison with regional tribal governments.

2017: Peggy Flanagan (1979–), White Earth Nation, became the first Native American woman elected as lieutenant governor in the country and the first Native person elected statewide in Minnesota. For several hours on June 20, 2019, from 12:30 P.M. until around 3 P.M., Flanagan served as active governor while Governor Tim Walz was under general anesthesia during a medical procedure, also believed to be a first for a woman and a Native American in the state's history. A member of the Democratic-Farmer-Labor Party (DFL), she served in the Minnesota House of Representatives (2015–2018) representing District 46A in the Twin Cities metropolitan area. On July 28, 2016, Flanagan became the first Native American woman to address the Democratic National Convention as an official speaker.

Peggy Flanagan

2018: Valerie Nurr'araaluk Davidson (1967–), Yup'ik, Democrat, became Alaska's first female Alaska Native lieutenant governor, serving in the position from October 16, 2018, to December 3, 2018. She was preceded by Byron Mallott, who had abruptly resigned the office. In April 2020, Davidson became the first woman to serve as president of Alaska Pacific University. Holding a law degree from the University of New Mexico, her earlier positions included senior director of legal and intergovernmental affairs for the Alaska Native Tribal Health Consortium, chair of the Tribal Technical Advisory Group to the Centers for Medicare and Medicaid Services, and Commissioner of the Alaska Department of Health and Social Services.

2018: Paulette Jordan (1979–), Coeur d'Alene, was the Democratic gubernatorial candidate in Idaho in 2018, becoming the first woman nominated to the position by a major party in that state and the first

Paulette Jordan

John Kevin Stitt

Native American woman nominated for governor in U.S. history. She lost the election to Republican governor Brad Little but garnered more votes than any Democratic gubernatorial or congressional candidate in Idaho history. Jordan served in the Idaho House of Representatives from December 1, 2014, to February 14, 2018. In 2008, after graduating from the University of Washington, she became the youngest person elected to the Coeur d'Alene Tribal Council. In February 2020, Jordan announced her candidacy to run for the U.S. Senate. She won the Democratic primary but lost in the general election to incumbent Republican senator Jim Risch.

2019: Wenona Singel, a citizen of the Little Traverse Bay Bands of the Odawa Indians, was appointed by Governor Gretchen Whitmer to serve as the deputy legal counsel to the Office of the Governor, the first American Indian to hold this position in Michigan. A magna cum laude graduate of Harvard College, Singel received a JD from Harvard Law School. Before her appointment, she served as an associate professor at Michigan State University College of Law and associate director of the Indigenous Law and Policy Center.

2019: John Kevin Stitt (1972–), Cherokee Nation, Republican, elected as governor of Oklahoma in 2018, became the first enrolled member of a tribal nation to serve in a governorship in the country. Governor Stitt, who graduated from Oklahoma State University with a degree in accounting, founded Gateway Mortgage Group in 2000.

◆◇◆

STATE JUDICIARY

1926: Jessie Elizabeth Randolph Moore (1871–1956), Chickasaw, became the first American Indian woman elected to a state office in Oklahoma, with her election as clerk of Oklahoma's Supreme Court.

1974: Abby Abinanti (1947–), Yurok, who attended the University of New Mexico School of Law, became the first Native American woman to be admitted to the State Bar of California. During her career, she was a San Francisco Superior Court commissioner, a judge or magistrate for several tribes, and a commissioner in the Unified Family Court for the San Francisco Superior Court. Abinanti, whose specialties include family court and juvenile dependency, returned to the Yurok Tribe to help set up its fishing court, later serving as a judge of the Yurok Tribal Court. She became the court's chief judge in 2007. Her other firsts include spearheading California's first tribal child support program, which allows tribal members to provide nonmonetary support such as food and labor. Judge Abinanti also created the country's first tribal program that helps members who have rehabilitated themselves clear their criminal records.

1975: Roy H. Madsen (1923–2017), Alutiiq, was the first Alaska Native to become a Superior Court judge, serving for 15 years. During his life, he worked to help pass the Alaska Native Claims Settlement Act and to form the Kodiak Area Native Association. The Kodiak courthouse was renamed the Roy H. Madsen Justice Center in his honor, and a documentary about his life premiered in 2017.

1978: Hawai'i's constitution recognized the Hawaiian language as an official language of the state along with English, making Hawai'i the first state in the union to recognize its native language as an official language.

1998: Carol Jean Vigil (1947–2009), Tesuque Pueblo, was the first woman elected as a state district judge in the United States. She was also the first Native American woman to be elected as a state court judge in New Mexico. Vigil, who completed her law degree at the University of New Mexico, was the first Pueblo woman to be admitted to New Mexico's state bar. She worked for the Indian Pueblo Legal Services, followed by private law practice and as an attorney for the Tesuque Pueblo. Vigil authored tribal codes for Taos Pueblo and Tesuque Pueblo. In 1995, she was named one of the "10 Who Made a Difference" by the *Santa Fe New Mexican*.

2000: Olin Jones, Chickasaw Nation, was named the first director of the newly created Office of Native American Affairs within the California Department of Justice. Jones had earlier worked for the Governor's Office of Criminal Justice Planning (OCJP) and served as a liaison to Native Americans. At OCJP, he developed California's first grant funding program specifically to benefit Native people on tribal lands.

2006: Leroy Not Afraid (1971–) became the first Crow Indian justice of the peace in Montana's Big Horn County. He previously served in the Crow Nation legislature (2004–2007) and as chairman of the Lodge Grass Public Schools Board of Trustees (2003–2007).

2012: Joey Jayne (1957–), Navajo, became the first Native female Justice Court judge in Montana history, serving as Northwestern Montana's Lake County justice of the peace. Born in Shiprock and raised in Tohatchi, New Mexico, Jayne attended the University of Montana School of Law intent on becoming a water rights attorney. She earned a

Indian Indenture Act in California

The first law passed after California became a state was the Indian Indenture Act, which was passed in 1850 by California's newly created legislature on April 19, 1850. The act was adopted to address worker shortages caused by the Gold Rush, allowing any white man to identify a Native American as vagrant, lazy, or drunk, thereby permitting law enforcement officials to arrest and fine him. Since most Native Americans could not pay the fines, a week's worth of their labor would be auctioned off, with the highest bidder paying the fines.

bachelor's degree in agricultural industry from Arizona State University and a master of science degree in watershed management and hydrology from the University of Arizona. Jayne also served as a Democrat in the Montana House of Representatives from the 15th district from 2000 to 2008.

2016: Anne K. McKeig (1967–), Ojibwe, became the first American Indian to serve on the Minnesota Supreme Court. She was appointed by Governor Mark Dayton as Minnesota's 94th associate justice. McKeig, a descendant of White Earth Nation, specializes in child protection and Indian welfare cases. McKeig had previously served as a district court judge and as a presiding judge in the Fourth District's Family Court.

2019: Raquel Montoya-Lewis (1968–), Pueblo of Isleta, became the first Native American to serve on the Washington Supreme Court. She was appointed by Governor Jay Inslee to replace retiring state Supreme Court justice Mary Fairhurst. Montoya-Lewis, born in Spain, earned her law degree at the University of Washington. She served as the chief judge for the Lummi, Nooksack and Skagit tribes and the Northwest intertribal courts. Her career also includes serving as an associate professor at Western Washington University and being elected and reelected to the Whatcom County Superior Court. As Supreme Court justices in Washington are elected, Montoya-Lewis had to run to keep her seat, winning a six-year term in 2020. Of being the first Native on the Court, she commented, "The most important thing is that I not be the last."

2019: On June 18, California governor Gavin Newsome issued Executive Order N-15-19, which formally apologizes for atrocities committed against Native Americans in the early days of California statehood. Besides mandating a first-of-its-kind formal apology, the order also established a Truth and Healing Council to address the historical relationship between the state and California Native Americans. The executive order acknowledged state-sponsored violence, exploitation, dispossession, and the attempted destruction of tribal communities.

2019: Matthew Scott, Lumbee, became the first American Indian district attorney in the state of North Carolina, serving Robeson County. A 2002 graduate of the University of Wisconsin–Madison School of Law and former paratrooper, former special assistant U.S. attorney, combat veteran, and U.S. Army Judge Advocate General Corps attorney, he was sworn in at the University of North Carolina–Pembroke on January 3, 2019.

Alaska's Anti-Discrimination Act, 1945

Alaska's Anti-Discrimination Act was signed into law on February 16, 1945, the first anti-discrimination law in the United States. Elizabeth Peratrovich, Tlingit, was instrumental in securing passage of the legislation, fighting to end "No Natives Allowed" and other pervasive racism against Alaska Natives. In 1988, Alaska's legislature established February 16 as Elizabeth Peratrovich Day, now an annual observance in the state. Other recognitions for Peratrovich include the renaming of a gallery of the Alaska House of Representatives in her honor, a bronze bust sculpted by her son Roy adorning the lobby of the State Capitol, and the U.S. Mint commemorating her on U.S. currency. In 2009, a documentary about Peratrovich's civil rights advocacy premiered as *For the Rights of All: Ending Jim Crow in Alaska*.

2021: Sonja McCullen (1969–), a Honolulu deputy prosecuting attorney, became the first Native Hawaiian appointed to a Hawai'i appellate court in decades. The Hawai'i Senate voted to approve her to serve on the Intermediate Court of Appeals. Appointed by Governor David Ige, McCullen has worked in the appellate division of the Honolulu Prosecutor's Office, clerked for Hawaii Supreme Court associate justice Paula Nakayama, and served as an attorney for United Public Workers. McCullen also taught Hawaiian studies and language while serving as a high school teacher.

STATE LEGISLATORS AND MORE

ALASKA

1924: William L. Paul Sr. (1885–1977), Tlingit, known as the "Father of Native Land Claims," was the first Alaska Native elected to the Alaskan Territorial House of Representatives. Paul attended the Carlisle Indian School in Pennsylvania and earned his baccalaureate degree at Whitworth College in Tacoma, Washington. After completing his law degree from La Salle University, he became the first Native attorney in Alaska. Paul helped build the Alaska Native Brotherhood (ANB), launching the newspaper *Alaska Fisherman* to advance ANB's work on behalf of civil rights.

1948: William E. Beltz (1912–1960) and Percy Ipalook (1906–1990) were the first Iñupiaq representatives elected to the Territorial Legislature in Alaska. Beltz, a Democrat, initially served as a member of the House and then successfully ran for a seat in the Territorial Senate in 1950, serving from 1951 to 1960. Following Alaska statehood in 1959, he was elected as the first president of the Alaska State Senate. Ipalook, an ordained minister, served in the House and was a member of the Alaska Statehood Committee from 1949 to 1959.

1956: Eben Hopson (1922–1980), Iñupiaq, was elected to the Alaska Territorial Legislature in 1956, and with Alaska statehood in 1959, he was elected to the state's first senate. In

1965, Hopson helped organize Alaska's first regional land claims organization, which entered an aboriginal claim to traditional lands of the Arctic Slope Inupiat. He became the first executive director of the Arctic Slope Native Association, which launched the Alaska Native Land Claims movement. In 1968, he became the executive director of the Alaska Federation of Natives (AFN). During that period, Hopson worked to secure the enactment of the Alaska Native Land Claims Settlement Act in 1971. He also became special assistant for Native affairs to Governor William A. Egan, helping to shape state policy with respect to land claims settlement. In 1972, Hopson became the first mayor of the newly organized North Slope Borough and was reelected in 1975.

1957: Constance Harper Paddock (1920–2011), Athabascan, was the first Alaska Native to serve as chief clerk of the Alaska House of Representatives. Raised in Fairbanks, Alaska, she attended Haskell Indian Junior College and earned a degree in business education. In 1942, Paddock moved to Juneau, where she worked for the Bureau of Indian Affairs. She was employed by the governor's office and then served as chief clerk.

1974: Brenda Itta (1943–), Inupiaq, became the first Alaska Native woman elected to Alaska's House of Representatives, serving until 1976. Itta was born in Barrow and attended a Bureau of Indian Affairs school. She later became active in the Alaska Federation of Natives and the Arctic Slope Native Association. Itta also served as an aide to Alaska's Senator Ernest Gruening, seeking to establish a working relationship between his office and Alaska Native villages. She was a lobbyist for the region in Washington, D.C. She was president of the Alaska Native Women's Statewide Organization, and as a state legislator Itta served on the House Finance Committee and chaired the subcommittee on Health and Social Services.

1993: Georgianna Lincoln (1943–), Athabascan, became the first Alaska Native woman to serve in the Alaska State Senate when she was sworn into office. Previously, she had served in the Alaska House of Representatives (1991 to 1992) as well as in the Alaska legislature for 14 years, her tenure lasting to 2005. During that period, the Democratic Lincoln championed a number of issues, including those that focused on women and children and natural resource management. In 1996, she became the first Native woman to be a candidate for the U.S. Congress from Alaska. Lincoln was the executive director of the Fairbanks Native Association and director at the Tanana Chiefs Conference. She served on the board of Doyon Corporation for more than 30 years.

2000: Glenn Godfrey (1949–2002), Aleut, became the first Alaska Native to serve as commissioner of the Alaskan Department of Public Safety. Appointed by Governor Tony Knowles, he remained in the position until retiring in 2002 after a 32-year career. Godfrey had also served as director of the Alaska State Troopers.

ARIZONA

1966: Lloyd L. House (1931–2015), Navajo/Oneida and a Democrat, became the first Native American elected to the Arizona State Legislature, serving in Arizona's House of Representatives (1967 to 1968). He was in the U.S. Marine Corps from 1950 to 1954 and the U.S. Air Force Reserves during the Vietnam War. After his term as a legislator, House earned his doctorate in higher education and business administration, becoming dean of instruction for Navajo Community College (Diné College). He was also the director of the Phoenix Indian Center and organized the first Social Security offices for the Navajo and Hopi tribal nations.

1997: Debora Lynn Norris (1950–), Navajo/Tohono O'odham, Democrat, was one of the first two Native American women to serve in the Arizona House of Representatives (1997–2002). A graduate of Stanford University, she represented the 11th district.

1997: Sally Ann Gonzales (1957–), Pascua Yaqui, Democrat, was one of the first two Native American women to serve in the Arizona House of Representatives (1997–2001), representing the 20th district. Gonzales also served in the Arizona House from January 2011 to January 2013, representing the 27th district, and from January 2013 to January 2019, representing the 3rd district. She became a member of the Arizona Senate from the 3rd district, assuming office in January 2019. Gonzales also served on the Pascua Yaqui Council in Arizona from 1992 to 1996.

2003: Jack Jackson Jr. and Jack Jackson Sr. (1933–), Navajo, Democrat, became the first father and son to serve together in the Arizona State Legislature. Jackson Jr. served in the House of Representatives from 2003 to 2005 while his father was serving in the State Senate (1998–2004). Jackson Sr. had earlier served in the Arizona House from 1985 to 1998, and Jackson Jr. represented Arizona's 2nd district in the State Senate from January 2011 to July 2013. He then took a newly created post in the U.S. Department of State, becoming the first liaison to Native American tribes on environmental issues.

2015: Norman Dodson, Navajo, was sworn in as the first Native American special deputy U.S. marshal–court security officer in the District of Arizona. Dodson, a 35-year veteran of Arizona's Tuba City Police Department, joined the Navajo Police Department in 1977.

2016: Jamescita Peshlakai (1968–), Navajo, became Arizona's first Native American woman senator with her election in 2016 to represent

Jamescita Peshlakai

legislative district 7. Peshlakai, a Democrat, formerly served in the Arizona House of Representatives (2013 to 2015). She holds a master's degree in educational psychology from Northern Arizona University and is an Army veteran, having served in the Persian Gulf War.

2020: Gabriella Cázares-Kelly (c. 1982–), a citizen of the Tohono O'odham Nation and a Democrat, was elected as Pima County recorder in Tucson, Arizona, becoming the first Native American elected to a Pima County seat and beating her Republican opponent with 60 percent of the vote. She is also the cofounder of Indivisible Tohono, which focuses on providing voter education and other civic engagement in her tribal nation.

ARKANSAS

2006: Donna Jean King Hutchinson (1949–), Blackfeet, Republican, was elected to the Arkansas House of Representatives and served until 2013. She represented the 98th district, which includes part of Benton County. Her twin sons, Jeremy Hutchinson and Timothy Hutchinson, also served in the Arkansas state legislature.

CALIFORNIA

2016: Todd Gloria (1978–), Tlingit-Haida, Democrat, became California's first Native American-Filipino-Puerto Rican-Dutch-LGBT assemblyman. He was elected to the California State Assembly from the 78th district, which includes a large area of San Diego, and assumed office on December 5, 2016.

2016: A section of State Highway 371 in Anza, California, was posthumously named for Frank Hamilton, Cahuilla, a Riverside County special deputy sheriff who served in the 1890s and is believed to have been the first law officer in the county killed in the line of duty. The measure designating Special Deputy Frank Hamilton Memorial Highway was enacted into state law on February 1, 2016.

2018: James C. Ramos (1967–), Serrano/Cahuilla, became the first California Indian to be elected to the California State Assembly. A Democrat representing the 40th District, he is a resident of the San Manuel Indian Reservation in San Bernardino County. Ramos has served as a supervisor and board chairman of San Bernardino County. He was the first Native American to be elected to the Board of Supervisors as well as to the San Bernardino Community College Board of Trustees. In 2011, with his appointment by Governor Jerry Brown, he became the first Native American appointed to the State Board of Education. Ramos has also served as chairman of the San Manuel Band of Mission Indians and in other leadership roles.

COLORADO

1976: The Colorado General Assembly established the Commission of Indian Affairs (CCIA) within the Office of the Lieutenant Governor. The commission serves as the official liaison between the Southern Ute Indian Tribe and the Ute Mountain Ute Tribe and the State of Colorado. It works on a government-to-government basis with the two federally recognized tribal governments, maintaining contact with the tribes and urban Indian communities in the state.

1982: Benjamin Nighthorse Campbell (1933–), Cheyenne, was the first Native American elected to the Colorado House of Representatives.

2021: Colorado governor Jared Polis rescinded an 1864 proclamation made by territorial governor John Evans that called for citizens to kill American Indians and take their property. The order was used to justify the Sand Creek Massacre, a brutal attack that left more than 200 Cheyenne and Arapaho people dead. Rick Williams, Lakota/Cheyenne scholar of Native American history, found the original order by Evans while researching the aftermath of an 1861 treaty.

HAWAII

1925: Rosalie Enos Lyons Keli'inoi (1875–1952), Native Hawaiian/Portuguese, became the first woman elected to the Hawaii Territorial Legislature. The only female member during her one term in office, she introduced sixteen bills, four of which were passed into law. One of them, Act 274, is considered a landmark piece of legislation for women's rights. It granted property rights to women, allowing them to sell and manage their own property without their husbands' approval. Keli'inoi's path-breaking election helped pave the way for other women to enter politics. She was ranked among a list of the most influential women in Hawaiian history by *Hawai'i Magazine* in 2017.

1978: The Office of Hawaiian Affairs (OHA) was created by the Hawaii State Constitutional Convention. Its provisions include a mandate to better the conditions of Native Hawaiians as well as the Hawaiian community in general. OHA was to be funded with a pro rata share of revenues from state lands deemed "ceded." It continues to work to improve the well-being of Native Hawaiians in areas that include education, health, housing, and economics.

IDAHO

1956: Joseph Garry (1910–1975), Coeur d'Alene, was the first Native American to be elected to the Idaho House of Representatives. A Democrat, he ran for the U.S. Senate in 1960 but was defeated. In 1966, he became the first Native American elected to the

Idaho state senate. Garry also served 25 years on the Coeur d'Alene tribal council, 13 of those years as chairman. Other leadership roles included serving as president of the National Congress of American Indians for six years. His life and work are documented in *Saving the Reservation: Joe Garry and the Battle to Be Indian* by John Fahey (2001).

1984: Jeanne Givens (c. 1951–), Coeur d'Alene, Democrat, was the first Native American woman elected to the Idaho House of Representatives, winning reelection in 1986. In 1988, she became the first Native American woman to run for Congress. Givens also served as the former chair of the Institute of American Indian Arts (IAIA) board of trustees.

1990: Larry Echo Hawk (1948–), Pawnee Nation, who served in Idaho from 1991 to 1995, was the first Native American elected as state attorney general in the United States. In 1992, he became the first American Indian to head a state delegation to the Democratic National Convention, also participating as a principal speaker. In 2009, President Barack Obama nominated Echo Hawk to serve as the U.S. assistant secretary of the interior for Indian affairs, and he was unanimously confirmed to the position by the U.S. Senate. In 1982, he won election to a seat in the Idaho State House of Representatives, serving for two terms.

KANSAS

2010: Ponka-We Victors (1981–), Tohono O'odham/Ponca, became the first Native American woman to be elected to the Kansas House of Representatives. A Democrat representing Kansas district 103, she was reelected to a sixth term in 2020. Victors earned a master of public administration degree from Wichita State University in 2008 and was influenced to go into politics from her work as a congressional intern. In 2013, she garnered national attention when she addressed Kansas secretary of state Kris Kobach and other advocates of a bill to deny in-state tuition to Kansas high school graduates who were undocumented immigrants, commenting: "I think it's funny, Mr. Kobach, because when you mention illegal immigrant, I think of all of you."

Stephanie Byers

2020: Stephanie Byers (1963–), Chickasaw Nation, was elected to the Kansas House of Representatives, the first openly transgender person to serve in the state legislature and also the first transgender Native American elected to such office in the country. Byers, a member of the Democratic Party, represents the 86th district in Kansas. An educator who earned degrees from Oklahoma Christian University and Kansas State University, she taught for 29 years before retiring in 2019. Byers, the recipient of the National Educator of the Year award by the Gay, Lesbian & Straight Education Network, assumed her Kansas House office in 2021.

2020: Christina Haswood (1994–), Navajo, was elected at age 26 to represent District 10 in the Kansas House of Representatives, one of the youngest members of the Kansas Legislature. A Democrat, Haswood earned a master's degree in public health management from the University of Kansas Medical Center. Haswood, who wore traditional Navajo dress during her swearing-in ceremony on January 11, 2021, recorded her preparations via TikTok, making national news.

Christina Haswood

KENTUCKY

2000: Reginald K. Meeks (1954–), Chero-kee/African American, Democrat, a member of the Kentucky House of Representatives, has represented District 42 for 21 years. Representative Meeks completed his juris doctor degree at the University of Iowa College of Law and previously served as alderman for the City of Louisville from 1982 to 2000. His civic work includes serving on the Kentucky Native American Heritage Commission and on the board of the Kentucky Native American Arts & Cultural Center.

MAINE

1999: Donna Loring (1948–), the Penobscot Nation's tribal representative in the legislature, was appointed by Governor Angus S. King Jr. as his aide de camp, which also included the rank of colonel. Loring, a Vietnam veteran, served as the chair of the legislature's Advisory Commission on Women Veterans. She conceptualized and advocated for the first State of the Tribes Address, observed by the state legislature for the first time in the state's history on March 11, 2002. Loring authored the Act to Require Teaching of Maine Native American History and Culture in Maine's Schools, signed into Maine state law in 2001.

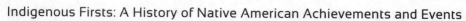

Donna Loring

2013: Henry John Bear (1956–), Maliseet, became the first elected Maliseet representative to the Maine legislature, which had previously been an appointed position. Although not permitted to vote, Bear and the other two tribal representatives (Passamaquoddy and Penobscot) can introduce and sponsor legislation. Bear, a member of the Houlton Band of Maliseets, previously worked as an attorney and as a municipal judge. In 2001, he was elected as tribal councilor of the Maliseet Nation at Tobique.

MASSACHUSETTS

1885: Watson F. Hammond (1837–1919), Montauk, was the first Native American elected to serve in the Great and General Court, the Massachusetts legislature. At age 7, following the death of his father, a Montauk tribal member from Long Island, New York, Hammond was sent to live with an uncle in Mashpee, Massachusetts. A seaman, he later became a cranberry farmer and inventor, patenting a cranberry separator in 1883. Hammond held all town offices in Mashpee, including town clerk, moderator, selectman, surveyor, and treasurer. As a Republican legislator, he represented Barnstable and Mashpee.

MICHIGAN

1924: Cora Reynolds Anderson (1882–1950), Chippewa descent, Republican, became the first woman and the first Native American elected to the Michigan House of Representatives and represented Baraga, Iron, Keweenaw, and Ontonagon counties during her 1925–1926 tenure. In Lansing, the Anderson House Office Building and Cora's Café within that building are named in her honor.

1982: Beverly Clark (1939–2013), Aamjiwnaang First Nation, Sarnia Reserve, was the first Native American commissioner for the Michigan Civil Rights Commission (1982–1991). In 1983, Clark also became the first female president of the Michigan Trial Lawyers Association (now called the Michigan Association for Justice).

2013: Matthew Wesaw (1953–), Pokagon Band of Potawatomi, was the first Native American to become executive board director of the Michigan Department of Civil

Rights. He retired as tribal chairman and president and CEO of the Pokagon Gaming Authority to take the position. Wesaw also had a 26-year career as a Michigan state police trooper and served as director for the Michigan State Police Troopers Association. In 2018, he was reelected chairman of the Pokagan Band for the third time; his earlier elections were in 2008 and 2012.

MINNESOTA

1990: Harold R. "Skip" Finn (1948–2018), Ojibwe, Leech Lake, Democrat-Farmer-Labor (DFL), became the first Native American elected to the Minnesota Senate, representing Minnesota's District 4 from 1991 to 1996. He was the first to receive a bachelor's degree in American Indian studies from the University of Minnesota, where he completed his law degree in 1979. His daughter, Jamie Becker-Finn, was elected to the Minnesota House of Representatives in 2016, representing District 42B, and was reelected in 2018 and 2020.

Mary Kunesh

Harold "Skip" Finn

2012: Susan L. Allen (1963–), Rosebud Sioux, Democratic-Farmer-Labor (DFL), became the first American Indian woman elected to the Minnesota state legislature and the first openly gay American Indian woman to win election to any state legislature. In 2018, she had served four terms in Minnesota's House of Representatives, but she did not seek reelection. An attorney, Allen has also served as a judge in the Prairie Island Indian Community's Children's Court and as an appellate judge for the Lower Sioux Indian Community. In 2019, Jacobson Law Group, which Allen joined in 2013, announced that Allen had been named a share-

Susan Allen

holder of the firm, which is in St. Paul, Minnesota. In her legal career, she represents tribal governments and tribal business entities on matters such as corporate governance, commercial transactions, contracts, and tax issues.

2020: Mary Kunesh (former name Kunesh-Podein; 1960–), Standing Rock Sioux, became the first American Indian woman elected to the Minnesota Senate, representing District 41. A member of the Democratic-Farmer-Labor (DFL) party, she also served in the Minnesota House of Representatives, representing District 41B from 2017 to 2020. Kunesh, a library media specialist, graduated from St. Catherine's University in St. Paul and St. Cloud State University. She was a founding member of the Native American and People of Color & Indigenous (POCI) caucuses. Her special legislative concerns include education, civil justice, environment, and American Indian issues.

MISSISSIPPI

1841: Greenwood LeFlore (1800–1865) was the first Choctaw elected to the Mississippi state legislature, serving as a senator from 1841 to 1844. Earlier, in 1830, he had been elected principal chief of his tribal nation. A proponent of removal, LeFlore was one of signers of the Treaty of Dancing Rabbit Creek, which provided for relinquishment of Choctaw lands in Mississippi and removal west of the Mississippi River. LeFlore's pro-removal stance was controversial with other Choctaws. He stayed in Mississippi, serving as a state senator and becoming wealthy as a planter and entrepreneur.

MONTANA

1932: Dolly Smith Cusker Akers (1901–1986), Assiniboine, elected to the Montana House of Representatives in 1932, was the first Native American to serve in Montana's state legislature and the only woman who served in the 1933–34 legislative session. As a legislator, she chaired the Federal Relations Committee and was a representative of Governor Frank Cooney to the U.S. secretary of the Interior. Cusker was elected as a Democrat but became an active member of the Republican Party. Born Dolly Smith, she attended school on Montana's Fort Peck Reservation and at Sherman Institute in Riverside, California. Her career included being the first woman elected to the Tribal Executive Board on the Fort Peck Indian Reservation and, in 1956, winning election as the first female chair. She also served as vice president of the National Congress of American Indians. Dolly Smith Cusker Akers remained active in tribal politics for some 40 years, often traveling to Washington, D.C., as a delegate representing her tribal nation.

2008: Denise Juneau (1967–), Mandan/Hidatsa/Arikara, Democrat, was elected superintendent of public instruction, becoming the first Native American woman elected to statewide office in Montana. In 2012 she won her election for a second term in office.

NEBRASKA

2016: Tom Brewer (1958), Lakota, became the first Native American elected to the Nebraska legislature. Brewer, who grew up on the Pine Ridge Reservation, earned a bachelor of arts degree from Nebraska's Doane University and attended the U.S. Army War College. He served in the U.S. Army for 36 years, including six tours in Afghanistan, and was awarded two purple hearts and a bronze medal. During his service, he was shot seven times, seriously injured by a grenade, and suffered traumatic brain and other injuries, retiring from the military as a colonel. A Republican, Brewer represents the 43rd district in the state legislature and has focused on veterans' issues.

NEVADA

1938: Dewey Sampson (1898–1982), Pyramid Lake Paiute, was the first American Indian elected to the Nevada legislature, serving one term and sponsoring legislation to benefit Native Americans in the state. Sampson graduated from the Stewart Indian School near Carson City, Nevada (1918), where he returned to teach music. He and his brother Harry provided leadership in the Reno-Sparks Indian Colony.

2011: John Oceguera (1968–), Walker River Paiute, Democrat, was the first-ever American Indian to serve as Speaker of the Nevada Assembly, holding the position in the 2011-2012 session. Oceguera represented Clark County District 16 until 2013. Earlier, he had a 20-year career with the North Las Vegas Fire Department, retiring as an assistant chief in 2011.

2018: Shea Backus (1975–), Democrat, is believed to be the first Native American woman elected to the Nevada State Assembly. Representing District 37, she served until November 4, 2020, when she lost reelection. An attorney certified in Indian law, she completed her law degree at Arizona State University's Sandra Day O'Connor College of Law.

NEW MEXICO

1966: Tom Lee, Navajo, a Republican, was the first Native American elected as a New Mexico state senator. Starting in 1967, he served three consecutive terms and then served several terms on the Navajo Nation Council.

1973: Nick L. Salazar (1929–2020), Ohkay Owingeh, a Democratic member of the New Mexico House of Representatives, was elected and represented District 40 until 2018. He was New Mexico's longest-serving lawmaker and one of the longest serving legislators in the nation. Salazar was known for wearing a red carnation on his lapel during legislative sessions. A veteran of the U.S. Air Force, other contributions included his work as a mechanical technician at the Los Alamos National Laboratory.

1985: James Roger Madalena Sr. (1948–), Jemez Pueblo, was the first member of his Pueblo elected to New Mexico's House of Representatives. A Democrat, he represented the 65th district from 1985 to 2017. Before becoming a state legislator, he served as a county commissioner. Madalena ran for his legislative seat again in 2020 but was defeated in the Democratic primary.

1988: Lynda Morgan Lovejoy (1949–), Navajo, Democrat, became the first Native American woman to be elected to the New Mexico House of Representatives, serving in the position for five terms until 1998. In 1999, she was appointed the first commissioner of the newly established New Mexico Public Regulation Commission, holding the position for three terms, the only American Indian woman on the commission. In 2007, Governor Bill Richardson appointed her to New Mexico's state senate, representing the 22nd district, the first American Indian woman to hold the position, and she was elected in 2008 for a full term until 2013. Lovejoy was the first woman to be a finalist for Navajo Nation president in 2006 but lost the election to incumbent President Joe Shirley Jr. She also ran for the office in 2010 but lost to Navajo Nation vice president Ben Shelly.

2008: Sandra D. Jeff (c. 1967–), Navajo, Democrat, was elected to serve in the New Mexico House of Representatives from the 5th district, serving until 2015. It represented the first time in New Mexico history that Native American women held seats in both the House and Senate. Lynda Morgan Lovejoy (Navajo), who had held the same House seat as Jeff, was then serving in the Senate.

2012: Georgene Louis (1978–), Acoma Pueblo, Democrat, was elected to the New Mexico House of Representatives and began serving in 2013 as the first Pueblo woman in the state legislature representing District 26, which includes part of Albuquerque. Besides working as an attorney, including as general counsel of the Pueblo of Tesuque, she has served as an adjunct professor at the University of New Mexico, her alma mater. Louis was reelected to a fifth term in 2020. On January 4, 2021, she announced her candidacy for New Mexico's 1st congressional district special election but was defeated on March 30, 2021.

NORTH CAROLINA

1973: Henry Ward Oxendine (1940–2020), Lumbee, became the first American Indian to serve in the North Carolina State House of Representatives. A Democrat, he served the 21st District and was appointed to the position following the death of state representative Frank White and then elected to the seat. Oxendine, an Air Force veteran and a 1973 graduate of North Carolina Central University College of Law in Durham, served in the North Carolina General Assembly until 1976. Later activities included appointments by Governor Jim Hunt to the 6th Highway Division on the North Carolina Secondary Roads Council and to the newly created North Carolina Board of Paroles. In 2008, Oxendine became a judge on the Supreme Court of the Lumbee Tribe.

1999: David T. McCoy (1952–), Turtle Mountain Band of Chippewa Indians, was the first American Indian to serve in multiple roles in North Carolina state government, including secretary of the North Carolina Department of Transportation (beginning in 1999), state budget director (2001–2008), and state controller (2008–2014). McCoy, who graduated in 1985, was also the first member of a federally recognized tribe to graduate from the University of North Carolina's School of Law, where he founded the UNC Native American Law Students Association.

NORTH DAKOTA

1970: Arthur Raymond (1923–2009), Oglala Lakota, Republican, was the first person of known American Indian descent to serve in North Dakota's state legislature. He was reelected to the state's House of Representatives in 1972 and 1974. Raymond was a member of the Rosebud Sioux Tribe and attended the Rosebud Boarding School. After serving in the Army during World War II, he graduated from Dakota Wesleyan University (DWU) in Mitchell, South Dakota. While at DWU, he worked for the *Mitchell Daily Republic* and was hired full time in 1953, becoming city editor the same year. Raymond continued his career in journalism in North Dakota at the *Williston Herald* and later at the *Grand Forks Herald*. Following the establishment of the Department of Indian Studies at the University of North Dakota (UND) by state law in 1971, he was hired as its first director and also taught a range of courses. He earned a master's degree in American culture from the University of Michigan in 1980 and pursued Ph.D. studies there, completing all but a dissertation in 1985. Raymond retired from UND in 1991.

2007: Richard Marcellais (1947–), Turtle Mountain Band of Chippewa Indians, Democratic-Nonpartisan League Party, assumed office in the North Dakota Senate, representing the 9th district. In November 2008, he was elected tribal chairman at Turtle Mountain, becoming the first person to hold office as

both a state senator and as tribal chairman in North Dakota and possibly the nation. In 2010, Marcellais was unsuccessful in a run for reelection to the tribal chairmanship. Running for reelection to his Senate seat, he defeated his Republican opponent and has continued to be reelected since then.

2018: Ruth Buffalo, Mandan, Hidatsa, and Arikara, became the first Native American Democratic woman elected to the North Dakota Legislature House of Representatives. From the 27th District, she defeated incumbent Randy Boehning (Republican), the primary sponsor of a voter ID law viewed as disenfranchising Native American voters. Buffalo's educational background includes a bachelor of science degree in criminal justice and three master's degrees.

OKLAHOMA

1979: Helen TeAta Gale Cole (1922–2004), Chickasaw Nation, Republican, was the first Native American woman elected to the Oklahoma state legislature, as a member of the House of Representatives until 1984 and as a state senator representing the 45th district from 1984 to 1986 and 1991 to 1996. Cole also served as the mayor of Moore, Oklahoma, in 1990. She was named a delegate to the Republican National Convention in 1968 and 1992. Cole was inducted into the Chickasaw Hall of Fame in 1999.

1987: Neal McCaleb (1935–), Chickasaw, a civil engineer, was named Oklahoma's first secretary of transportation by Governor Henry Bellmon, serving until 1993. Reappointed to the position in 1995 by Governor Frank Keating, he became the first person to serve as director of both the Oklahoma Department of Transportation and the Oklahoma Turnpike Authority, in addition to being secretary of transportation, until 2001. McCaleb also served in the Oklahoma House of Representatives from 1975 to 1983 and was elected minority floor leader in 1978.

1990: Sandy Garrett, Cherokee, became the first woman elected as the Oklahoma state superintendent of public instruction and the only woman to hold a statewide office for five consecutive terms. Born in Muskogee, Oklahoma, Garrett earned her bachelor's degree and master's degrees from Northeastern State University in Oklahoma. She served as a teacher and a gifted programs coordinator in Muskogee. Superintendent Barrett worked to implement Oklahoma's Education Reform Act of 1990. Her administration also saw to the development of the state's pre-kindergarten programs.

T. W. Shannon

2006: Al McAffrey (1948–), Choctaw Nation, Democrat, became the first openly LGBT person elected to serve in the Oklahoma legislature, serving in the state's House of Representatives from the 88th district until 2012. He then served in the Oklahoma Senate from 2012 to 2015.

Al McAffrey

2013: T. W. Shannon (1978–), Chickasaw/African American, made history by becoming the youngest Speaker of the Oklahoma House of Representatives and the first Chickasaw and first African American to hold the post. He was also the first African American Republican in the country to head a legislative body since Reconstruction. Shannon was first elected to Oklahoma's House of Representatives in 2006, serving until 2015. He ran for the Republican nomination in the special election to succeed Senator Tom Coburn in the U.S. Senate but lost to U.S. representative James Lankford in 2014. Shannon, an attorney, became chairman of the Future Major-

David Holt

ity Project, part of a recruitment effort of the Republican State Legislative Committee.

2018: David Holt (1979–), member of the Osage Nation, became the first Native American mayor of Oklahoma City, also the city's youngest mayor since 1923. Holt, a Republican, served in the Oklahoma Senate from the 30th district from 2010 to 2014, eventually as majority whip. A major achievement as mayor was the passage of MAPS 4 in 2019, a nearly $1 billion initiative that includes 16 priorities such as upgrades to all neighborhood parks, a new wellness center, transit upgrades, affordable housing to address homelessness, a new civil rights center, and a new multipurpose stadium. Holt's leadership culminated in a unanimous council vote for the measure and overwhelming approval by voters for an eight-year, one-cent sales tax to fund MAPS 4, the highest percentage of support for any sales tax in the city's history. In 2020, Holt was elected as a trustee of the U.S. Conference of Mayors and is the recipient of many honors, including the Visionary Award from OKC Black Chamber. An attorney, he is the author of *Big League City: Oklahoma City's Rise to the NBA* (2012).

2019: Lisa Johnson Billy (1967–), Chickasaw, Republican, became the first Native American to be named to the Oklahoma governor's Cabinet in the state's history, serving as the first secretary of Native affairs. She was named to the position by Governor Kevin Stitt, Cherokee, following his election to the governorship in November 2018. Billy's other political firsts include serving as the first Native American, the first woman, and the first Republican elected to the Oklahoma House of Representatives representing District 42 of the state. She was in office from 2004 to 2014, when she was "termed out" after serving twelve years. During her first term, Billy became a founding member of the House Native American Caucus. She also served in the Chickasaw Nation Legislature from 1996 to 2001, returning to that office in 2016.

OREGON

1990: Jacqueline S. Taylor (1935–2008), Citizen Potawatomi, was the first Native American elected to the Oregon Legislature. She was a Democrat and served in Oregon's House of Representatives until 2000, when term limits prevented her from running for reelection. Taylor was later elected to the Citizen Potawatomi Nation Tribal Legislature.

PENNSYLVANIA

2007: Barbara McIlvaine Smith (1950–), Sac and Fox Nation, Democrat, was the first Native American elected to the Pennsylvania House of Representatives, representing the 156th District from 2007 to 2010. Her win, by 23 votes, gave Democrats control of the state house for the first time in 12 years. In 2010, she was narrowly defeated for reelection by her Republican opponent, Dan Truitt. Earlier, Smith was elected to Pennsylvania's West Chester Borough Council, serving from 2002 to 2006, two of those years as vice president. In 2016, she was appointed as a board member to the Pennsylvania State System of Higher Education.

SOUTH DAKOTA

1970: John P. "Pat" Flynn Jr. (1922–1979), Lakota, became the first person of Native American descent to be elected to South Dakota's state senate. A descendant of Chief Spotted Tail, he served twenty-four years in the U.S. military in a career that spanned World War II, the Korean War, and the early years of the Vietnam War. Lt. Colonel Flynn was a POW, who endured 16 months in captivity in North Korea, suffering torture and long periods of solitary confinement. As a state senator, he was assigned to the Local Government, Natural Resources, and Taxation committees and served in office for one term as a Republican. His life is documented in *Chief: Marine Corps Warrior* by Sean J. Flynn (2003).

1982: Thomas Shortbull (1946–), Oglala Lakota, was the first elected state senator from a newly created legislative district that included Todd and Shannon counties as well as a portion of Bennett County. In 1981, South Dakota was required to create the district under section five of the Voting Rights Act. Shortbull, a Democrat, was instrumental in effecting the change against gerrymandering that had existed among three counties on the Rosebud and Pine Ridge reservations. Shortbull served three terms as state senator of legislative district 27, from 1983 to 1988. His legacy of achievement includes continuing to advocate for voting rights and serving as president of Oglala Lakota College from 1975 to 1979 and from 1995 to the present. He announced his intention to retire in July 2022. Shortbull was inducted into the South Dakota Hall of Fame in 2017.

1994: Robert D. Ecoffey, Oglala Lakota, became the first American Indian to serve as a U.S. marshall in South Dakota.

2004: Theresa B. "Huck" Two Bulls (1949–2020), Oglala Sioux, Democrat, became the first American Indian woman elected to the state legislature in South Dakota. She represented the 27th district in the state senate and served until 2008. Two Bulls was then elected as president of the Oglala Sioux Tribe of the Pine Ridge Reservation in South

Dakota, the second woman to hold the position, serving a two-year term, from December 2008 to December 2010. She also held other leadership positions on the tribal council. Two Bulls, an attorney, served on a U.S. Department of Justice task force seeking to reduce violence against American Indian women. In 2015, she became secretary-treasurer of the National Congress of American Indians.

2018: Troy Heinert (1972–), Rosebud Sioux, Democrat state senator, became the first Native American elected as Senate minority leader in South Dakota, assuming office on January 8, 2019. Heinert, a graduate of Sinte Gleska University, was first elected to South Dakota's House of Representatives from District 26A, comprising Todd and Mellette counties, in 2012 and served for one term, from January 2013 to January 2015. Following his election to the state senate in 2014, he was elected in 2015 as senate assistant minority leader. He was reelected as state senator in 2018 and 2020.

2021: Tamara St. John (1966–), Dakota, became the only Native American Republican in the South Dakota House of Representatives, after the retirement of Lakota Republican Steve Livermont. St. John, Sisseton-Wahpeton tribal archivist at Lake Traverse Reservation, was elected to South Dakota's House of Representatives from the 1st district in 2018.

TENNESSEE

2014: Bryan Terry (1968–), Choctaw Nation, Republican, was elected to Tennessee House of Representatives from the 48th district in 2014, becoming the only Native American serving in the state's legislative body. Terry, who graduated from the University of Oklahoma College of Medicine, worked as a doctor in Oklahoma and Tennessee. He was reelected in 2016, 2018, and 2020.

WASHINGTON

1898: William Bishop Jr. (1861–1934), Snohomish, Republican, was the first Native American to be elected to the state legislature in Washington, initially to the House of Representatives, where he eventually served four terms. After several tries, Bishop was elected to the state senate in 1918 and reelected in 1922. In 1926, he helped draft the constitution of the Snohomish Tribe of Indians, incorporating it in 1927, and serving as its first president. Bishop was reelected to the state senate in 1932 and served until his death.

1979: Lois J. Stratton (1927–2020), Spokane, became the first Native American woman to serve in the Washington state legislature. Stratton, Democrat, served in the state House of Representatives from the 3rd district until 1985 and in the state senate from 1985 to 1993.

WYOMING

1980: Scott "Scotty" Ratliff (1943–), Eastern Shoshone, Democrat, was the first Native American elected to Wyoming's legislature (House of Representatives); he served until 1992. A wounded Vietnam War veteran, he attended college on his return home from military service. Ratliff served as a member of the Wyoming State Council on Juvenile Justice and as president of the board for the Cowboy Hall of Fame. In 1990, he received the Human Rights Award from the Wyoming Counseling Association. Ratliff continued his service as a member of the Shoshone Economic Board, the Wyoming State Board of Tribal Economic, and the National Advisory Council on Indian Education. In 2002, he was hired by U.S. senator Mike Enzi to help improve the quality of life for people on the Wind River Indian Reservation and surrounding areas.

2016: Affie Ellis (1978–), Navajo Nation, Republican, was the first Native American elected to serve in the Wyoming State Senate and the first Native American woman elected to the Wyoming legislature. She defeated incumbent Democrat Floyd Esquibel in the general election and represented Wyoming's District 8. Ellis is a former assistant attorney general of Wyoming, owner of Ellis Public Affairs, and the former owner of Steamboat's Steak and Smokehouse until it closed in 2018. She was reelected in 2020.

Affie Ellis

came the first Native American woman elected to the Wyoming House of Representatives. Born and raised on the Wind River Reservation, she represents District 33, formerly held by her uncle, Patrick Goggles. Clifford became one of only nine Democrats in the 60-member House chamber and the first woman from the Wind River Reservation ever elected to Wyoming's legislature. She joined one other American Indian woman in the Wyoming legislature, Senator Affie Ellis, Navajo, Republican. Clifford was reelected in 2020.

2018: Andrea "Andi" Clifford (aka Andrea LeBeau), Northern Arapaho, Democrat, be-

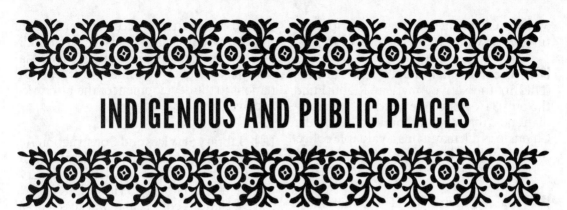

INDIGENOUS AND PUBLIC PLACES

"As a creative practitioner working in the public realm, I grapple with the disconnection between narratives surrounding public space and my reality as an Indigenous Dakota artist.... Public art, monuments, and historic markers that perpetuate defective views of Native American and Indigenous peoples are everywhere across America. Despite this reality, there is fertile ground for educating the public about Indigenous peoples through art and creating a strong Indigenous presence in these spaces that have historically excluded us.... How can we use social, political, and natural history to create space for justice? It is the responsibility of all practitioners working in the public sphere to address these issues in their works, as they are fundamental to the land occupied, the resources used, and the people and living things affected."

—Erin Genia, Sisseton-Wahpeton Dakota from *"Unseen Dimensions of Public Space: Disrupting Colonial Narratives,"* Boston Art Review, *Issue 04: Public Art Issue, Fall 2019.*

ARCHIVES AND LIBRARIES

—Sandra D. Littletree, Ph.D., Diné/Eastern Shoshone, from "Let Me Tell You About Indian Libraries": Self-Determination, Leadership, and Vision—The Basis of Tribal Library Development in the United States, 2018.

"Tribal libraries in the United States have become sites of cultural and language renewal, gathering places, and places to collect, preserve, and share Indigenous knowledge. After more than forty years of development, tribal libraries have become important sites of decolonization, where sovereignty and self-determination are paramount."

1958: The Colorado River Indian Tribes Library in Mojave, Arizona, was created and is thought to be the first tribal library. Apart from providing programs and lending materials to members, the library is devoted to the preservation and documentation of the

Mohave, Chemehuevi, Navajo, and Hopi cultures. A new library was dedicated in 1970.

1970: The National Indian Law Library (NILL) of the Native American Rights Fund, the only law library devoted to federal Indian and tribal law, was founded in Boulder, Colorado. NILL maintains a valuable collection of Indian law resources and assists people with Indian law-related research.

1973: Lotsee Patterson (1931–), Comanche librarian, educator, and cofounder of the American Indian Library Association, developed the first training program specifically for American Indian librarians. In 2005 the American Library Association (ALA) announced that it was naming Patterson as one of its honorary members, ALA's highest honor. She also received the Oklahoma Library Legend Award in 2007.

1975: Mary Nieball (1929–2008), Apache, earned a Ph.D. in library information services (LIS) from Texas Woman's University in Denton. She was the first Native American to earn a Ph.D. in LIS and one of the first to receive an advanced degree from Texas Woman's University.

1977: New York State passed the Indian Library Bill and became the first state to allocate permanent financial support for tribal libraries.

1977: The Bureau of Indian Affairs officially announced the first plan to improve library/media/information programs for American Indian people on or near reservations. The efforts led to the passing of the National Indian Omnibus Library Bill in 1979, which became the basis for federal funding for library services on reservations.

1978: Cheryl Metoyer (1947–), Cherokee, became the first editor of the new publication *American Indian Libraries Newsletter*

(AILN). Metoyer, who received her Ph.D. in library and information services from Indiana University in 1976, has assisted the Mashantucket Pequot, Cahuilla, and other tribal nations in the development of their libraries, archives, and museums.

1984: Library Services and Construction Act (LSCA) Title IV was the first federal legislation that earmarked money for library services for Indian tribes and Hawaiian Natives. Native Nations could finally access federal grants to use for the training and salaries of library employees and to buy library materials; operate special programs; build, purchase, or renovate library buildings; provide transportation to and from the library for patrons; disseminate information about the library; and assess tribal library needs.

1985: The Training and Assistance for Indian Library Services (TRAILS) was designed to assist American Indian tribes with library development and operations. The first of its kind, it was funded as part of Title II, Part B of the Higher Education Act.

1989: The Tribal College Librarians Institute (TCLI) held its first annual week-long program hosted by the Montana State University Library in Bozeman. TCLI is designed to provide continuing education, professional development, and networking opportunities for tribal college librarians. Today, around 35–60 participants from across the United States and Canada attend. Maori librarians from Australia and New Zealand have also participated.

1990: Robin Kickingbird (1956–), Kiowa, was named the first American Library Association Minority Fellow.

1994: Diné citizen Barbara Billey (1952–),who worked at San Juan College Library in Farmington, New Mexico, was the first Native

American librarian elected president of the New Mexico Library Association.

1995: X̱wi7x̱wa Library (Squamish word for echo) was founded by Gene Anne Joseph, a Wet'suwet'en Nadleh'dena First Nations librarian, on the Vancouver campus of the University of British Columbia. To date, it is the only Aboriginal branch of an academic library in Canada. In 2008, the library began digitizing materials so resources could be shared with Indigenous peoples worldwide. Joseph is the first librarian of First Nations descent in BC.

1999: The first International Indigenous Librarians Forum (IILF) convened in Auckland, Aotearoa/New Zealand. The biannual meeting provides networking, debate, discussion, and sharing for Indigenous librarians representing Indigenous communities around the world.

2001: The First Archivist Circle (FAC) was founded to support Native American archival materials and archivists. The office is in Salamanca, New York, on the Seneca Allegany Reservation.

2003: California hosted the first Western Archives Institute dedicated to training Native American and tribal archivists.

2004: The Huntington Free Library Native American Collection, based in the Bronx, New York, for many years, was transferred to Cornell University in Ithaca, New York. Components include exceptional materials documenting the history, culture, languages, and arts of First Peoples of the Americas as well as contemporary politics, education, and human rights issues. The collection features more than 40,000 volumes, including 4,000 rare books, significant manuscripts, photographs, artwork, and related materials.

2015: The Center for Digital Scholarship and Curation at Washington State University's (WSU) Libraries opened its doors to the first Tribal Stewardship Cohort participants for a year-long program covering the life cycle of digital stewardship. The training includes

Activism at the Library

Loriene Roy (1954–), Anishinaabe, White Earth Nation, professor at the University of Texas at Austin's School of Information, was elected president of the American Library Association (ALA) for the 2007–2008 term, becoming the first Native American elected to the position in the organization's 131-year history. As president, Roy created working circles in place of traditional task forces to ensure a climate of inclusivity and collaboration within ALA. She founded and directs the If I Can Read, I Can Do Anything national reading club for Native children and the Honoring Generations scholarship program for Indigenous students, which was funded by the Institute of Museum and Library Services. Roy has been active in the American Indian Library Association (AILA) and served as president from 1997 to 1998 and is a member of the Corazon de Tejas chapter of REFORMA and associate member of Te Ropu Whakahau/Maori in Libraries and Information Management. Roy received her doctorate from the University of Illinois at Urbana-Champaign and is the recipient of many awards, including the 2007 *Library Journal* "Mover & Shaker."

hands-on learning emphasizing the specific needs of tribal archives, libraries, and museums (TALMs). The first 12 cohorts were from tribal archives, libraries, museums, and cultural centers across the United States.

2018: Sandra D. Littletree, Diné/Eastern Shoshone, completed her thesis: *"Let Me Tell You About Indian Libraries": Self-Determination, Leadership, and Vision—The Basis of Tribal Library Development in the United States,* at the Information School at the University of Washington. It was the first time a doctoral student had done comprehensive research on American Indian libraries.

2019: The Institute of Museum and Libraries Services (IMLS) awarded the National Medal for Museum and Library Service to the Barona Band Mission Indians Cultural Center and Museum in Lakeside, California, and Jamestown S'Klallam Tribal Library in Sequim, Washington, a premier honor. The Jamestown S'Klallam Tribe was also the first in Indian Country to earn a designation as a "Bicycle Friendly Community" by the League of American Bicyclists.

GARDENS AND PARKS

"But it's more just to, you know, have a space where we can come [together] because we're never alone. ... To have this space—an open space to come and be ourselves with each other—is something that a lot of Native kids, a lot of Native youth, a lot of Native elders, and a lot of Native people in general in the city of Chicago are happy about."

—Anthony Tamez (Cree/Lakota/Black), copresident of Chi-Nations Youth Council, which facilitated the First Nations Garden (Chicago)

2001: The First Nations Garden was dedicated as part of the Jardins Botanique de Montréal. It is a contemporary garden with interpretation panels, interactive terminals, visitor activities, shows, special events, and the like. It boasts more than 300 different plant species—some 5,000 trees, shrubs, and grasses. Eleven First Nations peoples of Québec cooperated and are represented: Abenaki, Algonquin, Attikamek, Cree, Huron-Wendat, Innu, Malecite, Micmac, Mohawk, Naskapi, and Inuit. Spokesperson Florent Vollant, an Innu singer-songwriter, said that the First Nations Garden avoids stereotypes.

2001: Steele Indian School Park opened in Phoenix, Arizona, on the site of a former U.S. government boarding school for American Indian children. The Phoenix Indian School, like most others of the late nineteenth and twentieth centuries, was designed to force Indigenous children to assimilate Euro-American culture and values, creating decades of trauma, despair, and sorrow for Native communities. A sunken spiral garden—made of recycled concrete slabs from the paths on which Native American schoolchildren once walked—serves as an entry monument and modern-day labyrinth where many urban dwellers go each day to exercise. The Circle of Life promenade links three historic buildings with 28 custom-designed interpretive columns that tell the history of the school. The Phoenix Indian School Preservation Coalition, Inter Tribal Council of Arizona president John Lewis, Native American Heritage Society president Arlo Nau, and Native American Viet Nam Veterans president Tom Amiotte were key in making sure that the history and truth of the site is honored.

2010: Work began on the Native Gathering Garden in Thomas Cully Park in Portland, Oregon. The 36,000-square-foot garden provides a place for the community to gather, host cultural celebrations, and engage in Indigenous land practices, while reclaiming the urban forest. A novel idea for a city park, the project is rooted in respecting and educating through Indigenous cultural values.

2018: In a first-ever collaboration, the Chicago American Indian Center (AIC) and the City of Chicago partnered to create the First Nations Garden, located on Pulaski Road and Wilson Avenue in the Albany Park neighborhood. The garden's purpose is twofold: to serve as a healing space for Chicago's Indigenous community and as a teaching and learning hub for non-Native people to learn about Indigenous cultures. Chicago has over 75,000 Native citizens, the largest population in a Midwestern city and one of the largest urban Indian populations in the country.

2019: The two-acre Homestream Park opened in Winthrop, Washington, honoring both the original inhabitants, Interior Salish people called the Methow (also located in the Methow Valley), and the traditional cycle of the salmon. A meandering trail, lined by interpretive signs about fish and rivers, begins at the *Water Is Life* salmon-spawning sculpture by celebrated artist Virgil "Smoker" Marchand, a member of the Colville Confederated Tribes, and ends with his *Coming Home* salmon-encampment sculptures. Marchand designed a dozen sculptures for the park, shaping steel into striking images of First Peoples and animal life. His dazzling monuments are also on display along highways, parks, and buildings across the Pacific Northwest, Arizona, and Canada. The project initiated the novel idea of "spirit easement," a way for "any current landowners in the Methow Valley to acknowledge that their property is open and welcoming to all spirits of deceased Methow People and that as current landowners, with a good heart, you welcome those spirits to access, inhabit, or use in any other way this property as part of their Spirit Homeland." Like any legal easement, it is permanent and entitled "The People of the Methow Who Have Lost Their Spirit Homeland."

GOVERNMENT-SPONSORED MURALS, STREET ART, AND MOSAICS

"I create art that evokes the collective, drawing upon ancestral oral tradition as well as threads of modern mythology. My murals, multimedia projects, sculptures and canvas works establish a space for communal dialogue about history and imagination, magic and self-expression. I tell stories that seek to engage and inspire as many communities and individuals as possible."

—Paul Deo (Choctaw/Powhatan/Lenape)

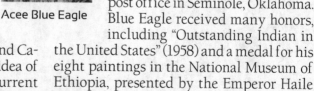

Acee Blue Eagle

1939: Acee Blue Eagle (1907–1959), Muscogee (Creek) Nation, was the first Native artist to have a mural commissioned by the Federal Arts Project during the Great Depression (1929–1939). The oil-on-canvas interior mural, *Seminole Indian Scene*, is still on display at the U.S. post office in Seminole, Oklahoma. Blue Eagle received many honors, including "Outstanding Indian in the United States" (1958) and a medal for his eight paintings in the National Museum of Ethiopia, presented by the Emperor Haile Selassie, another first.

1992: *Tableau,* a rare outdoor granite mosaic by Anishinaabe artist George Morrison (1919–2000), was installed at the Nicollet Mall in Minneapolis, Minnesota. Consisting of nearly 200 individual pieces cut from 14 colors of granite, the piece includes animal, bird, weather, and plant imagery—a beaver, bear, horse, leaves, lightning bolt, and suggestions of water and clouds. The mosaic can be read from all four directions; it has no top or bottom, left or right. Morrison is considered one of Minnesota's most important twentieth-century artists, with works in museum collections worldwide.

2009: Todd "Estria" Johnson made news when he became the first Native Hawaiian to be named Best Graffiti Artist by the *East Bay Express* in Oakland, California. In 2010, he gave a TEDx talk on the power of public art. Estria was honored for his art and community work by U.S. House minority leader Nancy Pelosi (2012). In 2013, he and two coartists jointly won *Miami New Times's* Best Mural award for their mural *Universal Aloha Wall*, at Wynwood Walls in Miami, Florida, an outside gallery composed of murals transforming ugly warehouse buildings. Estria has engaged youth and community members in his projects and founded the Estria Foundation in 2010.

2010: The first mural was revealed on the newly designated American Indian Cultural Corridor in Minneapolis, Minnesota. Local artist Bobby Wilson (1984–), Sisseton-Wahpeton Dakota, recruited American Indian youth to help create the massive project, which is considered one of the biggest murals in Minneapolis. Pictured on the side of the Minnesota Chippewa Tribe building are young people with three community elders

Art adorns the walls of Indian Alley in Los Angeles.

who are local heroes. The mural is part of "Paint the Ave," sponsored by the Native American Community Development Institute, and eventually the East Franklin Native community was decorated with more murals that can be seen from city trains.

2011: Indian Alley was named with an unofficial street sign in Los Angeles. The tiny lane is referred to as "one of the most famous public spaces in the country" among Native Americans. Before it moved, United American Indian Involvement, Inc. (UAII), an outreach center for American Indians that became an important center for social, spiritual, political, and rehabilitative activities for the Native community, was adjacent. Paintings and sculptures by renowned Los Angeles street artists depicting Native American leaders and social activists have made Indian Alley a significant site for Los Angeles street art. Contributors to the ongoing art project include muralists Votan, Maya/Nahuatl, and Jaque Fragua, Jemez Pueblo.

2013: Artist Andrew Morrison (1981–), Apache/Haida, achieved a milestone agreement with the Seattle Public Schools in Washington about the murals he painted at the Wilson Pacific school, formerly Indian Heritage High School, from 2001 to 2013. In 2013, the school was slated for demolition, and the colossal murals depicting several Indigenous luminaries were to be destroyed. But Morrison and the school district created a memorandum of understanding (MOU) and the murals were preserved, protected, and relocated to the new Robert Eagle Staff Middle and Cascadia Elementary school buildings. Morrison's stellar works grace many buildings in the state of Washington. The award-winning artist has also created permanent public masterpieces in Boston; Chicago; Anchorage, Alaska; Scottsdale, Arizona; and Ft. Belknap, Montana, as well as other sites.

2014: The mural *Honoring Our Origins* went up on Van Nuys Boulevard's "Mural Mile" in Los Angeles, California. The painting celebrates Toypurina, a Tongva medicine woman who helped lead a revolt against the San Gabriel Mission in 1785. The HOOD-sisters, a team of Native and Latina artists, created it and were the first women to have artwork on the busy strip of the major LA thoroughfare.

2017: *Ganawenjige Onigam*, loosely translated to "S/he takes care of Duluth" in Ojibwe, was unveiled in Duluth, Minnesota. It was painted by artists Votan Ikwas, Mayan; Derek Brown, Diné; and Leah Lewis, Pueblo. The vibrant mural of an Ojibwe jingle dress dancer combines different subjects: a water protector; Native American women in general; missing and murdered Indigenous women; and the Zapatista movement. Although the city has a large Indigenous population, there had been no representation of Indigenous residents in public art. The gargantuan painting graces an entire wall of the Dr. Robert Powless Cultural Center at the American Indian Community Housing Organization (AICHO).

2018: For the first time, a contemporary mural at Harvard University in Cambridge, Massachusetts, featured Wampanoag culture. Muralist Paul Deo (1961–), Choctaw/Powhatan/Lenape, painted the vibrant interactive depiction of the First Peoples of the area on the exterior wall of the Harvard Ed Portal building in the Allston neighborhood of Boston, Massachusetts. Deo is also the first muralist to honor May Edward Chinn, the first Native (Chickahominy) and African American doctor to practice at Harlem Hospital, with a mural in the hospital lobby. His masterpiece, the *Planet Harlem* mural on the corner of Malcolm X Boulevard and 126th Street in New York City's Manhattan, celebrates African American luminaries from Adam Clayton Powell Jr. to Harriet Tubman. Also a teaching artist, Deo has instructed dozens of young people to create the massive paintings that dot the city landscape. Deo, who also designs film and theater sets, was the first Native to be a member of International Alliance of Theatrical Stage Employees, Moving Picture Technicians, Artists and Allied Crafts of the United States Local 478 of New Orleans, Louisiana. Inspired by his work with refugee orphans from Guatemala and Honduras, Deo drew on his background in information technology to design MyndTeam, an intelligent personal assistant that allows users to create personalized teams of advisors in cyberspace.

2020: In an extraordinary venture, blight got turned into beauty at an abandoned motel north of Flagstaff, Arizona. Five Native muralists "artified" the eyesore building by changing its facade into the *american rent is due* installation. Dr. Chip Thomas, muralist and longtime physician serving the Navajo Nation, assembled Indigenous artists for the project. Thomas "Breeze" Marcus, Tohono O'odham/Adimel O'odham/Ponca/Otoe; Vyalone, Zuni/Raramuri/Chicano; Douglas Miles, Apache; Jerrel Singer, Diné; and Liv-A'ndrea Knoki, Diné, transformed the ugly exterior into a dazzling desert scene. Native heroes, calligraffitied writings, and colorful geometrics reclaim the landscape. Thomas has initiated other projects, including *Painted Desert* (2012), in an ongoing endeavor to beautify the Navajo Reservation by converting public eyesores into eye candy. Native street artists, muralists, and their allies have collaborated on masterpieces popping up on water towers, billboards, empty buildings, and markets, creating a vast outdoor art gallery.

2020: *Take Back the Power*, a massive 77-foot mural, looms over North Tejon Street in Colorado Springs, Colorado. Pyramid Lake Paiute artist and activist Gregg Deal (1975–) created the giant portrait of his daughter dressed in contemporary and traditional clothing with a red handprint across her face, a symbol referencing the Missing and Murdered Indigenous Women, Girls and Two-Spirit People (MMIWG2S) movement.

2021: La Barca Cantina set sail around Manahatta (Manhattan, NY) as New York City's first and only floating Mexican restaurant. Onboard are the murals of Tlisza Jaurique, Mexica/Yaqui, an award-winning multidisciplinary artist, scholar, and educator. She created an Indigenous feminine/ist aesthetic visual space on the water with quintuple murals featuring Mayahuel, goddess of the maguey (personification of agave, goddess of alcohol and fertility); Camazotz (bat essential to the pollination of the maguey); Aztectopus (eight arms, eight hidden talents); and other images related to the theme. Jaurique was the first Native artist to be commissioned by New York Cruise Lines and is best known for her intricate paintings and installations that address change, hermeneutics, power, and decoloniality. In 2008, Jaurique was the first Indigenous Mexican American woman to exhibit at the Metropolitan Museum of Art (NYC) and has had many exhibitions at the National Museum of the American Indian and other venues around the country. Among her many honors are an Artists' Fellowship Grant, NYC (2016), a National Museum of Natural History Native American Scholar Award, the NDN Collective Artist Grant, and the United States Artist Grant (2020).

MUSEUMS

"The work that I do at the museum is mostly education: educating the public around Native history, culture, the arts, spirituality, environment, and our life ways. At the museum we share a first-person perspective; we share our stories. The stories are a form of activism that share our history, the historical trauma that took place here, how it affects us today, and what we do to overcome these barriers that have been put in our way.... We have a very vast collection of our cultural belongings, which is a word we use to decolonize the word artifact, and our archival collections of pictures and maps and writings and things of that nature."

—*Lorén Spears, Narragansett, executive director of the Tomaquag Museum, Exeter, Rhode Island*

NATIVE MUSEUMS

1931: The Tantaquidgeon Museum opened in Uncasville, Connecticut, and is thought to be the first tribally specific museum. John Tantaquidgeon (1865–1949), Mohegan, and his family founded it at the height of the Great Depression as a way for visitors to experience the spirit of the Mohegan and the beauty of Native America from an Indigenous perspective. Today, it is a popular tourist stop for visitors from around the world.

1938: Osage Nation Museum in Pawhuska, Oklahoma, identifies itself as the "oldest tribally owned museum in the United States."

1972: The Institute of American Indian Arts (IAIA) Museum of Contemporary Native Arts (MoCNA) opened. It is the only museum in the country dedicated to exhibiting, collecting, and interpreting progressive works of art by contemporary Native American artists. Located in downtown Santa Fe, New Mexico, MoCNA stewards over 9,000 contemporary Indigenous artworks created from 1962 to the present.

1973: The American Indian Movement (AIM) Interpretive Center Inc. grew out of the Heart of the Earth Survival School. Located

in what is now the American Indian Corridor in Minneapolis, Minnesota, it was the first of its kind to chronicle the history of AIM, which started in Minneapolis. AIM holds thousands of historical records, media archives, photographs, and the testimony of those sharing the story of AIM. AIM Patrol jackets, minutes of the earliest AIM organizing meetings, photographs of victims of police beatings, and audio interviews with historic figures are all part of the collection.

1986: The Simon Paneak Memorial Museum, featuring both the local history of the Nunamiut (Inland Inupiat) and the ethnography of the central Brooks Range, opened in

The Tantaquidgeon Museum, owned by the Mohegan tribe, is the oldest Native-owned museum in America. It was founded in Uncasville, Connecticut, by the Tantaquidgeon family in 1931.

the village of Anaktuvuk Pass, Alaska. Not only is it the northernmost museum in the United States, but it is also only accessible by air. As the last remaining group of inland-dwelling Nunamiut, the people of Anaktuvuk Pass consider the museum an important resource for the elders and educators of the community. They can pass traditional knowledge, skills, and values on to their youth by working in close cooperation with the North Slope Borough's Inupiat History, Language, and Culture Commission and the North Slope Borough School District to develop historical and cultural information for classroom use.

1992: Located in Inukjuak, Quebec, Canada, on the eastern shore of Hudson Bay, the Dan-

The Tunica Treasure

In a landmark decision (1985), the Tunica Treasure was repatriated to its rightful owners, the Tunica-Biloxi of Louisiana, which helped put in motion the repatriation movement and the subsequent passing of the Native American Graves Protection and Repatriation Act of 1990 (NAGPRA). Before NAGPRA, Native people were not able to protect their cultural belongings; treasure hunters and grave looters stole Indian property and sold it to the highest bidders. Heirlooms were ripped away from communities, destroying history and traditions.

The Tunica Treasure, an extensive collection of Native American European trade items and tribal valuables, was buried in more than 100 graves by the Tunica from 1731 to 1764 on lands near present-day Angola Prison. At the time, the Tunica operated a vast trading network that stretched from Oklahoma to Florida and controlled salt production and supply until well after European and American encroachment. It was not a surprise that their holdings would be extensive and tempting to fortune seekers. Tunica colonial-era prosperity was evident in the fine European ceramics, guns, kettles, bells, beads, and other property buried with their owners. A local thief raided the graves and tried to sell the items to the Peabody Museum at Harvard University, but the tribe found out and waged a long and arduous legal battle to regain and conserve their historic belongings. The stolen property was not returned until 1989, and it was in terrible condition. The Tunica-Biloxi Tribe had raised enough funds to purchase two refrigerator truck trailers to serve as a conservation laboratory. Experts were brought in to evaluate the items and train tribal members how to properly restore their cultural belongings, saving the tribe thousands of dollars and turning the Tunica-Biloxi people into conservators for the collection. Archaeologists called the Tunica Treasure the greatest find in the lower Mississippi valley and one of the greatest archaeological finds of the twentieth century.

In 2011, the brand-new Tunica-Biloxi Cultural and Educational Resources Center (CERC) in Marksville, Louisiana, was dedicated. The Tunica Treasure was installed in its own exhibit in the 40,000-square-foot building that also includes a conservation and restoration laboratory, museum, gift shop, library, auditorium, classrooms, distance learning center, meeting rooms, and tribal government offices.

iel Weetaluktuk Museum opened. It is named for the first Inuit archaeologist and features contemporary Inuit artwork and archaeological and cultural belongings testifying to the origin of the Inuits in Nunavik. The domed ceiling of the mezzanine recalls the inside of a traditional igloo, a structure made of blocks of snow piled in a spiral that Inukjuak people used to build. Weetaluktuk (1951–1982) investigated several Inuit sites and advocated for stronger Inuit influence in cultural affairs.

2007: Nk'Mip Desert Cultural Centre, owned by the Osoyoos Indian Band of the Okanagan First Nations, was completed in Osoyoos, British Columbia, Canada. It is the only museum in the world whose main purpose is to steward the largest remnant of the Great American Desert, one of Canada's most endangered places. The visitors are treated to flora and fauna of the desert ecosystem. The facade of the eco-friendly building blends with the unique landscape and has received top awards for its environmentally innovative architectural design. Exhibits reflect the Okanagan culture as well as the surrounding environment.

2009: Ah-Tah-Thi-Ki Museum, opened and operated by the Seminole Tribe of Florida, became the first tribally governed museum to be accredited by the American Association of Museums.

2016: The Tomaquag Indian Memorial Museum in Exeter, Rhode Island, scored a National Medal from the Institute of Museum

The Tomaquag Indian Memorial Museum in Rhode Island is that state's first and only museum of Native history and culture.

Indigenous Firsts: A History of Native American Achievements and Events

and Library Services (IMLS). The award was presented by First Lady Michelle Obama. It was the first time a Native-operated museum took the top honor. Tomaquag was founded in 1958 by Mary E. Glasko Congdon (Princess Red Wing; 1896–1987), Narragansett/Pokanoket-Wampanoag, and was Rhode Island's first and only Native museum. Congdon was a culture keeper and conducted museum tours from an Indigenous perspective. She became the first Native woman to receive an honorary Doctor of Human Affairs from the University of Rhode Island (1975) and the first to serve as a member of the Speaker's Research Committee of the under secretariat of the United Nations (1947–1970). Today the Tomaquag Indian Memorial Museum is led by Lorén Spears, Narragansett, and offers a variety of experiences, exhibits, and an annual honoring that celebrates individuals for their contributions to Native cultures and communities.

2019: For the first time, the Institute of Museum and Library Services (IMLS) awarded a national medal to a tribally owned museum located on an Indian reservation. The Barona Band of Mission Indians was given top honors for its Barona Cultural Center and Museum in Lakeside, California.

2021: *USA Today* rated the Museum of Native American History (MONAH) in the top ten history museums—the only Native museum in the top list. David Bogle, a registered member of the Cherokee Nation, created the museum in his hometown of Bentonville, Arkansas. Bogle's private holdings are on display, along with a number of collections donated or on loan to the museum. Programming offers special events for both children and adults. An annual Native American "virtual" cultural celebration has presented a variety of topics about Indigenous America including "Four Directions. One Earth. Mission United," featuring Commander John Herrington (Chickasaw), the first Native Amer-

ican astronaut. The Indigenous Medicine Garden cultivates plants native to North America and is a joint project of MONAH, the Thaden School, Runway Group, Garden City Nursery, the Fay Jones School of Architecture at the University of Arkansas, and Dr. Daniel Wildcat, a Yuchi member of the Muscogee Nation of Oklahoma, from Haskell Indian Nations University.

2021: The First Americans Museum (FAM) opened in Oklahoma City, Oklahoma, to chronicle the peoples indigenous to the area as well as those removed from their homelands to Indian Territory, present-day Oklahoma. FAM programs and exhibits promote awareness about the 39 unique cultures, diversity, history, contributions, and resilience of the tribal nations in Oklahoma today. Funding for the $175 million, 175,000-square-foot museum is from a partnership between the Oklahoma City government and the Chickasaw Nation with financial support from the state as well. Designed to Smithsonian Institution standards, the museum features Smithsonian and Tribal Nations galleries.

NON-NATIVE MUSEUMS

1925: The Denver Art Museum began acquiring Native art; today, it has one of the largest collections in the country. Over 18,000 objects by artists from over 250 Indigenous nations represent both historical and contemporary artists.

1955: The seven-acre Caguana Ceremonial Park, the largest and most complex Taino ceremonial site in the West Indies, became a protected area under the administration of the Instituto de Cultura Puertorriqueña (ICP) and became a National Historic Landmark in 1993. The center consists of a large central plaza, a ceremonial dance area, 10 rectangular earth-and-stone–lined ball courts and plazas, petroglyphs carved on perimeter

The National Museum of the American Indian

In 1989, Senator Daniel Inouye, Native Hawaiian, introduced the National Museum of the American Indian Act, which passed as Public Law 101-185. It established the National Museum of the American Indian (NMAI) as "a living memorial to Native Americans and their traditions." The act also states that human remains, funerary objects, sacred objects, and objects of cultural patrimony be considered for repatriation to tribal communities, as well as items acquired illegally. The museum includes three locations: National Museum of the American Indian on the National Mall, Washington, D.C.; the George Gustav Heye Center, a permanent exhibition and education facility in New York City; and the Cultural Resources Center (CRC), a research and collections facility in Suitland, Maryland. On September 21, 2004, for the inauguration of the NMAI, Senator Inouye addressed an audience of around 20,000 American Indians, Alaska Natives, and Native Hawaiians, the largest gathering of Indigenous people in Washington, D.C.

Senator Inouye was prompted to take action on behalf of Indian leaders, who had discovered that the Smithsonian Institution had some 12,000 to 18,000 Indian remains in its collection. They protested that Native bodies had been objectified and human remains should not be part of any museum collection. After the National Museum of the American Indian Act was enacted, the Smithsonian repatriated about 5,000 individual remains. Additionally, thousands of sacred and cultural belongings have been repatriated, often with ceremony and celebration by the rightful owners.

The NMAI Act was a first and created many other firsts. For the first time, Native people were recruited as department heads and in many other positions.

- W. Richard West Jr. (1943–), Cheyenne/Arapaho/Southern Cheyenne, was the founding director of the National Museum of the American Indian (1990–2007) and the first Native to direct any Smithsonian museum.

- Martha de Montaño (1944–), Prairie Band Potawatomi, was first hired in 1984 to manage the Indian Information Center at the George Gustav Heye Museum of the American Indian in the Harlem neighborhood of New York City. After the NMAI, Act passed, the George Gustav Heye Center was merged with the Smithsonian NMAI and the Indian Information Center became the Cultural Resource Center (CRS) and given a new home in the U.S. Custom House in the Financial District at Manhattan's southern tip. Montaño was challenged to transform a cold area of caged windows and marble walls into a comfortable place of learning despite the rules restricting structural changes to a historic landmark. In 1994 visitors were welcomed into a warm quiet space that offered countless ways to study the past, present, and future of American Indians. Montaño then designed the resource center for the new NMAI facility on the Mall in Washington, D.C., and became its first director until retiring in 2007.

The National Museum of the American Indian (contd.)

- Jose Montaño was the first-ever Aymara cultural interpreter at NMAI. An educator and musician from Bolivia, Montaño is trilingual (Spanish/Aymara/English) and gave workshops, lectures, and museum tours during his tenure with the museum. He was a member of the internationally acclaimed Grupo Aymara, a Bolivian folk troupe that performs pre-Hispanic and contemporary music of the Indigenous peoples of the Andes using traditional flutes, panpipes, and drums as well as stringed instruments that originated in Spain.

- Annie Teamer, Cherokee, became the first-ever director of volunteers and was based at the George Gustav Heye Center in New York City (1994). She had been an educator with the Native American Education Program before going to the museum and built a strong volunteer department based on Indigenous values of reciprocity and sharing.

- Chef Freddie Bitsoie (1975), Navajo, was hired in 2016 as the first Native American chef of Mitsitam Native Foods Café, NMAI's eatery in the D.C. location. He trained at Le Cordon Bleu College of Culinary Arts (formerly the Scottsdale Culinary Institute) in Arizona. In 2011, he was named "a rising star in the constellation of young chefs" by *Native Peoples* magazine. Bitsoie was also the winner of NMAI's Living Earth Festival Native Chef Cooking Competition in 2013. Other work includes hosting his *Rezervations Not Required* TV show and attending to his consulting firm FJBits Concepts.

stones, and one circular plaza, as well as the remains of an oval-shaped structure and a sacred *cemi* mound. Located near Utuado, Puerto Rico, it is also operated by the National Park Service (NPS). In 2007, the United Confederation of Taíno People appealed to the NPS and ICP to better protect the site as thousands of visitors have destroyed some of the area. There are laws in the United States designed to protect Native American cultural properties, such as the Native American Graves Protection and Repatriation Act and sections of the National Historic Preservation Act, but these safeguards do not include the Taíno of Puerto Rico as they are not a federally recognized tribe.

1991: The Akta Lakota ("to honor the people") Museum & Cultural Center opened on the campus of St. Joseph's Indian School in Chamberlain, South Dakota. Housed in a former school, the octagon-shaped building has 14,000 square feet of display space featuring Lakota art, cultural belongings, and educational exhibits. The Collector's Gallery is a space for local artists to sell their work, and the outdoor Medicine Wheel Garden is filled with Indigenous plants and symbols significant to Lakota traditions.

1992: The Marion Steinbach Indian Basket Museum was established in Tahoe City, California, as the only museum devoted entirely to the art of Native basketry and their many uses. The world-class collection includes almost 900 baskets from 85 nations throughout California and western North America. In addition to baskets, the collection also features Native clothing, jewelry, tools, and pottery. Art created by several notable Washoe weavers like Dat-so-la-lee and Maggie Mayo James is on display.

2020: The Museum of Indian Culture in Allentown, Pennsylvania, partnered with the Delaware Nation, Oklahoma, to extend the Delaware Historic Preservation Office. It was the first official collaboration between the Delaware (Lenape) and an existing museum in their original territory. The goal is to raise public awareness of local Lenape history as well as contemporary Lenape life and culture.

COINS, STAMPS, FLAGS, AND LICENSE PLATES

"I hope that as a designer I can represent on a national scale the modernity of Native people—that we're engaged in modern culture while still carrying forward our traditional heritage."

—Rico Lanáat' Worl, Tlingit/Athabascan, the first Alaskan Native to design a U.S. postage stamp

1816: The first flag of the Kingdom of Hawaii was approved by King Kamehameha (c. 1736–1819). The Hawaii state flag has most of the original elements, making it the only U.S. state flag to have flown over a kingdom, a territory, a republic, and a state.

c. 1861: The Confederated States of America rallied for support from the tribal nations located within their states. The Confederacy promised equal and fair representation and inclusion in the government. They even created separate flags for their Indian allies:

Creek, Cherokee, Catawba, Choctaw, and Seminole. Tribal nations were reeling from the effects of forced removal and distrusted the United States; some tribal members were tempted to join the Confederacy while others considered the Civil War a white man's battle. Most of the Creek supported the Union army. The flags fell into obscurity and were not seen as the great gift that the Confederacy intended.

1927: When Alaska became a state in 1959, the flag of the territory of Alaska was adopted as the state flag. John Ben "Benny" Benson Jr. (1913–1972), Alutiiq, designed the flag for the territory when he was only 13 years old. A territory-wide contest was held for students in grades 7–12, and of more than 700 submissions, Benson's won first place. He was awarded $1,000, an engraved watch, and a trip to Washington, D.C. Benson looked to the sky for the symbols he included in his design. He submitted his art

Hawaii has been a kingdom, protectorate, territory, and then a state in the United States. The state flag is very similar to the older versions that were used over the history of the islands.

The Alaskan flag was designed by young "Benny" Benson Jr., who designed the flag at the age of 13 for a contest held in 1927, when Alaska was still a territory.

along with this description: "The blue field is for the Alaska sky and the forget-me-not, an Alaskan flower. The North Star is for the future state of Alaska, the most northerly in the union. The Dipper is for the Great Bear—symbolizing strength."

c. 1940: The Arapaho were one of the first nations to adopt a flag that honored their soldiers fighting in World War II. Flag symbols represented happiness, ceremonies, and long life.

1970: Kenojuak Ashevak (1927–2013) was the first female Inuit artist to have her work displayed on a Canadian stamp. Released by Canada Post in 1970, *The Enchanted Owl* was reproduced on a six-cent stamp to commem-

orate the 100th anniversary of the Northwest Territories.

1974: The Red Lake Band of Chippewa Indians issued the first tribal license plate. Upheld by the Minnesota Supreme Court, the practice opened a new dimension of tribal sovereignty among Native nations, and today dozens of nations issue their own plates.

1995: The Navajo Nation's flag was the first Native American flag taken to space when astronaut Bernard Harris carried it aboard the space shuttle *Discovery*.

1996: Keith Birdsong (1959–2019), Muscogee Creek/Cherokee, was the first American Indian to create stamps for the U.S. Postal Service (USPS) and the first artist to honor Native American dance forms on postage. The five-stamp series depicted the Fancy Dance, the Butterfly Dance, the Traditional Dance, the Raven Dance, and the Hoop Dance. Birdsong also designed the cachet that accompanied a 1994 U.S. Postal Service space-flown stamp portfolio. In addition, he was the first Native to illustrate the covers of *Star Trek* novels.

2004: The milestone "Art of the American Indian" postage stamp series was released. Graphics were chosen from various museum collections: Navajo jewelry, Mimbres bowl, Kutenai parfleche, Tlingit sculptures, Ho-Chunk bag, Seminole doll, Mississippian effigy, Acoma pot, Navajo weaving, Seneca carving, and Luiseño basket.

2006: The first stamp designed by a Chickasaw artist went on sale. Mike Larsen (1945–) created the stamp to commemorate the 2007 Oklahoma centennial, and it featured a sunrise over the Cimarron River.

2007: Pocahontas (c. 1596–1617), Powhatan, was the first Native American honored on a U.S. postage stamp.

The flag of the Navajo Nation was designed by Jay R. Degroat, a student from Mariano Lake, New Mexico, for a contest. It was adopted by the Navajo Nation in 1968.

2008: A picture of *Sacred Rain Arrow*, a sculpture on display at Tulsa's Gilcrease Museum, by Chiricahua Apache Allan Houser (1914–1994), became the first design by a Native artist on an Oklahoma license plate.

2009: Herb Kawainui Kāne (1928–2011) was the first Native Hawaiian to have his art featured on a postal stamp. The painting depicts a surfer riding a wave on a longboard, a popular choice among Native Hawaiian surfers for centuries. Next to him, two people paddle an outrigger canoe to shore. Kāne had extensive knowledge and experience in surfing and canoe construction, a skill he developed from building a traditional sailing canoe himself. Kāne, one of Hawaii's beloved Living Treasures and recipient of numerous cultural awards, also designed the 25th-anniversary

Herb Kawainui Kāne

Hawaii statehood stamp, featuring a voyaging canoe and the migratory bird, the golden plover.

2009: Nine of Oregon's federally recognized tribal nations added their flags to the Walk of Flags on the state's Capitol grounds in Eugene as a separate display. The tribes were: Burns Paiute Tribe; Confederated Tribes of Coos, Lower Umpqua, and Siuslaw; Coquille Indian Tribe; Cow Creek Band of Umpqua Tribe of Indians; Confederated Tribes of Grand Ronde; Klamath Tribes; Confederated Tribes of Siletz Indians; Confederated Tribes of the Umatilla Indian Reservation; and Confederated Tribes of the Warm Springs Reservation.

2019: Governor Doug Burgum announced that the flags of North Dakota's five tribal nations would be displayed at the state Capitol in Bismarck, a decision that Turtle Mountain Band of Chippewa chairman Jamie Azure called "monumental." The five flags now stand near the public entrance to Burgum's office in the Capitol. The tribal nations in North Dakota are the Mandan, Hidatsa, and Arikara Nation; Spirit Lake Nation; Standing Rock Sioux; Turtle Mountain Band of Chippewa Indians; and the Sisseton Wahpeton Oyate Nation.

2019: Nebraska's first license plate honoring Native peoples was designed by award-winning artist Donel Keeler (1952–2020), Dakota/Northern Ponca. The blue and gold plate depicts an eagle feather in one corner, a Native on horseback in another, and a leaping buffalo in the center.

2020: Tribal Flag Plaza was unveiled in front of the state Capitol in Helena, Montana, honoring Native Americans by flying the flags of Montana's eight tribal nations. At the unveiling, tribal members joined Governor Steve Bullock and Lt. Governor Mike Cooney in raising the flags permanently at the Capitol. Montana's tribes are the Blackfeet Nation, Chippewa Cree Tribe, Crow Nation, Confederated Salish and Kootenai Tribes, Fort Belknap Nakoda and Aaniiih Nations, Fort Peck Assiniboine and Sioux Tribes, Little Shell Chippewa Tribe, and the Northern Cheyenne Tribe.

2020: A new $1 coin was released by the U.S. Mint featuring civil rights leader Elizabeth Peratrovich (Tlingit), the first Alaska Native to be depicted on U.S. currency. The theme of the coin is Peratrovich and Alaska's Anti-Discrimination Law of 1945. The year 2020 marked the 75th anniversary of Peratrovich's testimony in support of the nation's first antidiscrimination law.

2021: Rico Lanáat' Worl, Tlingit/Athabascan, was the first member of the Tlingit Nation in Alaska to design a U.S. postal stamp.

Part of the Forever Stamp series, "Raven Story" depicts the bird flying through the sky among yellow stars and a shining full moon. In Juneau, the Sealaska Heritage Institute hosted the unveiling of the stamp with a ceremony in front of its building on July 30, 2021.

2021: The flags of the Treaty One Nation, Dakota Nations, Métis Nation, and the City of Winnipeg were raised together for the first time on September 15 at Winnipeg City Hall in Manitoba. The city said the flags will be permanent symbols to residents and elected officials of its mutual respect and understanding to move forward in a journey to reconciliation.

STATUES, MONUMENTS, AND MULTIMEDIA INSTALLATIONS

"There is no record of what he (Po'pay) looked like. No drawings. I'm just capturing his image as the stone speaks to me."

—Cliff Fragua, Jemez Pueblo, about his sculpture created for the U.S. National Statuary Hall in Washington, D.C.

c. 1937: Russell Spears (1917–2009), Narragansett, revitalized Narragansett stoneworking art. He left his creative stamp on walls, fireplaces, and outdoor structures throughout Rhode Island, Connecticut, and beyond. Spears was also a tribal leader and jewelry artist and taught the arts to his 12 children. He turned the most utilitarian household stone pieces into art. His fans clamored for Spears's creations as having a fireplace built by him increased house values by thousands. He was featured in the

PBS film documentary about Narragansett stone masons, *Stories in Stone* (2008).

1948: Allan Houser (1914–1994), Chiricahua Apache, was the first Native to create a public monument in the United States. The stone piece, *Comrade in Mourning*, at the Haskell Institute in Lawrence, Kansas, is a memorial to Indian servicemen who died during World War II. When Joe Biden began his presidency in 2021, a figural group created by Houser in 1990 was moved to the Oval Office from the National Museum of the American Indian and depicts a running horse and a Native male rider. Houser was one of the most renowned Native American painters and Modernist sculptors of the twentieth century and was named the first-ever Oklahoma Cultural Ambassador

(1984). His sons and grandson became successful artists, continuing his legacy. The family maintains a commercial gallery of Houser's work in downtown Santa Fe, New Mexico, and the Allan Houser Compound, a foundry and sculpture garden located south of Santa Fe.

1974: *The Keeper of the Plains* was erected adjacent to the Mid-America All-Indian Center on the confluence of the Arkansas and Little Arkansas rivers in Wichita, Kansas. The 44-foot Cor-Ten steel sculpture by Kiowa-Comanche artist Blackbear Bosin (1921–1980) is surrounded by multiple displays describing the original peoples of the area, as well as "Rings of Fire," several fire pits that illuminate the statue at night. Bosin, also known as Tsate Kongia, is the only American Indian to have

Completed in 1974 by sculptor Blackbear Bosin in Wichita, Kansas, *The Keeper of the Plains* stands 44 feet (13.4 meters) tall.

Indigenous Firsts: A History of Native American Achievements and Events

a public work in the tallest American statues category, which only lists statues over 40 feet. The other 27 listings include the Statue of Liberty in New York City and the U.S. Marine Corps War Memorial (Iwo Jima Memorial) in Arlington, Virginia.

1979: For the first time, a sculpture by a Yupik artist was commissioned by the City of Seattle, Washington, and installed at the King County International Airport. Lawrence Beck (1938–1994), Yupik, created the large outdoor stainless-steel piece *Poktalartok Inukshuk*, meaning "floating shape" in the Inuit language. Beck's works, found in museums worldwide, are often composed of "found" objects. The Inuit word for spirit, "Inua," is used in the name of each piece of his world-renowned mask exhibit. The various masks were fashioned with old rearview mirrors, baby moon hubcaps, discarded whitewall tires, surplus airplane rivets, kitchen implements, toys, and other found objects and brought Beck international acclaim.

1988: Artist Alvin Kanak, from Nunuvut, Canada, was the first Inuit to create a sculpture given by the Canadian government to another country. The *Inukshuk* sculpture was gifted to Brisbane, Australia, and is designed in the iconic style of the ancient stone sculptures found above the Arctic Circle. Historically used for navigation, these statues were built by the Inuit, Iñupiat, Kalaallit, Yupik, and others in an area with few natural landmarks. Inukshuks have become a symbol of Canada and are given to Mexico, Norway, Guatemala, and United States.

1990: *The Young Kamehameha* bronze sculpture was unveiled in front of the Grand Wailea Resort Hotel & Spa in Wailea, Hawaii, on

This Inukshuk designed by Alvin Kanak can be seen at Vancouver's English Bay. Inukshuks are stone landmarks used by peoples of the Arctic region for navigation and to help guide travelers.

The iron sculpture *Spirit Warriors* by artist Colleen Cutschall was erected at the Little Big Horn Battlefield in 2002.

the island of Maui. Native Hawaiian artist/writer/cultural preservationist Herb Kawainui Kāne (1928–2011) created the monumental statue, the first accurate representation of the famous King Kamehameha I, founder of the Kingdom of Hawaii. Kāne designed and named the Hōkūle'a, a seafaring and full-scale replica of a wa'a kaulua, a Polynesian double-hulled voyaging canoe (1975). He considered it a moving sculpture, and it still sails around the world with a staff that teaches about Indigenous Hawaiian culture. Kāne's art included illustrations, paintings, books, and even postal stamps. Many credit him as being the father of the renaissance of Native Hawaiian culture.

2000: For the first time in Canada, a national park was designated as both a park and a national historic site (1995). Five years later, a commemorative monument, designed by Mi'kmaw cultural traditionalist Kaqtukwasisip Muin'iskw (1961–2011), was unveiled at the Kejimkujik National Park and Na-

tional Historic Site in Caledonia, Nova Scotia. The shape is based on the traditional Mi'kmaw woman's peaked hat, which also appears in many of the park's petroglyphs. The statue bears Muin'iskw's words, "This monument is for all Mi'kmaw People. Let it be a reminder of the past, healing for the present, and a promise for the future."

2002: For the first time, a monument honoring Indigenous people went on display in the Battle of Little Big Horn Battlefield National Monument in Montana. Designed by Lakota artist Colleen Cutschall (1951–), the iron statue, *Spirit Warriors*, commemorates Native American warriors in the Black Hills War (1876).

2002: *The Guardian*, a three-ton, 17.5-foot-tall bronze representation of an American Indian man, was placed atop the Capitol building in Oklahoma City, Oklahoma. It was the first time a state capitol was topped by a Native American figure. Artist Enoch

Kelly Haney (1940–2022), Seminole/Muscogee Creek, designed the image to be a composite of material and spiritual cultural characteristics of Oklahoma's thirty-nine tribes. The dignified, muscular man carries a spear, attached to his waist by a strap and staked in the earth, to symbolize his commitment to stand his ground in a fight. HIs circular shield, representing the circle of life, features a cross and four feathers dangling from the shield, which symbolize the four seasons and directions.

2003: A colored bronze statue of Saint Kateri Tekakwitha, Mohawk, the first Native to be granted sainthood by the Catholic Church, was enshrined in front of Saint Francis Basilica in Santa Fe, New Mexico, the first time an American Indian sculpted the saint for public display. Internationally celebrated artist Estella Loretto, Jemez Pueblo, is one of

The statue of Saint Kateri Tekakwitha in Santa Fe, New Mexico, honors the first Native American to be granted sainthood by the Catholic Church.

the few, if not the only, Native woman working in bronze.

2005: Sculptor Cliff Fragua (1955–), Jemez Pueblo, became the first American Indian artist to have a sculpture placed in the U.S. Capitol's Statuary Hall. The seven-foot Tennessee marble statue depicts Po'pay (Tewa for "ripe pumpkin"), the esteemed leader of the Pueblo Revolt against the Spaniards in 1680.

2005: *The Passage*, a pedestrian link between downtown Chattanooga, Tennessee, and the Tennessee River at Ross's Landing, was opened to the public. It is the nation's largest public art project celebrating Cherokee history and culture. Created by the collective Artists Gadugi (Cherokee Artists Working Together) of Oklahoma, the installation features a "weeping wall" representing the tears shed as the Cherokee were driven from their homes and removed on the Trail of Tears. Seven six-foot ceramic disks relate thousands of years of Cherokee history in their Southeastern homelands. Seven 14-foot-tall stainless-steel sculptures of stickball players, depicting the Pleiades constellation, grace the wall facing the river, educating visitors about the game and its importance to Cherokee culture. *Little Water Spider*, a 12-foot-by-8-foot stainless steel sculpture, representing the Cherokee account of how fire came to the people, adorns the reflecting pool. Ross's Landing was established in 1816 by Cherokee Chief John Ross, and he operated it as a successful trading post until 1838 when the location served as a departure point for Cherokees driven west to present-day Oklahoma by the U.S. government. Artists on Team Gadugi are Bill Glass, Ken Foster, Gary Allen, Wade Bennett, Robby McMurtry, and Demos Glass, all citizens of the Cherokee Nation.

2006: The tallest statue (40 feet) ever created by a Canadian Native artist was erected at the Millbrook Cultural & Heritage Centre in Millbrook, Nova Scotia, owned by the

The statue of Po'pay at the U.S. Capitol's Statuary Hall is by artist Cliff Fragua.

Millbrook First Nation. The monument designed by Mi'kmaw artist Art Stevens pays homage to cultural hero Glooscap, a key figure in Mi'kmaq origin accounts.

2007: Nora Naranjo-Morse (1953–), Santa Clara Pueblo, unveiled her outdoor sculpture, *Always Becoming*, built on site at the National Museum of the American Indian in Washington, D.C. She is the first Native woman to have a public outdoor piece in that city. Based on Santa Clara Pueblo traditions, the work is comprised of five separate sculptures depicting family members Father, Mother, Little One, Moon Woman, and Mountain Bird. Ranging in size from seven and a half feet to sixteen feet tall, the pieces are constructed of clay, stone, black locust wood, bamboo, grass, and yam vines. The natural elements ensure that the sculptures will change over time, hence the name *Always Becoming*.

2007: Marvin Oliver (1946–2019), Quinault/Isleta Pueblo, made history as the first non-Italian artist to be commissioned for a public art piece in Perugia, Italy, sister city to Seattle, Washington. The mammoth bronze sculpture of an orca fin is on permanent exhibit at Porto Nova, one of the gateways to the city of Perugia, where it is viewed by thousands each year.

2009: *Indian Land Dancing* was the first public artwork designed by Native residents of Chicago, Illinois. The brightly colored mosaic, based on and including the poem "Indian Land Dancing," by E. Donald "Eddy" Two-Rivers (1945–2008), Ojibwe, is displayed on the walls of the Lake Shore Drive underpass at Foster Avenue in the Edgewater neighborhood.

2010: *P'oe iwe naví ûnp'oe dinmuu* (My Blood Is in the Water) was a commissioned outdoor installation, an Indigenous response to Santa Fe's 400th anniversary. It featured blood dripping from a taxidermied mule deer onto an amplified Pueblo drum, memorializing the animal as a spiritual mediator of the landscape and paying tribute to the traditional processes through which Indigenous people put food on the table. The work celebrates the continuity of past and present of Indigenous culture and community attached to the area.

2013: Artist Lillian Pitt (1944–), Confederated Tribes of Warm Springs, created the

Kalapuya sculpture installed near the Kalapuya Bridge along the Willamette River near Eugene, Oregon. She is the first Native woman to have a public monument displayed in the state. The 40-foot-long stainless-steel sculpture represents the spiritual and day-to-day connections between the Kalapuya people and the Willamette River. The massive work depicts a Kalapuya canoe, salmon, and trout in the river and camas and cattails that were vital food sources for the Kalapuya. The names of the major Kalapuya tribes from the Eugene area are inscribed in the skim coating of the structure. Eight thousand pounds of stainless steel were used in making the sculpture, which also showcases a crescent moon and stars cast in bronze. Besides being a sculptor, Pitt is also a mixed media artist, working in clay, bronze, wearable art, prints, and glass.

2015: *Repellent Fence* was erected as the largest binational land art installation in the country. Postcommodity, an Indigenous interdisciplinary arts collective based in Arizona and New Mexico, spent eight years developing the exhibit, which was comprised of 26 "scare-eye" 10-foot-diameter yellow balloons suspended 50 feet in the air over a two-mile span bisecting the U.S.-Mexico border. *Repellent Fence* flew for four days, rejoining the towns of Douglas, Arizona, and Agua Prieta, Sonora (Mexico), which, since 2012, have been separated by an 18-foot-high steel border fence. From the air, the installation looked like a "suture, reconnecting two bodies of land that had been divided," according to Postcommodity artist Kade L. Twist, Cherokee. Other members, both past or present, are Cristóbal Martínez; Steven Yazzie, Navajo; Raven Chacon, Diné; and Nathan Young, Delaware/Pawnee/Kiowa. Postcommodity refers to the "commodity era" of Native American art trading in the late 1800s and 1900s, with the "post" being in reference to their contemporary take on traditional Native art forms. Their

work has been exhibited nationally and internationally.

2017: Four bronze busts depicting Lakota luminaries Charles Eastman, Nicholas Black Elk, Oscar Howe, and Vine Deloria Jr. were installed in the new First Nations Sculpture Garden in Halley Park in Rapid City, South Dakota. Acclaimed Lakota sculptor Marilyn "Wasú Wasté" Helen Wounded Head (1952–2019) created them. The First Nations Sculpture Garden was first envisioned by Elizabeth Cook-Lynn, Dakota and member of the Crow Creek Sioux Tribe, retired professor of Native studies, and a longtime resident of Rapid City. Her goal was to create a quiet space where Native people could reflect on the contributions and achievements of their ancestors, a respite in an area dominated by monuments honoring white culture.

2018: The earthwork monument *Mantle* was revealed on historic Richmond, Virginia's Capitol Square. Honoring Virginia's Native nations, the sculpture is based on the spiral shell embroideries on the historic Powhatan's Mantle (c. 1608), believed to represent the nations of his confederacy. Designed and installed by internationally acclaimed New York–based artist and writer Alan Michelson, Mohawk, Six Nations of the Grand River, the winding path leading to the work is paved with local river stones and landscaped with indigenous plants from the region. The piece seems to be moving and is enhanced by symbols of Native history and religions. Richmond is known for its Monument Avenue with statues honoring Confederate figures; *Mantle* is the first work on the avenue conceived by Native people and created by a Native artist.

2019: Artist Doug Hyde (1946–), Nez Perce/Assiniboine/Chippewa, installed his bronze sculpture of a Nez Perce woman, *et-weyé·wise* ("I return from a hard journey"), on the Joseph, Oregon, Bronze Artwalk, a

Remembering Sand Creek

Renowned artist Edgar Heap of Birds (1954–), Cheyenne/Arapaho, and the Denver Art Museum (DAM) came to an agreement concerning the relocation of his seminal sculpture, *Wheel*. Dedicated in 2005, the commissioned piece was installed at the Gio Ponti–designed museum's north-facing entrance and references American Indian lodge and medicine wheel iconography with its circle of red, forked tree forms. It has been ceremonially blessed by Native holy people and represents a sacred site for Native Americans. Heap of Birds used the building's curved wall to mount the Cheyenne words "nah-kev-ho-eyea-zim," which mean "we are always returning back home again." Based on the Big Horn Medicine Wheel, a sacred site in northern Wyoming, as well as the circular form of a traditional Plains Indian Sun Dance lodge, he designed the multidisciplinary outdoor circular porcelain enamel on steel. Ten forked poles, or trees, are aligned with the summer solstice—on June 21, the sun rises in an opening to the east between the first and last poles. Each tree is covered with words and drawings that recount different events in the history of the area's American Indian peoples, from conflict over resources to global cooperation among Indigenous peoples. Because of the installation's role in healing past wrongs against the Native community, moving it was yet another blatant disregard of the importance of cultural belongings. DAM was renovating and felt that moving the piece was necessary. However, Heap of Birds and DAM came to an agreement to move the entire structure, including 12 inches of topsoil upon which it rests. The agreement is a benchmark for Native people's voices in public spaces.

The wheel was meant to be a gathering place. It has been the final destination of Cheyenne and Arapaho runners participating in the annual 173-mile Sand Creek Spiritual Healing Run commemorating those who were killed during the Sand Creek Massacre (1864) by the U.S. Volunteer Cavalry. Over a century ago, those same soldiers marched in a "heroes" parade through Denver, near this very place, sporting trophies of severed body parts from their slaughter.

showcase for the bronze foundries dotting Wallowa County. His is not the only statue depicting Indigenous subjects, but it is the only one created by a Native sculptor. The piece represents the Nez Perce's forced removal from their home valley and those who remained and returned. Hyde, recipient of several awards, casts his bronze sculpture from original stonework. Jurors from three reservations—Colville in Washington, Nez Perce in Idaho, and Confederated Tribes of the Umatilla in Oregon—selected Hyde's design as the best. Another of his monumental sculptures, *Code Talker* (1988), graces an office complex at Central Avenue and Thomas Roads in the downtown business district of Phoenix, Arizona.

2020: For the first time, a sculpture by a Native artist was dedicated on Indigenous Peoples Day. Chinook Indian Nation chairman and artist Tony A. (naschio) Johnson designed *Guests of the Great River*, an outdoor installation at the Burke Museum of

Natural History and Culture in Seattle, Washington. The piece, composed of 11 large-scale bronze paddles, represents the arrival of a Chinookan canoe carrying Indigenous cultural heroes and knowledge of the Columbia Region.

2020: The National Native American Veterans Memorial, named *Warrior's Circle of Honor,* was unveiled in Washington, D.C., on the grounds of the Smithsonian's National Museum of the American Indian.

2021: After years of negotiating between Native leaders and the Colorado state government, Native people won their bid to erect the *Sand Creek Massacre Memorial,* a statue of a grieving American Indian mother, in a prime location on the west steps of the Colorado State Capitol in Denver. The Sand Creek Massacre was the most brutal event in the state's history. On November 29, 1864, volunteers from the First and Third Colorado Cavalry regiments ambushed and slaughtered 230 Cheyenne and Arapahoe, mostly women, elderly, and children, although the 700 people living at the Sand Creek site had been promised peace and safety by the government. After the attack, the Army soldiers burned the camp and took trophies from the bodies, which they displayed in a parade through Denver, where they were initially hailed as heroes. Cheyenne/Arapaho artist Harvey Pratt, who designed the National Native American Veterans Memorial, created the memorial. Pratt, who had family members die in the massacre, felt the trauma experienced by his ancestors. He was taught to always have shoes by his bed in case he had to get up and run for his life in the night.

ORGANIZATIONS

1979: The American Indian Library Association (AILA) was created in conjunction with the White House Pre-Conference on Indian Library and Information Services on or near Reservations. An affiliate of the American Library Association (ALA), AILA advocates for the library-related needs of American Indians and Alaska Natives.

2010: The Estria Foundation was founded by Indigenous Hawaiian artist Todd "Estria" Johnson and social media pioneer Jeremy LaTrasse in Oakland, California, as a way to raise the social consciousness on human and environmental issues through public art projects, education, and community events across the globe. The first programs were the *Water Writes* mural series and the national art competitions of the Estria Battle, art competitions that took place in Harlem, Brooklyn, Chicago, Los Angeles, Honolulu, and Oakland. In 2013, the organization piloted the Mele Murals project at Kaimukī High School in Honolulu, Hawaii, on the island of Oahu, which sparked the Hālau Pāheona after-school program (2016). Mele Murals honors the last commands of King David Kalākaua, "Look to the keiki, teach them, groom them, show them wonder, and inspire them." The project provides a platform to teach young people to become storytellers, painters, and community leaders. Integrated into the curriculum at Kaimukī High School, students learn Hawaiian culture and history by designing and painting public art. In 2020, the Estria Summer Program created a virtual Kākaka Maoli curriculum where students learned how to connect with 'āina (the land) and Hawaiian values through virtual huaka'i (field trips), because of pandemic restrictions. The students, aged 9 to 12 years old, were eventually able to paint their mana'o (personal insight) at Kaimukī High School by maintaining social distancing. The mural pays homage to the universe and represents the heavens, the past, and how youth can stay connected in the present to Hawaiian culture.

2010: The Association of Tribal Archives, Libraries, and Museums (ATALM) was officially incorporated as an organization dedicated to serving the needs of cultural organizations worldwide, with an emphasis on Indigenous peoples in the United States. It is headquartered in Oklahoma City, Oklahoma, and hosts an annual conference. In 2007 before ATALM was officially incorporated, it started giving Guardian Awards in five categories. The first honorees were Dr. Lotsee Patterson, Comanche, professor emerita, School of Library and Information Services, University of Oklahoma, for the Lifetime Achievement Award; Alyce Sadongei, Kiowa/Tohono O'odham, Arizona State Museum, for the Leadership Award; the Dragonfly Project, a partnership between the Haines Borough Public Library in Alaska and the Chilkoot Indian Association, for the Outstanding Project Award; the St. Regis Mohawk Tribe, for the Archives Institutional Excellence Award; the Colorado River Indian Tribe (Amelia Flores), for the Library Institutional Excellence Award; and the Tamastslikt Cultural Institute, for the Museum Institutional Excellence Award. They have since added more categories.

MILITARY

> *"Native people are keenly aware of what we've given to this country. Across what would become the United States, Native people fought rapacious European powers and, when the time came, fought an expanding American government in order to protect themselves and their homelands. In the 19th century, the United States fought more wars against Indian tribes than it did against 'foreign' powers...."*

—*David Treuer*, New York Times, *August 31, 2021*

MILITARY ACADEMIES

1822: David Moniac (1802–1836), Muscogee Creek, was the first Native American to attend and graduate from the U.S. Military Academy at West Point. In addition, Moniac was the first minority to attend and the first student from Alabama to enroll at the Academy. He attended through a provision of the Treaty of New York (1790) in which the United States agreed to educate such Creek youth as agreed upon, not exceeding four at any one time. At his graduation, Moniac received a commission as Brevet Second Lieutenant in the 6th U.S. Infantry Regiment, but he later resigned. In 1836, he volunteered to lead a unit of Creek Volunteers from Alabama to aid the United States in Florida during the Second Seminole War and was commissioned as a captain by the Army. Moniac was promoted to major after commanding a successful charge but was later killed by a musket volley during the fighting.

1917: Joseph James "Jocko" Clark (1893–1971), Cherokee Nation, became the first American Indian to graduate from the U.S. Naval Academy. In 1953, he retired as a full admiral in the Navy, the first Native American naval officer to attain that rank. Clark's naval career began in 1913, spanning World War I, World War II, and the Korean War, with his experiences primarily in aircraft carrier combat. During his 40-year tenure in the military, his leadership included serving as commander of the new USS *Yorktown* (following the loss of an earlier one in the Battle of Midway), carrier task group commander, and commander of the Seventh Fleet. He was promoted to rear admiral in 1944. The highest-ranking naval officer of Native American descent in U.S. history, his military awards include the Distinguished Service Medal, Navy Cross, Silver Star, and the Legion of Merit. Clark was buried at Arlington National Cemetery. In 1980, the Navy named a guided-missile frigate the USS *Clark* in his honor.

Admiral Joseph James Clark

1922: Francis J. Mee (1899–1990), Chippewa, White Earth, graduated from the U.S. Naval Academy and was commissioned as ensign serving on the battleship USS *Tennessee BB-43*. Later, he advanced to rear admiral on the basis of combat citation in 1952. In 1918, Mee was appointed to the U.S. Naval Academy from the Ninth Congressional District. In 1927, Mee returned to Annapolis, Maryland, for instruction in mechanical engineering at the postgraduate school. He then earned a Master of Science degree from Columbia University. During his career, Mee received numerous awards, including the World War II Victory Medal and the Philippine Liberation Ribbon with one star.

Victor Joe Apodaca Jr.

1961: Victor Joe Apodaca Jr. (1937–1967), Navajo/Spanish American, was the first Native American graduate of the U.S. Air Force Academy. Assigned to the 389th Tactical Fighter Wing in Danang, South Vietnam, his F4 Phantom fighter jet was shot down over North Vietnam on June 8, 1967. Major Apodaca was missing in action for years. His remains were reportedly kept at the Central Identification Laboratory in Hawaii, held there since 1988, until they were identified through DNA in 2001 and returned to his family that year. One of Apodaca's sons escorted his father's remains from Hawaii via a commercial flight, but after landing in Minneapolis, all flights were grounded because of the September 11 attacks at the Twin Towers and the Pentagon. Two days later, with help from the military, Apodaca's remains arrived in Colorado, and they were buried with military honors at the U.S. Air Force Academy Cemetery.

1966: Donald Winchester, Cherokee, became the first known Native American graduate of the U.S. Coast Guard Academy in New London, Connecticut. Winchester also became the Coast Guard's first known

Medal of Honor: Indian Scouts

In 1869, Co-Rux-Te-Chod-Ish (Mad Bear), Pawnee, a U.S. Army scout, was the first Native American to receive the Medal of Honor (MOH). Awarded on July 8, 1869, the citation reads: "Ran out from the command in pursuit of a dismounted Indian; was shot down and badly wounded by a bullet from his own command." His actual name, Co-Tux-A-Kah-Wadde (Traveling Bear), was misinterpreted and the incorrect one cited. Fifteen other Native American Army scouts are identified as MOH recipients (Apache, 10; Black Seminole, 4; and Yavapai, 1).

The National Native American Veterans Memorial at the National Museum of the American Indian, which is part of the Smithsonian Institution in Washington, D.C.

Native American Veterans Memorial, National Museum of the American Indian

The Native American Veterans' Memorial Establishment Act of 1994 authorized the National Museum of the American Indian to construct and maintain a National Native American Veterans' Memorial in Washington, D.C. The legislation was amended in 2013, making it possible to bring the long-standing project to fruition. Artist Harvey P. Pratt, Cheyenne/Arapaho, a Vietnam veteran who served in the U.S. Marine Corps, designed the steel and stone structure, called the Warriors' Circle of Honor. Located outside the Smithsonian's National Museum of the American Indian on the Mall, it was dedicated on Veterans Day in 2020. Pratt, a self-taught forensic artist, is also a Southern Cheyenne chief for the Southern Cheyenne and Arapaho Tribes of Oklahoma. He said of the work, "I can't believe it will be one of the 12 national memorials in Washington, D.C."

Native American aviator. A decorated pilot who served in the Coast Guard for two decades, he logged more than 5,000 flight hours in various types of aircraft. Winchester retired from the Coast Guard with the rank of commander.

1970: Daucey Brewington, Lumbee/Coharie, became the first member of his tribe to graduate from the U.S. Air Force Academy. Brewington grew up in North Carolina, where he attended Indian-only schools before joining the Air Force. He said, "I saw the military as my way out. I have a history of service members in my family. I had family who fought from World War I through the Korean conflict." Brewington went on to become a C-130 pilot, leaving active duty as a colonel in 1979 and serving in the Reserve until 1992. "Natives have fought in wars in support of the U.S. since the Revolutionary War in 1774," he commented. "They have fought in almost every war since the country was founded. Natives played a major role in winning WWII with the Navajo Code Talkers, and they did all this before even being able to vote in 1948."

1972: Elary Gromoff Jr. (1949–2017), Aleut, was the first Alaska Native to graduate from the U.S. Military Academy at West Point. After serving more than 20 years in the U.S. Army Corps of Engineers, he returned to Alaska and worked with Native Corporations, including serving on the Aleut Corporation Board of Directors.

1981: Midshipman Sandra L. Hinds, unidentified tribe, became the first American Indian woman to graduate from the U.S. Naval Academy.

1982: Dolores Kathleen Smith, Cherokee, became the first Native American woman to graduate from the U.S. Air Force Academy. She became a training pilot and served in the Air Force until 1990, when she left with the rank of captain.

1984: Brigitte T. Wahwassuck Kwinn (1962–), Potawatomi, was the first American Indian woman to graduate from the U.S. Military Academy at West Point, where she earned a Bachelor of Science degree in math, science,

and engineering. Kwinn completed a Master of Science degree in systems engineering at the University of Arizona in 1994. She was an assistant professor at West Point from 1994 to 1997 and 2002 to 2006. Kwinn also became a lecturer at the Naval Postgraduate School in Monterey, California.

1988: Janet Emerson became the first known Native American woman to graduate from the U.S. Coast Guard Academy.

2021: Second Lt. Daniel Alvarado (Hiragija Wani'uga—"He Who Shields Them"), Winnebago Tribe of Nebraska, graduated from West Point Military Academy. He was the first known Native American to direct the 100th Night Show, a tradition at West Point since 1871, when the "Firsties" take a humorous look back at their four years at the academy. The cadets take a lighthearted poke at West Point, its cultural idiosyncrasies, and various events, circumstances, and people who shaped their class. Most of it is based in truth, some exaggerated, but all of it offered in the name of humor and entertainment. Alvarado directed the play "100 70 Days until Graduation: The Commissioning Factory," written by a classmate. He also received a very special gift from his family, who celebrated his graduation by giving him a prayer fan made of red-tailed hawk tail feathers, which are considered sacred and awarded for doing something exceptional.

◆◇◆

AMERICAN REVOLUTION

1770: Crispus Attucks (c. 1723–1770), Natick/African American, was identified as the first casualty of the Boston Massacre, the first in the cause of the American Revolution against the British. The Attucks surname has been translated as "deer" in the language of his mother's people. In 1888, the Boston Massacre Monument, also known as the Crispus Attucks Monument, was installed in Boston Common in his honor and that of other massacre victims.

1774: The Stockbridge Militia, composed primarily of Mahican, Wappinger, and Munsee Indians, was the first Native unit to fight against the British during the revolution.

Crispus Attucks

William McIntosh

WAR OF 1812

c. 1812: William McIntosh (1775–1825), Creek, was the first Native American to be commissioned brigadier general in the U.S. Army. Andrew Jackson bestowed the commission for McIntosh's contributions to Jackson's forces at the Battle of Horseshoe Bend and other contributions. He sent warriors to fight in the War of 1812, Creek War of 1812, and the first Seminole War of 1817–1818.

CIVIL WAR

"A little known but crucial part of the story was that more than 20,000 American Indians fought on both sides of the conflict. Many thought their participation would guarantee their survival, protect their lands, and enhance their autonomy. Instead, for them the post-war period was tragic. A reunited nation turned its vision towards westward expansion, overrunning Indian lands and decimating their populations."

—*From* American Indians and the Civil War

1863: Company K of the 1st Michigan Sharpshooters began serving in the Civil War, becoming the largest all-Indian regiment in the Union Army east of the Mississippi River. The Company consisted of 146 men, 139 of them Anishnaabek, Indigenous people of the Great Lakes. The Anishnaabek

Allies in War, Partners in Peace

Allies in War, Partners in Peace is a bronze sculpture in the National Museum of the American Indian (NMAI) that honors the friendship forged between the Oneida Indian Nation and the United States during the American Revolution. Sculptor Edward Hlavka created the monument depicting Oneida tribal members Chief Skenandoah and Polly Cooper standing alongside General George Washington. Cooper was among the Oneidas who walked hundreds of miles from their home in New York State to Valley Forge, Pennsylvania, to provide white corn and other vital supplies to Washington's Continental Army. She remained at Valley Forge to aid the troops. Chief Skenandoah played a crucial role in the decision to side with the colonists during the war. The Oneida Nation donated the monument, which is nearly 20 feet tall and weighs 1,925 pounds, to commemorate the opening of NMAI in 2004.

include Odawa/Ottawa, Ojibway/Chippewa, and Potawatomi tribal nations.

1863: Garrett A. Graveraet (1842–1864), Anishinaabe/German, was the only American Indian officer of Company K of the 1st Michigan Sharpshooters. Second Lt. Graveraet, who was fluent in Anishinaabemowin, English, and French, was a teacher at the government school in Harbor Springs, Michigan, and a talented musician. He recruited men, including his own father, Henry, into Company K, which then officially mustered in 1863. Lt. Graveraet, who was wounded at the Siege of Petersburg, died at the Armory Hospital in Washington, D.C., on July 1, 1864. He was later buried on Mackinac Island, Michigan, where his father, who died at the Battle of Spotsylvania Courthouse in May 1864, is also commemorated with a gravestone.

1864: Henry Berry Lowry (also Lowrie) (c. 1848–?), Lumbee, was the leader of a band that waged guerrilla war in North Carolina during the Civil War. He became a legendary figure among his people, compared to Robin Hood for helping the poor and fighting against oppression by the rich and powerful. During the war, the Lowry band included family members, other Indians, African Americans, and Union soldiers who had escaped from Confederate imprisonment. The band continued to operate until Lowry's disappearance in 1872 and the death of his brother Stephen the following year.

Henry Berry Lowry

1864: Stand Watie (Degataga, "he stands"; 1806–1871), Cherokee, was promoted to the rank of brigadier general in the Confederate army, the only American Indian to achieve that rank during the Civil War, and was named commander of the Indian Cavalry Brigade a short time later. The war occurred only a few decades after the tribe's removal to Indian Territory (present-day Oklahoma), rupturing the tribal nation between the Union and the Confederacy, with Watie leading the Confederate Cherokee. He was the last Confederate general to concede to the Union army, surrendering at Doaksville, Choctaw Nation, on June 23, 1865. Before retiring from public life, Watie served as a delegate in negotiations for the Cherokee Reconstruction Treaty in 1866.

1865: Ely S. Parker (Hasanoanda, later Donehogawa; 1828–1895), Tonawanda Seneca, student of law, civil engineer, and tribal leader, was the highest-ranking American Indian in the Union Army during the Civil War, a lieutenant colonel at the time of the Confederate surrender at Appomattox Court House, Virginia, in 1865. He served as General Ulysses S. Grant's military secretary, drafting the terms of surrender. General Robert E. Lee, noting Parker's American Indian identity, is said to have commented, "I am glad to see one real American here." Parker later recounted, "I shook his hand and said, 'We are all Americans.'" At the end of the war, Parker's rank became brevet brigadier general. After Grant was elected president of the United States, he appointed Parker to serve as U.S. commissioner of Indian affairs in 1869, the first American Indian to serve in that position.

1889: A Grand Army of the Republic (GAR) post was established on the Menominee Reservation in Wisconsin, the first American Indian GAR organization in the United States. A second, Oneida Post 228, was founded in Brown County, Wisconsin, in 1899. As with other such organizations in the country, these posts were established to benefit Civil War military veterans of the Union.

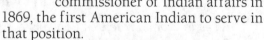

First Native American War Nurses, Spanish American War

Catholic nuns Susan Bordeaux (Mother Mary Anthony), Ellen Clark aka Ellen Clifford (Sister Mary Gertrude), Annie B. Pleets (Sister Mary Bridget), and Josephine Two Bears (Sister Mary Joseph) became known as the first Native American war nurses in 1898. They were part of a small religious order founded by Father Francis Craft, a Roman Catholic priest with medical training and military service, who worked in Dakota Territory (present-day North and South Dakota), notably at Rosebud, Standing Rock, and Fort Berthold.

By the time the Spanish American War broke out, Father Craft had offered his services and those of his order's four remaining nuns to the War Department. They initially nursed the sick in military hospital wards at Camp Cuba Libre in Jacksonville, Florida, for six weeks. After transferring to Camp Onward in Savannah, Georgia, they sailed to Camp Columbia in Havana, Cuba, in December 1898. Living in tents and paid $30 per month, the nuns provided nursing care to the sick and wounded. On October 15, 1899, Susan Bordeaux died of tuberculosis-related complications and was buried with military honors in the military cemetery at Camp Egbert in Cuba. Craft wrote: "This is the first time in the history of our Army that a Sister was buried by the Army with the honors of war, and it will be of interest to the Army that the first Sister so buried, was a granddaughter of Chief Spotted Tail, and a grandniece of Chief Red Cloud." By December 1899, Ellen Clark and Annie Pleets left religious life and returned home. The fourth nun, Josephine Two Bears, returned home in 1901.

WORLD WAR I

"By war's end, the U.S. War Department estimated that more than 17,000 Indian men registered. Sixty-five hundred were drafted. The rest volunteered. All in all, as much as 30 percent of the adult Indian male population participated in World War I, double the national average."

—*David Treuer,* New York Times, *August 31, 2021*

1917: Charlotte Edith Anderson Monture (1890–1996), Mohawk, Six Nations Reserve, who became the first Native Canadian registered nurse when she graduated from nursing school at New Rochelle Hospital in New York in 1914, joined the U.S. Medical Corps and served in the Army Nurse Corps during World War I. She also became the first female Status Indian and registered band member to gain the right to vote in a Canadian federal election. The Military Service Act of 1917 had provided wartime nurses with that right.

1917: Cora Elm (1891–1949), a member of the Oneida Nation, served as a nurse in France during World War I. Born in Wisconsin, she attended the Carlisle Indian School in Pennsylvania and graduated in 1913. Elm then trained as a nurse at the Episcopal Hospital in Philadelphia, graduating in 1916 and staying on as supervisor of wards. She sailed for Europe in 1917, reaching France on Christmas Day. Elm and other nurses were split among three hospitals as the base hospital was readied, opening in Nantes in April 1918. "Although I was in a base hospital," she later said, "I saw a lot of the horrors of war. I nursed many a soldier with a leg cut off, or an arm." Elm married James E. Sinnard in 1921 and later served as ward supervisor in a number of veterans hospitals, including Wood Veterans Hospital in Milwaukee, Wisconsin.

1917: Joseph Oklahombi (1895–1960), Choctaw Nation (Oklahoma), was the most highly decorated Native American soldier during World War I. He registered for the draft and volunteered on May 25, 1917, serving in Company D, 141st Regiment, 36th Infantry Division (Texas and Oklahoma National Guard). Oklahombi and fellow soldiers were recipients of the French Croix de Guerre for gallantry as well as the Silver Star for their actions during trench warfare in France, including rushing on German machine gun nests and capturing 171 prisoners. Oklahombi's military service also included contributions as a Choctaw code talker.

1918: Lula Owl Gloyne (1891–1985) was the first member of the Eastern Band of Cherokee Indians (EBCI) to become a registered nurse and the only member of the EBCI to serve as an officer in World War I. After graduating from Hampton Institute in Virginia in 1914 and teaching in South Carolina, Owl attended the Chestnut Hill Hospital School of Nursing in Philadelphia. In 1916, she graduated from Chestnut Hill, where she was awarded the gold medal in obstetrical nursing. As an EBCI officer in WWI serving as a second lieutenant in the U.S. Army Nurse Corps, Owl was a Red Cross nurse at a base hospital at Camp Lewis, Washington. Gloyne's later work included providing nursing care at EBCI, where she was instrumental in the founding of the first hospital there. She was later named Beloved Woman by her people and, in 2015, was in-ducted into the North Carolina Nurses Association Hall of Fame.

1918: Mathew B. Juan (1892–1918), Pima, who enlisted in the U.S. Army under the name Mathew B. Rivers, was the first American Indian and the first Arizonan to be killed in action during World War I. He died from machine gun fire in the Battle of Cantigny in France. Juan was interred there, but his remains were later returned home to Sacaton, Arizona.

1918: Regina McIntyre Early (1895–?), who served as an Army nurse in World War I, is believed to be the first female veteran of World War I who was an enrolled member of an American Indian tribe in Montana, the Confederated Salish and Kootenai Tribes. McIntyre (her surname at the time) served overseas from September 29, 1918, to July 20, 1919, in base hospitals that included those in Savenay and Caen, France. She was discharged from service on August 9, 1919.

1918: Samuel White Bear, Mato ska (c. 1899–1918), Lakota, was the first World War I soldier from the Pine Ridge Reservation in South Dakota to die in the service.

WORLD WAR II

1941: Melvin Kealoha Bell (1920–2018), Native Hawaiian, who enlisted in the U.S. Coast Guard (USCG) in 1938 and became a radioman, transmitted the first radio transmissions warning of the surprise attack on Pearl Harbor on December 7, 1941. Specializing in naval communications intelligence, he helped break the secret Japanese Imperial Navy code, contributing to saving countless lives during the war. In 1944, Bell became the first Pacific Islander to become a chief

Code Talkers became famous for their valuable work in World War II, but these Indigenous heroes date back to 1918, when Choctaw Indians became the first Code Talkers.

Choctaw Code Talkers

"You had this crazy situation where the Choctaw language was being used as a formidable weapon of war, yet back home children were being beaten at school for using it," says Judy Allen, senior executive officer of tribal relations with the Choctaw Nation of Oklahoma. "The two soldiers who were overheard by the officer probably thought they were in trouble rather than about to provide the answer to the army's communication problems."

During World War I, Choctaw soldiers assigned to the U.S. Army's 142nd Infantry Regiment, 36th Division, served as code talkers, their Native language identified as the first American Indian language to be used as part of the U.S. military communications system. These servicemen contributed to American Expeditionary Force victories in several key battles in the Meuse-Argonne campaign in France.

Two Choctaw officers were initially selected to oversee a communications system that soon included 18 other tribal members. The team began transmitting messages

Choctaw Code Talkers (contd.)

in their tribal language, wartime contributions deemed a success by Allied leaders. The Army continued to enlist soldiers from other tribes as Code Talkers, including Cheyenne, Comanche, Cherokee, Osage, and Sioux.

In 1989, the government of France presented the Chevalier de l'Ordre National du Merite (Knight of the National Order of Merit) to Choctaw and Comanche tribal leaders to recognize Code Talker contributions to the war effort in France during World Wars I and II. Nineteen Choctaw servicemen have been documented as World War I code talkers: Albert Billy, Mitchell Bobb, Victor Brown, Ben Carterby, Benjamin Colbert Jr., George Davenport, Joseph Davenport, James Edwards, Tobias Frazier, Ben Hampton, Noel Johnson, Otis Leader, Solomon Louis, Peter Maytubby, Jeff Nelson, Joseph Oklahombi, Robert Taylor, Walter Veach, and Calvin Wilson.

petty officer. In another first, he advanced to the first master chief in his rate in 1958, becoming the first minority master chief in the history of the U.S. Coast Guard. He retired a year later and became a civilian employee of the USCG. Bell later became a quality engineer with the Department of Navy and worked for years in the field of submarine-launched ballistic missiles. At his retirement in 2004, he had completed 65 years of combined military and federal civil service, one of the longest such careers in U.S. history. In 2019, the USCG announced that Bell would be the namesake of the 55 Fast Response Cutter.

1942: George Drapeaux (1916–2008), from the Yankton Sioux Reservation in South Dakota, was the first Native American Coast Guardsman to participate in World War II combat operations. He served as a gunner's mate on the Coast Guard–manned transport USS *Wakefield*. Drapeaux helped fight off Japanese aircraft while the transport evacuated civilians from Singapore. During his service, from 1940 to

Ira Hayes

1945, he also served aboard the USS *Saranac IV*. Drapeaux later served as vice chairman of the Yankton Sioux Tribe and in other leadership roles.

1942: Ira Hayes (1923–1955), Pima, who enlisted in 1942, was the first U.S. Marine paratrooper from his tribal nation. He also became one of the best-known Native Americans to serve in World War II. In 1945, he was one of the U.S. Marines who raised the American flag on the top of Mount Suribachi during the Battle of Iwo Jima in the South Pacific. The flag raising was captured in the famous Pulitzer Prize–winning photograph by AP photographer Joe Rosenthal. A sculpture based on the iconic image later became part of the Marine Corps War Memorial in Arlington, Virginia. Fame proved to be difficult for Hayes, who suffered from what is now known to be posttraumatic stress disorder. He succumbed to exposure and alcoholism, dying at the age of 32. Hayes was buried with full military honors at Arlington National Cemetery. He is memorialized at the Gila River Indian

Community, his home reservation in Arizona, and beyond.

1942: Joseph R. Toahty (1919–1997), Pawnee/Kiowa, who enlisted in the U.S. Coast Guard in 1941 and trained to become a landing craft coxswain, was the first Native American to participate in an offensive operation with U.S. naval forces during World War II. He participated in the initial landings at Tulagi and Guadalcanal.

1942: The Alaska Territorial Guard (ATG), informally called the Tundra Army (also

Lieutenant Colonel Wayne Don, 107th Civil Support Team commander in the Alaska Army National Guard, shows a photo of his uncle, Sam Herman, who served in the Alaska Territorial Guard during World War II.

Iroquois Declaration of War, 1942

We represent the oldest, though smallest, democracy in the world today. It is the unanimous sentiment among Indian people that the atrocities of the Axis nations are violently repulsive to all sense of righteousness of our people, and that this merciless slaughter of mankind can no longer be tolerated. Now we do resolve that it is the sentiment of this council that the Six Nations of Indians declare that a state of war exists between our Confederacy of Six Nations on the one part and Germany, Italy, Japan and their allies against whom the United States has declared war, on the other part.

"Uncle Sam's Men"), was a military reserve force composed primarily of Alaska Natives, first organized in 1942. Several thousand volunteers served to protect Alaska's vast territory from the threat of Japanese invasion during World War II. Organized by Army Air Corps Major Marvin R. "Muktuk" Marston and supported by Governor Ernest Gruening, the ATG recruited Natives from more than 100 communities throughout Alaska. Serving without pay, the members cooperated with the regular armed services, providing intelligence, scouting, reporting, and related defense measures. The ATG was disbanded in 1947, but U.S. veteran status for the members was not forthcoming until legislation, passed in 2000, made it possible. Participants were then able to obtain federal transcripts of military records, including discharge certificates. With the passage of time, many of the ATG members were no longer living, and efforts to locate survivors proved difficult.

Mary Greyeyes

1942: The Indian Division of the Civilian Conservation Corps (CCC-ID) became a civilian unit to assist the war effort, a division led by the military. It was reportedly the only such division requested to change from civilian to military status. Participants did work for the army as shipyard workers, ammunition factory workers, carpenters, truck drivers, radio operators, mechanics, stock inspectors, and other assignments on bases.

1942: Mary Greyeyes (1920–2011), Cree, Muskeg Lake Nation, Saskatchewan, who joined the Canadian Women's Army Corps (CWAC), was the first First Nations woman to enlist in the Canadian Armed Services. She appeared in an army publicity photograph that depicted her being blessed by her chief prior to leaving for service. The photo, which was staged and inaccurately captioned for years, became internationally famous. Greyeyes served in England, remaining there until her discharge in 1946.

1942: Thomas Oxendine (1922–2010), Lumbee, was the first Native American to complete Navy Flight School and to be commissioned as a Navy pilot. He served as a fighter pilot and flight instructor in World War II, Korea, and Vietnam. His honors include the Distinguished Flying Cross, which he earned for landing at sea under enemy gunfire and

Aleut Evacuation and Internment during World War II

During World War II, U.S. authorities responded to Japanese aggression in the Aleutian Islands by evacuating 881 Unangax̂ (Aleuts) from nine villages and relocating them to southeast Alaska, where they were crowded into internment camps, or "duration villages." They languished in these places, struggling to survive in an alien environment, lacking basic necessities, subsisting on poor camp food, and succumbing to illness. It would not be until nearly two years after the war ended that the people were able to return to their communities. Following years of debate, the U.S. government finally passed the Civil Liberties Act of 1988, to make restitution to Aleut residents of the Pribilof Islands and the Aleutian Islands for "injustices suffered and unreasonable hardships endured while Aleut residents were under United States control during World War II."

rescuing a downed pilot during World War II. Oxendine later recalled that his Navy flight training "was kind of a fluke, and I don't know of any others who came in until President Truman integrated the Armed Forces in 1947."

1942: Julia Nashanany Reeves (1919–1998), Forest County Potawatomi who joined the Army Nurse Corps in 1942, was assigned to one of the first medical units shipped to the Pacific. Her service included an assignment aboard the hospital ship *Solace* in New Caledonia before being transferred to Norwich, England, where she was stationed until V-J Day and subsequently returned to the United States. The first lieutenant mobilized with the 804th Station Hospital during the Korean War.

1943: Paul "Red Bird" Bitchenen, Cheyenne/Arapaho, was the first member of his Oklahoma tribal nation killed in action in World War II.

1943: Ernest Childers (1918–2005), Creek, was the first American Indian to receive the U.S. Medal of Honor in the twentieth century. He was also the first in the National Guard's 45th Division to receive the honor. Childers, a 2nd Lieutenant in the army, received the Medal of Honor on April 8, 1944, in Naples, Italy, for actions he performed against the enemy on September 22, 1943, in Oliveto, Italy. Childers, who attended boarding school at Chilocco in Oklahoma, joined Oklahoma's National Guard on May 8, 1937, and mobilized with the 45th Infantry Division of the U.S. Army on September 10, 1940. Following the war, he entered Advanced Officers' Training School to pursue a career in the army. Childers was the first of two Chilocco alumni to receive the Medal of Honor; the second was fellow 45th Infantry Division soldier Jack C. Montgomery, Cherokee, who received the honor in 1945. The new Ernest Childers Health Center,

Lieutenant Ernest Childers (left) shakes hands with General Jacob L. Devers.

opened in 2021, was constructed to provide Tulsa veterans with more access to VA care.

1943: Eva Mirabal (Eah Ha Wa, Green Corn or Fast Growing Corn; 1920–1968), Taos Pueblo, enlisted in the Women's Army Corps (WAC) and was commissioned to create a comic strip for the Corps newsletter, becoming the first female Native American cartoonist. Her strip, *G.I. Gertie,* gave voice to women in the military and also garnered commissions to create more artworks, including posters advertising war bonds and murals for the army. Mirabal contributed to *Bridge of Wings,* a mural at Wright-Patterson Air Force Base in Dayton, Ohio. After her discharge from the military, Mirabal studied at Southern Illinois University in Carbondale for a year and also taught as artist-in-residence. After several years away from

Joseph Medicine Crow, War Chief

Joseph Medicine Crow (1913–2016), Crow Nation, served in the 103rd Infantry of the U.S. Army during World War II. During his military service, he completed the tasks required to become a war chief among his people. He touched an enemy without killing him, took a weapon from the enemy, led a successful war party, and stole horses from the enemy (around 50 horses from German officers). Medicine Crow, who was awarded the Bronze Star Medal and the Légion d'honneur, became the last surviving war chief of his people. In 2009, he received the Presidential Medal of Freedom from President Barack Obama, who said of him, "Dr. Medicine Crow's life reflects not only the warrior spirit of the Crow people, but America's highest ideals." A historian and author, he wrote *From the Heart of the Crow Country: The Crow Indians' Own Stories* (1992), *Counting Coup: Becoming a Crow Chief on the Reservation and Beyond* (2006), and other works. Chief Medicine Crow lived to be 102.

home, Mirabal returned to Taos Pueblo and remained there for the rest of her life. The paintings she created there are deemed to be "among the first portraits of individuals by an American Indian artist." Mirabal also completed commissions at the Santa Fe Indian School, the Veterans' Hospital and Library in Albuquerque, and other locations.

1943: James Collins Ottipoby (1899–1960), Comanche, was the first American Indian chaplain to be commissioned in the U.S. Army. Born in Lawton, Oklahoma, he was the first Native American to graduate from Hope College in Holland, Michigan (1925). Ottipoby, who also attended Western Theological Seminary, became a pastor in the Reformed Church in America and served several Native American congregations. In 2013, his alma mater, Hope College, unveiled oil paintings of him and three other early graduates of the school (one African American and two Japanese). Called *Celebrating Early Faces of Inclusion*, each painting was commissioned from artist Paul Collins, who created the works from photographs of the men as students. The paintings, along with biographical sketches, are permanently displayed in the rotunda of the Martha Miller Center for Global Communication at Hope College.

1943: Minnie Spotted Wolf (1923–1988), Blackfeet Nation, was the first Native American woman to serve in the U.S. Marine Corps. Initially, she expressed interest in joining the army when she was 18 years old but was discouraged by a recruitment officer who advised her that the war was "not for women." Later, in July 1943, Spotted Wolf was accepted into the Marine Corps Women's Reserve, serving four years in California and Hawaii. Her duties included driving trucks loaded with heavy equipment and sometimes working as a jeep driver for visiting generals. Her service was featured in news stories as well as a comic book to promote the war effort. Following her discharge in 1947, Spotted Wolf returned to Montana, where she eventually attended college and became

Minnie Spotted Wolf

Navajo Code Talkers: The First 29

"The officer wasted no time. He looked around the room at each of us, the carefully selected Marine recruits of Platoon 382, and told us we were to use our native language to
devise an unbreakable code. I read expressions of shock on every face. A code based
on the Navajo language? After we'd been so severely punished as children for speaking
it at boarding school?" —Chester Nez, original Navajo Code Talker

In 1942, the first 29 Navajo Code Talkers were recruited by the U.S. Marine Corps (USMC)
to test the feasibility of using the Navajo language for combat communications. They
became Platoon 382, the first all-Navajo platoon in USMC history. The original group of
Navajo recruits developed the initial code of 200-plus terms (a number that later increased), including those for the English alphabet. The code proved to be successful, and
many other Navajo servicemen also became code talkers. The Navajo Code Talkers participated in every major Marine Corps operation in the Pacific theater, helping to win the
war. Marine Corps leadership, for example, noted that these servicemen were critical to
the victory at Iwo Jima. The code talker program was declassified in 1968. In 2000, Congress passed legislation to honor the Navajo Code Talkers with special medals, specify-
ing gold ones for the first 29 participants and silver for others.

The 2000 Navajo Code Talkers Congressional
Gold Medal

a teacher, teaching in reservation schools for
nearly 30 years.

1943: Brummett Echohawk (1922–2006),
Pawnee, served with Oklahoma's famed
45th Infantry Thunderbird Division during
World War II, creating "the war's first actual battle sketches to be drawn by a front-
line infantryman." Echohawk, honored for
his bravery in combat, was the recipient of
the Bronze Star, the Purple Heart, and a
posthumous Congressional Gold medal.
Drawings that he produced during the war
were published in *Yank, the Army Weekly*,
and were also syndicated in some eighty
newspapers. His cartoons were published
in *Stars and Stripes* newspaper. The Brummett Echohawk Project, which is online, includes a number of his combat sketches.
After the war, Echohawk studied at the Detroit School of Arts and Crafts, the Art Institute of Chicago, the University of Chicago, and the University of Tulsa.
Echohawk served as a staff artist for the
Chicago Daily Times and *Chicago Sun-
Times*. From 1957 to c. 1967, his *Little Chief*
cartoon strips appeared in the Sunday
edition of the *Tulsa World*. He also designed
the Pawnee Nation flag and seal. The flag
includes nine arrowheads that symbolize
the wars in which the Pawnees fought in
the service of the United States: Indian wars,
Spanish-American War, World War I,
World War II, Korean War, Vietnam War,

Pascal Cleatus Poolaw Sr.

Pascal Cleatus Poolaw Sr. (1922–1967), Kiowa, who is cited as the most decorated American Indian in the history of the U.S. military, was also a member of the Kiowa Black Legs (or Leggings) Warrior Society. After enlisting in the U.S. Army in 1942, his military service spanned three wars: World War II, Korea, and Vietnam. Poolaw earned 42 awards and medals, including four Silver Stars, five Bronze Stars, three Purple Hearts (one per war), and the Distinguished Service Cross. He had retired from the military but reentered in 1967 in an effort to prevent a son from having to deploy. First Sergeant Poolaw was killed in action in Vietnam on November 7, 1967. By then, he had served nearly 25 years in the military. Poolaw Hall is named in his honor at Fort Sill in Oklahoma.

Desert Storm, Operation Enduring Freedom, and Operation Iraqi Freedom.

1945: Louis Charlo (1926–1945), a member of the Confederated Salish and Kootenai Tribes, was among the U.S. Marines who were the first to raise an American flag at Iwo Jima. That event was overshadowed by the fame of the second flag raising, which occurred on the same day, February 23, and featured Ira Hayes, Pima. Charlo was killed in action on Iwo Jima on March 2, 1945, a short time after the flag raising, while trying to save fellow Marine Ed McLaughlin. Charlo was posthumously awarded a Purple Heart and Bronze Star Medal. In 2019, his sacrifice was memorialized with a highway sign at mile marker 7 on U.S. Highway 93 North in Montana.

1945: Harvey Natchees (1920–1980), Ute, was featured in many newspapers as the first American to enter Germany's capital, Berlin, in the final days of World War II. He enlisted in the U.S. Army in 1942 and served in a reconnaissance battalion in the 3rd Armored Division. Natchees fought in many battles, and his valor was recognized with a Silver Star, Bronze Star, and a Purple Heart with oak leaf cluster. While in Berlin, he took United Press journalists on a jeep tour of conquered territory. After his discharge from the Army in October 1945, Natchees returned to the Uintah-Ouray Reservation in Utah. The following year, he and his wife rode in Salt Lake City's Pioneer Day parade to the cheers of thousands.

2021: Julia Kabance (1910–2021), Prairie Band Potawatomi, celebrated her 111th birthday, making her the oldest known living female American veteran of World War II. Kabance joined the U.S. Women's Army Corps in 1943, at age 32, serving until she became a disabled veteran after suffering hearing loss due to measles in 1945. However, she continued working for the U.S. Army Corps of Engineers as an accountant until her retirement in 1972. Throughout her life, Kabance found great joy in volunteering and working with veterans, particularly at the Colmery-O'Neil VA Medical Center in Topeka, Kansas. She received the Good Conduct Medal, the World War II Victory Medal, and the American Campaign Medal. In November 2019, Kabance became the first Native American to receive the Distinguished Citizen Medal from the Daughters of the American Revolution. On Kabance's 110th birthday, Combat Vets Association made her feel special with a surprise socially distanced parade for her.

◆◇◆

KOREAN WAR

"Then perhaps we can all understand what my grandfather said to me: 'The real warrior is the one who fights to defeat war itself.'"

—*Joseph M. Marshall III, from* Walking with Grandfather: The Wisdom of Lakota Elders

1951: Mitchell Red Cloud Jr. (1925–1950) was posthumously awarded the Medal of Honor, becoming the first (and only) member of the Ho-Chunk Nation in Wisconsin to receive the honor. He served in the U.S. Marines during World War II and in the U.S. Army during the Korean War. Red Cloud was killed in battle near Chonghyon, Korea, on November 5, 1950. The citation reveals Red Cloud's heroic actions, which included wrapping his arm around a tree to continue firing at enemy forces while

Mitchell Red Cloud Jr.

he was severely wounded, after which he died. He prevented the enemy from overrunning his company's position, providing needed time to evacuate the wounded and to reorganize. Tributes in his name include Camp Red Cloud, a U.S. Army camp in Korea, renamed on May 18, 1957; a Wisconsin historical marker, located on Highway 54; and an infantry rifle range bearing his name at Fort Benning, Georgia. The U.S. Navy christened the USNS *Red Cloud* (T-Akr 313), a transport ship, in Corporal Red Cloud's honor on August 7, 1999.

1952: Charles George (1932–1952) was the first (and only) member of the Eastern Band of Cherokee Indians (EBCI) to be awarded the Medal of Honor, which was pre-

sented posthumously. Serving in the U.S. Army as a private first class, he was killed in combat in Korea on November 30, 1952. George was a rifleman in Company C of the 179th Infantry Regiment of the 45th Infantry Division participating in a raid behind enemy lines to capture a prisoner for interrogation. He died after throwing himself on a hand grenade to save two fellow soldiers. The VA Medical Center in Asheville, North Carolina, was renamed the Charles George VA Medical Center in his honor. Other tributes include the Charles George Memorial Arena at Cherokee High School, the Charles George Bridge on the reservation, and the establishment of the Charles George Beloved Veterans Hall, which officially opened on Veteran's Day, November 11, 2019, in the Museum of the Cherokee Indian in Cherokee, North Carolina. In 2012, two schoolboys recovered George's Purple Heart, Bronze Star, and Good Conduct Medal in an antique shop in New York, and the medals were returned to his family.

1952: Herbert Kaili Pilila'au (1928–1951) was the first Native Hawaiian to be awarded the Medal of Honor. Born and raised on the island of O'ahu, Pilila'au, who was drafted into the Army, was sent to Korea in March 1951. Serving as private first class with Company C, 23rd Infantry Regiment, 2nd Infantry Division, he voluntarily remained behind to cover his unit's withdrawal from the Battle of Heartbreak Ridge on September 17, 1951. PFC Pilila'au held off enemy forces with his automatic weapon and grenades until his ammunition was exhausted, and then he engaged the enemy in hand-to-hand combat until he was mortally wounded. He was posthumously awarded the Medal of Honor for his actions. Pilila'au was buried at the National

Herbert Kaili Pilila'au

Cemetery of the Pacific in Honolulu on February 26, 1952.

1998: James E. "Jim" Amerson, Chickasaw, who served as a combat tank commander in the 45th Infantry Division in Korea, was the first Native American to be elected commander of the State American Legion in Oklahoma.

2008: Master Sergeant Woodrow "Woody" Wilson Keeble (1917–1982), Sisseton Wahpeton Dakota, was posthumously awarded the Medal of Honor for acts of "extraordinary courage, selfless service, and devotion to duty" during the Korean War, the first full-blood Sioux Indian to receive the honor. A veteran of both World War II and Korea, he was one of the most highly decorated soldiers in North Dakota history. Keeble once commented: "There were terrible moments that encompassed a lifetime, an endlessness when terror was so strong in me that I could feel idiocy replace reason. Yet I have never left my position, nor

Master Sergeant Woodrow "Woody" Wilson Keeble

have I shirked hazardous duty. Fear did not make a coward out of me." The Sisseton Wahpeton Oyate Health Care Center changed its name to the Woodrow Wilson Keeble Memorial Health Care Center on May 14, 2009, to honor the memory of Master Sergeant Keeble.

VIETNAM WAR

1962: James Gabriel Jr. (1938–1962) was the first Special Forces soldier and the first Native Hawaiian to be killed in the Vietnam War. "The Ballad of the Green Berets," the number one song in 1966, was written by then Staff Sgt. Barry Sadler, in part, to honor Gabriel.

1966: James Elliott ("Willie") Williams (1930–1999), Cherokee, who earned the Medal of Honor for demonstrating conspic-

Billy Walkabout

Billy Walkabout (1949–2007), Cherokee Nation, became regarded as the most decorated Native American soldier in the Vietnam War. Born in Cherokee County, Oklahoma, he enlisted in the U.S. Army in 1968 after graduating from high school. Walkabout was a combat infantryman in Vietnam, serving in Company F, 58th Infantry, which was attached to the 101st Airborne Division. During a long-range reconnaissance patrol in a region southwest of Hue on November 20, 1968, he was seriously wounded when he and fellow soldiers came under enemy fire for hours. Walkabout received the Distinguished Service Cross for valorous actions during the mission that included simultaneously returning fire, helping his comrades, and boarding other injured soldiers onto evacuation helicopters. He retired as a second lieutenant, later suffering from complications associated with exposure to Agent Orange defoliant used in Vietnam. Walkabout also suffered from posttraumatic stress disorder, suicidal thoughts, and self-isolation. Besides the Distinguished Service Cross, his awards included Silver Stars, Bronze Stars, and the Purple Heart. Walkabout, who died on March 13, 2007, is buried at Arlington National Cemetery.

uous gallantry on October 31, 1966, while serving as a patrol boat commander in Vietnam, became the most decorated enlisted man in Navy history.

1981: The first powwow to honor Vietnam veterans specifically was held in Anadarko, Oklahoma. It became an annual event sponsored by the Vietnam Era Veterans Inter-Tribal Association.

1984: Donna Loring (1948–), Penobscot, Vietnam veteran, was the first woman police academy graduate to become a police chief in Maine, serving the Penobscot in that position from 1984 to 1990. She served in Vietnam as a communications specialist in 1967 and 1968, processing casualty reports from throughout Southeast Asia. In 1999 Maine governor Angus King commissioned Loring to the rank of colonel and appointed her to be his advisor on women veterans' affairs.

GULF WAR, OPERATION DESERT STORM

"Native Veterans are highly regarded within tribal communities for their dedication and commitment to serving in the Armed Services throughout America's history and up to the present day. American Indian and Alaska Native people serve in the US Armed Services at a higher rate than any other group."

—*National Congress of American Indians*

Lori Piestewa

1991: Stephen Eric Bentzlin (Wicahpi Etan, Came from the Stars; 1967–1991), Sisseton-Wahpeton Sioux, was the first Native American killed during Operation Desert Storm's first ground attack. He died on January 29, 1991, while serving with the 3rd Light Armored Infantry Battalion, 1st Marine Division's screening force during its engagement with an Iraqi armored convoy near Khafji, Saudi Arabia. During the course of the battle, his vehicle was accidently destroyed by friendly fire from an Air Force missile. Corporal Bentzlin, who grew up in Minnesota, was reportedly one of four Native Americans who lost their lives in the Gulf War.

IRAQ AND AFGHANISTAN

2003: Private First Class Lori Piestewa (1979–2003), Hopi, who served with the U.S. Army Quartermaster Corps, was the first woman killed in action during Operation Iraqi Freedom and was the first known American Indian female soldier to die in combat in a foreign war while serving in the U.S. military. A landmark mountain in Phoenix, Arizona, was renamed Piestewa Peak in her honor. In 2011, the U.S. Army named its Directorate of Training Sustainment headquarters at Fort Benning, Georgia, Piestewa Hall. That year, the American Legion Post No. 80 on the Hopi Reservation was renamed the Lori Piestewa Post. Other honors include the annual Lori Piestewa National Native American Games.

2004: Sergeant Lee D. Todacheene (1974–2004), an Army medical specialist attached to the 1st Battalion, 77th Armor Regiment, Infantry Division, was killed on April 6, 2004, while on guard duty in Balad, Iraq, becoming the first Navajo tribal member to be killed in the Iraq war. Sergeant Todacheene's funeral mass was held at Saint Isabel Church in

Lukachukai, Arizona, and he was buried in the St. Isabelle Community Cemetery on April 12, 2004.

2004: An intertribal powwow was held at Al Taqaddum Air Base located in central Iraq during Operation Iraqi Freedom, the first documented powwow to take place in a combat zone. Held on September 17 and 18, 2004, it was organized by Sergeant Debra K. Mooney, Oklahoma Choctaw, and other troops from the Oklahoma National Guard unit on base. The participants made a drum from a 55-gallon oil drum cut in half and covered with canvas from a cot. Desert Storm, a Cherokee drum group that provided the music, wore ribbon shirts also fashioned from found materials on base.

2005: James D. Fairbanks (1952–2011), Anishinaabe, White Earth Nation, was the first Native American to serve as force master chief, the highest-ranking enlisted Navy Seabee. When he was promoted to the position, there were approximately 20,000 Seabees in the Naval Construction Battalions. "If leaders put their people first," Fairbanks commented, "they will always succeed." His advice for junior sailors included this: "Stay focused on your goals, find friends who are positive and want to succeed too. There is no limit to the good you 'Can Do.'" Fairbanks, who was force master chief until 2008, had a career that encompassed more than 28 years in the military, starting with two years in the U.S. Marine Corps after graduating from high school, the rest in the U.S. Naval service. Serving during the war eras of Vietnam, the Gulf War, and the Iraq War, his tours of duty included extensive international travel. Fairbanks earned more than 40 awards and ribbons, including the Bronze Star, and the love and respect of the troops. In 2019, Fairbanks became the first person honored under

Becker County's memorial roadway program in Minnesota. County Highway 26 was dedicated on November 11 of that year as Force Master Chief James D. Fairbanks Memorial Highway.

2006: Lucas T. White (1978–2006), Confederated Tribes of the Umatilla Reservation, was the first American Indian from the Yakima Valley killed while serving in Operation Iraqi Freedom. Sergeant White, a U.S. Army soldier from Moses Lake, Washington, was leading a striker patrol in Baghdad, Iraq, when his unit was ambushed by enemy forces. White was buried at Arlington National Cemetery.

2015: Joshua L. Wheeler (1975–2015), Cherokee Nation, a member of the elite U.S. Army Special Forces Operational Detachment-Delta (known as Delta Force), was killed in Iraq during Operation Inherent Resolve. He was the first known American service member killed in action in the operation. Master Sergeant Wheeler died in the Iraqi city of Irbil, helping to secure the release of 70 hostages held by the enemy. He had 14 deployments to Iraq and Afghanistan and was highly decorated, the recipient of eleven Bronze Star Medals and many other honors.

Master Sergeant Joshua L. Wheeler

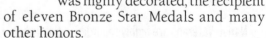

AIR FORCE

1942: Hiawatha Ow-Altu "Bob" Mohawk (1921–2006) joined the Air Force in December 1942, becoming a fighter pilot. The son of Ota-ah-ka Mohawk from Quebec and Hazel Levert Smith, he was born in Florida and graduated from the Pearl River County Agricultural High School in Poplarville, Mississippi. Mohawk worked as a welder prior to entering the military. He flew more than 47 successful missions in Europe during World War II and was awarded the Distinguished Flying Cross in 1945.

1942: Clarence L. Tinker (1887–1942), Osage, was the first Native American to attain the rank of major general in the U.S. Army Air Forces. After the Japanese attacked Pearl Harbor in 1941, he was appointed commander of the Air Forces in Hawaii to reorganize air defenses. Leading a force during the Battle of Midway in June 1942, his plane went down and was lost in the ocean. Tinker, who died on June 7, 1942, with his crew, became the first U.S. Army general to be killed in World War II. The recipient of many honors, he was posthumously awarded the Distinguished Service Medal. Oklahoma City Air Depot was named Tinker Field in his honor and became known as Tinker Air Force Base. Tinker's family members and tribal nation continue to honor him as well, including with a song written as a tribute to him, "one of their most honored heroes."

1944: Ola Mildred Rexroat (1917–2017), Oglala Lakota, was the first (and only) Native Amer-

Clarence L. Tinker

Ola Mildred Rexroat

ican woman to serve in the Women Airforce Service Pilots (WASP). After earning a bachelor's degree in art from the University of New Mexico in 1939, she became interested in flying and attended WASP training, graduating at Sweetwater, Texas. Rexroat then spent time towing targets for live fire exercises by aerial gunnery students and helping to transport personnel and cargo. After the war drew to a close and the WASPs were disbanded, she joined the Air Force, serving for ten years as an air traffic controller at Kirkland Air Force Base in New Mexico, work she also did for the Federal Aviation Administration for 33 years. In 2007, she was inducted into the South Dakota Aviation Hall of Fame. On March 10, 2010, the WASPs, including her, were honored with a Congressional Gold Medal for their service to the nation. Rexroat, who lived to be 99, was buried at Arlington National Cemetery. Following her death, the airfield operations building at Ellsworth Air Force Base in South Dakota was named in her honor.

1953: The Thunderbirds, the name attributed to Native American influences, were officially formed as an aerobatic squadron at the Luke airbase in Maricopa County, Arizona.

Lauren Arnett Campbell

Staff Sergeant Lauren Arnett Campbell, Native American, became the first female aerial gunner in the Air Force Reserve. Deployed to Afghanistan, she flew over 145 combat sorties with a helicopter rescue unit. She is one of the veterans featured in "Experiencing War: Stories from the Veterans History Project" by the Library of Congress. In her oral history interview, she describes a schedule of flying alternating 12-hour shifts and her impressions of Afghanistan. Campbell's service locations included Patrick Air Force Base, Florida; Helmand Region, Afghanistan; and Kirtland Air Force Base, New Mexico.

2021: Captain Haida StarEagle, Matinecock, became the first female Native American intelligence officer of the U.S. Space Force. A 17-year veteran of the Air Force, she served as a flight commander of training with the 36th Intelligence Squadron at Joint Base Langley-Eustis (JBLE), Virginia. StarEagle, a Brooklyn native, was chosen in December to change branches and was slated to remain with the 36th until her new duty title and station were approved. She was inducted into the Space Force at JBLE on March 12, 2021.

ARMY

1866: The enlistment of Indian scouts was first authorized by Congress as part of a reorganization bill for the Army. The provision stipulated: "The President is authorized to enlist and employ in the Territories and Indian country a force of Indians not to exceed one thousand to act as scouts, who shall receive the pay and allowances of cavalry soldiers, and be discharged whenever the necessity for further employment is abated, at the discretion of the department commander." By 1891, Army General Order No. 28 reduced the number of Indian scouts to 150. The last four scouts retired at a formal ceremony at Fort Huachuca, Arizona, in 1947.

1891: War Department General Order No. 28, issued March 9, 1891, authorized Native Americans to be enlisted in the Regular Army and serve in Indian Companies within Regular Army infantry and cavalry regiments.

1981: Vickie Morgan Jones (c. 1954–), Seneca-Cayuga, Quapaw, was the first Native American woman to graduate from the Army Aviation Center and School at Fort Rucker in Alabama. She was the first American Indian woman in the nation to become a helicopter pilot as well as the first woman to complete air assault school. Jones is depicted in a portrait, *Heritage of Valor*, painted by visual artist and Oklahoma state senator Enoch Kelly Haney. In 2018, Major (retired) Vickie Morgan Jones became the first female Native American inducted into the Oklahoma Officers Candidate School Hall of Fame.

2010: Kina Swayney (1960–2017) retired as a U.S. Army lieutenant colonel after 24 years of service; she was the highest-ranking member of the Eastern Band of Cherokee Indians (EBCI) in the tribe's history. A combat veteran, she served deployments in Bos-

Native American Numbers in Military Service

It may come as a surprise that in spite of the historical oppression and genocide of Native Americans by the U.S. military, many American Indians have served in the military since colonial times. In recent decades, they have served at a higher rate in proportion to their population than any other ethnic group. There is much speculation as to the reasons why: some serve to reaffirm treaty alliances, others may perceive military service as an extension of their warrior traditions, several are citizens of Native nations that have declared war independently on foreign enemies of the United States, many see the military as a career opportunity, and others serve for sheer love of home and country. Arab Americans have the second highest percentage of any ethnic group to serve in the military.

nia/Kosovo, Kuwait, Iraq, Afghanistan, Egypt, and Kazakhstan. In 2009, Swayney was the only American Indian serving as head of the U.S. delegation to the U.S. Army while deployed to Kazakhstan. She earned a long list of commendations, including outstanding service during two terms as company commander of the 765th Transportation Battalion. In 2015, she created the Cherokee Civil Action Team, a community organization to promote ethical leadership in tribal government. In 2018, Lt. Col. Swayney was posthumously named a Beloved Woman by the EBCI.

2021: Keith Wayne Colbert (1954–), Creek Nation, was inducted into the Order of the White Plume on March 25, 2021, for his outstanding service, leadership, and contributions to the U.S. Army, becoming the first Native American to receive the prestigious award. The White Plume award, which was established in 1982, is the Army's highest medal for achievement in support of Army Family and MWR (Morale, Welfare, and Recreation) programs. Colbert, who served some 40 years, became the 467th in the line of awardees to receive the lifetime achievement award.

COAST GUARD

1927: Harold A. Tantaquidgeon (1904–1989), Mohegan, became the first Native American chief petty officer in the Coast Guard. He also became officer-in-charge of the 75-foot cutter CG-289, the first Native American to command a Coast Guard cutter. Tantaquidgeon, who enlisted on board the vessel *Pequot* in 1921, served until 1930, three of those years commanding CG-289 in Prohibition law enforcement operations. He then returned to the Mohegan Tribe in Uncasville,

Connecticut, where he and his family co-founded the Tantaquidgeon Museum. From 1952 to 1970, Tantaquidgeon was chief of the Mohegan.

1942: Howard J. Kischassey (1903–1991), Little Traverse Bay Band of Odawa Indians, was promoted to warrant radio electrician, becoming the Coast Guard's first Native American warrant officer. Kischassey, who had transferred from the Navy, began his career in the Coast Guard in 1921. By 1938, he had become a chief radioman and was serving as officer-in-charge of the Coast Guard Station at Dam Neck, Virginia, overseeing a crew. By the time he retired in March 1947, Kischassey was the first Native American to serve as a warrant officer, lieutenant junior grade, and lieutenant.

2015: Michelle Roberts, Tlingit, became the first identified female Alaska Native to achieve the rank of chief petty officer in the U.S. Coast Guard.

2020: Canada's first Indigenous coast guard auxiliary was launched in British Columbia. The auxiliary consists of 50 volunteer members from five First Nations along the B.C. coast—Ahousat, Heiltsuk, Gitxaala, Nisgaa, and Kitasoo. The Indigenous Canadian Coast Guard Auxiliary works in tandem with the Canadian Coast Guard to complete missions. Besides having extensive knowledge of territorial waters, the Indigenous auxiliary can respond to areas in its vicinity more quickly.

MARINE CORPS

2018: Leandra Begay (c. 1997–), Navajo, a combat soldier in the U.S. Marine Corps who completed training at Camp Geiger, North Carolina Infantry Training Battalion, was sent to her first duty, becoming the first woman in her combat unit. The great-great-granddaughter of Navajo Code Talker Jimmie Clark, Begay is believed to be the first female Native American Marine in a combat role. She is a member of the 1st Battalion 2nd Marine Division at Camp Lejeune, North Carolina; her military occupational specialty (MOS) is 03-11, known as the infantry rifleman (in her case, riflewoman).

Captain Anneliese Satz

2019: Anneliese Satz (c. 1990–), Shoshone-Bannock, became the first female pilot of the F-35B jet fighter in the U.S. Marine Corps (USMC) after being the first woman to complete USMC's F-35B Basic Course. Before joining the Corps, Captain Satz earned her commercial pilot license flying helicopters. U.S. senator Mike Crapo (R-Idaho), who submitted a Congressional Record Statement honoring her on September 9, 2019, noted her first operational unit as the Green Knights of Marine Fighter Attack Squadron 121 in Iwakuni, Japan.

NATIONAL GUARD

2005: LaRita A. "Rita" Aragon (1947–), Choctaw and honorary Citizen Potawatomi, became the first woman of Native American descent to hold the rank of brigadier general in the U.S. Air National Guard. In a career with multiple firsts, she was also the first female commander of Oklahoma's Air National Guard and the first woman to serve as secretary of military and veteran affairs for the state of Oklahoma. She was inducted into the Oklahoma Hall of Fame in 2016.

2008: Crystal N. Ralston, Cherokee/Apache/Paiute, became a U.S. Air Force technical sergeant in the Air National Guard, Indiana, the first Native woman to hold the position of an airman in that state. She had served for three years in the Missouri National Guard before reenlisting with the 122nd Fighter Wing as a services troop.

2016: Joane "Joni" K. Mathews, Lac du Flambeau Band of Lake Superior Chippewa Indians, became the first female brigadier general in the Wisconsin Army Guard and the first female Native American general officer in the entire Army National Guard. She was also the first female commander of the Wisconsin Army Guard's 1st Battalion, 147th Aviation Regiment; the first female brigade commander in Wisconsin Army Guard history; the Wisconsin Army Guard's first nonmedical female colonel; and the first female chief of staff in the organization's history. Mathews earned a bachelor of arts degree in aviation administration, advanced degrees, and completed numerous military courses. Mathews served nearly 11 years on active duty, which included flying missions and supporting the no-fly zone in northern Iraq. In 2020, she was nominated for promotion to major general.

Joane K. Mathews

NAVY

1860: The first U.S. Navy ship to be named for Pocahontas, the famous daughter of Virginia's Chief Powhatan, was a steamer that was originally built in Boston, Massachusetts, in 1852 and purchased by the U.S. Navy in 1855. Originally commissioned as the USS *Despatch* on January 17, 1856, the vessel was recommissioned and renamed the USS *Pocahontas* in 1860. The USS *Pocahontas*, which was decommissioned in 1865, saw action in the American Civil War.

1908: The first U.S. naval ship named in honor of the Navajo was commissioned. *Navajo I* (Tug) was built in 1907 and operated in the Hawaiian Islands performing towing and docking operations. Stricken from the Navy list in 1937, *Navajo* was later placed in service in 1942 for use during World War II. Following wartime service, the tug was stricken again in 1946 and sold for scrap in 1948.

1942: For the first time, a naval vessel was named in honor of a Native woman. The Maritime Commission acquired and christened a harbor tug, *Sacagawea* (YT-241), named after the Shoshone guide for Lewis and Clark. However, it was never commissioned by the Navy.

1953: Solomon Atkinson (1930–2019), Metlakatla Indian Community, was the first Alaskan Native to join the Underwater Demolition Teams (UDT), the precursor to Sea-Air-Land (SEAL) teams of the Navy's elite special warfare community. He was on the very first SEAL team created by President John F. Kennedy in 1962 and helped train new recruits. Atkinson also trained 48 astronauts, including Neil Armstrong, Buzz Aldrin, and Jim Lovell, in underwater weightlessness simulations. He completed three combat tours in Vietnam, earning awards and medals for personal valor, including the Bronze Star and the Purple Heart. Fellow SEALs said of him: "Sol's story will continue to be told by the men he trained, by the officers who relied on him, by the Frogmen who all respect him. An officer, a gentleman, an athlete, a friend, Sol Atkinson is all of these; but of all these traits, he is first

a Frogman." After 22 years of service in the Navy (1951–1973), Atkinson retired and returned to Metlakatla, where he was instrumental in starting and leading the first veteran organization. He also served as Metlakatla's mayor for two terms, working to improve roads, houses, and other services for the community.

1957: Dr. George Blue Spruce (1931–), Laguna/Ohkay Owingeh Pueblo, American Indian dentist, then serving in the U.S. Navy Submarine Fleet, received a special assignment to perform dental work for the crew members of the USS *Nautilus*, the world's first operational nuclear-powered submarine. The dentistry was essential to preparing the teeth of crew members to withstand the high pressures they would experience on a path-breaking journey to the North Pole.

1998: Misty Dawn Warren (1974–1999), Choctaw, was the first American Indian woman and only the eighth female to achieve designation as naval test parachutist. She enlisted in the U.S. Navy in January 1998 and later that year attended Basic Airborne School at Fort Benning, Georgia, where she earned her Basic Parachutist Jump Wings. Warren's dream was to enter the space program after completing her tour of duty in the Navy, but she experienced equipment failure during her 75th jump and died on June 15, 1999.

2003: The USNS *Benavidez*, a Bob Hope-class roll-on/roll-off vehicle cargo ship of the U.S. Navy, became the first ship named in honor of Army Master Sergeant Raul "Roy" P. Benavidez (1935–1998), Yaqui/Mexican, recipient of the Medal of Honor. The *Benavidez* was activated for Operation Enduring Freedom and arrived in the Persian Gulf with replacement equipment for units in Iraq. Master Sergeant Benavidez received the Medal of Honor in 1981 in recognition of his "daring and extremely valorous actions" in combat as a staff sergeant during the Vietnam War.

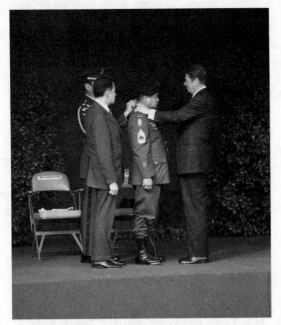

President Ronald Reagan presented Master Sergeant Roy P. Benavidez with the Medal of Honor in 1981.

2019: The U.S. Navy announced that towing, salvage, and rescue ships (T-ATS) would be known as the Navajo-class of ships to honor the contributions of Navajo people to the armed forces. Vessels in this class are named for Native American tribal nations or prominent Native Americans. They include USNS *Navajo*, USNS *Cherokee Nation*, USNS *Saginaw Ojibwe Anishinabek*, and the 2021-announced USNS *Muscogee Creek Nation*.

2020: Cherokee Federal Red Wing was selected to join the first multibillion-dollar contract awarded by the U.S. Navy's Commander, Fleet Readiness Centers (COMFRC). COMFRC awarded the 10-year, $6.1 billion contract among 42 small business industry partners, enabling the U.S. Navy, government customers, and international partners to procure aircraft maintenance services and other support more quickly. Cherokee Federal's engineering and manufacturing service is a subsidiary of Cherokee Nation Businesses and has provided aerospace and defense services for more than 50 years.

LEGISLATION/RECOGNITION

1919: As enacted by Congress on November 6, 1919, American Indian veterans of World War I were granted the right to petition for U.S. citizenship. The legislation stated in part: "That every American Indian who served in the Military or Naval Establishments of the United States during the war against the Imperial German Government, and who has received or who shall hereafter receive an honorable discharge, if not now a citizen and if he so desires, shall, on proof of such

The USNS *Navajo* T-ATS 6 coat of arms

discharge and after proper identification before a court of competent jurisdiction ... be granted full citizenship...."

2008: The Code Talkers Recognition Act of 2008 was enacted by Congress to require the issuance of medals to recognize the service of Native American code talkers to the United States. It identified specific tribes to consult for names of applicable servicemen: Assiniboine, Chippewa and Oneida, Choctaw, Comanche, Cree, Crow, Hopi, Kiowa, Menominee, Mississauga, Muscogee, Sac and Fox, and Sioux. The legislation also specified means of providing future information to accommodate updates.

2013: Thirty-three tribes were recognized in Emancipation Hall at the U.S. Capitol on November 20, 2013, for the dedication and valor of Native American code talkers to the U.S. Armed Services during World War I and World War II. Of the tribal nations recognized, 25 were presented with Congressional Gold Medals.

2021: Governor Doug Ducey signed legislation making National Navajo Code Talkers Day an official state holiday in Arizona every year on August 14. State senator Jamescita Peshlakai sponsored the legislation to honor the code talkers for their crucial service during World War II. If National Navajo Code Talkers Day falls on a day other than Sunday, the Sunday following August 14 is to be observed as the holiday. The Navajo Nation observes August 14 as a tribal holiday, commemorating the day Japan announced it would surrender to Allied forces.

WHY WE SERVE

"I'll only say that in the memory of our brave fathers I will try and be like one of them, who used to stand single-handed against the foes."

—*William Pollock, Pawnee, Rough Rider*

"We serve this country because it's our land. We have a sacred purpose to protect this place."

—*Jeffrey Begay, Diné (Navajo) veteran*

"I am an Indian and never had any experience in a war before, but I realize that I was doing my duty as a patriot and was fighting to save democracy and do hope that in the future we Indians may enjoy freedom which we Indians are always denied."

—*Joe High Elk, Cheyenne River Sioux, World War I veteran*

"We wanted to do our share in the big fight, and we tried to do it."

—*Charles Sorrell, Shoshone, World War I veteran*

"In our heart, this is still our land, so we're fighting still for our land."

—*Mitchelene BigMan, Apsaalooke (Crow)/ Hidatsa, veteran and founder of Native American Women Warriors organization*

MEMORIALS

1921: Chief Plenty Coups (1848–1932), Crow, was invited to represent Native Americans at the dedication of the Tomb of the Unknown Soldier at Arlington National Ceremony in Washington, D.C. on November 11, 1921. During the ceremony, he placed his eagle feather headdress and coup stick at the tomb. "I am glad to represent all the Indians of the United States" at the dedication, Plenty Coups said, noting that each eagle feather "represents a deed of valor by my race."

1926: The Haskell Archway leading to the stadium at Haskell Institute (now Haskell

Crow Nation chief Plenty Coups attends a burial at the Tomb of the Unknown Soldier in 1921.

Indian Nations University) in Lawrence, Kansas, was dedicated as the first World War I memorial in the United States and drew thousands of people. The event, the largest in Lawrence history, included Haskell's first intertribal powwow. Haskell alumni Agnes Quapaw and Alice Beaver Hallam, both Quapaw, contributed to a capital campaign to build the Haskell Stadium, designating their funds for an archway to the facility. More than 2,500 tribal peoples donated 250,000 to Haskell's capital campaign, which was used to build the stadium.

1947: Commissioned by the Haskell Alumni Association in 1947, Chiricahua Apache artist Allan Houser (1914–1994) created *Comrade in Mourning,* a memorial to those who gave their lives during World War II. The sculpture, which was dedicated on January 28, 1949, was the first public monument in the United States by a Native American. It remains on display at Haskell Indian Nations University, one of the memorials that honor veterans.

1998: The Pentagon held the first ceremony recognizing the military service contributions of Native Americans. The American Indian and Alaska Native Veterans Recognition Ceremony, which was observed in honor of Veteran's Day and Native American Heritage Month, marked "the first time that Native American veterans from all services have been honored together in the Pentagon."

1999: *Ka Lehua Helele'i* (The Scattered Lehua Blossoms) went up in front of the Fort De-Russy Army Museum in Waikiki, Hawaii. Rocky Ka'iouliokahihikolo'Ehu Jensen (1944–), acclaimed Native Hawaiian sculptor, artist, and cultural practitioner, carved the monumental *kukalepa* (memorial to fallen Hawaiian warriors) from Native ohia logs, the largest he had ever seen. Jensen designed the five statues to be a Hawaiian Stonehenge, rising from the ground like fingers from a hand, each piece similar but with differences. Each column represents a different face of the Hawaiian god of war, Kunuiakea. Never before had Native Hawaiian military history been publicly honored.

2000: A previously unnamed bridge on Alaska's George Parks Highway was named the Alaska Native Veterans' Honor Bridge to commemorate Alaska Natives who have served in the U.S. Armed Forces and had not been formally recognized before by the state. The bridge was chosen in part because it "symbolizes that the distinct culture of all Alaska Natives and non-natives are bridged by their common service to country."

2001: The National Aboriginal Veterans Monument, the first such monument honoring all Indigenous veterans of Canada, was unveiled in Confederation Park in Ottawa, Ontario, Canada. Artist Lloyd Pinay, Pee-

The Haskell Arch at Haskell Indian Nations University was dedicated on October 30, 1926, to the 415 Haskell students who served during World War I.

Indigenous Firsts: A History of Native American Achievements and Events

peekisis First Nation, designed the bronze statue to represent all Aboriginal peoples who served in war and peacekeeping operations from World War I to the present. The monument depicts a golden eagle (symbolic as both the Creator and the spirit of Indigenous peoples) as the messenger between the Creator and man. Four human figures, facing the four cardinal points, represent First Nations, Inuit, and Métis. Female figures honor the role of women; the human depictions hold both war and spiritual items. Each of the four animal figures, one on each corner, symbolizes a special attribute: a wolf (family values); a buffalo (tenacity); an elk (wariness); and a bear (healing powers).

2002: For the first time, a monument honoring Indigenous people went on display in the Battle of Little Big Horn Battlefield National Monument in Montana. Designed by Lakota artist Colleen Cutschall (1951–), the iron statue, *Spirit Warriors*, commemorates Native American warriors in the Black Hills War (1876).

2007: Vernon Tsoodle (1931–2011), Kiowa, was the first Native American to be inducted into the Oklahoma Military Hall of Fame. As a teenager, Tsoodle joined the all-Indian company of the 45th Infantry Division and served in World War II. In 1949, he enlisted in the U.S. Marine Corps and the following year was deployed to Korea, where he participated in the defense of the Puson Peninsula and was later awarded the Bronze Star for his actions. Tsoodle also served as communications chief for an artillery battery in the Vietnam War. In 1996, Tsoodle was instrumental in the development of the Native American Marine Corps Veterans Organization.

2008: The Choctaw Nation of Oklahoma became the first American Indian tribe to re-

The American Indian Veterans National Memorial is located at the Heard Museum in Phoenix, Arizona. It was designed by John Douglas Architects in Phoenix and debuted in 2012.

ceive the Secretary of Defense Employer Support Freedom Award. It is the highest recognition given by the U.S. government to employers that provide outstanding support of employees serving in the National Guard and Reserve. The Choctaw Nation has a veterans advocacy program and other services to assist their service member employees and troops. *

2012: The American Indian Veterans National Memorial, "the first and only known national memorial to American Indian veterans of many conflicts," opened to the public at the Heard Museum in Phoenix, Arizona. It features pieces by acclaimed sculptors Allan Houser, Chiricahua Apache, and Michael Naranjo, Santa Clara Pueblo, as well as panels noting Native service and sacrifice spanning more than three centuries. Naranjo, a Vietnam War veteran who suffered an injury that caused him to become blind, carves his sculptures by touch.

2013: Jeremiah "Jerry" Wolfe (1924–2018) was designated the first Beloved Man of the Eastern Band of Cherokee Indians (EBCI) in over 200 years, the first since Little Turkey, who died in 1801. Wolfe was honored for his military service in the U.S. Navy during World War II, which included participating in the Normandy invasion on June 6, 1944, and for extensive other contributions. He was one of the veterans featured in connection with the Charles George Beloved Veterans Hall, which officially opened

Charles Shay

at the Museum of the Cherokee Indian on Veterans Day in 2019. In 2020, the North Carolina Board of Transportation approved a resolution to dedicate a stretch of highway between U.S. 19 and U.S. 74 as the Beloved Man Dr. Jerry Wolfe Highway. Western Carolina University had honored Wolfe with an honorary doctorate of humane letters degree in May 2017.

2015: The Fort Hall Reservation, home of the Shoshone-Bannock Tribes, became the first reservation in the United States to be recognized as a Purple Heart Reservation. The Military Order of the Purple Heart (MOPH) held a recognition ceremony at the Tribal Business Center in Fort Hall. The designation and event honor veterans. Fort Hall officials received plaques identifying the reservation's status as a Purple Heart Reservation during the ceremony.

2016: Honor Flight Nevada, a nonprofit organization with the mission of transporting military veterans to Washington, D.C., to tour the nation's capital and visit veteran memorials, organized the first all–Native American Honor Flight. The three-day trip, with some 43 Native veterans from the Great Basin area participating, visited the National Museum of the American Indian as well as monuments such as the National World War II Memorial, Vietnam Veterans Memorial, and the Iwo Jima Marine Memorial.

2017: Charles Shay Indian Memorial Park was dedicated at France's Saint-Laurent-sur-Mer to honor all North American Indians who landed in Normandy on June 6, 1944, as part of the Allied invasion to liberate Western Europe. The park is named for Charles Norman Shay, Penobscot, one of two American Indian combat medics to survive the war and one of the last living World War II veterans. The Charles Shay Memorial honors the 175 American Indian soldiers who landed on Omaha Beach on D-Day, some 55 of whom have been identified. An estimated 500 Native Americans participated in Operation Neptune (D-Day) as paratroopers or ground troops landing on the beaches. Shay traveled to Normandy in 2007 and has returned nearly every year after that. His other honors include being inducted into the Légion d'Honneur by

Four members of the Native American Women Warriors: U.S. Army: Capt. Calley Cloud, Crow; Spc. Krissy Quinones Cloud, Crow; Retired Sfc. Mitchelene BigMan, Crow, the group's president and founder; and Sgt. Lisa Marshall, Cheyenne River Sioux.

Native American Women Warriors

The Native American Women Warriors (NAWW), the first all–Native American female color guard, was founded in 2010 by Mitchelene BigMan, Apsáalooke (Crow)/Hidatsa (1965–), to recognize female veterans and their contributions to the military and the nation. NAWW members, dressed in specially designed jingle dresses, marched in President Barack Obama's inaugural parade in January 2013 and have served as color guards at other events. BigMan served in the military from 1987 to 2009, including tours of duty in Germany, Korea, and Iraq. NAWW, a nonprofit organization, works to raise awareness about Native American women veterans and to assist them with support services. BigMan, NAWW's president, was honored as a Champion of Change at the White House in 2014.

France's then-president Nicolas Sarkozy. Shay is the author of *Project Omaha Beach: The Life and Military Service of a Penobscot Indian Elder*.

2018: A 37-foot totem pole, raised at Alaska's Prince of Wales Island to honor veterans, is believed to be the first for this purpose. Some 30 years in the making, the Veterans Totem Pole was fostered by Aaron Isaacs Jr., a former Alaska Army National Guardsman and U.S. Army 82nd Airborne paratrooper, who worked with carver Jon Rowan, a U.S. Marine Corps veteran, to design the totem. It depicts service branches and a Prisoner of War/Missing in Action insignia as well as other representations and was raised at a ceremony on August 18, 2018.

2018: Actor and producer Wes Studi (1947–), Cherokee, delivered a historic and moving tribute to veterans at the Academy Awards ceremony; he is believed to be the first American Indian to present at the Oscars, and part of his speech was in the Cherokee language, another first. Studi, a Vietnam veteran, commented: "I think that it was high time that veterans were honored, as well as it was high time the academy had a Native as a presenter." In 2019, he became the first Native American to receive an Honorary Oscar for his storied career in film.

2018: The Canadian Forces Leadership and Recruit School (CFLRS) in Saint-Jean-sur-Richelieu, Quebec, Canada, inaugurated the first permanent Canadian Armed Forces Indigenous Spiritual Lodge in the history of the Canadian Armed Forces. During an inaugural ceremony on December 7, 2018, Lieutenant-Commander Martin Poëti, chaplain of the Canadian Forces Leadership and Recruit School, noted: "The Saint-Jean Garrison now has a chapel for Catholics and Protestants, a multifaith centre for Jews and Muslims, and a Place for Peace—an Indigenous Spiritual Lodge. Although the spiritual lodge is open to everyone regardless of spiritual, religious, or philosophical affiliation, it is designed and built to meet the needs of Indigenous military personnel who wish to celebrate their ancestral practices and rich spiritual heritage."

VETERAN CEMETERIES

2013: Yurok Veterans Cemetery was completed on the Yurok Indian Reservation in Weitchpec, California, one of the first Veterans Administration (VA)-funded cemeteries in the nation. It includes 500 burial sites, a solar-powered committal shelter, a maintenance building, an avenue of flags, and a memorial kiosk. It also includes design elements reflecting Yurok culture, such as a native plant landscape incorporating the tribe's ethnobotany.

2013: Sicangu Akicita Owicahe Tribal Veterans Cemetery (also known as Rosebud Sioux Tribe Veterans Cemetery), deemed the first National Native American Cemetery, opened on Memorial Day on the Rosebud Sioux Reservation in Mellette County, South Dakota. It was made possible by a grant from the Department of Veterans Affairs and was the first cemetery in the nation established jointly by the VA and a federally recognized tribe. It is the first of its kind to be awarded to a sovereign tribal nation. The cemetery's Lakota name, Sicangu Akicita Owicahe, is translated as Rosebud Tribal Veteran. Rosebud "has more than 4,000 U.S. military veterans, the highest per capita of any ethnic group, and the cemetery serves to honor them as both US veterans and Lakota warriors." It was designed in the shape of a turtle, which symbolizes life, longevity, and fortitude in Lakota culture.

2016: Joseph Medicine Crow (1913–2016), the Crow Tribe's last surviving war chief and a widely renowned historian, was the first person to be buried in the Apsaalooke Veterans Cemetery, newly created by the Crow Tribe in 2015.

2017: The Houlton Band of Maliseet Indians in Maine dedicated its tribal veterans cemetery, the first located east of the Mississippi River. It was completed with a grant from the U.S. Veterans Administration's National Cemetery Program.

2020: The U.S. Department of Veterans Affairs (VA) broke ground on the first American Indian Veterans Memorial at a VA national cemetery. Located at Riverside National Cemetery in California, it is the VA's first major monument honoring American Indian, Alaska Native, and Pacific Islander veterans. The memorial, which is being paid for with funds raised by the Riverside National Cemetery Support Committee, consists of a plaza and walkway centered on *The Gift*, a bronze statue representing an American Indian.

Joseph Medicine Crow

◆◈◆

VETERAN ORGANIZATIONS AND SERVICES

1927: The All Indian American Legion Post 38 was formed in White Eagle, Oklahoma, and named after Alfred Little Standing Buffalo, Ponca, a World War I combat veteran. Buffalo Post 38, as it is also known, was reported to be the first post in the nation comprised entirely of American Indians. After World War II, the post became inactive but was reactivated in 1946. Today, it is the oldest veterans' organization in the Ponca community.

1943: The Otoe War Mothers in Oklahoma became the first all-Indian Chapter of the American War Mothers Organization. The founding members were mothers of Otoe children who were serving in the Armed Services. The nonprofit, nonsectarian, nonpolitical organization has continued to provide services, such as sending care packages, hosting dinners on Memorial Day and Veterans Day, and assisting those in ill health.

1997: Iva Good Voice Flute (1968–), Oglala Lakota, Air Force veteran, founded an American Legion Post, Legion Post 321, of Native women military veterans on the Pine Ridge Reservation in South Dakota. She was joined by Darlene Yellow Cloud, who served as commander, and Jerlene Arredondo, post vice commander, and other veterans. Good Voice Flute, who served as post adjutant, also provided oral history for the Women in the Military Service Memorial project.

2006: The Muskogee Veteran Administration Medical Center in Oklahoma became the first VA facility to be renamed in honor of a Native American. The new name honors World War II Medal of Honor recipient Jack C. Montgomery, Cherokee Nation.

2009: Maine became the first state to commemorate its Native American veterans, establishing Native American Veterans Day to be observed every June 21. Charles Norman Shay, Penobscot elder and decorated World War II veteran, said the annual commemoration would "remind the general public, as well as our own Native communities, about Native American contributions and sacrifices to the spirit of freedom, and to honor those who have served or are now serving our country."

2010: Pedro "Pete" Molina (Pascua Yaqui) became the nation's first assistant secretary for Native American veterans affairs when he was sworn in by Roger Brautigan, the director of the California Department of Veteran Affairs. California created the new position to administer services to Native American veterans in the state, reportedly the largest population of American Indian veterans in the country.

2016: The first Tribal Housing and Urban Development-Veterans Affairs Supportive Housing (HUD-VASH) program was launched to assist Native American veterans who are homeless or at risk of homelessness. The demonstration program, which aims to end homelessness among veterans on tribal lands, provided for 5.9 million in assistance to some 26 tribes.

2018: The Lumbee Tribe launched what it identified as the first American Indian program to aid disabled veterans, the outcome of a partnership among the tribe, the U.S. Department of Labor, and the North Carolina Department of Commerce. The focus is to assist disabled veterans in finding careers where they can earn a decent income and improve their quality of life.

SOVEREIGNTY, LAND, AND THE ENVIRONMENT

"... all treaties made, or which shall be made, under the authority of the United States, shall be the supreme law of the land...."

—*U.S. Constitution, Article VI*

TREATIES

1613: Two Row Wampum, or the Guswenta, was the first treaty recorded between the Haudenosaunee and Europeans, an agreement of mutual respect and noninterference with the Dutch who entered Iroquois territory.

1778: The Treaty with the Delawares, which was negotiated by commissioners of the United States and Delaware leaders, was the first formal treaty between a Native American nation and the newly established U.S. government. Signed at Fort Pitt in Pennsylvania on September 17, 1778, it is considered a treaty of "peace and friendship" between sovereign nations.

1830: The Treaty of Dancing Rabbit Creek, negotiated at Dancing Rabbit Creek in Mississippi with the Choctaw tribal nation, was the first of the removal treaties between the U.S. government and American Indians after the passage of the Indian Removal Act of 1830. The treaty marked the final cession of Choctaw lands east of the Mississippi River and outlined terms of removal. The Choctaw Nation was the first American Indian tribe to be removed by the federal government from its ancestral homeland to present-day Oklahoma.

1868: The Navajo became the only Native Nation to use a treaty with the federal government to escape removal and return to their homeland. Written on paper from an army ledger book, it was called *Naal Tsoos Sani* ("Old Paper") in the Navajo language. The treaty went on display at the Smithsonian's National Museum of the American Indian and later traveled to the Navajo Nation Museum in Window Rock, Arizona, in 2018. During that period, the Navajo Nation received a contribution of one of three originals of the document known to exist, the gift believed to make it "the first tribe to possess an original copy of its treaty with the government" according to Navajo Nation Museum director Manuelito Wheeler.

1913: The Northwest Federation of American Indians (NFAI), the first intertribal treaty rights organization, was founded by Thomas G. Bishop, Snohomish, in Washington State.

1977: The first conference to be held at the United Nations on Indigenous Populations of the Americas was organized by the International Indian Treaty Council (IITC).

2000: On March 18, 2000, Johnny M. Lehi Sr., president of the San Juan Southern Paiute Tribe, and Kelsey Begaye, president of the Navajo Nation, signed the first treaty that the two tribal nations had signed with each other in 160 years. The treaty allows the Paiutes approximately 5,400 acres of land of their own.

2014: American Indian and First Nation tribal nations made history by signing a cross-border Indigenous treaty for the first time in 150 years, establishing an intertribal alliance to restore bison to 6.3 million acres of land between the United States and Canada. The treaty signing occurred on September 23, 2014, on Blackfeet Territory in Montana and included the Blackfeet Nation, Blood Tribe, Siksika Nation, Piikani Nation, Assiniboine, and Gros Ventre Tribes of Fort Belknap Reservation, Assiniboine and Sioux Tribes of Fort Peck Indian Reservation, Salish and Kootenai Tribes of the Confederated Salish and Kootenai Indian Reservation, and Tsuu T'ina Nation. Often called the "buffalo treaty," other nations have since joined the agreement of cooperation, renewal, and restoration to preserve prairie ecosystems and Indigenous cultural and spiritual relationships with buffalo.

2020: Hundreds of Native American treaties were conserved and digitized for the first time by the U.S. National Archives in Washington, D.C., and the Museum of Indian Arts and Culture in Santa Fe, New Mexico. The online collection features 374 ratified Indian treaties from the National Archives' holdings. These documents, many in fragile con-

Suzan Shown Harjo

Suzan Shown Harjo, Cheyenne/Hodulgee Muscogee leader, writer, and activist, became the first woman to receive an honorary doctor of humanities degree from the Institute of American Indian Arts in 2011. She was the first Vine Deloria Jr. Distinguished Indigenous Scholar at the University of Arizona in 2008, the first person to be awarded back-to-back fellowships by the School for Advanced Research in 2004, and the first Native woman to be honored as a Montgomery Fellow at Dartmouth College in 1992. Honored with a Presidential Medal of Freedom in 2014, Harjo was awarded the National Conference on Race and Ethnicity in American Higher Education's first Activist for Systemic Social Justice Award in 2015. She edited *Nation to Nation: Treaties between the United States and American Indian Nations*, the companion volume to an exhibition by the same name that opened at the National Museum of the American Indian in 2014.

dition, are of ongoing importance to tribal nations, representing binding legal agreements. The digitization project was completed with funding from an anonymous donor, making access to these highly significant documents possible. Viewers can use Indigenous Digital Archive (IDA) Treaties Explorer, a tool optimized for searching and studying the materials.

TRIBAL GOVERNMENT

"Indian Tribes are distinct political communities, retaining their original rights as the undisputed possessors of the soil from time immemorial ... The very term *nation*, so generally applied to them, means a people distinct from others, having territorial boundaries, within which their authority is exclusive, and having a right to all the lands within those boundaries, which is not only acknowledged but guaranteed by the United States."

—1832 U.S. Supreme Court ruling
Worcester v. Georgia

1827: The Cherokee Nation adopted its first modern constitution.

1861: While allied with the Confederate States of American during the U.S. Civil War, Choctaws in Indian Territory (present-day Oklahoma) became the first U.S. tribe to adopt a flag. It was used between 1861 and 1864 and continued to inspire later Choctaw flags.

1935: The Confederated Salish and Kootenai Tribes of the Flathead Reservation in Montana adopted the first tribal constitution drafted under the Indian Reorganization Act of 1934.

1936: Hydaburg became the first village in Alaska to form an Indian Reorganization Act (IRA) Council after the IRA was amended to include Alaska Natives.

1971: The Muscogee elected a principal chief without presidential approval, the first time since the partial dismantling of their national government.

1974: The Red Lake Band of Chippewa Indians in Minnesota became the first tribal nation in the country to issue its own vehicle license plates. The vehicle-licensing authority, an exercise of tribal sovereignty, was upheld by the Minnesota Supreme Court.

1981: The Menominee Indian Tribe was the first tribal nation in Wisconsin to enter into a reciprocity agreement with the state, operating in cooperation with the Wisconsin Department of Transportation, Division of Motor Vehicles. The full-service licensing department, which follows Tribal Ordinance 85-21, provides Menominee Nation license plates, vehicle titles, and registration and related services.

1984: The first joint council meeting in nearly a century and a half was held between the Eastern Band of Cherokee and the Cherokee Nation of Oklahoma, the historic gathering taking place in Red Clay, Tennessee.

1989: The Centennial Accord was developed and signed by 26 federally recognized tribes and the State of Washington, marking the first such relationship to strengthen tribal and state government-to-government relations in the nation. The Snoqualmie, the Samish, and the Cowlitz later signed the accord after becoming federally recognized. The Yakama and Kalispel tribes, who believed their primary relationship was with the federal government, declined to sign the agreement. The Warm Springs, Umatilla, and Nez Perce tribes, out-of-state tribes with treaty-reserved rights within Washington State, became party to the accord in 2004.

1995: Charles W. Blackwell (1942–2013), Chickasaw, was named Chickasaw Nation ambassador to the United States during a ceremony in Washington, D.C., becoming the first American Indian tribal ambassador to the U.S. government. A graduate of the University of New Mexico School of Law, Blackwell was nationally known for his advocacy of tribal sovereignty and work on behalf of Native people. Chickasaw Nation governor Bill Anoatubby appointed Blackwell as a delegate to the United States in 1990.

2002: Tribal chiefs in Maine addressed a joint session of the state legislature on March 11, 2002, the first time in Maine's legislative history.

2008: The Coquille Indian Tribe in Oregon passed a law allowing same-sex marriage, believed to be the first tribal nation to enact a marriage equality measure. The legalization went into effect in 2009, with Kitzen Branting and her partner Jeni Branting becoming the first same-sex couple to have their marriage recognized by the tribe. The Coquille law requires tribal membership by at least one partner.

2008: The Coushatta Tribe of Louisiana became the first Native American tribe to sign an affirmation of friendship with the State of Israel, according to Asher Yarden, Israel's consul general. The signing ceremony was held on the reservation in Elton, Louisiana, with some 300 people in attendance. Representatives hoped to develop business relationships and exchanges.

2009: The Confederated Tribes of the Umatilla Indian Reservation (CTUIR) in Oregon became the first tribal nation in the country to comply with, and implement, the Sex Offender Registration and Notification Act (SORNA) passed by Congress in 2006. CTUIR and the state of Ohio were the first two jurisdictions in the country to comply with SORNA (aka the Adam Walsh Act).

2014: The governing body of the Three Affiliated Tribes of the Fort Berthold Indian Reservation in North Dakota (Mandan, Hidatsa, Arikara, or MHA Nation) approved the Human Trafficking Code (Loren's Law), the first tribal code that addresses both labor and sex trafficking.

2014: Washington's Tulalip, Oregon's Umatilla, and Arizona's Pascua Yaqui, participants in a Department of Justice pilot program, became the first tribal nations to meet the legal requirements to begin prosecuting non-Natives under provisions of the 2013 reauthorization of the Violence against Women Act (VAWA). The Pascua Yaqui Tribe made history on March 26, 2014, by becoming the first tribal nation to prosecute non-Natives for domestic violence under the new legislation.

2015: The Pamunkey, located near Richmond, became the first American Indian tribe in the Commonwealth of Virginia to be federally recognized. The tribal nation, historically the largest tribe within the Powhatan Chiefdom when the English arrived at Jamestown in 1607, signed treaties with the English in 1646 and 1677. The Pamunkey, with ancestral ties to Pocahontas, now have over 200 members and some 1,200 acres of land. The tribe sought federal recognition through the Bureau of Indian Affairs, a difficult process that took more than 30 years to complete. In 2015, the Pamunkey were officially notified of the determination of their recognition petition, and it became final the following year. Consequently, the tribal nation became the 567th federally recognized tribe in the United States.

2015: The Suquamish Tribe and the State of Washington entered a marijuana compact, the first in both the state and the nation. The agreement allows for the tribal nation to cultivate, process, and sell marijuana within the state's regulated marijuana system. The compact was negotiated with the tribe by the Washington State Liquor and Cannabis Board on behalf of the state.

2016: Blackfeet Law Enforcement Services Department officer Misty Keller Salois, Blackfeet, was the first American Indian woman to become a U.S. marshall. At ceremonies celebrating her advancement, Salois was presented with an eagle feather and given the name "Crane Woman" by Chief Earl Old Person.

2016: The Cocopah Indian Tribe in Arizona signed a memorandum of agreement that made it the first tribe in the nation to become an Integrated Public Alert & Warning System (IPAWS) Collaborative Operating Group (COG). As a COG, an agency authorized by FEMA to create emergency alerts and warnings through IPAWS, Cocopah helped to enhance the tribal nation's ability to prepare for, respond to, and recover from emergencies.

2018: Trudie Jackson (1967–), Navajo, became the first out transgender and two-spirit Native woman to run for president of the Navajo Nation. Jackson is also the founder of the Southwest American Indian Rainbow Gathering, which addresses health disparities of American Indians who identify as two-spirit (2SLGBTQ). Pursuing a doctorate with a focus on American studies at the University of New Mexico, she hoped to open the first American Indian Transgender Clinic in the Southwest.

2018: The Oglala Sioux Tribe Department of Public Safety, under the direction of Police Chief Robert D. Ecoffey, became the first Native American law enforcement agency to join First Net, a program of the federal government and AT&T focused on improved communications for first responders. The program prioritizes first responders' phone calls when there are large crowds, such as powwow events, or an emergency, such as attack or weather threats.

2018: The North Dakota Indian Affairs Commission, a state agency, hosted the Strengthening Government to Government Relationships and Partnerships Conference, the first of its kind in North Dakota. The event drew more than 300 tribal, state, and federal officials and sought to rebuild relationships in the wake of the Dakota Access Pipeline protests.

2019: Albuquerque became the first city in America to recognize tribal sovereignty by establishing government-to-government relations with its adjacent tribal communities. Albuquerque's City Council voted unanimously to pass a bill amending the originating ordinance of the Commission on American Indian and Alaska Native Affairs to recognize and formalize relations between the city and surrounding pueblos and tribes. Mayor Tim Keller and tribal representatives signed the first-of-its-kind bill into law on March 12, 2019.

2019: The Bay Mills Indian Community, based in Brimley, Michigan, became the first tribe in Michigan to legalize marijuana. Its tribal ordinance is consistent with state law with respect to personal possession, cultivation, and use. Recreational marijuana use was approved by Michigan voters for the state in November 2018.

2019: The Blackfeet Nation hosted the first Murdered and Missing Indigenous Women (MMIW) tribunal in the United States on October 4 and 5 at the Blackfeet Community College in Browning, Montana. Organized by the Global Indigenous Council in association with the Rocky Mountain Tribal

Leaders Council and supported by Carlyle Consulting, it provided a forum for testimony from MMIW survivors and victims' families. The tribunal provided needed attention to "an Indian Country tragedy, and a national and international disgrace."

2019: The Cherokee Nation named Kimberly Teehee as its first delegate to the U.S. House of Representatives. The nonvoting position, which had never been filled, is one of the provisions of the 1835 Treaty of New Echota. Article 7 of the treaty stipulates that the Cherokee Nation "shall be entitled to a delegate in the House of Representatives of the United States whenever Congress shall make provision for the same."

2019: The Oglala Sioux Tribe approved a same-gender marriage ordinance in a 12–3 vote with one abstention in July 2019, becoming the first tribal nation in South Dakota to legalize same-sex marriage. Tribal members Monique "Muffie" Mousseau and Felipa De Leon successfully petitioned for the action after finding they could not be married on the reservation in 2015. The U.S. Supreme Court legalized same-sex marriage in 2015, but federally recognized tribes have the right to make their own decisions on the issue.

2019: The Winnebago Tribe of Nebraska celebrated tribal member Anthony Walker as a "Ho Chunk Hero," the first such recognition the tribal nation had bestowed. A federal officer, Walker helped save 39 people from a burning building on the Spirit Lake Reservation in North Dakota in April 2019. The tribal council proclaimed June 14 as Anthony Walker Day in Winnebago and the event started with a first responder escort into town. The honoring included a celebration at the reservation, where Walker was presented with gifts, and a meal and powwow were held for the entire community.

2020: Acoma Pueblo in New Mexico became the first Native American tribal nation in the United States to coordinate and conduct court-mandated alcohol monitoring using the Minneapolis-based AB Kiosk system, which fully automates the process. The Acoma Tribal Court installed the kiosk in the Pueblo of Acoma Law Enforcement Center, greatly reducing the time and expense of administering monitoring.

DIPLOMACY AND INTERNATIONAL RELATIONS

"Simple apologies are not sufficient. There needs to be a real reckoning."

—*Steven Newcomb, Shawnee/Lenape, on the Vatican response to the Doctrine of Discovery*

1804: The Otoe and Missouria were the first tribal groups to hold council with Meriwether Lewis and William Clark, leaders of the Corps of Discovery expedition authorized by President Thomas Jefferson to explore the West. The first formal meeting was held on August 3, 1804, at a site Clark called Council Bluff, near present-day Fort Calhoun, Nebraska. The leaders promoted U.S. sovereignty and sought tribal cooperation and allegiance.

1847: The Choctaw people, despite living in hardship and poverty after being removed to Indian Territory, donated money halfway across the world to aid the Irish people suffering from the great famine. Although the exact sum is not known, estimates are from four to twenty thousand dollars in today's currency. In 2020, Irish people donated over a million dollars raised through a Go Fund

Doctrine of Discovery

The Doctrine of Discovery established a spiritual, political, and legal justification for colonization and seizure of land not inhabited by Christians, especially if it resulted in material gains and more converts for the Catholic Church. The basic elements of the Doctrine of Discovery are outlined in a series of decrees, issued by popes starting in the 1100s and named the "papal bulls." They include sanctions, enforcements, authorizations, expulsions, admonishments, excommunications, denunciations, and expressions of territorial sovereignty for Christian monarchs supported by the Catholic Church. There are two papal bulls that were and remain particularly damaging to aboriginal peoples: Pope Nicholas V issued "Romanus Pontifex" in 1455, granting the Portuguese a monopoly of trade with Africa and authorizing the enslavement of local people; and Pope Alexander VI issued the Papal Bull "Inter Caetera" in 1493 to justify Christian European explorers' claims on land and waterways they allegedly discovered, and promote Christian domination and superiority; it has been applied in Africa, Asia, Australia, New Zealand, and the Americas.

The Doctrine of Discovery fueled white supremacy in that white European settlers were (and are) designated as "instruments of divine design and cultural superiority." An ideology developed that, indeed, European settlers were "sanctioned by God" to bring Christian order to the world even if it supported the dehumanization of those living on the land and their dispossession, enslavement, murder, and forced assimilation. In the 1800s, the Doctrine of Discovery was the basis for the Monroe Doctrine, which declared U.S. domination over the Western Hemisphere, and Manifest Destiny, which justified American expansion westward to the Pacific and beyond. In an 1823 Supreme Court case, *Johnson v. McIntosh*, the Doctrine of Discovery became part of U.S. federal law and was used to dispossess Native peoples of their land. Chief Justice John Marshall wrote "that the principle of discovery gave European nations an absolute right to New World lands." As recently as 2005, Supreme Court justice Ruth Bader Ginsburg ruled against the Oneida Indian Nation in the Supreme Court case *Sherrill v. Oneida Indian Nation*. The Oneida Nation had purchased some of the same land that had been illegally taken from them over a century before; the nation refused to pay real estate taxes to the town of Sherrill, New York, as the property was no longer under the town's administration and was now part of the reservation and a sovereign nation. Sherrill lost its case in lower courts. However, Ginsburg's opinion was based upon a long and flawed history, and she ruled in Sherrill's favor. She drew upon the so-called "discovery doctrine" and Chief Justice John Marshall's opinion in the 1823 *Johnson v. McIntosh* case. Tribal sovereignty, the Court implied, was a quaint and antiquated notion not worthy of its consideration. For years, Native leaders have asked for the pope to rescind doctrines; many Catholics have agreed. In July of 2021, Bishop Douglas J. Lucia of Syracuse, New York, requested a meeting with the Vatican to ask that the pope repudiate theological teachings used for centuries to justify the subjugation of Indigenous peoples.

Me campaign to help the Navajo and Hopi nations, devastated by the COVID pandemic. Organizer Vanessa Tulley said, "173 years later, the favor is returned through generous donations from the Irish people to the Navajo Nation during our time of crisis."

1923: The Haudenosaunee issued its first passports. The first person to use one was Cayuga statesman Deskaheh to travel to the League of Nations headquarters in Geneva, Switzerland. Although Canada and Great Britain do not recognize the passport, some other countries do, including Japan, who accepted a Haudenosaunee delegation to attend the World Congress of the International Association for the History of Religions in 2005. In July 2010 the United Kingdom did not accept the tribal passports of the Iroquois Nationals field lacrosse team for travel to the UK for the 2010 World Lacrosse Championship. The U.S. government offered to immediately issue U.S. passports to the team members, and several days after this offer was rejected, they issued waivers that would allow the team back into the United States; however, the UK continued to refuse to issue visas. The Indian world was shocked as Indigenous peoples invented the game. Speculation was that it was an effective way to limit the competition in favor of Europeans.

1977: The first delegation of Native American leaders went to a United Nations meeting in Geneva, Switzerland. The Haudenosaunee addressed the Western World in an address called "A Basic Call to Consciousness."

1989: Tonya Gonnella Frichner (1947–2015), Onondaga, founded and served as president of the American Indian Law Alliance, an Indigenous Peoples advocacy group based in New York City and an NGO with consultative status to the United Nations Social and Economic Council. She served a three-year term (2008–2010) as the North American representative to the United Nations Permanent Forum on Indigenous Issues and was key in the drafting, negotiations, and passage of the United Nations Declaration on the Rights of Indigenous Peoples (2000).

2002: The first meeting of the Permanent Forum on Indigenous Issues at the United Nations was held in New York City.

2007: The United Nations approved the UN Declaration on the Rights of Indigenous Peoples. In 2010, the Declaration was endorsed by the United States.

2015: The Turkish International Cooperation and Development Agency donated $200,000 to build a water tank for the Confederated Tribes of Warm Springs Reservation of Oregon. This grant is to ensure clean drinking water for 10 years for a reservation elementary school.

2016: David Archambault II, chairman of the Standing Rock Sioux tribe, delivered a speech against the Energy Transfer Partners' Dakota Access oil pipeline to the Human Rights Council at the United Nations in Geneva, Switzerland. He tried to garner international support for his nation's fight against the pipeline that threatened the health of his community. Supporters from all over the world stood in solidarity, and thousands traveled to South Dakota to support the movement.

TRIBAL GOVERNMENT LEADERS

1841: Edmund Pickens (1789–1868), Chickasaw, was elected the first chief of the Chickasaw District of the Choctaw Nation. He also became the second controlling chief financial official and treasurer and, in 1847, was elected tribal captain. Chief Pickens was inducted into the Chickasaw Hall of Fame in 1992.

1856: Cyrus Harris (1817–1888), Chickasaw, was elected the first governor of the Chickasaw Nation under its newly established constitution as a republic, initially serving from 1856 to 1858, followed by terms of 1860–1862, 1866–1868, 1868–1870, and 1872–1874. In 1837, Harris and his family started their journey to Indian Territory (present-day Oklahoma), part of the removal of tribal nations from their southeastern homelands. His bilingual skills and leadership role contributed to the rebuilding of the tribal nation.

Henry Chee Dodge

1922: Alice Brown Davis (1852–1935), Seminole (Tiger Clan), was the first female principal chief of the Seminole Tribe of Oklahoma and was appointed to the post by President Warren G. Harding, serving from 1922 until her death. Besides raising a large family, Davis also served as an educator, rancher, postmistress, and interpreter. She was inducted into the Oklahoma Hall of Fame in 1930, Davis House was named for her at the University of Oklahoma in Norman in 1950, and a bronze bust of her was unveiled at the New York World's Fair in 1964.

1922: Lucy Tayiah Eads (1888–1961), Kanza and Potawatomi, was the first woman to serve as principal chief of the Kaw Nation. Orphaned as young children, Eads and her brother were adopted and raised by tribal leader Chief Washungah. Eads attended Haskell Institute in Lawrence, Kansas, where she trained as a nurse. As principal chief, Eads made education a priority for her people and worked to reestablish the Kaw Agency. She was reelected, eventually serving as principal chief until 1934.

1922: Jose Sotero C. Ortiz (Oh-pah Too-weh; 1877–1963), Ohkay Owingeh, became the first elected leader of the All-Indian Pueblo Council, a reorganization of the modern nineteen Pueblos in New Mexico. The leaders joined together to oppose the Bursum Bill, legislation detrimental to Pueblo land and resource rights.

1923: Henry Chee Dodge (Hastiin Adiits'a'ii, "Mister Interpreter"; c. 1957), Navajo, served as the first tribal chairman of the Navajo Business Council from 1922 to 1928 and chairman of the then Navajo Tribal Council from 1942 to 1946. After becoming separated from his mother during the Long Walk of 1864, he was raised by an aunt and learned English from his Anglo-American step-uncle. Chee Dodge eventually served as an official Navajo interpreter to the U.S. military. He also became the last official head chief of the Navajo Tribe, serving from 1884 to 1910. His family included six children, among them Thomas Dodge, who served as tribal council chairman from 1932 to 1936, and Annie Dodge Wauneka, who received the Presidential Medal of Freedom in 1963 for her life of service. Chee Dodge Elementary School and Chee Dodge Boulevard in New Mexico are named in the Navajo leader's honor.

1937: Edith J. Parks (1903–1982), Tulalip, was the first woman elected to the Board of Directors of the Tulalip Tribes of Washington, serving as board secretary and certifying the tribal nation's amended constitution of 1948. In 1939, Harriette Shelton Williams Dover was elected to the board, serving for 14 years, part of that time as chairwoman, the first woman to do so.

1940: Viola Jimulla (Sicatuva, "Born Quickly"; 1878–1966), Yavapai, became the first chieftess of the Yavapai-Prescott tribe in Arizona, a position she held until her death. She and her husband, Sam Jimulla, who died in 1940, worked to have land set aside for the reservation. The Yavapai-Prescott Tribal Council was formed under Viola Jimulla's leadership. Jimulla, who was inducted into the Arizona Women's Hall of Fame in 1986, was also a master basket maker.

1946: Lilakai (Lily) Julian Neil (1900–1961), Navajo, became the first woman elected to the Navajo Tribal Council, serving in the position until 1951. She is also associated with the founding of La Vida Mission, a Seventh-day Adventist center, in Farmington, New Mexico. Lily Neil Memorial Chapel at the mission is named in her honor.

1959: Virginia S. Klinekole (1924–2011), Mescalero Apache, was the first woman elected president of the Mescalero Apache Tribe in New Mexico, serving two terms in that office and then remaining on the tribal council until 1986. During her presidency, she set up a loan program for tribal members through a local bank and led the tribal government in providing homes for residents. Klinekole also promoted economic development and stressed the importance of education. Fluent in Apache, Spanish, and English, she helped to develop an Apache language dictionary.

1962: William "Buffalo" Tiger (1920–2015), Miccosukee, became the first elected tribal chairman of the Miccosukee Tribe of Indians of Florida, following federal recognition of the tribal nation. Prior to that, he was the tribe's spokesperson, serving as liaison between the tribe and the state and federal governments. In 1959, Tiger had accepted an invitation from Fidel Castro to visit Cuba, tribal diplomacy that garnered the attention of state and federal authorities and ulti-

Betty Mae Tiger Jumper

mately contributed to federal recognition for the tribal nation. He remained tribal chairman until 1985, was a founding member of what became the United South and Eastern Tribes (USET), and was named president emeritus of the organization in 2010. He wrote his autobiography, *Buffalo Tiger: A Life in the Everglades* (2002), with historian Harry A. Kersey, Jr.

1967: John Borbridge Jr. (Duk saa.aat'; 1926–2016), Tlingit, was elected as the first full-time president of the Central Council of Tlingit and Haida Indian Tribes of Alaska. He was responsible for opening Central Council's first office and worked to implement the tribe's Six Point Plan and to help settle Alaska Native land claims. Borbridge was later elected as the first president and chairman of Sealaska Corporation's Board of Directors (1972 to 1978).

1967: Betty Mae Tiger Jumper (Potackee; 1923–2011), Seminole, became the first woman elected to chair the Seminole Tribe of Florida, a position she held until 1971. She was also the first Seminole (along with a cousin) to graduate from high school, continuing her education by pursuing nursing at the Kiowa Indian Hospital in Lawton, Oklahoma. In 1957, Tiger Jumper was a member of the first tribal council that helped secure federal recognition of the Seminole Tribe. She also launched a tribal newspaper that became the *Seminole Tribune*. In 1970, Tiger Jumper was one of two women appointed by President Richard Nixon to the National Council on Indian Opportunity. A tribal storyteller, she authored books and other works.

1971: William Wayne "W. W." Keeler (1908–1987), of Cherokee descent, was elected principal chief of the Cherokee Nation, the tribal nation's first elected chief since Oklahoma statehood. Initially appointed by President

Harry Truman to the position in 1949, he also became the last presidentially appointed leader to the office. Keeler was a chemical engineer who had a long career with Phillips Petroleum Company, eventually serving as chief executive officer of the company.

1971: Harry J. W. Belvin (1900–1986) was the first principal chief elected by the Choctaw Tribe of Oklahoma following an act of October 22, 1970 (84 Stat. 1091) authorizing each of the Five Civilized Tribes to select their principal chief by popular vote. Previously, under the Dawes Act, chiefs of those tribal nations had been appointed by the president upon recommendation from the Bureau of Indian Affairs. Before his election in 1971, Belvin had already served as principal chief of the Choctaw Tribe for 23 years, becoming the longest serving leader in the role. He represented the 20th District in the Oklahoma House of Representatives from 1955 to 1961 and in the state senate from 1961 to 1965.

1971: Overton James (1925–2015), Chickasaw, became the first governor of the Chickasaw Nation elected by the Chickasaw people since Oklahoma statehood in 1907. Earlier, he was appointed to the governorship by President John F. Kennedy in 1963, becoming the youngest man to serve in the position. James held office until 1987; that same year, he became the first Chickasaw inducted into the tribal nation's hall of fame.

1976: Mildred Imoch Cleghorn (En-Ohn or Lay-a-Bet; 1910–1997), Fort Sill Apache, who was born a prisoner of war at Fort Sill, Oklahoma, became the first tribal chair of the newly organized Fort Sill Apache Tribe, serving until 1995. Besides her leadership roles, she was a noted artist of traditional dolls representing tribes she had encountered in her teaching career. Cleghorn's numerous awards include the Ellis Island Award in 1987 and the Indian of the Year Award in 1989.

1985: Wilma Mankiller (1945–2010), Cherokee, became the first woman to serve as principal chief of the Cherokee Nation and the first woman to lead a large American Indian tribal nation. She served in the position until 1995, working to build new clinics, improved infrastructure, community services, education programs, economic revenues, and self-government. Following her retirement from politics, Mankiller continued her advocacy, authored books, and lectured on a range of topics. Her autobiography, *Mankiller: A Chief and Her People* (written with Michael Wallis), was published in 1993. The recipient of numerous honors, she was awarded the Presidential Medal of Freedom in 1998.

1987: Verna Williamson Teller (1950–), Isleta Pueblo, became the first female governor of Pueblo of Isleta. Following her tenure as governor, she served as her tribal nation's chief justice, president of the tribal council, and council member. In 2019, she became the first Native American to deliver the invocation in the history of the U.S. House of Representatives.

1988: Twila Martin-Kekahbah (1947–), Chippewa-Cree, became the first woman elected chairperson of the Turtle Mountain Band of Chippewa in North Dakota. A graduate of

Wilma Mankiller received the Presidential Medal of Freedom from President Bill Clinton in 1998.

the University of North Dakota and Penn State University, she served three terms, 1988 to 1990, 1990 to 1992, and 1994 to 1996.

1990: Peterson Zah (1937–), Navajo, was elected the first president of the Navajo Nation and sworn into office on January 15, 1991. Born in Keams Canyon, Arizona, Zah attended Phoenix Indian School and later Arizona State University (ASU), where he graduated with a bachelor's degree in education in 1963. He became director of the DNA People's Legal Services program, providing vital support to tribal members. In 1983, Zah was elected chairman of the Navajo Tribal Council, holding that office until 1987. After serving as Navajo Nation president (1991 to 1995), he became special advisor to the president on American Indian affairs for ASU. In 2005, ASU honored Zah, one of the 100 most important Native Americans in the last century, with an honorary degree. He is the coauthor of *We Will Secure Our Future: Empowering the Navajo Nation*, with Peter Iverson (2012).

Chief G. Anne Richardson

1990: Kay "Kaibah" C. Bennett (1922–1997), Navajo, teacher and author, was the first woman to run for the presidency of the Navajo Nation. Her candidacy was challenged because she lived in Gallup, New Mexico, and not on the reservation, but she was able to prevail in court. Bennett held jobs as a teacher, interpreter, and head of special education at the Phoenix Indian School (1947 to 1952) and served on the Inter-Tribal Indian Ceremonial's board of directors from 1974 to 1982. Her books include *Kaibah: Reflection of a Navajo Girlhood; A Navajo Saga*, the story of a family living in the 1880s; and *Keesh, the Navajo Indian Cat*, a children's book.

1995: Joyce Dugan (c. 1952–), Cherokee, was the first female principal chief of the Eastern Band of Cherokee Indians in North Carolina,

until 1999. A graduate of Western Carolina University, she earlier served as superintendent of Cherokee Central Schools for five years. During her tenure, Principal Chief Dugan reacquired land in which Kituwah, the Cherokee mother town, is located. She is the coauthor of *The Cherokee* (2002).

1998: Emily Cheromiah (1952–), Laguna Pueblo, was elected as tribal secretary, the first woman to hold public office in the Pueblo of Laguna. A referendum before the voters in 1996 approved having women run for tribal offices, resulting in a change to centuries-long traditional all-male leadership. Serving as tribal secretary was a full-time position with a two-year term, requiring Cheromiah to relinquish her job as a vocational rehabilitation counselor.

1998: G. Anne Richardson (1956–), Rappahannock, was sworn in as chief of the Rappahannock Tribe in Virginia, the first woman to hold that position since early in the eighteenth century. She has also served as assistant chief, helped the Rappahannock win official state recognition, and directed Mattaponi-Pamunkey-Monacan, Inc., a consortium providing training and employment services for Virginia Indians. Other endeavors included efforts to achieve federal recognition of Virginia's tribes as well as community revitalization and development. In 2006, Richardson was named one of the Virginia Women in History.

2004: Cecelia Fire Thunder (1946–), Lakota, nurse and community health planner, was elected as the first female president of the Oglala Sioux Tribe of the Pine Ridge Reservation in South Dakota. She served until she was impeached on June 29, 2006, several months before the end of her two-year term of office. Fire Thunder had earlier announced her intention to create a Planned

Parenthood clinic at Pine Ridge, in response to the state legislature's passage of a law banning virtually all abortions in South Dakota. The tribal council impeached her for proceeding without gaining their consent. Fire Thunder founded community-based health clinics during an earlier period of her life when she lived in California. After returning to Pine Ridge, she became a founder of the Oglala Lakota Women's Society. Fire Thunder also worked at a domestic abuse shelter and became the coordinator of the Native Women's Society of the Great Plains. In addition, she is an artist known for creating award-winning dolls and other work.

2004: Erma Vizenor (1944–), Anishinaabe, was the first woman elected to lead the White Earth Nation, the largest tribe in Minnesota, serving until her resignation in 2016. She also served as secretary-treasurer, a position she was appointed to in 1996, elected to in 1997, and held until 2002. Vizenor, born and raised on the reservation, was a teacher and school administrator for twenty years. Her educational background includes a Bachelor of Science degree in elementary education, a master of science degree in guidance and counseling, and a second master's degree. She also earned a Doctor of Education degree in administration, planning, and social policy from Harvard University. As tribal leader, Vizenor's efforts included pursuing constitutional reform. In 2013, she oversaw the drafting of a new constitution that encompassed a number of changes, including qualifications for tribal membership. The new constitution was approved by a referendum vote, but it was not implemented following the election of new tribal council members, who opposed it. The ensuing political struggle over the issue sparked Vizenor's resignation.

2005: The first State of the Tribe address in Wisconsin's state legislature was delivered by Ray Deperry, chair of the Red Cliff Band of Lake Superior Chippewa and president of the Great Lakes Inter-Tribal Council, on March 8, 2005. Deperry, representing the state's 11 tribal nations, deemed the occasion the start of new and improved relationships with elected officials of Wisconsin.

2006: Glenna J. Wallace (c. 1938–), Shawnee, was the first woman to be elected chief of the Eastern Shawnee Tribe in Oklahoma. Besides serving on the tribe's business committee for 18 years, she also worked as a teacher and administrator at Crowder College in Missouri for 38 years.

2010: Paula Pechonick (1941–), Delaware, was the first woman elected as chief of the Delaware Tribe of Oklahoma.

2011: Phyliss J. Anderson (1961–), Choctaw, was the first woman elected tribal chief of the Mississippi Band of Choctaw Indians (MBCI). Anderson, who had earlier served on the tribal council, was the fourth tribal chief to be elected since 1945, when the MBCI was reorganized and federally recognized. In 2016, President Barack Obama appointed her to serve on the National Advisory Council on Indian Education. Anderson, who served two four-year terms as tribal chief, was recognized with the 2019 Tribal Leader of the Year Award by the Native American Finance Officers Association.

2012: For the first time, women were elected to the tribal council at San Ildefonso Pueblo in New Mexico. Prior to that, council members were appointed, but a new policy allowed female tribal members to vote and run for office in the Pueblo's first elections. Irene Tse-Pe and two other women were elected to the 10-person council.

2013: Earl J. Barbry Sr. (1950–2013), who served as tribal chairman and tribal administrator of the Tunica-Biloxi Tribe of Louisiana from 1978 until his death, was honored with the first lifetime achievement award by the United South and Eastern Tribes (USET), an inter-tribal organization that represents member tribes. In 2006, Chairman Barbry was named a Louisiana Legend by Louisiana Public Broadcasting in recognition of his contributions to the region, the first American Indian to receive the honor.

2017: Maulian Dana (1984–) became the first Penobscot Nation ambassador following her appointment to the position by Chief Kirk Francis. Dana, who was elected to the Penobscot Nation Tribal Council in 2016 for a four-year term, presents issues to Native and non-Native audiences in her role as ambassador. Two of her goals were realized in 2019 when the Maine legislature voted to ban the use of Native American mascots in public schools and the governor of Maine signed legislation to replace Columbus Day with Indigenous People's Day.

Maulian Dana

2017: The tribal election of the Tulalip Tribes of Washington garnered the first female-majority board in its history. Marie Zackuse (1948–), Tulalip, who served as a member of the Board of Directors for 24 years, was elected as chairwoman of the tribal nation.

2018: Gwendena Lee-Gatewood became the first chairwoman of the White Mountain Apache Tribe in Arizona. A few months later, she was selected as the president of the Apache Alliance Summit, which is comprised of nine Apache tribes from Arizona, New Mexico, and Oklahoma, formed in the 1970s to work for the collective benefit of the member tribal nations.

2020: Alicia Mousseau (1982–), Lakota, was elected vice president of the Oglala Sioux Tribe and is believed to be the first openly LGBTQ person elected to the tribal nation's executive council. Mousseau grew up on the Pine Ridge Reservation in South Dakota. She has a Ph.D. in clinical psychology from the University of Wyoming and previously worked for the National Native Children's Trauma Center at the University of Montana.

2020: In a historic first, the Northern Cheyenne Tribe in Montana elected women for all its open tribal council seats. Donna Marie Fisher was elected tribal president and Serena Brady Wetherelt won as tribal vice president. Five other council seats were won by Melissa Rae Fisher, Norma Gourneau, Silver Little Eagle, Gwen Talawyma, and Debra Waters Charette. With the election, a record high of seven of ten of the council members were women.

TRIBAL JUDICIARY: COURTS AND LAW

1808: The Cherokee Nation established a law code.

1822: The Cherokee Nation established the Cherokee National Supreme Court.

1822: John Martin Jr. (1781–1840), Cherokee, was one of the first men to serve on the newly established Cherokee Tribal Court in 1822. He was also the tribal nation's first treasurer and helped write and sign the first Cherokee Constitution in 1827. Martin served as a circuit judge for two tribal districts in Georgia as well. After removal to Indian Territory, he became the first chief justice of the Cherokee Supreme Court reestablished there in 1839. In 2013, the Cherokee honored Judge Martin, the tribal nation's first chief justice, with a monument at the Cherokee Courthouse in Tahlequah, Oklahoma.

1883: Courts of Indian Offenses were initiated by Secretary of the Interior Henry M. Teller, whose goal was to eliminate "heathenish practices" among Indians. Acting on Teller's directive, the commissioner of Indian affairs established a tribunal at all agencies, "except among the civilized Indians," to be known as the court of Indian offenses. The courts became general tribunals for handling certain offenses on reservations.

1905: Julia Wades in Water (also Sta-Ti-Pi-Ta-Ki, Wades-in-the-Water; 1872–?), Blackfeet, was the first woman to serve as an officer in the Indian Police. Hired shortly after the turn of the century, she worked at Montana's Blackfeet Agency for 25 years and retired in the 1930s. Her duties included housekeeping and cooking as well as handling female prisoners. Wades in Water and her husband both had their portraits done by artist Winold Reiss in the summer of 1943.

1931: Thomas "Ted" Leo St. Germaine (1885–1947), Lac du Flambeau Ojibwe tribal attorney and professional football player, became the first Native American admitted to the State Bar in Wisconsin and the first Native American to practice law in the state. Years earlier, he had become licensed to practice law in Iowa but instead went on to study at the University of Wisconsin Law School, intent on playing football there. St. Germaine also attended Yale Law School, graduating with a Bachelor of Laws degree in 1913. After returning to the Lac du Flambeau reservation in Wisconsin, he championed Indian treaty rights and environmental stewardship, work that saw fruition many years later.

1970: John EchoHawk (1945–), Pawnee, was the first graduate of the University of New Mexico's (UNM) special program to train Indian lawyers, earning his JD degree. While studying at UNM, he was a founding member of the American Indian Law Students Association. In 1970, EchoHawk also helped found the Native American Rights Fund (NARF) and has been with the organization since its inception. In 1977, he became the executive director of NARF and has served continuously in the leadership role for more than 40 years. EchoHawk was recognized as one of the 100 most influential lawyers in America by the *National Law Journal*, one of many accolades for his leadership in the Indian law field.

1983: Tillie Hardwick (1924–1999), Pomo, was instrumental in reversing the U.S. government's California Indian Rancheria termination policy. Born Tillie Myers, she grew up on the Pinoleville Indian Rancheria, near Ukiah, California. In 1979, assisted by California Indian Legal Services, Hardwick filed a lawsuit that became a class action case. In a 1983 decision on the case, a U.S. district court restored the status of 17 California rancherias.

1983: Juanita Jefferson (?–2011), Choctaw, was the first woman to serve as a tribal judge for the Choctaw Nation of Oklahoma and served nearly 23 years before retiring.

1985: Tom Tso (1945–), Navajo, was the first chief justice of the Supreme Court of the Navajo Nation, serving until 1991. That judicial authority is an outgrowth of the Navajo Tribal Court of Appeals, dating back to 1959, part of the Navajo Nation's establishment of the judiciary as a separate branch of tribal government. The Supreme Judicial Council, a political body that could hear appeals, existed between 1978 and 1985, when it was eliminated. At that time, the Navajo Tribal Court of Appeals became the Supreme Court of the Navajo Nation, serving as the court of last resort.

1994: Ron Whitener (1969–) graduated from the University of Washington Law School and was hired as the first in-house legal counsel by the Squaxin Island Tribe, where he is a tribal member. Whitener held the position until 2000, advising on issues related to treaty rights, tribal governance, Indian health, and economic development. He then joined the faculty of the University of Washington Law School, heading the Indian Law Clinic, which later became the Tribal Court Public Defense Clinic. Whitener has also served as an associate justice on the Northwest Intertribal Court of Appeals and as the chief judge for the Confederated Tribes of the Chehalis Indian Reservation. In 2009, he became a founding member of the Whitener Group in Olympia, Washington, providing legal expertise to businesses and clients.

1995: Mary Jo Brooks Hunter, Ho-Chunk, who completed her law degree at the UCLA School of Law in 1982, was elected as the first chief justice of the Ho-Chunk Nation Supreme Court in Wisconsin. Reelected numerous times since then, she has also served on other tribal courts and engaged in teaching.

2011: Bishop William Wantland (1934–), Seminole, became the first chief justice of the Seminole Nation Supreme Court in Oklahoma. The court was reinstated for the first time since Oklahoma's statehood in 1907. Wantland, a law school graduate, earned a doctorate in religion in 1976, and in 1980 was elected bishop of the Diocese of Eau Claire, Wisconsin.

2017: The Cherokee Nation filed a lawsuit in tribal court against six top drug distributors

Chief Justice Robert Yazzie, Justice Eleanor Shirley, and Justice Wilson Yellowhair (by special designation) are shown here presiding over a case in 2011 for the Navajo Nation.

The National Congress of American Indians meets in Albuquerque, New Mexico.

National Congress of American Indians

The National Congress of American Indians (NCAI) is an American Indian and Alaska Native rights organization. It was founded in 1944 to represent tribal nations and protect them from termination and assimilationist policies. The organizational structure of the NCAI is composed of a general assembly, an executive council, and seven committees. Officers include a president, vice president, first vice president, recording secretary, treasurer, plus an executive board consisting of 12 area vice presidents and twelve alternative area vice presidents. Each nation is allotted a number of votes based on its size. In its almost 80 years, NCAI has successfully challenged such issues as antidiscrimination in federal jobs, creation of the Tribal Advisory Commission to advise Congress, protection for Alaska Natives after statehood, and blocking states from having civil and criminal jurisdictions over Indians. NCAI continues to protect programs and services to Indian people, particularly those targeting Indian youth and elders; promotes and supports pre-K through postsecondary and adult education; enhances Indian health care, including prevention of juvenile substance abuse, HIV-AIDS prevention, and other major diseases; supports environmental protection and natural resources management; protects Indian cultural resources and religious freedom rights; promotes economic rights, both on and off reservations; and promotes the rights of all Indian people

National Congress of American Indians (contd.)

to decent, safe, and affordable housing. Both federally recognized and state-recognized Indian tribes can be members of NCAI.

In 1944, Napoleon B. ("N. B.") Johnson, Cherokee Nation, became the first president of the National Congress of American Indians.

Ruth Muskrat Bronson with President Calvin Coolidge (left)

In 1944, Ruth Muskrat Bronson (1897–1982), Cherokee, became the first woman to serve as executive director of the newly formed National Congress of the American Indians (NCAI), a position she held until 1948. She also edited the NCAI's publication, *Washington Bulletin*, and, in 1949, became one of the three original trustees of the organization's nonprofit educational affiliate, ARROW (Americans for the Restitution and Righting of Old Wrongs). In earlier firsts, Bronson became the first Indian woman to graduate from Mount Holyoke College in Massachusetts in 1925 and the first guidance and placement officer in the Bureau of Indian Affairs in 1930.

Veronica Murdock

In 1977, Veronica Murdock (1944–), Shasta/Mohave, became the first woman president of the National Congress of American Indians, serving in the position until 1979. A member of the Colorado River Indian Tribes (CRIT), which is headquartered in Parker, Arizona, Murdock's leadership has included serving as CRIT's vice chair from 1969 to 1979. Born Veronica Lee Homer, she also worked for the Bureau of Indian Affairs in various capacities from 1980 to 2004, including as superintendent of the Salt River Agency from 1994 to 2004. In 1961, she became Miss Indian Arizona and had the opportunity to serve as a majorette for the John F. Kennedy inaugural. Murdock became one of the founders of Women Empowering Women for Indian Nations (WEWIN), an organization to foster tribal women to serve as leaders and role models.

Fawn R. Sharp

In 2003, Tex Hall (1956–), Mandan, Hidatsa, Arikara Nation, president of the National Congress of American Indians, presented the first State of American Indian Nations address on January 31, 2003. The presentation has been delivered annually since that time to members of Congress, government officials, tribal leaders and citizens, and the larger public. The speech raises major issues, outlines goals and priorities, and advances the nation-to-nation relationship with the United States.

In 2020, Fawn R. Sharp (1970–), Quinault, president of the Quinault Indian Nation and president of the National Congress of American Indians (NCAI), became the first female president of NCAI to give a State of Indian Nations address. She presented the address at the George Washington University in Washington, D.C., on February 10, 2020.

in the United States seeking to decrease the flood of opioids into the tribe's communities across 14 counties in Oklahoma. It represents the first time an Indian nation filed suit against pharmaceutical companies for damages done to tribal citizens from powerful drugs such as oxycodone and hydrocodone. In 2018, a federal judge ruled that the Cherokee Nation lacked the jurisdiction to try the case in the tribe's court system.

TRIBAL LAND

"I'd like it if people stopped thinking that the United States somehow 'gave' reservations to Indians, or Native Americans. Fact: it was the other way around."

—Louise Erdrich

1758: The first American Indian reservation was created by European colonists in what would be Shamong Township, New Jersey. Created on August 29, 1758, for the Lenni Lenape (Delaware) and called the Brotherton reservation, it consisted of 3,000 acres of land. In the late 1700s the Lenape began giving sanctuary to Cherokee Indians fleeing the land-hungry colonists in the South. New Jersey sold the reservation in 1801, with a portion of the proceeds going to the former residents. Some residents remained in New Jersey and became the Sand Hill Band of Lenape and Cherokee Indians, named for the area where many tribal members lived, but the majority were dispersed to other areas of the country.. In 1948, Chief Crummel accepted a New Jersey Governor's Proclamation for the right to remain in New Jersey.

1853: The Sebastian Indian Reservation (aka Tejon Reservation) was the first Indian reservation in California. It was established by Edward F. Beale, superintendent of Indian affairs for California, on Rancho El Tejon lands in the San Joaquin Valley. In 1863, Beale bought Rancho El Tejon for private use, and by then, the number of Native people living there had diminished from more than 2,000 to approximately 100.

1937: The Lone Pine Paiute-Shoshone Reservation, located near Lone Pine, California, was established via a land exchange between the U.S. Department of the Interior and the City of Los Angeles. The rapidly growing city took over most of Owens Valley Paiute land, and the tribal band resettled on acreage in nearby Big Pine.

1965: Eben Hopson (1922–1980), Inupiat, was the first executive director of the Arctic Slope Native Association, which helped launch Alaska's Native land claims movement.

1971: The Alaska Native Land Claims Settlement Act (ANCSA), the largest land claims settlement in U.S. history, was signed into law by President Richard Nixon on December 18, 1971. It created 12 regional profit-making Alaska Native corporations, allocated land to over 200 village, group, and urban corporations that ultimately encompassed some 45.5 million acres, and made a cash payment of approximately a billion dollars. A 13th regional corporation headquartered in Seattle, Washington, was later established for qualifying Alaska Natives who lived outside of the state of Alaska. Since its passage, ANCSA has been amended by Congress many times to refine the terms of the settlement and to address Alaska Native rights and jurisdictional issues.

Eben Hopson

1974: The first land transfer under the Alaska Native Land Claims Settlement Act was 4,267 acres of land to the Kenai Natives Association.

1992: Taos Pueblo in New Mexico was designated a UNESCO World Heritage Site in 1992, the only living Native American community with the designation. The Pueblo became a National Historic Landmark in 1960 and was added to the National Register of Historic Places in 1966.

2012: Some 79 acres of land were placed into federal trust by the Mississippi Band of Choctaw Indians in Henning, Tennessee, for a longstanding Choctaw community, which became the first federally recognized tribal land base in Tennessee.

2017: Ryan Sundberg (1975–), Yurok, was the first Native American to be appointed to the 12-member California Coastal Commission (CCC) in its 41-year history. The CCC has been described as one of the most powerful land use agencies in the country. Initially created in 1972 and made permanent by the 1976 Coastal Act, the CCC was designed to protect California's approximately 1,100 miles of coastline. In 2010, Sundberg was elected to the Board of Supervisors in Humboldt County. He has also served on the Trinidad Rancheria tribal council for many years.

2020: The Rosebud Economic Development Corporation (REDCO), with support from the World Wildlife Fund and Rosebud Tribal Land Enterprise, announced the inaugural transfer and release of 100 plains bison from the National Park Service to the newly established Wolakota Buffalo Range

Taos Pueblo was designated a UNESCO World Heritage Site in 1992.

on the Rosebud Indian Reservation in South Dakota. This 27,680-acre area, when it reaches capacity, is slated to become North America's largest Native American–owned and -managed bison herd. The initial 100 bison were transferred from Badlands National Park and Theodore Roosevelt National Park, the first of as many as 1,500 of the animals to be transferred to the Wolakota range.

TRIBAL LAND RETURN

"The loss of land plays out in our everyday lives and it shapes how we look at things and how we feel about ourselves. We've spent 15 years in the Bay Area doing community organizing in the Indian community. And honestly, all the issues we're struggling with come down to land. You know, the land was taken and that was such a deep soul wound. The taking of the land, the heart of the people, was the cause of a lot of problems. And I believe that with the land trust, and you know, the land itself, I think that's really going to help us to find our way back."

—*Johnella LaRose,*
cofounder/director of Sogorea Te' Land Trust

1921: The Hawaiian Homes Commission Act of 1920 (HHCA) was passed to repatriate land to Native Hawaiians, and the Department of Hawaiian Home Lands (DHHL) was instituted. Homestead leases (for 99 to 199 years at an annual rental of $1) are for residential, agricultural, or pastoral purposes and available. Aquacultural leases are also authorized, but none have been awarded to date. The intent of the homesteading program is to provide for economic self-sufficiency of Native Hawaiians through the pro-

vision of land. However, the program is underfunded and usually requires vigorous legal action for any Native Hawaiians to acquire lands as the government has not been responsive. About 200,000 acres of land across the Hawaiian Islands are reserved solely for Native Hawaiians, who can prove they are of 50 percent or more Hawaiian blood, which is problematic. Also, the lands are often not accessible or arable, or they have natural resources, making it hard to get a mortgage for any kind of buildings. Today, almost 30,000 people are on the waiting list and countless have died in the past century without realizing their dream of getting back even a small plot to call home.

1970: Blue Lake and lands surrounding it in New Mexico were returned to the Taos Pueblo, the first land return to a tribal nation for religious purposes by the U.S. government. Taos tribal members had fought for

President Richard Nixon signed the Blue Lake Bill in 1970.

the restoration of their sacred lands for 64 years, finally achieving the return with legislation by Congress signed by President Richard Nixon.

1997: The Susanville Indian Rancheria in California became the first tribe to regain land from the U.S. Army. Working with the Sierra Army Depot and Lassen County Local Reuse Authority, the rancheria secured over 120 housing units, the return of 73 acres to its land base, and the use of the Sierra Army Depot military health clinic.

2004: Selected by the Bureau of Indian Affairs, the Confederated Salish and Kootenai Tribes (CSKT) became the first self-governance tribe in the nation to receive funding for the Indian Land Consolidation Project (ILCP). The ILCP was intended to fund tribal purchase of undivided fractional interests, percentages of ownership in land parcels, to improve the economic development potential of such lands for the benefit of tribal members.

2015: The Kashia Band of Pomo Indians reacquired part of its ancestral lands, the purchase restoring their people unfettered access to a coastal area in what is now Sonoma County, California, for the first time in more than 150 years. The Kashia Coastal Reserve is owned and managed by the tribe, believed to be the first time that a tribe in the United States had held a private deed and management rights to their ancestral lands.

2015: Sogorea Te' Land Trust was founded by Corrina Gould, Lisjan Ohlone, and Johnella LaRose, Shoshone Bannock/Carrizo, as an urban Indigenous women-led land trust based in the San Francisco Bay Area in California. It works to facilitate the return of Indigenous land to Indigenous people. The name comes from Sogorea Te', a 3,500-year-old Karkin Ohlone village and burial site, a sacred place in need of protection from desecration.

2020: The Esselen Tribe in California, one of the smallest Native tribes in the country, was able to obtain ancestral land back with support from a $4.52 million grant from California Natural Resources Agency. "This is one of the first times a tribe has gotten its land back," commented Tom Little Bear Nason, who heads the Esselen Tribe of Monterey County, a nonprofit set up to accept ownership of the tract. The land, along the Little Sur River, will once again serve as a refuge for tribal members.

TRIBAL LAND USE

1986: The InterTribal Sinkyone Wilderness Council was founded by tribes in California's Mendocino and Lake counties as the first intertribal cultural land protection organization.

2014: The Seneca Nation of Indians of New York approved a measure ensuring that new landscape planting in public spaces on Seneca lands will be exclusively composed of local indigenous species, the first U.S. tribe to establish such a policy. Owners of private property at the Seneca Nation are encouraged to reintroduce Native species and remove invasive Eurasian plants. Its ongoing efforts included planting over 445 native trees and shrubs and reintroducing 25 different species into the landscape.

2015: The Suquamish signed the first tribal marijuana compact in Washington State as well as in the nation. The 10-year agreement with the Washington State Liquor and Cannabis Board allows the tribe to grow, process, and sell marijuana statewide.

2017: The Confederated Tribes of the Colville Reservation was the first tribe in Washington to receive a permit from the state department of agriculture authorizing hemp cultivation and marketing under the U.S. Agricultural Act of 2014. The tribal nation began by planting a 60-acre plot and researching the marketability of seed and fiber.

2017: The Squaxin Island Tribe broke ground for Native Sun Grown in March 2017, the first tribal marijuana grow site in the state of Washington. Located on the Olympic peninsula northwest of Olympia, the site consisted of five-plus acres.

PARK LANDS AND OTHER PROTECTED AREAS

1932: Francis X. Guardipee (Ah-koo-in-slak-mi Chief Lodgepole; 1885–1970) was the first Blackfeet tribal member to work as a park ranger, serving at Montana's Glacier National Park from 1932 to 1948. In 1916, Guardipee founded Boy Scout Troop 100, believed to be

The Navajo Nation Zoological and Botanical Park in Window Rock, Arizona, is the only Native American zoo in the United States. It is home to about 50 different species that are native to Navajo lands.

the first Native American troop in Montana. At Glacier, in 1973, Chief Lodgepole Peak, located in the Two Medicine area of the park, was named in his honor. In 2017, Glacier National Park featured a photo of Guardipee on its annual pass. In 2018, Guardipee was named to the Montana Cowboy Hall of Fame.

1977: The Navajo Nation Zoological and Botanical Center became the first Native American owned and operated zoo in the country. Initially located at the tribal fairgrounds, the facility was later moved to Tse Bonito Tribal Park in Window Rock, Arizona. The zoo began with a single orphan black bear donated to the Navajo Nation, expanding with other animals and resources over time.

1978: The Spiro Mounds Archaeological State Park, with assistance from the Oklahoma Archaeological Survey, opened an interpretive center as the first Oklahoma precontact American Indian archaeological site open to the public.

1982: The Confederated Salish and Kootenai Tribes in Montana officially established the first tribal wilderness area in the nation. Its Mission Mountain Tribal Wilderness Area includes some 92,000 acres of reservation land and, within it, a 10,000-acre grizzly bear conservation zone.

1989: Barbara Booher Sutteer (c. 1941–), Uintah-Ouray Ute, became the first American Indian woman to be appointed superintendent in the National Park Service, overseeing the Custer Battlefield National Monument (renamed Little Bighorn Battlefield National Monument in 1991) in Montana. Her appointment triggered letters of protest from Custer fans but was lauded by supporters of change and a more balanced view of the historic battle.

1989: Grand Portage State Park, which was established in 1989, lies within the reserva-

MapUp

The National Congress of the American Indian (NCAI) and Google held the first ever Indigenous Mapping Day in honor of the United Nation's International Day of the World's Indigenous Peoples on August 9, 2013. Besides NCAI, participants included Google Map Maker, Google Earth Outreach, and the Google American Indian Network. The MapUp was held to improve mapping information, making it possible for tribal participants to add or identify roads, schools, health facilities, offices, businesses, and more. Mapping could also be done in Native languages supported by Google Map Maker, including Cherokee, Navajo, Inuktitut, Inupiaq, Kalaallisut, and Hawaiian.

tion of the Grand Portage Band of Chippewa Indians in Minnesota. It is the only one of Minnesota's state parks not owned by the state; it was created and implemented through collaborative efforts with the tribal nation, which leases the land for the site.

1997: The first intertribal wilderness area in the country was established by the Inter-Tribal Sinkyone Wilderness Council, a non-profit land conservation consortium comprised of ten federally recognized tribes with cultural and ancestral ties to the Sinkyone region in California. The council purchased the 3,845-acre parcel of redwood forestland, a small portion of Sinkyone's indigenous territory, from the Trust for Public Land.

2011: Frog Bay Tribal National Park, owned by the Red Cliff Band of Lake Superior Chippewa in Wisconsin, became the first tribally owned and controlled park in the United States. Located along the shore of Lake Superior on the Red Cliff Indian Reservation in Wisconsin's Bayfield County, it began with an original 89-acre parcel of land reacquired by the tribal nation. Another 82-acre private parcel of land was acquired in 2017, protecting the lower estuary and mouth of Frog Creek and restoring former reservation lands to tribal ownership. The area includes Frog Bay Tribal National Park

and Frog Creek Conservation Management Area. The park is open to both tribal members and the general public, with part of the conservation area only open to designated uses by Red Cliff tribal members.

2013: Park ranger Joni Mae Makuakane-Jarrell (1956–) became the new chief of interpretation at Hawaii Volcanoes National Park (HVNP), the first Native Hawaiian to serve in the position. Makuakane-Jarrell, a 32-year park service veteran, worked at all five national park units on the island of Hawaii during her career. She initially served as an interpretive ranger at HVNP through the Young Adult Conservation Corps program, working her way through the ranks to become the park's supervisory ranger. "One of my visions for the park," Makuakane-Jarrell commented, "is sharing all the traditional Hawaiian names of places here. Hawaiians are very keen observers, and when they name things, it usually tells the story or history of the area."

2014: Kukutali Preserve, the first tribal state park in the United States to be co-owned and jointly managed by a federally recognized Indian tribe and a state government, opened to the public on June 16, 2014. Located within the Swinomish Reservation in Washington, it encompasses 84 acres on Kiket Island and

Population

The 1860 federal decennial census was the first to clearly identify any Native Americans for enumeration, or not. The instructions for enumerators that year specified: "Indians *not taxed* are not to be enumerated. The families of Indians who have renounced tribal rule, and who under state or territorial laws exercise the rights of citizens, are to be enumerated. In all such cases write 'Ind.' opposite their names, in column 6, under heading 'Color.'"

In 2020, Lizzie Chimiugak, Yup'ik, 90, became the first person counted in the 2020 U.S. Census on January 21, 2020. The Census, held every ten years, started in rural Alaska, in part out of necessity, to help reach residents before spring melt. After the count at Toksook Bay, Chimiugak and others participated in a celebration featuring an Alaska Native dance group and Alaska Native foods.

Flagstaff Point and nine acres on Fidalgo Island. Washington State Parks, with help from the Trust for Public Land, acquired the land in 2010 and the state-tribal partnership was worked out over four years.

2019: The Santa Rosa Band of Cahuilla in California received a $10,000 donation from the Soboba Band of Luiseño Indians to create its first park on the reservation. It will be some 28,000 square feet, located on a vacant lot next to tribal administration buildings, and feature playground equipment and tetherball and volleyball courts.

ENVIRONMENTAL ISSUES

1949: The Mescalero Apache in New Mexico sent the first all-Indian fire crews to battle an off-reservation fire in the Lincoln National Forest. The Mescalero Red Hats, named for their unique helmets, initiated a tradition of national service across reservations in the western United States.

1970: Tohono O'odham Utility Authority (TOUA) was one of the first tribally owned and operated electric utilities in the country. It was created by the Tohono O'odham Nation in Arizona to provide utility services to the tribe.

1989: Forester/ecologist/conservationist Michael DeMunn (Da hà dá nya), Seneca, organized the Finger Lakes Land Trust in the central New York State Finger Lakes region. The only known Seneca forester, he has dedicated his life to managing and improving forests in all aspects like erosion control, restoring abundance and diversity of native plant and animal life, and convincing owners to conserve their lands in perpetuity/public trust. Most of his forestry work is done with just simple tools and bare hands. DeMunn locates old-growth stands and protects them; to date, he has saved over 30,000 acres in New York State and northern Pennsylvania. A member of the Hawk Clan, his Seneca name means "he protects all things that come from the forest." His clan mother (Allegheny Seneca) was an herbalist and healer; DeMunn helped her gather plants for many years. An educator, lecturer, and workshop facilitator for colleges and organizations, he has also consulted for state parks, the National Park Service, lawyers, and real estate companies. Saving sacred sites is another passion of DeMunn's, who is also an artist and author. His children's books, *The Earth Is Good: A Chant in Praise of Nature* and *Places of Power,* help young people learn to appreciate the Earth's gifts and that they, too, are part of nature.

1990: The InterTribal Bison Cooperative was founded to encourage tribal nations to raise buffalo on their lands again. Fred Dubray, Cheyenne River Lakota, and five member nations helped start the work with some 1,500 buffalo. In 1997, the National Wildlife Federation signed a memorandum of understanding with the InterTribal Bison Cooperative, the first conservation agreement between an environmental organization and an intertribal group, to advocate for the return of bison to tribal lands.

1993: Honor the Earth was established by Anishinaabe environmentalist Winona LaDuke and Indigo Girls folk rock band members Amy Ray and Emily Saliers to create awareness and support for Native environmental issues. Headquartered in Calloway, Minnesota, it is a national organization that works to raise public awareness and to raise and direct funds to grassroots Native environmental initiatives. Its model, deeply rooted in community, history, and long-term struggles to protect the earth, is based on strategic analysis of what is needed to forge change in Indian country.

1993: Melissa K. Nelson, Turtle Mountain Chippewa, was named as the first Native executive director of the Cultural Conservancy.

1994: William Yellowtail Jr. (1948–), Crow, appointed by President Bill Clinton, became the regional administrator for the Environmental Protection Agency's Region 8 office in Denver, the first Native American and the first non-Coloradoan to hold the position. The post involved oversight of federal environmental programs in six states and for 27 tribes. Yellowtail had earlier served as a member of the Montana Senate for eight years.

1994: Corbin Harney (1920–2007), spiritual leader of the Western Shoshone Nation, founded the Shundahai Network to address spiritual and environmental concerns associated with nuclear threats. He also established Poo Ha Bah, a Native healing center in Tecopa, California. Harney, who traveled nationally and internationally as a spiritual leader and activist, was the recipient of numerous awards, including the Nuclear-Free Future Award in 2003. He wrote *The Way It Is: One Water, One Air, One Mother Earth* (1995) and *The Nature Way* (2009).

1997: The Louden Tribal Council of Galena, Alaska, created the first tribally owned corporation in Alaska—Yukaana Development Corporation (YDC), a for-profit environmental remediation business. It led a successful effort to clean up the contamination caused by a local military base. YDC also provides training and employment opportunities across the rural region.

1999: The Pueblo of Zuni in New Mexico was the first tribe in the country to propose plans for a sanctuary to house nonreleasable eagles for cultural and religious use. The Pueblo then opened the first Native American–owned and –operated eagle sanctuary. The award-winning Zuni Eagle Sanctuary, which revived the ancient practice of eagle husbandry and became a source of molted eagle feathers for tribal members, also initiated community education and raptor care training programs.

2001: Arnell Abold (1964–), Oglala Lakota, became the first Native woman to serve as

The Fish Wars of Washington State

Billy Frank Jr. (1931–2014), Nisqually tribal member, was a treaty rights activist and environmental leader. He is best remembered for his part in the grassroots movement in Washington state known as Fish Wars, where for decades he hosted a series of "fish-ins" protesting the state's refusal to honor fishing rights granted by the Treaty of Medicine Creek. The Nisqually, Puyallup, and Muckleshoot nations were all impacted from the 1960s through the 1970s. Frank's perseverance culminated in the Boldt Decision, which affirmed that Washington state tribes were entitled to half of each year's fish harvest. As a lifelong activist and the chairman of the Northwest Indian Fisheries Commission for over thirty years, Frank promoted cooperative management of natural resources. He was posthumously awarded the Presidential Medal of Freedom by President Barack Obama in 2015. The following year, a national refuge was renamed in his honor to the Billy Frank Jr. Nisqually National Wildlife Refuge.

Billy Frank Jr.

executive director of the InterTribal Buffalo Council (ITBC), an organization whose mission it is to restore buffalo to Indian Country. Established in 1992, ITBC is headquartered in Rapid City, South Dakota, and its membership has grown to include representation from over 60 federally recognized tribes. Abold previously served as fiscal director for the organization and has also worked for the Oglala Sioux Tribe, Red Cloud Indian School, and American Horse Indian School.

2001: Andrea Gilham (1965–), Blackfeet, became the first Native American woman to head a Bureau of Indian Affairs fire office at her home in Browning, Montana. She attended college at the University of Montana in Missoula, fighting fires during the summer. From 1989 to 1991, Gilham worked on a hotshot crew, an elite unit, in the Flathead National Forest. After earning her degree and moving into management, she continued to work fire lines every summer.

2003: The Rosebud Sioux Tribe in South Dakota became the first tribal nation in the country to sell wind power. In 1998, the tribe

had applied for a cooperative grant from the U.S. Department of Energy to build a commercial utility turbine, ultimately negotiating the first U.S. Department of Agriculture Rural Utilities Service loan to a tribe for a commercial wind energy project. Rosebud has sold excess clean energy to Basin Electric, with a multiyear sale of "green power" to Ellsworth Air Force Base in South Dakota. The tribe also negotiated the first tribal sale of renewable energy credits to NativeEnergy of Vermont.

2005: The Bad River Band of Lake Superior Chippewa was the first tribe in Wisconsin to be granted authority under the Clean Air Act to protect the nation's vital air resources as a sovereign partner with the U.S. Environmental Protection Agency.

2006: The Iowa Tribe of Oklahoma, which completed an eagle aviary in January 2006, became the first tribal nation in the country federally permitted through the U.S. Fish and Wildlife Services to rehabilitate injured eagles. It had received the first Eagle Aviary—Live permit in Oklahoma and a tribal wildlife grant for construction of an aviary in December 2005. The Iowa Tribe's Grey Snow Eagle House protects and rehabilitates injured bald and golden eagles from the state of Oklahoma and provides education, research, and other services.

2006: Lakota Solar Enterprises (LSE), one of the first 100 percent Native American–owned and –operated renewable energy companies, was founded by Henry Red Cloud, Oglala Lakota, on the Pine Ridge Reservation in South Dakota. LSE was followed by Red Cloud Renewable Energy Center (RCREC), which Red Cloud created to provide technical training and hands-on green job skills to tribal members. In 2013, he and Trees, Water & People opened the Sacred Earth Lodge, a dormitory and training facility that hosts hundreds of guests each year.

2008: The Augustine Band of Cahuilla Indians was the first tribe in Southern California to develop a major solar energy project approved by the U.S. Bureau of Indian Affairs. The tribe installed a 1.1-megawatt photovoltaic plant, located in the Augustine Solar Energy Park. The installation powers a major percentage of the energy needs of the tribe's business operations.

2009: The Lummi Nation, located northwest of Bellingham, Washington, developed the first tribally owned and operated commercial mitigation bank in the United States, designating a percentage of reservation land to the Lummi Nation Wetland and Habitat Mitigation Bank. The bank sells mitigation credits to tribal and nontribal projects, helping the tribal nation balance development and preservation goals for its lands.

2009: The Ramona Band of Cahuilla, which became the first fully "off grid" reservation with 100 percent renewable energy for all its facilities, was one of eight Southern California organizations recognized by the U.S.

Environmental Protection Agency in 2009 for efforts to protect and preserve the environment.

2010: The Chickasaw Nation opened the first tribally owned and operated compressed natural gas (CNG) fueling station in Oklahoma. "CNG not only lowers the cost of fuel and maintenance," Chickasaw governor Bill Anoatubby observed at the ribbon cutting, "it is better for the environment, boosts the Oklahoma economy and moves the U.S. closer to energy independence." The tribe plans to convert its vehicle fleet to have more that run on CNG.

2010: The Comanche Nation and Fish and Wildlife Service met to formally establish the first permitted and tribally managed noneagle feather repository in the country. Based in Cyril, Oklahoma, it became operated by Sia: The Comanche Nation Ethno-Ornithological Initiative. "Sia" is a Comanche word meaning "feather."

2010: *Qapirangajuq: Inuit Knowledge and Climate Change*, directed by Inuk filmmaker Zacharias Kunuk and Dr. Ian Mauro, became the world's first Inuktitut-language film about climate change. It explores Inuit environmental knowledge as well as the future of the Arctic.

2011: Kayenta Township in Arizona, a political subdivision of the Navajo Nation, became the first tribal community in the country to adopt the International Green Construction Code (IGCC), a regulatory code established to aid in the construction of sustainable buildings. The IGCC's goals include reducing energy usage while preserving natural and material resources.

2011: The Turtle Mountain Band of Chippewa Indians in North Dakota became the first tribe in the nation to ban hydraulic fracturing from its homelands. Called fracking, the method is used to extract oil and gas from deep beneath the earth, injecting chemical liquids into rocks at high pressure to make them break apart for petroleum to flow.

2013: The Indigenous Food and Agriculture Initiative was founded at the University of Arkansas at Fayetteville.

2013: The Quapaw Tribe in Oklahoma negotiated a remedial response cooperative agreement with the Environmental Protection Agency (EPA) Region 6 to self-perform the remediation of a culturally significant tribal property known as Catholic 40, the first tribal-led Superfund Site in the nation.

2015: The Confederated Salish and Kootenai Tribes (CSKT) in Montana became the first tribal nation in the United States to own a major hydro-electric facility. CSKT bought Kerr Dam on the Flathead River from Northwestern Energy and now operates it under Energy Keepers, Inc., an award-winning tribal entity. Initially called the Salish Kootenai Dam, the name was changed to Seli's Ksanka Qlispe' Dam to reflect the Native language names of the Salish, Kootenai, and Pend d'Oreille, all three parts of CSKT.

2016: LaDonna Brave Bull Allard (Ta Mak'a Wast'e Win, Good Earth Woman; 1956–2021), Standing Rock Sioux Tribe, founded the Sacred Stone Camp, the first resistance camp of the #NoDAPL movement to fight against the construction of the Dakota Access Pipeline. The camp was located on her land, some of the closest tribally owned land to the construction site, and drew thousands of water protectors. The #NoDAPL movement became one of the most powerful Indigenous rights movements in recent times.

2016: Louisiana's Isle de Jean Charles received a grant of $48 million from

LaDonna Brave Bull Allard

the U.S. Department of Housing and Urban Development, the first allocation of federal tax dollars to move an entire community away from the increasingly adverse impacts of climate change. Dubbed the nation's first climate change refugees, the island's residents include mostly Biloxi–Chitimacha–Choctaw tribal members but also those from the United Houma Nation. The plan, no longer supported by tribal leadership, would resettle residents at a location purchased by the state 40 miles north in Schriever.

2016: Native Renewables was cofounded by Navajo (Diné) tribal members Wahleah Johns and Suzanne Singer on the Navajo Reservation. The organization's stated mission is to empower Native American families to achieve energy independence by growing renewable energy capacity and affordable access to off-grid power. In 2021, President Joseph Biden appointed Johns to head the U.S. Department of Energy Office of Indian Energy Policy and Programs. Singer, executive director of Native Renewables, is a former staff engineer and post-doc at Lawrence Livermore National Laboratory.

2016: The St. Regis Mohawk removed the Hogansburg Dam, the first removal of an operating hydroelectric dam in New York State and, according to federal officials, the nation's first decommissioning of a federally licensed dam by a Native American tribe. The measure was part of the tribal nation's long struggle to restore territory despoiled by industrial pollution.

2017: The Moapa Southern Paiute Solar Project became the first utility-scale solar power plant to be built on tribal land. Constructed and operated by First Solar, it is located on the Moapa River Indian Reservation some 30 miles north of Las Vegas, Nevada. The project has a long-term power purchase agreement with the Los Angeles Department of Water and Power to bring clean, renewable energy to the city's residents. It can generate enough energy to power an estimated 111,000 homes.

2017: Solar Bear was founded by Robert Blake, a member of the Red Lake Band of Chippewa, in Minneapolis, Minnesota. The American Indian–owned solar installation company installed solar panels on the Red Lake Nation Government Center in 1918, the start of a process to make the tribal nation energy independent. In 2020, Blake started a second company called Native Sun Community Power Development, a nonprofit that promotes renewable energy and helps participants transition to clean energy.

2018: The Affiliated Tribes of the Northwest Indians (ATNI) and eight northwestern tribal nations were among the first tribes to join We Are Still In, a coalition of U.S. leaders confronting climate change in the aftermath of President Donald Trump's decision to withdraw the United States from the Paris Agreement. Tribal nations joining the coalition include Blue Lake Rancheria in California, Nisqually, Quinault, Hoh, Jamestown S'Klallam, and Suquamish tribes of Washington, Confederated Tribes of the Umatilla Indian Reservation in Oregon, and Confederated Salish and Kootenai Tribe of Montana.

2018: The White Earth Band of Ojibwe in Minnesota adopted the Rights of Manoomin to protect wild rice and the freshwater sources essential to its survival, the first law to recognize legal rights of plant species. White Earth and the 1855 Treaty Authority, a treaty rights organization, established legal personhood for the rice. They drew from the Rights of Nature, an international concept that says nature should have the same rights as humans. Attorney Frank Bibeau, executive director of the 1855 Treaty Authority

and a White Earth citizen, defines the rights as an extension of Ojibwe treaty rights.

2019: CannonBall Community Solar Farm, the first and largest solar energy farm in North Dakota, was built in the community of Cannon Ball on the Standing Rock Reservation. Representing approximately half of the state's solar power, the enterprise was a joint effort of solar energy nonprofits and the Lakota tribal nation. The solar farm is located about three miles from the Dakota Access Pipeline, which generated massive protests in 2016 concerning issues related to the pipeline's environmental impact.

2019: The first Tribal Multi-Hazard Mitigation Plan was created by the Scotts Valley Band of Pomo Indians, Big Valley Band of Pomo Indians, Elem Indian Colony, Habematolel Pomo of Upper Lake, and Robinson Rancheria of Pomo Indians in the wake of devastating fires in northern California in 2018. The plan identifies hazards, assesses risk, and proposes strategies that members can implement to protect their respective tribal communities.

2019: The Yurok Tribe in California declared rights of personhood for the Klamath River, likely the first such action for a river in North America. The declaration, part of a growing Rights of Nature movement, is aimed at protecting the environment.

2020: The Minnesota Legislature approved a $46 million appropriation for the Prairie Island Net Zero Project, which is envisioned to create an energy system that results in net-zero emissions, a first for the Prairie Island Indian Community (PIIC). The funding comes from the state's renewable development account, which was established as a stipulation to allowing Xcel Energy to temporarily store nuclear waste in dry casks outside its nuclear power plant located adjacent to PIIC.

2020: The Nevada Department of Wildlife and the Pyramid Lake Paiute Tribe reintroduced more than 20 bighorn sheep into the Pyramid Lake Range, marking the first time since the early 1900s that the species had been seen. The sheep population had once thrived in the mountain range but had been wiped out.

2020: The New York State Department of Environmental Conservation (DEC) and the Saint Regis Mohawk Tribe (SRMT) announced the first state-tribal partnership for Area of Concern (AOC) on the U.S. side of the Great Lakes. The historic cooperative agreement will help to accelerate the restoration of natural resources and traditional Native American uses within the St. Lawrence River AOC near Massena, New York, and the Akwesasne Territory.

VOTING RIGHTS

Obstacles at Every Turn: Barriers to Political Participation Faced by Native American Voters, released June 4, 2020, "provides detailed evidence that Native people face obstacles at every turn in the electoral process: from registering to vote, to casting votes, to having votes counted."

—*Native American Rights Fund*

1912: Wilhelmina Kekelaokalaninui Widemann Dowsett (1861–1929), Native Hawaiian, founded the National Women's Equal Suffrage Association of Hawaii, the first women's suffrage organization in the Territory of Hawaii. She actively fought for the right of women to vote, encouraging other Hawaiians to join the effort.

1924: The first Indian League of Women Voters was founded in the community of Odanah on the Bad River Band of Lake Superior Chippewa Reservation in Wisconsin. Established in October 1924, the League was composed of 86 Odanah women. Cecelia Rabideaux, one of the founders, served as chair.

1934: Lucille Roullier Otter (1916–1997), Salish, was hired to work at the Dixon, Montana, headquarters of the Indian Division of the Civilian Conservation Corps (ICCC), the first woman to work in an administrative capacity in the Indian CCC. Besides being in charge of budgeting ICCC projects, she oversaw accounts, payroll, and purchase orders. Otter later became known for her efforts to encourage tribal members to vote, initially working to register women. Over time, working against barriers preventing Indians from voting, she registered over a thousand voters on the Flathead reservation. In 1988, Otter was awarded an honorary degree by Salish Kootenai College.

1948: Miguel Trujillo Sr. (1904–1989), also called Michael Trujillo, Isleta Pueblo, won the right for Native Americans to vote in New Mexico. Trujillo attended the Albuquerque Indian School and the Haskell Institute in Lawrence, Kansas, before earning a bachelor's degree from the University of New Mexico. A veteran of World War II, he'd been a Marine sergeant in the military. Trujillo, who was working on a master's degree from UNM, filed suit for the right to vote. Although the federal government had granted citizenship to Native Americans in 1924, the state constitution still barred them from voting. The U.S. District Court of New Mexico sided with Trujillo in *Trujillo v. Garley.* "We are unable to escape the conclusion that under the Fourteenth and Fifteenth Amendments," the ruling found, "this constitutes discrimination on the ground of race."

1983: *Windy Boy v. Big Horn County, Montana,* filed in 1983, was the first Indian case outside the South undertaken by the Voting Rights Project of the American Civil Liberties Union. Janine Pease (then Janine Windy Boy), a member of the Crow Nation, and seven other plaintiffs sued Big Horn County because of vote dilution and voter suppression tactics. In 1986, U.S. district judge Edward Rafeedie ruled that the county's election system violated the Voting Rights Act, finding, "Past and present discrimination against [the Northern Cheyenne and Crow] makes it more difficult for [them] to participate in the political process."

2015: Advance Native Political Leadership was founded, the first Native organization working to increase the representation of Native leaders in U.S. politics. The co-founders include Chrissie Castro, Diné/Chicana; Anathea Chino, Acoma Publo; Kevin Killer, Oglala Lakota; and Minnesota lieutenant governor Peggy Flanagan, White Earth Nation.

2019: The Native American Voting Rights Act passed the Washington State legislature and was signed into law by Governor Jay Inslee on March 14, 2019. The provisions include allowing Native Americans to use nontraditional addresses if living on a reservation and permitting tribes to request more election resources from the state.

RELIGION

"In the beginning, we were told that the human beings who walk about on Earth have been provided with all things necessary for life. We were instructed to carry a love for one another and to show a great respect for all the beings of this Earth. We were shown that our life exists with the tree life, that our well-being depends on the well-being of the vegetable life, that we are close relations of the four-legged beings. In our ways, spiritual consciousness is the highest form of politics...."

—*Chief Leon Shenandoah, message delivered to the General Assembly of the United Nations, October 24, 1985*

1799: Handsome Lake Religion or Longhouse Religion was a new religious movement founded by Ganioda'yo (Handsome Lake), a Seneca leader, healer, and prophet, that emerged among the Seneca, in the northeastern United States, one of the Six Nations of the Haudenosaunee (Iroquois Confederacy). While severely ill, he received spiritual revelations that became the foundation of the Gai'wiio, or Good Message of the religion. Handsome Lake devoted the rest of his life to preaching the beliefs among the Six Nations. His teachings were later recited as the Code of Handsome Lake by those qualified to do so.

1870: Ghost Dance of 1870 was a religious movement founded by the prophet Wodziwob and originated among the Northern Paiute of the Walker River Reservation. It arose

at a time of great suffering and privation from loss of land and means of subsistence as well as calamitous drought, starvation, and illness epidemics. Wodziwob's prophecies included the restoration of conditions that existed before the arrival of Europeans in the region. Elements associated with the Ghost Dance were curing and increase rites, use of a traditional Paiute Round Dance, and a number of ceremonies. The movement spread to other tribal nations in the region and local variations developed.

1881: The Indian Shaker Religion was founded by John Slocum (1838–1897), a member of the Squaxin Island Tribe in Washington. In 1881, during an illness in which he was reportedly near death, he had a vision in which he was instructed in the

An illustration of the first Indian Shaker church, circa 1892, which was located in Mud Bay, Washington.

new religion. Sometime later, Slocum became ill again and was cared for by his wife, Mary Thompson Slocum, who started shaking uncontrollably in his presence. John Slocum interpreted her shaking as a spiritual manifestation saving him from dying. Shaking was then incorporated into the religion and hence its name, a way to dispel illness or bad feelings. Slocum and other adherents were regularly punished, including imprisonment, for opposing government restrictions against tribal cultural and religious practices. On June 7, 1892, the Shaker Church was organized as an association at Mud Bay, Washington, and incorporated in nearby Olympia, on June 20, 1910. It was also incorporated in Oregon and California.

Late 1880s: William Faw Faw (1854–1924) was an Otoe-Missouria prophet who started a new religious movement that was believed to be influenced by the Drum Dance (Dream Dance) introduced to his people by the Potawatomi. He began his new religious practices after receiving a spiritual message from a vision he had while ill. A ceremony initiated by Faw Faw included the planting of cedar trees, tobacco offerings, gift exchanges, and presents for the poor. It also included distinctive design elements, such as cedar trees, in clothing. Faw Faw's coats with beaded designs are part of some museum collections. His religious movement was short lived, believed to have lasted from at least 1891 to 1895. The leader, who opposed land allotment, encouraged his followers to return to Native traditions and reject European ways.

1890: Wovoka (c. 1856–1932), Northern Paiute, was known as the prophet who founded or revitalized the Ghost Dance of 1890. Born near Walker Lake in present-day Esmeralda County, Nevada, he was the son of visionary leader Tavibo (also Numu-tibo'o). Wovoka was influenced by a neighboring white farmer, David Wilson, and his family, who gave him the name Jack Wilson. Wovoka's Ghost Dance revelation occurred in 1889, following an experience of death and rebirth, during which he received powers from the Creator, including prophecies. Wovoka also received teachings for his people, advising them to live in peace. If they followed the instructions he imparted, they would be reunited with family members and friends in the other world, one without illness or death. Wovoka also taught a sacred dance, which the people were to perform. From his teachings, the Ghost Dance religion emerged and soon spread to other tribal groups. It was opposed by government agents and missionaries, who worked to suppress it, ending in tragedy among the Lakota with the Wounded Knee massacre in Dakota Territory on December 29, 1890.

Wovoka

c. 1904: Jake Hunt (Titcam Nashat) 1804–1913), Klikitat, founded the Waptashi or Feather Religion, also referred to as the Feather Dance or the Spinning Religion, a revitalization movement in the Pacific Northwest. Hunt's instructions for it came from visions he had when he fell asleep during a period of mourning. Upon awakening, he set in motion the spiritual instructions he had received. Hunt's actions included building a ceremonial longhouse and taking a new name, Titcam Nashat, meaning Earth Thunderer. He expanded the use of eagle feathers in the religion, included mirrors, and held ceremonies on Sundays. Hunt prohibited alcohol use by members of the faith and adopted curing, where followers were able to treat illnesses. Hunt also sought to spread the religion to

seven nations, as he had been spiritually instructed to do.

1932: Pretty-Shield (1856–1944), Crow medicine woman, became one of the first to have her life story recorded. Author Frank Linderman initially published Pretty-Shield's story as *Red Mother* and then as *Pretty-shield: Medicine Woman of the Crows*.

1961: Mountain Wolf Woman (Xéhachiwinga; 1884-1960), Ho-Chunk (Winnebago), shared her life story with her adopted niece, ethnologist Nancy Oestreich Lurie, who published it as *Mountain Wolf Woman: Sister of Crashing Thunder*. Recorded by Lurie in 1958, it became one of the earliest firsthand accounts of the experiences of a Native American woman. Mountain Wolf Woman, born in Wisconsin, grew up in the traditional religion of her people, eventually participating in Christian services in boarding school and beyond. She became an adherent to the Peyote Religion, providing an account of her conversion and practice in her autobiography.

1975: Frank Fools Crow (c. 1890–1989), Oglala Lakota spiritual leader and medicine man, was the first holy man of a Native religion to deliver an invocation in the U.S. Senate. He said the prayer in Lakota, and it was translated into English.

1991: *Chiefly Feast: The Enduring Kwakiutl Potlach* at the American Museum of Natural History was the first comprehensive survey of Kwakiutl art by a U.S. museum. It was also the first exhibition the museum did with the assistance of Native people since George Hunt, Kwakiutl/English, came to New York in 1901. The display included 120 objects acquired by the museum between 1897 and 1902 by anthropologist Franz Boas, assistant curator at the museum.

1991: In a novel gesture, the U.S. Bureau of Prisons published a booklet to educate its staff on Indian ceremonies. The booklet said a sacred Indian pipe should be accorded the same respect as the Bible, Koran, or Torah. Laws for Indigenous ceremonies vary from state to state, yet prisoners from all other religions are allowed to observe their traditions. In some states, Indigenous prisoners have had their hair cut against their will—for many, hair cutting is part of a grief ritual—and have been denied access to sacred herbs like tobacco used in ceremonies.

1997: Thomas J. Stillday Jr. (1934–2008), Ojibwe from the Red Lake Nation, became the first American Indian and the first spiritual leader outside the Judeo-Christian tradition to serve as chaplain in the Minnesota Senate, a two-year term. His historic first meant that an Indigenous religion was officially represented there for the first time in 139 years of statehood. Born in his family's home at Red Lake, Stillday served in the army for 12 years and was a combat engineer in the Korean War, where he and fellow Ojibwe used their tribal language in coded radio communications. Known for his expertise in his Indigenous language, culture, and religion, he was also a championship grass dancer and singer. Stillday, who was often sought after for his counsel, also served as tribal council member, school board member, and in other leadership roles.

2005: *Po'pay: Leader of the First American Revolution* was published, the first time Pueblo historians recounted the history of the Pueblo Revolt of 1680 in book form. Edited by Joe S. Sando, Jemez Pueblo, and Herman Agoyo, Ohkay Owingeh (formerly San Juan Pueblo), the authors drew on oral history and other sources to discuss the momentous history. Po'pay (?–1690) was a visionary leader, a medicine man from San Juan Pueblo known for leading the 1680 rebellion against oppressive Spanish rule.

PEYOTE RELIGION/NATIVE AMERICAN CHURCH

"The U.S. Supreme Court reversed a long line of settled cases in order to rule that the use of the sacrament of Native American worship, the holy medicine, peyote, is not protected under the First Amendment of the constitution. They said, in our case, our religious exercises, our form of worship, the use of our holy sacrament, is not protected by the Constitution. The Court said that Native Americans, who have enjoyed religious liberty on this land since before the pilgrims fled here, are no longer entitled to religious liberty. This trampling of Native American religious liberty is intolerable. Our people have been using the holy medicine, peyote, for thousands of years, thousands of years."

—*Reuben A. Snake Jr.,*
September 29, 1990, U.S. Capitol

1500s: Peyote use was first documented by Franciscan missionary Bernardino de Sahagún, who described its use among the Chichimeca tribal group in Mexico. According to him, the Chichimeca called the plant *peiotl* and believed that its powers included protection from danger.

1620: During the Spanish Inquisition, inquisitors issued an edict banning Peyotism as an act of superstition. They decreed that those who disobeyed would face repercussions. Over the next 265 years, hearings involving court cases prosecuted under the edict were held in some 45 Spanish settlements or towns.

c. 1880s: Quanah Parker (Kwaina, "Fragrant"; c. 1848–1911), Comanche, an influential peyote leader, is considered the originator of the half-moon ceremony in Indian Territory (present-day Oklahoma). His father was Peta Nocona (Noconi, "Wanderer"), chief of the Comanche's Kwahadi (Quahada) division, and his Euro-American mother, Cynthia Ann Parker, had been captured as a child and later became Nocona's wife. Parker's involvement with peyote is believed to have started in the 1880s, when peyotists successfully used it to treat a wound or illness. As a roadman, or leader, he was a proponent of the half-moon ceremony taught to him by Lipan Apaches Billy Chiwat and Pinero. The ceremony, with its half-moon-shaped altar, became known as the Comanche Way, the Kiowa Way, and the Quanah Parker Way. An influential chief, Parker served as a judge on the Courts of Indian Offenses after the tribal court system was organized at the consolidated Kiowa, Comanche, and Wichita Agency in 1886. Federal officials approved his appointment although he practiced tribal traditions they generally punished, including Peyotism and polygamy. Parker defended the Peyote Religion. He and other peyotists testified openly before the Oklahoma Constitutional Convention in 1907 in defense of the legal religious use of peyote. "The White man goes into his church and talks about Jesus," Parker said. "The Indian goes into his tipi and talks with Jesus."

Quanah Parker

c. 1880s: John Wilson (Nishkû'ntu, "Moon Head"; c. 1840–1901), Caddo/Delaware/French, referred to as "the Revealer of Peyote," introduced a new peyote ceremony in Indian Territory (present-day Oklahoma) in the 1880s. He was Lenape and French but is said to have identified himself as Caddo and spoke that language. Initially a medicine man, he experienced peyote and became

John Wilson

a roadman, or leader. His ritual became known as the Big Moon, also called the Wilson Way and Cross Fire. In contrast to the Half-Moon peyote ceremony, Wilson's ritual included a larger, horseshoe-shaped altar and ceremonial differences. The cross, representative of the four directions in tribal cultures, later became associated with the Christian cross. Wilson was also an active leader in the Ghost Dance of 1890 in Indian Territory but returned to Peyotism as a full-time leader and practitioner.

1899: The first statute law prohibiting the use of peyote was enacted in Indian Territory (present-day Oklahoma). The law's Section 2652 deemed it "unlawful for any person to introduce on any Indian reservation or Indian allotment situated within this Territory or to have in possession, barter, sell, give, or otherwise dispose of, any 'Mescal Bean,' or the product of any such drug to any allotted Indian in this Territory." It also specified penalties, including fines and/or imprisonment.

c. 1901: John Rave (1856–1917), Winnebago from Nebraska, introduced the Peyote Religion among the Winnebago people. Rave experienced Peyotism for the first time in Indian Territory (present-day Oklahoma) in the late 1800s and began practicing it when he returned home. He attributed positive changes in his life, such as recovery from a serious illness, to the healing power of peyote. Rave's ceremony became known as the John Rave Cross Fire ritual and included Christian symbols and other elements.

1912: Jesse Clay (1878–1928), Winnebago and a peyote roadman, introduced the Half-Moon Ceremony of the Peyote Religion to the Winnebago people. Clay observed the ritual during a visit in Oklahoma with Jock Bull Bear, Arapaho. A year later, Bull Bear visited Clay's home in Nebraska and conducted the ceremony. After learning it, Clay served as its roadman. The Half-Moon Peyotism was the second branch of the religion among the Winnebago after the Cross Fire ritual.

1914: The Peyote Society or Union Church Society, the first Peyotism church on record, was referred to in a U.S. court hearing. Little is known about the society, and it is likely that it was not legally incorporated.

1914: Jonathan (also Johnathan) Koshiway (1886–1971), Sac and Fox (also identified as Otoe), founded the First Born Church of Christ, the second peyote church and the first one to be legally incorporated. Koshiway, who was born on the Sac and Fox Reservation in Kansas, attended the Chilocco Indian School in Oklahoma and Haskell Institute in Kansas. His first experience using peyote occurred on the Otoe reservation, where he married an Otoe woman. Koshiway, a roadman described as "the Grand Old Man of Peyote," worked for more than 40 years advancing the religion.

1918: The Native American Church, established in Oklahoma by intertribal adherents of the Peyote Religion, was first incorporated. The purpose as defined in the articles of incorporation included fostering and promoting religious belief with the practice of the Peyote Sacrament. The action provided legal definition for the Peyote Religion and a means for Peyotists to protect it. Following the initial incorporation, the Native American Church was founded in other states. The 1918 charter was amended in 1944 and became the Native American Church of the United States. Later, the national organization changed its name to the Native American Church of North America to include Canadian adherents.

1921: The Peyote Church of Christ was incorporated in Thurston County, Nebraska, by Winnebago peyotists, the first such church incorporated outside the state of Oklahoma. Thirty-eight people, including leaders such as Albert Hensley and Jesse Clay, signed the charter.

1944: Frank Takes Gun (1908–1988), Crow, was elected vice president of the Native American Church of the United States, one of the organization's first officers and the only official chosen from outside the state of Oklahoma. He was reelected until 1956, when the organization held its first election as the Native American Church of North America and he became president. Takes Gun worked to establish and maintain religious freedom, encouraging members to incorporate peyote churches under the laws of their states to enhance protection. He assisted with incorporations in Utah, New Mexico, Arizona, Colorado, California, Nevada, and Canada. Takes Gun spent years seeking legalization of Peyotism on the Navajo Reservation.

1954: The Native American Church of Canada was incorporated in Red Pheasant, Saskatchewan, Canada.

1966: The Native American Church of Navajoland was formed. The founders applied to be incorporated within the state of Arizona in 1970 and 1971. However, they were denied as the state opposed the use of peyote. In 1973 it was incorporated by the state of New Mexico.

1990: Reuben A. Snake Jr. (1937–1993), Winnebago, became the official spokesperson for the Native American Church (NAC), following the Supreme Court decision in *Employment Division, Department of Human Resources of Oregon v. Smith* that held that the Free Exercise Clause permits the state to prohibit sacramental peyote use and to deny unemployment benefits to persons fired for such use. Snake, a prominent roadman and internationally known leader, was tasked with leading the battle to protect the sacramental use of peyote. He organized and coordinated the Native American Religious Freedom Project, working tirelessly for federal legislation that would amend the American Indian Religious Freedom Act (AIRFA). Snake did not live to see the outcome of his hard work—the AIRFA amendments passed into law in 1994, allowing the traditional use of peyote by American Indians for religious purposes. An account of Snake's life appears in *Reuben Snake, Your Humble Serpent: Indian Visionary and Activist*, as told to Jay C. Fikes (1996).

NON-NATIVE RELIGION

"This Lakota world view meshes with the Baha'i world view. The same Creator that sent Moses and Jesus also sent the White Buffalo Calf Woman and Baha'u'llah—the prophet founder of the Baha'i faith. So it's not difficult for me to reconcile the teachings of the White Buffalo Calf Woman and Baha'u'llah. I see it—Baha'u'llah's teachings—as the next step of Lakota ways. Only now we take our place in the world community, with all Indian people united."

—Jacqueline Left Hand Bull, Lakota, first American Indian elected chairperson of Baha'i National Spiritual Assembly

1643: Hiacoomes (c. 1610–1690), from Noepe (Martha's Vineyard), became known as the first Wampanoag to convert to Christianity. He was influenced by English pastor Thomas Mayhew Jr., who instructed him in Puritan beliefs and doctrines. Assisted by Mayhew, Hiacoomes began preaching to his fellow Wampanoag. In 1670, he was ordained a minister, and the first Indian church was created at Martha's Vineyard.

1651: Puritan missionary John Eliot established the first of 14 Indian "praying towns" in Natick, Massachusetts. The endeavor dislocated Indigenous Algonquian people from their own homes and communities to convert them to Christianity and English lifeways in such towns. Participants became known as "Praying Indians," following Christian teachings and living under English law.

1663: *Mamusse Wunneetupa-natamwe Up-Biblum God*, developed by Puritan missionary John Eliot, was published in the Massa-

Rowley of Roanoke Island

A Roanoke Island man known as Rowley became the first Native American to be baptized and buried in England. He traveled to that country with Englishmen returning there from the land area they called Virginia. Rowley, who was presented at the court of Queen Elizabeth, was baptized on March 12, 1588. He died the following year, on April 7, 1589, and was buried at St. Mary's Church graveyard in Bideford, England. In 1984, the town of Manteo, North Carolina, requested that Rowley be honored; the request was granted and a memorial plaque in Rowley's honor was placed at the Bideford church.

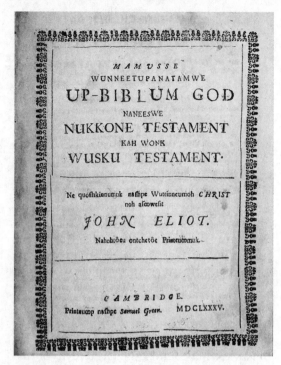

MAMUSSE
WUNNEETUPANATAMWE
UP-BIBLUM GOD
NANEESWE
NUKKONE TESTAMENT
KAH WONK
WUSKU TESTAMENT·

Ne quoſhkinnumuk naſhpe Wuttinneumoh *CHRIST*
noh aſoowefit
JOHN ELIOT.
Nahohtôeu ontchetôe Priſteuôomuk.

CAMBRIDGE.
Printeuôop naſhpe *Samuel Green.*   MDCLXXXV.

Also known as the *Eliot Indian Bible,* the *Mamusse Wunneetupa-natamwe Up-Biblum God* was translated by John Eliot from the Geneva Bible into the Massachusett language. Released in 1661 with only the New Testament, a new edition came out in 1663 with both the Old and New Testaments.

rian Colin Calloway writes, "He was, in effect, Dartmouth's first development officer."

1769: Founded on July 16, 1769, Mission San Diego de Alcalá was established by Franciscan missionary priest Junípero Serra in present-day San Diego, California. It was the first in a series of 21 missions built by Spanish Franciscans stretching more than 500 miles between San Diego and Sonoma. The purpose of the mission system was to Christianize and colonize Native peoples in Alta California (today's state of California). California Indians are erroneously called "Mission Indians." Serra is considered the architect of the brutal system, which was devastating to Native people.

1815: Henry ʻŌpūkahaʻia (often spelled Obookiah) (1792–1818) became identified as the first Native Hawaiian to convert to Christianity. While a child, his parents were slain by Hawaiian warriors, leading him to eventually secure passage onboard an American merchant ship. During the journey, a sailor befriended ʻŌpūkahaʻia and taught him English. He arrived in New Haven, Connecticut, in 1809, where he was introduced to Christianity by the Reverend Timothy Dwight and others. Ultimately, ʻŌpūkahaʻia's experiences influenced the founding of the Foreign Mission School, initially located in New Haven, and then Cornwall, Connecticut. By 1817, six Hawaiians were among a dozen or so students enrolled at the school. In 1818, ʻŌpūkahaʻia died of typhus fever and was buried in Cornwall. Years later, at the request of descendants, his remains were repatriated to Hawaii. The reburial was held at Kahikolu Congregational Church and Cemetery in Napoʻopoʻo on August 15, 1993. ʻŌpūkahaʻia's legacy includes inspiring Christian missions, translating the Book of Genesis into a phonetic Hawaiian alphabet, and a posthumously published memoir.

chuset language, the first Bible printed in British North America. Eliot, whose first Algonquian teacher and translator was Cockenoe, Montauk, was assisted by him as well as Job Nesutan, Massachusetts; John Sassamon, Massachusett; and James Printer, Nipmuc, to translate and create the first alphabetic writing system for a Native American language.

1766: Samson Occom (1723–1792), Mohegan, was the first American Indian minister to visit Britain, a trip he undertook to help raise money for American Indian students to attend Moor's Charity School in Lebanon, Connecticut, and what became Dartmouth College in Hanover, New Hampshire. As histo-

Henry Obookiah

The Mission San Diego de Alcalá was established, for one reason, to convert Native peoples to Christianity.

1823: Peter Jones (Kahkewaquonaby, Sacred Feathers; 1802–1856), Mississauga (Ojibway), born in Burlington Heights above Lake Ontario in Canada, became the first Native Methodist missionary to the Ojibway following his conversion to Christianity in 1823. Also a translator, his linguistic work included work on the earliest translations of the Bible into the Ojibway language. He translated hymns, prayers, and other materials as well, his efforts benefitting non-Indian missionaries such as James Evans and Thomas Hurlburt, who began to compete against him for assignments and credit. In addition to his religious leadership, Jones served as chief to the Credit River Mis-

Peter Jones

sissauga, his mother's people, and to another band. He fought for Native land rights, traveling to Britain to do so. In 1845, Jones was photographed in Edinburgh, Scotland, believed to be the first photographic study of a Canadian Indigenous person. His writings include *Life and Journals* (1860) and *History of the Ojebway Indians* (1861), published posthumously.

1833: Jesse Bushyhead (Unaduti; 1804–1844), Cherokee, was the first ordained Cherokee Baptist minister. He became the pastor of his own church at Amohee in Tennessee, also helping to spread the gospel and found new churches. Bushyhead was an associate of the Reverend

Indigenous Firsts: A History of Native American Achievements and Events

San Estevan del Rey Mission Church was a base for Spanish colonization. Centuries later, it was listed on the National Register of Historic Monuments.

San Estevan del Rey Mission

In 1629, the Franciscans founded the San Estevan del Rey Mission Church to control and acculturate the people at the Acoma Pueblo people (in present-day New Mexico) and to establish a base for Spanish colonization. In 2007, it became the first building in a Native American community to be named a National Trust for Historic Preservation site. Both the Pueblo and the mission are listed on the National Register of Historic Monuments. The mission has also been named a Save America's Treasures site and one of 100 endangered sites by the World Monuments Fund and is the oldest and largest intact adobe mission in North America.

Evan Jones, the superintendent of the Baptist Mission to the Cherokee, serving as an assistant missionary. He worked with Jones to translate sermons, the Book of Genesis, and other religious works into the Cherokee language. In 1834, Bushyhead was appointed as a justice of the Cherokee Supreme Court. He also held other high tribal offices and served as a delegate to Washington, D.C., at times. Bushyhead also assisted with removal, leading Cherokees from their southeastern homeland to Indian Territory (present-day Oklahoma) during the forced migration. He and Evans resumed their religious efforts in the new location near present-day Westville, Oklahoma, establishing a Baptist mission. In 1840, Bushyhead became chief justice of the Cherokee Nation, serving until his death.

1833: Charles Journeycake (Neshapanacumin; 1817–1894) was the first Delaware (Lenni Lenape) west of the Mississippi River to be converted to Christianity. His conversion occurred shortly after the removal of his people from Ohio to Kansas. In 1841, Journeycake became a charter member of the newly organized Delaware and Mohegan Baptist Mission Church at their new home. He preached in a number of languages, including Delaware, Shawnee, Wyandot, Seneca, and Ottawa.

Charles Journeycake

Journeycake later helped negotiate a new homeland for his people in Indian Territory (present-day Oklahoma) following Euro-American pressures for them to leave Kansas. In 1867, the tribal group did relocate and again had to rebuild. Journeycake, a recognized chief, continued in his leadership role. He was ordained in 1872 and served as a pastor until the end of his life.

1834: Pablo Tac (1822–1841), Luiseño, enrolled at the Collegium Urbanum de Propaganda Fide in Rome with fellow tribesman Agapito Amanix, the first seminarians from California missions. During the course of his studies, Tac created a written form of Luiseño, producing a groundbreaking manuscript of his people's language, history, and oral traditions. Both students died while studying in Rome, Amanix in 1837 and Tac in 1841. It would take nearly a century before Tac's manuscript was published.

1839: *Ka Palapala Hemolele* (The Holy Scriptures), the first edition of the complete Bible in the Hawaiian language, was published in 1839. In 2012, a new edition called *Ka Baibala Hemolele* (The Holy Bible), with modern Hawaiian orthography using complete diacritics, was finished and released for the first time.

1840: Joseph Napeshnee (Napeshneeduta; c. 1800–1870) was the first full-blood Dakota male to convert to Christianity. He was baptized at Lac qui Parle Mission (a French translation of the Indigenous Dakota name, meaning "lake that speaks"), located near present-day Montevideo, Minnesota, on February 21, 1840. Christened Joseph Napeshnee, he eventually served as a ruling elder in the Presbyterian Church for nearly ten years. The first written Dakota language alphabet and dictionary were created at Lac qui Parle, which was a site for missionary work to Dakotas for almost 20 years.

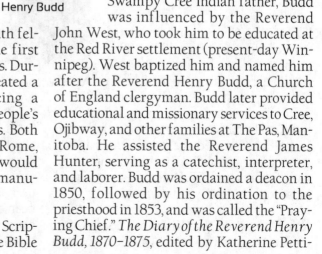
Henry Budd

1853: Henry Budd (Sakacewescam, "Going Up the Hill"; c. 1812–1875), Cree, was the first North American Indian to be ordained to the priesthood by the Church of England. The son of a Métis mother and a Swampy Cree Indian father, Budd was influenced by the Reverend John West, who took him to be educated at the Red River settlement (present-day Winnipeg). West baptized him and named him after the Reverend Henry Budd, a Church of England clergyman. Budd later provided educational and missionary services to Cree, Ojibway, and other families at The Pas, Manitoba. He assisted the Reverend James Hunter, serving as a catechist, interpreter, and laborer. Budd was ordained a deacon in 1850, followed by his ordination to the priesthood in 1853, and was called the "Praying Chief." *The Diary of the Reverend Henry Budd, 1870–1875,* edited by Katherine Petti-

In 1942, the WPA rebuilt the Lac qui Parle Mission, which was originally erected in 1835.

pas, was published in 1974. The Henry Budd College for Ministry at The Pas, Manitoba, Canada, trains theologians.

1855: James Chrysostom Bouchard (Watomika, Swift Foot; 1823–1889), Delaware, was the first American Indian to be ordained to the Roman Catholic priesthood in the United States. Following a conversion to the Presbyterian faith, he converted to Catholicism. In 1848, he entered the Jesuit Order at Florissant, outside of St. Louis, Missouri, and was ordained in 1855. During his priesthood, he served primarily in California.

1855: Allen Wright (Kiliahote; 1826–1885), Choctaw, was the first American Indian

Allen Wright

from Indian Territory (present-day Oklahoma) to be awarded a master of arts degree from the Union Theological Seminary in New York City. He was then ordained to the Presbyterian ministry, became an honorary member of the American Board of Commissioners of Foreign Missions, and returned home to work among his people. Following service in the Confederate Army during the Civil War, Wright was elected principal chief of the Choctaw, holding the office from 1866 to 1870. By then, he had already served on the Choctaw Council and as treasurer of the Choctaw Nation. Wright has also been credited with the Choctaw words (okla humma) to name the state of Oklahoma, often translated as "red people."

1865: John B. Renville (c. 1831–1903) was the first Dakota to be ordained a minister by the Presbyterian Church. He was the son of Mary and Joseph Renville Sr., a trader at Lac qui Parle in Minnesota Territory. After attending mission school there, he attended college in Illinois. Renville later served as a teacher at the Upper Sioux Agency in Minnesota Territory. During the Dakota War of 1862, Renville and his wife were taken captive but later released. Other family members also became ministers, among them Isaac Renville and Victor Renville.

1867: Enmegahbowh (He That Stands before His People; 1813–1902), aka the Reverend John Johnson, Anishinaabe, was ordained, becoming the first American Indian priest in the Episcopal Church. Enmegahbow helped found St. Columba's church at Minnesota's Gull Lake and later St. Columba's on the newly established White Earth Reservation, where he served until his death. He is commemorated on June 12 on the Episcopal Calendar of Saints.

1871: John Eastman (Mahpiyawakankida; 1849–1921), Santee Sioux, was the first Native American student at Beloit College in Wisconsin, attending its preparatory school from 1871 to 1872. Eastman, his family, and other tribal members were part of the maelstrom of the Dakota War of 1862, facing perilous exile, prison, and loss of family, homes, and livelihoods. They were influenced by missionaries, including the Stephen Riggs family, during that period. In 1870, Eastman walked some 170 miles from Flandreau, South Dakota, to the newly founded Santee Normal Training School (SNTS) in Santee, Nebraska. There he was taught by the Reverend Alfred L. Riggs, SNTS's founder, who paved the way for him to attend Beloit. Ordained in 1876, Eastman's work included serving 30 years as pastor of Flandreau's Presbyterian Church. In 1915, he became general missionary for Presbyterian Churches in South Dakota.

1874: The Bureau of Catholic Indian Missions was established in Washington, D.C., primarily to protect and advance missionary work among Native American Catholics. Its work has included supporting building projects, staffing schools, enabling parish religious education programs, raising awareness about Native American and Alaska Native Catholics, and calling others to share the bureau's mission. The bureau was originally founded as the office of the commissioner for Catholic Indian Missions.

1879: Robert Williams (?–1896) was the first Nez Perce to be ordained a Presbyterian minister. He was influenced by Susan Law McBeth, a missionary among his people, attending a school she opened and completing the theological training she provided. Williams became a pastor at Kamiah, the first church established among the Nez Perce. Organized on December 25, 1871, the First Indian Presbyterian Church of Kamiah, the oldest Protestant church in Idaho still in use, was added to the National Register of Historic Places in 1976.

1884: John Henry Kilbuck (1861–1922) became the first Lenape (Delaware) to be ordained as a Moravian minister. Born in Kansas, he was the great-grandson of the Lenape principal chief, Gelelemend, who signed the Treaty of Fort Pitt (1778), the first American Indian treaty with the United States. Kilbuck (also Killbuck), who was encouraged by Moravian missionaries in Kansas to continue his education in the East, studied at the Nazareth Boys' School and later at the Moravian College and Seminary in Bethlehem, Pennsylvania. Following his marriage to Edith Romig, the newlyweds and another missionary couple traveled to Alaska to establish the first Moravian mission station there, named Bethel. The Kilbucks served as missionaries and educators in Alaska for most of their lives, working with the Yup'ik and adopting their language as that of the Moravian Church in Alaska.

1890: Edward Cunningham (1862–1920), from Alberta, became the first Canadian Métis to be ordained a Roman Catholic priest. Born in Edmonton, Alberta, into a family of eleven children, he began his schooling at St. Albert. Cunningham attended the University of Ottawa from 1882 to 1885 and then entered the Novitiate of Lachine. He continued his education at the Scolasticat Saint-Joseph in Ottawa and completed his theology studies at Lac La Biche, Alberta. After Cunningham was ordained, he became known as a renowned speaker who served missions in Alberta.

1898: Edward Marsden (1869–1932), Tsimshian, was the first Alaska Native to be ordained to the ministry. Born in Metlakatla, British Columbia, he became a protégé of Presbyterian missionary Sheldon Jackson, who encouraged him to attend the Carlisle Indian School in Pennsylvania. In 1891, Marsden attended Marietta College in Ohio, receiving his degree in 1895. In 1894, he became a U.S. citizen, reportedly the first Alaska Native to do so. Marsden continued his training at Lane Theological Seminary in Cincinnati, Ohio, graduating in 1898. He then returned to Alaska, where he ministered to Tlingit near Ketchikan, expanding his religious work to include many small communities in southeastern Alaska. Marsden helped build boats, homes, churches, schools, and orphanages. Earlier in his life, he had mastered an array of trades, including carpentry and brickmaking. In 1888, he had also become a licensed marine steam engineer and navigator, his skills all serving him as missionary leader and educator.

Edward Marsden

1903: Albert Negahnquet (1874–1944), Citizen Potawatomi, is considered to be the first full-blood American Indian to be ordained a Roman Catholic priest. After enrolling in Sacred Heart Mission in Indian Territory (present-day Oklahoma), he eventually attended seminary in Rome and was ordained there. His clerical name was Father Dom Bede, and he returned to the United States to work among Indian people in Oklahoma and Minnesota.

1903: Cornelius Hill (1834–1907) became the first Oneida deacon in the Episcopal Church in 1895 and, in 1903, the first member of his tribal nation to be ordained an Episcopal priest. In 1843, he was taken to the newly

Cornelius Hill

established Nashotah House, an American theological seminary in Nashotah, Wisconsin, for schooling. Hill, who became a chief of the Oneida Nation at a young age, championed Native rights, including the retention of tribal lands. For many years, he served as an organist and interpreter for Episcopal services and was a highly respected leader.

1912: Edward Ahenakew (1885–1961), Plains Cree, became the first Native to be ordained an Anglican priest. He studied theology at Wycliffe College in Toronto, Ontario, and at Emmanuel College in Saskatoon, Saskatchewan, graduating and becoming ordained. In the aftermath of the flu epidemic of 1918, Ahenakew studied medicine at the University of Alberta but had to leave his studies after three years because of impoverishment and ill health. He worked in communities across Canada and was involved with the Indian League of Canada. Ahenakew also published a newsletter in Cree and English and collaborated on a Cree-English dictionary. He was awarded an honorary Doctor of Divinity by Emmanuel College. Ahenakew wrote *Voices of the Plains Cree*, which was published posthumously in 1973.

1925: Edward Goodbird (Tsaskaka-sakis; c. 1871–1938), principal informant and translator for anthropologist Gilbert L. Wilson on Hidatsa life, became the first member of the Fort Berthold Reservation in North Dakota to become an ordained minister. *Goodbird the Indian: His Story*, told to Wilson and first published in 1914, became lauded as a landmark in anthropological writing for its early use of biography to portray another culture. Goodbird, who was baptized when he was about 35 years old, preached in the Hidatsa language and built a chapel at Independence on the Fort Berthold Reservation. Wilson's extensive work with Goodbird and his other relatives resulted in a rich portrait of one family. The best-known account of Goodbird's mother's life was published as *Buffalo Bird Woman's Garden: Agriculture of the Hidatsa Indians*.

1933: William Henry Pierce (1856–1948) wrote *From Potlatch to Pulpit* (1933), identified as the first published book by a Tsimshian author. Pierce, the son of a Tsimshian mother and a Scots father, was born at Fort Rupert in British Columbia. He was converted to Christianity by Methodist missionary Thomas Crosby, later serving as his interpreter. Ordained in 1886, Pierce worked to convert other Native people and served as a missionary for many years. His memoir includes information about Tsimshian culture and religious beliefs.

1939: Moroni Timbimboo (1888–1975), Shoshone, became the first Native American Mormon bishop and, with his counselors, the first Native bishopric or district. He served as leader of the Washakie Ward Chapel from 1939 to 1945. Timbimboo was the grandson of Sagwitch (meaning "orator"), who was chieftain of a band of Northwestern Shoshone and survivor of the Bear River Massacre. During the massacre, U.S. Army troops killed hundreds of Shoshone men, women, and children near present-day Preston, Idaho, on January 29, 1863. A decade later, Sagwitch and members of his band were baptized into the LDS faith. By then ordained an LDS elder, he and his wife were the first American Indians to have their marriages sealed in the church. Timbimboo was ordained a bishop by LDS president George Albert Smith the same year the Washakie Ward Chapel in Utah was dedicated. He also served as bishop's counselor for 26 years.

1940: Walter Soboleff (Kaajaakwtí; 1908–2011), Tlingit, earned a master's degree in divinity from the University of Dubuque in Iowa, becoming one of the first Alaska Natives ordained to ministry in the Presbyterian Church. He then established a church in Juneau and opened it to all people, the first pastor to do so at a time when segregation prevailed. Soboleff was also the first Alaskan to have his sermons broadcast live on radio, extending his message beyond his church. In 1951, he began a twenty-year term as Alaska National Guard chaplain. In 1962, after 22 years, state and church authorities ordered his church closed and demolished. Soboleff then became an itinerant preacher, serving Southeast Alaska villages. During his long lifetime, he also served as chair of Sealaska Heritage Institute, president of the Alaska Native Brotherhood, and held leadership posts in education. A fluent speaker of Tlingit, he worked to preserve Native language and culture. The Sealaska Heritage Institute opened the Walter Soboleff Building, a cultural and research center, in Juneau in 2015. Congress honored him by creating the Alyce Spotted Bear and Walter Soboleff Commission on Native Children in 2016. Soboleff, also the recipient of honorary doctorates, passed away at the age of 102.

1941: Percy Ipalook (1906–1990) was the first Inupiat to be ordained as a minister in the Presbyterian Church. After attending Sheldon Jackson High School in Sitka, Alaska, he completed academic and theological training at the University of Dubuque in Iowa.

1943: James Collins Ottipoby (1899–1960), Comanche, was the first American Indian chaplain to be commissioned in the U.S. Army. Born in Lawton, Oklahoma, he graduated from Hope College in Holland, Michigan, in 1925, the college's first Native American graduate. Ottipoby, who attended Western Theological Seminary, was a pastor in the Reformed Church in America and served several Native American congregations.

1943: Philip B. Gordon (Tibishkogijik, "looking into the sky"; 1885–1948), Ojibwe, became the first ordained American Indian priest to offer the invocation at the convening of the U.S. House of Representatives. Father Gordon was the first Ojibwe to be ordained a priest and the second Native American priest in the United States after Albert Negahnquet, Potawatomi. Born in Gordon, Wisconsin, Gordon attended St. Paul Seminary School of Divinity, the Catholic University of America, the American College in Rome, St. John's University in Minnesota, and other schools. Ordained in 1913, Gordon served as an assistant director of Catholic Indian Welfare for the Bureau of Catholic Missions in Washing-

The Walter Soboleff Building in Juneau, Alaska, is named after a renowned leader who was one of the first Alaskan Natives to be ordained in the Presbyterian Church.

ton, D.C., as well as pastor of churches in Wisconsin's tribal communities. Known for his activism, Gordon was called "Wisconsin's Fighting Priest." In 1923, he became president of the Society of American Indians and a member of the Committee of One Hundred, a reform group advising on Indian policy. His request for an Indian parish rejected by Catholic superiors, his final placement was at a non-Indian church. For many years, he was the only Native American Catholic priest in the country.

1948: B. Frank Belvin (1914–1999), Choctaw, earned a doctorate degree from Eastern Baptist Theological Seminary in Philadelphia, Pennsylvania, becoming the first American Indian to earn a Ph.D. in theology. During some 40 years with the Baptist Home Mission Board, he served as a missionary to Apache, Creek, Kiowa, Seminole, and other Indian people and was also responsible for building mission churches. Belvin, who was appointed to the National Council on Indian Opportunity by President Richard Nixon, was named to the Bacone College Hall of Fame and the American Indian Athletic Hall of Fame.

1952: Gloria Ann Davis (1933–2000), a Navajo/Choctaw Catholic nun, became the first American Indian in the Order of the Blessed Sacrament, making her first profession of vows in 1955 and her final vows in 1960. She held a BA degree in education at Xavier University in New Orleans and an MA degree at Loyola University. Davis was a member of Sisters of the Blessed Sacrament for 48 years, serving in numerous locales.

1953: Edwin Lani Hanchett (1919–1975) became the first Native Hawaiian to become an ordained priest of the Episcopal Church, the first suffragan (assistant) bishop in 1967, and the first bishop in 1970. He attended the University of Hawaii and the Church Divinity School of the Pacific in Berkeley, California. Hanchett, the son of the first Native Hawaiian medical doctor to practice in Hawaii, was originally a premed student. He later presided as vicar of St. George's, Pearl Harbor, and as rector of St. Peter's, Honolulu.

1954: Vine Deloria Sr. (1901–1990), Yankton Dakota, was appointed to a national executive post in the Episcopal Church, the first American Indian named to a top executive position by a major Protestant denomination. His career included serving as an Episcopal archdeacon of South Dakota.

1961: Charles Kekumano (1919–1998), Native Hawaiian, was named by Pope John XXIII as an honorary chaplain of the papal household, with the title of monsignor, the first Native Hawaiian to hold the honor.

1962: David Salmon (1912–2007), Gwich'in Athabascan, became the first Athabascan ordained an Episcopalian priest, a first in Alaska history. He was also the first traditional chief of the interior and a founding member of the Tanana Chiefs Conference (TCC) and Denakkanaaga, a nonprofit elders organization. The Reverend Chief Salmon was a master musician and toolmaker as well.

1963: Marvin Fox (Omahksipiitaa, Big Eagle; 1935–2018), Blood, was ordained at St. Mary's Catholic Church on the Blood Reserve near Cardston, Alberta, becoming the first treaty Indian in Canada to become a Catholic priest. Fox, said to have later left the priesthood, received BA and BEd degrees from the University of Ottawa, and studied linguistics at the University of Alberta, community development at St. Francis Xavier (Coady International Institute), and management at the University of Calgary. He worked for his community and Treaty 7 First Nations for some 30 years. Fox held a range of positions throughout his career, including dedicated efforts to preserve the Blackfoot language and culture.

1963: John Snow (1933–2006) was the first ordained minister of the United Church of Canada from the Stoney Nakoda Nation in Alberta. Born and raised on the reserve in Morley, Alberta, he was given the name Intebeja Mani (Walking Seal) by his great-grandfather. From 1958 to 1962, Snow attended the Cook Christian Training School in Phoenix, Arizona, and, upon graduating, became the first member of his tribal band to earn a postsecondary diploma. After returning home, he enrolled at St. Stephen's College in Edmonton and was ordained in the spring of 1963. Snow was elected chief of the Nakoda-Wesley First Nation, serving from 1968 to 1992 and from 1996 to 2000. He is the author of *These Mountains Are Our Sacred Places*, published in 1977.

1968: West Cross Street Baptist Church was chartered in Baltimore, Maryland, by Lumbee Indians. The founding pastor of West Cross was the Reverend James Miller Dial, Lumbee. Earlier, the members had been meeting in homes and storefronts. In 1984, the congregation purchased a building with a seating capacity of 700 and closer to the community served, called South Broadway Baptist Church.

1972: Harold S. Jones (1909–2002), Dakota, who had a long career in the ministry of the Episcopal Church, became the first American Indian to be elevated to the office of bishop by any Christian denomination. He was consecrated suffragan bishop of the Episcopal Diocese of South Dakota on January 11, 1972. In 1935, he graduated from Northern State University (NSU) in Aberdeen, South Dakota, becoming the school's first Native American graduate. Jones then attended Seabury Western Theological Seminary in Evanston, Illinois, graduating with a master of divinity degree in 1938 and received an honorary doctor of divinity degree from there in 1973. He began his ministry at Wounded Knee, South Dakota, on the Pine Ridge Reservation. His

life story is told in *Dakota Cross-Bearer* (2000) by Mary E. Cochran.

1975: George P. Lee (1943–2010), Navajo, was the first American Indian to be appointed as a full-time member of the First Quorum of the Seventy, a general authority of the Church of Jesus Christ of Latter-day Saints. In 1989, church authorities excommunicated Lee, who attributed the action to disagreements with other leaders over a range of issues, including the role of American Indians in the Latter-day Saints religion. It was the first excommunication in 46 years imposed against a Mormon general authority. Lee's autobiography, *Silent Courage*, was published in 1987.

1978: The first Baha'i Native Council was held on the Yakama Indian Reservation in Washington State. Attendees were from across the United States and Canada.

1983: Anna Frank (1939–), Athabascan, was the first Alaska Native woman to be ordained to the Episcopal priesthood. In 2019, she was honored with a traditional potlatch by Denakkanaaga and other Alaskan organizations. Frank's honors include an honorary Doctor of Laws degree from the University of Alaska Fairbanks in recognition of her years of service as a community health aide, counselor, and priest.

1983: The Reverend Homer Noley (1932–2018), Choctaw Nation, was the founder of the National United Methodist Native American Center (NUMNAC), which focused on strengthening the self-sufficiency and self-determination of Native American churches and ministry. Noley was the author of *First White Frost*, which documented the activities of Methodist missionaries with respect to Native Americans. He was also a coauthor of *A Native American Theology* (2001) with Clara Sue Kidwell and George E. Tinker. Noley served as executive director of NUM-

NAC in Claremont, California, at the end of his career, retiring in 1999.

1983: Sister Verna Fowler (1942–), Menominee/Stockbridge-Munsee, helped found A New Genesis, a religious community in Green Bay, Wisconsin. After taking vows as a Franciscan Sister of Christian Charity in 1964, she taught in Catholic schools for more than a decade. In 1970, Sister Fowler was granted a sabbatical to work in Washington, D.C., where she helped lobby for the Menominee Restoration Act to reverse termination policies for the Menominee. She also served as an aide to Menominee leader Ada Deer, the chair of the Menominee Restoration Committee. In 1992, Fowler, who completed her Ph.D. from the University of North Dakota, was hired by the Menominee Tribe of Wisconsin to establish a tribal college. Fowler did so and served as president of the College of Menominee Nation for 24 years, one of the longest-serving presidents in the tribal college movement.

1985: David Pendleton Oakerhater (Okuhhatuh; Making Medicine; c. 1847–1931), Southern Cheyenne, was named a saint of the Episcopal Church, the first Native American to achieve sainthood in the religion. A former warrior who had been imprisoned in St. Augustine, Florida, and famed ledger artist, he became an ordained deacon in the Episcopal Church in 1881. The Anglican Communion celebrates his feast day on September 1.

David Oakerhater

1985: The complete Bible was translated into the Navajo language for the first time as *Diyin God Bizaad: The Holy Bible in Navajo* and published by the American Bible Society in 1985. The work, which began before the end of World War II, was done by missionaries and their guides who organized themselves into a group called Navajo Bible Translators. A new version, also published by the American Bible Society, was completed in 2000.

1985: Collins P. Jordan (1917–2004) was the first Oglala Lakota in the Diocese of Rapid City in South Dakota to be ordained a Catholic priest.

1989: Steven Tsosie Plummer (1944–2005) became the first Navajo bishop of the Episcopal Church, assuming office in 1990. Born in Coal Mine, New Mexico, he was baptized at Good Shepherd Mission in Fort Defiance, Arizona, in 1949. Plummer attended boarding school in Albuquerque and the Church Divinity School of the Pacific. He was ordained a deacon in 1975 and a priest in 1976. Plummer served as a curate at Fort Defiance, vicar of St. John the Baptizer in Montezuma Creek, Utah, and became the regional vicar of the San Juan area. He also served as the presiding elder of the Navajoland Area Mission.

1989: Lois V. Glory-Neal, Cherokee Nation, of the Oklahoma Indian Missionary Conference became the first Native American woman to be ordained elder. In 1992, she became the first Native American district superintendent. In 2020, Saint Paul School of Theology, located in Oklahoma and Kansas, announced that Rev. Dr. Glory-Neal was the recipient of its 2020 Distinguished Graduate Award honoring her years of service.

1990: Donald E. Pelotte (1945–2010), Abenaki, was the first American Indian to become a Roman Catholic bishop in the United States. He served 22 years in the Diocese of Gallup, New Mexico, where his leadership included developing training programs for Native American deacons and lay ministers. In 1999, Bishop Pelotte ordained his own twin brother, Dana Pelotte, to the priesthood, another first in known Catholic history.

1992: Stan McKay (1942–), Fisher River Cree Nation, Manitoba, was elected to serve as moderator of the United Church of Canada, the first Native person to lead a mainline denomination in the country. At his 1971 ordination at Fisher River, he was also the first Cree-speaking minister of the denomination to be ordained within his own community. McKay was instrumental in advancing the principle of reconciliation, leading to the establishment of a "Healing Fund" and ultimately to an apology to former students of United Church Indian Residential Schools.

Archbishop Charles Joseph Chaput

1993: Patricia Locke (1928–2001), Hunkpapa Lakota/White Earth Ojibwe, who accepted the Baha'i faith later in her life, was the first Native American woman to be elected to an office of the National Spiritual Assembly of the Baha'is of the United States. She served until 2001, becoming vice chair in 2001.

1996: Bertram Bobb (1924–2015), Choctaw, was appointed as the Choctaw Nation of Oklahoma chaplain, the only person to serve the position for a lifetime. He received a bachelor's degree in accounting/business management at Northeastern Oklahoma State University and attended the Dallas Theological Seminary in Texas. Bobb was ordained at Scofield Memorial Church in Dallas, Texas. In 1963, he founded and directed the Christian Indian Ministries in Antlers, Oklahoma, serving until his death. Bobb was chaplain to the Inter-Tribal Council of the Five Civilized Tribes for 27 years and a member of the Choctaw Code Talkers Association for 20 years.

1997: Agnes Tyon (1933–2015), who studied at the Vancouver School of Theology in Canada, became the first Oglala Lakota woman to be ordained a priest in the Episcopal Church. Her religious leadership included serving churches on the Pine Ridge Reservation in South Dakota. She was also employed at the Bureau of Indian Affairs and the Oglala Sioux Tribe for many years.

1997: Charles J. Chaput (1944–), Prairie Band Potawatomi, became the first Native American archbishop appointed by Pope John Paul II. Ordained to the Catholic priesthood in 1970, Chaput became the second Native American bishop in the United States in 1988 when he was named to serve Rapid City, South Dakota. He has served as archbishop of Denver and archbishop of Philadelphia. Chaput is the author of *Living the Catholic Faith* (2001) and *Render unto Caesar* (2008).

1999: Steven Charleston (1949–), Choctaw, became the president and dean of the Episcopal Divinity School in Cambridge, Massachusetts, the first person of color to lead an Episcopal seminary. He has also served as the national director for the Episcopal Native American Ministries, as a tenured professor of Systematic Theology at Luther Seminary, and as bishop of Alaska. In 2014, Trinity College in Hartford, Connecticut, named a building after him in recognition of his work in interfaith cooperation. Charleston is the author of daily meditations and books through Red Moon Publications.

2000: Clinical psychologist Eduardo Duran, Ph.D., Apache/Tewa, released his book *Buddha in Redface*. Duran was the first to write about Natives who follow Buddhism. Known for his success in treating Native Americans and for his specialty in healing historical trauma, he combines Buddhist and traditional Native practices in his psychotherapy. "I see the Buddha as a tribal person. I find that revealed in his deliberate action just before he became enlightened, when he reached down and touched the Earth, saying,

'The Earth is my witness.' The Buddha was keenly aware that the Earth has consciousness and can even bear witness to karma."

2001: Carol J. Gallagher (1955–), Cherokee Nation, was elected suffragan (auxiliary) bishop in the Episcopal Church's Diocese of Southern Virginia, the first Native American woman to become a bishop of a major Christian church. A 1989 graduate of the Episcopal Divinity School in Cambridge, Massachusetts, she became a priest in 1990. Gallagher has served on the editorial board of the *First Peoples Theology Journal* and the church's Council of Indian Ministries.

2007: Jacqueline Left Hand Bull (formerly Delahunt; 1943–), Rosebud Sioux, became the first American Indian and the third woman elected to lead the National Spiritual Assembly of the Baha'is of the United States. As chair, she headed a nine-member board overseeing some 150,000 members of the faith in the United States. Left Hand Bull, who joined the religion in 1981, previously served as vice chair of the governing body for five years. She is the co-author of *Lakota Hoop Dancer*, a children's book.

2007: Mark L. MacDonald (1954–), of Native descent, became the Anglican Church of Canada's first National Indigenous Anglican bishop. He had earlier served as bishop of the U.S. Episcopal Diocese of Alaska for ten years. In 2019, the General Synod of the Anglican Church of Canada voted to approve steps to enable a self-determining Indigenous church within its ranks. Following the change, Bishop MacDonald received the title and status of archbishop.

2007: Phyllis Hicks (1947–2015) was the first member of the Monacan tribe in Virginia to be ordained an Episcopal priest and the first Native American woman to be ordained a priest in the state. The ordination service was held at St. Paul's Bear Mountain Episcopal Church in Amherst, Virginia, with a sermon by Carol J. Gallagher, the first Native American female bishop in the faith. Hicks, who continued to serve her community during her preparations for ordination, was able to take over the primary role of celebrating Sunday services at St. Paul's after being ordained. She was also known for her leadership efforts to establish the Monacan Ancestral Museum and for helping to secure federal recognition for the Monacan tribe.

2008: The Church of Gichitwaa Kateri, formerly known as the Office of Indian Ministry, was incorporated as a parish of the Catholic Archdiocese of St. Paul and Minneapolis in 2008. The community was founded through cooperation with Dakota and Ojibwe elders and spiritual leaders, both Catholic and non-Catholic. Both Dakota and Ojibwe songs are used in the liturgy.

2010: Maurice Henry Sands (1955–), Ojibway/Odawa/Potawatomi from Bkejawanon Walpole Island First Nation in Ontario, became the first Native person appointed as a consultant to the U.S. Conference of Catholic Bishops' Secretariat of Cultural Diversity. Father Sands, based in Michigan and noted as a gifted multilingual speaker, was serving as pastor of St. Alfred Parish in Taylor. In 2005, he had become the archdiocese of Detroit's first Native priest. Father Sands served on the board of the Tekakwitha Conference, an organization representing some 1.5 million Indigenous Catholics in the United States and Canada (2006 to 2009).

2012: Kateri Tekakwitha (1656–1680), "Lily of the Mohawks," was the first Native North American to be named a saint by the Roman Catholic Church. She was born to an Algonquin mother and a Mohawk father in 1656 in what is now New York State, surviving smallpox as a child and converting to Christianity at the age of 20. Taunted and threatened in her home village for her beliefs, Tekakwitha fled to a new mission, where she cared for elders and the ill. In the winter of 1680, she became ill and died. For years after her death, people reported miracles after praying to her. In 1943, the Catholic Church venerated Tekakwitha and beatified her, or declared her blessed, in 1980. The canonization of Kateri Tekakwitha as a saint was held on October 21, 2012, with thousands traveling from the United States and Canada to Rome to witness the event. Pope Benedict XVI said at the service: "In her, faith and culture enrich each other! May her example help us to live where we are, loving Jesus without denying who we are." St. Kateri Tekakwitha has long been honored, including with shrines and places dedicated to her in both the United States and Canada, such as Our Lady of Martyrs Shrine at her New York birth place and the Saint Katerie Tekakwitha Shrine in Kahnawake Mohawk Territory in Quebec. Many artworks have been created in her name, including a bronze figure at St. Patrick's Cathedral in New York City. In 1939, the Tekakwitha Conference was organized, meeting annually since its first conference in Fargo, North Dakota. At the conferences, people gather in Kateri Circles, named in her honor, to pray in her name.

2012:   The entire Bible was translated into Inuktitut, also called Eastern Arctic Inuktitut, signifying the first time in Canada that a translation of the whole Bible was accomplished entirely by Native language speakers rather than by white missionaries. The massive linguistic task, which started in 1978, included participation by the Reverend Jonas Allooloo, an Inuk priest and canon of the Anglican Church of Canada, who worked on the project the entire time.

2012:   Deloria Bighorn, Chickasaw/Yankton Sioux, was elected as the first Native American woman to serve as chair of the Canadian National Spiritual Assembly, the national governing body of the Baha'i Community of Canada.

2013:   R. Guy Erwin (1958–), Osage Nation, became the first Native American and first publicly identified gay to be elected bishop of the Southwest California Synod of the Evangelical Lutheran Church in America (ELCA) in 2013. Although he had served congregations in the ELCA for over twenty years, Erwin chose not to be ordained until the denomination's policy on gay ministers changed. With ELCA's vote on LGBTQ ordination in 2009, he became one of the first publicly identified gay pastors in the denomination. Bishop Erwin, who holds a bachelor's degree from Harvard University and a doctorate from Yale University, was appointed as president of United Lutheran Seminary in Pennsylvania in 2020.

2016:   Phyllis Mahilani "Mahi" Beimes (1948–) became the first woman of Hawaiian ancestry to be ordained a priest in the Episcopal Church. She and three other Native Hawaiians were ordained to the transitional diaconate in Honolulu in 2015. They were in the first graduating class of Waiolaihui'ia, a local formation program that began in January 2013. Beimes, who served as the vicar at St. Matthew's Episcopal Church in Waimanalo, retired from her priestly duties on July 31, 2020. Before turning to the ministry, she had worked for 38 years at the Pearl Harbor Naval Shipyard.

2017:   Louis Butcher Jr., Lakota from Eagle Butte, South Dakota, addressed the national conference of the Islamic Circle of North America held in Baltimore, Maryland. Butcher, a Muslim, shared the similarities between traditional Lakota spirituality and Islam. He discussed the growing number of Indigenous converts to the Islamic faith. Support groups for Indigenous Muslims include Turtle Island Muslims and the Coalition of Indigenous Muslims. Although there are not

Church Apologies

In 1992, the Anglican Church offered an apology. Words by Primate Archbishop Michael Peers included the following: "I am sorry, more than I can say, that we were part of a system which took you and your children from home and family. I am sorry, more than I can say, that we tried to remake you in our image, taking from you your language and the signs of your identity. I am sorry, more than I can say, that in our schools so many were abused physically, sexually, culturally, and emotionally. On behalf of the Anglican Church of Canada, I present our apology."

In 2001, Pope John Paul II issued an apology to the Indigenous peoples of Australia, New Zealand, the Pacific Islands, and Oceania for abuses and injustices committed by the church. He asked for forgiveness where members of the church had been or still participated in such wrongs and condemned incidents of sexual abuse by clergy in Oceania.

In lower Manhattan, where Dutch colonizers built the first Collegiate Church in 1628, known as the Reformed Protestant Dutch Church, at Fort Amsterdam, one of the nation's first Protestant churches held a healing ceremony in 2009 to apologize to Native Americans. Collegiate representatives said: "We consumed your resources, dehumanized your people, and disregarded your culture, along with your dreams, hopes, and great love of this land." They continued: "With pain, we the Collegiate Church, remember our part in these events."

In a 2015 visit to Bolivia and an encounter with Indigenous groups, activists, and Evo Morales—Bolivia's first Indigenous president—Pope Francis apologized to the Indigenous Peoples of America for the Catholic Church's role in the brutalities of colonization for the first time. "I humbly ask forgiveness, not only for the offenses of the church herself, but also for crimes committed against the Native peoples during the so-called conquest of America."

many publications about the contact between Muslims and American Indians, anecdotal information recounts centuries of encounters, particularly of enslaved Muslims being given sanctuary by Native nations.

2017: Roxanne Jimerson-Friday, Shoshone/Seneca, became the first Native American woman from the Wind River Indian Reservation in Wyoming to be ordained to the priesthood of the Episcopal Church. Her ordination was held at Our Father's House Episcopal Church in Ethete, Wyoming, with the Right Reverend John S. Smylie, bishop of the Episcopal Diocese of Wyoming, presiding. Jimerson-Friday, who lived in New York until she was 10, is Seneca on her father's side of the family and Shoshone on her mother's side. She lives with her husband Aaron in Ethete, where she serves Our Father's House Episcopal Church and Fort Washakie's Shoshone Episcopal Mission.

2017: Margherita Mele (1980–) became the first enrolled Seneca to convert to Islam. A resident of Salamanca, New York, on the Allegany Indian Reservation, her children were the first Native Americans to attend the Universal School, a Muslim elementary and upper school in Buffalo, New York.

2021: The Jews of Color Initiative, based at Stanford University, California, released *Beyond the Count: Perspectives and Lived Experiences of Jews of Color*, an unprecedented study of the Jews of Color community. Native Americans from many different tribal nations who practice the Jewish faith were included. Survey respondents all said that they faced discrimination from Euro-American Jews and often had difficulty being accepted in their local synagogues.

LEGISLATION

1883: Rules were formulated by the U.S. government prohibiting a number of Native religious practices. As modified in 1892, these included: "Dances, etc.—Any Indian who shall engage in the sun dance, scalp dance, or war dance, or any other similar feast, so called, shall be deemed guilty of an offense,

and upon conviction thereof shall be punished for the first offense by the withholding of his rations for not exceeding ten days or by imprisonment...."

Native religious leaders and practitioners were subject to harassment, arrest, fines, incarceration, the withholding of rations (paid for by tribal nations themselves via treaty agreements), and other punitive measures. A number of Indian people continued tribal religious observances in secret, but also under the cover of celebrations such as 4th of July events championed by government officials.

1884: The Potlatch, a ceremony integral to Northwest Coast and other tribal nations in Canada and the United States, was first banned by the Canadian government through an amendment to the Canadian Indian Act in 1884. The legal action took effect on January 1, 1885, and lasted until 1951. The potlatch was often held on the occasion of important events, including births, name-givings, puberty, marriages, house building, totem pole raising, investiture of heirs, and funerals. While the ceremony varied among practitioners, it generally lasted for several days and included praying, feasting, singing, dancing, theatrical demonstrations, and gift distribution. Native people were subject to arrest and incarceration and their ceremonial

American Indian Religious Freedom Act

"Now, therefore, be it Resolved by the Senate and the House of Representatives of the United States of America in Congress Assembled, That henceforth it shall be the policy of the United States to protect and preserve for American Indians their inherent right of freedom to believe, express, and exercise the traditional religions of the American Indian, Eskimo, Aleut, and Native Hawaiians, including but not limited to access to sites, use and possession of sacred objects, and the freedom to worship through ceremonials and traditional rites." —From Public Law 95-341, August 11, 1978 goods confiscated under the ban, leading to incalculable suffering, damage, and loss.

1934: Commissioner of Indian Affairs John Collier issued Circular No. 2970, Indian Religious Freedom and Indian Culture, which stated in part: "No interference with Indian religious life or ceremonial expression will hereafter be tolerated."

1978: The American Indian Religious Freedom Act (AIRFA) was passed by the U.S. Congress. The legislation stated that the policy of the United States would be to protect and preserve for American Indians their inherent right of freedom to believe, express, and exercise the traditional religions of the American Indian, Eskimo, Aleut, and Native Hawaiians. It included access to sites, use and possession of sacred objects, and the freedom to worship through ceremonials and traditional rites.

1990: The Native American Graves Protection and Repatriation Act (NAGPRA) was signed on November 16, 1990. It represented a federal shift from considering Native American human remains as "archaeological resources" or "federal property." The legislation included provisions to protect Indian gravesites from looting and to require the repatriation to tribes of culturally identifiable remains, sacred objects, and objects of cultural patrimony taken from federal or tribal lands if certain legal criteria are met. The law does not apply to burial remains found on state or private property.

1992: The National Historic Preservation Act Amendments of 1992 (PL 102-575-16 USC 470) required that federal agencies consult with tribes about the effect that their actions may have on traditional religious places. The amendments also include an enhanced role for Indian tribes in the national historic preservation program and greater protection for places of cultural significance.

1994: The American Indian Religious Freedom Act Amendments of 1994, P.L. 103-344, was signed into law by President Bill Clinton on October 6, 1994, to protect the traditional use of peyote by Indians for religious purposes.

1996: Executive Order No. 13007: Indian Sacred Sites sought to accommodate access to and ceremonial use of American Indian sacred sites by American Indian religious practitioners and avoid affecting the physical integrity of the sites in any adverse way. It was issued by President Bill Clinton on May 24, 1996.

1997: A draft rule issued by the Pentagon provided that Native American U.S. soldiers would be allowed to use peyote, the sacrament of the Native American Church, in religious ceremonies. The rule was drafted to make Pentagon policy consistent with the American Indian Religious Freedom Act Amendments of 1994 protecting Native American religious use of peyote. The draft rule barred the use or possession of peyote on military vehicles, aircraft, and ships and outlined other conditions.

ORGANIZATIONS

1890. The first YWCA for Native American women opened at the Haworth Institute in Chilocco, Oklahoma.

1917: Lucy E. Hunter (Winnebago) received an appointment from the YWCA's national board as a special worker among American Indian girls, the first time an Indian was appointed to such a position. After graduating from Hampton Institute in Virginia in 1916, Hunter attended the Training School for Christian Workers in New York City. She then took a summer course at the YWCA before being assigned to work in Oklahoma.

REPATRIATION

1938: The first successful repatriation of cultural belongings under the Historic Sites Act of 1935 was the Midipadi (or Waterbuster Clan Bundle) to the Hidatsa people of North Dakota by the Museum of the American Indian in New York. This act, which reinforced the Antiquities Act of 1906, sought to protect sites deemed sacred by tribes.

1971: Maria Pearson (Hai-Mecha Eunka, Running Moccasins; 1932–2003), Yankton Dakota, first began her advocacy on behalf of Native American human remains in 1971, contributing to the passage of the Iowa Burial Protection Act of 1976. She became known as "the Founding Mother of the modern repatriation movement" and "the Rosa Parks of NAGPRA" (Native American Graves Protection and Repatriation Act) in recognition of her work. A BBC documentary, *Bones of Contention*, featuring Pearson, was broadcast in 1995.

1976: The Iowa Burials Protection Act of 1976 was the first legislation in the United States to specifically protect Native American remains. It was a precursor to the Native American Graves Protection and Repatriation Act (NAGPRA), the federal law enacted in 1990 to address the rights of lineal descendants, Indian tribes, and Native Hawaiian organizations to Native American cultural items, including human remains and sacred objects.

1992: The American Indian Ritual Object Repatriation Foundation was founded by public historian and arts activist Elizabeth Sack-

ler. The nonfederally funded, not-for-profit organization assisted in the repatriation of cultural and religious works to American Indian people for more than 15 years.

SACRED SITES

1906: Devils Tower in Wyoming was the first national monument named by President Theodore Roosevelt under the American Antiquities Act of 1906. The site is sacred to many tribal nations, among them Arapaho, Crow, Cheyenne, Shoshone, and Lakota. English translations of Native names for the site include Bear's Lodge, Bear's Tipi, Tree Rock, and Grey Horn Butte.

1972: For the first time, a Native Hawaiian sacred area was preserved by the U.S. government. Pu'ukohola Heiau, meaning "Temple on the Hill of the Whale," on the Island of Kawaihae, was designated a National Historic Site, having been commemorated as a Historical Landmark by the Hawaiian Territorial Government in 1928. This National Historic Site is home to one of the largest restored heiau (temples) and is steeped in the history of how King Kamehameha I united the islands into the Kingdom of Hawaii. The massive temple was built to fulfill the prophecy that he would be successful.

1987: Following negotiations with the U.S. Department of Energy, the Yakama were permitted to hold their first religious service on Gable Mountain since before the federal government had created Hanford nuclear reservation in Washington State and encompassed the tribal nation's sacred site.

2003: The first National Days of Prayer to Protect Native American Sacred Places took place across the country. Organized by the

Devils Tower in Crook County, Wyoming stands 5,112 feet (1,558 meters) high. A sacred place to many Native peoples, it was named a national monument by President Theodore Roosevelt in 1906.

Located on the northwest coast of the Big Island of Hawaii, Pu'ukohola Heiau was a temple built by King Kamehameha in 1791 to gain the favor of the war god Kūka'ilimoku.

Indigenous Firsts: A History of Native American Achievements and Events

Morning Star Institute, participants gathered at educational and ceremonial events during summer solstice to emphasize the need to protect sacred lands from desecration and harm.

2016: Bears Ears National Monument in Utah, one of the most extensive archaeological areas on earth, became the first national monument created at the request of a coalition of Native American tribal nations. President Barack Obama, utilizing the Antiquities Act, proclaimed the national monument. Consisting of 1.35 million acres, about one million acres is public land managed by the Bureau of Land Management, and the remaining 290,000 acres are managed by the U.S. Forest Service. The Bears Ears National Monument is represented by a Native American Commission with an elected officer from the Hopi Nation, Navajo Nation, Ute Mountain Ute Tribe, Ute Indian Tribe of the Uintah Ouray, and Zuni Tribe. The Commission helps further the directive to provide access to Indigenous peoples for cultural and religious uses of the land.

SCIENCE AND MEDICINE

"The spread of Tuberculosis among my people is something terrible—it shows itself in the lungs, kidneys, alimentary track, blood, brain and glands—so many, many of the young children are marked with it in some form. The physical degeneration in 20 years among my people is terrible. I have talked with them and done all I could to prevent infection and contagion, but I want to know if the Gov't can't do for us what it did for the Sioux in preventing the spread of this White Plague. The financial outlay for any of these ... requests is but small compared to the amount of good it will bring forth to my people."

*—Susan La Flesche Picotte, M.D., letter to
Commissioner of Indian Affairs Francis E. Leupp, November 15, 1907*

◆◇◆ DOCTORS/PHYSICIANS

1844: Peter Wilson (Waowawanaonk; ?–1871), Cayuga, believed to be the first known Native American to earn a medical degree, graduated from Geneva Medical College in Geneva, New York. His name has various translations, including "They Hear His Voice" or "The Pacificator," and he was raised on the Seneca Buffalo Creek Reservation and educated in Quaker schools. Waowawanaonk is sometimes listed as a chief or sachem in records but may not have officially held the title. He worked as an interpreter on New York's Cattaraugus Reservation and served as a signatory on a land treaty that he later worked to have reversed.

1850: John Masta (1819–1861), Abenaki, St. Francis, earned a medical degree from Dartmouth Medical School, one of the first American Indian physicians trained in a U.S. school of medicine. As part of his studies, he wrote a thesis on pneumonia. Masta had initially studied medicine in Canada and at the Vermont Medical Institute. He became a physician in Barton, Vermont. Masta's brother Joseph also became a doctor.

The Susan La Flesche Picotte Hospital Center is located in Walthill, Nebraska.

1866: Peter Edmund Jones (Kahkewaquonaby; 1843–1909), Mississauga Ojibwa, received his medical degree at Queen's College at Kingston, likely the first Canadian status Indian to attain the degree. Jones practiced among the Mississauga of New Credit and also served as head chief from 1874 to 1877 and 1880 to 1886.

1889: Carlos Montezuma (c. 1865–1923), Mojave-Apache (Yavapai), named Wassaja ("gathering" or "beckoning") by his people, was one of the first Native Americans to graduate from medical school. He was kidnapped at age four and sold for $30 to a white man, Carlos Gentile, a photographer and artist, who renamed him Carlos Montezuma. Montezuma graduated from the University of Illinois with a degree in chemistry in 1884 and completed medical school at Northwestern University's Chicago Medical College in 1889 (a short time after Dr. Susan La Flesche Picotte). He then worked as a physician for the Office of Indian Affairs for a number of years, including at the Car-

Peter Edmund Jones

lisle Indian School in Pennsylvania. Montezuma eventually resigned to work in private practice in Chicago. An activist and founding member of the Society of American Indians, he also published his own newspaper, *Wassaja: Freedom's Signal for the Indians*, titled after his Yavapai name. Montezuma's activism included advocating for the abolishment of the Office of Indian Affairs and attacking those he viewed as exploiters of Native people.

1892: Matthew Puakakoilimanuia Makalua (1867–1929) graduated from King's College School of Medicine in London, becoming the first Native Hawaiian chosen by the Hawaiian king to study medicine abroad and the first Western-trained Hawaiian doctor. Because of the chaos in Hawaii with the overthrow of the Republic, he remained in England, where he was noted for his philanthropy and treating the poor.

1893: Isabel Cobb (1858–1947), Cherokee, who graduated from the Women's Medical

The First Native American Woman Physician

In 1889, Susan La Flesche Picotte (1865–1915), Omaha, became the first Native American woman to graduate from medical school. She attended the Women's Medical College of Pennsylvania, the first medical school in the United States established for women, and graduated valedictorian of her class. The daughter of Joseph La Flesche (Iron Eyes) and his wife Mary Gale (One Woman), she attended mission school at Omaha Agency in Nebraska and Elizabeth Institute for Young Ladies in New Jersey. In 1884, La Flesche enrolled at Hampton Institute in Virginia, graduating salutatorian of her class in 1886. She then enrolled in medical school, returning to Hampton in 1887 to teach summer school. After graduating from the Women's Medical College in 1889, she returned to the Omaha Agency, where she served as a physician to her people as well as non-Indians in the area. Working tirelessly, beset by chronic ill health, Picotte served multiple roles as doctor, teacher, spokesperson, and advisor. In 1894, she married Henry Picotte, Yankton Sioux, and the couple had two sons. After fundraising, she was able to open the first hospital on a reservation that was not funded by the government in 1913. Work is underway to restore the original hospital as the Dr. Susan La Flesche Picotte Center. Other tributes in her honor include a bronze statue unveiled at Centennial Mall in Lincoln, Nebraska, in October 2021.

College of Pennsylvania in 1892, became the first woman physician in Indian Territory (present-day Oklahoma). She specialized in treating women and children and practiced medicine in rural Wagoner County. With no hospitals in the area, she also performed surgery in her patients' homes.

Isabel Cobb

1899: Lillie "Rosa" Minoka-Hill (1876–1952), Mohawk/adopted Oneida, was the first Iroquois woman to become a medical doctor and the second in the country after Dr. Susan La Flesche Picotte, Omaha, to achieve credentials as a physician. She graduated from the Women's Medical College in Pennsylvania in 1899. In 1905, she married Charles Hill, Oneida, and moved with him to his tribal nation in Wisconsin. Dr. Minoka-Hill operated a "kitchen clinic" at home, providing medical care for the Oneida. In 1947, she was adopted by the

Oneidas and given the name Yo-da-gent, "she who serves." In 1949, the Wisconsin Medical Association voted to award Dr. Minoka-Hill a lifetime honorary membership. Near Oneida, a monument in her name includes the words, "I was sick and you visited me." Dr. Rosa Minoka-Hill School is named in her honor in Green Bay, Wisconsin.

1914: Dr. Alsoberry Kaumu Hanchett (1885–1932) was the first Native Hawaiian to graduate from Harvard Medical College. He was also the first Native Hawaiian physician to return home to Hawai'i to practice medicine. Other firsts include being the first City-County physician in Honolulu and the first doctor at the Shingle Memorial Hospital, Molokai. Hanchett also earned an AB degree at Harvard University in 1911. During World War I, he served in the Medical Corps at Schofield Barracks and Fort Shafter. Hanchett, who abbreviated his name to A. Kaumu, then entered private medical practice.

1926: May Edward Chinn (1896–1980), Chickahominy/African American, became the first Native and Black woman to intern at Harlem Hospital in New York City. She was also the first to graduate from Bellevue Hospital Medical College, now New York University School of Medicine, and the first woman to ride with Harlem Hospital's ambulance crew. In 2021, muralist Paul Deo, Choctaw/Powhatan/Lenape, was commissioned to paint a mural of Chinn in the Harlem Hospital lobby.

1943: Thomas St. Germain Whitecloud II (1914–1972), Lac du Flambeau Band of Lake Superior Indians, who completed his medical degree in 1943, is believed to be the first Native American graduate of Tulane University School of Medicine in New Orleans, Louisiana. Also a writer, his best known literary work is "Blue Winds Dancing." Whitecloud's son, Thomas St. Germain Whitecloud III (1940–2003; class of 1966), and grandson, Jacques (1970–2017; class of 1998), also completed medical degrees at Tulane.

1954: William C. Blueskye (1922–2004), a member of the Seneca Nation raised on the Cattaraugus Reservation in New York, was the first American Indian on record to graduate as a doctor of osteopathic medicine from A. T. Still University's Kirksville College of Osteopathic Medicine in Missouri. The son of Bertram and Harriet (Halftown) Blueskye, Blueskye served in World War II as a technician third grade. At ATSU, he became a member of a coed service fraternity, and following graduation, he set up practice in Mentor, Ohio. More recently, the National Center for American Indian Health Professions (NCAIHP) at ATSU honored Blueskye with information about his life in an exhibit.

1955: Connie Redbird Pinkerman-Uri (1930–), Choctaw/Cherokee, who received her medical degree at the University of Arkansas in 1955 and a law degree from Whittier College in 1979, was the first Native American woman to earn degrees in both medicine and law. She became known for her investigative attention to the sterilization of American Indian women in the federal Indian Health Service without their informed consent.

Dr. Kona Williams, Forensic Pathologist

Kona Williams (c. 1978–), Cree/Mohawk, was named Canada's first First Nations forensic pathologist with her appointment to that position at the Centre of Forensic Sciences in Toronto, Ontario, in 2016. She is the daughter of Gordon Williams, Cree, Peguis First Nation, and Karen Jacobs-Williams, Mohawk, Kahnawake. Williams completed 14 years of postsecondary education, including four years of medical school and five years as an anatomical pathology resident at the University of Ottawa. She said there were no physicians in her family and that her first weeks of medical school "were like drinking from a fire hose." She also said: "I like to work with my hands, I move around a lot. I ended up being really good at forensic cases—finding out how somebody died. I really like answers and I thought here is this specialty that will provide me with all the answers, not that it does all of the time."

1956: James W. Hampton (1931–), Chickasaw/Choctaw, who graduated from the University of Oklahoma College of Medicine, became the first Native American medical oncologist in the nation. The Hampton Scholars, a scholarship program in his name, was established by the American Indian/Alaska Native Initiative on Cancer's Spirit of EAGLES in 2001.

1958: Taylor McKenzie (1931–2007), Navajo, who earned his medical degree in 1958, was the first Navajo to become a medical doctor and surgeon. He had a 30-year career in the Indian Health Service on the Navajo Nation. McKenzie served as vice president of the tribal nation from 1999 to 2003, credited with building new clinics and working to reauthorize the Indian Health Care Improvement Act. In December 2005, he was appointed to serve as the Navajo Nation's first medical officer.

1958: Charles Byron Wilson (1929–2018), Cherokee, who graduated first in his class at Tulane School of Medicine in 1954, became the first neurosurgical resident at the VA Medical Center of New Orleans in 1958. His medical career, in which he was dubbed the "Baryshnikov of Brain Surgery" and served as a founder of the field of neuro-oncology, included many firsts. In 1963, Wilson was recruited to become the first chair of a new division of neurosurgery at the University of Kentucky, where he organized one of the first national conferences devoted to brain tumors. Becoming chairman of the Division of Neurosurgery at the University of California, San Francisco in 1968, he established the Brain Tumor Research Center, the first such center approved by the National Cancer Institute. In later years, Wilson cofounded the Global AIDS Interfaith Alliance (GAIA), a nonprofit organization that delivers healthcare programs in Africa. *Cherokee Neurosurgeon*, a biography by Brian T. Andrews, was published in 2011.

1959: Lionel DeMontigny (1935–2007), Turtle Mountain Chippewa, was the first American Indian student to graduate from the University of North Dakota's School of Medicine and Health Sciences. In 1962 he joined the Commissioned Corps of the U.S. Public Health Service, later becoming the first American Indian appointed as assistant surgeon general in the United States. DeMontigny, who retired from the Corps in 1984, is credited with designing some of the first medical care delivery systems that combine Western and Traditional Indian health practices. He was also instrumental in developing programs to prepare Native students for medical school.

1964: Linwood "Little Bear" Custalow (1937–2014), Mattaponi, who graduated from the Medical College of Virginia, became the first American Indian to graduate from a medical college in Virginia. He lived in Newport News, Virginia, where he specialized in ear, nose, throat, facial plastic surgery, and allergy, and practiced for 38 years. Custalow was also the historian of the Mattaponi Tribe and the coauthor of *The True Story of Pocahontas: The Other Side of History*.

1966: Richard Kekuni Blaisdell (1925–2016) was the founding chairman of the Department of Medicine at John A. Burns School of Medicine (JABSOM) at the University of Hawai'i, the first Native Hawaiian to chair a department of medicine in a U.S. medical school. He graduated from Kamehameha Schools and received his medical degree from the University of Chicago's School of Medicine in 1948. During his 37-year career at JABSOM, Blaisdell worked tirelessly to improve Native Hawaiian health and mentored countless physicians. He was the force behind the critical study "E Ola Mau," documenting the health needs of Native Hawaiians. Blaisdell, who was known as the first Hawaiian hematologist, was also recognized for his knowledge of Hawai'i's medical history. He was honored as a Living Treasure of Hawaii by the Honpa Hongwanji Mission of Hawaii in 1990 and was the recipient of numerous other awards.

1968: Roberta Apau Ikemoto, Native Hawaiian, was the first Native Hawaiian woman to become a physician. She graduated from Kamehameha Schools in 1960 and received her medical degree from the University of California's School of Medicine in San Francisco in 1968. She specialized in radiology, becoming board certified in both radiology and nuclear medicine.

1970: Benjamin Bung Choong Young became the first Native Hawaiian psychiatrist when he graduated from Howard University College of Medicine in Washington, D.C. He did his residency at the University of Hawaii Medical School (John A. Burns School of Medicine, or JABSOM), where he eventually was appointed dean of students (1972–1986). Young is an advocate of increasing the numbers of Native Hawaiian health professionals and founded programs to recruit, train, and support Native medical students, including creating the Ben and DeDe Young Endowed Scholarship for Native Hawaiian medical students. He also practices neurology, treating a variety of conditions in his Kailua and Honolulu offices. In 1971, Young helped form the Polynesian Voyage Society and in 1976 served as the onboard physician for Hokule'a's maiden voyage. He established the Imi Ho'ola program, helping Native Pacific Islanders learn pre-med science courses to gain admission to medical school, while serving as chief of staff at Castle Medical Center. Known as the premier historian of Hawaiian medicine, Young was honored as a Distinguished Historian by the Hawaiian Historical Society for a lifetime of significant contributions to the preservation and perpetuation of Hawaii's history. He has received many other awards, including the prestigious Native Hawaiian Chamber of Commerce 'Ō'ō' Award in 2011.

1973: Lois Steele (1939–), Assiniboine, Fort Peck, became the first director of the Indians into Medicine Program (INMED) at the University of North Dakota, which was founded to increase the number of American Indians in medicine and other health professions. Steele completed her medical degree at the University of Minnesota in 1978.

1976: Ted Mala (c. 1946–), Inupiaq, became the first Alaska Native to become a medical doctor, earning his Doctor of Medicine and Surgery M.D. degree from the Autonomous University of Guadalajara in Mexico. Mala, the son of actor Ray Mala, also earned a Master of Public Health degree from Harvard University in 1980 and became the first Alaska Native commissioner of health and social services in 1990.

1976: Michael T. Vandall, Yankton Sioux, became the first graduate of the INMED Program at the University of North Dakota School of Medicine, where he completed his medical degree. He later specialized in obstetrics and gynecology, eventually serving as deputy chief of obstetrics at the Public Health Service hospital in Tuba City, Arizona, as well as in private practice.

1978: David Baines (1955–), Tsimshian and Tlingit, was the first American Indian student accepted into the Mayo Medical School, graduating from there in 1982. Baines worked in family practice on reservations in Idaho, at a community health center for American Indians and Alaska Natives in Seattle, and in other roles. He also served on the faculty at the Alaska Family Medicine Residency and became the first Alaska Native to become a full professor at a major American medical school.

1980: Clayton D K Chong graduated from the University of Hawaii John A. Burns

School of Medicine (JABSOM) and became the first Native Hawaiian oncologist. He specializes in hematology oncology in Honolulu and attended the Kamehameha Schools for Native Hawaiians.

1981: Lulumafuie Fiatoa received his medical degree from the University of Hawaii John A. Burns School of Medicine (JABSOM), becoming the first Samoan pediatrician.

1982: Emmett Chase (1952–), Hoopa Valley Tribe, became the first California Indian and first Hoopa Valley tribal member to become a physician with his graduation from the Stanford University School of Medicine in 1982. Chase helped Hoopa Valley gain its own acute care hospital, serving as the founding CEO of the K'ima:w Medical Center. The first California Indian to complete the preventive medicine residency at UCLA, he received his MPH in community health sciences there in 1990.

1982: Everett R. Rhoades (1931–), Kiowa Tribe of Oklahoma, who graduated from medical school at the University of Oklahoma in 1956, became the first American Indian director of the Indian Health Service (IHS; 1982 to 1993), serving in the position with the rank of rear admiral and assistant surgeon general of the Public Health Service Commissioned Corps. In 1971, Rhoades became a founding member of the Association of American Indian Physicians (AAIP). He was also instrumental in the development of the Oklahoma City Indian Clinic, which opened in 1974 and grew into one of the largest urban Native American health centers in the country. Rhoades became professor emeritus of medicine at the University of Oklahoma Health Sciences Center. His many contributions include work with the Strong Heart Study, a path-breaking study of cardiovascular disease among American Indians. In 2012, Rhoades was the recipient of the American Medical Association Foundation Award for Excellence in Medicine.

1982: Naleen Naupaka Andrade (1954–), who graduated from the University of Hawai'i John A. Burns School of Medicine (JABSOM) in 1982, was the first Native Hawaiian woman to become a psychiatrist and the first Native Hawaiian woman to lead a department of psychiatry at a U.S. medical school. She served as chair of psychiatry at JABSOM from 1995 to 2012 and served as national president of the American College of Psychiatrists in 2012. Andrade coedited *Peoples and Cultures of Hawai'i* with John McDermott. In 2017, while serving as professor and director of JABSOM's National Center on Indigenous Hawaiian Behavioral Health, she was honored with the American Academy of Child and Adolescent Psychiatry's Jeanne Spurlock Lecture and Award on Diversity and Culture.

1983: Kathleen Annette (1955–), White Earth Nation, became the first Anishinaabe woman in Minnesota to become a physician. In 1990, she also became the first woman to serve as director of the Bemidji Area Office of the Indian Health Service in Minnesota. In 2011, Annette was named president and CEO of the Blandin Foundation, a private foundation that works to strengthen rural communities in Minnesota, serving in that leadership role until 2020.

1986: Joseph Bell, Lumbee, graduated from the University of North Carolina, Chapel Hill, School of Medicine, becoming the first Lumbee pediatrician and the first Native American pediatrician in the state of North Carolina. His work includes serving as medical director and pediatrician at Pembroke Pediatrics and pediatrician with the Catawba Indian Health Service Unit.

1987: Frances Owl-Smith (1950–), Cherokee, was the first woman of the Eastern Band of

Cherokee Indians in North Carolina to become a physician. She completed her medical degree at the University of North Carolina at Chapel Hill School of Medicine and originally envisioned a career in family practice but ultimately chose to become a pathologist.

1988: Susan Veronica Karol (1957–), Tuscarora, who graduated from the Medical College of Wisconsin, became the first woman of the Tuscarora Indian Nation to become a surgeon. From 1988 to 1990, she served as chief of surgery and anesthesia at the Shiprock Indian Hospital in New Mexico. In 1996, Karol was the first woman to become chief of surgery at Beverly Hospital in Beverly, Massachusetts.

1989: Mary DesRosier, Blackfeet, who graduated from the University of North Dakota (UND) School of Medicine in 1989, was the first Blackfeet woman to become a medical doctor. After graduating, she completed a family medicine residency at UND-Minot in 1992. Returning home to Montana in 1995, she became the first Blackfeet medical doctor to practice medicine on the Blackfeet Reservation. In 2010, DesRosier, who is also the mother of eight children, was the recipient of the 2010 Dr. George Saari Humanitarian Award.

1989: Sharon M. Malotte (1955–), TeMoak Band of Western Shoshones, completed her medical degree at the University of North Dakota School of Medicine and Health Service, becoming the first Indigenous Nevadan to become a physician. Named Miss Indian Nevada in 1977, she was also the first in that role to become a doctor. Her work experience includes serving as medical director of the Pyramid Lake Paiute Tribal Health Clinic in Schurz, Nevada.

1991: Robert J. Sciacca (1944–), Stockbridge-Munsee, otolaryngologist, founded Alabama ENT Associates and spearheaded the completion of Medplex Medical Complex in Hoover, Alabama. A decorated Vietnam combat veteran, Sciacca entered the University of North Dakota School of Medicine through the INMED Program in 1974, completing a two-year B.S. degree in medicine program. He then transferred to the University of Alabama, where he completed his medical degree in 1978 and his ENT residency in 1982. Sciacca became board certified by both the American Academy of Otolaryngology Head and Neck Surgery and the American Academy of Otolaryngic Allergy.

1991: Walter Hollow (1947–), Assiniboine-Sioux, who became the first Native American to graduate from the University of Washington (UW) School of Medicine in 1975, was instrumental in the establishment of the Native American Center of Excellence (NACOE) at UW. In 1992, he founded the Indian Health Pathway (IHP) within NACOE to help prepare Native and non-Native medical students for careers in American Indian/Alaska Native health. Hollow was also a founding member of the Seattle Indian Health Board, one of the first clinics in the country to address urban Indian health needs.

1992: Joseph J. Jacobs (c. 1947–), Caughnawaga Mohawk/Cherokee, a Columbia University graduate (class of 1973), Yale Medical School-trained pediatrician (class of 1977), and Wharton School MBA (class of 1985), was appointed the first director of the newly established Office of Alternative Medicine at the National Institutes of Health. Earlier, Jacobs joined the Indian Health Service in 1980 and was assigned to the Gallup Indian Medical Center. His work included serving as an instructor and as a staff pediatrician.

1994: Lori Arviso Alvord (1958–) became the first Navajo woman to become board certified in surgery. She graduated from Dartmouth College in 1979, later attending Stanford University Medical School, where she earned her MD in 1985. Alvord completed a six-year residency at Stanford University Hospital before becoming board certified. Her autobiography, *The Scalpel and the Silver Bear*, has sold over 50,000 copies. In 2013, Alvord was nominated to serve as the U.S. surgeon general.

1994: Michael H. Trujillo (1944–), Laguna Pueblo, MD, MS, MPH, became the first U.S. president–appointed and U.S. Senate–confirmed director of the Indian Health Service and served two four-year terms. As director, he was an assistant surgeon general/rear admiral (2008) in the U.S. Public Health Service. In 2002, Trujillo was appointed to the Office of Surgeon General, Department of Health and Human Services (DHHS), working to improve the health status and disparities in health care of minority and underserved populations. After 29 years of federal service, he retired (2003) and became the associate dean and professor for the Outreach and Multicultural Affairs program of the University of Arizona College of Medicine–Phoenix.

1997: Nadine Caron (1970–), Ojibway, who graduated at the top of her class, was the first First Nations woman to graduate from the University of British Columbia's medical school and also became Canada's first female First Nations general surgeon. "I was the first not because I was special," Caron later commented, "but because of where we are as a society in Canada."

Dr. Nadine Caron

1998: Cathy K. Bell became the first Native Hawaiian "triple-boarded psychiatrist in Hawai'i," trained in three specialties—pediatrics, general psychiatry, and child and adolescent psychiatry. She completed her studies at Yale University (BS, biology), the University of Hawaii John A. Burns School of Medicine (1995, MD), and her residency at the University of Hawaii in 1998. Bell is the great-granddaughter of Alsoberry Kaumualii Hanchett, the first Native Hawaiian to graduate from Harvard Medical College and the first to return home to Hawaii to practice medicine. Her work as a physician includes cofounding the Kahala Clinic for Children and Family in Honolulu, which specializes in family therapy, parenting for challenging behaviors, and behavioral management and consultation.

2000: Patricia Nez Henderson (1965–), Navajo, was the first American Indian woman to graduate from Yale University School of Medicine. She was also the first to receive the Patricia Nez Award, an annual award given to recognize a Yale School of Medicine graduate committed to improving health among American Indian populations.

c. 2000s: Angela M. Pratt (1962–) became the first woman and the first Native Hawaiian to head the obstetrics and gynecology department at Kapi'olani Center in Honolulu. She graduated from the University of Hawai'i John A. Burns School of Medicine (JABSOM) with her medical degree in 2002. Earlier experiences included competing in beauty pageants to earn scholarship money to help pay for medical school, serving as Miss Honolulu 1986 and Mrs. Hawaii USA 1992. Pratt also worked as a flight attendant for Hawaiian Airlines, when she saw firsthand the poor state of health and living conditions of Indigenous communities while traveling the Pacific.

2003: Chiyome Leinaala Fukino (1951–) became the first Native Hawaiian and the first woman to serve as director of the Hawaii State Department of Health when she was appointed to the position by the state's governor, Linda Lingle. Fukino's stated priorities for the department included addressing

Azee' ąąh ál'į bee dabi'diszįį'ii atah azee' ááh ásh'įį doo díí binahjį':

Kodóó dinisingo dóó shił nilįįgo bee haasdziih díí bíla'ashdla'ii kót'éego bá na'anish she'iina doo;

The Physician's Pledge

Or, in English, "As a member of the medical profession: I solemnly pledge to dedicate my life to the service of humanity." Lines from the Physician's Pledge were said in Diné Bizaad, the Navajo language, at the University of New Mexico Health Sciences Center graduation for the first time in the spring of 2019.

long-term care, substance abuse, and mental health. She graduated from University of Hawaii's John Burns Medical School in 1979. In 2009, she became the first recipient of the Hawai'i Medical Association's President's Award.

Yvette Roubideaux

2007: Evan Adams (1966–), Coast Salish, actor and physician from the Tla'amin First Nation (formerly Sliammon) near Powell River, British Columbia, became the first Aboriginal health physician advisor for the province of British Columbia, from 2007 to 2012. Adams, who completed his medical degree at the University of Calgary in 2002, is best known internationally for his film roles as Thomas Builds-the-Fire in *Smoke Signals* and Seymour Polatkin in *The Business of Fancy Dancing*. In 2014, Adams became the chief medical officer of the First Nations Health Authority in British Columbia.

2009: Yvette Roubideaux (1963–), Rosebud Sioux, who received her undergraduate, medical, and public health degrees at Har-

vard University, became the first woman to lead the Indian Health Service (IHS), an agency within the U.S. Department of Health and Human Services. Confirmed by the Senate to a four-year term, Roubideaux administered a health care delivery program responsible for serving approximately two million American Indians and Alaska Natives in hospitals, clinics, and other settings throughout the nation. In previous positions, her work included research in diabetes and its prevention among American Indians and Alaska Natives. Although President Barack Obama nominated her for a second term at the helm of the IHS, the Senate failed to act and she served as acting director for a time before leaving office in 2015. Roubideaux later became vice president for research and director of the Policy Research Center at the National Congress of American Indians. She is a past president of the Association of American Indian Physicians and coeditor of *Promises to Keep: Public Health Policy for American Indians and Alaska Natives in the 21st Century* (2001).

2010: Shaquita Bell (1979–), Cherokee/African American, was the first Native American to be appointed chief resident at Children's Hospital in Seattle, Washington. Bell completed medical school at the University of Minnesota in 2006 and a pediatric residency at the University of Washington in 2009. A Minnesotan, she has pointed out that she's a "two-fer" as the daughter of a Cherokee mother and an African American father. Bell joined the Committee on Native American Child Health of the American Academy of Pediatrics in 2013, becoming chair in 2016.

2011: Maile Taualii (1975–) was the first Native Hawaiian appointed a member of the executive board of the American Public Health Association (APHA), the oldest and largest public health organization in the world, in its 139-year history. Taualii, who received her Ph.D. in health services from the University of Washington, became the founding director of the Native Hawaiian Epidemiology Center housed at Papa Ola Lokahi, the Native Hawaiian health board. She also served as the scientific director for the Urban Indian Health Institute, an Indian Health Service designated Tribal Epidemiology Center for nearly a decade. Taualii joined the University of Hawaii Mānoa faculty in May 2011, also serving as an assistant professor in Hawaii's John A. Burns School of Medicine.

2014: Joseph Keawe'aimoku Kaholokula, Ph.D., was granted tenure at the John A. Burns School of Medicine (JABSOM), University of Hawaii at Mānoa. A licensed clinical psychologist with a specialty in behavioral medicine, he is the director of the Department of Native Hawaiian Health, the first clinical department in any medical school in the United States dedicated entirely to the improvement of the health of native people.

2015: Amanda Bruegl (1980–), Oneida/Stockbridge-Munsee, completed a fellowship in gynecologic oncology at the University of Texas MD Anderson Cancer Center, becoming one of the first Native American gynecologic oncologists in the country. In 2007, she received her MD from the University of Washington School of Medicine and an MS from the University of Texas Graduate School of Biomedical Sciences in 2013. Her work includes serving as the director of tribal engagement for the Northwest Native American Center of Excellence at the Oregon Health and Science University School of Medicine in Portland. Bruegl researches gynecologic cancer preventions of Native American women, examining why they have one and a half times the rate of cervical cancer and twice the rate of death from cervical cancer.

2016: Dakotah Lane (c. 1981–), Lummi Nation, who completed his medical degree at New York's Weill Cornell Medicine at Cornell University in 2013, became the Lummi

Annie Dodge Wauneka

Annie Dodge Wauneka (1910–1997), Navajo, was the first Native American to receive the Presidential Medal of Freedom. She was awarded the medal in 1963 by President Lyndon Johnson, who cited her election to the Navajo Tribal Council and her long crusade for improved health programs. He said, "She has helped dramatically to lessen the menace of disease among her people and to improve their way of life."

Nation's first physician from its own community in Washington State. In March 2020, Lane was in self-quarantine after determining he was exposed to the first person at the reservation to test positive for coronavirus. As medical director of the Lummi Nation's health service, he helped the tribal community respond to the pandemic early.

2020: Kristine Thomas-Jones received a doctorate in public health from Walden University in Minnesota. She is the first Wampanoag to earn both a Ph.D. and a doctor of chiropractic degree and also has a master of science degree in molecular cell biology. Thomas-Jones and her husband, Bobby Thunderhawk Jones, Narragansett, own M'Askeaht Herbs, based in Sarasota, Florida. M'Askeaht Herbs is well-known on the powwow circuit in the Eastern states.

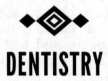

DENTISTRY

"If you want to be a leader, you must get into the game. You cannot do it standing on the sidelines. Do not waste your time. Once you have made up your mind, do not waiver from that goal, no matter how difficult the challenge may be. Remember, you have been born because your Native people need you."

—Dr. George Blue Spruce

1904: Louis R. Bruce (1877–1968), Mohawk, St. Regis, completed his Doctor of Dental Surgery (DDS) degree at the University of Pennsylvania Dental School in 1904, becoming one of the first Native American dentists. He played major league baseball for a time, debuting with the Philadelphia Athletics in 1904, completing one season. Bruce studied theology at Syracuse University in New York and, in 1910, established a dental practice in Syracuse and began a ministry on the nearby Onondaga reservation. In 1917, Bruce returned as a minister to St. Regis before retiring from the Methodist ministry in 1949. He helped organize the National Congress of American Indians and was a proponent of the citizenship bill to extend suffrage to American Indians. His son, Louis R. Bruce Jr., later became the second American Indian to serve as U.S. commissioner of Indian affairs.

1904: Caleb Sickles (1880–1950), a member of the Oneida Nation from Wisconsin, completed his dentistry degree at Ohio Medical University in 1904, becoming one of the first Native American dentists. He graduated from the Carlisle Indian School in Pennsylvania (1898) and attended Dickinson College Preparatory School, known as an athlete at both. At Ohio Medical University, Sickles served as captain of the 1903 football team and later worked as a coach at Heidelberg University in Tiffin, Ohio. He practiced dentistry in Tiffin, providing a description of his dental practice as well as a photo of his office for publication in Carlisle's *The Red Man*, in 1910. During World War I, Sickles was inducted into the military after the armistice was signed and served as a 1st lieutenant in the U.S. Army 11th Battalion. He practiced dentistry in Tiffin until his death.

1907: James E. "Jimmy" Johnson (1879–1942), Stockbridge, became one of the first Native American dentists. He entered the Carlisle Indian School in Pennsylvania in 1897, graduating with the class of 1901. In Carlisle, Pennsylvania, Johnson also completed Dickinson College Preparatory School in 1902 and attended Dickinson College for two years. An athlete, he played football at Carlisle, becoming an All-American quarterback and team captain. After leaving Pennsylvania in 1904, he enrolled in dental school at Northwestern University (NU) in Evanston, Illinois, and continued to play football, becoming captain of the squad at NU. After completing his DDS degree in 1907, Johnson initially worked as a dentist in Chicago, Illinois, in 1908, but moved to San Juan, Puerto Rico, and practiced dentistry there from 1909 to 1916. Johnson was married to Florence Welch, Wisconsin Oneida, and, like him, a Carlisle graduate (class of 1905). In 1969, he was inducted into the College Football Hall of Fame.

1956: George Blue Spruce Jr. (1931–), Laguna/Ohkay-Owingeh, the first American Indian to graduate from Creighton University School of Dentistry in Omaha, Nebraska, has a lifetime of firsts. "For nearly two decades," he said in an interview, "I was the only identified Indian dentist until numbers started picking up when federal programs began to open up dental schools to increase the numbers of Indian and other minority dentists." Blue Spruce served as assistant U.S. surgeon general from 1981 to 1986. Founder of the Society of American Indian Dentists, he later became the organization's president emeritus. Blue Spruce is also credited with writing the original draft of federal statutes for the Indian Health Care Improvement Act. His life story, *Searching for My Destiny*, was published by the University of Nebraska Press in 2009.

1973: Michael Claymore, Cheyenne River Sioux, entered the Indians into Medicine Program (INMED), then in its first year of operation at the University of North Dakota in 1973, completing his pre-dental work in 1976. He then entered the Creighton University School of Dentistry, where he completed his DDS degree in 1980. Claymore was the first dentist to graduate through the INMED Program.

1975: Jessica A. Rickert (1950–), Prairie Band Potawatomi, became the first female American Indian dentist in the country upon graduating from the University of Michigan's School of Dentistry. In 1982, she began a private practice in Interlochen, Michigan, and in 1983, Rickert published a book titled *Exploring Careers in Dentistry*, part of her effort to encourage young people to pursue dental careers. She also worked to establish an intertribal dental clinic in Detroit. In 2009, Rickert was inducted into the Michigan Women's Hall of Fame, which cited her achievements in dentistry and Native American rights.

1985: Darlene Sorrell (1959–) became the first Navajo to graduate from dental school, completing her degree at the Oregon Health and Science University School of Dentistry. She has been clinical director at the dental clinic at Second Mesa on the Hopi Reservation, completed a general practice residency in Anchorage, Alaska, and worked as clinical director at Southwestern Indian Polytechnic Institute (SIPI) and at the Albuquerque area dental program.

1990: The Society of American Indian Dentists (SAID) was founded in 1990 by George Blue Spruce Jr. and five other Creighton University alumni dentists. The first meeting was held at the University of Colorado Health Sciences Center. SAID was organized to address the needs of American Indian dentists, dental students, and dental auxiliaries, improving the status for American Indian/Alaska Native (AI/AN) dentists within the profession of dentistry and educational pathways for AI/AN students.

2002: Charles W. Grim (1958–), Cherokee Nation, was the first dentist to serve as director of the Indian Health Service (IHS). Grim, who graduated from the University of Oklahoma's College of Dentistry in 1983, was appointed director of the Division of Oral Health for the Albuquerque area of the IHS in 1992. President George W. Bush later appointed Grim, who received unanimous Senate confirmation, as IHS director to administer the principal federal health care service for American Indians and Alaska Natives. After his tenure at IHS from 2002 to 2007, Grim served in leadership roles in Oklahoma, first for the Cherokee Nation health system and then for the Chickasaw Nation, where he was appointed secretary of health in 2018.

2004: Alaska's first Dental Health Aide Therapists (DHATs) were a group of students who were trained in New Zealand in 2004. On their return home, they helped address the need for regular oral health care, providing access to mid-level dental care and prevention services for Alaska Native people in rural areas across the state. In 2007, Alaska Dental Therapy Education Program (ADTEP) welcomed its first class in Anchorage, and by 2015 ADTEP was partnering with Ilisagvik College to offer AAS degrees in dental therapy.

OTHER HEALTH PRACTITIONERS

1940: Alexander Ka'önohi (1905–1960) opened Kaonohi Naturopathic Clinic in Hawaii, becoming the first Native Hawaiian to operate his own clinic. A pioneer in integrating traditional and western healing modalities, he graduated from the ICS School of Pharmacy in Philadelphia, Pennsylvania (1922), and the Standard and National College of Naturopathy and Drugless Medicine in Chicago, Illinois (1932). Also a botanist, Dr. Ka'önohi was descended from a long line of Indigenous Hawaiian healers and created a pharmacology of almost 250 herbs from the islands. He was the first licensed naturopath and herbologist in the Territory of Hawaii and sponsored many Native Hawai-

ians through nursing and medical schools. In 1988, the Native Hawaiian health organization Papa Ola Lōkahi created the Ka'önohi Award to honor those Native Hawaiians who contribute to the health of Native Hawaiians, including traditional Kapuna modalities. Ka'önohi was an integral part of the community and often received payment in fruit or sugar cane.

1981: Reginald KHD Ceaser (1951–), Matinecock/Montauk—Turkey Clan Chief, became the first Native instructor as well as the first Shiatsu instructor at the Swedish School of Massage in New York City. He later became the head of the department. In 1984, he was also the first Indigenous person to serve on the New York State Board of Massage Therapists. Chief Ceaser is certified in Chinese herbal medicine and has a private practice in Queens, New York.

2018: Laura Clelland opened Salt Woman, LLC in Winslow, Arizona, becoming the first Navajo to operate a professional foot service business. She also may be the first Native person to be certified in pedorthics; her practice offers holistic treatment for issues including diabetes, fungal infections, and other foot maladies.

HEALTH MEASURES

1832: The U.S. Congress enacted the Indian Vaccination Act, the first piece of federal legislation designed to address an American Indian health problem, epidemic smallpox. As a result, between 40,000 and 50,000 Native Americans were vaccinated.

1836: Kuhina Nui Elizabeth Kaho'anoku Kina'u (wife of King Kamehameha II) (c. 1805–1839) ordered screening for smallpox of all foreign vessels arriving into Honolulu harbor, the first documented public health measure in Hawai'i.

1839: King Kamehameha III (c. 1813–1854), monarch, established quarantine laws, also the first records of vital statistics in the Hawaiian Islands.

1850: King Kamehameha III appointed the first Board of Health in Hawai'i to address epidemics and other health issues and to protect public health.

1866: The O'ahu Insane Asylum opened at Kapālama, Hawai'i, in 1866, a facility that the legislature of the Hawaiian kingdom had voted to establish in 1862. By 1900, it had an average of 140 patients. The facility closed in 1930 and most of the patients were transferred to a new Oahu hospital built the same year.

1929: The Office of Indian Affairs established its first preventive health program, emphasizing maternal and infant care.

1952: The Bureau of Indian Affairs established the Sanitarian Aide Program, the first hands-on public health program for American Indian communities. Tribal members took eight-week training courses at the Communicable Disease Center (renamed the Centers for Disease Control) aimed at implementing environmental sanitation programs locally. It addressed areas such as food sanitation, drinkable water supply, insect control, waste disposal, and community clean-up campaigns.

1957: The Indian Health Service (IHS) issued the "Gold Book," its first annual report to Congress documenting its efforts to improve the health of American Indians.

1988: Don Coyhis (1943–), Mohican Nation, founded and became the president of White Bison, a nonprofit organization that assists Native Americans affected by substance abuse. White Bison is the facilitator of the Wellbriety Movement, which Coyhis started in 1994 to help participants find sobriety from addictions to alcohol and other substances.

2014: The Healthy Diné Nation Act of 2014 (HDNA), the first junk tax in the country, was enacted by the Navajo Nation. The tribal council approved a 2 percent sales tax on foods of minimum to no nutritional value, such as pastries, desserts, chips, and soda, sold on the Navajo Nation. The legislation also removed previous taxes on healthy foods. Eighty percent of the revenue from the HDNA tax increase provides direct funding for community wellness projects such as the development of fitness centers, hiking trails, and vegetable gardens.

2018: On January 26, the Coyote Valley Band of Pomo Indians in California filed suit in

Medical Cannabis

In 2018, Seven Leaf in Akwesasne, Ontario, became the first Indigenous-owned and -operated producer of medical cannabis licensed by Health Canada under the Access to Cannabis for Medical Purposes Regulations. Located in the Akwesasne Mohawk Territory on Cornwall Island in Ontario, the company includes a team with diverse expertise in law, horticulture, business administration, and pharmaceuticals.

San Francisco against prescription drug manufacturers, distributors, and pharmacies for their role in the nation's opioid epidemic. Michael Hunter, chairman of the tribal nation, commented, "So far only six tribes have stepped up to take on Big Pharma and they are very large population tribes far off from California." He continued, "I am proud to say we are the first tribe in the West to sue." Hunter further noted that all tribal governments have been harmed by the opioid crisis and deserve to be compensated for the losses and costs involved.

MEDICAL FACILITIES AND PROGRAMS

1870: King Kamehameha V authorized a "premedical" school to prepare Native Hawaiians to study medicine in the United States and Great Britain. Ten students were in the first class, but the school was short lived. During his reign, the king focused on health issues, including having a medical text published. One of his advisors, Dr. Gerrit P. Judd, authored the *Anatomica*, the first medical text published in the Hawaiian language. Judd also translated government papers into that language from English while serving as the king's advisor. The University of Hawai'i Press reprinted *Anatomica* in 2003.

1877: The Cherokee Home for the Insane, Deaf, Dumb, and Blind, which was established by the Cherokee National Council, opened in Indian Territory (present-day Oklahoma).

1909: The U.S. Leprosy Investigation Station was opened at Kalawao, Hawai'i, and served as a research hospital for Hansen's disease, the first hospital in the United States author-

ized to research a specific disease. Hansen's is an infection caused by slow-growing bacteria that can affect nerves, skin, eyes, and nose lining. The hospital was closed in 1913, deemed a failure for a range of reasons, including inhumane treatment of patients.

1912: The first hospital built on an Indian reservation with funding from private sources was constructed for physician Susan La Flesche Picotte (Omaha) in Walthill, Nebraska, on the Omaha Indian Reservation. Picotte, the first American Indian woman to become a medical doctor, raised funds for it from a range of sources. The hospital served the community until the 1940s and was later used for other purposes. Known as the Dr. Susan La Flesche Picotte Memorial Hospital, it was declared a National Historic Landmark in 1993.

1928: The first air service to transport the sick and injured for medical care began in Alaska, with the initial patients traveling from Bethel to Anchorage. Alaska's vastness and the lack of roads in many areas made such flights essential.

1960: The Indian Medical Center in Gallup, New Mexico, established the first pharmacy residency program in the Indian Health Service. It represented the first time that advance training for Native pharmacists became available directly on or adjacent to an American Indian reservation. Gallup borders the Navajo Nation.

1971: The Indian Health Board (IHB) of Minneapolis was created in Minnesota, becoming one of the first urban Indian health care programs in the United States. The IHB was created to reduce health disparities and to provide health care for community members. In 1973, Congress provided funds to study unmet urban Indian health needs in Minneapolis. The findings documented a range of barriers to health care, leading to

Hiawatha Insane Asylum

In 1902, Congress opened the Hiawatha Insane Asylum in Canton, South Dakota, as the first and only such institution for American Indians in the United States. It was also called the Canton Asylum for Insane Indians and had a more insidious side than institutions that treated white Americans. Those Indians who rejected government policies and stood up for their rights were often diagnosed as mentally unfit and forced into Hiawatha or jails. Often people were dumped there who had tuberculosis or epilepsy. For the 30 years Hiawatha existed, it averaged four deaths per month; bodies were rarely repatriated to their loved ones. Patients were chained to their beds or confined to a strait jacket for years, choked, beaten, sexually assaulted, and had no proper toilet facilities, although the building had modern conveniences. Families were not allowed to visit, but the administration conducted paid tours so people could see the "crazy Indians." The staff was not trained, and there was no psychiatric treatment. There were few patient records or medical notes.

In 1929, an investigation revealed that the Hiawatha Asylum had a corrupt administration and torturous conditions for Native people. It was found to be a place of all around "intolerable conditions," with the "poorest kind of medical care," whose cleanliness was "very much below the standard of a modern prison." The chief medical director of the Office of Indian Affairs responded to this report by committing 150 more people. In 1933, John Collier became commissioner of Indian Affairs and met with patients of families, plus he read the earlier report. Collier closed the asylum with great protest from the town of Canton. Of the 69 Natives transferred to Saint Elizabeth's in Washington, D.C., only 16 were eventually freed, and they were thought to have been sterilized against their will before they were released.

congressional appropriations to support urban Indian clinics in selected cities. In 1976, Congress passed the Indian Health Care Improvement Act, establishing the urban Indian health program under Title V.

1971: The National Aeronautics and Space Administration (NASA) launched the first satellite dedicated to telemedicine in partnership with the Indian Health Service and the Papago Tribe (now, Tohono O'odham) in Arizona. The Space Technology Applied to Rural Papago Advanced Health Care (STARPAHC) utilized a modified recreational vehicle traveling among reservation communities to beam vital data from patients via a telecommunications network to physicians monitoring hospital consoles. STARPAHC made it possible for health professionals to interact with patients, diagnose illnesses, and specify treatments to be performed in the Mobile Health Unit. NASA's participation was operational from 1973 to 1977, but the project continued into the 1980s.

1976: The Puyallup Tribal Health Authority in Washington was the first ambulatory health clinic to enter into a contract with the Indian Health Service through the Indian Self-Determination and Education Assistance Act of 1975.

1977: The Menominee Indian Tribe of Wisconsin successfully raised funds to construct the Menominee Tribal Clinic, the first tribally owned and operated health facility in the United States. Since its establishment, the Menominee Tribal Clinic has been expanded several times, and since 1989 it has been an accredited clinic.

1978: Established by the Ramah Navajo School Board, Inc., Pine Hill Health Center in Pine Hill, New Mexico, became the first community-controlled health care system in the United States to operate under Public Law 93-368, the Indian Self-Determination and Education Assistance Act of 1975. The law provided for government agencies such as the Department of the Interior to enter into contracts with, and make grants directly to, federally recognized tribal nations.

1992: The Porcupine Clinic, the first community-owned and -operated clinic on an Indian reservation, achieved state certification as a rural health facility. Cofounded by Lorelei DeCora, RN (Winnebago/Lakota), it is located in the Porcupine community of the Pine Ridge Reservation in South Dakota.

1993: Anna Albert, Turtle Mountain Chippewa, director of Phoenix Indian Medical Center, was the first Native American, first female, and first nonphysician to direct an American Indian medical center in the nation. She earned a master's degree in public health administration from the University of Oklahoma.

1998: The Fort Belknap Health Center, located at the Fort Belknap Agency in Harlem, Montana, became the first Indian Health Service critical access hospital in the nation. Initially a pilot program, the six-bed facility became part of a nationwide program called critical access hospitals in August 1998.

1999: The Choctaw Nation of Oklahoma became the first tribe to build its own hospital with its own funding. Located in Talihina, Oklahoma, the Choctaw Nation Health Care Center was constructed as a 140,000-square-foot facility with 44 hospital beds for inpatient care and 52 outpatient exam rooms. It became the hub of health care services, covering $10 \frac{1}{2}$ counties of southeastern Oklahoma.

2002: The Department of Native Hawaiian Health was first established as a program of the John A. Burns School of Medicine (JABSOM) at the University of Hawai'i in 2002, becoming a clinical department the following year. Two preexisting JABSOM programs became part of the of the newly formed de-

The First Medical School in Indian Country

The Cherokee Nation in partnership with Oklahoma State University (OSU) Center for Health Sciences broke ground for the first medical school in Indian Country on the W. W. Hastings campus in Tahlequah, Oklahoma, in 2019. Cherokee principal chief Bill John Baker said of the planned OSU College of Osteopathic Medicine, "Our Native American doctors that are trained in Indian Country—it's going to change us from being a desert of primary care physicians to an oasis." The inaugural class of 54 students in the new medical school began their studies in fall 2020, their education initially taking place both virtually and socially distanced in person because of the coronavirus pandemic.

partment's medical education. Dr. Marjorie Mau served as the founding chair of the new department, which grew to become the only clinical department in a U.S. medical school dedicated to the health of an Indigenous population.

2015: The Puyallup Tribe opened the Salish Integrative Oncology Care Center, the first American Indian–owned cancer care center in the country according to the tribe. Located in Fife, Washington, the center combines traditional and natural healing to expand cancer care to help close the existing health care gap for its service population.

2016: Cherokee Nation Health Services in Tahlequah, Oklahoma, was awarded five-year accreditation by the Public Health Accreditation Board, the first tribal health department in the country to achieve that national designation.

2016: The Spirit Lake Nation became the first tribe in the Great Plains Area to enter a self-governance compact with the Indian Health Service (IHS). The tribal nation became responsible for running the Spirit Lake Health Center in Fort Totten, North Dakota.

2019: The House of Hope, the first cancer treatment center on the Navajo Nation, opened in Tuba City, Arizona. The culturally adapted cancer care center at Tuba City Regional Health Care provides oncology services to Navajo and Hopi people. It was developed to address high cancer rates as well as help patients who must travel hundreds of miles to receive treatment.

2020: North Dakota's State Board of Higher Education approved the first doctoral program in Indigenous health, and it is located at the University of North Dakota (UND). Dr. Don Warne, Oglala Lakota, director of the Indians into Medicine (INMED) and Master of Public Health programs at UND,

led the drive for the new program, cited as the first in the world. The Ph.D. degree in Indigenous health was launched in 2020.

MENTAL HEALTH

"… AI/AN [American Indian/Alaska Native] populations have disproportionately higher rates of mental health problems than the rest of the US population. High rates of substance use disorders (SUDs), posttraumatic stress disorder (PTSD), suicide, and attachment disorders in many AI/AN communities have been directly linked to the intergenerational historical trauma forced upon them, such as forced removal off their land and government-operated boarding schools which separated AI/AN children from their parents, spiritual practices, and culture."

—*"Mental Health Disparities: American Indians and Alaska Natives," American Psychiatric Association, 2017*

1952: Carolyn Lewis Attneave (1920–1992), Delaware/Scandinavian, graduated from Stanford University with a Ph.D. in psychology, becoming one of the first Native American psychologists in the country. She became known for founding network therapy and for other path-breaking work, including accomplishments in cross-cultural areas. In 1970, she founded and solely administered a newsletter, called *Network of Indian Psychologists*, that became a precursor to the Society of Indian Psychologists, established in 1975. The organization honors Attneave's internationally renowned work with a memorial scholarship in her name. The American Psychological Association presents a Carolyn Attneave Diversity Award, recognizing the promotion of diversity in family psychology. In 2019 Stanford University renamed Serra House, where the Clayman Institute for Gender Research is located, the Carolyn Lewis Attneave House.

1958: Herbert G. Fowler (1919–1977), Santee Sioux, established the first mental health clinic on an Indian reservation, at the Ute Reservation in Utah. Fowler, a genetic psychiatrist and the grandson of early physician Charles Alexander Eastman, served as the clinic's director for six years. He had been the first director of the Whitecloud Center, a pioneering mental health research project for American Indians and Alaska Natives, at the University of Oregon Health Sciences Center in Portland. Fowler was awarded the Lenin Science Prize in 1976.

1964: Marigold Linton (1936–), Cahuilla/ Cupeno, who earned a Ph.D. in psychology at the University of California, Los Angeles in 1964, has had a lifetime of firsts. A member of the Morongo Band of Mission Indians, she became the first California Indian to leave a reservation for college when she entered the University of California at Riverside in 1954. Linton found herself the only American Indian student on campus, persevering to graduate in 1958. After earning her Ph.D., she worked at the University of Utah, where she was the first woman hired as a full professor; Arizona State University, where she fostered a partnership between ASU and the Indian Health Service in Phoenix; and the University of Kansas, where she raised more than $18 million in grants in support of a partnership with Haskell Indian Nations University. Linton is a founding member of the National Indian Education Association (NIEA) and the Society for Advancement of Chicanos and Native Americans in Science (SACNAS). The Office for Diversity in Science Training at the University of Kansas established the Marigold Linton Scholarship in Biomedical Science in her honor. Linton's research specialty is long-term memory.

1966: Arthur McDonald, Oglala Lakota, became the first American Indian man to earn a Ph.D. in psychology upon graduating from the University of South Dakota. Besides teaching at Montana State University, he worked on the Northern Cheyenne Reservation, where he was instrumental in the founding of Dull Knife Memorial College (now Chief Dull Knife College). McDonald helped establish the INPSYCH program to counter the underrepresentation of Native Americans in the field of psychology. In 2000, he was awarded the Presidential Citation by the American Psychological Association for his invaluable contributions.

1974: Ronald G. Lewis (1941–2019), Cherokee Nation, was the first American Indian to receive a Ph.D. in social work with his graduation from the University of Denver in 1974. He became known as the "Father of American Indian Social Work" and was also the first American Indian to be tenured in the University of Wisconsin system and to become a social work dean in Canada. Known for his expertise on federal policy and social issues, Lewis contributed to the creation of the Indian Child Welfare Act of 1978. A psychiatric social worker, he also developed mental health programs for American Indians in Oklahoma.

1976: Diane J. Willis (1937–), Kiowa, was the first woman to serve as president of the Society of Pediatric Psychology, founded in 1969. She was the first editor of the *Journal of Pediatric Psychology*. She established the first psychology clinics at the Clinton Indian Hospital in Clinton, Oklahoma, and at the Cheyenne-Arapaho Indian Health Services Clinic in El Reno and Concho, Oklahoma. Willis is credited with helping to form the Child Protection Committee at OU Children's Hospital, the first program of its kind to systemically train medical personnel to detect signs of abuse and neglect in children.

1978: Catharine Gail Kincaid (1939–2013), Eastern Sioux descent, was the first American Indian to receive a fellowship from the National Institute of Mental Health/American Psychiatric Association. A graduate of Creighton University School of Medicine, she completed a fellowship in psychiatry at Massachusetts General Hospital. In 1991, Kincaid was named medical director for the state of New Mexico. Following this work, in 1994 she founded New Mexico's Delphi Unlimited to help employers deliver health care services to their employees.

1982: Johanna Ghe-e-bah Clevenger (1937–2012), Navajo, became the first woman elected president of the Association of American Indian Physicians, presiding over the organization again in 1992. She was board certified in psychiatry and neurology as well as certified in addiction medicine by the American Society of Addiction Medicine. She is on Harvard University Medical School's roll of "Women of Color as Leaders in Public Health and Health Policy."

1992: Maria Yellow Horse Brave Heart, Hunkpapa/Oglala Lakota, established the Takini Network, a Native nonprofit organization dedicated to healing the wounds inflicted on Native Americans through the experiences of intergenerational trauma. Her model of healing historical trauma has been customized to meet the specific recovery needs of Indigenous peoples throughout the world. A research associate professor at the University of New Mexico Department of Psychiatry and Behavioral Sciences, Brave Heart also serves as director of Native American disparities research in the university's Center for Rural and Community Behavioral Health. She earned her Ph.D. in clinical social work from Smith College School for Social Work in Northhampton, Massachusetts.

1998: Cornelia "Nel" Wieman (1964–), Anishinaabe, Little Grand Rapids First Nation in Manitoba, completed her training in psychiatry at McMaster University in Hamilton, Ontario, becoming the first female Indigenous psychiatrist in Canada. She has served as a psychiatrist in a community-based mental health clinic on the Six Nations of the Grand River territory, codirected the Indigenous health research development program at the University of Toronto, and worked as staff psychiatrist at the Centre for Addiction and Mental Health in Toronto. In 2018, Wieman joined the First Nations Health Authority in British Columbia as a senior medical officer for mental health and wellness. Her leadership also includes serv-

Logan Wright: The Father of Pediatric Psychology

In 1986, Logan Wright (1933–1999), Osage, became the first known American Indian to serve as the president of the American Psychological Association (APA). He received his doctorate in clinical psychology from Vanderbilt University in 1964. Wright, who coined the term "pediatric psychology," was referred to as the father of pediatric psychology. He was associated with the University of Oklahoma Health Sciences Center (Oklahoma Children's Memorial Hospital), where he worked in the department of pediatrics. Wright authored *The Encyclopedia of Pediatric Psychology* and other works. His many honors include the Distinguished Service Award from the Society of Pediatric Psychology.

ing as president of the Indigenous Physicians Association of Canada.

2018: Victoria O'Keefe, Cherokee/Seminole, clinical psychologist and faculty member, became the first Native American woman to win the APA/American Psychological Association of Graduate Students Award for Distinguished Graduate Students in Professional Psychology. O'Keefe is also the first Native woman to become a tenured professor at Johns Hopkins Bloomberg School of Public Health. Her work with tribal communities includes suicide prevention, mental health promotion, and wellness. In 2020, she was recipient of the Cherokee Nation Community Leadership Individual Award. In 2021, she was the named the first holder of the inaugural Mathuram Santosham Chair in Native American Health, a five-year faculty leadership chair, at the Bloomberg School of Public Health.

2018: Nagi Nunpa Hocoka, the Two Spirit Circle, became the first official safe place for young people who are lesbian, gay, bisexual, transgender, and queer or questioning (LGBTQ) on the Pine Ridge Reservation in South Dakota. Working to reduce the high rate of suicide and substance abuse on the reservation, Nagi Nunpa Hocoka is funded by the Substance Abuse and Mental Health Services Administration.

NURSING

1930: Sage Memorial Hospital School of Nursing on the Navajo Reservation, founded by Presbyterian medical missionary Dr. Clarence G. Salsbury in 1930, became the first accredited nursing program for American Indian women in the United States. In 1933, Ruth Henderson and Charlotte Adele Slivers, both Navajo, became the program's first graduates. Before it closed in 1951, Sage Memorial Hospital School of Nursing had graduated approximately 150 women from 50 tribal nations with nursing degrees. Located in Ganado, Arizona, the facility was designated a National Historic Landmark on January 16, 2009. Author Jim Kristofic documents Sage in his book *Medicine Women: The Story of the First Native American Nursing School* (University of New Mexico Press, 2019).

1935: The Kiowa Nurse Aide School/Kiowa School of Practical Nursing, located in Lawton, Oklahoma, is viewed as the first organized effort by the Indian Service to train American Indian women in nursing. In 1951, the school changed its name to the Kiowa School of Practical Nursing and was approved by the National Association of Practical Nurse Education. Four years later, the program moved from Oklahoma to Albuquerque, New Mexico, and changed its name to the Indian School of Practical Nursing, maintaining that name until the school's closing in 1974.

1981: Lynda Hunter (1952–), Shinnecock, became the head nurse of the Behavioral Health floor at Jacobi Medical Center in the Bronx, New York, the first time a Native person was awarded the position in any department at the prestigious institution, also a teaching hospital. It may also be the first time ever at any New York state medical facility. In 2005, Hunter was promoted to supervisor of the Behavioral Health Department.

1987: Josephine T. Waconda (1935–2013), Laguna/Isleta Pueblo, who received her diploma from Regina School of Nursing in Albuquerque, New Mexico, in 1955 and her BSN from the University of New Mexico in 1975, became the first American Indian woman to receive the rank of rear admiral (RADM) in 1987. Waconda managed a large health care program covering four states and serving numerous tribal nations. Her contributions included establishing the first diabetes clinics in the Indian Health Service and initiating some of the first wellness programs, including child abuse prevention and suicide prevention task forces. As assistant surgeon general, she accepted additional duties and responsibilities at multiple service levels. In 1991, Waconda became the first American Indian in public health service to receive flag officer rank. The recipient of many honors, she was named NMCNE Nursing Legend in 2004 and designated Pueblo Woman of the Year in 2008. Waconda was the daughter of Miguel H. Trujillo, who won the right to vote for American Indians in New Mexico. Her brother, Michael Trujillo, served as director of the Indian Health Service. She and her husband, John Waconda, had four children.

1995–96: The American Indian Program at Northern Arizona University, located at St. Michaels, Arizona, became the first reservation-based bachelor of science program in nursing in the United States. It was established to help address the critical shortage of nurses in the Navajo Nation.

2002: Susie Walking Bear Yellowtail (1903–1981), Crow, became the first American Indian nurse to be inducted into the American Nursing Association Hall of Fame, a posthumous honor. Yellowtail graduated from Boston City Hospital's School of Nursing in 1923 and completed her training at Franklin County Public Hospital in Greenfield, Massachusetts. In 1927, she became the first registered nurse of Crow descent, among the first of her people to achieve a higher education. After returning home to the Crow Reservation, she married fellow tribal member Thomas Yellowtail, worked at the hospital at Crow Agency, and traveled to other reservations as a consultant for the Public Health Service. Throughout her ca-

reer, she was a tireless advocate for improved living conditions and health care for American Indians.

2015: Navajo nurse-midwife Nicolle Gonzales (1980–) founded the first Native American–led birth organization, the Changing Woman Initiative, in Santa Fe, New Mexico. Its efforts include working to reinstate culturally supported births, fostering public awareness concerning overlooked issues of Native American maternal health, and increasing Indigenous representation within midwifery in the United States. The initiative became a 501(c)(3) nonprofit organization in 2018 and undertook a strategic planning process to explore sustainable ways to ensure access to culturally centered healthcare and traditional childbirth options for Native women.

2017: The first Indigenous nursing research center was dedicated at the Florida State University (FSU) College of Nursing in Tallahassee, Florida. The Center for Indigenous Nursing Research for Health Equity aims to attain health equity in part by partnering with Indigenous peoples and supporters globally. The center's executive director, John Lowe (Cherokee), was named the McKenzie Endowed Professor for Health Disparities Research at FSU. In 2016, he was honored with the American Nurses Association's Luther Christman Award, which recognizes the contributions of men in nursing.

ORGANIZATIONS

1973: The Society for Advancement of Chicanos/Hispanics and Native Americans in Science (SACNAS) was founded and later, in 1986, was incorporated. The organization is dedicated to fostering the success of scientists, from college students to professionals, to attain advanced degrees, careers, and positions of leadership in science. Its national office is in Washington, D.C.

1976: The National Indian Council on Aging (NICOA) was founded by members of the National Tribal Chairmen's Association (NTCA) to advocate for improved comprehensive health, social services, and economic well-being of American Indian and Alaska Native elders. Led by President Wendell Chino, the NTCA sponsored the first National Indian Conference on Aging in Phoenix, Arizona, from June 15 to 17, 1976. Some 1,500 American Indians and Alaska Natives representing 171 tribal nations attended.

1977: The American Indian Science and Engineering Society (AISES) was officially created, with mechanical engineer Al Qöyawayma, Hopi, becoming the founding chairman, and chemical engineer A. T. "Andy" Anderson, Mohawk, the founding executive director. AISES, now headquartered in Albuquerque, New Mexico, was founded as a national nonprofit organization with the mission of substantially increasing the representation of Indigenous peoples of North America and the Pacific Islands in science, technology, engineering, and math (STEM) studies and careers.

1994: The National Resource Center on Native American Aging (NRCNAA) was founded, receiving funding from the Administration on Aging. Its services include developing community-based solutions to improve the quality of life and the delivery of support services to the Native aging population. NRCNAA is located at the Center for Rural Health at the University of North Dakota in Grand Forks. In 2003, the National Resource Center for American Indian, Alaska Native, and Native Hawaiian Elders opened in Anchorage, Alaska; and in 2006, Hā Kūpuna (National Resource Center for Native Hawaiian Elders) opened in Honolulu, Hawaii.

2000: Michael E. Bird (1951–), Kewa Pueblo/Ohkay Owingeh, was elected as the first American Indian and the first social worker to serve as president of the 50,000-member American Public Health Association. Bird worked for the Indian Health Service (IHS) for 20 years as well as other agencies during his career. He served as past president of the New Mexico Public Health Association and on the boards of many organizations. Bird was also the first American Indian to serve on the National Policy Council of the American Association of Retired Persons (AARP). In 2018, he was recognized by the University of California, Berkeley School of Public Health as one of 75 Most Influential Alumni in the 75-year history of the School of Public Health.

2016: Seven Directions, supported by a grant from the W. K. Kellogg Foundation, became the first national public health institute in the United States to focus solely on Indigenous health and wellness. Located at the University of Washington, the organization also became a member of the National Network of Public Health Institutes. Myra Parker, Mandan/Hidatsa, JD, MPH, PhD, a faculty member in the Center for the Study of Health and Risk Behavior in the UW School of Medicine's Department of Psychiatry, serves as the chief executive officer of Seven Directions.

CORONAVIRUS, COVID-19 PANDEMIC

"Over four centuries, nine out of 10 Native Americans

perished from war or disease. Now our people are dying from COVID-19 at extraordinarily high rates across the country.... As COVID-19 takes a fearsome toll on our people, it also threatens the progress we have made to save our languages. The average age of our speakers— our treasured elders who have the greatest knowledge and depth of the language—is 70. They are also those who are at most risk of dying from COVID-19."

—*Jodi Archambault, "How Covid-19 Threatens Native Languages,"* New York Times, *January 24, 2021*

2020: Merle Dry (1964–2020), Cherokee Nation, diagnosed with COVID-19 on March 17, 2020, and dying a day later, was identified as the first coronavirus death in Oklahoma. A citizen of the Cherokee Nation, Dry was a groundskeeper at Oral Roberts University and a pastor at the Metro Pentecostal Church in Tulsa.

2020: Gloria Jane Merculief (1956–2020), Athabascan, was the first known person to die from COVID-19 in Alaska. Merculief died at the Alaska Native Medical Center in Anchorage within days of falling ill.

2020: Don Osceola (1942–2020), Seminole/ Miccosukee, who died on April 29, 2020, is believed to be the first Native American in Florida to succumb to the novel coronavirus disease. Born a Seminole, Osceola became a member of the Miccosukee Tribe of Indians of Florida when he married a member of that tribe. He was a highly decorated Vietnam War veteran, serving in the U.S. Marine Corps and earning the Purple Heart and many other medals for meritorious service. Osceola, who attended Florida International University in Miami, worked for the National Park Service. He also completed police academy training and worked as a police officer with the Miccosukee Police Department.

2020: Michael Lee (1970–2020), Navajo, was the Navajo Nation's first law enforcement officer to die from COVID-19. Lee, who began his law enforcement career in 1990, was a 29-year veteran of the Navajo Police Department, serving in the Window Rock district for his first seven years and his remaining years in the Chinle district. He fought on the front lines to combat the coronavirus pandemic, which had a devastating impact on the Navajo Nation.

2020: Doctors Without Borders, known for its work internationally, sent a team of medical professionals to help the hard-hit Navajo Nation in its efforts to combat COVID-19. The organization's assistance there is believed to be a first.

2020: Air Serv International, which normally conducts humanitarian relief efforts overseas, partnered with the Navajo & Hopi Families COVID-19 Relief Fund to transport critical humanitarian relief items by plane to remote Navajo and Hopi communities to help residents in their fight against the coronavirus. The organization implemented the Navajo Air Bridge Program, the first of its kind on domestic soil, with support from the ISTAT (International Society of Transport Aircraft Trading) Foundation. "We are shocked by how strikingly similar the disparities in resources are for Navajo and Hopi to those faced by our developing world beneficiaries," commented Danielle Payant, director of communications for Air Serv.

2020: The Indian Health Service (IHS) regional office in Bemidji, Minnesota, which serves tribal nations in Minnesota, Wisconsin, and Michigan, was the first IHS office in the country to receive COVID-19 vaccines. Following the Pfizer vaccine's arrival on December 14, health care workers in Cass Lake were the first IHS staffers, and among the first people anywhere in Minnesota, to be vaccinated. Drivers delivered doses to several tribal nations across Minnesota, and a Coast Guard helicopter transported the vaccine to Michigan and Wisconsin tribes.

2021: U.S. Air Force tech sergeant Michael Morris (1984–2021), a member of the Leech Lake Band of Ojibwe in Minnesota, passed away from COVID-19 while stationed at Aviano NATO Base in Italy. He is believed to be the first member of the U.S. Air Force to die of COVID-19 while on active duty. Morris, who had served 14 years at the time of his passing, is also identified as the first American Indian to die of the illness while on active duty. He and his wife Amanda had three children.

FOOD SOVEREIGNTY/NUTRITION

"When we talk about Indigenous Foods we're ultimately talking about relationship. We're talking about the foods that have historically nurtured and shaped our bodies, our cultures, and our traditions as Indigenous Peoples of this land base we know as Turtle Island from our (Anishinaabeg) creation stories.

"Other tribes have different names for this land base. In turn, the history of each of our Indigenous Foods is also tied to this land, and to us. Our histories are a shared one. This is what makes people, plants, and animals Indigenous to a place—a historical 'upbringing' if you will, in a shared space on our Maamaa Aki, Mother Earth."

—*Culinary Indigebotanist
Tashia Hart, Red Lake Nation*

1959: Claire Ku'uleilani Hughes (1936–) became the first Native Hawaiian registered dietitian. Her years of work included serving as chief of the nutrition branch of Hawaii's State Department of Health. She was named one of 2011's Living Treasures of Hawaii by the Honpa Hongwanji Mission of Hawaii in honor of her advocacy for health programs, including attention to the benefits of returning to a more traditional Hawaiian diet.

1992: The Traditional Native American Farmers Association (TNAFA) was formed, an outcome of an intertribal meeting of Native farmers and elders representing 72 farming families from 17 different Native communities in Arizona and New Mexico. Its stated mission centered on revitalizing traditional agriculture for spiritual and human need. Since its inception, TNAFA has addressed concerns such as the preservation and conservation of traditional and heirloom seeds.

2003: *Foods of the Southwest Indian Nations* (Ten Speed Press, 2002) by Lois Ellen Frank, Kiowa, was the first Native American cookbook to win the James Beard Award.

2006: The American Indian Health and Diet Project (AIHDP) was founded by Professor Devon Mihesuah, citizen of the Choctaw Nation of Oklahoma. The website is based on her book *Recovering Our Ancestors' Gardens: Indigenous Recipes and Guide to Diet and Fitness* (University of Nebraska, 2005). The revised edition won the 2021 Best in the USA Indigenous Book from Gourmand International. Mihesuah also coedited *Indigenous Food Sovereignty in the United States: Restoring Cultural Knowledge, Protecting Environments, and Regaining Health* (University of Oklahoma, 2019), which Gourmand named as the Best in the World University Press Book in its 2020 World Cookbook Awards.

2011: At a White House gathering, First Lady Michelle Obama and American Indian children planted the Three Sisters—corn, beans, and squash—together for the first time in the

First Lady Michelle Obama plants traditional crops with Native children in this 2011 photograph. At left, wearing glasses, is National Congress of American Indians President Jefferson Keel.

White House kitchen garden. Obama commented, "Today's a big day for us in the garden because it's the first time we're going to use native seeds of corn, beans and squash in the way they've been planted for thousands of years."

2012: Carl "White Eagle" Barnes (1928–2016), Cherokee, became known for originating a unique rainbow-colored corn that became known as Glass Gem. Barnes, who earned his Bachelor of Science in agriculture education at Oklahoma State University, worked for years with heritage corn, enabling many tribal groups to recover ancestral seeds. He and his family worked a farm and operated an organization called CORNS. Barnes often repeated the words "the seed

remembers," summing up his philosophy and teaching.

2016: The first scientific conference on Native American nutrition was held in Prior Lake, Minnesota. Cosponsored by the Shakopee Mdewakanton Sioux Community and the University of Minnesota's Healthy Foods, Healthy Lives Institute, it brought together more than 450 leaders, researchers, and health workers to address dietary factors contributing to Native health disparities. Held annually, the event is cited as "the only conference in the world devoted to food and nutrition for indigenous peoples."

2017: The Quapaw Nation in Oklahoma opened a 25,000-square-foot meat-packing plant, the first USDA-inspected reservation processing plant owned and operated by a tribe. Designed to adhere to humane animal handling, the tribe processes bison and cattle that it raises on open pastures. As a USDA-inspected facility, meat can be shipped across state lines and sold in public markets. Besides processing their own animals, the Quapaw process cattle for nearby ranchers from Oklahoma and Missouri.

2017: I-Collective, a national group of Indigenous food activists, chefs, and educators, was founded and began organizing events to create awareness of Indigenous foods. Members gathered for the first time in the kitchens of The Pixie and The Scout in New York City to prepare a pop-up dinner centered on Native cuisine "to rewrite Thanksgiving history." Its participating chefs include Oaxacan Neftali Duran, the National Museum of the American Indian's Native American Chef of the Year in 2014 and 2015; Brian Yazzie, aka Yazzie the Chef, Navajo; Hillel Echo-Hawk, Pawnee and Athabaskan; and Brit Reed, Choctaw, the Seattle-based founder of Food Sovereignty Is Tribal Sovereignty.

2018: The first Southwest Intertribal Food Summit was held in Taos, New Mexico, by the Native American Food Sovereignty Alliance, Taos Pueblo, the Taos County Economic Development Corporation, Red Willow Farm, and the Traditional Native American Farmers Association. Participants gathered on October 26 and 27 to learn and share knowledge of Indigenous foods, traditional food processing, seed saving, Indigenous plants, and cultural ways of Southwest tribal nations.

2018: The Native American Agriculture Fund (NAAF) was founded as an outgrowth of the historic *Keepseagle v. Vilsack* class action case, which was settled after more than 18 years in federal litigation over discrimination against Native American farmers and ranchers in the U.S. Department of Agriculture farm and ranch loan program and in the servicing of loans. The mission of NAAF, a private charitable trust, includes funding the provision of business assistance, agricultural education, technical support, and advocacy services. It became the largest philanthropic entity in the country whose purpose is to support the success of Native farmers and ranchers.

2020: The Cherokee Nation (CN) became the first tribal nation in the United States to send traditional heirloom seeds to the Svalbard Global Seed Vault, a long-term seed storage facility located at a remote site in Norway. The Oklahoma-based tribe's Natural Resources office collected nine samples of crops to send, including Cherokee White Eagle Corn, Cherokee Trail of Tears Beans, and Cherokee Candy Roaster Squash. All nine varieties selected predate European settlement. The Svalbard Global Seed Vault preserves seed and crop diversity in case of an agricultural hardship or global catastrophe. Representatives of Indigenous Andean communities in South America have also participated, depositing 750 potato seeds in 2015.

SCIENCE AND TECHNOLOGY

"I know from personal experience how changes in landscape and place can affect families for generations. I have learned that sense of place is as vital to humans as it is to plants and animals. In scientific terms, you might think of this sense of place as a niche in the eco-system, or the way a community of plants and animals interact with their environment."

—Robin Kimmerer,
Potawatomi, botanist and author

c. 1886: George Bushotter (Otaga, Strong; 1864–1892), Lakota, Lower Brule, who worked at the Smithsonian's Bureau of American Ethnology with James Owen Dorsey, became known as the first Lakota ethnographer. He provided firsthand accounts of his culture, writing pioneering texts in Lakota and assisting in the preparation of language materials later used in the *Handbook of American Indians*, edited by Frederick W. Hodge.

1929: Bessie Coleman (1892–1926), Cherokee/African American, was the first woman to earn an international aviation license, becoming the world's first licensed black aviator. She was born in Texas to Susan Coleman, who was African American, and George Coleman, Cherokee. Coleman, one of thirteen children, and her family lived as sharecroppers. She attended a segregated, one-room school, where she loved to read and excelled at math. Coleman eventually attended a missionary church school on scholarship and later Oklahoma Colored Agricultural and Normal University for one term. She read about the air war in Europe during World War I and became interested in flying. Prevented by race and gender from gaining admission to a flying school in the United States, she looked into training possibilities in Europe. Coleman learned to speak French and earned enough money to travel to Paris to pursue her dream. Overcoming daunting difficulties along the way, she ultimately earned her license at the Fédération Aéronautique Internationale on June 15, 1921. On her return to the United States, Coleman began teaching other black women to fly. She gave lectures, performed at flying exhibitions, and gained fame as an air circus performer in a surplus Jenny Trainer plane. Coleman, who be-

Bessie Coleman

came known as "Queen Bessie," died on April 30, 1926. She was thrown from a plane and fell to her death while practicing for an air show in Jacksonville, Florida. Coleman was the recipient of numerous honors, including becoming the first African American woman pilot honored with a U.S. stamp as part of a Black Heritage series in 1995.

1930: Mary Riddle (1902–1981), Clatsop/Quinault, was the first tribally enrolled Native American woman to earn a pilot's license and, a short time later, a commercial license. After seeing her first plane as an 11-year-old, she became mesmerized with flight. Although public opinion held that women could never be successful pilots, Riddle was determined to prove otherwise. She saved money to attend the Rankin School of Flying in Portland, Oregon, flying solo for the first time on May 10, 1930. Best known as a performing parachutist, she was pictured on the cover of *The 99er*, a publication of the Nine-Nines organization and the first magazine devoted to women fliers, in June 1934. After a back injury caused her to stop parachuting in 1938 and following restrictions on civilian aircraft during World War II, Riddle began working as part of the U.S. Air Force's Civil Service. "I just had to be near airplanes," she commented, "even if I could not fly them."

1935: Arthur C. Parker (1881–1955), Seneca, noted archaeologist, historian, folklorist, and

Arthur C. Parker

museologist, became the first president of the Society of American Archaeology. By then, he had also served as president of the Society of American Indians. Other work included serving as director of the Rochester Museum of Arts and Sciences from 1924 to 1945, developing its holdings and research during his tenure. Since 1998, the Society of American Archaeology has annually awarded the Arthur C. Parker Scholarship, which provides support to Native Americans for training in archaeological methods.

1942: Mary Golda Ross (1908–2008), Cherokee Nation, was the first woman engineer at Lockheed Aircraft Corporation (now Lockheed Martin) and six years later was an integral part of what became known as the "space race." She was the great-great granddaughter of Chief John Ross, who led the Cherokee Nation during the Indian Removal period of the 1830s and the resulting relocation of tribal members from their southeastern homeland to present-day Oklahoma. Mary Ross was the first Native aerospace engineer and a member of the top-secret team involved with the early years of space exploration. She was inducted into the Silicon Valley Engineering Hall of Fame in 1993. A 2019 Native American $1 coin by the U.S. Mint, with the theme *American Indians in the Space Program*, features Ross and an example of a mathematical equation she would have used in her calculations for interplanetary space travel. The coin also includes an image of an astronaut in space, a reality that Mary Ross helped make possible.

1966: Jerry C. Elliott (1943–), Cherokee/Osage, one of the first Native Americans to earn a degree in physics at the University of Oklahoma, became one of the first Native Americans to work at NASA. An aerospace engineer, he became the lead retrofire officer (earth/moon trajectory specialist) in the high-risk rescue of the crew of Apollo 13 after an oxygen tank exploded on board the spacecraft. Elliott was awarded the Presidential Medal of Freedom, the nation's highest U.S. civilian honor, by President Richard M. Nixon, in connection with that mission, in 1970. He was recognized for his duties at NASA Mission Control Center for Apollo 13, resulting in the safe return of the flight crew. Elliott computed the spacecraft

trajectory to enable the return to earth. A 2019 Native American $1 coin by the U.S. Mint, with the theme *American Indians in the Space Program*, honors Native Americans, including him. Elliot also had the name "High Eagle" bestowed on him by Native American elders.

1966: William R. Pogue (1930–2014) was the first person of Native American descent (Choctaw) to become an astronaut. Born and educated in Oklahoma, he enlisted in the U.S. Air Force after graduating from college and served for 24 years. He flew combat during the Korean War and also served as a flight instructor and mathematics professor. Accepted into NASA in 1966, he later served as command module pilot for *Skylab 4*, and he was launched into space in 1973. Pogue spent 84 days there, a duration record that was not broken for more than 20 years. He is the author of *How Do You Go to the Bathroom in Space?* and the coauthor (with Ben Bova) of *The Trikon Deception*, a science fiction novel.

1974: Madine Pulaski (1936–2005), Cherokee Nation, pioneering aviator, was the first woman to be appointed to the California Civil Aeronautics Board, receiving her appointment from then-Governor Ronald Reagan. Born Etha Madine Waltrip in Oklahoma, she began her career as a flight attendant with Trans World Airlines in 1957 and married pilot Walt Parsel. Pulaski, who earned her pilot's license in 1960, also worked as a flight instructor and became a founding member of the Orange County Chapter of the 99s, an international association of female pilots. In 1968 she married her second husband, Dennis Carpenter, who served two terms in the California State Senate, traveling with him to the White House and meeting President Richard Nixon as well as future presidents Gerald Ford and Ronald Reagan. In 1984, she married architect Rolly Pulaski, who collaborated with her on restoration projects. The Madine's Wings Foundation was established in Pulaski's honor.

1976: Edna Lee Paisano (1948–2014), Nez Perce/Laguna Pueblo, statistician, was the first American Indian to be hired by the U.S. Census Bureau as a full-time employee. She addressed the undercount of Native Americans and developed enumeration formulas that changed the way tribal nations were funded.

1979: Ellen Evak Paneok (1959–2008), Inupiaq, was the first Alaska Native woman to become a pilot. She began flying lessons at the age of 16, and by the time she was 23, she had her commercial and flight instructor certificates. In 1983, her first pilot job was in Kiana, Alaska, flying a Piper Cherokee Six. Working as a commercial pilot in Alaska for 17 years, Paneok "ferried everything from dynamite to live wolverines, the U.S. mail, passengers, and medical patients." She also served as an operations inspector for the Federal Aviation Administration and as an aviation safety coordinator for the Alaska Aviation Safety Foundation. In addition, Paneok was an author and an artist. In 1997, she was one of 37 pilots profiled in *Women and Flight*, an exhibition at the National Air and Space Museum. Paneok was inducted into the Alaska Women's Hall of Fame in 2012.

1993: T. David Petite (1956–), Fond du Lac Band of Lake Superior Chippewa, who is best known for being one of the key inventors of wireless networking technology, founded SIPCO, LLC (formerly Stat Signal Inc.), inventing fundamental technology covering various wireless mesh network protocols. He is also a founder of the Native American Intellectual Property Enterprise Council, a nonprofit organization helping Native American

Astronaut John Bennett Herrington

inventors and communities. A list of Petite's inventions can be found at Patent Genius or by a search at the U.S. Patent Office. He has approximately 100 issued patents and over 50 U.S. patents pending.

2001: Sam Dupris (1933–), Cheyenne River Sioux, was the first Native American inducted into the South Dakota Aviation Hall of Fame. After serving as a paratrooper in the U.S. Army and fighting in the Korean War, he pursued a career in aviation. Following his discharge from the military, Dupris completed flight training, becoming the first Native American to be employed as a pilot in the Federal Aviation Administration (FAA), eventually rising in the ranks to become an aircraft commander (captain) and then an operations officer (chief pilot). In 2010, Dupris was inducted into the South Dakota Hall of Fame.

2002: John Bennett Herrington (1958–), Chickasaw Nation, became the first enrolled member of a Native American tribal nation to travel in space. Born in Wetumka, Oklahoma, Herrington received a bachelor's degree in applied mathematics from the University of Colorado in 1983 and, in 1984, was commissioned as an ensign in the U.S. Navy at the Naval Air Station in Pensacola, Florida. The following year, he was designated a naval aviator, transitioning from student to patrol plane commander and instructor pilot. In 1990, Herrington attended the U.S. Navy Test Pilot School in Maryland and, after graduation, served as a test pilot at the U.S. Navy Force Warfare Aircraft Test Directorate from 1991 to 1993. In 1995, he completed an M.S. in aeronautical engineering from the U.S. Naval Postgraduate School. The following year, NASA selected him as an astronaut, and after two years of training and evaluation he received an assignment as a mission specialist. Herrington traveled to the International Space Station in the space shuttle STS-113 *Endeavour*, launching on November 23, 2002, from Kennedy Space Center in Florida. During the journey, he carried eagle feathers, the flag of the Chickasaw Nation, and other Native American items. Herrington accomplished three space walks tallying 19 hours and 55 minutes. NASA thus considers him, as an enrolled tribal member, to be the first American Indian astronaut to accomplish space travel and a space walk. The recipient of many honors, Herrington was inducted into the Chickasaw Hall of Fame in 2002 and the Oklahoma Aviation and Space Hall of Fame in 2007.

2006: Robin W. Kimmerer (1953–), member of the Citizen Potawatomi Nation, scientist and professor, became the founder and director of the Center for Native Peoples and the Environment in Syracuse, New York, the first of its kind in the Northeast. The establishment of the center at the SUNY College of Environmental Science and Forestry creates programs that draw on Indigenous and scientific knowledge to support goals of environmental sustainability. Kimmerer is the author of the acclaimed bestseller *Braiding Sweetgrass: Indigenous Wisdom, Scientific Knowledge and the Teaching of Plants*. Her first book, *Gathering Moss: A Natural and Cultural History of Mosses*, received the John Burroughs Medal for outstanding nature writing. Kimmerer, who holds an M.S. and Ph.D. in botany from the University of Wisconsin, is a SUNY Distinguished Teaching Professor of Environmental Biology.

2006: Lakota Solar Enterprises (LSE), located on the Pine Ridge Reservation in South Dakota, became one of the first Native-owned and -operated renewable energy businesses in the country. Owned and operated by Henry Red Cloud, Oglala Lakota, LSE builds solar air furnaces and provides green job training to Native American communities.

2007: Native Skywatchers was created by astrophysicist Annette S. Lee, Lakota, to record, map, and share Indigenous star knowledge. Its overarching goal is "to communicate the knowledge that indigenous people traditionally practiced a sustainable way of living and sustainable engineering through a living and participatory relationship with the above and below, sky and earth." Lee has served as an associate professor of physics and astronomy at St. Cloud State University since 2009. Members of Native Skywatcher's team include Carl Gawboy, Bois Forte Band of Chippewa, scholar and artist, who started research on Ojibwe Star Knowledge in the 1960s and is called the "Father of Ojibwe Indigenous Astronomy Revitalization."

Nancy B. Jackson

2007: Nancy B. Jackson (1956–2022), Seneca, chemist, became the founder and manager of the International Chemical Threat Reduction Department in the Global Security Center at Sandia National Laboratories in Albuquerque, New Mexico. Working with the U.S. Department of State, she was the first implementer in developing the Chemical Security Engagement Program (CSP), a program that works to improve chemical safety and security internationally. Jackson, who received her Ph.D. in chemical engineering at the University of Texas at Austin, became president of the American Chemical Society in 2011. In 2012 she was the recipient of the American Association for the Advancement of Science Award for Science Diplomacy.

2008: Robbie E. Hood (1955–), Cherokee, is an atmospheric scientist who became the first permanent director of the National Oceanic and Atmospheric Administration

(NOAA) Unmanned Aircraft Systems Program. A descendant of Chief John Ross, she spent much of her early years living in Neosho, Missouri, and Picayune, Mississippi, where she developed an interest in weather by witnessing the devastating effects of Hurricane Camille in 1969 and the Neosho tornado in 1974. Hood has worked as a mission scientist in National Aeronautics and Space Administration (NASA) research experiments studying hurricane genesis, intensity, precipitation, and landfall impacts.

2009: The Burns Paiute Tribe in Oregon became the first Native American tribal nation to complete full weatherization and installation of energy-efficient light bulbs in all reservation housing.

2010: David A. Close, Cayuse Nation, Confederated Tribes of the Umatilla Indian Reservation, zoologist, discovered a new corticosteroid hormone in the Pacific lamprey. The discovery of this stress hormone has scientific implications and application for lamprey conservation and management. Close, who received his Ph.D. in fisheries and wildlife from Michigan State University, has served as Distinguished Science Professor of Aboriginal Fisheries at the University of British Columbia in Victoria, Canada.

2011: The first plant experiment involving native seeds cultivated only by American Indians from the Western Hemisphere was implemented by Dakota astronomer and educator Jim Rock as a tiny part of the payload of the NASA space shuttle *Atlantis*. Rock, who worked with his wife, educator Roxanne Gould, Odawa/Ojibwe, and the Bella Gaia (Beautiful Earth) NASA education team, chose an 800-year-old cultivar of small leaf yellow tobacco for the trip, the tiny seeds chosen, in part, because of size restrictions. After returning to earth, the seeds

Kim TallBear

were taken to the Science Museum of Minnesota for observation.

2015: The Bear River Band of the Rohnerville Rancheria in Northern California became the first tribe in the state to install a hybrid solar, wind, and advanced energy storage microgrid for power generation.

2016: When the Laser Interferometer Gravitational-Wave Observatory (LIGO) announced the first evidence of gravitational waves, press releases were released around the globe in 20 or so different languages, one of them Blackfoot. Corey Gray, Siksika Nation, lead operator for the LIGO Hanford facility in Richland, Washington, asked his mother, Sharon Yellowfly, Siksika Nation, to do the translation, the first in a Native language. "This way she would be a poet for Einstein and astrophysics," Gray noted. "A code-talker for gravitational waves." Yellowfly had just two weeks to translate astrophysical jargon into Blackfoot, an inventive process, but did so before the deadline. She has since translated other press releases of LIGO discoveries.

2016: Kim TallBear (1968–), Sisseton-Wahpeton Oyate, became the first recipient of the Canada Research Chair in Indigenous Peoples, Technoscience, and Environment, which was awarded to her by the government of Canada. TallBear, who completed her Ph.D. at the University of California, Santa Cruz, serves as a faculty member at the University of Alberta in Manitoba, Canada. She is the author of *Native American DNA: Tribal Belonging and the False Promise of Genetic Science* (2013).

2019: The Navajo Nation became the first program to use mapping technology known as Plus Codes in the United States, the outcome of a partnership between the nonprofit

Rural Utah Project and Google. The six-digit codes allow first responders to find residences, many without street addresses, more quickly. The technology also helps on driver licenses, voter registration forms, and for other purposes. As of January 2020, 500 signs displaying Plus Codes had been installed on Navajo homes and businesses with plans to expand.

2021: The Shakopee Mdewakanton Sioux Community in Minnesota acquired 47 percent of Windward Engineers & Consultants, the first time the tribal nation has co-owned an engineering firm. The company provides a range of services, including design and building services, fire protection and code safety consulting, and life cycle cost analysis.

SPORTS AND GAMES

"My father and my uncle just threw me into the water from an outrigger canoe. I had to swim or else. I have no doubt the ancient Hawaiians used every stroke we know and perhaps had better swimming form than we'll ever have."

—Duke Kahanamoku

BASEBALL/SOFTBALL

1897: Louis Sockalexis (1871–1913), Penobscot, became the first Native American in the National Baseball League. He played outfielder with the Cleveland Spiders. From Old Town, Maine, Sockalexis was a stand-out athlete at an early age, and it was reported that he could throw a baseball across the Penobscot River from Indian Island to the shore of Old Town. The fans taunted him, screaming racist slurs when he was on the field. It was surprising when the Spiders changed their name to "Indians," ostensibly to honor Sockalexis.

Moses J. "Chief" Yellow Horse

1921: Moses J. "Chief" Yellow Horse (1898–1964) was the first Pawnee to play in the major leagues (Pittsburgh Pirates, 1921–1922). Because of injuries, he spent the last four years of his career pitching in the minors (Sacramento, Fort Worth, and Omaha). It is thought that he was the first Native American athlete to have a comic strip character modeled after him. Dick Tracy's originator, Chester Gould, who was also born on the Pawnee reservation, created the character Yellow Pony in the 1940s. He was based on stereotypes and hardly resembled Yellow Horse.

1931: Pepper Martin (1904–1965), Osage, was named the first-ever Associated Press Athlete of the Year. He played both third baseman and outfielder for the St. Louis Cardinals during the 1930s and early 1940s. He became known for his daring, aggressive base-running prowess and lauded for his heroics during the 1931 World Series, in which he was the catalyst in the Cardinals' upset victory over the Philadelphia Athletics.

1953: Charles "Chief" Bender (1884–1954), White Earth Chippewa, was the first American Indian to be inducted into the Baseball Hall of Fame. As the star pitcher for the Philadelphia Athletics for 16 seasons in the 1910s and 1920s, he amassed 212 wins in 16 seasons. Bender is credited with being the first to use the "nickel curve," now called the slider. He led his team to their first World Series Championship (1910). He may have been the first Native American to coach a major league team.

1964: Professional baseball player Kenneth Adair (1936–1987), Cherokee, was the first Native American to set two American League records for a second baseman while on the Baltimore Orioles team. He had the fewest errors in a season with 150 or more games and most consecutive errorless games. Adair's glove is in the National Baseball Hall of Fame.

1968: Johnny Bench (1947–), Choctaw, was the first catcher to win the National League Rookie of the Year Award as well as the 1968 National League Gold Glove Award for catchers, another rookie first. Bench played for the Cincinnati Reds from 1967 to 1983, is a member of the National Baseball Hall of Fame, a 14-time All-Star selection, and a two-time National League Most Valuable Player. His team won six division titles, four National League pennants, and two consecutive World Series championships. ESPN has called him the greatest catcher in baseball history.

Salt River Fields at Talking Stick in Scottsdale, Arizona, is home of the Salt River Rafters and serves as the spring training facility for the Arizona Diamondbacks and the Colorado Rockies.

1969: Phyllis "Yogi" Bomberry (1943–2019), Cayuga, a softball champion, was the first woman to win a Tom Longboat Award, named for the champion Onondaga runner.

1989: The all-Native "North Americans Fastpitch" softball team was founded by Frank LaMere, Winnebago. In the 1990s, LaMere organized 10,000 Sioux, Winnebago, and Omaha who lived in the Sioux City, Iowa, area to protest the proposed name for the Sioux City minor league baseball team, the Sioux City Soos. The name was changed to the Sioux City Explorers.

2011: Salt River Fields at Talking Stick became the first Major League Baseball spring training stadium complex erected on land owned by Indigenous people. The Salt River Pima–Maricopa Indian Community in the Scottsdale, Arizona, area hosts the stadium where the Arizona Diamondbacks and the Colorado Rockies train.

2011: Jacoby Ellsbury (1983–), Navajo, became the first Boston Red Sox baseball player ever to become a member of the 30-30 club, an elite group of Major League Baseball batters who have collected 30 home runs and stolen 30 bases in a single season. A center fielder, he was also the first Navajo to play on an MLB team (Red Sox and Yankees). He won the World Series two times.

2015: Kyle Lohse (1978–), Nomlaki, was the first Native American pitcher to defeat all 30 Major League Baseball teams. He was only the 14th pitcher ever to achieve this rare status.

2019: Trevor Boone (1997–), Osage, became the first Oklahoma State University (OSU) baseball player to record three three-homer games in his career. He was the only OSU player to collect All-Big 12 Conference First Team Honors and emerged as one of the nation's top sluggers.

BASKETBALL

"Being able to sage, just cleanse the energy, make sure that we're all balanced. I saged last game, and I plan to sage almost every game if the opposing team will allow me to.... I'm not going to bring too much of the spirituality into basketball, but yeah it's part of my native culture where I'm from."

—*Kyrie Irving, Lakota, professional basketball player*

1904: The Fort Shaw Indian School Girls' Basketball Team became World Champions at the 1904 Louisiana Purchase Exposition (better known as the St. Louis World's Fair). The team was made up of seven Native American students who attended the Fort Shaw Indian Boarding School in Fort Shaw, Montana. They defeated basketball teams

Members of the Fort Shaw Indian School Girls' Basketball Team that won the 1904 World Championships and became the subject for the 2009 movie *Playing for the World*.

from across the United States and beyond. Their story is told in *Playing for the World: 1904 Fort Shaw Indian Girls' Basketball Team,* which first aired in February 2009. It is also told by Linda Peavy and Ursula Smith in their book *Full-Court Quest: The Girls from Fort Shaw Indian School, Basketball Champions of the World* (University of Oklahoma, 2014).

1967: Lloyd "Sonny" Dove (1945–1983), Mashpee Wampanoag/Narragansett, was the first Native American to win the Haggerty Award, given to the All-New York Metropolitan NCAA Division I men's college basketball player of the year, presented by the National Invitation Tournament (NIT) and the Metropolitan Basketball Writers Association (MBWA). In that same year, he played on the U.S. basketball team in the Pan American Games in Winnipeg, Manitoba, Canada, where the United States took the gold medal. Dove was among the first ten men selected for "Basketball Legacy Honors" at St. John's University in Queens, New York, and in 2008 he was named to St. John's University "All-Century Team." In 2011, he was inducted into the New York City Basketball Hall of Fame and is thought to be the first Native American to earn the honor.

1967: Martin Waukazoo (1948–), Lakota, was the first American Indian in South Dakota to be selected All American and held the all-time South Dakota boys' basketball records in both Class AA single game scoring (individual) and top scoring games in South Dakota cage history. In 2013, Waukazoo was inducted into the South Dakota High School Basketball Hall of Fame.

1994: The SuAnne Big Crow Award was presented for the first time. Named for SuAnne Big Crow (1974–1992), Lakota, the annual award is given to a South Dakota high school senior athlete who excels at academics and is also a community activist. Big Crow was

a natural at basketball, and in 1989, she dominated in the state championship when she made the winning shot at the buzzer. She died in a car crash on her way to receive the Miss Basketball Award. Considered to be the best female player in South Dakota's history, Big Crow scored an average of 39 points per game and set a state record by making 67 points in a single game. Off the court, she united her Pine Ridge community and advocated for children. Her family took up her cause and campaigned for a Girls and Boys Club to be established at Pine Ridge, the first ever on a reservation. It is named for her. December 19 has been declared "SuAnne Big Crow Day" by the state of South Dakota, and she was inducted into the South Dakota Hall of Fame in 2017.

1997: Ryneldi Becenti (1971–), Navajo, became the first Native American to play in the Women's National Basketball Association (WNBA) when she signed with Phoenix Mercury. She was an All-Pac 10 First Team selection in both her seasons at Arizona State University, and a two-time honorable mention All-America honoree. Her team won the bronze medal for the United States at the 1993 World University Games in Buffalo, New York. She was the country's top junior college point guard in 1990–91. In her early career, Becenti played professional ball in Sweden, Greece, and Turkey. In 2013, she was the first women's basketball player to have her jersey (No. 21) retired by Arizona State University.

2000: Sam McCracken, Fort Peck Assiniboine and Sioux Tribes, a Nike employee and former high school basketball coach, became the manager of Nike's Native American Program and developed a plan for building relationships between Nike and the 250 Indian tribes that had received diabetes education grants and 188 schools that are enrolled in the Office of Indian Education Programs (OIEP). Nike's program collaborates with Indian Health Service (IHS) and the National

Indian Health Board (NIHB) on their "Just Move It" program, which promotes physical fitness on Indian reservations. In July of 2004, McCracken was honored with Nike's Bowerman Award, the annual award that honors the Nike employee who best exemplifies the legacy of tireless motivation, innovation, and inspiration.

2002: Kelvin Sampson (1955–), Lumbee, was the first Native American basketball coach (University of Oklahoma Sooners) to make it to the Final Four of the National Collegiate Athletic Association (NCAA). In 2003, his Sooners advanced to the Elite Eight. As coach of the University of Houston Cougars team, Sampson led his team to the 2021 Final Four.

2003: The Mohegan Tribe of Connecticut became the first Native nation to own a professional sports team after they purchased the Connecticut Sun, the Women's National Basketball Association (WNBA) team formerly known as the Orlando Miracle.

2005: The Sun Kings basketball team was purchased by the Yakama Nation of Washington State and renamed the Yakama Sun Kings. It was the first time a Native nation bought a pro men's basketball team.

2007: The Native American Basketball Invitational (NABI), launched in 2003, received NCAA certification, becoming the first Native-owned basketball tournament.

2007: The Lady Indians, the Sequoyah High School basketball team from Tahlequah, Oklahoma, became the first all-Indian school to be invited to the Nike Tournament of Champions. They earned the prestigious invitation by being three-time state champions and were ranked in the top ten in a *Sports Illustrated* national poll.

2007: Jason Alan Kapono (1981–), Native Hawaiian, was the first National Basketball Association (NBA) player to lead the league in three-point field goal percentage in two consecutive seasons, and he also won the Three-Point Shootout twice (2007 and 2008). Kapono won an NBA championship with the Miami Heat in 2006.

2011: Tahnee Robinson (1988–), Shoshone, was the first Wyoming-born player and the first University of Nevada player to be drafted by the Women's National Basketball Association (WNBA). She was also the first Shoshone.

2019: Ben Strong (1986–), Red Lake Band of Chippewa Indians, was hired as the first-ever Native American to be the staff development coach for the Phoenix Suns. A retired player (2016), Strong spent his basketball career playing abroad in the Netherlands, Israel, New Zealand, and Uruguay. His first coaching job was at Huntingdon College in Montgomery, Alabama, and he was the player development specialist for the Philadelphia 76ers' staff before being hired by the Suns.

2019: Jacqulynn Nakai (1991–), Navajo, became the first woman to be named the National Junior College Athletic Association All American twice and the first Pima Junior College woman to win the Arizona Community College Athletic Association Player of the Year. She signed to play for the University of Nevada as a guard.

2020: For the first time, the Mescalero Apache School (MAS) Lady Chiefs became the New Mexico 2A State Basketball Champions.

2020: Ada McCormack-Marks, enrolled member of the Coeur D'Alene Tribe, was named the Idaho Coach of the Year in her division. She led her Lapwai High School Girls Basketball Team to League, District, and State Championships. This was not only a first for a Coeur D'Alene but also the first for a new basketball coach, although McCormack-Marks coaches other grades and sports.

◆◇◆

FOOTBALL

"When it comes to building a nation, the foundation of making a strong nation is to make sure the young people are being raised in a manner that allows them to be successful."

—Teton Saltes, Oglala Lakota,
2020 recipient of the Wuerffel Trophy

1897: Frank Hudson (1875–1950), Laguna Pueblo, was the first American Indian chosen for football's Walter Camp for All-American Second Team as well as the first Native to be selected as an All-American football player.

1909: Albert Andrew Exendine (1884–1973), Delaware, was the first American Indian to become a head football coach for a college team. His championship teams included Otterbein College (1909–1911), Georgetown University (1914–1922), the State College of Washington (now Washington State University; 1923–1925), Occidental College (1926–1927), Northeastern State Teachers' College (now Northeastern State University; 1929), and Oklahoma Agricultural and Mechanical College (now Oklahoma State University; 1934–1935). While at Georgetown, Exendine earned a law degree at Dickinson School of Law and later practiced law in Oklahoma. He served with the Bureau of Indian Affairs. Exendine was a star player at Carlisle Indian Industrial School where he was an All-American end. An all-around athlete, Exendine was also the head

Albert Exendine

baseball coach at Oklahoma A&M from 1932 to 1933. He was inducted into the College Football Hall of Fame as a player in 1970.

1931: Henry "Honolulu" Thomas Hughes Jr. (1907–1963) was the first Native Hawaiian to play professional football. He first played for the Boston Braves and later was an original member of the Washington, D.C., football team (1933).

1997: Native Vision was founded in Baltimore as a partnership between Johns Hopkins Center for American Indian Health and the National Football League Players Association. NFL players and other professional athletes mentor reservation-based youth in fitness and wellness.

2004: Ronald Ekdahl (1986–) was the first Chippewa to play football for the Central Michigan University Chippewas. He helped lead his team to back-to-back Mid-American Conference (MAC) championships (2006–7). The former linebacker was one of the youngest people ever to be elected chief of the Saginaw Chippewa Indian Tribe (2017).

2006: The Whalers from Barrow High School in Utqiaġvik, Alaska, played the first official football game in the Arctic, against Delta High School from Delta Junction, Alaska. Utqiaġvik (formerly known as Barrow) is the northernmost town in the United States. The team won and celebrated by jumping into the Arctic Ocean, just a hundred yards from the field. In 2017, they won their first Division III state title.

2008: Samuel Jacob Bradford (1987–), Cherokee, was the first Native American and only the second sophomore to win the Heisman Trophy. He played quarterback for the Oklahoma Sooners and went on to play pro football with the St. Louis Rams, Philadelphia Eagles, Minnesota Vikings, and Arizona Cardinals.

2008: Kevin Mawae (1971–), Native Hawaiian, became the first Native person to be president of the National Football League Players Association and served until 2012; his tenure included the 2011 National Football League lockout. During his football career, he played offensive lineman for the Seattle Seahawks, New York Jets, and Tennessee Titans.

Sam Bradford

Kevin Mawae

2018: The National Football League selected seven young football players as ambassadors to represent their first Native American Youth Football Ambassador Program. The goals of the program are to celebrate Native football players playing throughout the country and to help those players generate interest in football within their communities. The ambassadors were selected using the following criteria: character; athletic ability; academic success; and community involvement. The youth represent a broad spectrum of outstanding achievement, from award winners in several different sports to membership in the National Honor Society. The ambassadors represented seven different nations: Clayton Franklin, Kashia Band of Pomo Indians, California; Edward Ono Po Hill, Pauma Band of Luiseno Indians, California; Dean Holyan, Navajo Nation, Arizona; Keynan Arnold, Iowa Tribe of Oklahoma; Jhadi Harjo, Choctaw Nation of Oklahoma; Frederick Fox, Three Affiliated Tribes, North Dakota); and Tyler Ogimaabinez Garza Moose, Mille Lacs Band of Ojibwe, Minnesota.

2020: Teton Saltes (1998–), Oglala Lakota, was named the 2020 recipient of the Wuerffel Trophy, an award that honors college football players who excel in community

service and celebrates their positive impact on society. He is thought to be the first Native to earn the honor. A two-time Wuerffel Trophy semifinalist, Saltes had been named the 2020 Allstate AFCA Good Works Team Captain. A senior at University of New Mexico, he was also the trophy's first recipient from the Mountain West Conference and the first to be awarded the trophy on the televised *Home Depot College Football Awards* on ESPN. In 2021, Saltes became the first football player (offensive lineman) from the Pine Ridge Reservation to vie for a spot on the New York Jets' roster.

GOLF

"I was praying he would make birdie just so I could say I beat Jack Nicklaus by one shot."

—Rodney Curl, Wintu professional golfer's comment about his 1974 win over Jack Nicklaus

1953: Jackie Liwai Pung (1921–1917) was the first Native Hawaiian to join the Ladies Professional Golf Association (LPGA) tour. During her 12 years on the LPGA circuit, Pung won nine major tournaments. After she retired from competition, she became the first woman director of golf at Mauna Kea Beach Hotel and then at Waikoloa Village Golf Course. The LPGA named her Teaching Professional of the Year in 1967. Pung was inducted into the first class of the Hawaii Golf Hall of Fame in 1988 and taught golf well into her 80s. Her life was chronicled in a 2005 biography, *Jackie Pung: Women's Golf Legend*, by Betty Dunn.

1968: Frank Dufina (1884–1972), Mackinac Bands of Chippewa and Ottawa Indians, was the first Native American to play golf on the professional circuit and competed in the Western Open in 1911 and 1922. Dufina was still playing in 1968, earning him the distinction of being named the "Longest Working Golf Professional in History" by *Golf Digest*. The annual Frank Dufina Match Play Championship is held in his honor at the Wawashkamo Golf Club on Mackinac Island, Michigan.

Ashton Locklear

1974: Rodney Curl (1943–), Wintu, became the first Native American professional golfer to win a Professional Golf Association (PGA) tour event. He won the Colonial National Invitation in Fort Worth, Texas, over runner-up Jack Nicklaus.

1998: Notah Begay III (1972–), Navajo, became the first Native American and the third ever professional golfer to shoot a 59 on a U.S. pro tour. He was a member of the Stanford University NCAA Division men's golf championship team, a three-time All-American, and a teammate of Tiger Woods. In 2005, he founded the Notah Begay Foundation to promote Native American youth fitness, and he hosts golf clinics for Native youth. In 2009, Begay was named one of *Golf Magazine*'s Innovators of the Year, and he is an analyst with the Golf Channel.

ships, and she is a two-time national champion on the uneven bars (2014 and 2016). Locklear was an uneven bars specialist and was an alternate for the 2016 Summer Olympics U.S. gymnastics team, the Final Five.

2021: Shawn N. Yazzie (2009–), Navajo/Sac and Fox/Comanche, became the youngest and probably first Native American to win the USA Gymnastics Arizona state championship. He took the gold in the pommel horse, rings, and vault events and the bronze in floor exercise, parallel bars, and the high bar. At the 2021 USA Gymnastics Development Program National Championships in Daytona, Florida, Yazzie won the third-place medal on floor and became No. 18 in the top 20 gymnasts in his age group, making him the 18th best 12-year-old gymnast in the nation. He was the only Native American in the competition.

"I like doing gymnastics because it helps me to get all of my energy out. I really enjoy it because I'm really good at it and I also enjoy doing it every day. My mom and dad have both invested a lot into me."

—*Shawn Yazzie, Navajo/Sac and Fox/Comanche, gymnast*

ICE HOCKEY

"Hockey is a great game and I love it. I am part of a fading generation that you will never have again. Every one of us is one of a kind, that will never be repeated. To all of my friends and acquaintances, thank you for your advice and direction, that helped make me who I am today—a very, very happy person."

—*George Armstrong, Ojibwe hockey player*

GYMNASTICS

2014: Ashton Taylor Locklear (1998–), Lumbee, was the first Native American to win a gold medal in gymnastics. She took top honors as a member of the U.S. team at the 2014 World Artistic Gymnastics Champion-

1953: Frederick "Fred" Sasakamoose (1933–2020), Cree, was one of the first First Nations players in the National Hockey League, playing 11 games with the Chicago Black Hawks during the 1953–54 season. He spent the remainder of his career in various leagues and worked to advance hockey among First Nations youth. Sasakamoose also served as chief of the Ahtahkakoop Cree Nation. He was inducted into four sports halls of fame and, in 2017, became a member of the Order of Canada. Sasakamoose passed away from COVID-19 a short time before the publication of his book *Call Me Indian: From the Trauma of Residential School to Becoming the NHL's First Treaty Indigenous Player* (2021).

1969: George Armstrong (1930–2021), Ojibwe, is a Canadian former professional ice hockey center who played 21 seasons in the National Hockey League (NHL), all for the Toronto Maple Leafs. He played 1,188 NHL games between 1950 and 1971 and was the Leafs' captain for 13 seasons. Armstrong was a member of four Stanley Cup championship teams and played in seven NHL All-Star games. He scored the final goal of the NHL's "Original Six" era as Toronto won the 1967 Stanley Cup. In 1969, Armstrong was the first person selected to receive the Charlie Conacher Humanitarian Award, given to an NHL player who made "outstanding contribution to humanitarian or community service projects." Armstrong organized floor hockey for developmentally delayed children and also served as the chairman of the Cerebral Palsy Association of Canada. He was inducted into the Hockey Hall of Fame in 1975, and the Maple Leafs honored his uniform number 10 in 1998 and officially retired it in 2016.

Jordin Tootoo

George Armstrong

1973: Henry Charles Boucha (1951–), Ojibwa, from Warroad, Minnesota, became the first Native to become the Detroit Red Wings rookie of the year (1972–73). He was inducted into the United States Hockey Hall of Fame in 1995.

2003: Jordin John Kudluk Tootoo (1983–) became the first Inuit player in the National Hockey League when he signed with the Nashville Predators. He was also the first Canadian player from Nunavut to play pro hockey. He started the first Native hockey camp in Nunavut, and in 2015 the New Jersey Devils chose Tootoo for the 2015 NHL Foundation Player Award. Tootoo kickstarted his organization, Team Tootoo Foundation, with the $25,000 he received. The main focus of the Team Tootoo Fund is to raise awareness for suicide prevention and antibullying programs for at-risk youth.

2008: Brigitte Lacquette (1992–), Saulteaux (Plains Ojibway), was the first First Nations hockey player to be named to the National Women's Team in Canada. Lacquette, from the Cote First Nation in Saskatchewan, was also the first Ojibway in University of Minnesota–Duluth hockey history. In 2018, she became the first First Nations woman to play for the Canadian women's Olympic hockey team. The Hockey Hall of Fame included her Olympic hockey stick in its diversity exhibit in 2018.

2018: Timothy Leif "T. J." Oshie (1986–), Anishinaabe, won the Stanley Cup as a member of the Washington Capitals. He is considered a shootout specialist in the NHL and is one of the top career leaders in goals scored and scoring percentage since the league adopted shootouts in overtime. Oshie graduated from Warroad High

School in Warroad, Minnesota, known globally as Hockey Town USA because it has produced seven Olympians, dozens of Division I players, an all-time point leader in the NHL, six total state high school hockey championships (four boys' and two girls'), and Oshie, a Stanley Cup winner.

T. J. Oshie

The town has fewer than 2,000 people. But Oshie is the only champion who ever brought hockey's biggest prize to Warroad. The mayor declared July 24 T. J. Oshie Day, the champion got a hero's welcome, and he was saluted by a Native American honor song in front of 2,500 fans. Oshie took to the stage and addressed the crowd, publicly thanking his family, former coaches, and teammates for the role they've played in his success.

2019: Craig Berube (1965–), Cree, led his team, the St. Louis Blues of the National Hockey League (NHL), to their first-ever championship. Although he had just been appointed the interim coach, Berube turned the failing team around to become the Stanley Cup champions, after which his position became permanent. Berube's playing career included 17 seasons in the NHL for the Philadelphia Flyers, Toronto Maple Leafs, Calgary Flames, Washington Capitals, and New York Islanders. He also served as scout for Team Canada's 2016 World Cup of hockey team.

LACROSSE

"Lacrosse is my medicine, it is happiness and I want to help others find their medicine."

—Jeremy Thompson,
Onondaga professional lacrosse player

1883: The Haudenosaunee (Iroquois) team demonstrated *Tewaaraton* (Creator's Game), ancestor of today's lacrosse, for the first time in the United Kingdom. The sport was used to entice the British to emigrate to Canada.

1949: The first World Series of Stickball was played during the Choctaw Indian Fair held near Philadelphia, Mississippi, home of the Mississippi Band of Choctaw Indians. The sport is thousands of years old, but the rules have changed in contemporary times. The early playing field could be miles long with 100 or even up to 1,000 players. There was no protective equipment, and sometimes games lasted for days, often played to settle disputes between nations instead of going to war. It is often referred to as "the little man of war" and the ancestor of modern lacrosse.

1960: Leon Miller (1895–1961), Cherokee, was the first American Indian to be inducted into the Lacrosse Hall of Fame. He served as the head football coach at the City College of New York (CCNY) in 1943 as well as the CCNY's head men's lacrosse coach from 1932 to 1960. He was a teammate of Jim Thorpe when they attended Carlisle Indian School.

2015: The Haudenosaunee Under 19 women's team won the 2015 Nike Cup—Orange Division championship, defeating STEPS Lacrosse Philly.

2015: Jeremy Thompson (1987–), Onondaga, was the first Native American athlete to have his banner hung at the Nike World headquarters near Beaverton, Oregon. He is a professional lacrosse player for the Panther City Lacrosse Club of the National Lacrosse League in Texas and a member of the Iroquois National Team with his brothers. The lacrosse award-winning brothers—Jeremy, Lyle, Miles, and Hiana—hold lacrosse clinics for youth.

The *Hōkūle* is a double-hulled Polynesian canoe known as a *wa'a kaulua*. In 1976, it famously navigated from Hawaii to Tahiti using only traditional navigation techniques.

Remembrance and Healing through Sports

In the 19th century, Native people began to commemorate violence perpetrated against Indigenous nations by holding a variety of walks, runs, horse and bike rides, and water events.

The Appaloosa Horse Club held the first annual Chief Joseph Trail Ride in 1965 to pay homage to the historical 1,300-mile route traveled by the Nez Perce Tribe while attempting to escape the U.S. Cavalry in 1877. When the Nez Perce surrendered, near starvation and exhaustion, they were less than 40 miles from the Canadian border. In 1986, Congress named the famous trek the Nez Perce National Historic Trail, which winds through portions of Oregon, Washington, Idaho, Wyoming, and Montana. Today riders honor Chief Joseph's valiant efforts to save his people from U.S. troops by riding 100 miles over a five-day period, which means it takes a total of thirteen years to complete the entire trail. The Nez Perce are credited with developing the Appaloosa breed.

Herb Kawainui Kāne, Native Hawaiian artist, historian, and cultural practitioner, founded the Polynesian Voyaging Society (PVS) in 1973. It led to the construction of

Remembrance and Healing through Sports (contd.)

Hōkūle'a ("Star of Gladness"), a replica of a traditional, double-hulled sailing canoe. Kāne disputed the Eurocentric supposition that Polynesian exploration and settlement was random instead of planned. Through computer simulations of wind patterns and ocean currents, Kāne and other scholars proved that a drifting canoe had no chance of reaching Hawaii, Easter Island, and New Zealand from other parts of Polynesia or Micronesia. To further confirm that the Hawaiian ancestors had the expertise and equipment to travel the Pacific Ocean in ancient times, the Hōkūle'a successfully completed its first trip using traditional navigation techniques in a 30-day, 2,500-mile trip from Maui to Tahiti. From 2013 to 2018, the Hōkūle and crew, under the direction of Pwo navigator Nainoa Thompson, PVS president, circumnavigated the globe, visiting over 150 ports, 18 nations, and eight of UNESCO'S Marine World Heritage sites. "The Worldwide Voyage has been a means by which we now engage all of Island Earth—bridging traditional and new technologies to live sustainably, while sharing, learning, creating global relationships, and discovering the wonders of this precious place we all call home."

The Remember the Removal bike ride was started in 1984 by the Cherokee Nation for Cherokee youth to retrace the Trail of Tears and understand the many hardships their ancestors endured when they made the same journeys on foot that ended 180 years before. Governors in the nine states along the 5,043-mile removal trek issued proclamations declaring it "Trail of Tears Remembrance Week" as cyclists crossed their respective states. It became an annual event in 2009, and the Eastern Band of Cherokee Indians joined the ride in 2011. Riders are selected through interviews and physical fitness tests; they train for six months. Cyclists visit many historical sites of the Cherokee people in the original homelands and along the route.

The Canoe Journey, an annual event in which Pacific Northwest Tribes travel the ancestral waterways of their cultures, began in 1998. Tribal nations from Oregon, Washington, Alaska, and British Columbia host the paddlers, following the ancient water routes around the Salish Sea, with feasts, ceremony, and events, as they come ashore for breaks. The Lummi, Squamish, Confederated Tribes of the Grand Ronde, Chinook, and other nations see the Canoe Journey as an affirmation of sovereignty. Indigenous people who share canoeing traditions from as far away as New Zealand have joined this culturally significant commemoration.

In the bitter winter of 1890, the Seventh Cavalry massacred Miniconjou Lakota leader Big Foot and 150 of his people at Wounded Knee, South Dakota, after they had traveled 300 miles hoping to find refuge on the Pine Ridge Reservation. It was one of the worst massacres in U.S. history. In 1986 Lakota elders founded the Sitanka Wokiksuye (Big Foot Memorial Ride), tracing Big Foot's route across the frigid plains to Wounded Knee.

Remembrance and Healing through Sports (contd.)

Meant to begin the process of healing, a "Wiping of the Tears" ceremony was held to mourn for loved ones. In 1992 the event was changed to the Oomaka Tokatakiya (Future Generations Ride) to also foster leadership qualities in youth. The two-week journey helps riders experience some of the hardships their ancestors endured, as a "physical, spiritual, and intellectual remembrance."

The 6,000-mile marathon Peace and Dignity Journey, held every four years, began in 1992, a significant date marking the start of a new cycle according to the Sacred Stone Calendar, and is meant to restore peace and dignity to Indigenous communities brutalized by colonialism. Participants share experiences and histories. Indigenous people of the Americas are invited, and runners start from Chickaloon, Alaska, in the North and Tierra del Fuego in the South. At times, a contingent starting from the Northeastern United States joins, and the final destination is Teotihuacan in Mexico. The run lasts several months; runners travel through Native and non-Native communities, rural and urban, stopping to pray and spread the spirit of peace and dignity. The event is also a recognition of the Eagle and the Condor, a prophecy throughout peoples of the Americas that foretold how people will reunite as one, like a body broken into pieces that is made whole again.

Lee Lone Bear, a Northern Cheyenne descendant of survivors of the 1864 Sand Creek Massacre, established the annual Sand Creek Spiritual Healing Run from Sand Creek to Denver, Colorado, in 1999. Cheyenne and Arapaho tribal members begin running from the Sand Creek Massacre National Historic Site in Eads, following the 173-mile route taken by soldiers returning to Denver after massacring 230 Cheyenne and Arapaho, mostly elders, women, and children. Troops of the 3rd Regiment, Colorado (US) Volunteer Cavalry, sported "trophies" from their slaughter as they paraded through downtown Denver on December 22, 1864.

Members of the Dakota tribe, joined by members of other tribal nations, initiated the first annual 330-mile Dakota Wokiksuye Memorial Ride from Crow Creek, South Dakota, to honor the hundreds of Native women and children who were massacred at Crow Creek over a century ago. The 2005 inaugural event brought attention to the Indigenous women in the present who are missing, abused, and murdered at 10 times the national average in both the United States and Canada.

In 2021, teenager Ku Stevens, Paiute, started the Remembrance Run to honor his great-grandfather, Frank "Togo" Quinn, who escaped three times from the Stewart Indian Boarding School near Carson City, Nevada. Quinn's first getaway was when he was just eight years old; the child made the 50-mile trek across the high desert all the way to his home on the Yerington Reservation. Stevens wanted to honor those memories as well as all of those who were removed from their families and sent to

Remembrance and Healing through Sports (contd.)

one of the 350 boarding schools across the United States and Canada created to force the assimilation of Native Americans.

Navajo president Jonathan Nez attended the ground-breaking ceremony for the Shasta Jim Rintila (SJR) Equine Ranch in 2021. SJR, founded by Shirlene Jumbo-Rintila, Navajo, is the first equine therapy program for Navajo veterans with PTSD. Horse therapy is popular in Native communities, particularly for those considered part of the Horse Nations.

The Tiwahe Glu Kini Pi (TGKP), "Bringing the Family Back to Life" in Lakota, is based on the Rosebud Indian Reservation and provides equine therapy for youth affected by trauma. Founder Grey Cloud, Lakota, said, "Oftentimes, these kids don't get to experience much love or attention in their homes, communities or schools, but they get it from the horses. And working with the horses, they learn boundaries, they learn Lakota values, how to show them, how to receive them."

MOUNTAINEERING

"It's not respectful to go climb a church. That's a mainstream cultural norm. But the idea of respecting native sacred spaces in the same way is a pretty new discussion, at least on a national level."

—*Len Necefer, Navajo mountaineer and CEO of Natives Outdoors*

1913: Walter Harper (1893–1918), an Athabascan mountain climber and guide, was the first person to reach the 20,320-foot summit of Alaska's Denali (Mt. McKinley), the highest peak in North America. In 2013, Congress changed the name of the Talkeetna Ranger Station in Talkeetna, Alaska, to the Walter Harper Talkeetna Ranger Station in his honor.

1971: Betty Ivanoff Menard, Inupiaq, reached the peak of Denali (Mt. McKinley) to become the first Native Alaskan woman to complete the epic climb.

2017: Len Necefer (1989–), Navajo, a mountain climber, began to restore Indigenous place names to sacred mountain sites that were first scaled by Natives long before the place names had been changed. He created new locations on Facebook and Instagram after he climbed peaks in the Navajo Nation: Sisnaajini (Blanca Peak) in Colorado; Dook'o'oosłííd Nuvatukya'ovi, and Wi:munakwa (the San Francisco Peaks) in Arizona; Dibe Ntsaa (Hesperus Mountain) in Colorado; and Tsoodził (Mount Taylor) in New Mexico. If Necefer is unable to find original Native place names, he creates them and has now given 40 mountains Indigenous names on social media. He is bringing attention to the appropriation of sites that have been important to Native communities for thousands of years and founded Native Outdoors as an online campaign that now makes clothing and partners with larger brands to spread the message. Necefer, who has a Ph.D. in engineering from Carnegie Mellon, said that "the creation of the first national parks, like Yellowstone and Glacier, was predicated on the forced removal of Indigenous populations from these areas. It created this myth that these are untouched wilderness areas."

OLYMPIAN/PARALYMPIAN MEDALISTS

"Winning this medal, to me this will mean that every Paralympics I've ever been to I've medaled. I'm very happy that I was able to pull that off."

—*Cheri Becerra Madsen, Omaha, bronze medalist, 2021*

1912: Duke Paoa Kahinu Mokoe Hulikohola Kahanamoku (1890–1968) became the first Native Hawaiian Olympian swimmer to win a gold medal in the 100-meter freestyle and a silver medal with the relay team. That same year, he introduced surfing to a spellbound audience at Coney Island, New York. It was the first time the sport had been seen on the East Coast and one of the first times it had been demonstrated in the United States. During the 1920 Olympics in Antwerp, Belgium, Kahanamoku won gold medals in both the 100 meters (bettering fellow Hawaiian Pua Kealoha) and in the relay. He finished the 100 meters with a silver medal during the 1924 Olympics in Paris, France, with the gold going to Johnny Weissmuller and the bronze to Duke's brother, Samuel Kahanamoku. He was 34 and this was his last Olym-

Duke Kahanamoku

Jim Thorpe

pic medal. However, Duke was an alternate for the U.S. water polo team at the 1932 Summer Olympics. He was the first Native to be inducted into the International Hall of Fame (1965).

1912: Louis Tewanima (1888–1969) Hopi, was the first American to win an Olympic medal in the 10,000-meter race. He earned the silver medal in the 1912 Olympics held in Stockholm, Sweden. Since 1974, the Louis Tewanima Association has sponsored the annual Louis Tewanima Footrace on the Hopi Reservation in Arizona.

1912: James Francis Thorpe (Wa-Tho-Huk; 1887–1953), Sac and Fox, was the first person to win the gold medal in the newly created Olympic decathlon event. He also took the gold for pentathlon during the same Olympics. An all-around athlete from the Carlisle Indian Industrial School, he excelled at every sport he played. Many sports analysts consider him to be the greatest athlete of the twentieth century and even the greatest athlete of all time.

1920: Warren Kealoha (1903–1972) became the first Native Hawaiian to win the gold medal in the Olympic Games men's swimming event, the 100-meter backstroke (Belgium). In the 1924 Olympics held in France, he repeated his gold medal performance. Kealoha set four world records in his career and was inducted into the International Swimming Hall of Fame as an "Honor Swimmer" in 1968.

1924: Clarence "Taffy" Abel (1900–1964), Sault Ste. Marie Chippewa, was the first American Indian to be the U.S. flag bearer at an Olympic opening ceremony. Abel performed the honors at the 1924 Winter Olympic Games in Chamonix, France. He was an ice hockey player and his team won the silver medal that year, with Abel scoring 15 goals. He had a long career in the National Hockey League (NHL) and was the first U.S. player to be an NHL regular (New York Rangers and Chicago Black Hawks). Abel's last five years were with the Black Hawks; they won the Stanley Cup in 1934. The Lake Superior State University hockey rink (Sault Ste. Marie, Michigan) is named after Taffy Abel, the first rink to be named for a Native player.

1948: Jesse Bernard "Cab" Renick (1917–1999), Choctaw, led the Americans to a gold medal victory in basketball in the 1948 Summer Olympics held in London, England. He was the first American Indian to be captain of an Olympics basketball team. He was the first Oklahoma State University two-time All-American selection (1947 and 1948). Renick was also the second tribal citizen, after Jim Thorpe, Sac and Fox, to win an Olympic gold medal.

1964: William Winston "Billy" Kidd (1943–), Abenaki, was the first American male to win an Olympic alpine medal. He took the silver in the slalom at the 1964 Winter Olympics in Innsbruck, Austria.

1964: William Mervin "Billy" Mills (1938–), Oglala Lakota, won the gold medal in the 10,000-meter run at the 1964 Summer Olympics in Tokyo, Japan. To date, he is the only American to do so. Mills is the co-founder of the nonprofit Running Strong for American Indian Youth, which aims to help Native American people fulfill their basic needs—food, water, and shelter—while also helping their communities gain self-sufficiency and self-esteem. The recipient of over 15 sports and humanitarian honors, he was awarded a 2015 President's Council Lifetime Achievement Award for his promotion of healthy lifestyles

Billy Mills

nationwide. Mills is the subject of the 1983 movie *Running Brave*.

1968: Rachel Kealaonapua "Keala" O'Sullivan (1950–) became the first Native Hawaiian to medal in diving at the Olympics, held in Mexico. She earned a bronze medal in three-meter springboard; O'Sullivan's Olympic career was short-lived because of lack of funds.

1972: Henry Charles Boucha (1951–), Ojibwa, was an American professional ice hockey center. He played for the American national team at two World Championships and at the 1972 Winter Olympics, where he won a silver medal. Boucha played in both the National Hockey League (NHL) and World Hockey Association (WHA) between 1971 and 1977; many sports analysts say he is the greatest hockey talent ever produced by the state of Minnesota. In 1977, he was playing for the Minnesota North Stars against the Boston Bruins when an opposing team member deliberately struck Boucha in the eye with a hockey stick, resulting in an eye injury that forced him to hang up his skates at the age of 26. He was inducted into the U.S. Hockey Hall of Fame in 1995, and in 2013, he published his autobiography, *Henry Boucha, Ojibwa, Native American Olympian*.

2000: Cheri Becerra Madsen (1976–), an Omaha Wheelchair Racer Olympian, took gold in the 100-meter and the 400-meter at the Paralympics in Sydney, Australia. She set a world record in the semifinals of the 200-meter, the only person to break under 29 seconds in the event. She claimed silver at the 2016 Paralympic Games in Rio de Janeiro, Brazil. During Madsen's career, she has competed in four Paralympics and two World Para Athletics Championships, medaling in each. In 2021, Madsen won the bronze in the women's 100m T54, crossing the line in 16.33 seconds, earning her tenth career medal at the Paralympic Games.

2002: Tom Reeves, Cheyenne River Sioux, was the first Native to serve as captain of the U.S. Olympic Rodeo team (Utah) and took the silver in the saddle bronc event. A star rodeo athlete and thought to be the best bronc rider of his generation, he went on to coaching after he retired. Reeves led Ranger College in Texas to the College National Finals Rodeo men's title in 2007, just two years after he was hired to revitalize the sport after at a 23-year hiatus. He was the first Native coach to receive the ProRodeo Hall of Fame Mentoring Award in 2007 for "dedicated leadership in serving youth as a treasured mentor and positive role model."

2008: Logan Maile Lei Tom (1981–), Native Hawaiian, led the indoor volleyball Team USA to win the silver medal and was named Best Scorer at the Olympics held in China. She won another silver medal at the 2012 Olympics (England). Tom was also awarded the Most Valuable Player of the 2004 FIVB World Grand Prix and is a four-time Olympian at the outside hitter position. At age 19, Tom became the youngest woman ever to be selected for an American Olympic volleyball team when she competed at the 2000 Olympic Games in Sydney, Australia. In 2021, Tom was inducted into the International Volleyball Hall of Fame, another first.

2008: Natasha "Tasha" Kanani Janine Kai (1983–) was the first Native Hawaiian woman to play for the National Women's Soccer Team and took Olympic gold in China. She was the first to play in the National Women's Soccer League (Sky Blue FC)

Cheri Madsen

and was a major contributor to her team's 2009 championship season. She was also the first player from Hawaii on the full Women's National Team and to make a Women's World Cup Team. Kai was part of the U.S. women's rugby sevens team that played in the first IRB Women's Sevens Challenge Cup held in Dubai, UAE, in 2011.

2012: Richard Peter (1972–), Cowichan Tribe, made history when he won his third Paralympics gold medal at the London 2012 Paralympics Games as a member of Team Canada Wheelchair Basketball. A five-time Paralympian, Peter also took a silver medal at the 2018 Paralympics in Beijing and medaled in several other international championships. He was inducted into the British Columbia Sports Hall of Fame in 2010, was awarded the national Tom Longboat Award (2000 and 2004), and was awarded the Indspire Award in the Sport category in 2012. For a few years, Peter played professionally in Europe.

Logan Tom

2012: Kaleo Okalani Kanahele Maclay (1996–), Native Hawaiian, won a silver medal with Team USA in her first Paralympics Games in London. She is the only Hawaiian Paralympics sitting volleyballist and has been part of several victories: Parapan American Championship, gold medal, 2010 and 2015; WOVD Championship, silver medal, 2010; ECVD Continental Cup, three gold medals, 2011 and 2012; and WOVD Championship, gold medal, 2014.

2014: Carey Price (1987–), Ulkatcho First Nation, led the Olympic Canadian hockey team to win the gold medal in the Winter Olympics held in Russia and was also voted the best goaltender in the competition by the International Ice Hockey Federation (IIHF).

A Canadian professional goal-tender for the Montreal Canadiens, he is considered one of the best goaltenders in the world by *Hockey News* and *EA Sports*. Price won a gold medal at the 2016 World Cup of Hockey plus many other awards.

2016: Kyrie Andrew Irving (Héla,

Carey Price

"Little Mountain" in Lakota; 1992–), enrolled member of the Standing Rock Sioux Tribe, became the first Lakota basketball player to win a gold medal in basketball in Rio de Janeiro, Brazil. He was also the first Native to be named the NBA Rookie of the Year (2011). He was chosen by the Cleveland Cavaliers with the first overall pick in the 2011 NBA draft and won an NBA championship with the Cavaliers in 2016. With the win, he became the first Native and the fourth member of Team USA to capture the NBA championship and an Olympic gold medal in the same year. In 2014, Irving helped lead Team USA to win gold in the FIBA Basketball World Cup and was named the tournament's MVP; he was then named the 2014 USA Basketball Male Athlete of the Year. Irving is also a seven-time All-Star. He signed with the Brooklyn Nets as a free agent in 2019. Irving is known for his philanthropy and support of the water protectors protesting the Dakota Access Pipeline in North Dakota.

2021: Carissa Moore (1992–), Native Hawaiian, won the gold medal in surfing at the 2020 Tokyo Olympics. Despite surfing being invented by Native Hawaiians centuries ago, Moore was the only Native Hawaiian in the competition. The Olympic medal was one of several awards Moore has earned in the sport. Her many achievements include the youngest surfer to reach a final of

Carissa Moore

an Association of Surfing Professionals (ASP; now called the World Surf League) World

Title Race event (2007); youngest winner of a Triple Crown of Surfing event, a 6-Star World Surfing Qualifying WQS Prime Event (2008); ASP Women's World Tour Gidget Pro Sunset Beach winner; and the youngest ever to be declared the ASP Women's World Champion who went on to win the title four more times. Moore wears the Hawaiian Kingdom flag instead of the U.S. flag when she competes for the United States at World Surf League international competitions. She was part of an unsuccessful bid to allow the Hawai'i surfing team to compete independently from the United States, which many Kānaka Maoli (Native Hawaiians) do not recognize as the legitimate government of Hawai'i.

RACING

"Just the speed we were carrying was really impressive and it's not often you see guys who can hold speeds of high 40s, lower 50s [kilometres per hour] for so long."

—*Neilson Powless, Oneida, professional road racing cyclist*

2000: Danny Ongais (1942–2022) was inducted into the Motorcross Hall of Fame and was the first Native Hawaiian to compete in the Indianapolis 500. The National Hot Rod Association ranked him 39th in the Top 50 Drivers, 1951–2000. He competed professionally in motorcycle, sports car, Formula One, and drag racing. Nicknamed the "Flying Hawaiian," Ongais competed in his first Indy in 1977; his auto racing career spanned 25 years. In 1963 and 1964, Ongais was the American Hot Rod Association AA Gas Dragster Champion, and in 1965 he was the National Hot Rod Association AA Dragster Champion. In 1969, he set 295 world land speed and endurance records at the Bonneville Salt Flats in Utah and was the Hawai'i State Motorcycle Champion in 1960.

2001: Cory Wetherill (1971–), a Navajo race car driver, was the first Native American to compete in the Indy 500. In 2002, he had 8 podium finishes and one win at Nashville Superspeedway.

2020: Neilson Powless (1996–) is an Oneida American professional road racing cyclist who currently rides for UCI World Team EF Education–Nippo. In August 2020, he was named in the startlist for the 2020 Tour de France, the first Native American to ever compete in the storied race. His debut was so strong that Powless was again named as part of the EF Team for the 2021 Tour de France.

Neilson Powless

Frontier Days outdoor rodeo and western celebration. At first, the fans and participants made fun of their clothing and dismissed them as not being much of a threat. Once the rodeo began, however, it was a different story. Twelve thousand spectators, an enormous number at that time, watched Purdy, Low, and Ka'au'a carry off top awards. Little did the surprised attendees realize that the Hawaiian *paniolos* (cowboys) came from a cowboying tradition much older than that of the American West. Purdy won the World's Steer Roping Championship—roping, throwing, and tying the steer in 56 seconds in a torrential downpour. Ka'au'a and Low took third and sixth place and all on borrowed horses. In 1999, Purdy was voted into the National Cowboy and Western Heritage Museum's Rodeo Hall of Fame and was the first inductee to the Paniolo Hall of Fame established by the O'ahu Cattlemen's Association. In 2007, Purdy was inducted into the Cheyenne Frontier Days Hall of Fame.

1976: Jackson Sundown (1863–1923), Nez Perce, was the first Native rodeo champion to be inducted into the Rodeo Hall of Fame at the National Cowboy and Western Heritage Museum in Oklahoma City, Oklahoma. He was the bronc-riding winner of the 1916 Pendleton (Oregon) Round-Up.

RODEO AND HORSE RACING

"Young Native Americans see other Native Americans succeed and this inspires them to work, train and take their chance."

—*Wiley Petersen, Shoshone Bannock tribe, coach for the Wolves, a bull-riding team*

1908: Ikua Purdy, Jack Low, and Archie Ka'au'a, Native Hawaiians, traveled to Cheyenne, Wyoming, to compete in the annual Cheyenne

Jackson Sundown

1976: The first annual Indian National Finals Rodeo Inc. (INFR) was held at the Salt Palace in Salt Lake City, Utah, bringing together several regional Indian Rodeo Associations from the United States and Canada. In 2006 the INFR Commission added INFR Tours as a way to qualify, and contestants travel thousands of miles competing in tour rodeos to earn points needed to qualify for the INFR. In

The horse relay in Pembleton, Oregon, is an intense sport originally designed to help train Indian warriors.

Indian Relay Racing: America's First Extreme Sport

No one is sure of the origins of Indian Relay, but it has been around for hundreds of years. Some believe that at one time it was a "war game" to hone warriors' skills for moving at breakneck speeds into battles. Others think it started as a relay used in hunting buffalo, and another theory is that it began as training to capture wild horses. And maybe all are true. But whatever the origin, it has been popular among Plains people for centuries, who sometimes refer to themselves as the Horse Nations. Little has changed since bygone eras, although now Indian Relay is an organized sport with governing associations, rules, and prize money.

Some Indian communities have relay venues, and the sport can often be seen at big events like the Calgary Stampede and Crow Fair. Indian Relay has grown from a bush-league pastime to a high-stakes competition, with purses worth tens of thousands of dollars. And hundreds of thousands of fans turn out to enjoy the thrill of America's first extreme sport.

The Indian Relay season from spring to the fall is grueling and a mix of high-speed competitions of courageous and superb horsemanship. Competitions take place ac-

Indian Relay Racing: America's First Extreme Sport (contd.)

ross Arizona, Idaho, Montana, Nebraska, North Dakota, Oklahoma, Oregon, South Dakota, Utah, Washington, Wyoming, and Canada and include teams representing what are called the "Horse Nations" as well as others: Comanche, Cheyenne, Arapaho, Lakota Crow, Gros Ventre, Nez Perce, and Crow. The off-season winter months are filled with rigorous training for both horse and human athletes. Even when there is snow, people and horses prepare with weightlifting, agility workouts, and stamina-building exercises.

Both men and women compete. Each team is made up of three racehorses and three humans. Every member has an important task that if not done properly can result in a catastrophe. The mugger is responsible for catching the first horse or the team will be disqualified. In between exchanges, the holders calm the horses before and after runs. Each team member is an outstanding athlete. It is dangerous, physical, and intensely competitive. Crossing the finish line first does not ensure a victory, as winners must be free of any of these penalties: failure to pay racing fees, loose horses on the track (rider falls off or mugger fails to catch horse), false starts, rider dismounted in another team's area, and striking another team's horse. Races are broken into heats, with four to six teams lined up on a racetrack. As in historic times, horses are decked out in finery at the races. The riders, too, are often dressed to match their steeds with painted symbols on themselves and their thoroughbreds.

At a typical event, the announcer introduces each team of three horses, one jockey, two horse holders, and one mugger. The crowd's cheers block out the drumming and singing. Each tall horse's human leads it around in a tight circle, showing off its painted symbols and smooth hard muscles. The horses paw the dirt with excitement. The teams of humans and horses are decked out in their finery with color coordinated outfits. No helmets. No protective vests. No saddles. No aluminum stirrups. Only reins and a crop. Above it all, a horn blasts, and horse and human are speeding around the dirt track as if they are one. Dust flies up from hooves, grass and hay seed sometimes gust around the two, but nothing stops them. They dash through it. At breakneck speeds, the racers are finishing the first lap, and the waiting animals dance around, barely able to contain their anticipation. The jockey soars from one horse to the other, hardly touching the ground, and they're off again. Often the exchange gets chaotic. Handlers can get knocked down, jockeys can miss their mark and plummet to the ground, and a horse may even take off on a wild gallop without his rider, while fans and handlers both try to contain it. But the race goes on no matter the injuries. One more galloping performance completes the second lap, and the jockey flies through the air again, onto the back of the second waiting, excited horse. The last lap is as thrilling and as grueling as the first, and finally the winner crosses the finish line, sometimes at over 40 miles an hour. Victory is met with more traditional drumming and singing plus roaring from the stands. And of course, the purse, which is sometimes thousands of dollars. This is the Indian Relay!

2010 the INFR Commission added junior and senior categories so that youth could participate and elders could be honored. Today, INFR is held in the fall at South Point Equestrian Center in Las Vegas, Nevada; champion Indian cowboys and cowgirls from 75 tribal nations compete in events like Saddle Bronc Riding, Steer Wrestling, and Tie-Down Roping. In addition, there is a celebration of those admitted to the Indian National Rodeo Finals Hall of Fame, and a Miss Indian Rodeo is crowned. The majority of the INFR members are also members of the Professional Rodeo Cowboys Association (PRCA).

2019: For the first time, a team made up of only Native Americans entered the Professional Bull Riders Global Cup (PBR)—the "Olympics of bull riding." Called the Wolves, the team took third place at the event held in Dallas, despite having never competed together before. The Wolves members had representatives from the Navajo, Cherokee, Sioux, and Chippewa tribal nations, including Cody Jesus, the 20-year-old Diné rider who was a contender for the PBR's 2019 Rookie of the Year. In a later competition, Jesus suffered an injury, which took him out of the sport for a year. He was rated #7 in the world. As of 2020, 17 Native Americans were rated in the top 30 PBR riders—one in every five.

RUNNING

"One can't be an athlete all his life, but he can use the same desire that made him. For clean living, for love of God and country."

—*Andy Payne, Cherokee,*
winner of the longest race in the world

c. 1861: Louis "Deerfoot" Bennett (1828–1897), Seneca, was the first Native American to be a running champion both in the United States and in Great Britain. After beating the best runners in the United States, he was lured to Great Britain to compete for rather large sums of prize money. Deerfoot raced professionally for two years; up to 15,000 spectators attended the British meets and wagered heavily. He returned to the United States a wealthy man and started a traveling circus of runners. Over Deerfoot's career, he set many records, like racing 12 miles in just over an hour.

c. 1876: Big Hawk Chief, Pawnee, was the first person recorded as running a mile in less than four minutes. U.S. Army officials not only marked off the course, but they also timed the race twice. Despite this official documentation of a sub-four-minute mile race, Big Hawk Chief never received official credit. Today, the Pawnee Nation of Oklahoma holds an annual Hawk Chief Run/Walk in his honor.

1904: Frank Pierce, Seneca Nation, was the first Native American contestant in track and field in the Olympics although little is known about him. At the St. Louis Olympic Games, he represented the Pastime AC (New York City) for the marathon. However, Pierce never contended in the race and there was no mention of him. No further details of his athletic career or life are known.

1907: Tom Longboat (1886–1949), Onondaga, was the first Native American to win the Boston Marathon. Setting a record of 2:24:24 over the old 24.5-mile course, he was four minutes and 59 seconds faster than any of the previous ten winners of the event. In the 1908 Olympic Games marathon, he and several other lead runners collapsed, and a rematch was organized the same year at Madison Square Garden in New York City. Longboat won this race, turned professional, and in

1909 at the same venue won the title of Professional Champion of the World in front of a sell-out crowd. Longboat was the best runner during his time and often clashed with his coaches over his style of training. He trained hard for a day and then rested, which was not the usual approach. Today's runners use the same method.

Tom Longboat

record for a U.S. Marathon (New York City), finishing under two and a half hours. She won the Honolulu Marathon four straight years (1978–81). Dillon is recognized by the International Association of Athletics Federations as having set world bests in the half marathon, 30 kilometers, and 20 kilometers.

1928: Andy Payne (1907–1977), Cherokee, won the inaugural Transcontinental Foot Race, the longest race in the world and sponsored by the new Route 66. The historic event started in Los Angeles and ended in New York for a distance of 3,423.5 miles, which he completed in 573 hours, 4 minutes, 34 seconds, 15 hours ahead of the runner-up. Payne went on to earn a law degree and be elected clerk to the supreme court in Oklahoma City, Oklahoma, six times. A commemorative statue of Payne graces a quiet spot on Route 66 in Foyil, Oklahoma. Another statue pays homage to the long-distance runner at the Cherokee Heritage Center in Tahlequah, Oklahoma. An Andy Payne Bunion Run is held every May in Oklahoma City, and in 1998 Payne was one of the first to be inducted into the Oklahoma Long Distance Running Hall of Fame in Tulsa.

1939: Ellison Myers "Tarzan" Brown Sr. (1913–1975), Narragansett, became the first Native American to win the Boston Marathon two times. He won in 1936 (2:33:40) and in 1939, when he also set the American men's marathon record (2:28:51). Brown once again set the marathon record in the 1940 Salisbury Beach, Massachusetts, race (2:27:30). He also participated in the 1936 Summer Olympics in Berlin, Germany. Brown was inducted into the American Indian Athletic Hall of Fame in 1973.

1980: Patti Catalano Dillon (1953–), Mi'kmaw, was the first American woman to set the

1988: Wings of America was founded to improve the lives of Native American youth through distance running. Primarily based in the Southwest, Wings hosts running and fitness camps in Native communities with almost 2,000 young runners. Participants represent Wings both as individuals and as a team in several marathons across the country.

1992: Phillip Castillo, Acoma Pueblo, won the NCAA Division II National cross-country championship, the first Native American to win an All-American collegiate cross-country title. He also led his teammates to the only perfect score of 15 in NCAA history. He competed for Adams State University, where he was a nine-time All-American. Castillo was inducted into the university's Hall of Fame in 2018.

2000: Kelsey Nakanelua (1966–), American Samoan, was the first to represent American Samoa in Olympic track and field. He competed in the 100-meter run in the 2000 Olympic Games held in Australia.

2018: RJ Lowdog (2003–), Assinaboine/Sioux, was the first Native American double amputee (and possibly first of any ethnicity) to take first in his 15–18 age group in the Montana Marathon. He was the Shriners Spokesperson of the Year in 2013, another first, and is a champion wrestler. Lowdog placed sixth in the Montana State Wrestling Championship and is expected to excel in wrestling as well as other sports.

SLEDDING, SKATING, SKATEBOARDING, SNOWBOARDING

"Growing up, I didn't see any Native pro-skaters. It was me creating for myself. It's just what I wish someone else would've done when I was a younger kid."

—*Doug Miles Jr., Apache professional skateboarder and filmmaker*

1974: Carl Huntington (1947–2000) was the first Alaska Native (Athabascan) to win the Iditarod Trail Sled Dog Race and took the prize in the second year of the annual event.

1975: Emmitt Peters Sr. (aka "Yukon Fox"; 1940–2020), Athabascan, was the first and only rookie to win the 1,049-mile Iditarod Trail Sled Dog Race. He and his lead dogs Nugget and Digger shattered the previous speed record by almost six days. In 2006, Peters was inducted into the American Indian Athletics Hall of Fame as a dog-musher.

1982: Rose Albert was the first Native Alaskan (Koyukon Athabascan) woman to compete in the Iditarod. With only five months to train, Albert took over the dogs of her deceased brother. There were many challenges as the team was used to her brother's commands and gave her a hard time. Still, Albert was able to place 32nd and completed the race. Also an artist, she graduated from the American Indian Institute of Arts (1981) in Santa Fe, New Mexico, and operates the Nowitna River Studios in Anchorage.

2001: The Tsha' Hoňnoňyeňdakwha (Where they play games) of the Onondaga Nation was built near Syracuse, New York. The 2,000-seat arena serves as a home to the Onondaga Nation's lacrosse team, the Onondaga Athletic Club (OAC) RedHawks, and as an ice arena from September through March. Local high schools and colleges as well as a youth hockey team (Onondaga Thunder) consider Tsha' Hoňnoňyeňdakwha their home ice, and the arena is also used for recreational skating.

2002: Naomi Lang (1978–), Karuk Tribe of California, was the first Native American woman to compete in the Olympic Winter Games (2002). A competitive ice dancer, she and skating partner Peter Tchernyshev are two-time Four Continents champions (2000 and 2002) and five-time U.S. National champions (1999–2003). Lang started skating when she was eight, after seeing Smurfs on Ice, and began competitive ice dance with John Lee, winning the 1995 U.S. Novice title and the 1996 U.S. Junior silver medal.

Naomi Lang with partner Peter Tchernyshev at a 2014 Russian skating event.

2006: Ross Anderson (1971–), Cheyenne/Arapaho/Mescalero Apache/Choctaw, is an FIS World Cup/professional alpine skier as well as Native American speed skier. In 2006, he became the first Native American to set a new world record by being the fastest alpine skier from the Western Hemisphere, at 154.06 mph (247.93 km/h); this placed him ninth in the world all-time ranking.

2010: Callan Chythlook-Sifsof (1989–) Yupik/Inupiaq, became the first Alaskan Native to win a spot on the U.S. Olympic Snowboarding Team. In 2007, she won the Visa U.S. Snowboardcross Championships and took third in the first World Cup of her career. Chythlook-Sifsof earned a silver medal at the Winter X Games and the second World Cup podium of her career in Switzerland (2011). In 2012, she took two top-ten World Cup finishes.

2011: John Baker (1963–) won the Iditarod, becoming the first Inupiat to do so. His first race was in 1996, and he consistently places in the top 10 during the long-distance Iditarod Trail Sled Dog Race. Baker won the 2011 Iditarod with a finish time of 8 days, 19 hours, 46 minutes, 39 seconds.

2018: Team Indigenous competed in the Roller Derby World Cup in Manchester, England. The 20-person team represented Indigenous nations from North and South America, New Zealand, and other parts of the world. The organizer of the team was Melissa Waggoner, Diné, a professional athlete who had skated on Team USA. She said that her Facebook supporters urged her to develop a team so that Indigenous skaters could have their own organization. The team welcomes Indigenous women and those who identify as women "to provide a space of solidarity, strength and love."

2019: The first Rides for the Res—Skateboard Trade-Up was hosted on the San Carlos Reservation in Arizona by Doug Miles of Apache Skateboards and Cowtown S.K.A.T.E. for the first time. Youth brought old, but skateable, skateboards and traded them for a brand new one. The old boards were refurbished and passed on to beginner skaters. A skate clinic was held and cash prizes given for the best tricks. Skateboarding has become a popular sport for Native American kids, especially those from rural areas.

2021: The Diné Skate Garden Project kicked off on February 14 with a live-streamed benefit concert hosted by singer Jewel and featuring guests Tony Hawk (professional skateboarder), Tia Wood (Cree/Salish Tik-Tok webstar), and community leaders from Two Grey/Toadlena Chapter of the Navajo Nation in New Mexico. The quest for a skatepark in the New Mexico section of the Navajo Nation caught the attention of Hawk, who is partnering with organizations Orenda Tribe, Inspiring Children, and Wonders Around the World to build the first skatepark in the Two Grey community. But what ramped up enthusiasm to build it was a video of Navajo skateboarder and artist Naiomi Glasses (1997–) riding her board down a mountain rock face dressed in a traditional long skirt, instead of the usual swirls and curves in a skatepark. Glasses rallies for skateboard parks in rural Indian communities because of the positive influence the sport had on her life. "I was the only girl my age I knew who skated. There were times kids would make fun of my appearance because of my cleft lip and I would look forward to the end of the school day when I could skate and focus on something that made me happy. I'm thankful to say, skateboarding has remained my happy place." An activist and skateboarder, Glasses is also a seventh-generation Navajo textile artist, who creates wearing and saddle blankets, bags, and other woven masterpieces. She donates much of her profits to Chizh for Cheii (Wood for Grandpa), an organization that provides free firewood to high-risk elders on the Navajo Nation and surrounding areas.

SOCCER

"I think I'm just trying to be the best advocate for myself and for Native American communities as I can. I'm an N7 ambassador, which is a branch of Nike that is a fund for indigenous communities and athletes. I'm hoping that through different forms of outreach, I can keep telling stories that are authentic representations of Native American communities. I want to start breaking down those really old stereotypes that have permeated American culture since forever.

—Madison Hammond, Navajo/San Felipe Pueblo, professional soccer player

2001: Brian Ching (1978–), Native Hawaiian, was the first player from Hawaii as well as the first Native Hawaiian to be drafted into Major League Soccer (MLS) when he signed with the Los Angeles Galaxy. During his tenure with the Houston Dynamo, he won the team's Golden Boot Award four times.

2012: Christopher Elliott (Wondo) Wondolowski (1983–), Kiowa, became the first Native American professional soccer player to be named the Most Valuable Player by Major League Soccer (MLS). Currently he is a forward for the San Jose Earthquakes. Wondo was the top scorer in the 2010 and 2012 seasons and one of the top strikers in MLS. With 161 goals in MLS, he is the highest scorer in the competition's history, as well as the only player in league history to score 150 or more regular-season

Brian Ching

goals. As of September 28, 2019, Wondo is also the only player in league history to have scored ten or more goals in ten consecutive seasons and holds the record for most MLS goals on the road and MLS game-winning goals (both home and away). A full international since 2011, Wondolowski represented the United States at three CONCACAF Gold Cups—winning the 2013 edition—and also played at the 2014 FIFA World Cup in Brazil.

2020: Madison Hammond (1997–), Navajo/San Felipe Pueblo, was the first Native American to sign with the National Women's Soccer League. A defender for the OL Reign (Tacoma, Washington), she was an honor student at Wake Forest College and played violin for the Wake Forest orchestra.

TENNIS, TABLE TENNIS, AND BOWLING

"You've got to love what you do, no matter what it is. There's always going to be ups and downs. It's the way sports is and the way life is. You've got to be able to learn from the bad. It tortures you when you can't win every time; you have to lose more than you win. You learn from the losing to try and better yourself."

—Mike Edwards, Cherokee/Choctaw/Chickasaw, professional bowler

1973: Angelita Rosal (1951–), Dakota table tennis champion, was the first woman to be inducted into the American Indian Athletic Hall of Fame. She was born on the Spirit Lake Reservation in North Dakota and won many national championships. The first was the U.S. Singles Championship, when she was only 12 years old, and she went on to win U.S. Doubles Championships. Rosal qualified for World Championships in 1973 in Yugoslavia and was inducted into the U.S. Table Tennis Hall of Fame in 1996.

1994: Mike Edwards (1961–), Cherokee/ Choctaw/Chickasaw, was the first Native person to win the Pro Bowlers Associations title at the Miracles Open in Toronto, Ontario, Canada. A champion professional bowler, he has bowled 26 perfect games—12 during a PBA tour and 14 sanctioned league and tournament events. In 1993, he was the coholder of the PBA Record for highest single match game score and was featured in an *ABC Bowling Magazine* article, "The Year of the Indian." Edwards was inducted into the American Indian Athletic Hall of Fame in 1997 and to date is the only bowler to be honored. In 2012, he won the U.S. Bowling Congress Senior Masters.

1995: Dawn Kelly Allen (1995–), Euchee/ Cherokee/Quapaw, was the first tennis player and one of the first women to be inducted into the American Indian Athletic Hall of Fame. A professional player, she won many championships in the North American Indian Tennis Association (NAITA) tournaments, more than any other woman. Allen was the Women's Singles Champion: 1976–1984, 1986, 1988–1991; the Women's Doubles Champion: 1977–1978, 1984–1986, 1990–1991; and the Mixed Doubles Champion: 1977–1978, 1984–1986, 1990–1991. She also scored the Women's Singles and Doubles championships in the World's Fair All-Indian Tennis Tournament in Phoenix, Arizona in 1979.

1996: George Blue Spruce Jr. (1931–), Laguna/San Juan, became the first male tennis player to be inducted into the American Indian Athletic Hall of Fame. From 1956 to 1958, he won several tennis championships during his tour of duty as a dentist in the U.S. Navy and was a tennis coach at the U.S. Merchant Marine Academy (1963–1966). Blue Spruce took the gold in both the Phoenix and Arizona State Senior Olympics in tennis in the 50–55 age category (1983 and 1984) and also won several tournaments in the North American Indian Tennis Championships tournaments. Blue Spruce has been past president of the North American Indian Tennis Association and has served on the board of directors.

2016: Amanda Stone, Cherokee Nation, became the first Native woman to be named the Mid-America Intercollegiate Athletics Association (MIAA) Tennis Coach of the Year and also won the next year. She was also the first Native woman to be a head tennis coach at a university (Louisiana Tech University) and the first to be the "all-time winningest head coach" in the history of the Lady Techster team.

WATER SPORTS

Rell's Definition of Aloha Spirit: "Simple, really. You give and you give and you give … and you give from here (the heart), until you have nothing else to give."

—*Rell Kapolioka`ehukai Sunn, Native Hawaiian, surfer*

1955: Robert Gawboy (1932–1987), Chippewa from Vermillion Lake Indian Reservation, Minnesota, became the gold medal winner in the 220-yard breaststroke at the Indoor National AAU Aquatic Meet at Yale University with a world record time of 2:38.0. Gawboy won many other swimming competitions and was the only swimmer ever inducted into the American Indian Athletics Hall of Fame (1980).

1968: Edward Ryon Makuahanai Aikau (1946–1978) was a Native Hawaiian lifeguard and surfer. In 1968 he became the first lifeguard hired by the City and County of Honolulu to protect the North Shore, and later he was the first lifeguard of Waimea Bay. Aikau saved over 500 people and became famous for his prowess on the big Hawaiian surf, winning several awards, including the 1977 Duke Kahanamoku Invitational Surfing Championship. Aikau was named Lifeguard of the Year in 1971. In 1978, Aikau became a crew member of Hōkūle'a, a traditional Polynesian double-hulled voyaging canoe, which was to follow the ancient route of the Polynesian migration between the Hawaiian and Tahitian island chains. The canoe capsized, and Aikau paddled for help on his surfboard. Although the crew was rescued by the U.S. Coast Guard, the hero who had saved so many was never seen again, and the search for Aikau was the largest air-sea search in Hawaiian history. In the 1980s, bumper stickers and T-shirts with the phrase "Eddie Would Go" spread around the Hawaiian Islands and to the rest of the world. According to maritime historian Mac Simpson, "Aikau was a legend on the North Shore, pulling people out of waves that no one else would dare to. That's where the saying came from— Eddie would go, when no one else would or could. Only Eddie dared." "The Eddie," formerly known as the Quiksilver Big Wave Invitational in Memory of Eddie Aikau, is held at Waimea Bay.

1976: Charles Nainoa Thompson (1953–) was the first Hawaiian to practice the ancient Polynesian art of navigation since the fourteenth century, having navigated two double-hulled canoes (the Hōkūle'a and the Hawai'iloa) from Hawai'i to other island nations in Polynesia without the aid of western instruments. He is the executive director of the Polynesian Voyaging Society.

1996: Rell Kapolioka`ehukai Sunn (1950–1998), Native Hawaiian, was the first Indigenous woman to be named "Woman of the Year" by the Surfer's Hall of Fame. With the passing of Duke Kahanamoku, she was credited with becoming the Surfing Ambassador of Aloha. In 1982, "Auntie Relli" won first place in the International Professional Surfing ratings, making a name for women in the sport.

1998: Norman Maktima (1979–), Laguna/Hopi/San Felipe, was the first Native American and the first person to win the gold medal in the first-ever World Youth Fly Fishing Championship held in Italy. He also led the U.S. team to win the silver. He was just seven years old. Since then, Maktima has won several championships, including the U.S. Fly Fishing Competition. He is a teacher and guide, and has an online presence teaching fly-fishing. Maktima owns and operates the High Desert Angler, the first Native American fly-fishing business.

WEIGHTLIFTING, WRESTLING, WEAPONRY, COMBAT SPORTS

"When I first started boxing, once I got on the national team, I found myself in a better place than I was when I started as a teenager. I wanted to start going back to my roots and giving back."

—Mary Spencer, Chippewas of Nawash Unceded First Nation, Ontario, Canada, professional boxer

1936: Chester J. Ellis (1913–1986), Seneca, won the national Golden Gloves Championship, bantamweight division. He followed that victory by winning the International Glovers Championship, the first Native to win both.

1956: Edmund Kealoha Parker (1931–1990), Native Hawaiian, was the first Indigenous American person to found a martial arts style, American Kempo Karate, which is taught by affiliated schools in 18 different countries including the United States, Canada, Mexico, Great Britain, Germany, Spain, Australia, and South Africa. He was an actor and a technical consultant for films like the *Perfect Weapon* (1991), released after Parker's death. In 1965, he founded the International Karate Championships tournament in Long Beach, California, the oldest major tournament in the country. His wife, Leilani Parker, published his biography, *Memories of Ed Parker: Sr. Grandmaster of American Kenpo Karate,* in 1997.

1961: Joe Tindle Thornton (1916–2019), Cherokee, became the first Native American World Archery Champion in Oslo, Norway, breaking three world records. He was also the first Native American to win the British International Trials Championship (1962) and a member of the U.S. archery team that earned the world championship (1967 and 1971). Thornton won the U.S. National Archery Championship (1970) when he was 54. He served on the board of governors of the National Archery Association, was president of the Oklahoma Archery Association, and was inducted into the American Indian Athletic Hall of Fame in 1978. Thornton was present at the dedication ceremony (2016) for the Joe Thornton Archery Range in Tahlequah, Oklahoma, the first range ever built on tribal lands.

1963: Ben Nighthorse Campbell (1933–), Cheyenne, scored a Native first when he became a three-time U.S. judo champion, win-

Ben Nighthorse Campbell

ning the gold medal in the Pan-American Games in 1963. He was captain of the U.S. Olympic Judo Team in the 1964 Summer Olympics in Tokyo. Later he coached the U.S. international judo team. Campbell is a politician who served as a U.S. representative from 1987 to 1993 and as a U.S. senator from Colorado from 1993 to 2005.

1972: Takamiyama Daigorō (born Jesse James Wailani Kuhaulua; 1944–), Native Hawaiian, was the first foreign-born *rikishi* (strong man or professional Sumo wrestler) to win the top division Sumo championship. His highest rank was sekiwake, and in 1986, he achieved another milestone as the first foreign-born wrestler ever to found a training stable (Azumazeki Stable). His most successful wrestler was fellow Hawaiian Akebono, who reached the highest rank of yokozuna in 1993, another first.

1976: Clifford Patrick Keen (1901–1991) was a Comanche wrestler who served as the head coach of the University of Michigan collegiate wrestling team from 1925 to 1970. He led the Michigan Wolverines to 13 Big Ten Conference championships and coached 68 All-American wrestlers. In 1976, he was the first Native American and one of the initial inductees into the National Wrestling Hall of Fame.

1996: Stephanie Murata (1970–), Osage, was the first Native woman to compete in a major wrestling championship, the Pan American Championship in San Juan, Puerto Rico. She went on to win the U.S. National Women's Championship eight times and was inducted into the National Wrestling Hall of Fame in 2018.

2000: Jay Dee "B. J." Penn (1978–) became the first non-Brazilian as well as the first Indigenous Hawaiian to win the black-belt division of the World Jiu-Jitsu Championship.

2001: Jordyn Brown (1988–), Cheyenne River Sioux, became the first-ever American Indian female inducted into the U.S. Martial Arts Hall of Fame; she was only in the seventh grade. She earned her black belt at 10, going on to win more than 100 awards.

2008: Jacob Deitchler (1989–), Ojibwe, became the youngest-ever Native American to win a place on the U.S. Olympic Wrestling Team. It had been 32 years since another high schooler had earned a berth on the Olympic team.

Jacob Deitchler

2010: Chadwick (Ugisata) Smith (1950–), Cherokee, was the first Native American to be inducted into the National Wrestling Hall of Fame in the Outstanding American category. Smith was an undefeated wrestler his senior year at Maplewood High School in Nashville, Tennessee, and went on to wrestle at the University of Tennessee–Martin. He served four terms as chief of the Cherokee Nation from 1999 to 2011.

2014: Kali Reis (1986–), Seaconke Wampanoag/Nipmuc/Cherokee/Cape Verdean, was the first Native American to win the International Boxing Association (IBA) middleweight crown, the first Native female to win a world championship, and the first Native American professional boxer from New England. She took both the Female Universal Boxing Federation (UBF) and the World Boxing Council (WBC) world middleweight titles in 2016. In 2020, Reis earned top honors again when she fought her way to the World Boxing Association (WBA) super lightweight world title. In 2021, she scored two more firsts when she became the super lightweight champion of both the WBA and the IBO. Since 2009, Reis has been a residential counselor and youth mentor. She travels to Native and non-Native communities to share her story and addresses different issues like suicide, missing and murdered Indigenous women (MMIW), LGBTQ issues, depression, addiction, and being a two-spirited person. Reis is both the star and cowriter of *Catch the Fair One*, a thriller about a former Native American boxer who searches for her missing sister. In 2021, the film was featured in the world-famous Tribeca Film Festival in New York City.

2015: Gayle Hatch (1939–), Delaware, became the first Native American to be presented the Alvin Roy Award for Career Achievement by the National Strength and Conditioning Association (NSCA). He received the award for producing champion athletes in Olympic weightlifting and football. The Gayle Hatch Weightlifting Team has won 49 USA weightlifting national championships. Gayle Hatch athletes have competed in weightlifting events at the 1984, 1988, and 1992 Summer Olympics and participated on 12 USA world teams. Hatch served as head coach of the men's USA Olympic weightlifting team at the 2004 Summer Olympics in Athens, Greece. He is an inductee of the USA Strength and Conditioning Coaches Hall of Fame, the USA Weightlifting Hall of Fame, and the American Indian Athletic Hall of Fame.

2021: Mary Spencer, Chippewas of Nawash Unceded First Nation, the most decorated amateur boxer in Canada, became a professional boxer. Spencer is a three-time world champion and five-time Pan American champion, an Indspire Award recipient in the sports category (2014), and the 2019 recipient of the Randy Starkman Award by the Canadian Olympic Committee.

COMPETITIONS, EVENTS, FESTIVALS, AND ORGANIZATIONS

1970: The first Arctic Winter Games were held in Yellowknife, Northwest Territories, Canada. The high-profile biennial circumpolar sport competition draws Indigenous athletes from communities in the Arctic Sea region, including the United States, Canada, Russia, Greenland, Norway, Sweden, and Finland. Team and individual competitions are held in alpine skiing, arctic sports and Dené games, badminton, basketball, biathlon, cross-country skiing, curling, dog mushing, figure skating, gymnastics, ice hockey, indoor soccer, snowboarding, snowshoe biathlon, snowshoe running, short track speed skating, volleyball, and wrestling. The U.S. (Alaska) teams have earned the Hodgson Trophy, awarded for fair play and team spirit, five times, more than any other country. The trophy is named for Stuart Milton Hodgson, former commissioner of the Northwest Territories.

1972: The first annual Native Youth Olympics (NYO) was held in Anchorage, Alaska. Organized by teachers, the goal of the event was to demonstrate Native games so the students would not forget their heritage. One hundred students from 12 boarding schools competed in the first Olympics. Today there are 10 events based on games past generations of Alaska Native people played as a way to test their hunting and survival skills, increase strength, and maintain endurance, agility, and the balance of mind and body. Although events are based on traditional Alaska Native activities, the competition is open to all Alaska students from seventh to 12th grades.

1972: The American Indian Athletic Hall of Fame was founded at Haskell Indian Nations University in Lawrence, Kansas. The first 14 athletes inducted included four different sports; some inductees selected played more than one sport: Alexander Arcasa, Colville, football, 1909–12; Charles "Chief" Bender, White Earth Chippewa, baseball, 1903–17; Wilson "Buster" Charles, Oneida, Olympic decathlon, 1927–31; Albert A. Exendine, Delaware, football, 1902–7; Joseph N. Guyon, Chippewa, football, 1911–27; Jimmie Johnson, Stockbridge-Munsee, football, 1899–1905; John Levi, Arapaho, football, 1921–25; John "Tortes" Meyers, Cahuilla, baseball, 1908–17; Allie P. Reynolds, Creek, baseball, 1942–54; Theodore "Tiny" Roebuck, Choctaw, football, 1923–27; Rueben Sanders, Tutuni/Rogue River, football, 1896–1941; Louis Tewanima, Hopi, track and field, 1907–12; Jim Thorpe, Sac and Fox, football/baseball/track, 1907–19; and Louis Weller, Caddo, football, 1929–31.

1977: The Lakota Nation Invitational (LNI) was founded and has grown annually. With a focus on Native youth, an abundance of teams from across the United States come together for friendly competitions in basketball, volleyball, cross-country, traditional hand games, cheerleading, wrestling, a pow-wow, Lakota language bowl, art show, knowledge bowl, chess, poetry slam, plus other events. It is the first such endeavor. Tens of thousands view the athletic, recreational, and educational activities in person or online. Held in Rapid City, South Dakota, the LNI puts a Lakota spin on sports and games.

1990: The North American Indigenous Games (NAIG) was founded as the first Olympic style sports event exclusively for Native peoples of Canada and the United States. Held in Edmonton, Alberta, Canada, it featured a cultural component as well as almost 20 sporting categories. Held every two to three years, the largest attendance

World Eskimo-Indian Olympics

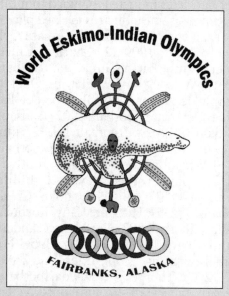

The logo for the World Eskimo-Indian Olympics.

The first World Eskimo-Indian Olympics (WEIO), held in Fairbanks, Alaska, in 1961, drew contestants and dance teams from Utqiagvik (formerly, Barrow), Unalakleet, Tanana, Fort Yukon, Noorvik, and Nome, Alaska. The event was a big success and has been held annually every July. Although it was a first, the competitive games were/are from historical times, when people had to be physically and mentally strong to live in the harsh Alaskan climate. They had to transfer physical fitness into survival.

For millennia, the same events played today at the WEIO taught people how to be tough and well-rounded to survive; the games challenged every part of the body. They were played at gatherings, sometimes celebrations of successful whale or seal hunts when the temperature outside the warm community house, built of driftwood, whale bone, and stone, could be 60 degrees below zero. But inside people were comfortable. Young men practiced amazing athletic feats while the whaling captains watched, searching for those who would be an asset on whaling and hunting teams. To be chosen, one had to be strong, fast, and have great balance and agility. The captains also needed their crew to be able to deal with pain and hardship. Like coaches today who scout athletes, captains observed the young men to see who had the best qualities.

Competitive Events at the World Eskimo-Indian Olympics:

- Knuckle Hop or Seal
- Four-Man Carry
- Ear Weight
- Ear Pull
- Drop the Bomb
- One-Foot High Kick & Two-Foot High Kick
- One-Hand Reach
- Alaskan High Kick

World Eskimo-Indian Olympics (contd.)

- Kneel Jump

- Indian Stick Pull

- Toe Kick

- Eskimo Stick Pull

- Arm Pull

- Nalukataq (Blanket Toss)

- Fish Cutting

- Seal Skinning

- Greased Pole Walk

- Bench Reach

Alaskan Indigenous communities are experiencing catastrophic effects of climate change. The WEIO events are based on skills needed to survive in a world of ice, snow, and freezing temperatures. Today, some villages are a storm away from being underwater, and the animals essential to the diet of Northern peoples are becoming extinct.

was at the 2006 NAIG held in Denver, Colorado, where 10,000 athletes from the United States and Canada represented more than 1,000 different nations. In addition to sporting events, the games include a parade and a variety of cultural performances.

1995: The Native American Sports Council (NASC) became an official member of the U.S. Olympic Committee. NASC promotes athletic excellence and wellness within Native American communities through sports programs that combine traditional Native American values with those of the modern Olympics.

1995: Bobby Letterman, Cherokee, founded the National Indian Sports Association.

2000: The online magazine *NDN Sports* was launched. It is first in reporting the latest news about Indian athletes and Native sports organizations at all levels.

2005: The Cherokee Nation hosted its first annual Traditional Native Games competition in Cherokee Territory, Oklahoma. The events included a cornstalk shoot, Cherokee marbles, horseshoes, hatchet throw, blowgun, and chunkey.

2007: The Montana Indian Athletic Hall of Fame was founded in Billings, Montana, to honor American Indian athletes from Montana. The first inductees: Malia Camel-Kipp, Blackfeet, the first Native American to play for University of Montana Grizzlies women's basketball team; Philip Red Eagle, Assinboine-Sioux, Indian baseball and basketball player and coach; Louis Herman Longee, Assinboine-Sioux; Marvin Camel, Confederated Salish and Kootenai Tribes of

Charlene Teters appeared in a Senate Committee on Indian Affairs meeting on May 5, 2011.

American Indians Are People, Not Mascots

The National Coalition against Racism in Sports and Media (NCARSM) was formed in 1989 to "fight the powerful influence of major media who choose to promulgate messages of oppression." The media reinforces the widely held misconceptions of American Indians in the form of sports team identities resulting in racial, cultural, and spiritual stereotyping. One of the founders and active members is Spokane tribal member Charlene Teters (1952), an artist and educator, who in 1988 was studying for a Master of Fine Arts at the University of Illinois at Urbana-Champaign. She attended her university basketball game and was horrified to see a European American student dressed as a stereotypical whooping Chief Illiniwek and performing a pseudo–Native American dance. This racist caricature was the school mascot. Teters and other American Indian students took action to have the mascot eliminated. She and others showed up at games silently holding a sign that read, "We are human beings, not mascots." Her life was threatened. She was spit on. Burning cigarettes were pelted at her. Soon hundreds of Native Americans showed up on Homecoming Day at the University of Illinois to protest with Teters. Non-native alumni and students maintained they were honoring Native people with the tradition of Chief Illiniwek and took a strong stand to keep the mascot. *In Whose Honor*, a documentary by Jay

American Indians Are People, Not Mascots (contd.)

Rosenstein, recounted the events and included other actions taken by the new coalition, NCARSM, to eradicate racist mascots. Its efforts have been largely successful, with the elimination of Chief Illiniwek (2007) and the Washington Red——s (2020), and dozens of schools have decided to change their names and mascots. However, there are still hundreds of sports teams at every level that continue to perpetuate racism by holding onto their fake Indian mascots.

In 2019, Maine became the first state in the nation to outlaw Native American mascots in all public schools, colleges, and universities. After she signed the bill, Governor Janet Mills said, "While Indian mascots were often originally chosen to recognize and honor a school's unique connection to Native American communities in Maine, we have heard clearly and unequivocally from Maine tribes that they are a source of pain and anguish." Maulian Dana, the tribal ambassador for the Penobscot Nation in Maine, told the *New York Times* that the new law "sends a message of truth and honor and respect. It is part of a big picture of historical oppression of Indigenous people," she said. "When you see people as less than people, you treat them accordingly. That actually points to the very core of it ... they make us invisible and turn us into stereotypes."

the Flathead Indian Reservation, first and also first Native to win the World Boxing Council World Cruiserweight (1980); Pete Conway, Blackfeet, standout basketball player from Eastern Montana College; and Larry Pretty Weasel, Crow, basketball player who holds several collegiate records at Rocky Mountain College.

2011: The newly formed Indian National Finals Rodeo Association Hall of Fame honored its first inductees: Dean C. Jackson, Navajo; Fred Gladstone, Blood; Pete Fredericks, Three Affiliated Tribes; Bob Arrington, Muscogee Creek; Jay Hardwood, Blackfeet; and Mel Sampson, Yakama.

2011: The Stronghold Society was founded by Walt Pourier, Oglala Lakota, artist, designer, and skateboarding activist, and Jim Murphy, writer, artist, skateboard company owner, and skateboarding activist, to promote healthy lifeways for youth of all races through skateboarding and athletic activities or events. They also build and maintain skateparks in Native communities like the Wounded Knee 4-Directions Toby Eagle Bull Memorial Skatepark on the Pine Ridge Reservation, South Dakota.

2017: Owen St. Clair (1972–), Pawnee/Navajo, became the first Native American selected to serve as a board member for the National Federation of State High School Associations, the governing body for the rules of competition for most high school sports and activities in the United States.

2018: The Pokagon Band of Potawatomi Indians based in Dowagiac, Michigan, held the first annual quadrathlon in the state of Michigan. The event is comprised of a 750-meter swim, a 20K bike ride, a 5K run, and a 2,000-meter kayak. Individuals and teams are invited to participate in one of three categories: beginner, competitor, and elder.

URBAN LIFE

"Since there is no place for Indians to assemble and carry on tribal ways and beliefs here in the white man's city, we, therefore, plan to develop: a center for Native American studies ... a great Indian University ... an Indian center of ecology ... an Indian school ... an Indian restaurant. We entered our land. We are the natural inhabitants. We cannot enter our land illegally."

—Activist Bernie Whitebear (1937–2000), Colville, from the Manifesto delivered to the City of Seattle on behalf of the United Indians of All Tribes Foundation to the City of Seattle, March 24, 1970

1911: The Will Rogers World Airport opened in Oklahoma City, Oklahoma, and was the first and to date only airport to be named after a Native American. Will Rogers, Cherokee, is sometimes referred to as the first "jetsetter," as he loved air travel and flew anywhere and any way he could, even on mail planes. As much as Rogers loved flying, he died in a plane crash in 1935.

1913: The City of Salamanca was incorporated on the Allegheny Seneca Reservation in New York and became the first city to be governed by an Indian tribe. Non-Seneca residents cannot own land but rather lease it from the Seneca Nation.

1915: Episcopalian priest Sherman Coolidge (1862–1932), Arapaho, helped found the Society of American Indians (SAI), forerunner of the National Congress of American Indians, in Columbus, Ohio, as a way to preserve Indigenous heritage and nurture pride in American Indians, devastated by the colonial practice of destroying the culture. On September 28, 1915, Coolidge issued a proclamation designating the second Saturday of each May as American Indian Day (AID) and urged Indians to observe it as a memorial to their "race." It was first celebrated in upper Manhattan's Inwood Park near the great tulip tree, which had become iconic of Indian New York. Native New Yorkers turned the annual serious event into a festival attracting thousands. Except for occasional interruptions, it has been observed right up to the present and is called Drums along the Hudson and is sponsored by Lotus Music and Dance, directed by Kamala Cesar, Mohawk.

1925: Will Rogers (1879–1935), Cherokee, was named the first honorary mayor of Beverly Hills, California, for one year; he was the president of the Beverly Hills governing body, but the city did not have a mayoral office. He was one of the earliest residents of the famed community and, along with actress Mary Pickford, was one of the new city's chief promoters. He rallied against annexation to Los Angeles, and today, Beverly Hills is still an independent municipality completely surrounded by LA. Rogers and Pickford attracted press coverage of Beverly Hills, and by 1928, Harold Lloyd, John Barrymore, Robert Montgomery, and Mary Hopkins had built residences there, part of the mass migration of those in the film industry. Rogers wrote of the land boom in 1923: "Lots are sold so quickly and often out here that they are put through escrow made out to the 12th owner. They couldn't possibly make out a separate deed for each purchaser; besides, he wouldn't have time to read it in the 10 minutes' time he owned the land." In 1929, horses were restricted to paths in Beverly Hills, causing Rogers to build a large ranch in Pacific Palisades so he could ride his horses "wild west style." In 1952, Beverly Hills's first municipal park (1915) was renamed Will Rogers Memorial Park.

1926: The first urban Indian association in the country was established by the Native community in New York City. Called the

Named after the famous Cherokee entertainer, Will Rogers Memorial Park in Beverly Hills, California, is about 5 acres (2 hectares) of beautiful grounds right off Sunset Boulevard and North Beverly Drive.

This rather famous 1932 *New York Herald-Tribune* photograph of ironworkers having lunch high above New York City as they sit on an I-beam doesn't tell the entire story of how many of these workers were Mohawks.

Mohawks Create the Modern Urban Landscape

In 1916, the first Mohawk high steel construction workers arrived in New York City to erect the Hell Gate Bridge. The Mohawk Nation ironworkers hailed from two communities: St. Regis Mohawk Reservation (aka Akwesasne), which straddles Ontario, Quebec, and New York State, and Mohawk Council of Kahnawá:ke, a reserve near Montreal, Quebec, Canada. The tradition of what is often called "skywalkers or cloud-walkers" began in 1886, when the Dominion Bridge Company, the construction firm responsible for building the Canadian Pacific Railroad's bridge across the Saint Lawrence River onto Mohawk land, hired Mohawks as day-laborers. But the Mohawk bridgemen were more interested in the unpopular and dangerous job of riveting, which paid more money. High-steel riveting is a rare skill, and Mohawks became experts in the field, handing down the proficiency for generations.

New York City was in a race to construct taller and taller buildings, and the Mohawk steel walkers were in great demand. But in the 1920s, immigration authorities chal-

Mohawks Create the Modern Urban Landscape (contd.)

lenged their right to work in the United States since most were from Canada. Court battles ensued, resulting in the ruling that because the Jay Treaty of 1794, between the United States and Great Britain, stated that Indians could pass freely and conduct commerce between the two countries, therefore Indians from Canada were *not* immigrants in the United States. The sovereign Mohawk Nation had been dissected by the two foreign countries without their consent, but the Mohawk People were still united.

Mohawks began to "walk iron" through the air, connecting the earth with the sky, and created the very bones of the Empire State Building, the George Washington Bridge, the United Nations, the Woolworth Building, 30 Rock, the Seagram Building, Lincoln Center, the Waldorf Astoria, and other iconic skyscrapers that mark the country's largest cityscape. Along with creating the famous buildings, Mohawks built their own community in Brooklyn in the 1930s, carving out ten square blocks in the North Gowanus neighborhood of the borough. At the heart of the area was the Local 361 of the Bridge, Structural and Ornamental Iron Workers Union on Atlantic Avenue. Soon the Brooklyn Gowanus neighborhood, a 12-hour car trip from the Kahnawake Reserve, was nicknamed Downtown or Little Kahnawake.

In "Downtown Kahnawake," businesses and organizations catered to the Mohawk community. One sign over a bar stated, "The Greatest Ironworkers in the World Pass through These Doors." The gathering spot served up Montreal beers to its Canadian Mohawk patrons. A Mohawk Sunday dinner was on the menu of the Spar Bar and Grill, and the local Presbyterian church became the first in its denomination to offer services in Mohawk as well as sponsor an annual powwow. Residents formed the Indian League of the Americas (ILOTA), which gave scholarships to Native youth; purchased land in Barryville, New York; and held a yearly powwow and hosted dances and other social events. Mohawks were active in the American Indian Community House, a social services and cultural institution, often serving in leadership positions.

The building boom slowed down in the late 1950s around the time of the opening of the New York Thruway, which cut the commute from Brooklyn to Mohawk homelands in half. Many families then chose to stay on the reservation; husbands drove the six hours to be home on weekends, renting rooms in New York City during the work week. Other places required the expertise of the iron workers; New York City was no longer the focal point for the industry. The last great skyscrapers that were built by the Mohawk experts in New York were the Twin Towers of the World Trade Center; they autographed the last beam they raised. After the Towers were demolished in 2001, the Mohawk builders assisted with the rescue and clean-up at Ground Zero. Many developed health problems and became disabled because of the toxins released into the air.

Today, New York City has almost 200,000 Native American residents. Statistics do not include Indigenous peoples from Canada, Mexico, the Caribbean, or South America. Al-

Mohawks Create the Modern Urban Landscape (contd.)

though the Mohawk population has declined, there are many well-known people who grew up in the five boroughs of the country's largest city. Alexandrea Kawisenhawe Rice (1972–), actress; Kahn-Tineta Horn (1940–), political activist/civil servant/former fashion model; Danielle Soames, actress/playwright/director; Kamala Cesar (1948–), dancer/director of Lotus Music and Dance; and Barbara Littlebear Delisle (1945–2017), artist/Mohawk language educator, are just a few of the notable Mohawks who grew up in New York City with ties to the famous iron workers.

American Indian Club, the members welcomed new people to the community, provided social and professional networking, and granted scholarships to Native youth.

1931: The "Exposition of Indian Tribal Arts" at Grand Central Art Galleries in New York City was billed as "the first exhibition of American Indian art selected entirely with consideration of esthetic value." It was the first exhibition of Native American Art held in New York City.

1947: The Phoenix (AZ) Indian Center opened as the first urban American Indian Center.

1954: Mauch Chunk (from the Munsee-Lenape language for "Bear Place"), Pennsylvania, was renamed Jim Thorpe in honor of the famed Sauk and Fox athlete, whom many sports historians believe to be America's top athlete ever. Thorpe (1887–1953) was born in Oklahoma, and his only connection to the area was that he attended Carlisle Indian Industrial School in Carlisle, Pennsylvania, a hundred miles southwest. However, his widow, distraught that the planned memorial in Shawnee, Oklahoma, had not happened, worked out an arrangement to bury his ashes in Mauch Chunk if officials there would rename their city and honor him in public monuments. Mauch

Chunk was searching for a way to improve the town's economy. The monument site contains Thorpe's tomb, two statues of him in athletic poses, and markers chronicling his life story. The grave rests atop mounds of soil from Thorpe's native Oklahoma and from the Stockholm Olympic Stadium in which he won his Olympic medals.

1958: Ella Pierre Aquino (1902–1988), Lummi/ Yakima, and others founded the American Indian Women's Service League, the first organization in Seattle, Washington, dedicated to resolving the problems of urban Indians. They dealt with critical situations affecting children, health, housing, and more and raised public consciousness of important urban Indian issues, brought Indian cultural traditions to the city, built a sense of community among Seattle Indians, and started an expansive network of essential social service organizations dedicated to helping urban Indians. Aquino was also a leading activist in the protection of Native children in the foster care system as well as tribal fishing rights. Her activism earned her the title "Give 'em Hell Ella," as she was photographed scaling a barbed wire fence in the struggle to take back Fort Lawton.

1968: The American Indian Movement (AIM) was formed in Minneapolis, Minnesota, to

Mauch Chunk, Pennsylvania, was renamed Jim Thorpe, Pennsylvania, as part of a deal with Jim Thorpe's widow to install the athlete's tomb (pictured) and two statues in the city.

combat violence and racism directed at Native people, particularly to protect people from the abuse meted out by the largely non-Indian police force. Founded by Clyde and Vernon Bellecourt, White Earth Ojibwe; Dennis Banks, Leech Lake Ojibwe; Herb Powless, Oneida; Eddie Benton-Banai, Lac Courte Oreilles Ojibwe; and others, AIM began to monitor police treatment of Native people. The efforts were successful as false and or unprosecuted arrests of Indians decreased by more than half in the first year of the organization's existence.

AIM became the front line in the struggle for civil and treaty rights, spreading to other cities and communities across the country where Native people were also being brutal-

ized by police, poverty, and racism. Although Indians had been organizing against and confronting colonialism, both historical and contemporary, for centuries, AIM and its call to activism restrengthened the resolve of Native people to survive on their own terms and brought that determination to the prime-time news so that all Americans became aware that Indigenous peoples were still here and part of the twentieth century. For the first time, America was paying attention to the history of 500 years of continuous struggle against the invasion of Indigenous homelands and the brutality against Indians that exists in contemporary times.

1972: Funding from the federal Indian Education Act, Title IV became available to urban school districts. A local educational association (LEA) with at least 10 Native students and in partnership with representatives from a local Native community (both parents and educators) created culturally appropriate educational programs to address dismal dropout rates. Some cities, like Buffalo, New York, created magnet schools for Indian students.

1972: The "survival school" philosophy was initiated by the American Indian Movement to address the holistic needs of urban Indian children, including life skills. The Heart of the Earth and Red School House survival schools were established in Minneapolis and St. Paul, Minnesota, to provide educational opportunities and support services for Native students from preschool to 12th grade living in the Twin Cities. Both were alternative Indian-controlled community schools started by parents seeking to curb the high drop-out and push-out rates of Native American students. A key purpose was to teach academics from a Native perspective and with culturally appropriate curricula. The Red School House was the last one to close in 1996.

1973: Little Earth of United Tribes was organized in South Minneapolis, Minnesota, as the nation's first public urban affordable housing project to give preference to Native peoples. Residents are from some 39 different tribes and have created programs for children, elders, job development, and the Little Earth of United Tribes Farm, which uses farming as a tool to teach youth the skills necessary for employment anywhere. Later the Little Earth Farm was started so residents could grow nutritionally dense, culturally relevant food and medicine to nourish and build community.

1976: The Los Angeles City/County Native American Indian Commission was created through the efforts of members of the Los Angeles Indian community and Los Angeles city and county governments. The commission's primary purpose is to increase the acquisition and application of funding resources to the socioeconomic challenges of American Indians in the city and county without duplication of effort.

1979: The American Indian Opportunities Industrialization Center (AIOIC) was founded in Minneapolis, Minnesota, to address the high unemployment rate of urban Indians. It was a novel and successful venture. The school offered job training but also provided participants with an education to give them a wide variety of employment options. Over 20,000 Native Americans gained employment in various sectors. Culturally based programs offered Natives a chance to build and/or enhance skills necessary to procure jobs without having to abandon their Indigenous values. AIOIC was nationally recognized in the workforce development field for its accomplishments.

1985: The nation's first extensive art exhibition on the topic of Native HIV/AIDS was held in New York City's only Indian owned and operated gallery, the American Indian Community House Gallery.

1985: Diosa Summer-Fitzgerald, Choctaw, was appointed as the first Native director of the renowned Jamaica Arts Center in Queens, New York, and she led it until her death in 1989. An artist, she taught traditional art forms and authored many museum guides, including "Native American Food," "Fingerweaving," "Narrative and Instruction," and "Ash Sapling Basketry."

1990: For the first time since the census began, more Native people were reported to be living in urban areas than on reservations or in rural regions. The urban Indigenous population was reported at 51 percent. In the 2020s, estimates range from 72 percent to

Part of the Reno-Sparks Indian Colony, the Reno-Sparks Tribal Health Center is a state-of-the-art medical provider for residents in Reno, Nevada.

The Indian Relocation Act of 1956

The Bureau of Indian Affairs (BIA) began an unofficial program to move people from reservations to cities for better economic opportunities in 1951. The Termination Era saw a reversal in policies from the Self-Government Era, and the federal government resolved to terminate the special trustee relationship tribes held with the United States. Although some thought that it appeared that Congress wished to liberate tribes from federal control, this policy became another means of controlling and erasing Native Americans' rights. The foremost method of terminating Native Americans' special status was through relocation from tribal lands. The 1952 Urban Indian Relocation Program was put into motion and then the Indian Relocation Act of 1956 was passed, making the policy a law. Many tribes were just "de-Indianized" overnight, losing their lands and tribal status. Many Indians were skeptical. Was it a nefarious scheme to destroy the sovereignty of tribal nations? Was it yet another way to force Native people to assimilate and give up tribal culture? Was it a plot to appropriate even more Native land?

The campaign to entice people to cities was strong, including seductive advertisements, promises of better living conditions, and fantastical and untrue "success"

The Indian Relocation Act of 1956 (contd.)

stories about families who had relocated. The BIA staffed job placement offices in Denver, Colorado; Salt Lake City, Utah; Los Angeles, Oakland, San Francisco, and San Jose, California: St. Louis, Missouri; Dallas, Texas; Cleveland, Ohio; Oklahoma City and Tulsa, Oklahoma; and Seattle, Washington.

Participants were given one-way tickets to an urban area, job placement and counseling, and subsistence funds until the first paycheck. Although some had successful outcomes in cities, a high number did not and returned to their homelands. Those who stayed often created Indian neighborhoods, organizations, and businesses. Some neighborhoods became part of the urban blight that affected other poor people as health, educational, housing, and training programs were terminated or downsized.

Sol Tax, anthropology professor at the University of Chicago, was dismayed at what he witnessed in Chicago as more and more Indians moved to the city. He emerged as an advocate for urban Indians and did his best to expose the unfair practices of the BIA. Tax wrote, "When Indians came to Chicago, they received relocation assistance for about six weeks. Indian families came on a train with a one-way ticket. Once they arrived, they had no place to go. They were met by somebody in the Bureau of Indian Affairs who took them to a rental house and found them a job. When Indians returned to the relocation office to say they had a problem, which they all did, they were told, we do not have anymore jurisdiction over you. We have rented you a home; if you want to move to another one, that is your problem. If you do not like your job, that is also your problem." Indians in Chicago, like other cities, were pushed into horrible areas and given jobs that no one else wanted, often temporary and without benefits or chance for promotions.

The BIA's intentions were to destroy tribalness and propel Indians into the dominant culture. Indeed, it was yet another attempt to demolish the connections to community and customs. But with all the problems, Indian people were resilient and crafted a new urban Indian culture, often preserving traditions while making new ones. Instead of becoming detached from the tribe, urban Indians created intertribalness.

Of course, Indigenous people were already living in cities, many occupying the same areas their ancestors settled before European contact. Most U.S. cities were incorporated on lands already "urbanized" by First Peoples for all the reasons towns exist: water, transportation routes, close proximity to food sources, building materials, and the like. Tragically as Anglo populations grew, Indigenous peoples were aggressively forced out of many cities. Still, many managed to remain in their traditional homelands, even owning parts of cities. The Agua Caliente Band of Cahuilla Indians are the largest landowners in Palm Springs, California; the Reno-Sparks Indian Colony is a major landlord in Reno, Nevada; and Utqiaġvik (formerly Barrow), Alaska, the

The Indian Relocation Act of 1956 (contd.)

northernmost town and the largest municipality in the United States, is an Inupiat community and also home to people from Korea, Mexico, Macedonia, and other countries.

The urban Indigenous population has been burgeoning for decades, yet Indian people are often still invisible to their non-Native neighbors. Today, almost every major city has some kind of Native organization that strives to serve the unique needs of Indians and support community and cultures.

83 percent, with the largest urban area reported to be Los Angeles County, California. However, statistics do not include Indigenous peoples with roots in other Western Hemisphere countries.

1991: The Picuris Pueblo made news when they opened the Hotel Santa Fe in New Mexico. They are the first tribe in the U.S. to partner with nontribal businesspeople to erect and operate an off-reservation hotel and the first to design an urban business with traditional Pueblo architecture.

1992: On the 500th anniversary of Christopher Columbus's first voyage, American Indians in Berkeley, California, celebrated the first "Indigenous Peoples Day." The Berkeley City Council replaced its observance of Columbus with a commemoration of Indigenous people. Each year, almost 200 cities and states have made the decision to not honor Columbus for his role in the devastation of the Americas and its original peoples. Cities from Newark, New Jersey, to Columbus, Ohio, to Seattle, Washington, now celebrate Indigenous Peoples Day.

1998: Garifuna Coalition USA was established in New York City, becoming the first organization to advocate for Garifuna immigrants. A unique blending of Caribbean Indigenous groups and enslaved Africans,

the Garifuna are a distinct ethnic group, with its own language, beliefs, and practices. Garifuna, which is still spoken in their city homes, is an Arawakan dialect with loanwords from Carib and different European languages. Because of the centuries of being pushed around the Caribbean and South America by colonial powers, they have often kept a low profile; many sought safe haven in New York beginning in the 1940s. The Garifuna Coalition operates the Bronx-based Garifuna Advocacy Center to provide social, educational, and cultural services to the community.

1998: The United Confederation of Taino People (UCTP) or La Confederación Unida del Pueblo Taíno was founded in New York City to unite the diaspora of Taíno people. Taíno homelands are in Caribbean countries, but like many other New Yorkers, they moved to the area seeking employment.

1998: Audrey J. Cooper (1948–2021), Cherokee/Sand Hill/Syrian, became the first director of the Multicultural Resource Center (MRC) in Ithaca, New York. Under her leadership, MRC grew to be an essential community treasure chest of projects, activities, and events that celebrated all people. Cooper founded the community forum "Talking Circles on Race and Racism" to develop intercultural literacy, to promote healing of racism and to create a culture of inclusivity. In 2008, she helped engineer the homecoming of the Tutelo Tribe to Ithaca, refugees from Southeastern colonialism who had been given sanctuary and adopted by the Cayuga in the 1753. The event grew into the First People's Festival, which has become a major commemoration of Indigenous peoples of the Americas in the Northeast.

2001: The first annual protest began against the Bay Street Shopping Mall in Emeryville, California. Every year, dozens of Ohlone people and allies gather at Shellmound Memorial Park to protest the desecration of a former burial site, which lies underneath the shopping center. In 2005, the documentary *Shellmound* chronicled the years of disrespect and destruction for the historical area. The huge mound that once rose 60 feet above the ground contained human burials and cultural objects until it was razed for a dance hall in the 1800s and then further decimated by a pigment plant (established in the 1920s) that polluted the area. The plant closed and the pollution was remediated for the construction of a shopping mall despite dissent from Native peoples and their allies. Nothing prepared the workers or the archaeologists supervising the site for the emotional discovery of hundreds of intact burials—or the extent of toxic contamination found at the site. But as it was once the largest and most extensive American Indian shellmound in the Bay area, protestors expected that there would be many buried in the massive cemetery. The Bay Street shopping mall on Shellmound Street draws hundreds of visitors every day; few are aware of the cultural significance of the land that lies beneath. Shellmound Memorial Park, a small area tucked into a corner of the mall, was a feeble attempt by developers to make amends with the Native community.

2001: The Lenape Cultural Center in Easton, Pennsylvania, was opened by the Lenape Nation of Pennsylvania, whose members are descendants of the area's first peoples, also called Delaware. In historic times, Easton was in Lenape territory, and although most Delaware were relocated to Indian Territory (present-day Oklahoma), some stayed behind. The Lenape Cultural Center chronicles that history and present-day lives of members, many who live in cities and towns in Pennsylvania, New York, New Jersey, and Delaware.

2005: The Residence Inn in Washington, D.C., made history when it took its first room reservation. It was a novel enterprise, as it is owned collaboratively by four different tribes: San Manuel Band of Serrano Mission Indians (California); Viejas Band of Kumeyaay (California); Forest Potawatomi Community (Wisconsin); and the Oneida Tribe of Indians (Wisconsin).

2006: The Children's Cultural Center of Native America (CCCONA) was founded by Nitchen, a Native organization in New York City. It became the first approved field-visit site for New York City public schools, wholly designed, operated, and staffed by Indian people. Classes from the New York City metropolitan area schools attend CCCONA to learn about the past, present, and future of Indigenous peoples in the region as well as from the Americas. Programming includes a puppet show featuring Lenape words and contemporary Lenape characters, Native Hawaiian songs, discussion of culture, and accurate information on First Peoples. CCCONA also offers teacher training and curriculum development.

2009: Filmmaker Eric Paul Maryea, Matinecock, premiered the film *The Lost Spirits.* The documentary chronicled the lives of contemporary Queens-based Matinecock and Montaukett families, previously ignored. The families managed to remain in their homelands despite overwhelming odds.

2010: President Barack Obama scored a first when he delivered an address to the 27th annual Gathering of Nations powwow held at the University of New Mexico in Albuquerque. His message was broadcast on the LoboVision video screen at the country's largest urban Native festival.

2011: All My Relations Arts Gallery opened in the American Indian Cultural Corridor along Franklin Avenue in Minneapolis. The gallery is an outgrowth of All My Relations Arts founded years earlier by Shirlee Stone as Mitakuye Oyasin (Dakota for All My Relations). Since its inception, it has created numerous exhibits featuring artists such as Frank Big Bear, Andrea Carlson, Gordon Coons, Jim Denomie, Sam English, Carl Gawboy, and Mona Smith.

2012: Mayan leader Don Tomás Calvo (from Guatamala), often referred to as the Mayan Pope, delivered an address to the United Nations, sharing the messages of his ancestors that the world was to enter a new cycle of a "monumental transition and an opportunity to realign priorities based on the feminine principles of love, gratitude, care and respect for both humanity and our environment." This message far differed from the popular interpretation that the world would end that year. Calvo and other Mayan elders led ceremonies with a focus on the over 90,000 Mayans dwelling in New York City. Thousands had fled to North America during Guatemala's decades-long civil war (1960–1996) to escape massacres by the government and wealthy landowners. Most Mayans (often called Amerindians) settled in Brooklyn working as day-laborers.

2015: The city of Bellingham, Washington, renamed a street in honor of Billy Frank Jr., environmental leader and treaty rights activist. In 2015, the Nisqually National Wildlife Refuge was also renamed in his honor, and he was posthumously awarded the Pres-idential Medal of Freedom by President Barack Obama. Frank (1931–2014), Nisqually, was a lifelong activist who was arrested more than 50 times during the Native American struggle for treaty fishing rights during the 1960s and 1970s. He also served as the longtime chairman of the Northwest Indian Fisheries Commission, leading the effort for the management and protection of natural resources.

2016: Mariana Vergara, Mapuche/Aymera, earned her doctorate in education from Teachers College at Columbia University in New York City. For the first time, a doctoral candidate used Indigenous methodologies to develop a transformative education program. The Mindfulness into Action (MIA) techniques are borrowed from various Native traditions and have been successfully adapted by activists to create community change in both non-Native and Indigenous community groups in cities in the United States and Ecuador.

2017: Tasha Cerda, Tohono O'odham Nation/African American, was the first woman and person of either African American or Native American descent to be elected mayor of Gardena, California. She is also the first Native American to be elected mayor in the state of California.

2017: On the Canadian government's behalf, Prime Minister Justin Trudeau donated the historical building at 100 Wellington Street in Ottawa as an embassy for Indigenous organizations, providing office and conference space to the Assembly of First Nations, the Métis National Council, and other Indigenous organizations.

2018: Ashley Minner, Ph.D., Lumbee, started to document the history of the Lumbee community in Baltimore, Maryland. While conducting a walking tour of the historic Native neighborhoods, she learned from Lumbee

The American Indian Cultural Corridor

In 2010, Franklin Avenue, the main thoroughfare of the south Minneapolis Native community, was named the American Indian Cultural Corridor, the first American Indian travel destination in the United States. It is one of the most densely populated urban Indian neighborhoods in the country. The Minneapolis-based Native American Community Development Institute (NACDI) conceptualized a plan to preserve the area and boost the economy through tourism. NACDI brought community members, Indian nonprofits, and Indian-owned businesses together to develop a plan with the central goal of teaching an often-ignored segment of the urban population how to become an economic and cultural power. NACDI encourages home and land ownership in a variety of business enterprises like entertainment venues, media outlets, health and wellness resources, and other areas known for job growth potential, opportunities for economic stability/development, and sustainability. NACDI has bought and renovated buildings for neighborhood businesses, art galleries, and offices with plans to establish an Indian-owned hotel and convention facility.

Indeed, the sights up and down Franklin Avenue prove that the neighborhood has been influenced by its Indigenous residents. Native artists have imprinted sidewalks with cultural designs. Businesses, tribal urban outreach offices, and apartment buildings are adorned with beautiful friezes and murals depicting Woodlands beadwork and ribbon work designs. Street light banners, bike racks, public art, and the designs/decals on bus shelters, benches, and recycling bins all celebrate Indian themes and images from the cultural traditions of the Dakota and Ojibwe, the major nations represented in the city. Boring metal electric boxes have been brought to life by Indigenous art and slogans. Aldi's Market and Dollar Tree share space with the Ancient Traders Market and the Native American Community Clinic right across the street from the All My Relations Gallery, featuring Native traditional and contemporary art. In the center of all the hustle and bustle is the Minneapolis American Indian Center, made beautiful by its wood collage facade fashioned by the world-renowned Grand Portage Ojibwa artist George Morrison.

elders that before gentrification, the area was chock full of Lumbee businesses, homes, and events, many more than Minner, a folklorist and professor at the University of Maryland, Baltimore County (UMBC), realized. The elderly Lumbees gathered around a map, pointing out entire blocks that thousands of Lumbee occupied before Baltimore began its urban revitalization efforts that displaced a large percentage of the Native population. Although Minner had lived her entire life in the city, it happened before her time. Minner was inspired to create the first archive of the Lumbees' long association with the city, which began over a century ago when citizens of the country's ninth-largest tribe started migrating to Baltimore from North Carolina in search of employment and relief from Jim Crow segregation. Her research has been so successful that her walking tour stops have tripled. Minner is also the inau-

The Daybreak Star Indian Cultural Center was once an abandoned military fort in Seattle, Washington.

The Center of Seattle's Indigenous Community

In the heart of Seattle, Washington's Magnolia neighborhood, the 21,000-square-foot Daybreak Star Indian Cultural Center is surrounded by 20 beautiful acres, mountain views, and an inspirational landscape. Located high atop a bluff overlooking the Puget Sound from Discovery Park, the Native-designed building, which opened in 1977, features giant cedar timbers, high ceilings, and a spectacular view. It is the first successful venture of its kind. The center is an urban base for Native Americans in Seattle and houses an art gallery, gift shop, social services offices, preschool, and several other programs and is used for events and conferences as well as being a popular venue for weddings and other celebrations. The Seafair Indian Days Powwow is hosted on the grounds every July. The 6,000-square-foot Bernie Whitebear Memorial Ethnobotanical Garden was cultivated in 2003, in memory of activist Whitebear. Over 40 different species of Coast Salish plants and other local species were selected from a variety of Pacific Northwest habitats—from open, seasonally dry meadows to old-growth rain forests as well as plants from other locales that highlight the trade and travel traditions of Indigenous peoples. Founded by the United Indians of All Tribes Foundation, one would think that Seattle was quite generous to and inclusive of its Native citizens by donating this prime piece of real estate to them. However, the acquisition of the lands and the building of the Daybreak Star Indian Cultural Center came about after a long struggle characterized by brilliant strategies,

The Center of Seattle's Indigenous Community (contd.)

dangerous confrontations, peaceful protests, "illegal" occupations, arrests, and the bravery and persistence of Indian people of all ages led by Native leaders Bernie Whitebear (1937–2000), Colville Confederated Tribes, Bob Satiacum (1929–1991), Puyallup Tribe, and others.

Whitebear and Satiacum became friends in the 1950s when Washington Nations, who had fished from time immemorial, were embroiled in legal battles with the state seeking to end their fishing rights. The two were actively involved in protests called "fish-ins." Their commitment to civil rights stayed with them far beyond their work with Nisqually and Puyallup struggles. Whitebear was involved with the Tacoma, Washington, Indian community, and when he moved to Seattle in 1966 to be closer to work, he sought to unite and mobilize his new urban Indian community. He promoted Native cultural events in the city but also took the lead in the campaign against the termination of the Colville tribe in 1969, when valuable timber on reservation lands spurred government officials to push for termination to make the timber publicly available. Tribal members, many of whom were very poor, were each offered $60,000 to give up their lands. Whitebear's efforts were triumphant, and the Colville voted unanimously against termination and retained the right to their land and cultural identity. Back in Seattle, Whitebear knew that to thrive, the people needed their own land—a new home away from home.

Whitebear and Satiacum were influenced by other Indian civil rights movements around the country, particularly with the Indian occupation of the out-of-service federal prison on Alcatraz Island in San Francisco, California. In 1969, Natives in the bay area had lost their cultural center to fire and were searching for a new facility. The protesters cited 1865 U.S. and Indian treaties granting surplus military lands to the original owners. Also, President Richard Nixon had signed a bill that granted nonfederal entities the ability to obtain surplus federal lands for below-market value. These leaders saw an opportunity for urban Indians to become land-based by acquiring surplus land created by the closing of federal prisons like Alcatraz in San Francisco and military bases like Fort Lawton in Seattle, which had recently been decommissioned. Whitebear and his followers, now organized as the United Indians of All Tribes Foundation, believed that the 1,100-acre fort could be reclaimed for the Native community. They voiced their plans to the Seattle government but were ignored. But Whitebear was ahead of the game and met with lawyers to seek options before the City of Seattle could gain title to the land. They tried different routes but concluded that the only way to be taken seriously would be by "storming the fort." They spent several months planning with other Seattle Indian leaders such as Joe DeLaCruz and Randy Johnson, working out the details of an invasion. By March of 1970, they were organized and ready.

Hundreds of Natives and their allies had arrived in Seattle, including Richard Oakes, Mohawk, leader of Alcatraz; actress Jane Fonda, known for her anti–Vietnam War

Bernie Whitebear talks to Senator Henry M. Jackson at the dedication ceremony for the Daybreak Star Indian Cultural Center.

The Center of Seattle's Indigenous Community (contd.)

protests; and Grace Thorpe, Sauk and Fox, daughter of athlete Jim Thorpe. The rounds of the military police were interrupted as Indian protestors clambered over a barbed wire fence while others rushed the front entrance shouting Red Power slogans. The invaders quickly set up a base camp inside the fort, and within minutes, over 50 teepees sprouted up on the base. More than a hundred activists had invaded the fort on the morning of March 8, 1970, with several hundred supporters, Indian and non-Indian, cheering them on and providing food and support. The army was not welcoming. Troops and MPs met the protestors with brute force and intimidation, dispersing several and arresting dozens. Whitebear was among those jailed.

The United Indians of All Tribes Foundation insurgency caught the attention of the national and international media. For the first time, people were hearing about the harsh conditions that Seattle's Indian citizens had to endure, and in the ensuing months, some 40 local non-Indian organizations came to support the UIATF's bid for the surplus fort

The Center of Seattle's Indigenous Community (contd.)

land. Meanwhile, Whitebear and Satiacum led a second invasion. On March 12, Indian activists once again stormed the front gate and once again were treated violently. The protestors set up "Resurrection City," a well-stocked camp right outside the front entrance to Fort Lawton, petitioning that the land be turned over for a multipurpose and education center. UIATF's legal representation advised Whitebear to head to the country's capital and present the case to the Bureau of Indian Affairs and to Congress.

The National Congress of American Indians (NCAI) supported the strategy, and Whitebear and a small group of UIATF members had an audience with the congressional committee that was considering Senator Henry Jackson's Fort Lawton bill, to turn the base into recreational grounds for Seattle. UIATF and the NCAI were able to get a temporary freeze on the Fort Lawton land in November of 1970, which prevented the City of Seattle from obtaining it. The city was then forced into negotiations with Whitebear and the UIATF. For the next year, the two groups conferred, and on March 29, 1972, two years after the original occupation, the UIATF was granted 20 acres of land on a 99-year lease, renewable at the end of the contract. Whitebear steered clear of labeling the new agreement with the city a treaty. "It's not a treaty. The white man doesn't keep treaties. It's a legal, binding, agreement." Daybreak Star Indian Cultural Center is not only beautiful, but it is also a constant reminder that Native people are a part of cities, too, and have the right to pursue Indigenous lifeways in an urban setting.

gural director of the minor in UMBC's public humanities program.

2018: Whitney Rencountre II, Dakota from the Crow Creek Sioux Tribe, was the first Native American to be the chairman of Visit Rapid City, South Dakota. He was named one of *605 Magazine*'s Young Leaders of 2017. He serves on the executive committee for the South Dakota Humanities Council and the board of directors for the Club for Boys in Rapid City. Rencountre is a spokesperson for Mniluzahan Okolakiciyapi Ambassadors, an organization working to improve race relations in Rapid City. He has been the director of the Ateyapi Program, a culturally based mentoring program in the Rapid City School District, and is the CEO of his graphic arts company, WITTGRAPHICS. Rencountre is a popular powwow emcee and has performed as a singer and dancer in Europe and South America.

2019: The Ain Dah Yung Center celebrated the grand opening of its new Mino Oski Dah Yung Permanent Supportive Housing facility, a first-of-its-kind development in St. Paul, Minnesota. Mino Oski Ain Dah Yung ("good new home" in Ojibwe) provides culturally responsive housing and services to Native American youth experiencing homelessness. Mike Laverdure, Turtle Mountain Band of Chippewa, served as the principal architect.

CITY GOVERNMENT

"When I first started it was difficult. I needed the help of the community. I needed to let them know that I meant business. When I needed help from the police and I didn't get it, I threw them in jail. Anyone who refused to help me got stuck in jail. I meant business."

—*Sadie Neakok*

1932: Judson L. Brown (1912–1997), Tlingit, was the first Alaska Native to be elected mayor of a town with a mixed population. He served two terms as mayor of Haines, Alaska.

2003: Elaine Fleming, Leech Lake Band of Ojibwe, was the first Native American elected as mayor of Cass Lake, Minnesota. She served two terms.

2012: Janeé Harteau (1964–), Ojibwe, Bad River Reservation, was appointed the chief of the Minneapolis Police Department, making her the first woman, first gay person, and first Native American to hold the post.

2017: Jenny Van Sickle, Tlingit/Athabascan, became the first Native woman to serve on the Superior City Council in Wisconsin, the only Indigenous person and the only person of color. In 2019, she received the first Community Choice Award, Women of Excellence. She was nominated for the award for her advocacy on behalf of Indigenous people and the LGBTQ community as well as her work on voter outreach.

2017: Arvina Martin (1979–), Ho-Chunk, was elected as the first Native American alder-

Sadie Neakok: Alaska's First Female Magistrate

In 1958, Sadie Neakok (1916–2004), Iñupiaq, was appointed the first female magistrate in Alaska and served in the state's Second Judicial District in Barrow (now named Utqiaġvik). She was met with incredible challenges. Neakok was caught between the demands of white law in a state emerging from federal jurisdictions and considering the needs of the Indigenous community that had long been ignored. She worked constantly to resolve clashes. She conducted court proceedings in both the English and Iñupiaq languages and had to fight for the right to include the Native language even though many defendants were not English speakers. Before a courthouse was erected, Neakok heard cases in her kitchen. Although she was a federal employee, she organized the Barrow Duck-In in 1961, a civil disobedience event to protest the federal ban on duck hunting, which threatened Iñupiat livelihood and food security. The Duck-In is considered a seminal protest, as it had significant influence over future subsistence regulation and Native claims laws in Alaska, such as the Alaska Native Claims Settlement Act. The disagreement was settled in an unusual way. Before U.S. Fish and Wildlife officers arrived on the scene, they would give ample notice to those communities that relied on subsistence hunting. No duck hunting would take place while the officers were in the area. The informal agreement lasted until 1997 when the law was overturned and subsistence hunting was no longer illegal. Neakok said that the best part of her job was "gaining the respect of my people." In 2009, five years after her death, Sadie Neakok was inducted into the Alaska Women's Hall of Fame.

woman in Madison, Wisconsin, representing District 11. Martin, a Democrat, is the former chair of the American Indian Caucus for the Democratic Party of Wisconsin. She ran for reelection to the Madison Common Council and won in the general election on April 6, 2021. Her current term ends in 2023. Martin was a 2018 candidate for Wisconsin secretary of state, but she lost the primary on August 14, 2018.

2018: David Holt, Osage, became the first Native American elected mayor of Oklahoma City in its 129-year history. Holt, a Republican, was elected to the state senate in 2010 from Oklahoma City's northwest District 30 and was serving in his second term at the time of his mayoral election. He resigned from that seat before being sworn in as the 36th mayor of Oklahoma City.

2018: Wendy White Eagle (c. 1960–), Ho-Chunk, became the first Native American trustee in the village of Campton Hills, Illinois, a suburb of Chicago. She served as the founding president and CEO of Native Capital Investment, near the village, for more than 15 years. In that role, White Eagle worked with local businesses to create self-sustaining business and communities.

2019: Chris Stearns, Navajo, was the first Native American to be elected to the city council in Auburn, Washington. Previously, he worked for 30 years as an attorney, government leader, and public policy advocate. Stearns was also appointed by President Bill Clinton as the first director of Indian affairs for the U.S. Department of Energy. In that position, he helped energy secretary Bill Richardson create a national Indian energy portfolio. Stearns also served as deputy counsel to the House Subcommittee on Native American Affairs, two terms as chairman of the Seattle Human Rights Commission, and president of the Board of Directors of the Seattle Indian Health Board.

2020: Matthew W. Beaudet, a citizen of the Montauk Tribe, was appointed commissioner of Chicago's Department of Buildings, becoming the first Native American to serve in the position.

2020: Roberta "Birdie" Wilcox Cano, Navajo, made history when she was elected to be the

The Exiles

The Exiles, a film about American Indians living in downtown Los Angeles in the 1950s, was shown at the Venice International Film Festival in 1961. Kent Mackenzie, a first-time filmmaker and recent graduate of the University of South California, served as the film's director. Young Indians, newly relocated from Indian reservations and living in the city, play versions of themselves. *The Exiles* was well received, earning praise from film critic Pauline Kael and others, but it quickly languished. Years later, it was restored by the Film and Television Archive at the University of California, Los Angeles, and released by Milestone in 2008. Author and filmmaker Sherman Alexie, who helped present *The Exiles,* commented: "It's a little problematic in that it's a white guy's movie about us. But in learning how the film was made, I think people will discover it was truly collaborative. The filmmakers ended up in the position of witness as much as creator."

first Native American mayor of Winslow, Arizona. Born and raised in Winslow, she worked for the Arizona Department of Corrections in Yuma.

2020: Todd Rex Gloria (1978–), Tlingit/Haida, was elected the mayor of San Diego, California. A Democrat, Gloria is the first Native and the first openly gay person to fill the top position of the country's eighth most populous city and California's second.

2020: Rebecca St. George, descendant of the Fond du Lac Band of Lake Superior Chippewa and the White Earth Nation, was appointed the City of Duluth's first female city attorney. She serves as the legal advisor and attorney for the mayor, city council, and all city departments. St. George's staff includes nine assistant city attorneys, four paralegals, a victim-witness specialist, and an insurance adjustor. Earlier, she was the staff attorney for the Fond du Lac band, representing and advising the tribal government on legal matters affecting the reservation. Before becoming an attorney, St. George worked with Mending the Sacred Hoop, a Duluth organization that works to end violence against Native women and children.

ORGANIZATIONS

1936: Scott N. Peters, Chippewa, spearheaded a group of Native American individuals, who had graduated from Flandreau Indian School and lived in Detroit, Michigan, in a first attempt to advocate for equal employment, services, and educational opportunities for urban Native women. It grew over the years from the humble North American Indian Club to the North American Indian

Association (NAIA), which today operates the Detroit Indian Center, providing a variety of services to the community. NAIA sponsors Michigan Indian Day, a celebration of unity; features an art gallery; and operates the Totem Pole Deli, which sells Native American cured meats.

1988: The Urban Native Youth Association (UNYA) was created to provide opportunities for urban Indigenous youth (Aboriginal, Métis, Inuit, First Nations, status, and non-status). UNYA operates over 20 programs, staffs almost 300 volunteers and staff, and has more than 300 community partners. It is based in Vancouver, British Columbia, Canada.

1998: The National Council of Urban Indian Health (NCUIH) was established in Washington, D.C., to represent the interests of urban Indian health programs before Congress and federal agencies, and to influence policies impacting the health conditions experienced by urban American Indians and Alaska Natives (AI/AN). NCUIH supports the development of quality, accessible, and culturally sensitive health care programs for AI/AN living in urban communities.

2000: The Urban Native Education Alliance (UNEA) was founded when a group of individuals decided to turn their shared interests into an official student organization. It is based in Redmond, Washington.

2003: The National Urban Indian Family Coalition (NUIFC) was created to advocate for American Indian families living in urban areas. NUIFC partners with Native organizations to research, understand, and raise awareness of the barriers, issues, and opportunities facing urban American Indian families. It is based in Seattle, Washington.

FURTHER READING

Abbott, Isabella. *La'au Hawai'i: Traditional Hawaiian Uses of Plants*. Honolulu: Bishop Museum Press, 1992.

Adams, David Wallace. *Education for Extinction: American Indians and the Boarding School Experience, 1875–1928*. Expanded edition. Lawrence: University Press of Kansas, 2020.

Alfred, Taiaiake. *Peace, Power, Righteousness: An Indigenous Manifesto*. Second edition. Toronto, ON: Oxford University Press Canada, 2009.

Álvarez, Noé. *Spirit Run: A 6,000-Mile Marathon through North America's Stolen Land*. New York: Catapult, 2020.

Alvord, Lori Arviso, and Elizabeth Cohen van Pelt. *The Scalpel and the Silver Bear: The First Navajo Woman Surgeon Combines Western Medicine and Traditional Healing*. New York: Bantam Books, 1999.

Anderson, Kim, Maria Campbell, and Christi Belcourt, eds. *Keetsahnak: Our Missing and Murdered Indigenous Sisters*. Edmonton: The University of Alberta Press, 2018.

Andrews, Brian T. *Cherokee Neurosurgeon: A Biography of Charles Byron Wilson, M.D.* CreateSpace Independent Publishing Platform, 2011.

Ash-Milby, Kathleen, David Penney and Kevin Gover, eds. *Kay Walking Stick: An American Artist*. Washington, DC: Smithsonian Books, 2015.

Austin, Raymond D. *Navajo Courts and Navajo Common Law*. Minneapolis: University of Minnesota Press, 2009.

Belin, Esther G., Jeff Berglund, Connie A. Jacobs, and Anthony K. Webster, eds. *The Diné Reader: An Anthology of Navajo Literature*. Tucson: University of Arizona Press, 2021.

Bellantoni, Nick. *The Long Journeys Home: The Repatriations of Henry ʻŌpūkahaʻia and Albert Afraid of Hawk*. Middletown, CT: Wesleyan University Press, 2018.

Bighorse, Tiana. *Bighorse the Warrior*. Edited by Noel Bennett. Tucson: University of Arizona Press, 1990.

Blackhawk, Ned. *Violence over the Land: Indians and Empires in the Early American West*. Cambridge, MA: Harvard University Press, 2006.

Blaeser, Kimberly M. *Gerald Vizenor: Writing in the Oral Tradition*. Norman: University of Oklahoma Press, 1996.

Blue Spruce, George Jr., as told to Deanne Durrett. *Searching for My Destiny*. Lincoln: University of Nebraska Press, 2009.

Boochever, Annie. *Fighter in Velvet Gloves: Alaska Civil Rights Hero Elizabeth Peratrovich*. Fairbanks: University of Alaska Press, 2019.

Boulley, Angeline. *Firekeeper's Daughter*. New York: Holt, 2021.

Bradley, David. *Indian Country: The Art of David Bradley*. Santa Fe: Museum of New Mexico Press, 2014.

Broker, Ignatia. *Night Flying Woman: An Ojibway Narrative*. St. Paul: Minnesota Historical Society Press, 1983.

Bruchac, Joseph, ed. *Returning the Gift: Poetry and Prose from the First North American Native Writers' Festival.* Tucson: University of Arizona Press, 1994.

Calloway, Colin G. *The Indian History of an American Institution: Native Americans and Dartmouth.* Lebanon, NH: University Press of New England, 2010.

Child, Brenda J. *Boarding School Seasons: American Indian Families, 1900–1940.* Lincoln: University of Nebraska Press, 1998.

Cochran, Mary E. *Dakota Cross-Bearer: The Life and World of a Native American Bishop.* Lincoln: University of Nebraska Press, 2000.

Conley, Robert J. *The Real People Series* (12 titles). New York: Doubleday, 1992–2002.

Cook-Lynn, Elizabeth. *Anti-Indianism in Modern America: A Voice from Tatekeya's Earth.* Champaign: University of Illinois Press, 2001.

Cummings, Denise K., LeAnne Howe, and Harvey Markowitz, eds. *Seeing Red—Hollywood's Pixeled Skins: American Indians and Film.* East Lansing: Michigan State University Press, 2013.

Curtice, Kaitlin B. *Native: Identity, Belonging, and Rediscovering God.* Grand Rapids, MI: Brazos Press, 2020.

Davies, Wade. *Native Hoops: The Rise of American Indian Basketball, 1895–1970.* Lawrence: University Press of Kansas, 2020.

Davids, Sharice, with Nancy K. Mays. *Sharice's Big Voice: A Native Kid Becomes a Congresswoman.* New York: HarperCollins, 2021.

DeJong, David H. *"If You Knew the Conditions": A Chronicle of the Indian Medical Service and American Indian Health Care, 1908–1955.* Lanham, MD: Lexington Books, 2008.

Deloria, Philip J. *Playing Indian.* New Haven, CT: Yale University, 1998.

Deloria, Vine, Jr. *For This Land: Writings on Religion in America.* New York: Routledge, 1998.

Dennis, Yvonne Wakim, and Arlene Hirschfelder. *A Kid's Guide to Native American History: More than 50 Activities.* Chicago: Chicago Review Press, 2009.

———. *Native American Landmarks and Festivals: A Traveler's Guide to Indigenous United States and Canada.* Detroit: Visible Ink Press, 2018.

Dennis, Yvonne Wakim, Arlene Hirschfelder, and Shannon Flynn. *Native American Almanac: More Than 50,000 Years of the Cultures and Histories of Indigenous Peoples.* Detroit: Visible Ink Press, 2016.

Diaz, Natalie. *Postcolonial Love Poem.* Minneapolis, MN: Graywolf Press, 2020.

Do All Indians Live in Tipis? Questions and Answers from the National Museum of the American Indian. Second edition. Washington, DC: Smithsonian Books, 2018.

Driskill, Qwo-Li. *Asegi Stories: Cherokee Queer and Two-Spirit Memory.* Tucson : The University of Arizona Press, 2016.

Echo-Hawk, Walter R. *In the Courts of the Conqueror: The 10 Worst Indian Law Cases Ever Decided.* Golden, CO: Fulcrum Publishing, 2010.

Echohawk, Brummett, with Mark R. Ellenbarger. *Drawing Fire: A Pawnee, Artist, and Thunderbird in World War II.* Lawrence: University Press of Kansas, 2018.

Emery, Jacqueline, ed. *Recovering Native American Writings in the Boarding School Press.* Lincoln: University of Nebraska Press, 2017.

Erdrich, Heid E., ed. *New Poets of Native Nations.* Minneapolis, MN: Graywolf Press, 2018.

Erdrich, Louise. *The Night Watchman: A Novel.* New York: Harper, 2020.

Estes, Nick. *Our History Is the Future: Standing Rock versus the Dakota Access Pipeline, and the Long Tradition of Indigenous Resistance.* New York: Verso, 2019.

Estes, Nick, et al. *Red Nation Rising: From Bordertown Violence to Native Liberation.* Oakland, CA: PM Press, 2021.

Fixico, Donald L. *Termination and Relocation: Federal Indian Policy, 1945–1960.* Albuquerque: University of New Mexico Press, 1986.

Flynn, Sean J. *Without Reservation: Benjamin Reifel and American Indian Acculturation.* Pierre: South Dakota Historical Society Press, 2018.

Ganteaume, Cécile R. *Officially Indian: Symbols That Define the United States.* Washington, DC: National Museum of the American Indian, Smithsonian Institution, 2017.

Greenlaw, Suzanne, and Gabriel Frey. *The First Blade of Sweetgrass.* Illustrated by Nancy Baker. Thomaston, ME: Tilbury House Publishers, 2021.

Gipp, Gerald E., et al., eds. *American Indian Stories of Success: New Visions of Leadership in Indian Country.* Santa Barbara, CA: Praeger, 2015.

Good Sky, Dianna. *Warrior Spirit Rising: A Native American Spiritual Journey.* Good Sky Global Enterprises LLC, 2021.

Gould, Janice. *A Generous Spirit: Selected Works by Beth Brant.* Toronto, ON: Inanna Publications, 2019.

Gura, Philip F. *The Life of William Apess, Pequot.* Chapel Hill: University of North Carolina Press, 2015.

Harjo, Joy, LeAnne Howe, and Jennifer Elise Foerster, eds. *When the Light of the World Was Subdued, Our Songs Came Through: A Norton Anthology of Native Nations Poetry.* New York: Norton, 2020.

Harjo, Suzan Shown, ed. *Nation to Nation: Treaties between the United States & American Indian Nations.* Washington, DC, and New York: National Museum of the American Indian in Association with Smithsonian Books, 2014.

Harris, Alexandra, and Mark G. Hirsch. *Why We Serve: Native Americans in the United States Armed Forces.* Washington, DC: National Museum of the American Indian, Smithsonian Institution, 2020.

The Harvard Project on American Indian Economic Development. *The State of the Native Nations: Conditions under U.S. Policies of Self-Determination.* New York: Oxford University Press, 2007.

Highway, Tomson. *From Oral to Written: A Celebration of Indigenous Literature in Canada, 1980–2010.* Vancouver, BC: Talonbooks, 2017.

Hirschfelder, Arlene, and Paulette Molin. *Encyclopedia of Native American Religions.* Updated Edition. New York: Facts-on-File, 2000.

Hirschfelder, Arlene, and Paulette F. Molin. *The Extraordinary Book of Native American Lists.* Lanham, MD: Scarecrow Press, 2012.

Hirschfelder, Arlene, Paulette Fairbanks Molin, and Yvonne Wakim. *American Indian Stereotypes in the World of Children: A Reader and Bibliography.* Second Edition. Lanham, MD: Scarecrow Press, 1999.

Hirschfelder, Arlene B., and Beverly R. Singer. *Rising Voice: Writings of Young Native Americans.* New York: Charles Scribner's Sons Books for Young Readers, 1992.

Holm, Tom. *Strong Hearts, Wounded Souls: Native American Veterans of the Vietnam War.* Chicago: University of Chicago Press, 1996.

Howe, Leanne, and Padraig Kirwan, eds. *Famine Pots: The Choctaw–Irish Gift Exchange, 1847–Present.* East Lansing: Michigan State University Press, 2020.

Hoxie, Frederick E. *This Indian Country: American Indian Activists and the Place They Made.* New York: Penguin Press, 2012.

Jensen, Toni. *Carry: A Memoir of Survival on Stolen Land.* New York: Ballantine Books, 2020.

Joinson, Carla. *Vanished in Hiawatha: The Story of the Canton Asylum for Insane Indians.* Lincoln: University of Nebraska Press, 2016.

Justice, Daniel Heath, and Jean O'Brien, eds. *Allotment Stories: Indigenous Land Relations under Settler Siege*. Minneapolis: University of Minnesota Press, 2022.

Kane, Herb Kawainui. *Voyagers*. Bellevue, WA: WhaleSong, 1993.

Kauffman, Hattie. *Falling into Place: A Memoir of Overcoming*. Grand Rapids, MI: Baker Books, 2013.

Keene, Adrienne. *Notable Native People: 50 Indigenous Leaders, Dreamers, and Changemakers from Past and Present*. California/New York: Ten Speed Press, 2021.

Kelsey, Penelope Myrtle, ed. *Maurice Kenny: Celebrations of a Mohawk Writer*. Albany: State University of New York Press, 2011.

Kennedy, Deanna M., et al., eds. *American Indian Business: Principles and Practices*. Seattle: University of Washington Press, 2017.

Kidwell, Clara Sue, Homer Noley, and George E. "Tink" Tinker. *A Native American Theology*. Maryknoll, NY: Orbis Books, 2001.

Kimmerer, Robin Wall. *Braiding Sweetgrass: Indigenous Wisdom, Scientific Knowledge and the Teachings of Plants*. Minneapolis: Milkweed Editions, 2013.

King, Thomas. *The Inconvenient Indian: A Curious Account of Native People in North America*. Minneapolis: University of Minnesota Press, 2013.

Kolstoe, John. *Compassionate Woman: The Life and Legacy of Patricia Locke*. Wilmette, IL: Baha'i Publishing, 2011.

Kristofic, Jim. *Medicine Women: The Story of the First Native American Nursing School*. Albuquerque: University of New Mexico Press, 2019.

Krouse, Susan Applegate. *North American Indians in the Great War*. Lincoln: University of Nebraska Press, 2007.

LaDuke, Winona. *All Our Relations: Native Struggles for Land and Life*. Cambridge, MA: South End Press, 1999.

———. *Recovering the Sacred: The Power of Naming and Claiming*. Cambridge, MA: South End Press, 2005.

LaDuke, Winona, with Sean Aaron Cruz. *The Militarization of Indian Country*. Calloway, MN: Honor the Earth, 2011.

LaPier, Rosalyn R., and David R.M. Beck. *City Indian: Native American Activism in Chicago, 1893–1934*. Lincoln: University of Nebraska Press, 2015.

LaPoe, Victoria L., and Benjamin Rex LaPoe II. *Indian Country: Telling a Story in a Digital Age*. East Lansing: Michigan State University Press, 2017.

Leary, J. P. *The Story of Act 31: How Native History Came to Wisconsin Classrooms*. Madison: Wisconsin Historical Society Press, 2018.

Lee, Winona K. Mesiona, and Mele A. Look, eds. *Ho'i Hou Ka Mauli Ola: Pathways to Native Hawaiian Health*. Honolulu: University of Hawai'i Press in Association with Hawai'inuiakea School of Hawaiian Knowledge, 2017.

Lewandowski, Tadeusz. *Ojibwe, Activist, Priest: The Life of Father Philip Bergin Gordon, Tibishkogijik*. Madison: University of Wisconsin Press, 2019.

Lindstrom, Carole. *We Are Water Protectors*. Illustrated by Michaela Goade. New York: Roaring Brook Press, 2020.

Loew, Patty. *Seventh Generation Earth Aspects: Native Voices of Wisconsin*. Madison: Wisconsin Historical Society Press, 2014.

Lomawaima, K. Tsianina. *They Called It Prairie Light: The Story of Chilocco Indian School*. Lincoln: University of Nebraska Press, 1994.

Loring, Donna. *In the Shadow of the Eagle: A Tribal Representative in Maine*. Gardiner, ME: Tilbury House Publishers, 2008.

Mailhot, Terese Marie. *Heart Berries: A Memoir*. Berkeley, CA: Counterpoint Press, 2018.

Mankiller, Wilma, and Michael Wallis. *Mankiller: A Chief and Her People*. New York: St. Martin's Press, 1993.

Marston, Muktuk. *Men of the Tundra: Eskimos at War*. New York: October House, 1969.

Martin, Joel W. *The Land Looks After Us: A History of Native American Religion.* New York: Oxford University Press, 2001.

Martinez, Xiuhtezcatl. *We Rise: The Earth Guardians Guide to Building a Movement That Restores the Planet.* Emmaus, PA: Rodale Books, 2017.

McClanahan, Alexandra J., ed. *A Reference in Time: Alaska Native History Day by Day.* Anchorage, AK: The CIRI Foundation, 2001.

McCool, Daniel, Susan M. Olson, and Jennifer L. Robinson. *Native Vote: American Indians, the Voting Rights Act, and the Right to Vote.* New York: Cambridge University Press, 2007.

McDougall, Brandy Nālani. *Finding Meaning: Kaona and Contemporary Hawaiian Literature.* Tucson: University of Arizona Press, 2016.

Meadows, William C. *The First Code Talkers: Native American Communicators in World War I.* Norman: University of Oklahoma Press, 2021.

Mihesuah, Devon A. *Recovering Our Ancestors' Gardens: Indigenous Recipes and Guide to Diet and Fitness.* Revised edition. Lincoln, NE: Bison Books, 2020.

Miles, Tiya, and Sharon Patricia Holland, eds. *Crossing Waters, Crossing Worlds: The African Diaspora in Indian Country.* Durham, NC: Duke University Press, 2006.

Miller, Robert J. *Reservation "Capitalism": Economic Development in Indian Country.* Lincoln: University of Nebraska Bison Books edition, 2013.

Miller, Robert J., Miriam Jorgensen, and Daniel Stewart, eds. *Creating Private Sector Economies in Native America: Sustainable Development through Entrepreneurship.* New York: Cambridge University Press, 2019.

Miranda, Deborah A. *Bad Indians: A Tribal Memoir.* Berkeley, CA: Heyday, 2013.

Momaday, N. Scott. *House Made of Dawn* (50th Anniversary Edition). New York: HarperPerennial Modern Classics, 2018.

———. *Earth Keeper: Reflections on the American Land.* New York: HarperCollins, 2020.

Morris, Kate. *Shifting Grounds: Landscape in Contemporary Native American Art.* Seattle: University of Washington Press, 2021

Moss, Margaret P. *American Indian Health and Nursing.* New York: Springer Publishing, 2015.

Nesteroff, Kliph. *We Had a Little Real Estate Problem: The Unheralded Story of Native Americans & Comedy.* New York: Simon & Schuster, 2021.

Nez, Chester, with Judith Schiess Avila. *Code Talker: The First and Only Memoir by One of the Original Navajo Code Talkers of World War II.* New York: Dutton Caliber, 2011.

O'Donnell, Michael, Joseph McDonald, and Alice Oechsli. *"Education, Leadership, Wisdom": The Founding History of Salish Kootenai College, 1976–2010.* Pablo, MT: Salish Kootenai College Press, 2018.

Orr, Jeff, Warren Weir, and the Atlantic Aboriginal Economic Development Integrated Research Program, eds. *Aboriginal Measures for Economic Development.* Winnipeg, MB: Fernwood Publishing, 2013.

Ortiz, Roxanne Dunbar. *An Indigenous Peoples' History of the United States for Young People.* Adapted by Jean Mendoza and Debbie Reese. Boston, MA: Beacon Press, 2019.

———. *Not "A Nation of Immigrants": Settler Colonialism, White Supremacy, and a History of Erasure and Exclusion.* Boston, MA: Beacon Press, 2021.

Oxendine, Joseph B. *American Indian Sports Heritage.* Champaign, IL: Human Kinetics Books, 1988.

Parker, Robert Dale, ed. *The Sound the Stars Make Rushing through the Sky: The Writings of Jane Johnston Schoolcraft.* Philadelphia: University of Pennsylvania Press, 2007.

Patsauq, Markoosie. *Hunter with Harpoon.* Translated from the Inuktitut by Valerie Henitiuk and Marc-Antoine Mahieu. Montreal: McGill-Queen's University Press, 2020.

Peavy, Linda, and Ursula Smith. *Full-Court Quest: The Girls from Fort Shaw Indian School, Basketball Champions of the World.* Norman: University of Oklahoma Press, 2008.

Pewewardy, Cornel, Anna Lees, and Robin Zapetah-hol-ah Minthorn, eds. *Unsettling Settler-Colonial Education: The Transformational Praxis Model.* New York: Teachers College Press, 2022.

Piatote, Beth. *The Beadworkers: Stories.* Berkeley, CA: Counterpoint, 2019.

Pickering, Verne, and Stephen Schaitberger. *Stands before His People: Enmegahbowh and the Ojibwe.* St. Paul, MN: Beaver's Pond Press, 2021.

Porter, Joy. *To Be Indian: The Life of Iroquois-Seneca Arthur Caswell Parker.* Norman: University of Oklahoma Press, 2001.

Powers-Beck, Jeffrey. *The American Indian Integration of Baseball.* Lincoln: University of Nebraska Press, 2004.

Prucha, Francis Paul, ed. *Documents of United States Indian Policy.* Third edition. Lincoln: University of Nebraska Press, 2000.

Ramirez, Renya K. *Standing Up to Colonial Power: The Lives of Henry Roe and Elizabeth Bender Cloud.* University of Nebraska Press/American Philosophical Society, 2018.

Red Eagle, Philip H. *Red Earth: A Vietnam Warrior's Journey.* Revised edition. United Kingdom: Salt Publishing, 2007.

Red Star, Wendy. *Wendy Red Star Delegation.* New York: Aperture, 2022.

Reséndez, Andrés. *The Other Slavery: The Uncovered Story of Indian Enslavement.* Boston: Houghton Mifflin, 2016.

Revard, Carter. *Winning the Dust Bowl.* Tucson: University of Arizona Press, 2001.

Rostkowski, Joîlle. *Conversations with Remarkable Native Americans.* Albany: State University of New York Press, 2012.

Round, Phillip H. *Removable Type: Histories of the Book in Indian Country, 1663–1880.* Chapel Hill: University of North Carolina Press, 2010.

Roy, Loriene, Anjali Bhasin, and Sarah K. Arriaga, eds. *Tribal Libraries, Archives, and Museums: Preserving Our Language, Memory, and Lifeways.* Lanham, MD: Scarecrow Press, 2011.

Rudnick, Lois P., with Jonathan Warm Day Coming. *Eva Mirabal: Three Generations of Tradition and Modernity at Taos Pueblo.* Santa Fe: Museum of New Mexico Press, 2021.

Ruffo, Armand Garnet. *Norval Morrisseau: Man Changing into Thunderbird.* Reprint. Madeira Park, BC: Douglas & McIntyre, 2018.

St. John, Jetty. *Native American Scientists.* No. Mankato, MN: Capstone Press, 1996.

Salamone, Frank A., ed. *The Native American Identity in Sports: Creating and Preserving a Culture.* Lanham, MD: Rowman & Littlefield, 2015.

Sando, Joe S., and Herman Agoyo, eds. *Po'pay: Leader of the First American Revolution.* Santa Fe, NM: Clear Light Publishers, 2005.

Sasakamoose, Fred. *Call Me Indian: From the Trauma of Residential School to Becoming the NHL's First Treaty Indigenous Player.* Viking Canada, 2021.

Saunt, Claudio. *Unworthy Republic: The Dispossession of Native Americans and the Road to Indian Territory.* New York: W.W. Norton, 2020.

Schilling, Vincent. *Native Athletes in Action!* Revised edition. Summertown, TN: 7th Generation Press, 2016.

Schroedel, Jean Reith. *Voting in Indian Country: The View from the Trenches.* Philadelphia: University of Pennsylvania Press, 2020.

Shay, Charles Norman. *Project Omaha Beach: The Life and Military Service of a Penobscot Indian Elder.* Solon, ME: Polar Bear, 2012.

Simpson, Leanne Betasamosake. *As We Have Always Done: Indigenous Freedom through*

Radical Resistance. Minneapolis: University of Minnesota Press, 2017.

Sleeper-Smith, Susan. *Indigenous Prosperity and American Conquest: Indian Women of the Ohio River Valley, 1690–1792.* Omohundro Institute of Early American History and Culture in Williamsburg, Virginia and the University of North Carolina Press in Chapel Hill, 2018.

Sleeper-Smith, Susan, et al., eds. *Why You Can't Teach United States History without American Indians.* Chapel Hill: University of North Carolina Press, 2015.

Smith, Cynthia Leitich, ed. *Ancestor Approved: Intertribal Stories for Kids.* New York: Heartdrum, 2021.

Smith, Linda Tuhiwai. *Decolonizing Methodologies: Research and Indigenous Peoples.* Third edition, London, UK: Zed Books, 2021.

Snyder, Michael. *John Joseph Mathews: Life of an Osage Writer.* Norman: University of Oklahoma Press, 2017.

Speroff, Leon, M.D. *Carlos Montezuma, M.D.: A Yavapai American Hero.* Portland, OR: Arnica Publishing, 2004.

Staeger, Rob. *Native American Sports and Games* (Part of the "Native American Life" series). Broomall, PA: Mason Crest, 2013.

Starita, Joe. *A Warrior of the People: How Susan La Flesche Overcame Racial and Gender Inequality to Become America's First Indian Doctor.* New York: St. Martin's Press, 2016.

Sterling, Shirley. *My Name Is Seepeetza.* Reprint. Toronto, CA: Groundwood Books, 1998.

Stewart, Omer C. *Peyote Religion: A History.* Norman: University of Oklahoma Press, 1987.

Sutton, Robert K., and John A. Latschar, eds. *American Indians and the Civil War.* United States Department of the Interior National Park Service, 2013.

Swift, Tom. *Chief Bender's Burden: The Silent Struggle of a Baseball Star.* Lincoln: University of Nebraska Press, 2008.

Swisher, Karen Gayton, and AnCita Benally. *Native North American Firsts.* Detroit: Gale Research, 1998.

Talaga, Tanya. *Seven Fallen Feathers: Racism, Death, and Hard Truths in a Northern City.* Toronto, ON: House of Anansi Press, 2017.

Tate, Juanita J. Keel. *Edmund Pickens (Okchantubby): First Elected Chickasaw Chief, His Life and Times.* Ada, OK: Chickasaw Press, 2009.

Tayac, Gabrielle, ed. *IndiVisible: African-Native American Lives in the Americas.* Washington, DC: Smithsonian Books, 2009.

Tiger, Buffalo, and Harry A. Kersey, Jr. *Buffalo Tiger: A Life in the Everglades.* Lincoln: University of Nebraska Press, 2002.

Tootoo, Jordin. *All the Way: My Life on Ice.* Penguin Canada, 2015.

Trafzer, Clifford E., ed. *American Indians/American Presidents: A History.* In Association with the National Museum of the American Indian. Washington, DC: Smithsonian Institution, 2009.

———. *American Indian Medicine Ways: Spiritual Power, Prophets, and Healing.* Tucson: University of Arizona Press, 2017.

Trask, Haunani-Kay. *From a Native Daughter: Colonialism and Sovereignty in Hawai'i.* Revised edition. Honolulu: University of Hawaii Press, 1999.

Treat, James, ed. *Native and Christian: Indigenous Voices on Religious Identity in the United States and Canada.* New York: Routledge, 1996.

Treuer, Anton. *The Language Warrior's Manifesto: How to Keep Our Languages Alive No Matter the Odds.* St. Paul: Minnesota Historical Society Press, 2020.

———. *Everything You Wanted to Know about Indians but Were Afraid to Ask.* Young Readers Edition. New York: Levine Querido, 2021.

Treuer, David. *The Heartbeat of Wounded Knee: Native America from 1890 to the Present.* New York: Riverhead Books, 2019.

Vecsey, Christopher. *Paths of Kateri's Kin.* Notre Dame, IN: University of Notre Dame Press, 1997.

Waggoner, Linda M. *Fire Light: The Life of Angel De Cora, Winnebago Artist.* Norman: University of Oklahoma Press, 2008.

———. *Starring Red Wing! The Incredible Career of Lilian St. Cyr, the First Native American Film Star.* Lincoln: University of Nebraska Press, 2019.

Weiden, David Heska Wanbli. *Winter Counts: A Novel.* New York: Ecco, 2020.

Wildcat, Daniel. *Red Alert!: Saving the Planet with Indigenous Knowledge.* Golden, CO: Fulcrum Publishing, 2009.

Wilkins, David E., and K. Tsianina Lomawaima. *Uneven Ground: American Indian Sovereignty and Federal Law.* Norman: University of Oklahoma Press, 2001.

Wilkins, David E., and Heidi Kiiwetinepinesiik Stark. *American Indian Politics and the American Political System.* Fourth edition. Lanham, MD: Rowman & Littlefield, 2018.

Williams, Maria Sháa Tláa, ed. *The Alaska Native Reader: History, Culture, Politics.* Durham, NC: Duke University Press, 2009.

Wilson, Diane, and Zibiquah Denny. *Voices Rising: Native Women Writers.* Duluth, MN: Black Bears & Blueberries Publishing, 2021.

Wilson-Raybould, Jody. *Indian in the Cabinet.* HarperCollins Canada, 2021.

Wimberly, Dan B. *Cherokee in Controversy: The Life of Jesse Bushyhead.* Macon, GA: Mercer University Press, 2017.

Witgen, Michael John. *Seeing Red: Indigenous Land, American Expansion, and the Political Economy of Plunder in North America.* Omohundro Institute of Early American History and Culture in Williamsburg, Virginia and the University of North Carolina Press in Chapel Hill, 2022.

Yohe, Jill Ahlberg, and Teri Greeves, eds. *Hearts of Our People: Native Women Artists.* Seattle: University of Washington Press, 2019.

SELECTED WEBSITES

Alaska Federation of Natives (AFN): https://www.nativefederation.org/

American Indian College Fund (AICF): www.collegefund.org

American Indian Higher Education Consortium: www.aihec.org

American Indian Library Association: https://ailanet.org/

American Indian Science and Engineering Society (AISES): www.aises.org

American Indians in Children's Literature (AICL): http://americanindiansinchildrensliterature.net

Assembly of First Nations (AFN): https://www.afn.ca/about-afn/

Association of Tribal Archives, Libraries, and Museums (ATALM): https://www.atalm.org/node/52

Association on American Indian Affairs (AAIA): www.indian-affairs.org

Center for Native American Youth (CNAY): https://www.cnay.org/

Council for Native Hawaiian Advancement: https://www.hawaiiancouncil.org/home

Cynthia Leitch Smith: https://cynthialeitchsmith.com/cynsations/

First Nations Development Institute: https://www.firstnations.org/

Four Directions: http://www.fourdirectionsvote.com/

Indian Affairs, U.S. Department of the Interior: www.bia.gov

Indian Country Today (ICT): https://indiancountrytoday.com/news

Indian Gaming Association (IGA): http://www.indiangaming.org/

Indian Health Service (IHS): www.ihs.gov

Indian Land Tenure Foundation (ILTF): https://iltf.org/

Indian Law Resource Center: https://indianlaw.org/

Intertribal Agriculture Council: https://www.indianag.org/

InterTribal Buffalo Council (ITBC): https://itbcbuffalonation.org/

Inuit Circumpolar Council (ICC): https://www.inuitcircumpolar.com/

National Association of Tribal Historic Preservation Officers (NATHPO): https://www.nathpo.org/

National Congress of American Indians (NCAI): www.ncai.org

National Council of Urban Indian Health (NCUIH): https://ncuih.org/

National Indian Child Welfare Association (NICWA): https://www.nicwa.org/

National Indian Council on Aging (NICOA): https://www.nicoa.org/

National Indian Education Association (NIEA): www.niea.org

National Indian Health Board (NIHB): https://www.nihb.org/

National Indian Justice Center (NIJC): https://www.nijc.org/

National Native American Boarding School Healing Coalition: https://boardingschool-healing.org/

National Native American Veterans Memorial: Honoring the Military Service of Native Americans: https://americanindian.si.edu/visit/washington/nnavm

National Native Hall of Fame: https://nativehalloffame.org/

National Urban Family Coalition (NUIFC): https://www.nuifc.org/about

Native American Journalists Association (NAJA): https://najanewsroom.com/

Native American Rights Fund (NARF): www.narf.org

Native Business Magazine: https://www.nativebusinessmag.com/

Native Forward Scholars Fund (formerly American Indian Graduate Center): https://www.nativeforward.org

Native Hoop Magazine https://nativehoop.org/

Native Knowledge 360° (NMAI): https://americanindian.si.edu/nk360/

Native Web: http://www.nativeweb.org/

NDN Sports: http://www.ndnsports.com/

PowWows: http://www.powwows.com/

Society for Advancement of Chicanos/Hispanics and Native Americans in Science (SACNAS): www.sacnas.org

United Nations Permanent Forum on Indigenous Issues (UNPFII): https://www.un.org/development/desa/indigenouspeoples/unpfii-sessions-2.html

NATIVE-OWNED MUSEUMS

Museums are a rich source of programming and resources including books, lectures, exhibits.

Accohannock Museum and Village
Accohannock Indian Tribe, Inc.
28380 Crisfield Marion Rd.
Marion Station, MD 21838
http://www.indianwatertrails.com/village.html

Agua Caliente Cultural Museum
219 S Palm Canyon Dr.
Palm Springs, CA 92262
www.accmuseum.org/

Ah-Tah-Thi-Ki Museum
34725 West Boundary Rd.
Big Cypress Seminole Indian Reservation
Clewiston, FL 33440
http://www.ahtahthiki.com/

Ak-Chin Him-Dak Eco Museum & Archives
47685 North Eco-Museum Rd.
Maricopa, AZ 85239
http://www.azcama.com/museums/akchin

Akwesasne Museum
321 State Route 37
Hogansburg, NY 13655-3114
www.akwesasneculturalcenter.org

Alutiiq Museum & Archaeological Repository
215 Mission Rd. #101
Kodiak, AK 99615
alutiiqmuseum.org/

Angel Decora Memorial Museum/Research Center
Winnebago Tribe of Nebraska
100 Bluff St.
Winnebago, NE 68071

http://www.winnebagotribe.com/cultural_center.html
Aquinnah Cultural Center
35 Aquinnah Circle
Aquinnah, MA 02535
http://wampanoagtribe.net/Pages/Wampanoag_ACC/index

Arvid E. Miller Memorial Library Museum
N8510 Moh-He-Con-Nuck Rd.
Bowler, WI 54416
http://mohican-nsn.gov/Departments/Library-Museum/

A:shiwi A:wan Museum & Heritage Center
Pueblo of Zuni
02 E Ojo Caliente Rd.
Zuni, NM 87327
http://ggsc.wnmu.edu/mcf/museums/ashiwi.html

Ataloa Lodge Museum/Bacone College
2299 Old Bacone Rd.
Muskogee, OK 74403
http://ataloa.bacone.edu/

Barona Cultural Center and Museum
1095 Barona Rd.
Lakeside, CA
www.baronamuseum.org/

Bernice Pauahi Bishop Museum
1525 Bernice St.
Honolulu, HI 96817
http://www.bishopmuseum.org/

Bois Forte Heritage Center
1500 Bois Forte Rd.
Tower, MN 55790
www.boisforte.com/divisions/heritage_ce
nter.htm

Cabazon Cultural Museum
84245 Indio Springs Pkwy
Indio, CA 92203
http://www.fantasyspringsresort.com/pro
d/cbmi

Catawba Cultural Preservation Project
1536 Tom Stevens Rd.
Rock Hill, SC 29730
www.ccppcrafts.com/

Cherokee Heritage Center
21192 S. Keeler Dr.
Park Hill, OK 74451
http://www.cherokeeheritage.org/

Cheyenne Cultural Center, Inc.
415 Gary Blvd.
Clinton, OK 73601
https://www.museumsusa.org/museums/
info/5980

Cheyenne Indian Museum
1000 Tongue River Rd.
Ashland, MT 59003
http://www.stlabre.org/

The Chickasaw Cultural Center
867 Cooper Memorial Dr.
Sulphur, OK 73086
http://chickasawculturalcenter.com/

Chitimacha Museum
155 Chitimacha Loop
Charenton, LA 70523
www.chitimacha.gov

Chugach Museum & Institute of History &
Art
560 East 34th Ave.
Anchorage, AK 99503-4196
www.chugachmuseum.org

The Citizen Potawatomi Nation Cultural
Heritage Center
1899 South Gordon Cooper Dr.
Shawnee, OK 74801
http://www.potawatomi.org/culture/cul
tural-heritage-center

Colville Tribal Museum
512 Mead Way
Coulee Dam, WA 99116
http://www.colvilletribes.com/colville_tr
ibal_museum.php

Comanche National Museum and Cultural
Center
701 NW Ferris Ave.
Lawton, OK 73507
http://www.comanchemuseum.com/

Fond du Lac Cultural Center & Museum
1720 Big Lake Rd.
Cloquet, MN 55720
http://www.fdlrez.com/%5C/Museum/in
dex.htm

Fort Belknap Museum
269 Blackfeet Ave.
Harlem, MT 59526
https://museu.ms/museum/details/15314
/fort-belknap-museum

Garifuna Museum
1523 W. 48th St.
Los Angeles, CA 90062
http://www.garifunamuseum.com/index.
php

George W. Brown, Jr. Ojibwe Museum &
Cultural Center
603 Peace Pipe Rd.
Lac Du Flambeau, WI 54538
www.ldfmuseum.com/

George W. Ogden Cultural Museum
Iowa Tribe of Kansas & Nebraska
3345 B Thrasher Rd.
White Cloud, KS 66094

Hana Cultural Center & Museum
4974 Uakea Rd.
Hana, HI 96713
http://hanaculturalcenter.org/

Harry V. Johnston, Jr. Lakota Cultural
Center
Cheyenne River Sioux Tribe
2001 Main St.
Eagle Butte, SD 57625
www.sioux.org

Hoo-hoogam Ki Museum
10005 E. Osborn Rd.
Scottsdale, AZ 85256
http://www.srpmic-nsn.gov/history_cul
ture/kimuseum.htm

Hoopa Valley Tribal Museum
CA-96
Hoopa, CA 95546
http://online.sfsu.edu/cals/hupa/Hoopa.
HTM

Hopi Museum (Hopi Cultural Center, Inc.)
AZ-264
Second Mesa, AZ 86043
http://www.hopiculturalcenter.com/

Huhugam Heritage Center
4759 N. Maricopa Rd.
Chandler, AZ 85226
http://www.huhugam.com

Huna Heritage Foundation
9301 Glacier Hwy.
Juneau, AK 99801-9306
http://www.hunaheritage.org

IAIA Museum of Contemporary Native
Arts (MoCNA)
108 Cathedral Place
Santa Fe NM 87501
https://iaia.edu/mocna/

The Indian Pueblo Cultural Center, Inc.
2401 12th St. NW
Albuquerque, NM
www.indianpueblo.org/

Ioloni Palace
364 S King St.
Honolulu, HI 96813
http://www.iolanipalace.org/

Inupiat Heritage Center
5421 North Star St.
Barrow, AK 99723
http://inupiat.areaparks.com/

Kanza Museum
698 Grandview Dr.
Kaw City, OK 74641
http://kawnation.com/?page_id=4188

Lenape Nation of Pennsylvania Cultural
Center
342 Northampton St.
Easton, PA 18042
http://www.lenapenation.org/cultureal
center.html

Lummi Records & Archives Center & Museum
2665 Kwina Rd.
Bellingham, WA 98226
http://www.lummi-nsn.org/website/dept
_pages/culture/archives.shtml

The Makah Cultural & Research Center
Neah Bay, WA 98357
www.makah.com/mcrchome.htm

Mashantucket Pequot Museum & Research
Center
110 Pequot Trail
Mashantucket, CT 06338-3180
http://www.pequotmuseum.org/Museum
Info.aspx

Mashpee Wampanoag Indian Museum
414 Main St.
Mashpee, MA 02649
http://www.mashpeewampanoagtribe.com
/museum

Mille Lacs Indian Museum & Trading Post
43411 Oodena Dr.
Onamia, MN 56359
www.mnhs.og/places/sites/mlim/

Monacan Ancestral Museum
2009 Kenmore Rd.
Amherst, VA 24521
http://www.monacannation.com/museum
.shtml

The Museum of the Cherokee Indian
589 Tsali Blvd.
Cherokee, NC 28719
https://www.cherokeemuseum.org/

Museum of Native American History
202 SW O St.
Bentonville, AR 72712
https://www.monah.org/

Museum of the Plains Indian
124 2nd Ave. N.W.
Browning, MT 59417
www.browningmontana.com/museum.ht
ml

The Museum at Warm Springs
Native Paths Cultural Heritage Museum
3300 Beloved Path
Pensacola, FL 32507
http://www.perdidobaytribe.org/about/
native-paths-heritage-museum-jones-
swamp

Nottoway Indian Tribe of Virginia Community House & Interpretive Center
23186 Main St.
Capron, VA
http://nottowayindians.org/interpretive
center.html

Navajo Nation Museum
Highway 264 and Loop Rd.
Window Rock, AZ 86515
http://www.navajonationmuseum.org/

Nohwike' Bagowa-White Mountain
Apache Cultural Center & Museum
Fort Apache, AZ 85926
http://www.wmat.nsn.us/wmaculture
.html

Oneida Nation Museum
County Rd. EE
Oneida, WI 54155
www.oneidanation.org/museum/

Onōhsagwë:de' Cultural Center (Seneca)
82 W. Hetzel St.
Salamanca, New York 14779
https://www.senecamuseum.org/

Osage Tribal Museum
819 Grandview Ave.
Pawhuska, OK 74056
http://www.osagetribalmuseum.com/

Pamunkey Indian Tribe Museum
175 Lay Landing Rd.
King William, VA 23086
http://www.pamunkey.net/museum.html

Penobscot Indian Nation
12 Downstreet St.
Indian Island, ME 04468
www.penobscotnation.org/museum/
Index.htm

The People's Center
53253 Hwy 93 W
Pablo, MT 59855
www.peoplescenter.org/

Poeh Museum and Cultural Center
78 Cities of Gold Rd.
Santa Fe, NM 87506
poehcenter.org/

Ponca Tribal Museum
2548 Park Ave.
Niobrara, NE 68760
http://www.poncatribe-ne.org/Museum

Potawatomi Cultural Center and Museum
1899 S Gordon Cooper Dr.
Shawnee, OK 74801

https://www.fcpotawatomi.com/culture-
and-history/

Pueblo of Acoma Historic Preservation Office
Sky City Cultural Center
1-40, Exit 102
Acoma, NM 87034
https://www.puebloofacoma.org

QuechanTribal Museum
350 Picacho Rd.
Winterhaven, CA 92283

Sac & Fox Nation of Missouri Tribal Museum
305 North Main St.
Reserve, KS 66434
www.sacandfoxcasino.com/tribal-museum
.html

San Carlos Apache Cultural Center
US-70 @ Milepost 272
Peridot, AZ 85542
www.sancarlosapache.com/San_Carlos_
Culture_Center.htm

Shakes Island
Wrangell Cooperative Association
104 Lynch St.
Wrangell, AK, 99929-1941
http://www.shakesisland.com/

Sheet'ka Kwaan Naa Kahidi Tribal Community House
456 Katlian St.
Sitka, AK 99835
http://www.sitkatours.com/

Shinnecock Nation Cultural Center & Museum
100 Montauk Hwy.
Southampton, NY 11968
www.shinnecockmuseum.com/

Shoshone Cultural Center
90 Ethete Rd.
Fort Washakie, WY 82514
https://www.wyomingtourism.org/things

-to-do/detail/Shoshone-Tribal-Cultural-
Center/8475

Shoshone-Bannock Tribal Museum
I-15 Exit 80, Simplot Rd.
Fort Hall ID, 83203
https://www.visitpocatello.com/sho
shone-bannock-museum/

Sierra Mono Museum
33103 Rd. 228
North Fork, CA 93643
www.sierramonomuseum.org/

Simon Paneak Memorial Museum
Anaktuvuk Pass, AK 99721
http://www.north-slope.org/depart
ments/inupiat-history-language-and-cul
ture/simon-paneak-memorial-museum/
our-museum

Six Nations Indian Museum
1462 County Route 60
Onchiota, NY 12989
www.sixnationsindianmuseum.com

Skokomish Indian Tribe
80 N Tribal Center Rd.
Skokomish, WA 98584
http://www.skokomish.org/culture-and-
history/

Southeast Alaska Indian Cultural Center,
Inc.
8800 Heritage Center Dr.
Anchorage, AK 99504
www.alaskanative.net/

Southern Ute Museum Cultural Center
77 Co Rd 517
Ignacio, CO 81137
www.succm.org/

Suquamish Museum
6861 NE South St.
Suquamish, WA 98392
www.suquamishmuseum.org/

Tamástslikt Cultural Institute
47106 Wildhorse Blvd.
Pendleton, OR 97801
http://www.tamastslikt.org/

Tantaquidgeon Museum
1819 Norwich New London Tpke.
Uncasville, CT
http://www.mohegan.nsn.us/

Three Affiliated Tribes Museum, Inc.
404 Frontage Rd.
New Town, ND 58763
http://www.mhanation.com/

Tigua Indian Cultural Center
305 Yaya Lane
El Paso, Texas 79907
https://www.ysletadelsurpueblo.org/tour
ism-hospitality/cultural-center

The Upper Missouri Dakota & Nakoda
Cultural Lifeway Center and Museum
Fort Peck Assiniboine & Sioux Indian Reservation
Poplar, MT 59255
http://www.fortpecktribes.org/crd/mu
seum.htm

Ute Indian Museum
17253 Chipeta Dr.

Montrose, CO 81401
http://www.coloradohistory.org/hist_site
s/UteIndian/Ute_indian.htm

Walatowa Cultural and Visitor Center
7413 NM-4
Jemez Pueblo, NM 87024
www.jemezpueblo.com/

Waponahki Museum & Resource Center
59 Passamaquoddy Rd.
Sipayik / Pleasant Point, MN 04667
http://www.wabanaki.com/museum.htm

Yakama Nation Museum
100 Spiel-yi Loop
Toppenish, WA 98948
www.yakamamuseum.com/

Yupiit Piciryarait Cultural Center
420 Chief Eddie Hoffman Hwy.
Bethel, AK 99559
http://bethelculturalcenter.com/

Ziibiwing Center of Anishinabe Culture &
Lifeways
6650 E. Broadway
Mt. Pleasant, MI 48858
http://www.sagchip.org/ziibiwing

INDEX

Note: (ill.) indicates photos and illustrations

L

S

T

X–Y

Z